THE PROCESS AND EFFECTS OF MASS COMMUNICATION

The Process and Effects of Mass Communication

edited by **WILBUR SCHRAMM**

UNIVERSITY OF ILLINOIS PRESS URBANA 1955

Second Printing

COPYRIGHT 1954 BY THE UNIVERSITY OF ILLINOIS
MANUFACTURED IN THE UNITED STATES OF AMERICA
LIBRARY OF CONGRESS CATALOG CARD NO. 54-9666

Foreword

This volume originated in the United States Information Agency's need for a book of background materials which could be used in training some of the agency's new employees in the field of research and evaluation. When the table of contents was made, however, it became clear that the book could be of much wider interest and usefulness than the original purpose required. Indeed, most of the readings had been tried out in classes of the Institute for Communications Research, at the University of Illinois, where the training was not aimed specifically at international communication. Therefore, the suggestion was made to the University of Illinois Press that this volume be offered for general sale.

Much of the background necessary for understanding the problems and practice of international communication is identical with the background necessary for making an intelligent approach to any other kind of social communication. That is, one must understand how the communication process works, how attention is gained, how meaning is transferred from one subjective field to another, how opinions and attitudes are created or modified, and how group memberships, role concepts, and social structure are related to the process. These problems take up the greater part of this volume, and, although illustrations come more often from international communication than from other areas, what is said about these subjects is equally applicable to any of the great laboratories in which social communication can be examined — for example, advertising, or domestic political campaigns, or adult education through the mass media.

When one applies this basic material to the laboratory of international communication, several aspects of the communication process assume greater importance. One is the problem of transferring meaning. Getting one's meaning understood by another individual, face to face, in one's own culture, is sometimes hard enough. When one communicates internationally, he has not only to transfer meaning between subjective individual fields but also between cultures which may be spectacularly different. One aspect of the communicator's equipment to which international communication must give special attention is, therefore, an empathic understanding of the cultures involved in the communication chain. This problem is discussed in the pages that follow, but of course there is no space in this volume for specific analysis of different cultures.

Another aspect of communication which bulks large for the international communicator, and especially for the person engaged in political or psychological warfare, is the organizational problem. The most important part of this is the relation of the communicator to sources of policy. There is also the problem of feedback, which is often highly difficult in international communication, and which in psychological warfare chiefly takes the form of intelligence. These are special problems which can only be suggested in the following pages, but which bulk large in the training of a student or practitioner of international communication.

For the student approaching international communication, therefore, this book of readings is designed as an introduction to the communication process and to the general problems of its use internationally — to be supplemented by the study of cultures and other special problems of the field.

For the student approaching other areas of communication, this book is an introduction to the communication process, illustrated by application to one of the most important communication laboratories of our time: communication between nations. Here, too, it should be supplemented by study of the particular problems of the area of communication in which the student plans to work.

In the making of the book, Mr. Ben Gedalecia, until recently chief of research and evaluation for USIA, has been helpful, as has Mr. Antonio Micocci, present chief of that division. Dr. Lewis Nixon, Mr. Richard Fitzpatrick, and Miss Phoebe Everett, all of whom had some responsibility for USIA training and training materials in the research and evaluation fields, have been consistently helpful. Debt must also be acknowledged to other members of USIA, such as Dr. Ralph White, who made suggestions and contributed a paper, to Mr. Joseph Klapper, who contributed several sections, and to Dr. Leo Lowenthal, who helped to structure this field in the important Winter, 1952-53, number of the *Public Opinion Quarterly*, which he edited. A great many persons made suggestions about the content of the book, and a great many authors and publishers were gracious in giving permission for the use of their materials. Among this latter class, Dr. Phillips Davison and Dr. Alexander George, who took time to revise their important paper especially for this volume, deserve special gratitude. And the University of Illinois Press, as usual, has been helpful in the planning, constructive in its criticism, painstaking in its handling of the copy, and patient.

Urbana, Illinois, January 17, 1954   Wilbur Schramm

Contents

THE PROCESS OF COMMUNICATION 1

  WILBUR SCHRAMM *How Communication Works* 3

THE PRIMARY EFFECT — ATTENTION 27

INTRODUCTORY NOTE: THE ANATOMY OF ATTENTION 29

WHY THEY ATTEND TO MASS COMMUNICATION 35

  BERNARD BERELSON *What "Missing the Newspaper" Means* 36

  KATHERINE M. WOLFE AND MARJORIE FISKE *Why They Read Comics* 48

  HERTA HERZOG *Motivations and Gratifications of Daily Serial Listeners* 50

  DOUGLAS WAPLES, BERNARD BERELSON, AND FRANKLYN R. BRADSHAW *Why They Read* 56

THE AUDIENCES OF MASS COMMUNICATION 68

  PAUL F. LAZARSFELD AND PATRICIA KENDALL *The Communications Behavior of the Average American: Some Tables* 69

  WILBUR SCHRAMM AND DAVID M. WHITE *Age, Education, and Economic Status as Factors in Newspaper Reading: Conclusions* 71

  VARIOUS SOURCES *Mass Communications and Their Audiences in Other Countries* 74

THE EFFECT OF DIFFERENT CHANNELS 85

INTRODUCTORY NOTE: THE NATURE OF CHANNELS 87

   JOSEPH T. KLAPPER *The Comparative Effects of the Various
Media* 91

GETTING THE MEANING UNDERSTOOD 107

INTRODUCTORY NOTE: THE MEANING OF MEANING 109

PERCEIVING THE MESSAGE 115

   DAVID KRECH AND RICHARD S. CRUTCHFIELD *Perceiving the
World* 116

   LEONARD DOOB *The Perception of Propaganda* 138

   GORDON ALLPORT AND LEO POSTMAN *The Basic Psychology
of Rumor* 141

COMMUNICATING TO ANOTHER CULTURE 156

   ALEXANDER H. LEIGHTON AND MORRIS EDWARD OPLER *Psychiatry
and Applied Anthropology in Psychological Warfare Against
Japan* 157

   BRUCE L. SMITH *Communications Research on Non-Industrial
Countries* 170

   RALPH K. WHITE *The New Resistance to International
Propaganda* 180

   WILLIAM BUCHANAN AND HADLEY CANTRIL *National
Stereotypes* 191

MODIFYING ATTITUDES AND OPINIONS 207

INTRODUCTORY NOTE: THE NATURE AND BEHAVIOR OF ATTITUDES 209

   EUGENE L. HARTLEY, RUTH E. HARTLEY, AND CLYDE HART
Attitudes and Opinions 216

   CHARLES E. OSGOOD AND PERCY H. TANNENBAUM *Attitude
Change and the Principle of Congruity* 251

   CARL I. HOVLAND, ARTHUR A. LUMSDAINE, AND FRED D. SHEFFIELD
*The Effect of Presenting "One Side" versus "Both Sides" in
Changing Opinions on a Controversial Subject* 261

   CARL I. HOVLAND AND WALTER WEISS *The Influence of Source
Credibility on Communication Effectiveness* 275

   JOSEPH T. KLAPPER *Mass Media and Persuasion* 289

   LEONARD DOOB *The Behavior of Public Opinion* 321

   BERNARD BERELSON *Communication and Public Opinion* 342

EFFECTS IN TERMS OF GROUPS 357

INTRODUCTORY NOTE: THE IMPORTANCE OF THE GROUP IN THE
COMMUNICATION CHAIN 359

   HERBERT BLUMER *The Crowd, the Public, and the Mass*......363

   ELIOT FREIDSON *Communications Research and the Concept
of the Mass*..380

   MATILDA WHITE RILEY AND JOHN W. RILEY, JR. *A Sociological
Approach to Communications Research*...................389

   STANLEY K. BIGMAN *Prestige, Personal Influence,
and Opinion* 402

   HADLEY CANTRIL *The Invasion from Mars*................411

   ROBERT K. MERTON *Mass Persuasion: The Moral Dimension*..424

**SPECIAL PROBLEMS OF ACHIEVING AN EFFECT WITH INTERNATIONAL
COMMUNICATIONS** 429

INTRODUCTORY NOTE: THE DIMENSIONS OF THE PROBLEM 431

   W. PHILLIPS DAVISON AND ALEXANDER L. GEORGE *An Outline
for the Study of International Political Communication*.....433

   HANS SPEIER *Psychological Warfare Reconsidered*...........444

   CHARLES Y. GLOCK *The Comparative Study of Communication
and Opinion Formation*..............................469

   DANIEL LERNER *Effective Propaganda: Conditions and
Evaluation*..480

   ERNST KRIS AND NATHAN LEITES *Trends in Twentieth
Century Propaganda* 489

   EDWARD A. SHILS AND MORRIS JANOWITZ *Cohesion and
Disintegration in the Wehrmacht in World War II*.........501

   LEONARD DOOB *Goebbels' Principles of Propaganda*..........517

   HAROLD D. LASSWELL *The Strategy of Soviet Propaganda*....537

   PHILIP SELZNICK *Problems of Counteroffense Against
International Communism* 548

100 TITLES FOR FURTHER READING 563

INDEX OF NAMES 573

INDEX OF SUBJECTS...578

The Process of Communication

▲ WILBUR SCHRAMM

*H*ow Communication Works

THE PROCESS

It will be easier to see how mass communication works if we first look at the communication process in general.

Communication comes from the Latin *communis,* common. When we communicate we are trying to establish a "commonness" with someone. That is, we are trying to share information, an idea, or an attitude. At this moment I am trying to communicate to you the idea that the essence of communication is getting the receiver and the sender "tuned" together for a particular message. At this same moment, someone somewhere is excitedly phoning the fire department that the house is on fire. Somewhere else a young man in a parked automobile is trying to convey the understanding that he is moon-eyed because he loves the young lady. Somewhere else a newspaper is trying to persuade its readers to believe as it does about the Republican Party. All these are forms of communication, and the process in each case is essentially the same.

Communication always requires at least three elements — the source, the message, and the destination. A *source* may be an individual (speaking, writing, drawing, gesturing) or a communication organization (like a newspaper, publishing house, television station or motion picture studio). The *message* may be in the form of ink on paper, sound waves in the air, impulses in an electric current, a wave of the hand, a flag in the air, or any other signal capable of being interpreted meaningfully. The *destination* may be an *individual* listening, watching, or reading; or a member of a *group,* such as a discussion group, a lecture audience, a football crowd, or a mob; or

▲ This paper, first published in the Shimbun Kenkyu of Tokyo and later in the 53rd Yearbook of the Society for the Study of Education, is a general introduction to the communication process.

an individual member of the particular group we call the *mass audience,* such as the reader of a newspaper or a viewer of television.

Now what happens when the source tries to build up this "commonness" with his intended receiver? First, the source encodes his
message. That is, he takes the information or feeling he wants to share
and puts it into a form that can be transmitted. The "pictures in our
heads" can't be transmitted until they are coded. When they are
coded into spoken words, they can be transmitted easily and effectively,
but they can't travel very far unless radio carries them. If they are
coded into written words, they go more slowly than spoken words,
but they go farther and last longer. Indeed, some messages long outlive
their senders — the *Iliad,* for instance; the Gettysburg address;
Chartres cathedral. Once coded and sent, a message is quite free of
its sender, and what it does is beyond the power of the sender to
change. Every writer feels a sense of helplessness when he finally
commits his story or his poem to print; you doubtless feel the same
way when you mail an important letter. Will it reach the right person?
Will he understand it as you intend him to? Will he respond as you
want him to? For in order to complete the act of communication the
message must be decoded. And there is good reason, as we shall see,
for the sender to wonder whether his receiver will really be in tune
with him, whether the message will be interpreted without distortion,
whether the "picture in the head" of the receiver will bear any
resemblance to that in the head of the sender.

We are talking about something very like a radio or telephone
circuit. In fact, it is perfectly possible to draw a picture of the human
communication system that way:

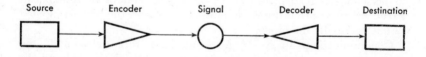

Source   Encoder   Signal   Decoder   Destination

Substitute "microphone" for encoder, and "earphone" for decoder
and you are talking about electronic communication. Consider that
the "source" and "encoder" are one person, "decoder" and "destination" are another, and the signal is language, and you are talking
about human communication.

Now it is perfectly possible by looking at those diagrams to predict
how such a system will work. For one thing, such a system can be no
stronger than its weakest link. In engineering terms, there may be
filtering or distortion at any stage. In human terms, if the source does
not have adequate or clear information; if the message is not encoded
fully, accurately, effectively in transmittible signs; if these are not
transmitted fast enough and accurately enough, despite interference

and competition, to the desired receiver; if the message is not decoded in a pattern that corresponds to the encoding; and finally, if the destination is unable to handle the decoded message so as to produce the desired response — then, obviously, the system is working at less than top efficiency. When we realize that *all* these steps must be accomplished with relatively high efficiency if any communication is to be successful, the everyday act of explaining something to a stranger, or writing a letter, seems a minor miracle.

A system like this will have a maximum capacity for handling information and this will depend on the separate capacities of each unit on the chain — for example, the capacity of the channel (how fast can one talk?) or the capacity of the encoder (can your student understand something explained quickly?). If the coding is good (for example, no unnecessary words) the capacity of the channel can be approached, but it can never be exceeded. You can readily see that one of the great skills of communication will lie in knowing how near capacity to operate a channel.

This is partly determined for us by the nature of the language. English, like every other language, has its sequences of words and sounds governed by certain probabilities. If it were organized so that no set of probabilities governed the likelihood that certain words would follow certain other words (for example, that a noun would follow an adjective, or that "States" or "Nations" would follow "United") then we would have nonsense. As a matter of fact, we can calculate the relative amount of freedom open to us in writing any language. For English, the freedom is about 50 per cent. (Incidentally, this is about the required amount of freedom to enable us to construct interesting crossword puzzles. Shannon has estimated that if we had about 70 per cent freedom, we could construct three-dimensional crossword puzzles. If we had only 20 per cent, crossword puzzle making would not be worth while).

So much for language *redundancy,* as communication theorists call it, meaning the percentage of the message which is not open to free choice. But there is also the communicator's redundancy, and this is an important aspect of constructing a message. For if we think our audience may have a hard time understanding the message, we can deliberately introduce more redundancy; we can repeat (just as the radio operator on a ship may send "SOS" over and over again to make sure it is heard and decoded), or we can give examples and analogies. In other words, we always have to choose between transmitting more information in a given time, or transmitting less and repeating more in the hope of being better understood. And as you know, it is often a delicate choice, because too slow a rate will bore an audience, whereas too fast a rate may confuse them.

Perhaps the most important thing about such a system is one we have been talking about all too glibly — the fact that receiver and

sender must be in tune. This is clear enough in the case of a radio
transmitter and receiver, but somewhat more complicated when it
means that a human receiver must be able to understand a human
sender.

Let us redraw our diagram in very simple form, like this:

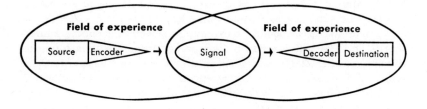

Think of those circles as the accumulated experience of the two individuals trying to communicate. The source can encode, and the
destination can decode, only in terms of the experience each has had.
If we have never learned any Russian, we can neither code nor decode
in that language. If an African tribesman has never seen or heard of
an airplane, he can only decode the sight of a plane in terms of whatever experience he has had. The plane may seem to him to be a bird,
and the aviator a god borne on wings. If the circles have a large area
in common, then communication is easy. If the circles do not meet —
if there has been no common experience — then communication is
impossible. If the circles have only a small area in common — that is,
if the experiences of source and destination have been strikingly unlike
— then it is going to be very difficult to get an intended meaning
across from one to the other. This is the difficulty we face when a
non-science-trained person tries to read Einstein, or when we try to
communicate with another culture much different from ours.

The source, then, tries to encode in such a way as to make it easy
for the destination to tune in the message — to relate it to parts of
his experience which are much like those of the source. What does he
have to work with?

Messages are made up of signs. A sign is a signal that stands for
something in experience. The word "dog" is a sign that stands for our
generalized experience with dogs. The word would be meaningless
to a person who came from a dog-less island and had never read of or
heard of a dog. But most of us have learned that word by association,
just as we learn most signs. Someone called our attention to an animal,
and said "dog." When we learned the word, it produced in us much
the same response as the object it stood for. That is, when we heard
"dog" we could recall the appearance of dogs, their sound, their feel,
perhaps their smell. But there is an important difference between the
sign and the object: the sign always represents the object at a reduced

level of cues. By this we mean simply that the sign will not call forth all the responses that the object itself will call forth. The sign "dog," for example, will probably not call forth in us the same wariness or attention a strange dog might attract if it wandered into our presence. This is the price we pay for portability in language. We have a sign system that we can use in place of the less portable originals (for example, Margaret Mitchell could re-create the burning of Atlanta in a novel, and a photograph could transport world-wide the appearance of a bursting atomic bomb), but our sign system is merely a kind of shorthand. The coder has to be able to write the shorthand, the decoder to read it. And no two persons have learned exactly the same system. For example, a person who has known only Arctic huskies will not have learned exactly the same meaning for the shorthand sign "dog" as will a person who comes from a city where he has known only pekes and poms.

We have come now to a point where we need to tinker a little more with our diagram of the communication process. It is obvious that each person in the communication process is both an encoder and a decoder. He receives and transmits. He must be able to write readable shorthand, and to read other people's shorthand. Therefore, it is possible to describe either sender or receiver in a human communication system thus:

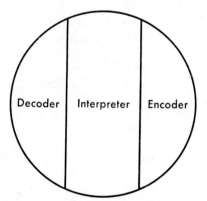

What happens when a signal comes to you? Remember that it comes in the form of a sign. If you have learned the sign, you have learned certain responses with it. We can call these mediatory responses, because they mediate what happens to the message in your nervous system. These responses are the *meaning* the sign has for you. They are learned from experience, as we said, but they are affected by the state of your organism at the moment. For example, if you are hungry, a picture of a steak may not arouse exactly the same response in you as when you are overfed.

But subject to these effects, the mediatory responses will then determine what you do about the sign. For you have learned other sets of reactions connected to the mediatory responses. A sign that means a certain thing to you will start certain other processes in your nerves and muscles. A sign that means "fire," for example, will certainly trigger off some activity in you. A sign that means you are in danger may start the process in your nerves and muscles that makes you say "help!" In other words, the meaning that results from your decoding of a sign will start you *en*coding. Exactly *what* you encode will depend on your choice of the responses available in the situation and connected with the meaning.

Whether this encoding actually results in some overt communication or action depends partly on the barriers in the way. You may think it better to keep silent. And if an action does occur, the nature of the action will also depend on the avenues for action available to you and the barriers in your way. The code of your group may not sanction the action you want to take. The meaning of a sign may make you want to hit the person who has said it, but he may be too big, or you may be in the wrong social situation. You may merely ignore him, or "look murder at him," or say something nasty about him to someone else.

But whatever the exact result, this is the process in which you are constantly engaged. You are constantly decoding signs from your environment, interpreting these signs, and encoding something as a result. In fact, it is misleading to think of the communication process as starting somewhere and ending somewhere. It is really endless. We are little switchboard centers handling and rerouting the great endless current of communication. We can accurately think of communication as passing through us — changed, to be sure, by our interpretations, our habits, our abilities and capabilities, but the input still being reflected in the output.

We need now to add another element to our description of the communication process. Consider what happens in a conversation between two people. One is constantly communicating back to the other, thus:

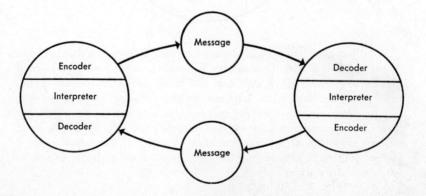

The return process is called *feedback,* and plays a very important part in communication because it tells us how our messages are being interpreted. Does the hearer say, "Yes, yes, that's right," as we try to persuade him? Does he nod his head in agreement? Does a puzzled frown appear on his forehead? Does he look away as though he were losing interest? All these are feedback. So is a letter to the editor of a newspaper, protesting an editorial. So is an answer to a letter. So is the applause of a lecture audience. An experienced communicator is attentive to feedback, and constantly modifies his messages in light of what he observes in or hears from his audience.

At least one other example of feedback, also, is familiar to all of us. We get feedback from our own messages. That is, we hear our own voices and can correct mispronunciations. We see the words we have written on paper, and can correct misspellings or change the style. When we do that, here is what is happening:

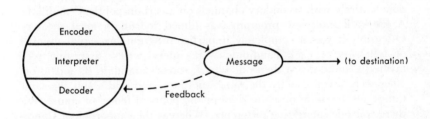

It is clear that in any kind of communication we rarely send out messages in a single channel, and this is the final element we must add to our account of the communication process. When you speak to me, the sound waves from your voice are the primary message. But there are others: the expression on your face, your gestures, the relation of a given message to past messages. Even the primary message conveys information on several levels. It gives me words to decode. It emphasizes certain words above others. It presents the words in a pattern of intonation and timing which contribute to the total meaning. The quality of your voice (deep, high, shrill, rasping, rich, thin, loud, soft) itself carries information about you and what you are saying.

This multiple channel situation exists even in printed mass communication, where the channels are perhaps most restricted. Meaning is conveyed, not only by the words in a news item, but also by the size of the headline, the position on the page and the page in the paper, the association with pictures, the use of boldface and other typographical devices. All these tell us something about the item. Thus we can visualize the typical channel of communication, not as a simple telegraph circuit, in which current does or does not flow, but rather as a sort of coaxial cable in which many signals flow in parallel from source toward the destination.

These parallel relationships are complex, but you can see their general pattern. A communicator can emphasize a point by adding as many parallel messages as he feels are deserved. If he is communicating by speaking, he can stress a word, pause just before it, say it with a rising inflection, gesture while he says it, look earnestly at his audience. Or he can keep all the signals parallel — except *one*. He can speak solemnly, but wink, as Lowell Thomas sometimes does. He can stress a word in a way that makes it mean something else — for example, "That's a *fine* job you did!" And by so doing he conveys secondary meanings of sarcasm or humor or doubt.

The same thing can be done with printed prose, with broadcast, with television or films. The secondary channels of the sight-sound media are especially rich. I am reminded of a skillful but deadly job done entirely with secondary channels on a certain political candidate. A sidewalk interview program was filmed to run in local theaters. Ostensibly it was a completely impartial program. An equal number of followers of each candidate were interviewed — first, one who favored Candidate A, then one who favored Candidate B, and so on. They were asked exactly the same questions, and said about the same things, although on opposite sides of the political fence, of course. But there was one interesting difference. Whereas the supporters of Candidate A were ordinary folks, not outstandingly attractive or impressive, the followers of Candidate B who were chosen to be interviewed invariably had something slightly wrong with them. They looked wild-eyed, or they stuttered, or they wore unpressed suits. The extra meaning was communicated. Need I say which candidate won?

But this is the process by which communication works, whether it is mass communication, or communication in a group, or communication between individuals.

COMMUNICATION IN TERMS OF LEARNING THEORY

So far we have avoided talking about this complicated process in what may seem to you to be the obvious way to talk about it — in the terminology and symbols of learning theory.[1] We have done so for the sake of simplicity. Now in order to fill in the picture it seems desirable to sketch the diagram of how communication looks to a psychologist of learning. If psychological diagrams bother you, you can skip to section 3.

Let's start with the diagram, then explain it.

[1] For the model in the following pages the author is indebted to his colleague, Dr. Charles E. Osgood. Dr. Osgood will soon publish the model in a more advanced form.

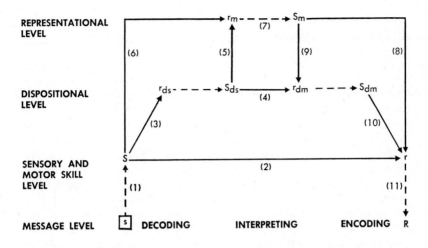

The diagram isn't as complicated as it looks. Remember that time in the diagram moves from left to right, and then follow the numbers and you won't get far off the road.

Begin with (1). This is the input. At the message level we have a collection of objectively measurable signs ⑤. These come to your sense organs, where they constitute a stimulus for action. This stimulus we call s. When the process gets as far as s, you are paying attention. The message has been accepted. It may not have been accepted as intended; s may not equal ⑤; the sensory mechanism may have seen or heard it incompletely. But everything else that happens as a result of the message in that particular destination will now necessarily be the result of the stimulus accepted by your sense organs.

Now look at number (2). The message may not have to go to any other level in order to bring about a response. If a man waves his fist near your nose, you may dodge. If he squeezes your hand, you may say "ouch!" These are learned, almost automatic, responses on the sensory and motor skill level.

But the stimulus may also bring about other kinds of activity within your nervous system. Look at number (3). The stimulus s may be translated into a grammatical response on your dispositional level — by which we mean the level of learned integrations (attitudes, values, sets, etc.) which make it so easy for you to dispose of the variety of stimuli that come to you in the course of a day. These are what we call the intervening variables. Suppose the stimulus stirs up activity in this area of intervening variables. Two things may happen. Look at number (4). The response may be so well learned that it doesn't even have to go to the level of thinking. You hear a line of a poem, and almost automatically say the second line. In that case the activity is through numbers (4) and (10).

More often, however, the activity goes through number (5). Here the original stimulus has been decoded into grammar, fed through the intervening variables, and sent up to the representational level of the central nervous system, where meanings are assigned and ideas considered. Occasionally a stimulus comes to that level without going through the intervening variables — as is number (6). These stimuli create activity in the central nervous system (r_m) which is the terminus of the decoding part of the process. This is equivalent to the meaning or significance of the signs $\boxed{S}$. What happens in number (7), then, is what we have been referring to as interpretation. The response r_m which we call meaning becomes in turn a stimulus which sets the encoding process in action, so that (7) is both the terminus of decoding and the start of encoding. We learn to associate meanings with desired responses. And so the encoding process moves through (8) or (9). That is, we give certain orders which either pass directly to the neuro-muscular system (through 8) or are passed through the intervening variables (through 9 and 10). In any case, all this activity of the nervous system finally results in a response on the motor skill level (r), which results in output (number 11). If the output is an overt response (R), then we have another message, which may offer itself as a collection of signs $\boxed{S}$ and be accepted by still another person as a stimulus (s).

This is what we believe happens when someone says to you, "cigarette?" and you answer "yes, please," or "no, thanks." If you are interested in doing so, you can translate all that is said about the communication process in this paper into the psychological symbols we have just been using. But to make the account simpler, we are going to shift gears at this point and talk about communication effects and mass communication in the terms we used in section 1.

HOW COMMUNICATION HAS AN EFFECT

The chief reason we study this process is to learn something about how it achieves effects. We want to know what a given kind of communication does to people. Given a certain message content, we should like to be able to predict what effect that content will have on its receivers.

Every time we insert an advertisement in a newspaper, put up a sign, explain something to a class, scold a child, write a letter, or put our political candidate on radio or television, we are making a prediction about the effect communication will have. I am predicting now that what I am writing will help you understand the common everyday miracle of communication. Perhaps I am wrong. Certainly many political parties have been proved wrong in their predictions about the effects of their candidates' radio speeches. Some ads sell goods; others don't. Some class teaching "goes over"; some does not.

For it is apparent to you, from what you have read so far, that there is no such thing as a simple and easily predictable relationship between message content and effect.

Nevertheless, it is possible to describe simply what might be called the conditions of success in communication — by which we mean the conditions that must be fulfilled if the message is to arouse its intended response. Let us set them down here briefly, and then talk about them:

1. *The message must be so designed and delivered as to gain the attention of the intended destination.*

2. *The message must employ signs which refer to experience common to source and destination, so as to "get the meaning across."*

3. *The message must arouse personality needs in the destination and suggest some ways to meet those needs.*

4. *The message must suggest a way to meet those needs which is appropriate to the group situation in which the destination finds himself at the time when he is moved to make the desired response.*

You can see, by looking at these requirements, why the expert communicator usually begins by finding out as much as he can about his intended destination, and why "know your audience" is the first rule of practical mass communication. For it is important to know the right timing for a message, the kind of language one must use to be understood, the attitudes and values one must appeal to in order to be effective, and the group standards in which the desired action will have to take place. This is relatively easy in face-to-face communication, more difficult in mass communication. In either case, it is necessary.

Let us talk about these four requirements.

1. *The message must be so designed and delivered as to gain the attention of the intended destination.* This is not so easy as it sounds. For one thing, the message must be made available. There will be no communication if we don't talk loud enough to be heard, or if our letter is not delivered, or if we smile at the right person when she isn't looking. And even if the message is available, it may not be selected. Each of us has available far more communication than we can possibly accept or decode. We therefore scan our environment in much the same way as we scan newspaper headlines or read a table of contents. We choose messages according to our impression of their general characteristics — whether they fit our needs and interests. We choose usually on the basis of an impression we get from one cue in the message, which may be a headline, a name in a radio news story, a picture, a patch of color, or a sound. If that cue does not appeal to us, we may never open our senses to the message. In different situations, of course, we choose differently among these cues. For example, if you are speaking to me at a time when I am relaxed and unbusy, or when I am waiting for the kind of message you have (for instance, that my friends have come to take me fishing), then you are more likely to get good

attention than if you address me when noise blots out what you say, or when all my attention is given to some competing message, or when I am too sleepy to pay attention, or when I am thinking about something else and have simply "tuned out." (How many times have you finished speaking and realized that your intended receiver had simply not heard a word you said?) The designing of a message for attention, then, involves timing, and placing, and equipping it with cues which will appeal to the receiver's interests.

2. *The message must employ signs which refer to experience common to both source and destination, in order to "get the meaning across."* We have already talked about this problem of getting the receiver in tune with the sender. Let us add now that as our experience with environment grows, we tend to classify and catalog experience in terms of how it relates to other experience and to our needs and interests. As we grow older that catalog system grows harder and firmer. It tends to reject messages that do not fit its structure, or distort them so that they do fit. It will reject Einstein, perhaps, because it feels it can't understand him. If an airplane is a completely new experience, but a bird is not, it may, as we have said, interpret the plane as a large, noisy bird. If it is Republican it will tend to reject Democratic radio speeches or to recall only the parts that can be made into pro-Republican arguments; this is one of the things we have found out about voting behavior. Therefore, in designing a message we have to be sure not only that we speak the "same language" as the receiver, and that we don't "write over his head," but also that we don't conflict too directly with the way he sees and catalogs the world. There are some circumstances, true, in which it works well to conflict directly, but for the most part these are the circumstances in which our understandings and attitudes are not yet firm or fixed, and they are relatively few and far between. In communicating, as in flying an airplane, the rule is that when a stiff wind is blowing, one doesn't land cross-wind unless he has to.

3. *The message must arouse personality needs in the destination and suggest some way to meet those needs.* We take action because of need and toward goals. In certain simple situations, the action response is quite automatic. When our nerves signal "pain-heat-finger" we jerk our fingers back from the hot pan. When our optic nerve signals "red traffic light" we stop the car. In more complicated situations we usually have more freedom of choice, and we choose the action which, in the given situation, will come closest to meeting our needs or goals. The first requisite of an effective message, therefore (as every advertising man knows), is that it relate itself to one of our personality needs — the needs for security, status, belongingness, understanding, freedom from constraint, love, freedom from anxiety, and so forth. It must arouse a drive. It must make the individual feel a need or a

tension which he can satisfy by action. Then the message can try to control the resulting action by suggesting what action to take. Thus an advertisement usually tells you to buy, what, and where. Propaganda to enemy troops usually suggests a specific action, such as surrender, subversion, or malingering. The suggested action, of course, is not always the one taken. If an easier, cheaper, or otherwise more acceptable action leading to the same goal is seen, that will probably be selected instead. For instance, it may be that the receiver is not the kind of person to take vigorous action, even though that seems called for. The person's values may inhibit him from doing what is suggested. Or his group role and membership may control what action he takes, and it is this control we must talk about now.

4. *The message must suggest a way to meet those needs which is appropriate to the group situation in which the destination finds himself at the time when he is moved to make the desired response.* We live in groups. We get our first education in the primary group of our family. We learn most of our standards and values from groups. We learn roles in groups, because those roles give us the most orderly and satisfying routine of life. We make most of our communication responses in groups. And if communication is going to bring about change in our behavior, the first place we look for approval of this new behavior is to the group. We are scarcely aware of the great importance our group involvements have for us, or of the loyalties we develop toward our several groups and institutions, until our place in the group or the group itself is threatened. But yet if our groups do not sanction the response we are inclined to make to communication, then we are very unlikely to make it. On the other hand, if our group strongly approves of a certain kind of action, that is the one we are likely to select out of several otherwise even choices.

You can see how this works in practical situations. The Jewish culture does not approve the eating of pork; the Indian culture does not approve the slaughter of cows, and the eating of beef. Therefore, it is highly unlikely that even the most eloquent advertisement will persuade an orthodox Jewish family to go contrary to their group sanctions, and buy pork; or an orthodox Hindu family, to buy beef. Or take the very simple communication situation of a young man and a young woman in a parked automobile. The young man communicates the idea that he wants a kiss. There isn't much likelihood of his not gaining attention for that communication or of its not being understood. But how the young woman responds will depend on a number of factors, partly individual, partly group. Does she want to be kissed at that moment? Does she want to be kissed by that young man? Is the situation at the moment — a moon, soft music from the radio, a convertible? — conducive to the response the young man wants? But then, how about the group customs under which the girl lives? If this is a first date, is it "done" to kiss a boy on a first date? Is petting condoned in the case of a girl her age? What has she learned from her parents and her friends about these things? Of course, she won't knowingly have a little debate with herself such as we have suggested here, but all these elements and more will enter into the decision as to whether she tilts up her chin or says, "No, Jerry. Let's go home."

There are two things we can say with confidence about predicting communication effects. One is that a message is much more likely to succeed if it fits the patterns of understandings, attitudes, values and goals that a receiver has; or at least if it starts with this pattern and tries to reshape it slightly. Communication research men call this latter process "canalizing," meaning that the sender provides a channel to direct the already existing motives in the receiver. Advertising men and propagandists say it more bluntly; they say that a communicator must "start where the audience is." You can see why this is. Our personalities — our patterns of habits, attitudes, drives, values, and so forth — grow very slowly but firmly. I have elsewhere compared the process to the slow, sure, ponderous growth of a stalagmite on a cave floor. The stalagmite builds up from the calcareous residue of the water dripping on it from the cave roof. Each drop leaves only a tiny residue, and it is very seldom that we can detect the residue of any single drop, or that any single drop will make a fundamental change in the shape or appearance of the stalagmite. Yet together all these drops do build the stalagmite, and over the years it changes considerably in size and somewhat in shape. This is the way our environment drips into us, drop by drop, each drop leaving a little residue, each tending to follow the existing pattern. This personality pattern we are talking about is, of course, an active thing — not passive, like the stalagmite — but still the similarity is there. When we introduce one drop of communication into a person where millions of drops have already fallen and left their residue, we can hardly expect to reshape the personality fundamentally by that one drop. If we are communicating to a child, it is easier, because the situation is not so firmly fixed. If we are communicating in an area where ideas and values are not yet determined — if our drop of communication falls where not many have fallen before — then we may be able to see a change as a result of our communication.

But in general we must admit that the best thing we can do is to build on what already exists. If we take advantage of the existing pattern of understanding, drives, and attitudes to gain acceptance for our message, then we may hope to divert the pattern slightly in the direction we want to move it. Let's go back to elections again for an example. It is very hard to change the minds of convinced Republicans or Democrats through communication, or even to get them to listen to the arguments of the opposing party. On the other hand, it is possible to start with a Republican or Democratic viewpoint and slightly modify the existing party viewpoints in one way or other. If this process goes on for long enough, it may even be possible to get confirmed party-men to reverse their voting pattern. This is what the Republicans were trying to do in the 1952 election by stressing "the mess in Washington," "time for a change," "the mistakes in Korea," and "the threat of Communism," and apparently they were successful in getting some ordinarily Democratic votes. But in 1952, as in every campaign, the real objectives of the campaigning were the new voters and the undecided voters.

The second thing we can say with confidence about communication effects is that they are resultants of a number of forces, of which the communicator can really control only one. The sender, that is, can shape his message and can decide when and where to introduce it. But the message is only one of at least four important elements that determine what response occurs. The other three are the situation in which the communication is received and in which the response, if any, must occur; the personality state of the receiver; and his group relationships and standards. This is why it is so dangerous to try to predict exactly what will be the effect of any message except the simplest one in the simplest situation.

Let us take an example. In Korea, in the first year of the war there, I was interviewing a North Korean prisoner of war who had recently surrendered with one of our surrender leaflets on his person. It looked like an open and shut case: the man had picked up the leaflet, thought it over, and decided to surrender. But I was interviewing him anyway, trying to see just how the leaflet had its effect. This is what he told me.

He said that when he picked up the leaflet, it actually made him fight harder. It rather irritated him, and he didn't like the idea of having to surrender. He wasn't exactly a warlike man; he had been a clerk, and was quiet and rather slow; but the message actually aroused a lot of aggression in him. Then the situation deteriorated. His division was hit hard and thrown back, and he lost contact with the command post. He had no food, except what he could find in the fields, and little ammunition. What was left of his company was isolated by itself in a rocky valley. Even then, he said, the morale was good, and there was no talk of surrendering. As a matter of fact, he said, the others would have shot him if he had tried to surrender. But then a couple of our planes spotted them, shot up their hideout, and dropped some napalm. When it was over, he found himself alone, a half mile from where he had been, with half his jacket burned off, and no sign of any of his company. A couple of hours later some of our tanks came along. And only then did the leaflet have an effect. He remembered it had told him to surrender with his hands up, and he did so.

In other words, the communication had no effect (even had an opposite effect from the one intended) so long as the situation, the personality, and the group norms were not favorable. When the situation deteriorated, the group influence was removed, and the personality aggression was burned up, then finally the message had an effect. I tell you this story hoping it will teach you what it taught me: that it is dangerous to assume any simple and direct relationship between a message and its effect without knowing all the other elements in the process.

THE NATURE OF MASS COMMUNICATION

Now let us look at mass communication in the light of what we have already said about communication in general.

The process is exactly what we have described, but the elements in the process are not the same.

The chief source, in mass communication, is a communication organization or an institutionalized person. By a communication organization we mean a newspaper, a broadcasting network or station, a film studio, a book or magazine publishing house. By an institutionalized person we mean such a person as the editor of a newspaper, who speaks in his editorial columns through the facilities of the institution and with more voice and prestige than he would have if he were speaking without the institution.

The organization works exactly as the individual communicator does. It operates as decoder, interpreter, and encoder. On a newspaper, for example, the input to be decoded flows in through the news wires and the reporters. It is evaluated, checked, amplified where necessary, written into a story, assigned headline and position, printed, distributed. This is the same process as goes on within an individual communicator, but it is carried out by a group of persons rather than by one individual. The quality of organization required to get a group of reporters, editors, and printers working together as a smooth communication unit, decoding, interpreting, and encoding so that the whole operation and product has an individual quality, is a quite remarkable thing. We have become so used to this performance that we have forgotten how remarkable it is.

Another difference between the communication organization and the individual communicator is that the organization has a very high ratio of output to input. Individuals vary, of course, in their output-input ratios. Persons who are in the business of communicating (preachers or teachers, for example) ordinarily have higher ratios than others, and so do naturally talkative persons who are not professional communicators. Very quiet persons have relatively higher input. But the communication institution is so designed as to be able to encode thousands — sometimes millions — of identical messages at the same time. To carry these, intricate and efficient channels must be provided. There have to be provisions for printing and delivering thousands of newspapers, magazines, or books, for making prints of a film and showing them in hundreds or thousands of theaters, for translating sound waves into electricity and distributing it through wires and through the air to millions of receiving sets.

The *destinations* of mass communication are individuals at the ends of these channels — individuals reading the evening paper, looking through the new magazine, reading the new book, sitting in the motion picture theater, turning the dial on the radio set. This receiving situation is much different from that which pertains in face-to-face communication, for one thing, because there is very little direct *feedback* from the receivers to the sender. The destination who, in a face-to-face situation, will nod his head and smile or frown while the sender is speaking, and then encode a reply himself, will very seldom talk back to the radio network or write a letter to the editor. Indeed, the kind of feedback that comes to a mass communication organization is a kind of inferential expression — receivers stop buying the publication, or no longer listen to the program, or cease to buy the product advertised. Only in rare instances do these organizations have an opportunity to see, more directly than that, how their messages are going over. That is one reason why mass communication conducts so much audience research, to find out what programs are being listened to, what stories are being read, what ads attended to. It is one of their few substitutes for the feedback which makes interpersonal communication so relatively easy to plan and control.

The following chapters will have something to say about the audiences of the different media, and we need not discuss them in any detail here. These audiences cluster, not only around a newspaper, magazine, or television station, but also around certain stories in the paper, certain parts of the magazine, certain television or radio programs. For example, Station A will not have the same audience at 8:00 as it had at 7:00, because some of these listeners will have moved to Stations B or C, and some of the listeners from B and C will have moved to A. Newspaper D will not have the same audience on its sports pages as on its society pages, although there will be some overlap. What determines which offering of mass communication will be selected by any given individual? Perhaps the easiest way to put it is to say that choice is determined by the Fraction of Selection —

$$\frac{\text{Expectation of reward}}{\text{Effort required}}$$

You can increase the value of that fraction either by increasing the numerator or decreasing the denominator, which is to say that an individual is more likely to select a certain communication if it promises him more reward or requires less effort than comparable communications. You can see how this works in your own experience.

You are much more likely to read the newspaper or magazine at hand than to walk six blocks to the news stand to buy a bigger newspaper or magazine. You are more likely to listen to a station which has a loud clear signal than to one which is faint and fading and requires constant effort from you to hear at all. But if the big game of the week is on that faint station, or if your favorite author is in the magazine at the news stand, then there is more likelihood that you will make the additional effort. If you were a member of the underground in occupied France during World War II, you probably risked your life to hear news from the forbidden Allied radio. You aren't likely to stay up until 2 a.m. simply to hear a radio program, but if by staying up that long you can find out how the Normandy invasion is coming or who has won the Presidential election — then you will probably make the extra effort just as most of the rest of us did. It is hardly necessary to point out that no two receivers may have exactly the same fraction of selection. One of them may expect more reward from Milton Berle than will the other. One of them may consider it less effort to walk six blocks to the news stand than does the other. But according to how this fraction looks to individuals in any given situation, the audience of mass communication is determined.

Unlike lecture audiences and small groups, mass communication audiences (with the exception of the people in a motion picture theater at the same time) have very little contact with each other. People in one house listening to Jack Benny don't know whether anybody in the next house is listening to him or not. A person reading an editorial in the New York *Times* has little group feeling for the other people in this country who read editorials in the New York *Times*. These audiences are individuals, rather than groups. But each individual is connected with a group or groups — his family, his close friends, his occupational or school group — and this is a very important thing to remember about mass communication. The more we study it, the more we are coming to think that the great effects of mass communication are gained by feeding ideas and information into small groups through individual receivers. In some groups, as you well know, it is a sign of status to be familiar with some part of mass communication (for example, in the teen-age group to hear the currently screamable crooner, or in some business groups to read the *Wall Street Journal*). In many a group, it is a news story from the radio, or an editorial from the *Tribune,* or an article from the *Times,* or an article from one of the big magazines, that furnishes the subject of conversation on a given day. The story, or article, or editorial, is then re-interpreted by the group, and the result is encoded in group opinion and perhaps in group action. Thus it may well be that the chief influence of mass communication on individuals is really a kind of secondary influence, reflected to the group and back again.

We are ready now to draw a diagram of mass communication, and to talk about the kinds of messages this sort of system requires and what we know about predicting their effects. This is the way mass communication seems to work:

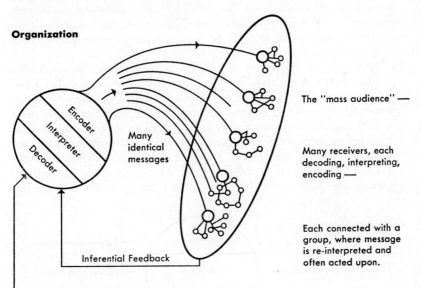

Organization

Encoder
Interpreter
Decoder

Many identical messages

Inferential Feedback

Input from news sources, art sources, etc.

The "mass audience" —

Many receivers, each decoding, interpreting, encoding —

Each connected with a group, where message is re-interpreted and often acted upon.

Now it is easy to see that there will be certain restrictions on the kinds of program which can be carried over these identical circuits to these little-known and changing audiences. The communication organization knows it is dealing with individuals, yet does not know them as individuals. Its audience research classifies, rather than individualizes, the audience. Audience research, that is, says that so many people are listening at a given time, or that so many men and so many women are likely to read a given kind of article, or that the readers of a given magazine are in the upper economic bracket and have had on the average 12 years of schooling. Whereas the individual communicator is dealing with individuals and able to watch the way his message is received and modify it if necessary, the organization is dealing only with averages and classes. It must pitch its reading level somewhere below the estimated average of its audience, in order not to cut off too many of the lower half of the audience. It must choose its content according to the best estimate it can make of what the broadest classes of receivers want and need. Whereas the individual communicator is free to experiment because he can instantly correct any mistake, the organization is loathe to experiment. When it finds an apparently successful formula, it keeps on that way. Or it changes the details but not the essentials. If one organization makes a great success with a given kind of message, others tend to copy it — not because of any lack of originality, but because this is one of the few kinds of feedback available from the mass audience. That is why we have so much sameness on the radio, why one successful comic strip tends to be followed by others of the same kind, one successful news or digest magazine by others, one kind of comedy program by others of the same kind, and so forth.

What can we say about the effects of these mass communication messages? For one thing, mass communication has pervasive effect because in many respects it has taken over the function of *society communicating*. Our society, like any other communication unit, functions as decoder, interpreter, and encoder. It decodes our environment for us, watches the horizon for danger and promise and entertainment. It then operates to interpret what it has decoded, arrives at a consensus so that it can put policy into effect, keep the ordinary interactions of communal life going, and helps its members enjoy life.

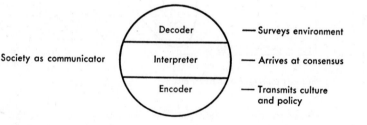

It also encodes — messages to maintain our relations with other societies in the world, and messages to transmit our culture to its new members. Mass communication, which has the power to extend our eyes and ears almost indefinite distances, and to multiply our voices and written words as far as we can find listeners or readers, has taken over a large share of the responsibility for this social communication. Newspapers, radio, television watch the horizon for us. By telling us what our leaders and experts think, by conducting a discussion or public issues, these media, and magazines and films as well, help us to interpret what is seen on the horizon and decide what to do about it. The textbook and educational films have led all the other media in encoding our culture so that the young persons coming into our society may learn as quickly and easily as possible the history, standards, roles, and skills they must know in order to be good members of society. This is not to say that all the media do not contribute in some degree to all these functions. For example, a book like *1984* may be as much a report of the horizon as the most current news story. And on the other hand, it is certainly true that a great deal of our culture is transmitted currently through television, radio, newspapers, and magazines. But the faster media are better equipped to be watchmen, and are more often so used. The slower, longer lasting media are better equipped to be teaching aids and are so used. The important thing is that *all* the mass media have important uses in providing the network of understandings without which the modern large community could not exist.

So much for the basic effect, which we see every day in the kind of customs around us, the people and problems talked about, and the language we speak. This is the slow, imperceptible effect. This is like building the stalagmite. But how about the specific effect of a given message transmitted by mass communication? How can we predict what the effect will be on the mass audience?

We can't predict the effect on the mass audience. We can only predict the effect on individuals. Communication organizations have developed group encoding, but there is only individual decoding. Therefore, we can predict the effect of mass communication only in the way we try to predict the effect of other communication — that is, in terms of the interaction of message, situation, personality, and group.

The first thing which becomes obvious, therefore, is that inasmuch as there are many different combinations of personality, situation, and group in any mass audience, there are likely to be many different kinds of effects. It is equally obvious that since mass communication doesn't know much about the individuals in its audience, predicting effects is going to be extremely difficult.

Nevertheless, there are certain things to be said. The problem of attention constantly faces mass communication. The average American (whoever he is) probably gives four or five hours a day to mass communication. If he lives in a big city, he gets a paper that would itself take half that time to read. (He doesn't read all of it.) He is offered the equivalent of two weeks of radio and television every day from which he can choose. He is offered a bewildering array of magazines and books and films. From these also he must choose. Other attractive ways to spend leisure compete with communication. He sometimes combines them — listening to music while he reads, playing cards or eating while he hears a newscast, playing with the baby while he watches television. Therefore, we can predict at least that any individual will have a fairly small chance of selecting any given item in mass communication, and that if he does select it, his level of attention may be rather low. This is responsible for many cases of "mis-hearing" radio. We know also that readership of the average newspaper story falls off sharply after the first few paragraphs, so that a member of the mass audience is likely not to see at all the latter part of a long newspaper story.

There are of course many cases in which markedly high attention is aroused by mass communication, and plentiful instances of listeners identifying closely with radio characters and adopting the mannerisms and language of movie heroes. It has been said that the mass media have brought Hollywood, Broadway, and Washington nearer than the next town, and there is a great deal of truth in this. There are also some cases in which very spectacular overt results have been accomplished by mass communication.

Let us recall one of them. Can you remember when CBS broadcast Orson Welles' performance of H. G. Wells' "War of the Worlds"? The script featured the invasion of the United States by armies from outer space. Perhaps you were one of the people who ran screaming for the hills, or armed yourself to wait for the invaders, or tried to call your loved ones long distance for a farewell talk. Or perhaps you were not. Perhaps you were one of those who heard the CBS announcers explain carefully that it was a play made from a book of fiction. Those who didn't hear those announcements were engaged in proving what we have just said about the low level of attention to some parts of mass communication.

But that doesn't entirely explain why people became hysterical and did things they were rather ashamed of the next day. And in truth, this is one of the really spectacular examples of mass communication effect. This happened without any specific reference to groups; it happened spontaneously in thousands of homes near the supposed scene of invasion. Why did it happen? Research men have studied the incident, and think they have put together the puzzle. For one thing, it was a tense time. People were full of anxiety, which could have been triggered off in many ways. In the second place, people trusted — still trust — radio news; the play was in the form of newscasts and commentaries. Therefore, the communication as it was interpreted really represented a spectacular change in the situation: the Martians were invading! Apparently the group element played no large part in this event, but the other three did. The message was accepted (minus the important identification as fiction). The listeners had a good deal of anxiety ready to be used. The message convinced them that the situation had indeed changed for the worse. Each according to his own personality and situation then took action.

As we have said, that was, fortunately, one of the few really spectacular examples of mass behavior. Another one was the Gold Rush that resulted in the 1890's when the newspapers brought word of gold in Alaska. Some people might say that what the Communists have been able to accomplish is a spectacular advertisement for the power of mass communication, and that subject is worth looking at because it shows us not only some of the differences between the ways we use the mass media and the way dictators use them, but also some of the principles of communication effect.

It is true that one of the first acts of the Communists, when they take over a country, is to seize the mass communication system. (That was also one of Hitler's first acts.) They also seize the police power and the control of productive resources, and they organize an intricate system of Party groups and meetings. I don't know of any case in which the Communists have put the whole burden of convincing people and gaining members on mass communications alone. They always provide a group structure where a convert can get reinforcement, and meetings to which a potential convert can be drawn. They use mass communication almost as an adjunct to these groups. In Korea and China, the mass media actually become texts for the groups. And the Communists do one thing more. If at all possible, they secure a monopoly on the mass communication reaching the people whom they are taking over. When they took Seoul, Korea, in 1950, they confiscated radio receivers wherever they found receivers despite the fact that they had captured Radio Seoul, intact, the most powerful transmitter in that part of Asia. They were willing to give up the use of Radio Seoul, if by so doing they could keep their subjects from foreign radio.

Now obviously, a state monopoly on communication, as well as control of resources and organization of a police state, is a long way from our system. And as long as our mass media are permitted free criticism and reporting, and as long as they represent more than one political point of view, we have little to worry about in a political way from them. But even though we may look with revulsion at the Communist way of using mass communication, still we can study it. And let us refer back to the four elements which we said were instrumental in bringing about communication effects — message, situation, personality, and group. The Communists control the messages. By their police power, control of resources (and hence of food and pay), they can structure the situation as they see fit. Their group organization is most careful, and offers a place — in fact compels a place — for every person. Thus they control three of the four elements, and can use those three to work on the fourth — the personalities of their receivers.

The Communists, who have now had 35 years practice in the intensive use of mass communication for accomplishing specified effects, are apparently unwilling to predict the results of their communication unless they can control three of the four chief elements which enter into the effect.

Let us take one final example. There is a great deal of violence in mass communication content today. Violence is interesting to children. Yet only a few children actually engage in acts of criminal violence. Most children do no such things. They sample the violent material, and decide they would rather play football. Or they attend faithfully to the violent material, use it to clear out vicariously some of the aggressions they have been building up, and emerge none the worse for the experience. Or they adopt some of the patterns in a mild and inoffensive way when they play cops and robbers. Only a few children learn, from the mass media, techniques of crime and violence which they and their pals actually try out. Now what is it that determines which of those children will be affected harmfully by those messages of violence, and which will not?

We can attempt to answer this question from cases we have studied. And the answer is simply that the other three elements — personality, situation, and group influence — will probably determine the use made of the message. If the child is busy with athletics, Scouts, church, or other wholesome activities, he is not likely to feel the need of violent and antisocial actions. On the other hand, if he is bored and frustrated, he may experiment with dangerous excitement. If he has a healthy personality, if he has learned a desirable set of values from his family group, he is less likely to give in to motivation toward violence. On the other hand, if his value standards are less certain, if he has lost some of his sense of belonging and being loved (possibly because of a broken home), he may entertain more hospitably the invitation to violence. If the group he admires has a wholesome set of standards, he is not likely to try an undesirable response, because the group will not reinforce it. On the other hand, if he belongs to a "gang" there is every reason to expect that he will try some of the violence, because in so doing he will win admiration and status in the group. Therefore, what he does will depend on the delicate balancing of these influences at a given time. Certainly no one could predict — except possibly on an actuarial basis — from merely seeing such a message exactly what the response to it would be. And it is entirely probable in the case we have mentioned that the community, the home, and the school — because they influence so greatly the other three elements — would have much more to do with the young person's response than would the message itself.

The all-pervasive effect of mass communication, the ground swell of learning that derives from mass communication acting as *society communicating* — this we can be sure of, and over a long period we can identify its results in our lives and beliefs. The more specific effects, however, we must predict only with caution, and never from the message alone without knowing a great deal about the situation, the personality, and the group relationship where the message is to be acted upon.

The Primary Effect — Attention

Introductory Note

THE ANATOMY OF ATTENTION

Communication is a buyer's market. Far more stimuli come to us than we are able to attend to. When we drive downtown, we notice very little about the houses and people on both sides of the street. Yet they are all the time offering stimuli to our senses. In other situations — for example, if we are looking for an address along the street — we may pay close attention. But when we drive downtown we are probably attending only to the traffic lights, automobiles, pedestrians at crossings, and other signals that help us drive safely where we want to go.

The signs of communication have to compete for an audience. You can see how this works for the mass media, and a little reflection will show you that it operates also in face-to-face conversation. How often, for example, do you have the undivided attention of the person you are talking to?

There is good reason to think that we scan our communication environment like an index, selecting among cues and concentrating our attention on the signs associated with the cues that specially attract us. You can see this operate when we scan the newspaper headlines, and sometimes when we use tables of contents. It seems also to be operative when we listen to voice radio. For example, experiments indicate that we habitually listen to a newscast at relatively low level of attention until a cue word or phrase awakens our attention and invites us to respond to the group of signs associated with the cue.

Furthermore, we tend to perceive the message in terms of the index cue. For example, the meaning we perceive in a picture often depends greatly on the caption. Two different newspaper headlines can result in two different impressions of the story. A word like "but" (as an experiment with public discussion indicates) can apparently index the material that follows it as "negative" regardless of the nature of the material.

Experimental work on this index function is in very early stages, and the process is not wholly understood as yet. Nevertheless, the idea promises to have important implications for encoders, who may find they should spend more effort devising index systems, spacing out and weighting their index cues.

The principles that determine whether a cue will attract attention may be described simply as follows:

(1) *Availability.* The first requisite is to deliver the signal, to make it easy to pick up. Other things being equal, you are more likely to tune in a program where the signal is strong and clear than one which fades and blurs and requires you to strain to hear. Other things being equal, you are more likely to look at a large billboard placed where you can conveniently see it as you stop for a traffic light, than you are to see a small placard on a house past which you drive at 60 miles an hour. Other things being equal, you are more likely to read the newspaper available when you are home and relaxed for the evening. *Other things being equal.* Of course, things are not always equal. During the Nazi occupation, Frenchmen who had radios were willing to strain to hear, if by so doing they could hear the BBC in place of the official Nazi radio. The few people in occupied Seoul during the summer of 1950 who had radios were willing to risk their lives in order to hear the UN radio for a few minutes a day, instead of the much more easily available Communist radio. But these things were done because of other motivations. Except for these motivations, the principle of least effort would have applied in those cases as it applies in the everyday commonplace act of discriminating among broadcasting stations, newspapers, theaters, and advertising signs.

(2) *Contrast.* Your attention is likely to be attracted to any signal which contrasts notably with the rest of your environment, providing that signal is readily available. Something that is noticeably louder, or brighter, or larger; a sudden movement in a static field; a sudden change in tone, intensity, pace, mass — all these things will serve to draw attention to themselves. Within the limits of ready availability, the converse will also hold. That is, a few seconds of silence in the midst of continuing sound, an autumn pastel in the midst of bright summer landscapes, a runner who suddenly stops in the middle of a race — these too will attract attention. This is one of the most valuable principles for the construction of advertising materials, and it has many implications.

But let us here record one point of caution in using the principle. It is easy to overdo loudness and size contrast and "novelty." It is easy for radio announcers and commentators, for example, to enter into an impossible competition for attention through loudness and excitement. The attention-drawing effect of loudness seems to operate on a kind of Weber's Law which, as you remember, is the psychophysical principle that constantly *increasing* differentials are required for discrimination among weights as the weights are increased. In other words, in a competition to attract attention through loudness, as the voices grow louder and louder, the intervals which separate the loudness of the speakers must be made greater and greater, if any difference is to be perceived. Low in the scale, the difference may be only one decibel; it may be 10 decibels, high in the scale of intensity. If loudness and excitement were the only tools with which radio commercials could compete, then soon radio announcers would be reduced to screaming. If intensity were the only means of attracting attention, then size would soon become impracticable, sound unsupportable, and brightness merely garish. Contrast must be attained by other means as well. A very good reason for using other means is the fact that if an intensity cue, once selected, does not adequately reward the selector, then the selector will be much less likely to respond to a similar cue the next time. The sensitivity, that is, may be decreased. Experiments have shown, for example, that words like "Flash!" and "Bulletin!" used indiscriminately, will at first raise the attention, but quickly lose their attention-gathering effect if the rewards are not proportional to the strength of the cues.

Repetition should also be mentioned under this head. Not only does it make a cue statistically more readily available, and in contrast with non-continuing cues; but also it seems to have the power of accumulating attention power — as a series of very small stimuli, for example, will finally trigger a nerve current.

(3) *Reward and threat.* This is perhaps too simple a way of trying to state the fact that the relation of a cue to a receiver's needs, wants, motivations, interests, habits, roles, frames of reference — however we want to codify his personality — will have a great deal to do with determining whether it attracts attention. A familiar name in a headline, a picture of one's own street, a story about the university football team in which one feels an almost personal pride, a story about a polio epidemic which may affect one's children, a story about a subject which has previously rewarded us and been remembered — cues like these will certainly attract attention. Similarly, we tend to be attracted to some cues because they fit the roles we play in society; they are the things that are "done," the things that are "read," the things we ought to be informed on. We respond to many cues simply because of habit (e.g., to turn on a certain radio program). In a sense, all this activity can be explained in terms of the reward or threat which the cues offer an individual scanner, or the habits that have grown out of rewarded responses.

A communicator is in the position of trying to arrange his index cues so that they will appeal to the personality needs of his audience. Some of these will be individual and personal; others will be widespread and general. For example, stories about Lindbergh in 1927 would have a personal-acquaintance appeal to a few hundred or thousand people, but vast numbers could enjoy the conflict situation of a man against an ocean, and could identify with the American boy who had that adventure and won the victory. The face-to-face communicator will therefore draw on all he knows about his listener, all that he can find out by feedback, in order to cue his message to the personal interests of the listener and thus get as much of the attention as possible. The mass communicator, on the other hand, will consider the general interests and needs of his audience, and try to cue his messages to the interests of large groups. This fact has been responsible for much of the dissatisfaction with mass communication, which, as it has grown larger, has been forced in the interests of economy to appeal to the interests of groups as large as possible, and thus to adopt what has been called a "lowest common denominator" approach, and ignore many specialized interests and needs.

The communicator tries to encode his material so as to give two dimensions of index information about it: intensity and subject matter. This is a delicate business, because if he gains attention by an intensity cue and then does not suitably reward the attention, or if he indicates (for example, by a scarehead) that a story has great reward or threat for the audience and the story does not live up to the head, he is in danger of extinguishing that response in his audience. Furthermore, if his headline does not accurately represent the story content, he may cause a misperception of the whole story. Therefore, the acts of indexing which seem most obvious to us — such as placing and headlining stories in a newspaper — are actually delicate problems in balancing intensity cues (headline size and blackness, position on the page, page in the paper, length of story, relation to pictorial material, etc.) against the predicted importance of the story to readers; and also constructing the headlines so as to indicate accurately what the content has to offer in response to the interests and needs of readers. If the signs of the story are themselves a kind of shorthand, then the headlines are shorthand for shorthand, and the weight of responsibility on the editor is very great indeed.

The audience, on its part, discriminates amongst the cues at hand, in terms of their relative availability (including economic availability), their contrast with environment, and the apparent reward or threat they offer. To a certain extent, as we have said, role and custom enter into the selection of an audience, but these also may be explained in terms of reward and learned habit.

We know something about how audiences organize themselves around the index cues of mass communication, although our information is better on gross problems (e.g., media audiences) than on finer questions (e.g., response to different kinds of cues). We know, for example, that in the United States two mass media (radio and newspapers) reach practically everyone, except the very young. Magazines reach about two-thirds of the people, motion pictures about one-half, books about one-fourth. Television is still not generally enough available to permit a fair comparison, although it seems destined to belong to the newspaper-radio group. There are great differences between countries of the world in respect to availability of mass media and therefore the size of audiences. In the United States, the circulation of daily newspapers is about 54 million, considerably more than one per average home. In Greece, where the population is about 8 million, the circulation of daily newspapers is about 800,000 or a little less than one paper for every two homes. In Burma, where there are 18 million people, the total daily circulation is about 100,000. In the United States there are about 95 million radios, or more than two per average home. In France, where the population is 41 million, there are 7.5 million receivers, a little less than one per home. In Ethiopia, where there are 17 million people, there are only 5,000 receiving sets.

In the United States, where our most detailed audience figures have been compiled, book reading and motion picture attendance fall off sharply after the teen years. After these years, school-motivation to use books is gone, and the social motivation to go to the movies is in competition with the more easily available entertainment at home. Newspaper reading seems to increase from the early teens through middle age, and radio listening appears to be on a high plateau during the middle years. People with more money or more education are likely to spend more time than others on mass media in general (except radio). And except for radio, and perhaps television, a kind of all-or-none law seems to be operative: that is, on the average, if an individual is above average in his communication time, he will also be above average in the amount of time he gives to each of the individual media.

If now we ask what materials different kinds of individuals select *within* the media, we come to a more complex situation. The first thing to be noted is that an individual selects only a small part of the mass communication material available to him. The average U. S. reader reads only one-fourth to one-third of the contents of a daily newspaper, chooses only a few per cent of the radio programs available to him. A very large proportion of attention to the mass media is to material which indexes itself as entertainment, or to pictures and other spectacular material which offers relatively easy going and a high level of excitement. The so-called "serious" use of mass communications (once past the textbook years) appears to be learned slowly, and to correlate highly with education and with pressing individual needs. Foreign political news, for example, is read by small percentages of

U.S. newspaper audiences unless it is couched in terms of conflict (as the 1952 Olympic Games were described, and as we tend increasingly to write of international diplomacy) or in terms that offer strong threat or reward to the reader or his family (for example, the threat of war or the promised reward of war's end). However, foreign political news will be read by larger percentages of college graduates than others, and by higher percentages of persons past the age of 30 than younger persons. Role differences account for some reading patterns, as for example the heavy male reading of sports, the heavy female reading of society news and fashion material. Likewise, the frame of reference is a powerful determinant, as can be seen in the heavy reading of local news in weekly newspapers, and in farmers' selection of agricultural material. However, it should be remembered that pictures and comics have highest readership in newspapers, comedians and thriller programs on the radio, a digest magazine and a picture magazine among periodicals.

Lest all this talk of mass communication throw perspective awry, we should mention here that the average person in the United States seems to devote only a little over four hours a day, about one-fourth of his waking hours, to mass communication. Most of his other waking hours are used, or are available, for individual communication — for conversations, telephone calls, letters, etc. If we then ask about the average person's *focus* of attention, we can assume that it decreases swiftly as it goes out from his primary group. That is, the greater part of his attention is given to communication with his family and close friends. Another part is devoted to business and acquaintances; a smaller part to the affairs of his town and state; a still smaller part to national and world events. Within his mass communication time, a considerable part of his attention is focussed on "escape" materials, which temporarily take him away from the threat or decision situations which surround his vote, his business, his health, or his home. There must be great individual differences, however, about which we know all too little, in the attention patterns of different individuals, and in different cultures. Actually this is a very important kind of knowledge, not only in the study of personality growth and communication practices, but also in the comparative study of cultures and the study of international relations. It is a matter of considerable importance to us at this moment, for example, to know what signals from the outside world come to the attention of the ordinary Russian or Chinese, Indian or Arab.

Why

They

Attend

to

Mass

Communication

The four following papers represent attempts by social scientists to find out why people read or listen to mass media. Dr. Berelson tries to find out some of the reasons why persons read newspapers by finding what they miss when they can't get newspapers. Using detailed interviews, Miss Wolfe and Miss Fiske analyze the reasons for reading comics, and Miss Herzog the gratifications that come from radio serial listening. Messrs. Waples, Berelson, and Bradshaw analyze in a broad way the reasons for reading.

▲ BERNARD BERELSON

What "Missing the Newspaper" Means

INTRODUCTION

In the late afternoon of Saturday, June 30, 1945, the deliverymen of eight major New York City newspapers went on strike. They remained on strike for over two weeks, and during that period most New Yorkers were effectively deprived of their regular newspaper reading. They were able to buy the newspaper *PM* and a few minor and specialized papers at newsstands, and they could buy copies over the counter at central offices of some newspapers. But the favorite papers of most readers were simply inaccessible to them for seventeen days.

These unusual circumstances presented a good opportunity for various interested parties — advertisers, newspaper publishers, radio executives, social scientists — to gauge public attitudes toward the newspaper, and at least three general polls of opinion were independently conducted during the strike. Some if not all findings of two polls have been made public, one by the Elmo Roper agency and the other by Fact Finders Associates, Inc. This article is a report on the third, an exploratory survey conducted for the Bureau of Applied Social Research, Columbia University.

According to the published findings, the Roper and Fact Finder organizations directed their efforts to determining what people had done in order to keep up with the news, what parts of the newspaper they particularly missed, and how much they missed the newspapers as the strike went on. On no specific question are their results strictly comparable, but in three ways they aimed at the same general atti-

▲ Dr. Berelson, who is director of the Behavioral Sciences Division of the Ford Foundation, first published this paper in *Communications Research, 1948-1949,* edited by Paul Lazarsfeld and Frank Stanton, published and copyright by Harper & Brothers (New York, 1949). It is reprinted here by permission of the publisher and copyright holder.

tudes or behavior, although in quite different ways. Both agencies attempted to get at the nature of the substitute for the newspaper, and in both cases respondents stressed that they listened to news broadcasts over the radio. Both attempted, in quite different ways, to discover what parts of the newspaper were particularly missed, and in both cases respondents stressed news (national, local, and war news) and advertising. Finally, both attempted to get at the degree to which the newspapers were actually missed, and in both cases respondents indicated that they missed the papers intensely.

Because the questions used by the two polling agencies differed greatly, the results are not strictly comparable. Furthermore, neither poll is able to interpret its data, which consist altogether of "surface facts," relevant only to the specific question at hand. Saying that one "misses the newspaper," or a part of it, can cover a variety of psychological reactions. What does "missing the newspaper" mean? Why do people miss it? Do they really miss the parts they claim, to the extent they claim? Why do they miss one part as against another? The Roper and Fact Finders polls bring little or nothing to bear on such questions, which are at the core of the basic problem, namely, to understand the function of the modern newspaper for its readers. Neither poll succeeds in getting at the more complex attitudinal matters operating in the situation.[1]

It was to attack this problem that the present study was conducted. At the end of the first week of the strike, the Bureau of Applied Social Research of Columbia University sponsored a quite different kind of study of people's reactions to the loss of their newspapers. Where the Roper and Fact Finders surveys were extensive, the Bureau's was intensive, designed to secure psychological insight in order to determine just what not having the newspaper meant to people. It is an axiom in social research, of course, that such studies can most readily be done during a crisis period like that represented by the newspaper strike. People are not only more conscious of what the newspaper means to them during such a "shock" period than they are under normal conditions, but they also find it easier to be articulate about such matters.[2]

Accordingly, the Bureau conducted a small number (60) of inten-

[1] On the necessity of "probes" to elicit the real "meaning" of straight replies, see Hadley Cantril and Research Associates, *Gauging Public Opinion* (Princeton: Princeton University Press, 1944), "Part One. Problems Involved in Setting the Issues."

[2] For an experiment designed to test the intensity of news interest of people relying primarily on newspapers and of those relying primarily on radio, see Paul F. Lazarsfeld, *Radio and the Printed Page* (New York: Duell, Sloan and Pearce, 1940), pp. 246-50. In this experiment, each group of respondents was deprived of its main source of news and their reactions to this situation were studied.

sive interviews.[3] The sample, stratified by rental areas in Manhattan, provided a good distribution by economic status although it was high in education. No attempt was made to secure statistically reliable data on poll questions of the Roper or Fact Finders sort (although for a few similar questions, such as what was missed in the papers, the results are the same as those from the Roper survey). Instead, the Bureau's interviews were designed to supply so-called qualitative data on the role of the newspaper for its readers, as that became evident at such a time. The results are not offered as scientific proof, but rather as a set of useful hypotheses.

In brief, then, the two polls on the subject present certain "surface facts," without knowing just what they mean. This study tries to suggest what "missing the newspaper" really means. Let us start with people's stereotyped responses to questions about missing the newspaper.

THE ROLE OF THE NEWSPAPER: WHAT PEOPLE SAY

Because of people's inclination to produce accepted slogans in answer to certain poll questions, there is always the danger that verbal response and actual behavior may not correspond. This danger was confirmed here. Intensive follow-up interviewing of the respondents demonstrated that practically everyone *pays tribute* to the value of the newspaper as a source of "serious" information about and interpretation of the world of public affairs, although not everyone uses it in that way. During the interview our respondents were asked whether they thought "it is very important that people read the newspapers or not." Almost everyone answered with a strong "Yes," and went on to specify that the importance of the newspaper lay in its informational and educational aspects. For most of the respondents, this specification referred to the newspaper as a source of news, narrowly defined, on public affairs.

However, not nearly so many people use the newspaper for this approved purpose, as several previous reading and information studies have shown. The general tribute without supporting behavior was evident in this study as well. When the respondents were given the opportunity to say spontaneously why they missed reading their regular newspapers, only a very few named a specific "serious" news event of the period (such as the Far Eastern war or the British elections) whereas many more answered with some variant of the "to-keep-informed" cliché or named another characteristic of the newspaper (e.g., its departmental features).

At another point in the interview, respondents were asked directly, "What news stories or events which happened last week (i.e., before

[3] A copy of the questionnaire appears in Appendix F, p. 309.

the strike) did you particularly miss not being able to follow up?" Almost half the respondents were unable to name any such story or event whereas others named such non-"serious" news stories as the then-current Stevens murder case. About a third of the respondents did cite a "serious" news event, most of them the Far Eastern war. Furthermore, directly following this question, the respondents were asked which of a list of six front-page stories of the week before they had missed "not being able to follow up in your regular paper."[4] Here, too, only a little more than a third of the respondents said that they had missed reading about the average serious event in this list. Thus, although almost all the respondents speak highly of the newspaper's value as a channel of "serious" information, only about a third of them seemed to miss it for that purpose.[5]

In brief, there seems to be an important difference between the respondents' *general* protestations of interest in the newspaper's "serious" purposes and their *specific* desires and practices in newspaper reading. The respondents' feeling that the newspaper "keeps me informed about the world" seems to be rather diffuse and amorphous, and not often attached to concrete news events of a "serious" nature. Again, for example, take the answer to our question, "Now that you don't read your regular newspaper, do you feel you know what's going on in the world?" Fully two-thirds of the respondents felt that they did not know what was going on although, as we have seen, only about half that many had any notion of what in the world they wanted more information about. To miss the newspaper for its "serious" news value seems to be the accepted if not the automatic thing to say.

[4] The six events were: Changes in President Truman's cabinet; developments in the Far Eastern War; the case of Mrs. Stevens; diplomatic events after the San Francisco Conference; the domestic food situation; the Langford murder case.

It should be mentioned in this connection that the strike occurred during a relatively quiescent news period. And this may have lowered the extent to which people missed reading about specific events.

[5] We attempted to get at the effect of the loss of newspapers upon the informational level of the respondents by asking them to identify a series of important news stories, pre-strike and intra-strike. On the whole, they were just as well informed about the intra-strike events as about the pre-strike events. However, this is inconclusive because it does not take into account either the fullness of information about such important stories or the extent of information about middle-sized and small news stories which do not get such extensive radio coverage.

Parenthetically, it is noteworthy that apparently no rumors gained currency during the newspaper strike. We tried to investigate the circulation of rumors by asking the respondents, "Have you heard from other people about any events or happenings which you haven't heard over the radio or read about?" This question drew a complete blank. Apparently access to the radio nipped any possible rumors in the bud.

But this does not mean that the newspapers were not genuinely missed by their readers. There were many spontaneous mentions of the intensity with which the respondents missed their papers, and several of those who missed them a good deal at the beginning of the strike felt even more strongly about it as the week wore on. The question is, *why* did people miss the newspaper so keenly. However, let us first review the several uses to which readers typically put the newspaper. This is the next step in our effort to put content into a check mark on a poll questionnaire by suggesting what "missing the newspaper" really means.

THE USES OF THE NEWSPAPER

The modern newspaper plays several roles for its readers. From the analysis of our intensive interviews, we have attempted to construct a typology of such roles, or functions, of the newspaper. Obviously the types enumerated here, while discrete, are not necessarily mutually exclusive for any one newspaper reader. Undoubtedly, different people read different parts of the newspaper for different reasons at different times. The major problem is to determine the conditions under which the newspaper fulfills such function as those developed here — and perhaps others — for different kinds of people. In this connection, the special value of a small group of detailed interviews lies in the identification of hypotheses which can then be tested, one way or the other, by less intensive methods. In other words, such "qualitative" interviews suggest the proper questions which can then be asked, in lesser detail, for "quantitative" verification.

In this section we shall mention briefly several immediate uses of the newspaper which we found in the interviews. The illustrative quotations are typical of those appearing in the interviews. Some of these uses correspond to acknowledged purposes of the newspaper, others do not.

For Information About and Interpretation of Public Affairs

There is a core of readers who find the newspaper indispensable as a source of information about and interpretation of the "serious" world of public affairs. It is important to stress, in this connection, that this interest is not limited simply to the provision of full information about news events. Many people are also concerned with commentaries on current events from both editorials and columnists, which they use as a touchstone for their own opinions. For example:

I don't have the details now, I just have the result. It's almost like reading the headlines of the newspaper without following up the story. I miss the detail and the explanation of events leading up to the news. I like to get the story behind and the development leading up to — it's more penetrating . . . I like to analyze for myself why things do happen and after getting the writers' opinions of it from the various newspapers, in which each one portrays the story in a different manner, I have a broader view and a more detailed view when I formulate my own opinion.

As a Tool for Daily Living

For some people the newspaper was missed because it was used as direct aid in everyday life. The respondents were asked, "Since you haven't been able to get your regular newspaper, have you found some things that you can't do as well without it?" Fully half of them indicated that they had been handicapped in some way. Many people found it difficult if not impossible to follow radio programs without the radio log published in the newspaper. Others who might have gone to a motion picture did not like the bother of phoning or walking around to find out what was on. A few business people missed such merchandising comments as the arrival of buyers; others were concerned about financial and stock exchange information. Several women interested in shopping were handicapped by the lack of advertisements. A few close relatives of returning soldiers were afraid they would miss details of embarkation news. A couple of women who regularly followed the obituary notices were afraid that acquaintances might die without their knowing it. Finally, there were scattered mentions of recipes and fashion notes and even the daily weather forecast in this connection. In short, there are many ways in which many people use the newspaper as a daily instrument or guide and it was missed accordingly.

For Respite

Reading has respite value whenever it provides a vacation from personal care by transporting the reader outside his own immediate world. There is no question but that many newspaper stories with which people readily identify supply this "escape" function satisfactorily for large numbers of people. Exhibit A in this connection is the comics, which people report liking for their story and suspense value. Beyond this, however, the newspaper is able to refresh readers in other ways, by supplying them with appropriate psychological relaxation. The newspaper is particularly effective in fulfilling this need for relief from the boredom and dullness of everyday life not only because of the variety and richness of its "human interest" content or because of its inexpensive accessibility. In addition, the newpaper is a good vehicle for this purpose because it satisfies this need without much cost to the reader's conscience; the prestige value of the newspaper as an institution for "enlightening the citizenry" carries over to buttress this and other uses of the newspapers.

When you read it takes your mind off other things.

It [the strike] gave me nothing to do in between my work except to crochet, which does not take my mind off myself as much as reading.

I didn't know what to do with myself. I was depressed. There was nothing to read and pass the time. I got a paper on Wednesday and felt a whole lot better.

For Social Prestige

Another group of readers seem to use the newspaper because it enables them to appear informed in social gatherings. Thus the newspaper has conversational value. Readers not only can learn what has happened and then report it to their associates but can also find opinions and interpretations for use in discussions on public affairs. It is obvious how this use of the newspaper serves to increase the reader's prestige among his fellows. It is not that the newspapers' content is good in itself but rather that it is good *for* something — and that something is putting up an impressive front to one's associates.

You have to read in order to keep up a conversation with other people. It is embarrassing not to know if you are in company who discuss the news.

Not that I am uneasy about what's happening but I like to know about the country so when people ask you questions you don't feel dumb and silly.

It makes me furious, absolutely furious, because I don't know what's going on and all my friends who are getting the papers do know.

For Social Contact

The newspaper's human interest stories, personal advice column, gossip columns, and the like provide some readers with more than relief from their own cares and routine. They also supply guides to the prevailing morality, insight into private lives as well as opportunity for vicarious participation in them, and indirect "personal" contact with distinguished people.

One explanation of the role of the human interest story is that it provides a basis of common experience against which urban readers can check their own moral judgments and behavior (the "ethicizing" effect).[6] The requirements for such stories are that they shall be understandable in terms of the reader's own experience and that they shall be "interesting." (One respondent who read the tabloids although he disliked them remarked that "the *Times* isn't written interestingly enough" and that "*PM* is the most honest paper but should have more interesting stuff like the *Journal-American*.") From the comments of a few respondents, it appears that the human interest stories and the gossip columnists do serve something of this purpose. In fact, a few respondents indicated that they missed the newspaper because, so to speak, some of their friends resided in its pages. A few women who read the gossip columnists and the society pages inten-

[6] An extensive speculative analysis of this role of the newspaper's human interest story for the urban masses is reported by Helen MacGill Hughes, *News and the Human Interest Story* (Chicago: University of Chicago Press, 1940).

sively seemed to take an intimate personal interest in their favorite newspaper characters and to think of them in congenial terms.

I miss Doris Blake's column [advice to the lovelorn]. You get the opinions in Doris Blake of the girls and boys and I find that exciting. It's like true life — a girl expressing her life. It's like everyday happenings.

I always used to condemn the mud-slinging in the *News* and *Mirror,* and many times I swore I'd never buy them if it weren't for the features I like. But just the other day I said to a friend of mine that I'd never, never talk like that about the papers again, because now I know what it is to be without them.

I missed them [favorite columnists] for their information, their news, their interviews with various people, their interaction with people. It is interesting to know people's reactions. If you read the background of individuals, you can analyze them a little better.

I like the *Daily News.* It's called the "scandal sheet" but I like it. It was the first paper that I bought when I came to New York. When you live in a small town and read the papers you know everybody who's mentioned in the papers. The *News* is the closest thing to them. The pictures are interesting and it makes up for the lack of knowing people . . . You get used to certain people; they became part of your family, like Dorothy Kilgallen. That lost feeling of being without papers increases as the days go on. You see, I don't socialize much. There's no place that you can get Dorothy Kilgallen — chit-chat and gossip — and Louella Parsons with Hollywood news.

THE DESIRABILITY OF READING

This brief review of some uses to which readers typically put the modern newspaper serves to introduce the following sections, in which we shall try to elaborate other (nonconscious) psychological reasons for the genuine interest in newspaper reading. Here again, we shall use material from our intensive interviews as illustrations.

There is some evidence in our interviews to indicate that *reading itself* regardless of content is a strongly and pleasurably motivated act in urban society. The major substitute followed during the period ordinarily given to the reading of the newspaper was some *other* form of reading, of a non-"news" character.[7] For the most part, the content of such substitute reading seemed to be quite immaterial to the respondents, so long as "at least it was something to read":

[7] The data on substitute activities were secured by asking the respondent to reconstruct the *first* occasion on which he missed his regular newspaper, with these questions:

"How did you feel the very first time you weren't able to get your paper(s)?"
"When was it that you first missed the newspaper?"
"What did you do then instead of reading the paper?"

Such questions not only help the respondent to recall his feelings and actions but also locate them in concrete behavior. We followed up by asking about substitute activities for the rest of the week.

I read some old magazines I had.

I read whatever came to hand — books and magazines.

I read up on all the old magazines around the house.

I read whatever was lying around and the others I hadn't had a chance to read before.

I went back to older magazines and read some parts I didn't usually read.

From such quotations one gets an impression that reading itself, rather than *what* is read, provides an important gratification for the respondents. The fact is, of course, that the act of reading carries a prestige component in American life which has not been completely countered by the rise of "propaganditis." After all, important childhood rewards, from both parent and teacher, are occasioned by success in reading and thus the act has extremely pleasant associations. Not only do the people of this country support libraries to promote the practice of reading; they also give considerable deference to the "well-read" man. In fact, the act of reading is connected with such approved symbols as "education," "good literature," "the full man," "intellectuality," and thus takes on its own aura of respectability and value.[8] And largely because of this aura, it is "better" to read something, anything, than to do nothing. For example, an elderly salesman told us:

Life is more monotonous without the paper. I didn't know what to do with myself. There was nothing to do to pass the time. It just doesn't work, nothing to pass the time.

One might speculate that in addition to the apparent desire of such people not to be left alone with their thoughts — in itself another

[8] The idea of reading as a nonconscious pleasurable activity can be pushed one step further in our data. There are a few references in psychoanalytic literature which associate reading with oral activity. The fullest development of this hypothesis appears in an article by James Strachey, "Some Unconscious Factors in Reading," *International Journal of Psychoanalysis,* XI (1930), 322-31, which deals with some oral associations with reading, some possible oral origins of the associations, and some unconscious functions of reading. Similar references appear in Edward Glover, "Notes on Oral Character Formation," *International Journal of Psychoanalysis,* VI (1925), 139. Some notes on the association between sucking activity and eye attention in the first few months of life appear in Margaret A. Ribble, *The Rights of Infants: Early Psychological Needs and Their Satisfaction* (New York: Columbia University Press, 1943), p. 29. In view of this hypothetical background, it is worth noting that one group of responses in the interviews seems to illustrate this notion. Occasionally, in their spontaneous answers to general questions about missing the newspapers, the respondents used a figure of speech in describing how much they missed the newspaper. In almost every such case, the figure was an oral one: "A glass of water . . . a cup of coffee . . . smoking . . . an appetizer to dinner (radio to the newspaper) . . . thirsty for news . . . I felt as though someone had taken candy away from me just as I was going to put it in my mouth." While these remarks are of course not conclusive, they do suggest that the act of reading may serve some persons as a socially acceptable source of oral pleasure. Thus reading material may serve the function of a pacifier for adults.

gratification of reading to which we shall return — the Puritan ethic
is at work in such cases. That is, such people may feel that it is somehow immoral to "waste" time and that this does not occur if one reads
something, because of the "worthwhileness" of reading. In short, in
explaining why people missed their regular newspapers, one must
start by noting that the act of reading itself provides certain basic
satisfaction, *without primary regard for the content of the reading
matter.*

ANOTHER USE OF THE NEWSPAPER

Within this context, what of the newspaper? Of the major sources
of reading matter, the newspaper is the most accessible. It is also cheap
and its contents can be conveniently taken in capsules (unlike the
lengthier reading units in magazines and books). All in all, the
newspaper is the most readily available and most easily consumed
source of whatever gratifications derive from reading itself. In addition, there are some other general bases for the *intensity* with which
people missed the newspaper.

References by several people to "not knowing what's going on" and
to "feeling completely lost" illustrate the sort of *insecurity* of the
respondent which was intensified by the loss of the newspaper:

I am like a fish out of water . . . I am lost and nervous. I'm ashamed to
admit it.
I feel awfully lost. I like the feeling of being in touch with the world at large.
If I don't know what's going on next door, it hurts me. It's like being in jail
not to have a paper.
You feel put out and isolated from the rest of the world.
It practically means isolation. We're at a loss without our paper.

In some way, apparently, the newspaper represented something like
a safeguard and gave the respondents an assurance with which to
counter the feeling of insecurity and anomie pervasive in modern
society.

This need for the newspaper is further documented by references
to the *ritualistic and near-compulsive character* of newspaper reading.
Many people read their newspapers at a particular time of the day
and as a secondary activity, while they are engaged in doing something else, such as eating, traveling to work, etc. Being deprived of
the time-filler made the void especially noticeable and especially effective. At least half the respondents referred to the habit nature of the
newspaper: "It's a habit . . . when you're used to something, you
miss it . . . I had gotten used to reading it at certain times . . . It's
been a habit of mine for several years . . . You can't understand it not
being there any more because you took it for granted . . . The habit's
so strong . . . It's just a habit and it's hard to break it . . ." Some
respondents used even stronger terms:

Something is missing in my life.

I am suffering! Seriously! I could not sleep, I missed it so.

There's a place in anyone's life for that, whether they're busy or not.

I sat around in the subway, staring, feeling out of place.

The strength of this near-compulsion to read the newspaper was illustrated in other ways. Such diverse newspapers as the tabloid *News* and the *Times* sold thousands of copies daily over the counter at their central offices. One respondent "went from stand to stand until I decided that it was just no use trying to get one." Another walked ten blocks looking for a paper; another went to her newsstand every night during the first week of the strike, hoping to get a paper. One young man reread out-of-date newspapers more thoroughly, "as a resort." Still other respondents admitted to reading the paper regularly even though they believed that they could spend their time more profitably:

It replaces good literature.

I usually spend my spare time reading the papers and put off reading books and studying languages or something that would be better for me . . . [Most of the paper] is just escape trash, except possibly the classified ads and I'm beginning to waste time reading them now, too, when there's no reason for it, just habit.

In this connection, the notion that knowledge is power sometimes appears. One man reported that he felt uneasy "because I don't know what I am missing — and when I don't know I worry." A few people even seemed to suggest that their being informed about the world had something to do with the control of it. A private secretary, for example, recognizing that she was "just a little cog in the wheel," remarked sadly that she "felt cut off" but that "things go on whether you know about it or not." Presumably, the regular contact with the world through the columns of the newspaper gave this person the feeling that she was participating in the running of the world. But when the newspaper was withdrawn, she realized that her little contribution was not being missed.

This sort of analysis throws a new light on the fact that about twice as many people missed the newspaper *more* as this week went on than missed it less. For such people, the absence of the daily ritual was only intensified as the week wore on. Something that had filled a place in their lives was gone, and the adjustment to the new state of affairs was difficult to make. They missed the newspaper in the same sense that they would have missed any other instrument around which they had built a daily routine.

Only a few respondents gave an affirmative answer to our question, "Are there any reasons why you were relieved at not having a newspaper?" But even they revealed the near-compulsive nature of newspaper reading. In some cases the fascinating attraction of "illicit" content seemed to constitute the compelling factor, e.g., in the case of the middle-aged housewife who reported:

It was rather a relief not to have my nerves upset by stories of murders, rape, divorce, and the war . . . I think I'd go out more [without the newspapers] which would be good for me. Papers and their news can upset my attitude for the whole day — one gruesome tale after the other. My nerves would be better without the paper.

The typical scrupulousness of the compulsive character is apparent in this case of a middle-aged waiter who went out of his way to read political comment with which he strongly disagreed:

I hate the policy of the *Mirror* [his only newspaper] . . . the editorial writer and also the columnist DeCasseres. It's a pleasure not to read him . . . I didn't have an opportunity of disagreeing with Winchell.

In still other cases, the compulsion resembled an atonement for guilt feelings about nonparticipation in the war; the comments of two women respondents suggest that they had forced themselves to read the war news, as the least they could do in prosecuting the war:

Under the stress and strain of wartime conditions, my health was beginning to fail and I enjoyed being able to relax a little.

I've been reading war news so much, I've had enough of it.

A young housewife felt that it was her duty to follow the developments of the war "for the boys — the spirit of it." And such respondents were gratified at the newspaper strike because it provided them with a morally acceptable justification for not reading the newspaper, as they felt compelled to do. Once the matter was taken out of their hands they were relieved.

SUMMARY AND CONCLUSION

In this article we have attempted to elaborate and "deepen" the answers to typical poll questions applied to a complex set of acts and feelings. We have tried to go beyond the general protestations of the newspaper's indispensability and seek out some basic reader-gratifications which the newspaper supplies. In doing so, we have noted certain typical uses of the modern newspaper — both "rational" (like the provision of news and information) and non-"rational" (like the provision of social contacts and, indirectly, social prestige). In addition, however, we have hypothesized that reading has value per se in our society, value in which the newspaper shares as the most convenient supplier of reading matter. In addition, the newspaper is missed because it serves as a (non-"rational") source of security in a disturbing world and, finally, because the reading of the newspaper has become a ceremonial or ritualistic or near-compulsive act for many people. In this way, we have progressively tried to define, in psychological and sociological terms, what missing the newspaper really means.

▲ KATHERINE M. WOLFE

▲ MARJORIE FISKE

Why They Read Comics

Children's experiences in comic reading fall into one of two patterns which differ qualitatively as well as quantitatively.

The normal child is a "moderate reader" who uses comics as a means of ego-strengthening. In the early or "funny animal" stage, he expands his ego-experience through projection. Later, in the "adventure" stage, he inflates his ego by identification with an invincible hero. Finally, he stands on his own feet, and employs "true" comics as a tool for the real adventure which is life itself. He may turn back to his earlier comic favorites, but he now reads them only as a means of relaxation. For the normal child, then, comics are a means of healthful ego-strengthening and anon a source of amusement.

Other children do not seem to be so eager to fortify themselves for the experience of life. They seem not yet to have emancipated themselves from their parents to any great degree and are both incapable and unwilling to assume responsibility on their own. But their belief in their parents seems nevertheless to have been shaken. The experiences of seven or eight years have apparently shown them that all human beings are imperfect, and that one cannot always rely on their insight, their justice, or their efficiency; they have apparently witnessed instances in which their parents manifested injustice, ignorance, or weakness.

They therefore search for a more perfect father-figure, a being who is omnipotent but, at the same time, tangible and feasible. And such a father-figure they find in Superman. These children become fans. The comics, by providing an authority and power which settles the

▲ This is the summary and conclusion of an article which appeared in *Communications Research, 1948-1949*, edited by Paul Lazarsfeld and Frank Stanton, published and copyright by Harper & Brothers (New York, 1949). It is reprinted here by permission of publisher and copyright holder.

more difficult or ultimate issues, enables these children to perform their daily tasks without too much anxiety.

For normal children, then, the comics function as an adaptation mechanism, and efficiently satisfy real developmental needs.

For the maladjusted child, the comics satisfy, just as efficiently, an equally intense emotional need, but here the need itself is not so readily outgrown. The religion of comics is not easily given up, for the child is frightened and no new religion beckons.

But the possible dangerous effects of comics on fans must not be overestimated. The child's problems existed before he became a fan, and the comics came along to relieve him. That he became a fan can no more be blamed upon the comics, than morphine can itself be blamed when a person becomes a drug addict. The drug addict, of course, might have found a better solution for his problems if there were no morphine available. Or, and perhaps better, there may be a drug which bestows the benefits of morphine without the dangers of morphine. And comics are, of course, more easily manipulated than are drugs.

▲ HERTA HERZOG

*M*otivations and Gratifications of Daily Serial Listeners

LISTENING GRATIFICATIONS

A preliminary study based on 100 intensive interviews suggests three major types of gratification experienced by listeners to daytime serials.

Some listeners seem to enjoy the serials merely as a means of emotional release. They like "the chance to cry" which the serials provide; they enjoy "the surprises, happy or sad." The opportunity for expressing aggressiveness is also a source of satisfaction. Burdened with their own problem, listeners claim that it "made them feel better to know that other people have troubles, too."

On the one hand, the sorrows of the serial characters are enjoyed as compensation for the listener's own troubles.

Thus a woman who had a hard time bringing up her two children after her husband's death, mentions the heroine of *Hilltop House* as one of her favorites, feeling that she "ought not to get married ever in order to continue the wonderful work she is doing at the orphanage." This respondent compensates for her own resented fate by wishing a slightly worse one upon her favorite story character: preoccupied by her own husband's death she wants the heroine to have no husband at all and to sacrifice herself for orphan children, if she, the listener, must do so for her own.

On the other hand, in identifying themselves and their admittedly minor problems with the suffering heroes and heroines of the stories, the listeners find an opportunity to magnify their own woes. This is enjoyed if only because it expresses their "superiority" over others who have not had these profound emotional experiences.

A second and commonly recognized form of enjoyment concerns the

▲ Miss Herzog, who is a member of the research staff of McCann-Erickson, first published the article of which this is a part in *Radio Research, 1942-1943*, edited by Paul Lazarsfeld and Frank Stanton, copyright by the authors, and published by Duell, Sloan, and Pearce (New York, 1944). It is reprinted here by permission of the author.

opportunities for wishful thinking provided in listening. While certain people seem to go all out and "drown" their troubles in listening to the events portrayed in the serials, others use them mainly to fill in gaps of their own life, or to compensate for their own failures through the success pattern of the serials.

Thus a rather happily married woman whose husband happens to be chronically ill, listens to *Vic and Sade* mainly for the "funny episodes," pretending that they happen to herself and her husband. A woman whose daughter has run away from home to marry and whose husband "stays away five nights a week," lists *The Goldbergs* and *The O'Neills* as her favorites, each portraying a happy family life and a successful wife and mother.

A third and commonly unsuspected form of gratification concerns the advice obtained from listening to daytime serials. The stories are liked because they "explain things" to the inarticulate listener. Furthermore, they teach the listener appropriate patterns of behavior. "If you listen to these programs and something turns up in your own life, you would know what to do about it" is a typical comment, expressing the readiness of women to use these programs as sources of advice.

DAYTIME SERIALS AS SOURCES OF ADVICE

The observations in this preliminary case survey were so striking that it was decided to test the matter on a larger scale. Therefore, in the summer of 1942, the respondents in the Iowa survey who listen to daytime serials were asked the following question:

Do these programs help you to deal better with the problems in your own everyday life?

Yes_____ No_____ Never thought about it that way_____ Don't know_____.

Of some 2,500 listeners, 41 per cent claimed to have been helped and only 28 per cent not to have been helped. The remainder held that they had never thought about it that way or that they did not know, or refused to answer the question.

On the basis of numerous tabulations designed to identify the types of women who consider themselves "helped" by listening to radio serials, two conclusions can be drawn. The less formal education a woman has, the more is she likely to consider these programs helpful. This corroborates a previous observation that less-educated women probably have fewer sources from which to learn "how to win friends and influence people" and are therefore more dependent upon daytime serials for this end.

We find also that on all educational levels those women who think they worry more than other people, more frequently find relief in listening to serials than women who say they worry less. Both results are summarized in Table 1. Each figure indicates, for the given class of listeners, the proportion of women claiming that the serials help them. It will be seen that the figures in the first line (worries more) are always higher than the corresponding figures in the second line (worries less), and that there is an increase from left to right, that is, with decreasing education of the respondents.

TABLE 1

Proportion of Listeners to Daytime Serials Who Are Being Helped by Listening to Them

(Classified by education and relative extent of worrying)

Worries in relation to other women	Proportion of listeners being helped by serials		
	College %	High School %	Grammar school %
More..........................	42	50	52
Less..........................	34	37	44

The proportion of those who feel helped also increases with the number of stories heard. Whereas among those who listen to one serial only, 32 per cent said they had been helped, 50 per cent of those who listen to six or more serials claim to have been helped. This is not surprising because we would expect those women who are more ardent listeners to impute beneficial effects to serial dramas.

But these over-all figures do not yet give us a clear idea of what women mean when they talk about such "help." For the respondents in the Iowa survey, we have no additional information. We can, however, draw upon the results of some 150 case studies of serial listeners in New York and Pittsburgh. Interviewers[1] were instructed to obtain complete examples of advice gleaned from daytime serials. They were cautioned to secure accounts of concrete experiences and not rest content with general assertions of aid derived from serials.

Judging from this information, the spheres of influence exerted by the serials are quite diversified. The listeners feel they have been helped by being told how to get along with other people, how to "handle" their husbands or their boy friends, how to "bring up" their children.

I think Papa David helped me to be more cheerful when Fred, my husband, comes home. I feel tired and instead of being grumpy, I keep on the cheerful side. *The Goldbergs* are another story like that. Mr. Goldberg comes home scolding and he never meant it. I sort of understand Fred better because of it. When he starts to shout, I call him Mr. Goldberg. He comes back and calls me Molly. Husbands do not really understand what a wife

[1] For the interviews we are indebted to Mrs. Clare Marks Horowitz of the Pennsylvania College for Women and to Mrs. Jeannette K. Green of Columbia University's Office of Radio Research.

goes through. These stories have helped me to understand that husbands are like that. If women are tender, they are better off. I often feel that if my sister had had more tenderness she would not be divorced today. I saw a lot of good in that man.

Bess Johnson shows you how to handle children. She handles all ages. Most mothers slap their children. She deprives them of something. That is better. I use what she does with my children.

The listeners feel they have learned how to express themselves in a particular situation.

When Clifford's wife died in childbirth the advice Paul gave him I used for my nephew when his wife died.

They have learned how to accept old age or a son going off to the war.

I like Helen Trent. She is a woman over 35. You never hear of her dyeing her hair! She uses charm and manners to entice men and she does. If she can do it, why can't I? I am fighting old age, and having a terrible time. Sometimes I am tempted to go out and fix my hair. These stories give me courage and help me realize I have to accept it.

In *Woman in White* the brother was going off to war. She reconciled herself, that he was doing something for his country. When I listened it made me feel reconciled about my son — that mine is not the only one. In the story the brother is very attached to the family — he tells them not to worry, that he would be all right and would come back.

They get advice on how to comfort themselves when they are worried.

It helps you to listen to these stories. When Helen Trent has serious trouble she takes it calmly. So you think you'd better be like her and not get upset.

They are in a position to advise others by referring them to the stories.

I always tell the woman upstairs who wants my advice, to listen to the people on the radio because they are smarter than I am. She is worried because she did not have any education and she figures that if her daughter grows up, she would be so much smarter than she was. I told her to listen to *Aunt Jenny* to learn good English. Also, you can learn refinement from *Our Gal Sunday*. I think if I told her to do something and something would happen, I would feel guilty. If it happens from the story, then it is nobody's fault.

The desire to learn from the programs is further confirmed by the fact that one-third of 100 listeners specified problems which they would like to have presented in a serial. A few quotations will serve to illustrate these choices:

When a man's disposition changes suddenly after being married for a long time. He starts gambling and to be unfaithful. What's the explanation?

I should like to know how much a daughter should give her mother from the money she makes. I give everything I earn to my mother. Do I have to?

Whether I should marry if I have to live with my mother-in-law.

A story which would teach people not to put things over.

About religious and racial differences.

Unquestionably then, many listeners turn to the stories for advice and feel they get it. Nonetheless, the matter is not quite so simple as it seems.

A question suggested by the quoted comments concerns the adequacy of the aid and comfort. The woman who has learned to deprive her children of something rather than "to slap them" seems to be substituting one procedure for the other without an understanding of the underlying pedagogical doctrine. It is doubtful whether the relationship between a wife and her husband is put on a sounder and more stable basis when she has learned to realize that "men do not understand what their wives have to go through." One might wonder how much the bereaved nephew appreciated, at his wife's death, the speech his aunt had borrowed from her favorite story.

A second question concerns the extent of the influence. Frequently the advice seems confined to good intentions without any substantial influence on basic attitudes. An example of this may be found in the following remarks of a woman who listens to serials because the people in them are so "wonderful":

They teach you how to be good. I have gone through a lot of suffering but I still can learn from them.

Yet, this same woman, when asked whether she disliked any program, answered:

I don't listen to *The Goldbergs*. Why waste electricity on the Jews?

Obviously, the "goodness" she was "learning" had not reached the point of materially affecting her attitude toward a minority group. In the same context, we may note that the advice derived from a serial is often doled out to other people, to sisters, or neighbors, thus providing the listener with the status of an adviser without its responsibilities.

Thirdly, the women who claim to have profited from the serials frequently think of quite unrealistic situations. Thus, one listener felt she had learned considerably from a story in which the heroine suddenly came into a great deal of money; the story character was concerned with keeping her children from profligate waste. Although the listener felt there was no prospect of ever having so much money herself, nonetheless she considered that this episode offered valuable advice:

It is a good idea to know and to be prepared for what I would do with so much money.

Very likely, the advice obtained from that story served as a substitute for the condition of its applicability. Similarly, the wistful thinking connected with such "potential" advice is brought out in the following account of a young housekeeper:

I learn a lot from these stories. I often figure if anything like that happened to me what I would do. Who knows if I met a crippled man, would I marry him? If he had money I would. In this story (*Life Can Be Beautiful*), he was a lawyer, so it was really quite nice. These stories teach you how things come out all right.

The over-all formula for the help obtained from listening seems to be in terms of "how to take it." This is accomplished in various ways. The *first* of these is outright wishful thinking. The stories "teach" the Panglossian doctrine that "things come out all right." In a less extreme form, a claim on a favorable turn of events is established by the listener's taking a small preliminary step which accords with a pattern established in a serial. This may be illustrated by the following comment of a middle-aged listener:

In Helen Trent the girl Jean is in love with this playwright. She used to be fat and he did not pay any attention to her. . . . I am fat and I got to get thin. That story taught me that it is dangerous to reduce all by yourself. Helen Trent took that girl to a doctor. That's just what I did. I went to the doctor last night. I am going to start the diet next week.

This listener actually saw a doctor about her weight. She postponed starting her diet for "next week." By following the serial's "advice" to this extent, she seems to feel assured of having taken sufficient steps to guarantee herself a result as romantic as that in the serial. (By reducing, Jean, the story character, won the love of a man who had not cared for her before.)

A *second* way in which the listeners are helped to accept their fate is by learning to project blame upon others. Thus one of the previously quoted listeners obtains "adjustment" to her marital problems by finding out that husbands never understand their wives. *Thirdly,* the listeners learn to take things by obtaining a ready-made formula of behavior which simply requires application. References such as "Don't slap your children, but deprive them of something" characterize this type of learning. Listeners, worried about problems confronting them, learn to take things "calmly," not to get "excited" about them. As one person said:

I learned that if anything is the matter, do not dwell on it or you go crazy.

Calmness in the face of crises is certainly a useful attitude. However, it is not always sufficient for a solution of the problems.

These data point to the great social responsibility of those engaged in the writing of daytime serials. There can be no doubt that a large proportion of the listeners take these programs seriously and seek to apply what they hear in them to their own personal lives. Much of this application seems somewhat dubious if measured by the yardstick of real mastery of personal problems. No mass communication can fully safeguard itself against abused application. On the other hand, the argument that the primary purpose of daytime serials is entertainment rather than education does not apply here. The writers of daytime serials must live up to the obligations to which the influence of their creations, however unintended, commits them.

▲ DOUGLAS WAPLES

▲ BERNARD BERELSON

▲ FRANKLYN R. BRADSHAW

Why They Read

As here used, the term "predispositions" includes all the personal conditions involved in the reading experience. Such conditions derive from various aspects of the reader's total personality. They range from broad traits like age and sex, through the reader's habitual attitudes as shaped by his primary group associations, to the most intimate feelings he has about himself at the moment. His feelings toward particular aspects of the environment are in a constant state of flux. But such feelings tend to cluster about more general attitudes which are relatively constant. Such feelings, attitudes, and motives combine to determine the reader's predispositions toward what he reads. Such predispositions are always an important factor in the effects of the reading.

The reader's predispositions are involved in the effects of reading in two ways. They condition the reader's selection of publications and they condition his interpretation of what he reads. Almost any phase of the reader's personality may be involved in the reading experience. His personal traits, subject interests, and reading ability may determine which of the accessible publications he will choose to read. And his attitudes, group memberships, and previous knowledge of the topic may determine not only what meanings he will take from the content but also how he will react to them. So it is that two readers of a novel like *The Grapes of Wrath* or *Native Son* may differ in the way each "takes" the book and will hence show different effects. One may read it for the sensational story. The other may read it for the sociological analysis. The difference can be explained only by differences in predispositions which may be fundamental or merely a temporary mood.

▲ This is a chapter from *What Reading Does to People,* published and copyright by the University of Chicago, (Chicago, 1940). It is reprinted here by permission of the publisher and copyright holder. When they wrote this book, the authors were on the faculty of the University of Chicago Graduate Library School.

The same predispositions are often involved in both the selection and the interpretation of reading, but they need not be. The reader may select his reading from one set of conditions and respond to it from a totally different set. In either case, his predispositions contribute to the resultant effects. Hence it is permissible to relate predispositions to both the selection and the interpretation of publications in the same discussion.

The expression of the reader's predispositions, and hence their influence, does not stop once the publication is in the reader's hands. Other acts of "selection" take place during the actual reading and affect the reader's interpretations. The reader's interest in and use of the publication, together with the content elements that offer pleasant or unpleasant stimuli, will determine how much attention he will give it. His methods of reading, which may range from a hasty skimming to a close analysis, naturally affect both his response to the publication and its effects on him. The more apparent differences between successful and unsuccessful college students, for example, have been found rather in *how* the student reads than in *what* he reads. The successful student is marked by his disposition to read beyond assignments, to re-read, and to apply his reading to his experience. The reader's total background of training and experience determines what meanings he will assign to particular words and passages; wide variations in such meanings have been revealed in recent studies.[1] And, finally, his previous knowledge and his previous attitudes influence his whole understanding of and response to the publication. How much of it he credits, what he accepts and rejects, the criticisms and the applications he makes — in short, his various responses to the publication are determined by the kind of person the reader is, i.e., by the nature of his predispositions.

Readers, like publications, may be described in many ways, the description depending on what the investigator wants to know about them. Booksellers should know the incomes of their clients before attempting to sell expensive books. Librarians should know the demands of their patrons, as a guide to better book selection. Publishers of textbooks should know the reading ability of the students for whom their texts are written. Propagandists should describe the attitudes of readers on their own issues, in order to aim their arguments effectively. Our description should cover the predispositions which explain why readers select certain publications and why they respond to them as they do. We shall describe the personal traits, the attitudes, and the motives involved, and we shall attempt to relate differences in readers' predispositions to differences in their uses of print and hence to differences in the effects of reading.

[1] I. A. Richards, *Interpretation in Teaching* (New York: Harcourt, Brace & Co., 1924).

Starting with the widest distinctions, we may divide people into readers and nonreaders, and environment into print and nonprint. Certain important facts about readers may be learned by studying the nonreader.[2] Some nonreaders simply cannot read, others simply will not. The first group may comprise the foreign-born, who do not read the language of available publications.[3] It comprises otherwise intelligent adults who do not understand publications on their special interests because they lack the necessary reading skills.[4] They may, of course, be physically or mentally incapable of reading. Persons who will not read are those who "can't find the time." This means that they begrudge time spent on reading because the resulting satisfactions come far short of substitute satisfactions obtained by other uses of their time. For the population at large the other competing uses are mainly conversation and radio-listening.

By passing over nonreaders and nonprint, we come to readers of print. Classing readers by sex shows that such differences affect readers' preferences for fiction and other broad types of print. Women read a larger proportion of fiction than men.[5] Boys prefer realistic adventure and girls prefer imaginative stories with a sentimental touch.[6] Sex differences persist when other factors like age are held constant.[7] Women are less interested in reading about business and politics than in topics like personality types, marriage, and travel. In short, both men and women are primarily interested in reading about themselves. The closer a topic fits one's personal problems or fantasies, the stronger its appeal.[8] Thus, women favor nonfiction about personalities, travel, self-improvement, and successful marriage. Men prefer nonfiction concerning laws and legislation, military preparedness, and business methods.

For our illustrative purposes readers and reading may be still further subdivided by corresponding differences in education and in the relative "maturity" of the publications read. For example, women of varying amounts of formal schooling read authors of corresponding

[2] Helen A. Ridgway, "Community Studies in Reading: III. Reading Habits of Adult Non-users of the Public Library," *Library Quarterly*, VI (1936), 1-33.

[3] Ethel M. Fair, "The Public Library versus Other Sources of Books" (unpublished Master's thesis, Graduate Library School, University of Chicago, 1935).

[4] Lyman Bryson, "Printed Materials for Use in Adult Education as Seen by the Consumer," *Journal of Adult Education*, VIII (1936), 371-72.

[5] Douglas Waples, *People and Print: Social Aspects of Reading in the Depression* (Chicago: University of Chicago Press, 1937).

[6] Douglas Waples and Ralph W. Tyler, *What People Want To Read About: A Study of Group Interests and a Survey of Problems in Adult Reading* (Chicago: American Library Association and University of Chicago Press, 1931).

[7] *Reading in General Education* (American Council on Education, 1939), chap. vii.

[8] Waples and Tyler, *op. cit.*

intellectual maturity within the general fiction class.[9] Seventy per cent of the readers of "classics" are college students.[10]

The more highly educated readers are attracted to more mature publications because their wider intellectual experiences enable them to share the authors' more mature attitudes toward life. But such publications are more easily misunderstood. Thus Richards[11] illustrates the different meanings brought to poetry by the student's comment on Millay's sonnet: "What's this of death, from you who never will die?" Here certain implications of immortality drew responses which obscured both the idea and the effect the poet intended to convey. Korzybski[12] and his school report many types of misunderstandings due to deficiencies in the experiences needed to interpret abstractions as the author intends. In addition to fuller experience of life, education supplies the study habits, the reading skills,[13] and the technical or precise vocabularies of those who prefer the more mature publications.

We may next class readers by occupation. As the central fact in most people's lives, occupation has an important role in the selection and interpretation of reading. Its importance, of course, varies with the occupation. First come the many occupations that are essentially literary and whose members are virtually paid to read — teachers, writers, editors, the clergy, and all sorts of students. Next come the professions like law, medicine, engineering, and the higher branches of applied sciences in which reading is necessary to keep abreast of new developments. Third come occupations like salesmanship, farming, and homemaking, which have an extensive literature rather because they include so many practitioners than because the literature contributes much to the readers' vocational efficiency. Thereafter vocational differences merge with the differences in intelligence and training the vocations imply. Occupational differences, as such, are clearly revealed in many subject classifications of publications. The nonfiction interests of men engaged in the professions, in skilled, semiskilled, and unskilled labor conform closely to type.[14] However, the reader's occu-

[9] Jeannette Howard Foster, "An Experiment in Classifying Fiction Based on the Characteristics of Its Readers" (unpublished Doctor's dissertation, Graduate Library School, University of Chicago, 1935). Abstracted: "An Approach to Fiction through the Characteristics of Its Readers," *Library Quarterly,* VI (1936), 124-74; Douglas Waples and Leon Carnovsky, *Libraries and Readers in the State of New York: The State's Administration of Public and School Libraries with Reference to the Educational Values of Library Service* (Chicago: University of Chicago Press, 1939).

[10] Foster, *op. cit.*

[11] I. A. Richards, *Practical Criticism: A Study of Literary Judgment* (New York: Harcourt, Brace & Co., 1929).

[12] Alfred Korzybski, *Science and Sanity: An Introduction to Non-Aristotelean Systems and General Semantics* (New York: Science Press Printing Co., 1933).

[13] Guy T. Buswell, *How Adults Read* ("Supplementary Educational Monographs," No. 45 [Chicago: University of Chicago Press, 1937]).

[14] Waples and Tyler, *op. cit.*

pation probably affects his general reading behavior most directly through the attitudes which the occupation develops.

Such gross distinctions among people are useful in designating equally gross distinctions among the publications they read. For the most part, however, the differences in reading result not from the personal trait as such but rather from the social groupings into which the trait tends to class the reader. For example, sex differences in reading taste, like sex differences in general, are less the effect of the sex trait as such than the effect of certain environmental expectations attached to the sex. Girls are supposed to be interested in the home and boys in business, and such continual and pervading suggestion leaves its mark on subject interests.[15]

Similarly, different ages read differently because people of various ages reflect the attitudes of the social, educational, and occupational groups of the corresponding age to which they belong and many of whose reading tastes they acquire by imitation and by community of interest.[16] When differences in education and in occupation are held constant, the differences resulting from age alone are slight. Children's subject interests in reading are highly uniform, largely because their experiences have been closely similar. Beyond the age of twenty, one must take intervals of fifteen years or more to show appreciable differences in the publications read by similar groups.[17] Older readers are typically given to retrospective subjects like history and religion and the arts. They likewise spend more time in reading than any other easily identified group, excepting students.[18]

But finer and more meaningful distinctions are needed to explain the selection and the interpretation of publications. Such distinctions are often provided by the wide variety of primary and secondary groups to which all individuals belong. An individual's loyalties to his family, his school or college friends, his vocational associates, his church, his club, his political party, his favorite sports and their adherents — each of these may explain his point of view toward the publications which he reads. Not only do such group identifications supply data useful in themselves but they also suggest some of the reader's effective predispositions which are seldom observable. Hence, the more of such group memberships we specify, the more accurately

[15] Lewis M. Terman and Margaret Lima, "Reading Interests," in Lewis M. Terman *et al., Genetic Studies of Genius,* Vol. I: *Mental and Physical Traits of a Thousand Gifted Children* (Stanford University, Calif.: Stanford University Press, 1925), pp. 441-54.

[16] Charles Bird, *Social Psychology* (New York: D. Appleton-Century Co., 1940); Edward K. Strong, *Change of Interests with Age; Based on Examination of More Than Two Thousand Men between the Ages of Twenty and Sixty, Representing Eight Occupations* (Stanford University, Calif.: Stanford University Press, 1931).

[17] Waples and Tyler, *op. cit.*

[18] Strong, *op. cit.*

we can predict the reader's stand on any issue of general social interest. Thus, a group of middle-aged Kansas farmers, members of the Methodist church and of the Republican party, with high-school education or less, and with incomes averaging two thousand dollars, will have many common attitudes upon important social questions. With some assurance, one can predict their reactions to any publication which takes a stand regarding a given current issue. Our concern with traits is to identify such like-minded groups for closer analysis of their reading responses in terms of their predispositions. Group memberships thus offer helpful objective descriptions of people in terms of their selection and interpretation of publications.

The practical importance of classing readers by their group memberships lies in the degree to which such memberships reflect attitudes relevant to their reading. To a large extent, attitudes derive from group memberships. Each group has common attitudes which its members might adopt *in toto* were they not opposed by the conflicting attitudes of other groups to which the same people also belong. Family and church groups are particularly influential in shaping radical attitudes, according to recent evidence;[19] but other groups based upon similarities in age, occupation, and education have been found mainly responsible for sex differences in interests and attitudes.[20] Genetic studies supply many examples of group influences upon religious, racial, political, and other attitudes.[21] An unusually thorough study reports that the most important influences upon radical-conservative attitudes are found in the attitudes held by the reader's parents and in the reading that he does. The habit of much reading not only disposed the readers to be radical but, over a period of five years, tended to increase the radicalism of the group. This is explained by the suggestion that "to be bookish in this era has meant to steep oneself in the disillusioned gropings of post-War thinkers, most of whom are clearly radical."[22]

With reference to such studies of attitude to date, it has been suggested by S. A. Stouffer and others that the attitude concept needs to be applied to the *large clusters* of attitudes which explain the characteristic differences between the Kansas farmer and, say, the New York retail merchant, as types. The research to define such attitude clusters

[19] Theodore Newcomb, "Determinants of Opinion," *Public Opinion Quarterly,* I (October, 1937), pp. 71-78.

[20] Lewis M. Terman and Catharine C. Miles, *et al., Sex and Personality: Studies in Masculinity and Femininity* (New York: McGraw-Hill Book Co., 1936).

[21] Gordon W. Allport, "Attitudes," in Carl A. Murchison (ed.), *A Handbook of Social Psychology* (Worcester: Clark University Press, 1935), pp. 798-844.

[22] Gardner Murphy and Rensis Likert, *Public Opinion and the Individual: A Psychological Study of Student Attitudes on Public Questions, with a Retest Five Years Later* (New York: Harper & Bros., 1938).

might well be patterned after the work of L. L. Thurstone to define
the "primary mental abilities," by means of a matrix of correlations
between each pair of abilities that have been tested. The tendencies
for certain attitudes of certain persons to be interdependent, i.e., to
form clusters, might thus be recognized.

An attitude is a tendency to act, a way of being "set" for or against
certain things. The reader with a given attitude tends to select reading to fit it and then to interpret the reading accordingly. Many communists read the *New Masses;* many capitalists read *Fortune.* And
they react to their reading as communists and capitalists. The reader's
selection of reading matter and, to some extent, his response to it are
by academic definition explained in the category of motives. Motives
are expected satisfactions. They represent a variety of attitudes backed
by various physiological conditions which produce "needs," "wants,"
"urges," or "demands,"[23] and modified by the environmental opportunities. Hence, combinations of the reader's various predispositions —
predispositions which lead him to expect certain kinds of satisfactions
from his reading — are best termed his motives for reading. In this
connection, readers of the *New Masses* are more clearly explained for
our purpose when we say they are motivated by a need for prestige
and social security than when we point to their attitudes favoring
communism.

Before discussing certain typical motives which cause readers to
select and respond to different publications, we must clarify some
verbal confusion. Only infrequently — and then in the simpler instances — does a motive appear singly and alone. The complexity of
the reader's predispositions ordinarily complicates his motivation.
Hence, it is usually permissible to speak of the *dominant* motive in a
particular situation as explaining the direction of the behavior.
Furthermore, the same motives may carry different labels, depending
on the depth of analysis attempted. Thus, "reading for curiosity" may
also be reading for understanding, for practical information, and for
much else. Some considerations were mentioned in chapter i relating
to the terminology herein used to describe the effects of reading.[24]
Similar considerations determine the choice of terms for motives.

Motives may be classified as intrapersonal and interpersonal. Intrapersonal motives impel the reader to publications likely to stimulate
his feelings about himself. Interpersonal motives impel the reader
toward publications involving his relationships with others. Of course,

[23] Daniel A. Prescott, *Emotion and the Educative Process: A Report of the
Committee on the Relation of Emotion to the Educative Process* (Washington,
D. C.: American Council on Education, 1938); Henry A. Murray *et al.,
Explorations in Personality; A Clinical and Experimental Study of Fifty Men
of College Age* (New York: Oxford University Press, 1938).

[24] See chap. i of the book from which this selection came: "Introduction and
Summary," pp. 18ff.

the satisfaction of either one type of motive often tends to satisfy the other. For example, desires for prestige which explain reading the Bible for intrapersonal satisfactions may also improve the reader's status with others, because of their respect for people who read the Bible. Since many motives are expressed in each category under different circumstances, a single discussion may cover both categories.

As already suggested, we may say a reader selects a book for a particular motive, like desire for prestige, when all the evidence points to it. For example, the reader himself says he likes to read what makes him feel important; the experienced analyst finds prestige a satisfactory explanation for the choice of reading; what we know about the book suggests that it was written to make people like the reader feel important; the reader seeks prestige in other situations, and his inferior status demands prestige. The cumulative evidence is convincing. Thus, we may impute a prestige motive to the boy who said he lived the part as he read about brave soldiers; who was a coward in physical sports, despising himself and being despised for his craven spirit; who constantly read stories about wars and brave soldiers; and who read for prestige according to the psychologist's report. By comparing several expressions of prestige motives, we may suggest how they normally operate toward the selection of reading matter.[25]

A common prestige motive toward reading is found in the reader's desire to put himself in the place of book characters who do things that win them admiration and success. The boy reading about soldiers selected publications which satisfied his need to identify himself with brave people. Fiction (*The Deerslayer*) and nonfiction (a set of volumes on the World War) served his needs equally well. Another boy with strong prestige needs identified himself with the heroes in Nick Carter's *Legacy* and in *Daisy, the Gentleman Burglar's Daughter*. He later succumbed to English teachers who were able to improve the quality of his reading by utilizing the same motive. The boy then likened himself to Byron, "who had cross feet and I've got cross eyes." Both cases are typical. Among boys, as represented by the several hundred case studies examined, Horatio Alger, Frank Merriwell, Jesse James, and Buffalo Bill are all selected on this pattern, and Byron is a common adult substitute. However, the adult normally demands characters drawn more closely to his likeness than the child demands.

The reader's need to identify himself with those who enjoy prestige regularly results in selecting and so interpreting publications at any level of maturity, on almost any subject, fiction or nonfiction, provided the reading presents famous people who resemble the readers in some respects. If their choice is severely limited, such readers do their best to make imaginary adjustments and compensations. One reader said, "You can imagine my strain in identifying myself with the leading characters in all those books, including the *Bride of Lam-*

[25] Evidence from several case studies is presented in the following discussion.

mermoor, read at age nine." Similar motivation, in reverse, is the desire for self-prestige by means of self-pity. A typical example is the "unloved, very lonesome girl of twenty, who collected poems about unrequited love and suicide."

Another expression of the motive leads to the reading of "good" or "new" or "best" books. The readers seek intrapersonal prestige by "self-improvement," by "keeping up with the latest titles," or by "reading what the critics recommend." They also usually anticipate praise from employers or teachers or associates because they have read such books. An example is the boy who made a valiant attempt to read *The Decline and Fall of the Roman Empire* because a relative was sure he could not read it. A common reason for avoiding the pulp magazines lies in the stigma attached to those who read them. Prestige readers may be distinguished from other readers of "good" books because they read few books by the same distinguished author, they select the better-known titles and resist the often stronger attractions of unknown or unfashionable titles, and they pay less attention to the content.

Other readers, seeking praise for the information they can display, select the "hard" rather than the "good" book. Here the rarity and complexity of the subject matter and the technical vocabulary are attractive qualities. Prestige motives often combine with the need to understand, whether for the sheer satisfaction of understanding, for the opportunity to apply the knowledge, or because of a desire to persuade or to "manage" other people. The first appears in readers who "like to consider themselves intellectually curious," who "have a keen interest in tracking down ideas, in understanding for its own sake," and the motive leads toward theoretical subjects. The second appears largely in vocational or practical-hobby reading. The reader typically selects only one book or one type of book. Most commonly the motive is found among students reading textbooks for the sole purpose of high marks; both their selection and their use of publications are frankly pragmatic. The third motive — the desire to understand people in order to manage them more effectively — is expressed mainly by parents, teachers, and salesmen. They choose such reading as the *Parent's Magazine,* or *Classroom Management,* or *How To Win Friends and Influence People.* Since women must manage servants, children, and husbands, the women's magazines cater directly to this interest.

Another group of motives may be labeled "respite" motivation. They imply a search for whatever publications will diminish anxiety or boredom by intensifying aesthetic experience, supplying vicarious adventure, or merely diverting the readers' attention from their personal cares. It is no accident that more people read the comic strips than read any other kind of print. The comics are as far removed from real life as they can be and still escape utter nonsense. They allow the reader to assault and overcome a prize collection of comic villians, thus relieving his aggressions toward the people and conditions which thwart him in "real" life. The more vigorous pulp magazines also serve to relieve the reader's frustrations by promoting the vicarious expression of his aggressive tendencies.[26] Almost any sort of print may afford respite and may be selected and read for that purpose. The scientist may find respite in detective stories, and the executive whose day is spent in administrative routine may find respite in treatises on scientific theory. As in most other experiences, respite in reading results from variety, from a change in the focus of attention. And it is by such changes in attention that the respite motive produces the important social effect of distracting people from their "serious" problems. Hence the satisfaction of the respite motive provides a sort of safety valve for social tensions and thus serves to maintain the *status quo*.

Desires for respite may find expression in reading literature of high artistic merit. Writers naturally describe writing as a fine art. Teachers represent the reading of belles-lettres as a means of intensifying aesthetic experience, comparable to any other fine art. Certain observers impute to the reading of belles-lettres a "relief of general tension and adjustment toward fundamental problems and conditions of environment and life." Such recommendations encourage such reading. Under what conditions the reading of what publications by what readers will afford the most respite we do not know. Nor is the question very important, since means other than reading are so numerous. But we can say with confidence that most readers desire more varied and more intense experience than daily routines afford and that a convenient vicarious source of such experience is found in a wide range of publications, from the human interest item in the daily press to the plays of Shakespeare. The satisfaction of the respite motive doubtless depends on the comprehensibility of what is read,[27] and it increases with familiarity.[28] The research literature on this area is rather barren. The subjects are usually school children; the motive, "reading for aesthetic appreciation," is usually more fittingly described as reading for approval by the teacher who assigned the reading. Systematic analyses of publications widely read by selected groups of readers and corresponding analyses of the readers' motivation are needed to relate reading for respite to other reading motives.

Another group of motives implies a need for greater sense of

[26] John Dollard *et al., Frustration and Aggression* (New Haven: Yale University Press, 1939).

[27] Helen K. Mackintosh, *A Critical Study of Children's Choice in Poetry* (University of Iowa Studies in Education, Vol. VII, No. 4 [Iowa City: University of Iowa Press, 1932]).

[28] J. E. and M. A. Mendenhall, *The Influence of Familiarity upon Children's Preferences for Pictures and Poems* (New York: Columbia University Press, 1933).

security. People may feel insecure in a wide variety of ways. Economic insecurity is perhaps the most uniform in its motivation of typical reading. But since such reading has already been noticed in connection with reading for practical information, we may comment instead upon the reading motivated by considerations of physical and social security.

Readers who need reassurance concerning their sanity or their strength are typically too timid or too poor to consult doctors and too uninformed to be critical of their reading. Accordingly, they select pseudo-scientific articles on psychology and health. They are attracted to publications with nontechnical vocabularies, which offer a quick and sure cure for most ailments, and which make strong appeals to prestige by citing medical authorities freely. Over a period of time the selections of such readers may incline to more extreme types of pseudoscience, astrology, numerology, or religious tracts. One is led to suspect that need for sense of physical security results from a deeper emotional insecurity.

Readers motivated by a need for greater social security may seek to improve their status within their family or social class or may try to exchange their social class for another social class. The former are commonly adolescents who seek reading on family conflicts. They aggressively avoid or aggressively select novels dealing with more placid home life. If the adolescent is attempting to break away from the family, his insecurity may be expressed by selection of books on philosophy and religion or of "philosophical" novels. Such readers tend to emphasize passages which involve their own particular problems — lack of parental affection, impending divorce in the family, overprotection, and the like. Among older people, and especially among college students, there is a shift from need for family security to need for social security. This leads to reading on various social problems and current events, whether in novels or nonfiction books or magazines and newspapers.

Some psychologists find the drive toward such reading to be a need for personal emotional security as well as a need for social security. The case studies imply an equally close relation between the needs for social security and for prestige. One reads up on socialism because "I felt ashamed to know so little when the members of the socialist club knew so much." Also, the "radicals" may do much heavy reading to win arguments with conservative friends and to enjoy the resulting prestige. The group studies show concentration upon books in history, economics, and political science by many faithful readers of liberal publications. Evidently the various other motives we have mentioned are involved to a degree that requires combined study of the readers and analysis of the content before the motivation can be clearly described. Here motives become highly complex. The age, sex, occupation, income, and family background traits of college students are interrelated to form both radical attitudes and needs for personal as well as social security. These in combination determine the selection and interpretation of reading. Such interrelationships are shown by many group studies of radicalism as well as by case studies of individual readers.[29]

The combinations of traits and motives in different readers, and from time to time in the same reader, attract them to different types of content. Some "radical" groups, for example, seek publications on economic theory which they select for their "reasonableness, freedom from dogmatism, precision of terms, impersonality, deference to facts, comprehensive goals, and lack of logical fallacies or rhetorical stunts." When readers so disposed encounter the opposite type of publication, they are repelled, despite their sympathies with the theory. Thus, a reader who had accepted the ideology of communism read the *Daily Worker* and was "repelled by the language. I threw away my first copy of the *New Masses* after a few editorials. I thought the line can't be valid since all their comments were critical of the *status quo* and since there must be something good in the present system." For further example, we find a Jewish boy, frightened into a serious interest in politics by the rise of the Nazis to power, who "scurried after Lenin's works." While he, too, preferred the more deliberate, rational type of reading because of his intelligence and training, his combined motives urged him toward publications stressing urgency of solution, sudden persuasion, and specific goals.

At the opposite extreme we have the lonely, inferior, introverted reader, dissatisfied with herself, her family, and the social order, who "has never read anything but the *Daily Worker* and the *New Masses* — no theoretical stuff"; who especially enjoyed "the letters from workers and readers . . . was moved by the feeling of conviction being so widespread." Here the rhetorical devices, the familiarity of setting and language, and the intimacy of appeal went home and developed a taste for more such. We conclude that this reader's sex, limited schooling, low occupational status, and other handicaps explain her attitudes of inferiority and insecurity. These attitudes developed needs for compensation through channels acceptable to her friends and associates. The communist publications yielded such compensations more effectively than other reading matter she could obtain and understand.

Readers' predispositions represent the least understood and probably the most important of the four major factors to which in combination we ascribe the social effects of reading. Closer attention to such group predispositions as can more safely be inferred from obtainable evidence will greatly refine the present knowledge of reading effects.

[29] Newcomb, *op. cit.;* Murphy and Likert, *op. cit.;* Bernard J. Breslaw, *The Development of a Socio-economic Attitude* ("Archives of Psychology," No. 226 [New York: Columbia University Press, 1938]) ; Solomon Diamond, *A Study of the Influence of Political Radicalism on Personality Development* ("Archives of Psychology," No. 203 [New York: Columbia University Press, 1936]).

The

Audiences

of

Mass

Communication

The three following selections are illustrative samples of the very extensive research literature on mass media audiences. Dr. Lazarsfeld's and Miss Kendall's tables present some facts on radio, magazine, motion picture, and book audiences in the United States. Messrs. Schramm and White analyze United States newspaper reading by age, education, and sex. Finally, a few examples from USIA studies are presented to show some of the differences between media availability and audiences in the United States and other countries.

▲ PAUL F. LAZARSFELD

▲ PATRICIA KENDALL

*T*he Communications Behavior

of the Average American: Some Tables

TABLE 1

Movie-Going and Radio-Listening Behavior

Number of Movies Seen in Previous Month:

No movies	39%
1-3 movies	37
4 or more movies	24
Total	100%

Amount of Radio Listening on Average Weekday Evening:

Less than 1 hour	26%
1-3 hours	49
3 or more hours	25
Total	100%

TABLE 2

Book and Magazine Readership

Book reading:

Read no books during past month	74%
Read at least one book during month	26
Total	100%

Magazine reading:

Read no magazine regularly	39%
Read at least one magazine regularly	61
Total	100%

▲ These tables are from *Radio Listening in America,* published and copyright by Prentice-Hall (New York, 1948). They are printed here by permission of publisher and copyright holder. The data for these and other tables in the book came from a national probability-sample survey of 3,529 persons in the United States, conducted by the National Opinion Research Center, of the University of Chicago, in the fall of 1947. Dr. Lazarsfeld is professor of sociology at Columbia University. Miss Kendall, formerly a member of the staff of the Bureau of Applied Social Research, is now Mrs. Lazarsfeld.

(Tables 3, 4, 5, and 6 have been omitted.)

TABLE 7

Proportion of Magazine and Book Readers According to Education

	College	High School	Grade School
Proportion who read magazines regularly........	86%	68%	41%
Proportion who read at least one book in previous month...................................	50	27	11

TABLE 8

Proportion of Radio and Movie Fans According to Education

	College	High School	Grade School
Proportion who listen to the radio three hours or more in the evening.........................	21%	29%	22%
Proportion who saw four or more movies in previous month...................................	25	28	16

TABLE 9

Movies Seen During Previous Month According to Age

Movie Attendance	21-29	30-39	40-49	50-59	60+
No movies..................	19%	31%	36%	51%	73%
One movie..................	15	18	16	15	9
Two or three movies..........	26	26	27	18	9
Four or five movies...........	23	16	14	11	6
More than five movies........	17	9	7	5	3
	100%	100%	100%	100%	100%

TABLE 10

Movie Attendance According to Size of Community

Movies Seen During Previous Month	Metropolitan Districts Over One Million	Metropolitan Districts Under One Million	2,500 to 50,000	Rural Nonfarm (Under 2,500)	Farm
No movies.............	32%	36%	36%	49%	52%
1-3 movies.............	40	39	38	33	35
4 or more movies.......	28	25	26	18	13
Total..............	100%	100%	100%	100%	100%

▲ WILBUR SCHRAMM

▲ DAVID M. WHITE

*A*ge, Education, and Economic Status as Factors

in Newspaper Reading: Conclusions

Insofar as these data are representative, the following conclusions seem to be indicated:

1. In general, the amount of news reading tends to increase with age, with education, and with economic status. News reading increases very rapidly through the teens, reaches a peak somewhere between the ages of thirty and fifty, and thereafter drops off slightly. High school educated persons read markedly more news in the paper than grade school educated persons, and college educated persons read a little more than high school persons.

2. A young reader seems to be introduced to the newspaper by its pictorial content. Among readers ten to fifteen, comics are by far the most read items in the paper, followed by news pictures and public affairs cartoons. Readership of news is far below the readership of these pictorial features. And in this entire sample, not one single person between the ages of ten and fifteen was found who had read *any* of the editorials.

3. Men's reading of news seems to come to a peak at an earlier age than does women's.

4. Education seems to make a greater difference in women's reading than in men's.

5. Economic status seems to make a greater difference in men's reading than in women's.

6. Teen-agers, persons who have had only grade school education,

▲ These conclusions are based on data gathered by a readership study made in January, 1949, in an Illinois city of approximately 100,000 population. The probability sample included 746 readers, and the survey dealt with the local evening paper which has approximately 65,000 circulation. The paper from which these conclusions come was first published in the *Journalism Quarterly,* and later in *Mass Communications,* copyright by the University of Illinois Press, 1949. The paper is reprinted here by permission of the copyright holder.

and persons in the lower economic groups are more likely to read crime and disaster news than any other broad class of news. Reading of crime news increases with age until the decade of the thirties, after which it remains relatively level. It remains unchanged or slightly decreases with rising economic status, and decreases with more education.

7. Reading of public affairs and editorials increases with age, with education, and with higher economic status.

8. Reading of comics is at its height in the teens, and decreases steadily from the age of fifteen on. It decreases also with more education and with higher economic position.

9. Reading of news pictures apparently begins as early as comics, but increases (instead of falling off as comics do) after fifteen, reaches a peak in middle life, and remains relatively high. It increases slightly with education and higher economic status.

10. Reading of political and editorial cartoons begins strongly in the teens, increases slightly, then tapers off. It seems to increase significantly with economic status.

11. Reading of society news is low in the teens and thereafter rises to a high plateau between the ages of thirty and sixty. In the case of women, it increases significantly with economic status.

12. Reading of sports news is at its height in the twenties, thereafter tapers off. It increases with economic status, and there is considerable increase between grade school and high school educated groups.

13. Older readers are more likely than younger readers to read letters to the editor.

14. Dividing news into two classes — that which gives an immediate reward psychologically (crime, corruption, accidents, disasters, sports, society, human interest, etc., which we shall call Class I) and that which gives a delayed reward (public affairs, economic matters, social problems, science, education, etc., which we shall call Class II) — it appears that:

a. Reading of Class I news comes to a peak at an earlier age than reading of Class II (Table V).

b. Reading of Class I news is higher among the high school educated segment of the population than in the college segment; Class II, higher in the college educated group (Table IV).

c. Reading of Class II news is more likely than reading of Class I to increase with rising economic status (Table VI).

15. People tend to read farther into Class I news than into Class II news. There seems to be no significant correlation of depth of reading with age, education, or economic status.

16. Summarizing reading patterns by age, it appears that a reader comes in later years to use a newspaper less and less for entertainment, more and more for information and serious viewpoints on public

affairs. There are noteworthy declines of comics and sports with age, noteworthy increases in the reading of public affairs news and editorials. Editorials, which are near the bottom in the ten to twenty bracket, are second only to news pictures in the over-sixty bracket.

17. Summarizing reading patterns by education it appears that readers on the lower end of the educational curve tend to use the newspaper for entertainment, sensational news, and pictorial material. Those at the top of the educational curve tend to use it less for entertainment, more for information on public affairs.

18. Summarizing reading patterns by socio-economic status, it appears that as comic reading declines, so reading of editorials and public affairs news increases with higher economic status. However, in some important respects the pattern for reading by socio-economic groups is not like the two patterns just described in 16 and 17. There is no decline in picture and cartoon reading with higher economic status, and there is a marked increase, with higher status, in the reading of sports and society news.

Mass Communications and Their

Audiences in Other Countries

Differences in availability of mass communications and in the audiences which gather round these media in different countries are often spectacular. Some of these differences may be illustrated from USIA and related studies.

AVAILABILITY

As might be expected, the greatest concentrations of mass media are in countries where per capita wealth and industrial development are high. For example, over 85 per cent of all radio receiving sets, over 80 per cent of all daily newspaper circulation, over 70 per cent of all cinema seats, are in Europe and North America. Over half the radio receivers of the world, about one fourth of the circulation of daily newspapers, and about one third of all the cinema seats are in the United States.

The following table will show the wide variation in availability of print, radio, and film in some representative countries:

	Newspapers— Copies daily per 1000 inhabitants	Receiving sets per 1000 inhabitants	Cinema seats per 1000 inhabitants
France	259	179	64
Italy	98	55	87
Egypt	17	12	10
Syria	19	15	7
India	6	1	4
Japan	224	106	8
Philippines	25	4	(?)
Brazil	30	51	20
Mexico	48	31	57
United Kingdom	596	244	86
United States	350	620	78

(Source: UNESCO figures, in some cases updated)

There is also a considerable variation within the Soviet orbit, as these figures will show:

	Copies daily per 1000 inhabitants	Receiving sets per 1000 inhabitants	Cinema seats per 1000 inhabitants
USSR	161 (?)	67	(?)
China	10 (?)	3	1
Czechoslovakia	193	188	56 (?)
Poland	122	49	9
Romania	141	17	7
Hungary	108	57	15
Bulgaria	112	29	13

(Source: UNESCO figures)

It should be pointed out that in some of these countries, notably the USSR, there is considerable wired redistribution of radio programs.

LITERACY

The map of world literacy divides into three large areas. North America, Western Europe (except Spain), Australia, New Zealand, and parts of Southeast Asia have less than 10 per cent illiteracy. On the other hand, China, India, the Moslem countries, and practically all of Africa have more than 80 per cent illiteracy. Between these two extremes — in the band between 10 and 80 per cent illiteracy — are Central and South America, Spain, and the vast expanse of Eurasia dominated by the Soviet Union.

Illiteracy in the United States is about 2 per cent. Here are the figures for certain other representative countries where data are available:

Percentage of Illiteracy

	Both sexes	Male	Female	
Belgium (1930)	5.6	5.2	6.0	(age 7 and over)
Brazil (1940)	56.1	49.7	62.4	(age 15 and over)
Bulgaria (1934)	31.4	19.5	43.3	(age 10 and over)
Burma (1931)	59.8	38.6	82.5	(age 10 and over)
Egypt (1937)	85.2	76.6	93.9	(age 10 and over)
France (1946)	3.4	3.2	3.6	(age 10 and over)
Greece (1928)	40.9	23.5	58.0	(age 8 and over)
Hungary (1941)	7.4	6.4	8.4	(age 6 and over)
India (1931)	90.9	84.7	97.6	(age 10 and over)
Italy (1931)	21.6	17.8	25.2	(age 10 and over)
Mexico (1940)	54.0	50.0	57.9	(age 10 and over)
Philippines (1948)	38.7	35.6	41.7	(age 10 and over)
Turkey (1945)	69.5	55.5	90.1	(age 10 and over)

(Source: *Progress of Literacy in Various Countries* — UNESCO monographs on fundamental education)

It is apparent that the general pattern is for somewhat higher percentages of illiteracy among females, and that in some countries (for example, the Moslem countries) the literacy differential between the sexes is considerable. There are also other differentials. One of these is racial. For example, only 47 per cent of white Brazilians are illiterate, compared to 79 per cent of black Brazilians. In Hungary (in 1930) the German speaking group had the lowest rate of illiteracy, followed by the Hungarian and Slovak speakers in that order. Among the larger language groups in Turkey, the Turkish speaking people had a significantly lower rate of illiteracy than either the Arabic or the Kurdish speaking people.

Another differential is by residence in city or country. In general, illiteracy is higher among rural residents. Thus, in Greece in 1928, the illiteracy among urban persons was 29 per cent, among rural persons 47 per cent. In Bulgaria, in 1934, it was 19 per cent among urban, 35 among rural.

OTHER EXAMPLES OF AVAILABILITY: NEWSPRINT AND FILM PRODUCTION

For examples of other factors entering into the availability of mass communications, we can consider newsprint and film production. It is a striking fact that the United States consumes almost two thirds of the world's annual production of newsprint. No other country consumes 15 per cent as much as does the United States. Compared to the United States' annual consumption of five *million* metric tons of newsprint, the United Kingdom uses just under 700,000 tons, and USSR about half that much. France uses a little over 200,000 tons; Japan, 100,000; Egypt, around 14,000; India, about 50,000; Czechoslovakia about 40,000; Hungary, about 20,000; and China, an estimated 60,000.

A large part of the world's film production has also been centered for a number of years in the United States. Thus, until recently the United States has been making over 400 feature films a year. India has been making about 250, Japan and France each slightly over 100, Italy and the United Kingdom about 75, and China between 50 and 75. Such countries as Belgium, Greece, and Hungary have been making 10 or less per year. The exact size of Soviet film output is not known.

MEDIA DIFFERENCES

Even beyond availability, however, there are important differences in the attention paid by media in different subjects to world events. This can be illustrated by a table compiled from Jacques Kayser's *One Week's News* (Paris, 1954), which examines the coverage given particular news stories by 17 dailies in 17 countries during the week of 5-11 March, 1951. In the following table, an *x* indicates that the story was *not* covered in the particular newspaper.

Borba (Yugoslavia)	The Times of India	La Nacion (Argentina)	Al Misri (Egypt)	Hurriyet (Turkey)	Rand Daily Mail (South Africa)	Daily Express (United Kingdom)	La Prensa (Mexico City)	Il Nuovo Corriere della Sera (Italy)	Pravda (USSR)	New York Daily News	Le Parisien libere (France)	Rude Pravo (Czechoslovakia)	O Estado de Sao Paulo (Brazil)	Ta Kung Pao (China)	Dagens Nyheter (Sweden)	Daily Telegraph (Australia)	
																	Korean War
						x			x			x		x			MacArthur's Declaration
																	Big Four Deputies Meeting
x												x		x			Razmara's Assassination
											x						Moroccan Situation
																	Ministerial Crisis in France
														x			Bevin's Resignation
x	x		x	x	x		x	x			x			x			Australian Court Decision (on Communist Party)
	x							x		x	x	x		x			Conspiracy in Pakistan
x	x		x	x	x		x			x	x			x			Conflict over La Prensa
x	x		x	x	x		x							x	x	x	Vote on Soviet Budget
x	x		x		x	x	x	x	x		x			x			Western European Communists Decreasing, U.S. Declares
x		x	x	x		x	x	x	x			x		x			Czech Ambassador to India Abandons Post
		x						x				x		x			Eisenhower Names Nato General Staff
x			x	x	x	x		x	x	x	x			x		x	Italy Votes Military Credits
						x	x	x		x		x		x	x	x	Resignation of Turkish Cabinet
x		x		x			x	x	x	x	x	x	x	x	x	x	Franchise Bill in South African Parliament
x	x		x	x	x	x			x			x		x			Charles-Wolcott Boxing Match

Another way to illustrate media differences, with newspapers, is in terms of size and distribution of space. Here is another table compiled from Kayser's study:

Newspaper	Total Ave. Space	Adver- tising	Foreign News	Acci- dents, Crimes, etc.	Sports	Eco- nomic, Finan- cial, Social, etc.
		Percentage devoted to:				
Borba (Yugoslavia)	1,194 sq. in.	0%	22%	0%	8%	19%
The Times of India	3,255	53	14	2	5	12
La Nacion (Argentina)	3,100	54	12	5	5	5
Al Misri (Egypt)	2,635	23	24	6	1	4
Hurriyet (Turkey)	2,015	31	22	2	4	1
Daily Mail (South Africa)	4,650	53	6	5	5	7
Daily Express (London)	1,860	32	8	11	8	6
La Prensa (Mexico City)	5,890	37	6	12	11	7
Corriere della Sera (Italy)	2,170	33	16	13	4	2
Pravda (USSR)	1,705	1	30	0	1	32
New York Daily News	10,230	66	2	7	4	1
Le Parisien Libere (Paris)	2,790	33	7	14	14	4
Rude Pravo (Czechoslovakia)	1,860	6	25	0	9	28
O Estado (Brazil)	11,625	68	6	2	4	9
Tao Kung Pao (China)	1,798	18	12	1	0	27
Dagens Nyheter (Sweden)	4,650	36	8	7	8	7
Daily Telegraph (Australia)	3,410	39	5	3	4	12
London Times	3,776	29	25	7	8	31
Izvestia (Moscow)	1,276	0	51	0	0	27
New York Times	14,285	46	16	9	10	41
Le Monde	2,508	23	50	0	1	23

In the table above, the figures on all except the last four papers are averages for the week of March 5-11, 1951; for the last four papers, they are for the day of 11 January, 1952. The advertising figure is a percentage of total space, whereas the remaining figures are percentages of editorial space. These differences must be kept in mind in reading the table; for example, the New York Times which devotes only 16 per cent of its copy to foreign news actually carries considerably more foreign news than Izvestia, which devotes 51 per cent of its copy to that category.

AUDIENCES: NEWSPAPERS

In the United States, around 90 per cent of adults regularly see daily newspapers. The figure is also very high in the United Kingdom, Germany, and Scandinavia. In France, a recent survey showed the corresponding figure to be 56 per cent, and in Italy 39 per cent. A small survey in the Philippines showed that 73 per cent of Manila respondents, but only 34 per cent of a nearby small town, read daily newspapers. The Japan Newspaper Publishers Association estimates that 70 per cent of Japanese read dailies, and throughout the Arab world about 70 per cent of the adults are thought to see dailies or hear them read more or less regularly. A small-sample survey in Hong Kong came up with the figure of 79 per cent daily newspaper readers. These studies, of course, were not all made with precisely the same techniques or at the same times, and therefore the comparisons should not be pressed too far.

In general, newspaper reading increases with education. Here are figures for two Moslem countries:

	Education		
	Elementary	*High School*	*College*
Percentage of Syrian readers who see papers almost daily	46	68	65
Percentage of Egyptian readers who see papers almost daily	65	75	95

(Source: Study by Bureau of Applied Social Research)

In the Philippines, the less educated persons have been shown to go to motion pictures as often as the more educated, but to read fewer books, newspapers, and magazines. This functional relationship between education and readership seems to be general.

Amount of education also helps to determine what parts of the newspaper an audience selects to read. We have already seen how this works for an American audience. Here are comparable figures for Japan:

	Education		
Per cent reading	Primary	Middle	College, High School
Foreign news	16.9	23.0	54.2
Political news	24.7	25.3	65.6
Economic news	10.1	20.7	40.0
Police news	52.8	47.1	60.0
Cultural news	7.9	23.0	37.0
Comic strips	56.2	52.9	57.1
Book reviews	4.5	17.2	34.2
Display ads	13.5	32.1	14.3

(Source: Odahara survey, 1952)

Most studies have indicated that the average American (if there is such a person) spends about 40 minutes a day with his newspaper. This is slightly higher than the figures we have been able to obtain from other countries. In France, for example, the two largest groups of readers seemed to average about 15 and 30 minutes, respectively. In Hong Kong the mode of the surveyed time was 30 minutes, but there was a secondary peak between 15 and 20 minutes. Most estimates of newspaper reading time in the United Kingdom have been about 25 to 30 minutes. It need hardly be pointed out that American papers, as a rule, are considerably thicker.

In many countries of the world there is much greater difference by sex in the amount of newspaper reading and the kind of newspaper read, than in the United States. For example, a survey by the Nippon Shimbun Kyokai showed that about 46 per cent of the male readers, but only 6 per cent of the female readers, were accustomed to reading domestic political news. The figures for reading of foreign news were 33 and 6 per cent, respectively. Comparable differences in amount and kind of reading apparently are to be found in southern Asia and the Arab crescent.

AUDIENCES: RADIO

In the United States, of course, radio goes into nearly every home. In France, the comparable figure is about 75 per cent of the homes; in Italy, about 60 per cent. In the Moslem countries and in Southeast Asia, the figures are much smaller. But these rough figures, which are generally parallel to the "sets per thousand" table given earlier, do not tell us as much as certain other data. For one thing, radios tend to be concentrated in cities rather than rural regions. Thus, in Paris about 83 per cent of homes have radios, but in places under 5,000 the comparable figure is 69 per cent. The big cities of Italy reported about 82 per cent of their homes equipped with radios, but only 41 per cent of homes in rural regions so equipped. In countries of the world, the scarcity of radio receivers is partly compensated for by using receivers outside the home. In the Arab countries, for example, where sets run as low as 2 per 1000 in some lands, fully 30 per cent of the radio audience listens outside the home. A large proportion of these listen in coffee houses, and the coffee house thus becomes one of the important centers of information input and discussion. Similarly in the Philippines, 91 per cent of the radio audience in Manila said they listened in their own homes; but in the village of Argao only 25 per cent listened at home. The others listened with friends or at some public places. In the Communist countries, government-provided loudspeakers supplement the individually-owned radios.

The radio audience in this country contains more females than males. Present research results do not indicate whether this is generally true throughout the world. In France, 52 per cent of the men, 59 per cent of the women said (in 1952) that they listened to the radio "quite a bit." In Italy, however, that question was answered affirmatively by 66 per cent of the men, 61 per cent of the women. In the Moslem countries and in India, where the culture makes for an educational and communication differential between men and women, the men both read more and listen to radio more.

Quite generally, however, radio listening seems to increase with education and economic status. This has proved to be true wherever tested. Furthermore, education makes a considerable difference in what the listener selects from his radio. Here, for example, are favorite radio programs of Arab listeners (Egypt, Syria, Jordan, and Lebanon) arranged according to education of the listeners:

Favorite program	Illiterate	Elementary	High School	College
News	45%	54%	60%	57%
Arab music	59	51	32	29
Western music	1	8	30	42
Koran readings	44	37	15	12
Talks and lectures	11	20	19	23
Unspecified music	13	18	24	26

(Source: Bureau of Applied Social Research study)

And here is a comparable set of figures from a survey by the Japanese radio NHK, asking listeners to name some of their favorite programs. Public affairs discussion programs and classical music programs entered into the voting as follows:

Audience, by education	Public affairs	Classical music
College	55%	67%
Middle school	35	30
Less than middle school	20	17

AUDIENCES: FILMS, MAGAZINES, BOOKS

In the United States, radio and newspapers (with television on the way) are almost universal media, with magazines, motion pictures, and books following in that order. The radio and newspaper audiences are usually figured at between 90 and 100 per cent of the adult population, with the magazine audience being estimated at between 60 and 70 per cent, the motion picture audience at between 50 and 60, and the book audience somewhere near 30.

This seems to be the general pattern in other countries, except that seldom are these figures so high, and also that in some places there are important differences stemming from the local culture or situation. In France, about 42 per cent, in Italy 23 per cent say they never go to movies; 18 and 38 per cent, in the two countries respectively, say they go once a week. In the same countries, 27 and 26 per cent, respectively, say they never read magazines; 44 and 36 per cent say they read them regularly. In Hong Kong, 54 per cent of the adults surveyed said they read magazines regularly. In a small Philippine village, where radios are scarce and newspapers probably hard to come by, 95 per cent of the adults said they sometimes read magazines; this compares to 83 per cent who sometimes heard radio, 53 per cent newspapers, 50 movies, and 41 books.

In most countries, as in the United States, motion picture attendance seems to decrease with age after the teens. In the Arab countries,

Christians are more likely than Moslems to go to the movies. In France and Italy more women than men read magazines. In Hong Kong, however, both magazine and book reading are nearly double among male readers. This is true also in the Philippines. In this case, as in the others, communication patterns are a reflection of the culture in which they operate.

AUDIENCES: THEIR TRUST IN THE MEDIA

Audience opinion of and trust in the different media is apparently a local matter, born of the nature of the local media, the culture itself, and the tensions existing. In the United States, several opinion surveys during the last fifteen years have seemed to show that people had a great deal of faith in the trustworthiness of radio news as compared to newspapers, and this has been used to explain a number of phenomena, including the panic reaction to Orson Welles' "War of the Worlds" broadcast. And it is true that in four Arab countries surveyed recently, 63 per cent of the respondents favored radio over newspaper as a reliable source of news. Likewise, other surveys have appeared to favor radio, but the questions have not always been clear or comparable. And even in these surveys there are important local differences. For example, Egypt (one of the four Arab countries surveyed) is highly positive toward newspapers, whereas Syria is negative. Egyptian dailies have a history and tradition of strength. Syrian papers are "party papers"; they depend on support from the faction they represent, and for the most part do not appeal widely. Therefore, Syrian readership is not very high, but in Egypt even a large percentage of the illiterates arrange to have parts of the newspaper read to them.

Similarly, in the Philippines there are important differences between ideas of media reliability in the cities and the villages. In Manila, only 19 per cent of respondents in a recent survey named the newspaper as the "best" (most reliable?) media source of information; whereas, in Argao, 53 per cent named the newspaper. In Manila, 57 per cent named the magazine; in Argao, only 13. In Manila, 32 per cent named books; in Argao, 4. In Manila, 6 per cent named radio; in Argao, 25. It is clear that either the media, or the situation, or the tastes, or the needs, or all of them, are quite different as between Manila and Argao, and that being the case, an average of the two places in respect to relative trust in radio or newspaper would be meaningless.

SUMMARY

By way of summing up, we can say that there are certain patterns of mass media use which seem to have general applicability throughout the world, but these are powerfully modified in any given place by the local situation and culture. In general, radio and newspapers tend to be the most widely spread media, with magazines, films, and books trailing behind. Media use increases with education and with economic status, and the amount of education correlates well with what a person chooses to read or listen to. So far as we can tell, a person who uses one medium more than average tends to be above average in his use of *all* media. In general, media use tends to increase from child-hood to middle age, with the exception of motion picture attendance, which decreases after the teens. Older people, better educated people, tend to choose more "serious" materials. And media use tends to be greater in urban than in rural places.

But having said that, we have to turn to cultural and situational differences to explain the important differences in media use in differ-ent countries. For example, why do western European women listen more to radio, read more magazines than men, whereas women in the Arab countries and southeast Asia both read and listen much less than men? Obviously, the answer is to be found in the different status of women in the several cultures. Why are the coffee house audiences in the Arab countries more likely to be Moslem than Christian, even on a basis proportional to the population? Why are the newspapers of Egypt more respected by their readers than the newspapers of Syria by theirs? Obviously, we have here a situational and cultural difference of some importance.

And when we turn back to a study of the situation and cultures in these different countries, we are reminded that when we study the media as information channels in many countries of the world, we are ignoring large segments of the population. A third of the people in the Arab countries get their information by word of mouth. The figure is even larger for India and probably for China. Therefore, the coffee house in the Arab countries, the bazaar in Asia, the opinion leader, the traveler, the story teller in all these countries are an important link in the chain of communication, and the dissemination and group dis-cussion that goes on far beyond the mass communication chain are important for us to know about.

In conclusion, it should be pointed out that for very few places in the world is there any such detailed information on mass media content and uses as we have for the United States. This must have been clear from the scarcity of examples in the paper we are just now concluding, but it is worth saying here because until we do get some of this in-formation and interpret it in light of the country's culture, we shall be handicapped in trying to talk to many of the peoples of the world.

The Effect of Different Channels

Introductory Note

THE NATURE OF CHANNELS

The choice and combination of channels is another practical decision which the communicator must make. In the day-to-day pattern of communicating with one's primary group, this decision does not often enter: the other group members are at hand, and one can talk to them face to face. But when one is separated from his primary group — even by a short business trip out of town — then he often has to make a decision about channels. Shall it be telephone, telegram, or letter? Is the matter important enough that he should rush home to talk face-to-face about it? Whereas the choice is relatively simple in this level of communication, in such an activity as planning persuasive communication for large groups of people, the choice is exceedingly complicated and often difficult. Sometimes availability and audience capability help to determine it; for example, where the audience is illiterate, one must use pictures and the spoken word. Where the audience does not have radios, obviously one cannot depend on radio channels. But in the most usual situation, where radio and print and pictures all reach the intended audience, then one must make a decision complicated by a number of factors: What is the relative availability of the channels to the communicator? What use is the audience accustomed to make of the different channels, and how much is he likely to trust each of them? What can one channel do better than another? How can several channels best be combined so that they will reinforce each other? What use of the mass media channels will be most likely to trigger off the small-group communication which helps an idea enter into the norms of a society?

It must be admitted that these difficult matters are not well understood. Klapper, in the chapter which follows, summarizes much of the available experimental knowledge. This, together with the availability of the channels and a clear knowledge of the target audience, must guide the communicator — unless, like the Communist party in the sovietized countries, he is able to control the whole environment of his audience, and thus to put his message on all media, reinforce it with face-to-face communication engineered by professional agitators, and reinforce both of those by exercising his police power and his ability to give or withdraw material rewards. Since that condition does not pertain outside totalitarian countries, it may be helpful to put down a few notes here on the differences, as we see them, among channels.

We can differentiate channels on a number of useful scales. Here are four of these:

(1) *Space-time.* Printed materials, still pictures, and art objects are space-organized. A radio broadcast and a telephone conversation are time-organized. Face to face communication, sound films, television are time-and-space-organized.

We learn great skill in assimilating groups of sign vehicles and interpreting their meaning. This is the case whether the signs are verbal or pictorial, seen or heard. One of the most dramatic examples of this skill, however, is learning to read. Here we very soon progress beyond the stage of reading single words. We become able to grasp contexts swiftly, form larger groupings, and assimilate the meaning of the whole sentence, as our eyes leap along the lines in the normal reading process. When we are working with a familiar language (as compared to a foreign language) or a familiar visual context (as compared, for example, to an abstract painting) we can do this very efficiently. The eye can handle more information than the ear, and there is reason to think that grouping of words is more difficult by ear, especially in fast speech. Certainly larger grouping is possible only to the extent that the audience remembers information already given. When one is reading he can set his own pace, turn back whenever he wishes to check the relation of one page, one paragraph, one sentence to others. In listening, however, he is at the mercy of the communicator. He cannot control the pace or turn back.

Because of this difference, the space-organized media appear to offer more favorable conditions for difficult concepts, for masses of detail, for criticalness, discrimination, and selectivity on the part of the audience. On the other hand, the time-organized media appear to offer some advantages for rote learning of simple material (slogans, for example), and for encouraging suggestibility in an audience. The communicator's ability to control the pace is apparently a factor in this latter quality. It must be admitted, however, that there is little research evidence bearing on the point.

Pictorial media, either space- or time-organized, excel in their ability to present many concrete descriptive details and to encourage recognition of such details.

Space-and-time media share the advantages and disadvantages of space media and time media. They do not permit the audience to control the pace, but do have the great advantage of reinforcing one sense with another, and of being able to represent movement and concrete details along with the human voice and other vehicles of sound.

There are apparently eye-men and ear-men — that is, individuals who are especially skillful in receiving space- or time-organized communication. Supposedly, this differential skill is learned rather than being innate with the sensory equipment. It is not known how such individuals are distributed in the culture, or whether the changing use of media (e.g., the great increase in radio use after 1920, or in television use after 1950) changes the distribution. More important from the viewpoint of international communicators, there is little information on the distribution of such skills in different cultures.

(2) *Participation.* As Cantril and Allport have shown, it is possible to characterize the media as to whether they permit much or little participation on the part of the audience. Thus, a media scale might be created, running from most participation to least participation, something like this:

> personal conversation
> discussion groups
> informal meetings
> telephone
> formal meetings
> sound motion pictures
> television
> radio
> telegraph
> personal correspondence
> form letters
> newspapers
> billboards
> magazines
> books

Higher degrees of social participation tend to create a sense of involvement, a group bond, a circular pattern of influence and decision making. They provide maximum feedback. Thinking back to the social functions of mass communication stated earlier in this volume, the high-participation media would seem to commend themselves particularly for the task of correlating society's response, for the process of exchanging and sharpening opinion. Low-participation media would seem to commend themselves for swift and widespread communication of information to individuals — for example, as newspapers and radio communicate latest information on the environment, and as books transmit condensed information on the culture to the culture's new members.

(3) *Speed.* Timeliness is maximum in television and radio. There

is considerable sense of timeliness in newspapers; some in magazines; less in motion pictures; least in books. Media at the more timely end of the spectrum naturally lend themselves to the news function — the communicating of information about the environment. Media at the slow end naturally lend themselves to study and reflective purposes — that is, to communicating the culture to students. It might be expected that media in the middle of the spectrum would be most effective in the process of correlating society's response — a job that requires less speed and greater reflectiveness than the news function, more speed and less study than the teaching function.

(4) *Permanence.* Books probably give the greatest sense of permanence. Next come motion pictures and magazines. There is but a small amount of permanence in newspapers. Least permanent are radio and television. It stands to reason that the more permanent media are likely to be used for principle and organized meaning, the less permanent for report or persuasion.

But far more important for the international communicator than these broad general laws are the specific details of how a given channel is regarded and used in a given culture. This, as we know, can vary significantly from country to country.

Perhaps the best summary of the literature on media differences is the 1949 memorandum by Dr. Klapper, which follows.

▲ JOSEPH T. KLAPPER

*T*he Comparative Effects of the Various Media

LIMITS OF THE DISCUSSION

A complete discussion of the effects of any one mass medium, let alone all mass media, is obviously impossible within the scope of this memorandum. Whatever happens as a result of the media's existence or whatever happens to an individual as a result of reading, listening, or watching may be termed an effect of the media. The area of effects thus includes not only the subjects of all four of these memoranda but further involves or touches upon literally all individual or social human behavior and a host of technological and commercial developments. Obviously, therefore, only an arbitrarily defined section of this vast field can here be discussed.

With the objectives of the Public Library Inquiry in mind, the Director of the Inquiry and the present author have therefore agreed to limit the present memorandum to what might be called the comparative *effectiveness* of the various media as instruments of informal pedagogy and of persuasion. Such other effects as the Director considers particularly pertinent to the objectives of the Inquiry are given separate attention in the other memoranda.

Even within this delimited field, however, certain exclusions must be formally announced. Thus studies and conjectures bearing on the media's effects upon the behavior or upon the morals of their audi-

▲ This is a memorandum written for the Public Library Inquiry. It is published here by permission of the Bureau of Applied Social Research of Columbia University, by whom it was reproduced and copyrighted in 1949. The author is a member of the evaluation staff of the United States Information Agency. To save space and make a simpler presentation, reference notes have been omitted in this reprinting. Readers who wish to turn to the original publication of this memorandum (entitled *The Effects of Mass Media*) will find an extensive summary bibliography.

ences will be ignored, at least in the present memorandum. We will be here concerned almost exclusively with those differences in pedagogical and persuasive effectiveness which arise from the fact that the different media present different sensory stimuli, that one is perceived visually, another aurally, and the like. Mention will also be made of the more important differences in distribution of the media, since such differences render the various media more and less effective in given areas of pedagogy or persuasion. We will not, however, be here concerned with the direction in which the media affect audience values. To the degree that this topic is pertinent to the specific areas of effect cited by the Director of the Public Library Inquiry, it is covered in the other memoranda.

A further and more conspicuous exclusion will bar from the present memorandum all discussion of the comparative effectiveness of the various media in *formal* pedagogy, i.e., in the classroom. A vast and variegated literature on this subject has accrued through a multitude of experiments conducted in various schools of education. Massive as it is, the literature is in general valid only for the specific curricular situations described. The findings vary, as indeed they must, with the subject of pedagogy, the relationship between the text and film, and the like. A comparison, for example, of the relative pedagogical effectiveness of a printed description of plant growth and a film portraying the process by time-lapse photography is a very different thing from a comparison of the effectiveness of a text on civics and a pertinent, although not precisely comparable film. An adequate treatment of the comparative effectiveness of the media in the classroom would require a volume in itself, and the findings reported would have little to do with the effectiveness of the media in out-of-school persuasion. The subject will therefore not be treated in this memorandum.

APPLICABILITY OF EXPERIMENTAL FINDINGS

A notable number of experimenters have undertaken to measure the comparative effectiveness of the various media as indicated by degree of retention of material, changes in audience attitude and the like. Before the findings of these experiments are presented, a word of caution must be given regarding the use of the data. To put the warning briefly, the empirical evidence must not be assumed to be valid in situations dissimilar to those described in the specific experiment.

Most of the investigations in which two or more media are compared were conducted under laboratory conditions which differ markedly from the situation in which the public at large listens to or looks at the products of mass media. Three differences between the laboratory and the social situations are of particular importance.

1. The controlled experiment ordinarily involves highly motivated

attendance. Often the subjects are students who are compelled to read, listen or watch by faculty command. Sometimes the subjects are paid to be spectators. Their awareness and reactions are thus likely to be quite different from those of the housewife or worker who reads, watches, or listens to what he wishes, when he wishes, and where he wishes.

2. The controlled experiment ordinarily involves identical texts presented through different media. Outside the laboratory, however, one is not likely to hear over the radio the exact words of a magazine article or advertisement. Data pertaining to identical texts cannot be assumed to be valid in relation to vaguely similar texts.

3. The controlled experiment ordinarily controls the frequency and length of exposure. The subjects see, hear, or view the material a given number of times, which is ordinarily equal for the several media. In daily life, however, a man may read something in the paper once and hear similar material over the air seven times, or twice, or not at all. In short, neither balanced exposure nor its results necessarily occur in the work-a-day world.

Yet the findings of controlled experiments must not be ignored in our present discussion. By indicating what may be expected when all conditions but one are equal they help us to identify those conditions which are not ordinarily equal and so to develop our understanding of the nature and results of given communicational situations.

Within the limits set in the first section, and keeping in mind the cautions noted above, we shall now consider the evidence and conjectures regarding the comparative effectiveness of the media. We shall first consider material in which different media are actually compared. Thereafter we shall note some of the unique advantages frequently attributed to each of the media.

ACTUAL MEDIA COMPARISONS

(1) *Print and direct or transmitted voice as devices to elicit retention*

A series of experimenters have investigated the relative retention of identical material presented in print or aurally, i.e., either by direct voice, a record, or a speaker. The findings seem remarkably consistent in regard to simple and brief material, and somewhat less consistent as regards complex or lengthy material.

As regards simple material, retention is apparently highest when both methods are used. Aural presentation alone, however, elicits, on the whole, longer and better retention than does print alone. The superiority of aural over printed presentation appears to be greater among less intelligent persons, including the mentally retarded. In reference to persons of exceptional intelligence or reading ability, the findings vary, the weight of existing evidence suggesting that the visual presentation elicits better retention among such subjects.[1]

In reference to complex or lengthy material, the various controlled experiments present wholly contradictory findings. Thus, Russell, Carey, and Young obtained findings substantially similar to those obtained with simple materials. However, Lumley, Green, and Carver, Larsen and Feder, and Goldstein all found that the complex material was the better retained after visual presentation.

The present author is not aware of any investigation in which the retention of complex material presented *both* visually and aurally was compared with retention afforded by only one type of presentation. It is at least a reasonable conjecture, however, that such double presentation would be more effective than presentation by either method alone.

Although the inconsistency of the laboratory findings regarding complex material cannot be resolved here the findings of certain adjacent researches suggest one possible clarifying factor. Lazarsfeld has demonstrated that in actual daily life, people on higher cultural levels "prefer print to radio for the communication of comparable subject matter" and that this preference is the greater according as the reading skill of the group is greater, and/or according as "their interest in [the] given subject matter is the greater." Radio, on the other hand, is the preferred source of most persons with less than high school education. Those who prefer radio and those who prefer print attribute precisely the same advantages to their favored medium (e.g., "easier to understand," "more absorbing," etc.). Lazarsfeld proposes that each of the groups is merely asserting that they find their favored medium a more efficient means of communication. It is of course not surprising that listening should be the more efficient process for most persons whose formal education is relatively slight.

Lazarsfeld recognizes the bearing of these data upon the experiments comparing the effectiveness of print and voice. He hopes his

[1] It is often stated by social scientists that the various experiments on this subject yield contradictory results. Some writers, e.g., Goldstein, attribute these differences to insufficiently refined experimental procedures.

The present author has observed that if the experiments using simple and brief material are distinguished from those using lengthy and complex material (short advertisements as opposed to "factual geography selections," 2,500 word essays on psychological topics and the like) the experiments bearing on simple material reveal no important inconsistencies.

In regard to simple and brief material, for example, findings essentially similar to those noted above were obtained by Carver, Stanton, DeWick, Elliott, Willen, Miller, Lass, and Goldstein.

The experiments *do* reveal contradictory findings as regards the *immediate* recall of material, but not as regards retention over a period of time. Carver furthermore differs from Lass and Goldstein in finding that aural presentation maintains its superiority among the more highly academically trained subjects.

analysis will help, furthermore, to clarify somewhat the much confused controversy regarding "eye versus ear." The experimental literature on this topic is full of contradictory statements: for every study which shows that the ear is more receptive, another study can be quoted which attributes that the perception is itself of only small importance in the communication of idea; what counts is the situation in which communication occurs — the reading and listening habits of the respondent and the character of the subject matter in question.

We have already noted in this memorandum that classifying the experiments according to "character of the subject matter" removes most of the inconsistencies in regard to simple and brief material. It is quite possible that the inconsistent findings regarding lengthy or complex material may reflect differences in the reading skill of the participating persons. The suggestion is offered merely speculatively. To test it would require a complex comparison of the educational level *and* reading skills of the subjects in each of the several experiments, a process too involved to be undertaken and reported upon in this survey of the literature.

In summary, the investigations of comparative retention afforded printed and spoken (actual, transmitted, or recorded voice) material present contradictory findings. All the experiments involving simple and short material, however, agree that presentation by both methods is most effective,[2] but that aural presentation alone is superior to visual presentation alone for most persons. In regard to more highly complex material, the weight of available evidence slightly favors print, but the conflicting findings are not yet reconcilable. It appears that other factors are at work and must be identified before the situation can be properly examined. Degree of reading skill may very probably be one such factor. Although no supporting evidence is available, it seems a reasonable conjecture that multiple media exposure to complex material would be more effective than single media exposure.

(2) *Face-to-face discourse, transmitted voice, and print, as instruments of persuasion*

The findings of several experiments agree on the relative persuasive power of "speech, radio, and print" in the transmission of identical texts. The typical procedure and findings are exemplified in the work of W. H. Wilke, who exposed three matched groups of university students to texts on war, religion, birth control, and economic issues. The identical material was presented to one group by a lecturer, to another group via a wired speaker, and to the third group in printed form. The lecturer was found to be the most effective in modifying opinions, the wired speaker next most effective, and the printed material least effective. Similar findings were obtained by Knower under roughly

---

[2] Not all the cited experiments actually include multiple exposure. Those that do agree on its superior effectiveness.

similar circumstances. Allport and Cantril, after a survey of several experiments, also lend their support to the apparently unanimous opinion, viz., personal address is superior in persuasive power to mechanical aural appeal, which is in turn superior to printed appeal.

The relative effectiveness of these media, demonstrated in laboratory situations, seems also to hold true in more normal social situations. Two major studies attribute this relative persuasive efficiency not to mere technological differences in the media, but rather to differences in content, audience coverage, or psychological aspects of the communicational situation.

Lazarsfield, Berelson, and Gaudet conducted an elaborate study of "how the voter makes up his mind in a presidential campaign." During seven months prior to the 1940 elections, 2,400 residents of Erie County, Ohio, were interviewed between two and seven times each. Research was directed upon various topics, among them the relative effectiveness of personal influence, radio, and newspapers upon persons' voting plans. The investigators found that

In comparison with the formal media of communication, personal relationships [i.e., casual conversation, *not* formal addresses] are potentially more influential for two reasons: their coverage is greater and they have certain psychological advantages over the formal media. . . .

Whenever the respondents were asked to report on their recent exposure to campaign communications of all kinds, political discussions were mentioned more frequently than exposure to radio or print. On any average day, at least 10% more people participated in discussions about the election — either actively or passively — than listened to a major speech or read about campaign items in a newspaper. And this coverage 'bonus' came from just those people who had not yet made a final decision as to how they would vote. Political conversations, then, were more likely to reach those people who were still open to influence.

For example, people who made up their minds later in the campaign were more likely to mention personal influences in explaining how they formed their final vote decision. Similarly, we found that the less interested people relied more on conversations and less on the formal media as sources of information. Three-fourths of the respondents who at one time had not expected to vote but were then finally 'dragged in' mentioned personal influence. After the election, the voters were given a check list of 'sources from which they got most of the information or impressions that caused them to form their judgment on how to vote.' Those who had made some change during the campaign mentioned friends or members of their family relatively more frequently than did the respondents who kept a constant vote intention all through the campaign.

Personal relationships, the investigators believe, not only achieve greater audience coverage than radio or newspapers but possess "certain psychological advantages which make them especially effective." Lazarsfeld, Berelson, and Gaudet mention "five such characteristics," viz:

(1) it is more casually engaged in, often nonpurposive, and thus less self-selective than mass media material which largely attracts persons already sympathetic to the view expressed.

(2) it is "flexible when countering resistance."

(3) it provides "immediate and personal . . . rewards for compliance" or punishment for noncompliance, being in itself capable of expressing social pleasure or displeasure.

(4) it may be exerted by a trusted or "intimate source."

(5) it may accomplish its ends without first instilling conviction. "The lady where I work wanted me to vote," reports one respondent. "She took me to the polls and they all voted Republican so I did too."

As between the radio and the newspaper, Lazarsfeld, Berelson, and Gaudet found radio to be the apparently more important persuasive agent for the majority of the respondents.

Asked which medium helped them to make their decision, the voters mention radio and newspaper about equally. When they are asked for the "most important" source, however, radio gets a clear lead.

Radio was also established as the more common agent for *changes* in vote intention. The investigators suggest three reasons for radio's superior effectiveness.

In the first place, a considerable amount of political material appears in the press from the beginning to the end of the campaign with few notable variations. In time, the claims and counter-claims of the parties as they appeared in cold print came to pall upon the reader who had been exposed to essentially the same stuff over an extended period. The campaign on the radio, however, was much more cursory in its early phases and became vigorous and sustained only toward the close.

Secondly, the radio campaign consists much more of 'events' of distinctive interest. A political convention is broadcast, and the listener can virtually participate in the ceremonial occasion: he can respond to audience enthusiasm, he can directly experience the ebb and flow of tension. Similarly with a major speech by one of the candidates: it is more dramatic than the same speech in the newspaper next morning.

And thirdly, the listener gets a sense of personal access from the radio which is absent from print. Politics on the air more readily becomes an active experience for the listener than politics in the newspaper does for the reader. It represents an approach to a face-to-face contact with the principals in the case. It is closer to a personal relationship, and hence more effective.

Lazarsfeld, Berelson, and Gaudet thus find that in a social setting personal influence is a more effective persuader than radio which is in turn more effective than print. These findings tend to confirm the findings of laboratory experiments, although the situations and tentative explanations differ. It will be remembered, for example, that in the laboratory situation "face-to-face discourse" refers to a formal speech while in the Erie County study the phrase refers to casual social conversation. In addition, the various differences between laboratory experiments and social situations, as cited above, all apply here.

Stouffer, reporting on his study of radio and newspaper preferences among news-consumers, brings a somewhat new point of view of the question of the relative persuasive, or suggestive, efficacy of the two media. Noting that suggestibility is higher among people on comparatively low cultural levels, Stouffer points out that these persons are proportionately more prevalent in the radio audience than in the newspaper audience. It would thus appear that, regardless of which of the media is more persuasive for the same persons,

the potential radio listener . . . is . . . more suggestible than the potential reader . . . Of all the facts that make radio a powerful social institution, probably the most imposing one is that radio is the preferred medium of the more suggestible man.

(3) *The screen compared with print and other media as regards rentention of material*

That material presented in motion picture or filmstrips is recalled in some detail, has been demonstrated by at least three studies. The present author has, however, been able to discover only one relatively recent comparison of the retention elicited by the screen as opposed to other media.

H. E. Jones tested the retention elicited in children by various novels and by commercial motion picture versions of the same books. His findings, reported in insufficient detail to permit any real evaluation, award the palm to the motion pictures.

An elaborate study made in the early thirties by Holoday and Stoddard, under Payne fund auspices, demonstrated that motion pictures elicited high and accurate recall in children of various ages. Children of 8 recalled 60% of the items remembered by superior adults, children of 11 to 12 remembered 75%, and the 15 to 16 year olds recalled 91% of the material recalled by their superior elders. Retention was quite lasting.

In general the second-third-grade children at the end of six weeks remember 90 per cent of what they knew on the day following the show. Three months after seeing the picture they remember as much as they did six weeks after seeing it. In some cases, as with 'Tom Sawyer,' they remember more at the end of six weeks and still more at the end of three months. At all ages including the adults the slow drop of the curve of forgetting is striking.

The investigators assert that "curves of retention are considerably higher than those obtained by previous investigators," but the investigations they cite in support of this position deal exclusively with the motivated memorization of nonsense syllables and poetry, and were all completed prior to 1918. The data presented by Holoday and Stoddard thus merely indicate that movies are recalled in detail, but do not indicate that the screen elicits any greater retention than do other media.

An elaborate series of studies recently made under War Department auspices indicate that films are highly effective in imparting factual information, but reveal no such degree of long term retention as is claimed by Holoday and Stoddard. Against the latter's claim of 90% recall six days after exposure and no further loss over six months, must be placed the War Department's findings of an approximate 50% loss of factual information between the first and ninth week following exposure. The findings of the two studies are, however, hardly comparable, Holoday and Stoddard having dealt with ordinary entertainment films while the army investigators were concerned with documentaries, or training films; i.e., with cinematic purveyors of factual information. Hovland, Lumsdaine, and Sheffield, who report upon the War Department investigation, make no mention of any attempt to compare retention of screen presented material with retention of material presented by other media.

(3a) *Motion pictures compared to filmstrips as purveyors of factual information*

The relative effectiveness of a film and a filmstrip in the teaching of map reading was investigated in the course of the War Department studies. The film failed to show the expected superiority, pedagogical effects of the two devices being found to be to all intents and purposes identical.

UNIQUE ADVANTAGES ATTRIBUTED TO THE SEVERAL MEDIA

Various social scientists and public opinion specialists have attributed to each of the media certain advantages as instruments of pedagogy and persuasion which are not shared by the other media. Although these attributions of advantage are rarely supported by objective data, they nevertheless represent the careful thinking of acute observers and are often so patently valid as to be beyond the need of objective demonstration. Some of the major advantages attributed to each medium will therefore be here cited.

Print

Five advantages of print are variously noted or emphasized by such writers as Lazarsfeld, Doob, Waples, and Berelson.

(a) *The reader controls the exposure.* Whereas radio and the screen place the audience in a spectator role and present the material at a set pace, print alone leaves the reader capable of proceeding at whatever pace he may find consistent with his capabilities and interests. He may scan, skip, or plod, as he pleases, and thus need not suffer the boredom or bewilderment which the pace and content of the other media may engender. Further he may read at such times as he pleases, stop when he pleases, and resume when and if he pleases. All in all, the reader may expose himself to print at the time when he is most amenable to such exposure.

(b) *Exposure may be and often is repeated.* Unlike the other media, printed matter is not necessarily limited to a single occasion of reaching its audience. Radio programs, with a few very rare exceptions, are produced only once. Motion pictures run for a period of some weeks but are rarely seen twice by the same person. Printed matter, however, remains available and readers commonly return to material already read to confirm their memory, to reconsider the content, or simply to reexperience the pleasure once obtained. Cumulative effect and availability for reference are thus more possible in print than in other media.

(c) *Treatment may be fuller.* Print alone may develop a topic to whatever degree and whatever length seems desirable. Radio programs and films are of predetermined and relatively brief duration, and to continue the development of a topic in a series of programs and films is rendered largely unfeasible by the nature of audience habits. Complex discussions are thus more fit for presentation in print than by other media.

(d) *Specialized appeal is possible.* Print continues to be less standardized in over-all content than are the other media. Despite the trend toward insuring the widest possible appeal and the corollary reluctance to offend anyone, material of an unorthodox nature can be more readily found in print than on the air or screen. Within the medium of print, such material can be found more often in books and specialized magazines than in newspapers or the mass circulation magazines. Print thus remains the medium in which minority views can most easily find voice.

Further, the specialized publications which are thus possible are potentially highly powerful persuasive agents. The audience for specialized publications apparently regard the publication as voicing their own personal interests and are thus the more likely to accept its advices. Lazarsfeld, Berelson, and Gaudet, for example, found that

In Erie County in 1940, the *Farm Journal* was mentioned as a concrete influence upon changes in vote intention as frequently as *Colliers,* despite their great difference in circulation, and the Townsend publication as frequently as *Life* or the *Saturday Evening Post.*

(e) *Possible greater prestige.* Although all mass media, by virtue of their very massiveness, are regarded as possessing prestige, print is *believed by some authors* to possess the highest prestige. Doob suggests that special prestige may be attached to specific publications by their habitual readers and that a man will be especially amenable to influence from "his paper." The fact that print is the oldest of the mass media has also been proposed as a reason for its peculiar prestige, as has the fact that print and "culture" are traditionally associated.

If print indeed possesses most prestige for most people, then that fact would contribute to its greater persuasive effectiveness. Recent researches, however, throw doubt upon this conjectured extra prestige. It has been shown that print is not the preferred medium of the less cultured and is in fact little used by many persons on the lower cultural levels. Whether they therefore attach more or less prestige to print is a matter of conjecture. In the absence of specific evidence the whole question of the relative prestige of print and other media must likewise remain a matter of conjecture.

Summary. Print, unlike the other media, permits its audience to set their own pace, allows for repeated exposure, allows for treatment of any length. Less reluctantly than the other media, print gives expression to minority views. Publications designed for minority or special-interest groups are peculiarly effective persuasive agents. In addition print is believed by some authors to possess greater prestige than the other media, but this belief can not at present be either substantiated or disproved.

Radio

Several of the unique advantages attributed to radio have been cited in the course of the foregoing discussion on taste. Thus we have already noted that radio reaches persons who are not often reached by print nor movies, and that this audience tends to be less cultured and more suggestible than the audience of other media. The possibilities of exploiting these facts, for good or ill, are fairly obvious, but ambitions must be tempered by the inevitable process of audience selection which programs themselves set in motion. We have also noted the speculations of Lazarsfeld, Berelson, and Gaudet to the effect that radio permits its audience "virtually to participate in ceremonial occasions" and that the "listener gets a sense of personal access from the radio" which thus "represents an approach to a face-to-face contact."

To these three unique advantages (audience structure, dramatic participation, and resemblance to face-to-face contact), we may add two others, proposed by Doob, and both purely conjectural.

Doob proposes that the radio possesses a unique advantage over other media by virtue of its speedy distribution of news. Because the radio can report an event almost immediately upon its occurrence, Doob believes that many persons first learn of the event via the radio. Whatever slant the radio may give that news, Doob believes, will be particularly susceptible of belief and not susceptible of contradiction due to this "fact of primacy."

Studies on the formation of attitude and belief, however, do not attribute any very great advantage to such primary framing. At least one study, in fact, suggests that people's first interpretation of a given matter is particularly *easy* to change.

Doob also proposes that radio listeners may envisage themselves as members of a gigantic group simultaneously engaged in listening to the same material and that this group feeling may increase the suggestibility of the audience. Here again, no objective data can be offered in proof or denial. It may be noted, however, that Coughlin's success has been attributed at least in part to his using local face-to-face contact in conjunction with radio speeches. The two avenues of influence are believed to have stimulated local and national in-group feelings among his audience, contributing to their feelings of immediate social security and prestige.

Screen

Surprisingly few unique advantages have been attributed to the commercial or semi-commercial screen as an instrument of persuasion or informal pedagogy.

(a) A vague or implicit belief that picturization is generally uniquely effective seems present in various works and is explicitly expressed by several writers including Doob and Blumer. That this is true in regard to some matters and doubtful in regard to others is beyond question.

(b) We have already noted that the motion pictures elicit a high degree of recall. That this recall is greater than that elicited by other media has been alleged, but not yet convincingly demonstrated.

(c) Holoday and Stoddard discovered that most children and many adults tend to accept unquestioningly all presumably factual information in commercial films. Inaccurate statements or pictures are apparently accepted as truth. Whether this blind trust in screen material is any greater than that inspired by other material has not been investigated.

(d) On the basis of personal reports, Blumer postulates that commercial films exercise a peculiarly deep "emotional possession" of children (*not* of adults). He attributes this possession to the facts of concrete setting, deliberate emotional stimulation, and attractive scenes. The child, Blumer postulates, imaginatively enters into the pictured world. Noting this phenomenon of "emotional possession" in conjunction with the unquestioning trust cited above, Charters believes that

All of these factors and probably others produce a condition that is favorable to certain types of learning. This is the quality of authority.

It must be again noted, however, that the Payne studies, which include both the Holoday-Stoddard and the Blumer studies, merely assert the *fact* of motion picture influence without attempting to compare the *power* of that influence with that exercised by other media.

Face-to-face Discourse

That face-to-face discourse is a far more effectual instrument of pedagogy and persuasion than any impersonal medium is the heavy consensus of opinion among social scientists and public opinion experts. The unique advantages attributed to this mode of communication derive directly from the fact of inter-personal relationship and are therefore likely to be the stronger as the situation is more individual, the less as the situation becomes formal or involves a large audience. To attempt to enumerate all these advantages seems a somewhat unnecessary undertaking. Of the five advantages cited by Lazarsfeld, Berelson, and Gaudet and noted above, the second and third (flexibility and immediate provision of reward or punishment) are particularly emphasized by writers primarily concerned with the psychological analysis of communicative processes. Hovland, for example, enters into some detail regarding the possibility of the speaker's recognizing the more effective stimulus, the immediate provision or promise of appropriate rewards and the like.

Mass Media Supplemented by Face-to-face Contact

The extreme pedagogical and persuasive effectiveness of mass media supplemented by face-to-face contact has been demonstrated by controlled experiments. Hovland, Lumsdaine, and Sheffield, for example, report that a lesson in map reading consisting of an army training film supplemented by a face-to-face lecture was far more pedagogically effective for its military audience than was the film alone. Whether the lecture was presented as an introduction or as a review was found to be of no significance, the mere fact of face-to-face supplement being the factor apparently responsible for increased effectiveness. Audience participation, which might be regarded as a kind of highly activated face-to-face contact, was likewise found to increase the pedagogical effectiveness of a film-strip designed to teach the phonetic alphabet.[3]

The combined use of mass media and face-to-face contact has characterized several highly successful propaganda campaigns. The propaganda successes of Father Coughlin, the Nazis, and the Soviet Union are cases in point. Several social observers, in particular Lazarsfeld and Merton, regard this combination of mass media appeal and face-to-face contact as in itself an especially powerful persuasive technique. Their analysis of its peculiar power emphasizes the manner in which such a combination provides the audience with certain psychological requisites of suggestibility. Their analysis, in other words, deals not so much with the media as with the psychology of the audience. Accordingly, the analysis is more pertinent to the memorandum on persuasion than to the present discussion of the comparative effectiveness of the media itself. We thus reserve further discussion of this point for the later memorandum, noting here only the fact that mass media supplemented by face-to-face contact has characterized several highly successful propaganda campaigns and *may* be in itself a superior persuasive device.

---

[3] It is to be noted that increasing the motivation of the soldiers to learn the material, accomplished by merely announcing that a quiz would be administered, increased learning as effectively as did audience participation.

SUMMARY

1. Laboratory experiments, which due to their rigid conditions of control differ markedly from social situations, indicate
   a. that combined use of aural and visual presentation elicits better retention of simple and brief material than does the use of either method of appeal alone;
   b. that aural presentation of whatever sort elicits better retention of simple and brief material than does visual presentation;
   c. conflicting findings regarding the relative effectiveness of visual and aural presentation in eliciting retention of lengthy or complex material. Other, extra-laboratory researches suggest that the reading skill of the audience may be a major criterion. It is possible that for the highly educated or for those with high reading skills, print may be the more effective medium while radio may be more effective for those of lesser reading skill. Further and more refined experimentation is needed to settle this question;
   d. that face-to-face discourse is a more effective persuasive agent than is transmitted voice, which in turn is more effective than print.
2. Researches carried out in more normal social situations confirm the laboratory findings cited in 1,d, above. These researches point to differences in the audience structure and psychological appeal of the various media as contributory factors.
3. Objective studies indicate that the screen elicits a high degree of recall, but only one study, reported in extreme brevity, suggests that this degree of recall is any greater than that elicited by other media. No generalizations on the comparative effectiveness of the screen as to other media can be substantiated by adequate empirical evidence.
4. Each of the media is ascribed certain unique advantages by various writers. Some of these attributions of advantage have been empirically demonstrated, some are patently true, and others are wholly conjectural. In general,
   a. *Print* permits the reader to govern the pace and occasions of exposure, permits successive re-exposure, and allows for treatment at any length. Of all mass media, print is apparently the least reluctant to give expression to minority views, and publications specially designed for such expression are extremely effective persuasive agents.
   b. *Radio* reaches an audience not as often reached by the other mass media, and tending to be more poorly cultured and more suggestible than the audience of other media. Radio affords the spectator some degree of participation in the actual event being

broadcast and thus approaches face-to-face contact. Radio has been alleged to possess unique persuasive capabilities because of its often being the first medium to communicate given material to the audience, and because of a group feeling alleged to be experienced by the audience. These last two allegations are neither supported nor disproved by existing empirical evidence.

c. The *screen* is believed to enjoy unique persuasive and pedagogical advantages by virtue of its presenting concrete visual material. These concrete settings and other factors are believed by some investigators to render the films capable of taking "emotional possession" of children. While it is established that children tend to accept without question information presented in films the pedagogical and persuasive implications of this trust have not been made clear nor has it been shown that other media do not achieve similar effects.

d. Face-to-face discourse is generally regarded as the most effective instrument of pedagogy and persuasion by virtue of such capabilities as flexibility, immediate provision of reward or punishment, and other characteristics deriving directly from the personal relationship involved.

e. The use of one or more mass media supplemented by face-to-face contact has characterized several highly successful propaganda campaigns and is believed by some observers to be in itself a superior persuasive device. But this is conjecture rather than proven fact. Controlled experiments in the army demonstrated the pedagogical advantage of film plus lecture for instruction in map reading. Further discussion of this combined face-to-face and mass media approach appears in Memorandum IV.

Getting the Meaning Understood

Introductory Note

THE MEANING OF MEANING

Walter Lippmann introduced his pioneering book on public opinion with a famous chapter entitled "The world outside and the pictures in our heads." He argued that, although men live in the same world, they think and feel in different worlds. Every man imposes a "pseudo-environment," said Lippmann, between himself and his real environment. Man does not deliberately falsify his environment, of course. But one observer's experience is never exactly like that of other observers, and he interprets his new experience in terms of his previous experience. Furthermore, a great part of his experience is already filtered before it comes to him. This is the part that passes through news services, textbooks, reports, tradition, custom, gossip, and rumor. In the way of a full and accurate picture of the world are "the artificial censorships, the limitations of social contact, the comparatively meager time available in each day for paying attention to public affairs, the distortion arising because events have to be compressed into very short messages, the difficulty of making a small vocabulary express a complicated world, and finally the fear of facing those facts which would seem to threaten the established routine of men's lives."

This is an insightful picture of the conditions under which communication tries to modify the "pictures in our heads." We are talking now about perception and meaning, for perception is the interpretive process through which we pass all the stimuli that we accept from our environment, and meaning is what comes out of this process — the "picture in our heads." We can also call it the end product of the decoding or, in the terms we used earlier, the mediating response which a stimulus arouses in us, and which in turn arouses the kind of self-stimulus which triggers off activity that leads to an overt response. We can't see meaning or observe perception. Everything we know about it has to be inferred backward from overt response and forward from stimulus. And yet we are able to put together a surprisingly workable picture of the interpretive function. Hardly any kind of knowledge about the communication process is more important to the communicator.

What happens in the interpretive process?

First of all, we can say that we perceive the world in terms of its *meaning* to us. We can't tolerate meaningless experience. As F. C. Bartlett said, "It is fitting to think of every human cognitive reaction — perceiving, imagining, thinking, and reasoning — as an effort after meaning." It is characteristic of people everywhere that they want to live in an organized world, where sense data will mean something and new experiences can be related to something already known. When something new, different, strange is encountered, the easiest way is to react to it in a way that will give it a meaning which will let the person respond to it with a learned reaction. This dispels insecurity, makes one feel at home.

Therefore, we *structure* experience so as to make it meaningful to us. We select, add, distort, relate. But the question is, what guides the way we structure it? And the broadest answer here is that we structure it according to our *frames of reference*.

Consider, for example, how differently a garage mechanic and a physician would perceive an automobile accident. Although both would be receiving essentially the same physical stimuli, still those stimuli would be producing far different interpretive responses inside the two men. Now bring to the scene an insurance adjuster, a new car salesman, a reporter, and a priest, and consider how differently they would be likely to perceive it.

Each observer would be to some extent *selecting* a part of the experience — the doctor, the broken human bodies; the mechanic, the broken cars; and so forth. In so doing he would *distort* the experience by emphasizing parts of it unequally. He may *add* to the experience; many a witness to an accident, in his excitement, has perceived something which has not happened. And he would certainly *relate* this experience back to his frame of reference — what he knows, what he needs, what he values. The doctor would relate it to his medical training, the mechanic to his mechanical experience, the salesman to his occupation of selling new cars, the priest to his vocation of saving souls.

Krech and Crutchfield give the example of an aviator who lands in a primitive country where no airplane and no white man have ever been seen before. How will the natives perceive this strange arrival? They will at once relate it to such frame of reference as they have to explain it. Perhaps the flying machine will seem to them a kind of a bird. Perhaps the strange man will seem to them a god. They may be unable to understand a supercharger or a dihedral, but they will still classify and interpret this new experience in terms of its meaning to them.

Or take the example from the same authors of an American tourist and a native Mexican at a bullfight. What will each perceive? The American (say K and C) "is likely to perceive and stress the pain to the animal, the messiness of the scene, and the flies. The Mexican fan, on the other hand, might perceive and stress the skill of the performer, his daring or fearlessness, the fine technical points involved, and even the fine spirit of the bull in putting up such a good fight."

A slightly different way to describe what is happening in these examples is to say that we tend to structure experience *functionally* — so that it works for us. There is a great deal of research evidence to back this up. McClelland and Atkinson used three groups of sailors, one group of whom had been fed only an hour before, another had gone four hours without food, and a third had gone 16 hours hungry. They were told that the experiment was to find out what objects they could see in poor light. In a darkened room they faced a screen on which an operator projected exactly nothing, although he went through the motions of operating a projector. Five seconds after each "slide" had been exposed, the experimenter gave the subjects a broad hint, for example: "Three objects on a table. What are they?" Or, "All the people in this are enjoying themselves. What are they doing?" The answers showed that the longer the respondents had been without food, the more food-related responses they were likely to give. That is, the "people" were likely to be enjoying themselves eating; the three objects on the table were likely to be hamburgers. Furthermore, hunger increased the apparent size of the food objects.

The Bruner, Goodman, Postman experiments come into this group, as does Murray's experiment on the different ways children perceive the picture of a strange man, before and after playing a game of murder. In each case, the experience is being perceived in such a way as to work for the perceiver — to match up to his needs, values, and expectations.

If now we ask what all this means in practical terms to the communicator, we can answer that it means he must give up any idea he may have of communicating impartial and unassailable "facts." As Krech and Crutchfield say, "There are no impartial 'facts.' Data do not have a logic of their own that results in the same perceptions and cognitions for all people. Data are perceived and interpreted in terms of the individual perceiver's own needs, own emotions, own personality, own previously formed cognitive patterns."

Practically speaking, then, these are some of the workings of perception a communicator must expect, and, so far as possible, allow for, as he tries to communicate his meaning:

1. *The receiver will interpret the message in terms of his experience and the ways he has learned to respond to it.* The tribesmen, seeing the airplane, interpreted it as a bird; that was the only experience within

which the aircraft had meaning for them. A picture of a bull, seen by a Hindu, would probably be classified in terms of a religious frame of reference; seen by a Korean farmer, it might be organized in terms of farm work; seen by a Spaniard, it might be put into a sporting frame of reference; whereas to a Texan it might be seen against an experience of cattle-raising.

Therefore, a communicator must consider how his audience's experience will enable them to interpret and respond to the signs he communicates. Will his message mean anything to them, or will their experience give it a different meaning from the one intended? Is he "talking over their heads"? Is he making the funny or dangerous little mistakes that a city man sometimes makes in the country or a traveler makes in another country? Is he "putting his meaning over"? Is he "striking responsive chords"? These old phrases take on a new importance when we see how important it is for a communicator to take into account his audience's frame of reference.

In this connection, we should mention language skills, because we can perceive word signs only in terms of the language responses we know. Language also relates back to experience, and people who have different experiences have to some extent different languages. Consider, for example, the different languages of labor and management, of Communists and non-Communists, of returning combat veterans after World War II and the civilians they left behind them.

2. *The receiver will interpret the message in such a way as to resist any change in strong personality structures.* Studies of pre-election propaganda indicate that strong Democrats tend to ignore Republican campaign propaganda, and vice versa. Presented a story containing both viewpoints, or news favorable to both sides, each reader tends to remember the points favorable to his side.

The dramatic result of the "Mr. Biggott" studies (Cooper and Jahoda) was that the very cartoons designed to ridicule prejudice were distorted so as to reinforce prejudice. For example, the cartoon showing the hospitalized Mr. Biggott demanding "only sixth generation American blood" for his transfusion was seen by prejudiced persons as a socially inferior person striving for social status. Allport and Lepkin give an example out of rumor studies: people who opposed rationing during World War II were more prone than others to believe and repeat rumors alleging extravagant use of gasoline by high officials, rumors of extravagant use of butter at army bases, etc. In other words, these rumors were given a more or less favorable reception according to how they agreed or disagreed with the strong structures of values, needs, goals, role-concepts the recipients were trying to defend.

3. *The receiver will tend to group characteristics in experience so as to make whole patterns.* A picture of a hat protruding over a fence

tends to be perceived as a person wearing a hat and standing behind a fence. Lines, dots, masses on a paper tend to group themselves into familiar geometrical or pictorial patterns.

More important, we tend to "make meaning" by grouping the characteristics of objects within a common class. Americans tend to think of English as stuffy, and English to think of Americans as crude. Americans tend to think of Orientals as "inscrutable," and white Americans tend to think of Negroes as musical, carefree, able to stand deprivation better than whites (Blake and Dennis). These ready-made reactions save time in evaluating new people and new social situations. It is much easier to classify the new English resident down the block in terms of this "picture in our heads" than to make an individual study of him. As a matter of fact, if we meet the Englishman and he turns out to be friendly and homespun we probably classify him as an "exception."

This trick of stereotyping is the basis for some most insidious propaganda. The Communists can evoke an instant and negative reaction by calling the name "Capitalist," just as we can by calling the name "Communist." The word "socialism" has begun to assume for us a stereotyped meaning which is quite at variance with the meaning evoked by the same word, for example, in England. In contrast, we tend to respond very favorably whenever we hear "the American way" or "free enterprise" or "America First" or "freedom of opportunity." We have built in these ready-made reactions, and tend to use them as a kind of tent to cover a variety of possible experience. That is why a propagandist finds it so effective to associate something he wants to tear down with some hated symbol (as the Nazis constantly associated the American government with Jews) or to associate something he wants to build up with a favorable symbol (a hero, a flag, the fathers of the country).

The phenomenon of perceptual grouping, however, has another important significance for communicators. When people group experiences that occur closely together, they very often fail to discriminate between coincidence and causal effect. In complex modern life, people are not able to look very closely at cause and effect. They tend therefore to assume a causal relation whenever they observe contiguity.

More especially, people are willing to associate someone whom they perceive as "bad" with almost any "bad" event which happens in his proximity; or someone "good" with a nearby "good" event. Zillig's experiment, using two groups of children, one liked, one disliked by the audience, the disliked one trained to perform gymnastic events perfectly whereas the liked group was trained to make mistakes — this experiment revealed that the audience remembered almost all the mistakes as having been made by the *disliked* group. This was not malicious or dishonest; it was merely an illustration of the way perception works. That is why the Nazis were able to blame most of the ills of the world on the Jews, and why the Communists have been able to blame most of the ills of Asia on the western powers.

This does not mean, of course, that coincidence can be substituted for causality with all people at all times. The more the person has been taught to be critical, the less he is likely to be compelled by strong needs or drives to accept a perceptual organization uncritically, the more likely he is to look behind the label or the suggestion and try to isolate the facts. The moral for the communicator trying to get his meaning across is the same we have been repeating throughout this section: that one must know as much as possible about the frames of reference, needs, goals, languages, and stereotypes of his receiver, if he hopes to design a message to get his meaning across.

Perceiving

the

Message

*The four following selections all treat aspects of mean-
ing and the problems of conveying it. The Krech and
Crutchfield selection is a classic treatment from the
Gestalt point of view. The chapter by Doob relates
perception to propaganda problems, and the paper by
Allport and Postman discusses the psychology of rumor,
which is one of the best laboratories for observing perceptual processes and patterns.*

▲ DAVID KRECH

▲ RICHARD S. CRUTCHFIELD

*P*erceiving the World

TWO MAJOR DETERMINANTS OF PERCEPTION

The principles of organization are frequently grouped into two major categories: the principles relating to the *structural* factors of perception and those relating to the *functional* factors involved in perception. Experimental and theoretical literature in perception psychology is replete with discussions as to the relative importance of these two sets of factors.

Structural Factors

By *structural* factors are meant those factors deriving solely from the nature of the physical stimuli and the neural effects they evoke in the nervous system of the individual.[1] Thus, for the Gestalt psychologist, perceptual organizations are determined primarily by the physiological events occurring in the nervous system of the individual in direct reaction to the stimulation by the physical objects. Though not denying the influence, under certain conditions, of motivation and mental set, they emphasize that the sensory factors are primary in accounting for the "look of things."

To use a very simple and common example, the Gestalt psychologist would point out that our perception of the dots in Fig. 1*a* is perforce a perception of two horizontal groupings and not, say, an ungrouped collection of dots or five vertical groups, etc. Furthermore, they would insist that the factors which force this organization derive from the

[1] The term *autochthonous* is frequently used by the Gestalt psychologist when referring to these factors.

▲ These selections are from *Theory and Problems of Social Psychology*, published and copyright by McGraw-Hill (New York, 1948). They are printed here by permission of the publisher and copyright holder. The authors are professors of psychology at California and Swarthmore, respectively.

spatial relationships among the physical dots themselves as faithfully projected in the sensory region of the brain and are relatively independent of our reasoning, needs, moods, past learning, etc. To repeat: Those sensory factors which are independent of the perceiving individual's needs and personality and which force certain organizations in his cognitive field are referred to as "structural factors of perception." The isolation of these factors, their careful description, and the

Fig. 1

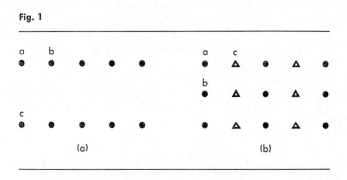

(a)   (b)

laws of their operation have led to the formulation of the "laws of organization."

Functional Factors

The *functional* factors of perceptual organization, on the other hand, are those which derive primarily from the needs, moods, past experience, and memory of the individual.[2] Thus, for example, in an experiment performed by Bruner and Goodman (1947), two groups of children (one a poor group from a settlement house in one of Boston's slum areas and the other a rich group from a "progressive school in the Boston area, catering to the sons and daughters of prosperous business and professional people") were asked to judge the size of various coins. The differences in the perceptions of the two groups of children were striking, with the poor group overestimating the size of the coins considerably more than did the rich group. The experimenters suggest that these results indicate the effect of need upon perception, and they formulate the following two hypotheses as possible general laws:

1. *The greater social value of an object, the more will it be susceptible to organization by behavioral determinants.*

[2] The term *functional* as applied to these factors was first suggested by Muenzinger (1942). In their treatment of these same factors, Bruner and Goodman (1947) suggest the term "behavioral determinants" which they define as ". . . those active, adaptive functions of the organism which lead to the governance and control of all higher-level functions, including perception. . . ."

2. *The greater the individual need for a socially valued object, the more marked will be the operation of behavioral determinants.*

Another illustration of the operation of functional factors is found in an experiment by Levine, Chein, and Murphy (1942). In that experiment, ambiguous drawings, when presented behind a ground-glass screen to hungry college students, were more frequently perceived as food objects (ham sandwiches, salads, etc.) than when presented to college students who had just finished eating. The different perceptions of the hungry and not-hungry students could not be due to "structural" factors, since the same pictures were presented to both groups but could be due only to the differences in need or motivation of the members of the two groups.

While quantitative laws of how these "functional" factors actually operate in perception are lacking, a great deal of experimental work is available that demonstrates their pervasive influence in perception.

. . . .

PROPOSITION I

The perceptual and cognitive field in its natural state is organized and meaningful

This first proposition affirms that the cognitive field, except perhaps in rare pathological conditions, is never a "blooming, buzzing confusion" of discrete impressions, unrelated experiences and unitary sensations. Whether we are discussing the initial sensory stimulations of the infant or the experiences of the adult when confronted by new and even bizarre objects and events, the individual's cognitive fields are organized and meaningful. A few examples may clarify the meaning of this proposition.[3]

"Simple" Perception

A baby is presented, for the first time in his life, with a red balloon on a white table. Considered purely physically, the "balloon" and the "table" can be described only as a visual field consisting of discrete pin points of stimuli consisting of light of varying wave lengths. What is the infant's resulting experience from this conglomeration of physical stimuli? Is it a mosaic of indifferently related kaleidoscopic sensations of reds and whites merging into one another, without form and without clearly defined boundaries, or is the child's experience better described as a perception of a red object having form and solidity against a background of a white object with its own form and

---

[3] For a discussion of the distinction between organized perceptions "without meaning" and organized perceptions "with meaning," see Tolman's (1933) paper. He characterizes the first concept as that held by the "pure Gestaltist," the second as that held by the "sign-Gestaltist."

solidity? Proposition I would require that the latter situation hold. The infant's perceptual field would consist of at least two discriminable, meaningful structures. The meanings might be extremely simple and might even be wrong — but there would be meaning. Thus, the red object might have the meaning that "this object if inserted in the mouth can be chewed and swallowed," and the white object may mean "this object, if pushed, will jiggle." The important thing is that the baby's experiences will be organized and meaningful.

Proposition I does not assert how much of this cognitive structure is due to the previous experiences of the baby or if the meanings are conditioned by hunger and activity needs. All we are concerned with is the nature of his cognitive field when he is stimulated by the balloon and the table.

The Strange and Bizarre

Or take another example. A savage who has never seen a white man or any of the paraphernalia of the white man's civilization sees an Army airplane descend from the skies and make a three-point landing and sees Second Lieutenant Arbuthnot come out of the plane. Obviously our savage will see the airplane and Arbuthnot as organized objects, but will they, because he has never seen their likes before, be completely meaningless to him? Again, the meaning he experiences may be wrong, but there will be meaning. He may experience the meaning of a "bird" as part of his purely visual precept of the airplane; he may ascribe the meaning of "God" or its equivalent to Arbuthnot, 2nd Lt. AUS. He will not have to wait until he is given instructions or until he has had further and extended experiences with these strange objects before his cognitive field is organized into a meaningful one.[4]

Forming an Impression of a Personality

A final example: In an experiment reported by Asch (1946) an attempt was made to determine how people form impressions of personality through hearing simple descriptions of the personality.[5] The experimenter read to his subjects (college students) a number of discrete characteristics which were said to belong to an unknown person. He then instructed his subjects to write a brief description of the impression the subject had gained of this unknown person. One

[4] The American school child who listened to his teacher sing various Christmas carols in foreign tongues and when asked to join with her sang "Atomic Bomb, Atomic Bomb" to the tune of "O Tannenbaum, O Tannenbaum" is an amusing and at the same time a somewhat horrifying illustration of the tendency to perceive strange sounds meaningfully. Akin to this is the youngster's remark, who after hearing the hymn that starts "Gladly the Cross I'd bear," asked "Why was the bear cross-eyed?"

[5] This experiment of Asch's is an interesting and valuable illustration of an experimental attempt to apply principles of "pure" perception to social material.

such list, for example, was: "energetic, assured, talkative, cold, ironical, inquisitive, persuasive." The list was read with an interval of approximately five seconds between the terms. Then the reading was repeated. Below are reproduced two of the typical sketches obtained from the subjects:

He is the type of person you meet all too often: sure of himself, talks too much, always trying to bring you around to his way of thinking, and with not much feeling for the other fellow.

He impresses people as being more capable than he really is. He is popular and never ill at ease. Easily becomes the center of attraction at any gathering. He is likely to be a jack-of-all-trades. Although his interests are varied, he is not necessarily well versed in any of them. He possesses a sense of humor. His presence stimulates enthusiasm and very often he does arrive at a position of importance.

Note how the discrete terms of the list have been organized into a living, meaningful, and even colorful personality. Not only have the individual terms *energetic, assured, talkative,* etc., been perceived in an organized way with an organized meaning, but the resulting organization of the terms has permitted the subject to "perceive" characteristics that were not even mentioned ("He possesses a sense of humor"). Asch summarizes the results of his experiments as follows:

When a task of this kind is given, a normal adult is capable of responding to the instruction by forming a unified impression. Though he hears a sequence of discrete terms, his resulting impression is not discrete. All subjects . . . of whom there were over 1,000 fulfilled the task in the manner described. . . . Starting from the bare terms, the final account is completed and rounded.

General Comments

What is true about our experiences with objects and people is also true about our experiences with events and ideas. Strange and new social mores, taboos, and relationships are not seen by us as meaningless but are immediately perceived with meaning. We cannot help doing this. Man is an organizing animal. This accounts, in many instances, for our misinterpretation or misunderstanding of the customs, habits, values and institutions of foreigners and strangers. We cannot say to ourselves, "Hold off any interpretation until you collect all the facts." As soon as we experience *any* facts, they will be perceived as organized into some sort of meaningful whole. This is a universal characteristic of the cognitive process and not a weakness of the impatient or prejudiced individual. In the experiment of Asch's referred to above, an experimental demonstration of the immediacy of this process is provided. In one of his experimental setups Asch read two different lists of traits to two different groups of subjects and again asked for personality descriptions. The two lists were identical with regard to the traits used but differed in the order of succession. For example, one group heard the following list: "intelligent, industrious, impulsive, critical, stubborn, envious." The other group heard the same words, but in reversed order: "envious, stubborn, critical, impulsive, industrious, intelligent." The descriptions obtained from the two groups of subjects differed markedly, leading Asch to conclude that "When the subject hears the first term, a broad, uncrystallized but directed impression is born. The next characteristic comes not as a separate item, but is related to the established direction.

Our perception of the dots in Fig. 1*a* as two sets of horizontal lines and the over-all impression we form of a man's personality from knowing only one or two facts about him are both instances of the same fundamental process of cognitive organization. This principle also helps us to understand the tenacity with which people hold on to "disproved" scientific theories or economic and political dogmas. No matter how much evidence one can bring to bear that a scientific theory does not fit the known facts, scientists are reluctant to give it up until one can give them another integration to take the place of the old. Merely attacking a well-integrated theory cannot be very effective. The old theory does integrate facts for people, does organize discrete experiences. In the absence of some other way of organizing facts, people will frequently hold on to the old, for no other reason than that.

PROPOSITION II

Perception is functionally selective

No one perceives everything that there is "out there" to be perceived. Our mental apparatus is not an indifferent organizing machine ready to accord equal importance to all stimuli that impinge upon our sense organs. The factors that determine the specific organization of our cognitive field and select out only certain stimuli to integrate into that field are frequently at work even before we are exposed to the physical stimuli. Typically, only certain physical stimuli are "used" in making up the organized perception, while other stimuli are either not used at all or are given a very minor role. This is what is meant by saying that perception is "selective."

Proposition II, however, also indicates that this selectivity is functional. The objects that play the major role in the organized perception, the objects that are *accentuated, are usually those objects which serve some immediate purpose of the perceiving individual.*[6] As our

[6] It should be clear that this does not necessarily mean that *only* those stimuli which serve some function or other will be noticed or seen by the subject. This statement affirms that the functionally significant stimuli will be given the major role to play, although other stimuli may be noticed peripherally, as it were. Bruner and Goodman (1947) make the further interesting suggestion that with habitual selection, the stimuli which are thus selected for major attention tend to become progressively more vivid and achieve greater clarity.

first motivational proposition has indicated, our basic, most useful unit in understanding the social behavior of the individual is the molar unit — a unit in terms of needs, tensions, and goals. To ask the question, then, "Why are certain objects selected to play a major role in most cognitive organizations?" is to ask the question, "What function does any cognitive organization serve?" The answer to this question not only will tell us what objects will be selected for perceptual organization but will also indicate the meaning with which those objects will be perceived.

Functional Selectivity of Perception and Dynamics of Behavior

Illustrations of the effects of needs, mental sets, moods, etc., in selecting out certain objects for a major role in perception are commonplace. So, too, are illustrations of the effect of these dynamic processes on the meanings given to the resulting perceptions.

Needs. — Let us take the simple example of two men seated at a lunch-room counter surveying the posted menu on the wall. One is very hungry; the other, only thirsty. Both are exposed to the same physical objects, yet the first will notice the hamburger and tomato-and-lettuce sandwiches, while the "tea, coffee, beer, pepsi-cola" items will be neglected or relatively so. The second man will react in the opposite manner. Ask both men to tell you what they "saw" on the menu, and the first will respond with a list of food items "and other stuff"; the second will enumerate the drink items "and other things." In one case the food items have been clearly and specifically perceived and organized against a background of nondifferentiated "other stuff"; in the second case the figure-ground relationships have been reversed.

That needs, rewards, and punishments can even determine in simple visual perception which aspect of a visual field will be selected out as the figure and which as the ground has been demonstrated by an experiment of Schafer and Murphy (1943). In that experiment two somewhat ambiguous figures were presented momentarily to the subjects. Each figure was so designed that part of the picture could be seen as an outline of a human face. Every time one of these faces was presented and seen as a face, the subject was rewarded (with money); every time the other figure was presented and seen as a face, the subject was punished (some of his money being taken away). The technique, in other words, was to build up a strong association between certain visual patterns and rewards and between other visual patterns and punishments. After this was done, the "rewarded" pattern and the "punished" pattern were combined into one picture in such a manner as to make it possible to perceive either face as the figure or as the ground. A significantly higher number of the faces that had previously been rewarded, when perceived alone, were not perceived as the *figure* in this combined picture than were faces that had been punished. Fifty-four out of sixty-seven perceptions were perceptions of the rewarded faces as figures.

That the meaning of what is selected for major attention in perception is influenced by needs is also apparent. We have already seen both in Levine, Chein, and Murphy's experiment and in Bruner and Goodman's experiment that the immediate perception of ambiguous objects is shaped by the hunger needs of the subjects and that the perceived size of a coin is determined by the differential goal character of the coins for the poor and rich children. On a more complicated level, Sanford (1936, 1937) has shown that the need for food, in children and in adults of college age, has a significant effect upon word association, interpretation of "neutral" pictures (*i.e.,* pictures having nothing to do, directly, with eating or with food), chain associations, completion of drawings, and completion of words where only the first two letters of a word were given. For example, a picture of a baby, a finger of whose hand was extended, was interpreted to mean "He's sticking his finger in the pie" by some of the hungry subjects, while some of the nonhungry subjects interpreted it as "He's pointing to a toy."

The successful diagnosis of individual need structures by the "projective technique" provides dramatic illustrations of the principles we have been discussing here. For the very use of this technique depends upon the fact that the specific perceptual and cognitive organizations with which the individual responds to pictures and words reflect his basic needs.

Mental Set. — Here, too, illustrations abound in everyday experiences. We see hundreds of men, every day, wearing different suits of clothing — suits that differ in cut, material, color, styling, number of buttons, etc. But usually all we perceive is that they are wearing clothes, and our resulting perceptual organization is not a very clear cut and differentiated one. What is the mental picture you have, for example, of the suit you saw your friend wear yesterday? But if we are on the way to a store to buy a suit, our perceptions of the clothes worn by friends and even strangers change rather remarkably. We notice the colors of the suits; we see shapes of pockets, cuts of lapels, presence or absence of pocket flaps which we never perceived before. With our changed mental set different objects are selected out for perception, and our resulting cognitive structures become much more differentiated and detailed.

A simple experiment by Murray (1933) has indicated how the mental set of the individual influences the meaning of what he perceives. Using girls as his subjects, Murray asked them to describe the picture of a man under two conditions — before these subjects had played a game of "murder" and after. In the latter instance the subjects tended to see much more maliciousness in the man's features than they did in the former instance.

The policeman, the social worker, the ward politician, and the foreign visitor walking through the same slum district not only interpret what they see differently but actually perceive different objects. The mental set of the perceiver can sometimes be of absolute importance in determining selective perception.

Mood. — An ingenious experiment of Leuba and Lucas (1945) provides some striking illustrations of how the mood or temperament of an individual operates to select out different stimuli for perceptual organization and tends to determine the meaning of the stimuli so selected.

The experiment involved the description of six pictures by three subjects when in each of three different moods: happy, critical, and anxious. Each of the three subjects was first hypnotized; the first mood was then induced by the appropriate hypnotic suggestions; and then the pictures were shown. After the subject had observed each picture, he was asked to describe what he had seen. When the six descriptions had been obtained, the subject was allowed to rest for a while, the first mood was removed by suggestion, he was brought back to his "normal" hypnotic state and told that he would forget having seen the pictures and what he had said about them. Then the next mood was induced, and the procedure repeated.

The final hypnotic suggestions for the different moods were as follows:

HAPPY MOOD: "Now you are feeling very happy and you are in a cheerful and joyous mood. You feel as if everything is rosy and you are very optimistic. You have a comfortable feeling of well-being; nothing is worrying you. You feel perfectly at peace with everything and everyone. You are in a very happy, cheerful, and optimistic mood."

CRITICAL MOOD: "Now you are very critical; you are quick to find fault and to condemn unfavorably. Your judgment of others is very harsh and severe. You see failings and faults very clearly. You are very critical and fault finding."

ANXIOUS MOOD: "Now you are quite anxious. You are disturbed over some possible misfortunes. You are disquieted and concerned as to something in the future. You are a little fearful and mildly alarmed. You have a feeling as if you were expecting something disagreeable to happen, yet were not sure that it would. You are quite anxious."

Following are three descriptions that one of the subjects gave for a picture showing "four college men on a sunny lawn, typing, listening to radio." In the happy mood his description read:

"Complete relaxation. Not much to do — just sit, listen and relax. Not much at all to think about."

When this subject was in a critical mood he observed or paid attention to or perceived, different things. Now his description ran:

"Someone ruining a good pair of pressed pants by lying down like that. They're unsuccessfully trying to study."

When in an anxious mood, still other items were perceived:

"They're listening to a football game or world series. Probably a tight game. One guy looks as if his side wasn't winning."

Notice how in the happy mood there seems to be little attention to details. The perceptual structure seems to be fairly simple and undifferentiated. In the critical mood a specific detail — the crease in one man's trousers — seems to occupy a central role in the perceptual field, an item which had not been reported at all in the first description. In the final mood, anxious, the details of the facial expression of one of the men are closely observed and interpreted, and now the cognitive field includes something that is not even physically present — a football or baseball game.

The different moods of the subjects had a directive effect not only on *what* was observed but, even more strongly, on the meaning of what was perceived. Thus, in analyzing some of the descriptions obtained from the subjects, the experimenters write:

The meanings and feelings attached to the activities shown in the pictures and the probable causes and results of those activities are usually different from mood to mood. In a happy frame of mind the Ss see the soldier in picture III (wounded man being carried on a litter by soldiers to aeroplane) as being "well taken care of" and as being taken "back to safety" or "a transport plane." When in an anxious mood these same Ss say the soldier "is in bad shape," "may not live," "an emergency case," "it frightens me."

Things are very rarely what they seem. The emotions, moods, personalities, and temperaments of people color and determine what they see "out there." The entire cognitive world of the individual who has an overriding need for security will be organized on quite a different basis from the individual who does not seek constant reassurances. "Wishful thinking" and "wishful perception" have similar sources. The man who fears a war and seeks peace will perceive political events, people, speeches, diplomatic forays, and production figures quite differently from the man who welcomes a war. The selectivity of perception is in large measure determined by the dynamics of behavior.

Functional Selectivity of Perception and Culture

What we perceive, as well as how we interpret what we perceive, is not only a function of those processes which can be specifically defined as motivational ones. Our immediate perceptions are also a function of the "higher order" cognitive organizations — of beliefs, of social ideals, of morals, of cultural frames of reference. The effect of these higher order cognitive organizations will be examined in more detail when discussing Proposition III, but for purposes of completeness a simple illustration at this point might be helpful.

Take, for example, the perceptions of an American tourist and a native Mexican at a Mexican bull fight. The American is likely to perceive and stress the pain to the animal, the messiness of the scene, and the flies. The Mexican fan, on the other hand, might perceive and stress the skill of the performer, his daring or fearlessness, the fine technical points involved, and even the fine spirit of the bull in putting up such a good fight.

What is selected out for perception not only is a function of our perceiving apparatus as physiologically defined but is partly a function of our perceiving apparatus as colored and shaped by our culture.

Functional Selectivity of Perception and Structural Factors

We must always remember, however, that in addition to the various factors discussed above, the physical distribution and qualities of the stimuli also help determine which stimuli, of the welter of stimuli impinging on our sense organs, will be selected out for perception. The familiar figure-on-background or "isolation" experiment of the perception laboratory illustrates this factor in operation. A single red dot, among many black dots, will "stand out" in perception. A single Negro in a crowd of white people is much more likely to be noticed by a neutral perceiver than if that individual were seen among many other Negroes. The slogan most frequently repeated (and most loudly) is also more likely to come to the attention of the individual than the infrequently mentioned one.

The "structural" factors involved in the creation and presentation of propaganda and educational material are sometimes quite important in determining what perceptions the "victims" or "students" will experience, as we shall see when we discuss those subjects. We must be constantly on guard against neglecting these structural factors in our attempt to pay proper attention to the functional factors. The physiological functioning of the nervous system in response to the nature of the distribution of the physical stimuli in space and time also operates so as to make perception selective.

General Comments

The failure to understand the implications of Proposition II, that perception is functionally selective, has led to much misguided effort and heartbreaking disappointment on the part of teachers, parents, religious missionaries, and leaders of "causes." Take a child on a slumming trip to teach him the facts of social life, and show him how haggard, lean, scrawny, and undernourished the children are, and what does he "see"? He may perceive only the interesting alleys and inviting fire escapes that these children have to play with as com-

pared with the clean, sterile, and uninteresting playrooms he has at
his disposal. Show a documentary film of life in Russia to an insecure
and hostile American, presenting pictures of Russian factory workers
doing the same sort of things that Detroit factory workers do, Russian
farm hands going through actions similar to those of Iowa farm hands,
Russian traffic policemen gesticulating very much the way New York
City "cops" do. Will he perceive all these similarities? Probably not.
He will have noticed the large tractor factories which could so easily
become converted to tank factories, he will have been impressed with
the "militaristic" bearing of the policemen and with the "ruthless
scowl" on the face of the Russian general who appeared for a few
feet in the film.

On the occasion of the 1946 reprinting of Upton Sinclair's *The
Jungle,* R. L. Duffus, reviewing the book in *The New York Times* of
Oct. 13, 1946, gives an interesting illustration of how functional
selectivity of perception can subvert the best intentions of the social
reformer. Duffus writes:

After this book appeared, four decades ago, quite a number of Americans
temporarily stopped eating meat. . . . They just didn't care for meat after
they had read young Mr. Sinclair's fictionalized account of how meat was
handled in the Chicago stockyards. This was not Mr. Sinclair's intention.
He was a socialist and an ardent friend of the underpaid and overworked. He
did not forsee that the American people, after reading of the misfortunes of
his Lithuanian hero, would clamor, not for a cooperative commonwealth,
but for a pure food law. . . . Young Mr. Sinclair admired the strong
peasant stock that was pouring into this country so hopefully at the turn of
the century. He hated to see it abused, as it was. He hated the cruelty which
ground the lives out of men. He hated child labor. He hated the growling
tyranny that fired and blacklisted when men formed unions to better their
lot. He hated the cheating and the foul corruption that battened on the
innocent. So he spent some seven weeks observing how people lived "back
of the yards" and then wrote this book. . . . He . . . threw into it his burning indignation, lighted it with his ingenuous hopes of a world redeemed by
socialism, and got it into print . . . it became a best seller, it has been
translated into twenty-seven languages, it led to reforms in the handling
of meat.

Upton Sinclair was a socialist, and the facts he perceived demonstrated, to him, the need for socialism. So he saw them, and so he
wrote them down. The vast majority of his readers, however, were not
socialists, but they were meat eaters, and they perceived his facts in
their own way and read therefrom their own lesson. They selected out
for major attention, not the stories about the little Stanislovs who were
forced to work in the packing houses or the men like Jurgis who
averaged a weekly salary of $6.65, but the other stories — about the
workmen and stockyard rats who had fallen into lard vats and had
gone out to the world as "pure leaf lard." Accordingly, his readers

did not conclude from Sinclair's facts that the world must be redeemed by socialism but merely that a new pure food act was required.

There are no impartial "facts." Data do not have a logic of their own that results in the same perceptions and cognitions for all people. Data are perceived and interpreted in terms of the individual perceiver's own needs, own emotions, own personality, own previously formed cognitive patterns.

PROPOSITION III

The perceptual and cognitive properties of a substructure are determined in large measure by the properties of the structure of which it is a part

To know that experience in its natural state is organized and meaningful (Proposition I) and that the nature of the organization is determined functionally (Proposition II) is not enough. Our mental world is a structured or organized one, and it can also be seen as broken down into hierarchies of structures. Our cognitive field does not consist of completely independent organized structures; each of our perceptions is not an experience that "lives a life of its own," as it were. Every perception is embedded in an organization of other percepts — the whole going to make up a specific "cognitive structure." Each of these cognitive structures, in turn, can be broken down into several related substructures. Thus, when we perceive a politician, our perception of that particular politician is influenced by all our other percepts involving politicians. But the major structure, politicians, may have substructures: Democratic politicians, Republican politicians, honest politicians, etc. What we need for an adequate understanding of any one perception is knowledge about the interrelationships among the structures and substructures of our cognitive fields. Proposition III is designed to answer the questions raised by this point and states that the perception of a single object or group of objects is determined by the nature of the cognitive whole in which the percepts of these objects will be embedded.

Illustrations from Simple Visual Perception

Figure 2 is usually perceived as a simple figure of three lines meeting at a center point O. Each angle made by any two adjacent lines, say angle AOC, can be described as a substructure of the figure. That is, the perception of that angle is of an organized figure "in its own right," but it is also perceived as a part of a larger figure — the whole of Fig. 2. Each of these angles is usually perceived as an obtuse angle, *i.e.*, larger than a right angle. What would happen to our perception of angle AOC if we added a few lines so as to induce a change in our perception of the *whole* structure without in any way changing the lines that make up angle AOC? The answer is immediately given if we

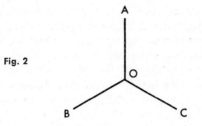

Fig. 2

look at Fig. 3. Now we perceive the substructure, angle *AOC*, as a right angle! Although we have not done anything physically to angle *AOC*, it "looks" different. It looks different because the *whole* figure, of which angle *AOC* is a part, looks different.

The same dependence of the perceptual properties of a part on the whole is seen in the *contrast* and *assimilation* experiments in visual perception. The results of these experiments can be summarized by the following statements: (1) Substructures of a major structure will tend to look either as much alike as possible (assimilation) or as much unlike as possible (contrast). (2) Assimilation appears when the differences between the substructures and the major structures are small; contrast appears when the differences are large. Thus, a series of black dots, in a single row, will all appear equally black despite the existence of minor differences in shade among them. Each dot, as a substructure of the row of dots, is assimilated, and the minor differences in blackness are not usually perceived. Conversely, if one dot were much brighter than the others, then that dot would be perceived as a light gray by virtue of being a member of a black contrasting series.

Now suppose that all you could see were angle *AOC* of Fig. 2 or only the single dot in our last illustration and you were told that a given person insisted that he perceived angle *AOC* as a right angle or that another individual perceived the dot as light gray. Would it not appear to you either that these people had defective vision or that they were inaccurate in their descriptions of their own perceptions? This would be a logical deduction if you could not see the whole of

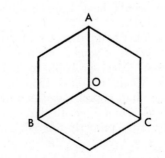

Fig. 3

Fig. 2 of which angle *AOC* was a part or if you could not see the entire set of dots. What is true for simple visual perception is also true for other instances of perceptual organization. We cannot understand an individual's perception, or interpretation of an event that is part of a larger organization for *him*, unless we also know what that larger organization is. This frequently accounts for the apparently incomprehensible perceptions and judgments of people and our failure to "understand" such people.

Perceiving Traits of Individuals and of Groups

A reformulation of this whole-part principle, in more specific social terms, might be helpful at this point. Such a reformulation is given in the following statement: *When an individual is apprehended as a member of a group, each of those characteristics of the individual which correspond to the characteristics of the group is affected by his group membership, the effect being in the direction of either assimilation or contrast.* Among other uses, this formulation can be helpful in aiding us to understand why, in our perception of people, we frequently are "biased" or "unjust."

Assimilation and contrast. — Suppose you were told that Arbuthnot is a member of the Communist party. Now suppose, also, that your cognitive field corresponding to "Communists" consists of the following characteristics: Communists speak with foreign accents, are always ready to incite to riot, and are unkempt in their appearance and dress. Let us now assume that Arbuthnot is, actually, somewhat poorly dressed. How will you perceive his dress? Most probably (if you do have that simple and stereotyped picture of Communists) you will perceive his clothing as "unkempt"; whereas if you had apprehended Arbuthnot as a member, say, of the "genteel poor," you might have perceived his dress as being "worn, but neatly and cleanly patched." What you would have done in the first instance is to have perceived Arbuthnot's dress in terms of the corresponding characteristics of the larger group of which he is a part (Communist), and, by assimilation, you would have ascribed the qualities of the group to the individual. In the second instance, your perceptual processes would have been of the same order, only this time your perception of Arbuthnot's dress would have been assimilated to a group having different characteristics.

Suppose, on the other hand, that Arbuthnot were dressed in the neat and intact dress of most of your acquaintances. Now, how would you perceive Arbuthnot? Most probably as being a "very well-dressed Communist." You would not have thought to use the phrase "very well-dressed" if you had apprehended Arbuthnot as a member of the Republican National Committee. In that case you would merely have perceived that he was "properly dressed." But since you know that

Arbuthnot is a Communist, you have perceived his dress in terms of the corresponding characteristics of the group of which he is a part; and this time by contrast, he would seem "very well-dressed."

In the same way do we judge the personality traits and motivations of individual Jews, Republicans, Negroes, Catholics, Russians, etc. Because so many Americans ascribe characteristic personality traits to these groups, as groups, their perceptions of the individual members of these groups usually show typical biases. Thus, many Americans, through the operation of the assimilation phenomenon, tend to overestimate the shrewdness of a particular Jew, or the inscrutability of a somewhat reticent Russian — because they believe Jews to be shrewd and Russians to be inscrutable. Because of contrast, they tend to overestimate the intelligence of a Negro who is normally intelligent and to underestimate the religious conservatism of a Catholic who is liberal in some of his religious views. Again, the reason appears to be due to the stereotyped notion that Negroes are stupid and that Catholics are extremely conservative believers. The common observation, during the war, of the tendency of the American soldier to regard any normally decent German as a "very good guy" is an instance of the contrast phenomenon, since many of our soldiers had been indoctrinated concerning the extreme ruthlessness and inhumanity of the Nazi and had generalized it to Germans.

. . . .

Frames of Reference

The whole-part principle can be summarized in still another way: Any stimulus is perceived in relation to other stimuli with which it is organized. This formulation, as Sherif and Cantril (1947) point out, is the basic definition of the term *frame of reference,* a term that they define as follows: "The term 'frame of reference' is simply used to denote the functionally related factors (present and past) which operate at the moment to determine the particular properties of a psychological phenomenon (such as perception, judgment, affectivity)."

Sherif (1935, 1936) has made this formulation of our Proposition III his major concept in social psychology and has generalized it to account for many varied processes. As Sherif and Cantril point out, in the volume cited above,

The scale of magnitudes against which subsequent stimuli of a similar kind are judged, the organized perceptual whole which determines the particular relative properties of its parts, the established social status in relation to which responses to other individuals and groups are shaped are all specific cases of frames of reference.

Illustrations of the frame-of-reference phenomenon abound in psychophysical experiments. Thus, for example, Wever and Zener (1928) have shown that when subjects are required to judge the weight of a series of objects as "light," "heavy," etc., the judgment of each weight is a function of the total series, since if the series itself is changed from a light series to a heavy one, the same object that was formerly judged heavy will now be judged as light.

Similar results are obtained when the judgments to be made are of a much more complicated sort and are directly related to social material. As an instance of such experiments the work of McGarvey (1943) can be cited. McGarvey had her subjects rate the "social prestige" of various occupations and found that the judged desirability of any given occupation was determined by the entire series of occupations to be judged.

Helson (1947) has attempted to treat this phenomenon of relativity of perception and judgment in terms of his theory of adaptation and has suggested a carefully worked-out mathematical formulation to help understand and predict the "universality of shifts in scale-value with change in comparison-stimulus." Because his theory goes beyond the mere observation that the perception of any single stimulus is changed as the related stimuli are changed, and because his theory is designed to predict some specific properties of the perception of certain stimuli, it is of some importance to see the implications of his formulation for social psychology. Briefly, his theory can be stated in the following way:

The effects of stimulation result in an organized perception (our Proposition I). For every such organized perception there is assumed a stimulus that represents the pooled effect of all the stimuli that gave rise to the organized perception. The individual may be said to be "attuned or adapted" to this central stimulus. That is, stimuli that are near this value (in intensity or affective value, etc.) will be perceived as "indifferent, neutral, doubtful, equal, or the like, depending upon the context . . ." of the judgment involved. Stimuli that are perceived in that way or judged in that way are said to be at "adaptation level." Stimuli that are above the adaptation level "are assumed to establish positive gradients" with respect to the adaptation-level stimulus and will be perceived as "good," "loud," or "strong." Similarly, stimuli that are below the adaptation level "establish negative gradients" with resulting perceptions of the opposite kind. If, now, new stimuli are introduced, which are above the adaptation-level stimulus, a new adaptation-level stimulus will gradually be established and all subsequent stimuli will then be perceived in terms of this new level.

The value of the above formulation to social psychology can be indicated by applying the adaptation-level theory to an analysis of certain propaganda techniques designed to change judgments of people. What would be the effect of publicizing *extreme* statements concerning any social issue? Let us choose racial prejudice, and let us assume that the stated opinions and beliefs available to an individual (opinions and beliefs that are publicly held by other people) range from an extremely prejudiced set to a rather mildly tolerant one. His adaptation level will then be such as to lead him to perceive a rather weak prodemocratic statement as "adequate, acceptable, or reasonable." Now, if the range is altered by adding extreme prodemocratic statements, it is highly likely that the individual will acquire a new adaptation level and he will judge as "acceptable and reasonable" a more strongly stated prodemocratic proposition than he formerly had. In other words, the sheer reiteration and publicity of strong, prodemocratic expressions can result in a shift in scale, or "framework," that can change a person's judgment in the direction of democracy.

Proposition IV

Objects or events that are close to each other in space or time or resemble each other tend to be apprehended as parts of a common structure

If we are to know just why certain perceptions are organized together with other perceptions to make one cognitive structure, we must have some general understanding of what determines why an individual will organize the perceptions of object *A* with that of object *B* into one common structure rather than the perception of object *A* with that of object *C*. Why, for example, do some people have a cognitive structure in which socialism and Christianity are organized together, while other people have a cognitive structure in which socialism and atheism are found together? Proposition IV attempts to indicate the major factors that determine the contents of a single structure.

Proximity and Similarity

In visual perception, experimental literature is replete with demonstrations that proximity and similarity are important organizing factors. Fig. 1*a*, which was used to illustrate the structural factors in perception, can serve to illustrate that in simple perception those objects which are close to each other in space (proximity) tend to be organized together in perception. Dot *A* is perceived as belonging to dot *B* rather than to dot *C* simply because *A* is closer to *B* than it is to *C*. A simple measurement of the physical distances among the different dots, everything else being equal, would permit us to predict, with a high degree of accuracy, which dots would be organized with which other dots. Similarly, Fig. 1*b* can be used to illustrate the principle of similarity. Here, dot *A* will be organized with dot *B* rather than with dot *C* because *A* is more similar (in shape) to *B* than it is to *C*.

This does not mean that Proposition IV is a purely "structural" proposition, that we can predict which organization will eventuate in the cognitive field of the individual merely by a description of the physical stimulus or the physical relationships existing among the stimuli. The terms *proximate* and *similar* must always be understood, of course, in a psychological sense, *i.e.,* as perceived by the individual. Two novel objects that are perceived as similar by one individual will not necessarily be perceived as similar by another individual and will therefore not give rise to the same cognitive structure. All the factors that we have discussed in the previous propositions will affect the perception of any object and therefore the nature of the resulting structure. The needs of the perceiver, his moods, his past training, etc., often play a determining role in defining what is proximate and what is similar. Thus, for example, a zoologist, because of his mental set and his previous cognitive organizations, might select out for perception, when viewing a new species of animal, the presence or absence of mammaries. All animals having this anatomical feature would be perceived as "similar," and so, in the cognitive field of the zoologist, horses, human beings, and whales might be organized together. Other people might see no similarity among these instances of land animals, human beings with souls, and fish. Or take another illustration: The child who has just received a spanking at the hands of his father may organize "fathers, bullies, and castor oil" into one structure of "evil" because these three objects have been perceived with a common characteristic. Yet if his father had never spanked him, such an organization might never take place. The individual who has read about the Nazis' racial theories and who has experienced racial prejudice at the hands of an American court might also perceive the Nazi and the American policeman as similar.

Culture and similarity cues. — The specific cues that are selected by us for major attention and will therefore determine our cognitive structures are, in turn, a function of our culture. Thus, if our culture and training emphasize signs of wealth as important cues to perceive at all times, we will perceive those cues most readily and will group people according to similarity of "wealth signs" — the kind of houses they live in, the automobiles they ride in (*e.g.,* "the station-wagon set"), the schools they send their children to, etc. If our culture or educational influences emphasize pigment of skin, we will group people into Negroes and whites; if the Maori culture emphasizes the importance of tattoo marks, people who have similar tattoo marks will be seen as similar and will be organized together in the perceiver's cognitive field.

The similarities, obviously, need not rest on visual signs alone. If similar *labels,* or descriptive words, are applied to different people, there will be a tendency to organize those people together in perception. If different people or objects play the same frustrating role in our experience, we may tend to perceive them together.

Proximity. — Proximity in time and space also works in very much the same way. The birth of twin cows occurring at the same time as a calamitous flood can be organized together as indications of the work of the devil. An increase in the divorce rate of a country, occurring about the same time as the outbreak of war, can be organized into one picture of Divine retribution.

Perceiving Cause and Effect

Perhaps one of the most important kinds of cognitive structures is that involved in "casual organization," *i.e.,* our perception of one object or event as a "cause" of another object or event. Some people perceive the Jews as the "cause" of depressions; others perceive the munitions manufacturer as the "cause" of war; still others perceive the current political administration as the "cause" of every national difficulty and calamity. What determines which cause will be organized together with which effect in our cognitive field? This is an extremely important question because so much of our social action is shaped by the way we perceive cause and effect.

Proximity and perception of cause and effect. — Duncker (1945), in his analysis of the thinking process, gives some compelling illustrations of how proximity may determine our perception of causations:

Someone comes home of an evening. A gust of wind slams the door shut behind him. At the same moment at the other end of the corridor, the light goes on in a room whose door is ajar. Although one knew ever so well that no causal connection exists between the door's blowing shut, and the light's going on, that rather someone in that room has turned on the light, by chance at exactly the same moment — still he would be unable to escape the compelling impression of causal relations . . . *the time and place of cause coincide phenomenally with the time and place of the effect.*

The point is not that all of our final or sophisticated statements of cause and effect are unequivocally determined by the temporal coincidence of two events but that in a new situation or in an ambiguous one, our immediate perception of cause and effect is largely determined by this factor. Knowing this, we can predict fairly accurately the causal relations that will be perceived by the child and the unsophisticated — whether we are concerned with the individual's perception of the cause of a "licking," the cause of war, or the cause of economic depressions.

Similarity and the perception of cause and effect. — For an illustration of the factor of similarity in the perception of causality, we can again quote from Duncker:

At least as important for man's dealing with causation as those spatial and temporal correspondences of *position* are certain correspondences of *form* between cause and effect. . . . An example of temporal correspondence of form: the rhythm of the sounds of knocking corresponds to the rhythm of the motions of knocking . . . heavy things make "heavy" noises, dainty things move daintily.

On a more complicated level, as in the perception of "human causation," Fritz Heider (1944) in his very helpful analysis of the perception of causality points out that the perception of responsibility (*i.e.,* the attribution of a crime to a person) can be due to several types of similarity:

A crime can be blamed on a person because of a physical similarity "he looks as if he could have committed this crime." Or he can be held responsible for it because of "spiritual" similarity, that is, a similarity between a crime as a moral event and the natural disposition of the "responsible". . . .

In his discussion, Heider refers to the well-known experiment by Zillig (1928) to illustrate this point. In that experiment two groups of children performed calisthenic exercises before an audience of their classmates. One of the performing groups was composed of children who were almost uniformly disliked by their classmates, and the other group, of children who were liked. The experimenter had trained the liked group to make mistakes deliberately and the disliked group to perform the calisthenics letter perfect. At the end of the two performances the experimenter discovered that the audience had "seen" the disliked group as having made the mistakes. A mistake, it appears, is much more likely to be organized together with disliked people than with liked people. As Heider says, "A bad act is easily connected with a bad person." The perception of cause and effect, in other words, is very definitely determined by our value judgments, our needs, our emotional reactions.

General Comments

The politician and the propagandist seem frequently to illustrate in their actions their awareness of our Proposition IV. In a critical political or economic situation, the politician may seek to avoid taking power and refuse a seat in the government. Why? Because he knows that if his administration coincides with a disastrous national occurrence, both of these events (his being in power and the national calamity) will tend to be perceived by many people as causally related — no matter how conclusively he can demonstrate that he was not at fault. He will be perceived as having been responsible for the military defeat or the economic depression just as certainly as Duncker's man perceived the door's being shut as the cause of the light's going on. The Jew or the Republican or the Catholic, if he is regarded as a "bad" person, will be perceived as the cause of a "bad" event.

This tendency to organize objects or events together on the basis of proximity or similarity is a universal one. It is not something that only the poor logicians do. This does not mean that we can never change our perceptions of causality and integrate objects and events originally perceived as unlike into a common structure, but it does mean that initially and prior to any corrections, our cognitive structures will be organized in terms of objects or events which are perceived as similar or in proximity.

SUMMARY

The fundamental importance of perception for social psychology is clearly indicated when we realize that all of man's molar action is shaped by his "private" conceptions of the world. This sets two major problems for the social psychologist: (1) the description of the social world as perceived by the specific individual (or individuals) whose social behavior we are interested in understanding and (2) the discovery of general principles of perception and cognition.

Without the description indicated in (1) above, the psychologist cannot interpret correctly the formalized expressions of beliefs and attitudes (whether verbally obtained or through observation of action) of the people whom he is studying. It is at this point that many current "attitude" and "opinion" studies are limited in their usefulness.

▲ LEONARD DOOB

$\mathcal{T}$he Perception of Propaganda

The individual is perpetually reacting to stimuli in the external and internal environment. Light reaches his eyes, sounds strike his ears, odors drift into his nose, air currents touch his skin, pangs contract his stomach, urine distends his bladder, substances have contact with his tongue, glandular secretions pour into his blood stream, and even thoughts occasionally affect him. In any case these stimuli innervate nerve endings which then produce action within the corresponding nerves. Many but not all of the nervous impulses reach the higher centers of the brain and at this point, it might be added, they may become conscious. When these physiological changes are disregarded, the first response to a stimulus can be said to be the perception of that stimulus. Thereafter changes may occur and learning can begin.

The perceptual response, however, is neither strictly mechanical nor passive. Even a camera cannot be said to record the environment in undistorted fashion. What this instrument reproduces depends not only on the object in front of the lens, but also on the nature of the lens, the aperture and speed of the shutter, the distance of the lens from the film, and the type of film in the camera. Physiologists and psychologists have long noted discrepancies between what the individual consciously perceives and what is known to be the nature of the stimulus in the environment. Railway tracks appear to converge as they approach the horizon — and no amount of hard thinking and no amount of training can prevent this illusion from occurring. Similarly a motion picture does not move and, if the projecting machine is functioning properly, not even the most perverted member of the audience can perceive the light upon the screen as a discrete series of motionless

▲ This is a chapter from the author's *Public Opinion and Propaganda,* copyright by Henry Holt and Company (New York, 1948), reprinted by permission of the copyright holder. Dr. Doob is a professor of psychology at Yale.

exposures which differ slightly from one another. The nature, then, of the stimulus and sense organ which mediates the energy from that stimulus affects the perceptual response. The sense organ's nature, moreover, may be temporarily affected by immediately preceding experiences. It is difficult to perceive much of a darkened environment after emerging from a brightly lighted room; eventually, as the eyes become adapted, many more perceptual responses can be made. Or, to recall the trite but pointed illustration, the same pail of water at medium temperature, into which two hands are dipped, is perceived as hot when the right hand has been previously submerged in water of low temperature and simultaneously is perceived as cold when the left hand has been in water of high temperature.

The perceptual response may also be markedly affected by other responses which the individual is making simultaneously and which therefore may cause him to fail to make that response, to distort or simplify it, or to project his own personality upon it. The pain from a toothache is less likely to be perceived when the unfortunate person, for example, is engaged in an interesting conversation than when he is attempting to fall asleep. The paranoid person, filled with anxiety for reasons not clear to himself and not infrequently unknown to his psychiatrist, reacts with suspicion and fright to an innocent greeting. The identical criticism of a political institution may be considered an illustration of the functioning of democracy in peacetime and an act of treason during a war. There is, therefore, no one-to-one relation between a perceptual response and its stimulus: perception is a response of the individual to a stimulus that is transmitted by particular sense organs.

The factors determining each perceptual response are variously weighted. No matter how brightly illuminated a visual stimulus is and no matter how determined the individual is to perceive it clearly, his perception may be vague or blurred if he is almost but not completely blind. No matter how distinct the sound is to other people and no matter how perfect his sense of hearing is, the individual may not perceive that sound if at the moment he is thoroughly engrossed in some other activity like reading a book. And no matter how hard the individual tries to perceive a part of a stimulus situation and no matter how keen his eyesight, he may not perceive that part of the stimulus if — like a needle in a haystack or, better, the figure of an animal concealed in a puzzle picture — it is embedded in a confusing or complicated context.

From the interrelationship and interaction of these factors two guiding principles emerge. In the first place, the perceptual response depends to a greater extent on the sense organs and on past habits when the stimulus is not part of a previous gradient, *i.e.*, when it is unstructured. A stimulus like "PFXEY" is vague and undifferentiated.

Similarly the type of ink-blot employed in a modern Rorschach test to measure personality characteristics is deliberately unstructured; it cannot easily be discriminated as part of one gradient rather than another; for this reason, the report of what the subject says he perceives is thought to be symptomatic of drives functioning within him. In contrast, other stimuli are so well structured that variability in perception is reduced to a minimum. A drop of ink on a white handkerchief is immediately visible, regardless of the other responses that ensue thereafter.

Then, secondly, the ongoing response which affects perception is an internal response with drive properties. If reinforced, it becomes a habit and subsequently functions the way any other habit does. After being evoked by a stimulus falling along its gradient, for example, it is likely to be decisive in determining perception. Cattle-breeders perceive steers not as romantic creatures but as reproductive organisms of particular capabilities.

Propaganda must be perceived before it can possibly have any effect. The advertiser must reach people with his message, or else they may never know of the existence of the product. The politician must speak to his constituents or have his own acts and promises portrayed by others or in the press if he is ever to win an election. The biased school teacher must have students to teach if his or her point of view is to be transmitted. The war propagandist seeks desperately to break through the perceptual barriers which the enemy erects to prevent the home and fighting fronts from hearing or seeing anything which might be demoralizing. The propagandist who does not reach his prospective audience is a failure from the outset.

In any society there is always a host of stimuli to which the individual can respond. Even the blessed savage of folklore fame who is supposed to lead a simple life is faced with a variety of stimuli: as he stands under the blue sky, cool breezes stroke his face, flowers give forth their scent, animals bestir themselves, and his family speaks to him in words of love and understanding. The lonely hermit may not perceive the bird on the tree because he has an itch or he may not scratch his skin because he is watching the bird. Stimuli, as it were, continually compete with one another to be perceived by people.

In modern society stimuli bombard the individual on all sides. From the physical environment come lights and scenery. From the internal environment come aches and drives and feelings. From the social environment come competing advertisements, competing political plans, competing social philosophies, and in general competing pressures. In the midst of all these stimuli appears some propaganda which therefore may not automatically be perceived. Means must be devised to have prospective propagandees perceive that propaganda stimulus.

▲ GORDON ALLPORT

▲ LEO POSTMAN

$\mathcal{T}$he Basic Psychology of Rumor

RUMORS IN WARTIME

During the year 1942, rumor became a national problem of considerable urgency. Its first dangerous manifestation was felt soon after the initial shock of Pearl Harbor. This traumatic event dislocated our normal channels of communication by bringing into existence an unfamiliar and unwelcome, if at the same time a relatively mild censorship of news, and it simultaneously dislocated the lives of millions of citizens whose futures abruptly became hostages to fortune.

This combination of circumstances created the most fertile of all possible soils for the propagation of rumor. We now know that *rumors concerning a given subject-matter will circulate within a group in proportion to the importance and the ambiguity of this subject-matter in the lives of individual members of the group.*

The affair of Pearl Harbor was fraught with both importance and ambiguity to nearly every citizen. The affair was important because of the potential danger it represented to all of us, and because its aftermath of mobilization affected every life. It was ambiguous because no one seemed quite certain of the extent of, reasons for, or consequences of the attack. Since the two conditions of rumor — importance and ambiguity — were at a maximum, we had an unprecedented flood of what became known as "Pearl Harbor rumors." It was said that our fleet was "wiped out," that Washington didn't dare to tell the extent of the damage, that Hawaii was in the hands of the Japanese. So widespread and so demoralizing were these tales that, on

▲ This paper was first published in the *Transactions of the New York Academy of Sciences* in 1945, and copyright by the Academy. It is printed here by permission of the publisher and copyright holder. Dr. Allport is a professor in the Department of Social Relations at Harvard; Dr. Postman is a professor of psychology at Indiana.

February 23, 1942, President Roosevelt broadcast a speech devoted entirely to denying the harmful rumors and to reiterating the official report on the losses.

Did the solemn assurance of the Commander in Chief restore the confidence of the people and eliminate the tales of suspicion and fear? It so happens that a bit of objective evidence on this question became available to us almost by accident. On the twentieth of February, before the President's speech, we had asked approximately 200 college students whether they thought our losses at Pearl Harbor were "greater," "much greater," or "no greater" than the official Knox report had stated. Among these students, 68 percent had believed the demoralizing rumors in preference to the official report, and insisted that the losses were "greater" or "much greater" than Washington admitted. Then came the President's speech. On February 25 an equivalent group of college students were asked the same question. Among those who had not heard or read the speech the proportion of rumor-believers was still about two thirds. But among those who were acquainted with the President's speech, the number of rumor-believers fell by 24 percent. It is important to note that, in spite of the utmost efforts of the highest authority to allay anxiety, approximately 44 percent of the college population studied were too profoundly affected by the event and by the resulting rumors to accept the reassurance.

The year 1942 was characterized by floods of similar fear-inspired tales. Shipping losses were fantastically exaggerated. Knapp records one instance where a collier was sunk through accident near the Cape Cod Canal. So great was the anxiety of the New England public that this incident became a fantastic tale of an American ship being torpedoed with the loss of thousands of nurses who were aboard her.[1]

Such wild stories, as we have said, are due to the grave importance of the subject for the average citizen and to the ambiguity to him of the objective situation. This ambiguity may result from the failure of communications, or from a total lack of authentic news, a condition that often prevailed in war-torn countries or among isolated bands of troops who had few reliable sources of news. Again, the ambiguity may be due to the receipt of conflicting news stories, no one more credible than another; or it may be due (as in the case of the Pearl Harbor rumors) to the distrust of many people in the candor of the Administration and in the operation of wartime censorship. As the war progressed, a higher degree of confidence in our news services was rapidly achieved, and rumors concurrently subsided.

In addition to the fear-rumors of 1942, which persisted until the tide of victory commenced to turn, there was a still more numerous crop of hostility-rumors whose theme dealt always with the short-

[1] R. H. Knapp, "A Psychology of Rumor," *Pub. Op. Quart.*, 1944, VIII, 22-37.

comings, disloyalty, or inefficiency of some special group of cobelligerents. The Army, the Navy, the Administration, our allies, or American minority groups were the most frequent scapegoats in these rumors. We were told that the Army wasted whole sides of beef, that the Russians greased their guns with lend-lease butter, that Negroes were saving icepicks for a revolt, and that Jews were evading the draft.

These hostility rumors were the most numerous of all. An analysis of 1,000 rumors collected from all parts of the country in 1942[2] revealed that they could be classified fairly readily as:

Hostility (wedge-driving) rumors = 66 percent
Fear (bogey) rumors   = 25 percent
Wish (pipe-dream) rumors   = 2 percent
Unclassifiable rumors   = 7 percent

To be sure, the proportion of fear and wish rumors soon altered. As victory approached, especially on the eve of V-E and V-J day, the whirlwind of rumors was almost wholly concerned with the cessation of hostilities, reflecting a goal-gradient phenomenon whereby rumor under special conditions hastens the completion of a desired event. But, throughout the war, and continuing to the present, it is probably true that the majority of all rumors are of a more or less slanderous nature, expressing hostility against this group or that.

The principal reason why rumor circulates can be briefly stated. It circulates because it *serves the twin function of explaining and relieving emotional tensions felt by individuals.*[3]

The Pearl Harbor rumors, for example, helped to *explain* to the teller why he felt such distressing anxiety. Would his jitters not be justified if it were true that our protecting fleet was "wiped out" at Pearl Harbor? Something serious must have happened to account for his anxiety. Families deprived of sons, husbands, or fathers vaguely cast around for someone to blame for their privation. Well, the Jews, who were said to be evading the draft, were "obviously" not doing their share and thus the heavy burden falling on "good citizens" was explained. True, this draft-evasion charge did not last very long, owing, no doubt, to the inescapable evidence of heavy enlistments among Jews and of their heroic conduct in the war. But when short-

[2] R. H. Knapp, *ibid.*, 25.
[3] This brief formula leaves out of account only the relatively few rumors which seem to serve the purpose of "phatic communication" — a form of idle conversation to facilitate social intercourse. When a lull occurs in a conversation, an individual may "fill in" with the latest bit of gossip that comes to mind, without being motivated by the deeper tensions that underlie the great bulk of rumor-mongering.

In this paper we cannot enter into a fuller discussion of the reasons why people believe some rumors and not others. This question is carefully studied by F. H. Allport and M. Lepkin, "Wartime Rumors of Waste and Special Privilege: Why Some People Believe Them," *J. Abnorm. & Soc. Psychol.*, 1945, XL, 3-36.

ages were felt, the traditional Jewish scapegoat was again trotted out as a convenient explanation of the privations suffered. Their operation of the black market "explained" our annoying experiences in the futile pursuit of an evening lamb chop.

To blame others verbally is not only a mode of explanation for one's emotional distress, but is at the same time a mode of *relief*. Everyone knows the reduction of tension that comes after administering a tongue lashing. It matters little whether the victim of the tongue lashing is guilty or not. Dressing down *anyone* to his face or behind his back has the strange property of temporarily reducing hatred felt against this person or, what is more remarkable, of reducing hatred felt against any person or thing. If you wish to deflate a taut inner tube you can unscrew the valve or you can make a puncture. Unscrewing the valve corresponds to directing our hostility toward the Nazis or Japanese, who were the cause of our suffering. Making a puncture corresponds to displacing the hostility upon innocent victims or scapegoats. In either case, the air will escape and relaxation follow. To blame Jews, Negroes, the Administration, brass hats, the OPA, or the politicians is to bring a certain relief from accumulated feelings of hostility, whatever their true cause. Relief, odd as it may seem, comes also from "bogey" rumors. To tell my neighbor that the Cape Cod Canal is choked with corpses is an easy manner of projecting into the outer world my own choking anxieties concerning my son or my friends in combat service. Having shared my anxiety with my friend by telling him exaggerated tales of losses or of atrocities, I no longer feel so much alone and helpless. Through my rumor-spreading, others, too, are put "on the alert." I therefore feel reassured.

EXPERIMENTAL APPROACH

Leaving now the broader social setting of the problem, we ask ourselves what processes in the human mind account for the spectacular distortions and exaggerations that enter into the rumor-process, and lead to so much damage to the public intelligence and public conscience.

Since it is very difficult to trace in detail the course of a rumor in everyday life, we have endeavored by an experimental technique to study as many of the basic phenomena as possible under relatively well controlled laboratory conditions.

Our method is simple. A slide is thrown upon a screen. Ordinarily, a semidramatic picture is used containing a large number of related details. Six or seven subjects, who have not seen the picture, wait in an adjacent room. One of them enters and takes a position where he cannot see the screen. Someone in the audience (or the experimenter) describes the picture, giving about twenty details in the account. A second subject enters the room and stands beside the first subject who proceeds to tell him all he can about the picture. (All subjects are under instruction to report as "accurately as possible what you have heard.") The first subject then takes his seat, and a third enters to hear the story from the second subject. Each succeeding subject hears and repeats the story in the same way. Thus, the audience is able to watch the deterioration of the rumor by comparing the successive versions with the stimulus-picture which remains on the screen throughout the experiment.

This procedure has been used with over forty groups of subjects, including college undergraduates, Army trainees in ASTP, members of community forums, patients in an Army hospital, members of a Teachers' Round Table, and police officials in a training course. In addition to these adult subjects, children in a private school were used, in grades from the fourth through the ninth. In some experiments, Negro subjects took part along with whites, a fact which, as we shall see, had important consequences when the test-pictures depicted scenes with a "racial angle."

All of these experiments took place before an audience (20-300 spectators). By using volunteer subjects, one eliminates the danger of stage fright. There was, however, a social influence in all the audience situations. The magnitude of this influence was studied in a control group of experiments where no one was present in the room excepting the subject and the experimenter.

At the outset, it is necessary to admit that in five respects this experimental situation fails to reproduce accurately the conditions of rumor-spreading in everyday life. (1) The effect of an audience is considerable, tending to create caution and to shorten the report. Without an audience subjects gave on the average twice as many details as with an audience. (2) The effect of the instructions is to maximize accuracy and induce caution. In ordinary rumor-spreading, there is no critical experimenter on hand to see whether the tale is rightly repeated. (3) There is no opportunity for subjects to ask questions of his informer. In ordinary rumor-spreading, the listener can chat with his informer and, if he wishes, cross-examine him. (4) The lapse of time between hearing and telling in the experimental situation is very slight. In ordinary rumor-spreading, it is much greater. (5) Most important of all, the conditions of motivation are quite different. In the experiment, the subject is striving for *accuracy*. His own fears, hates, wishes are not likely to be aroused under the experimental conditions. In short, he is not the spontaneous rumor-agent that he is in ordinary life. His stake in spreading the experimental rumor is neither personal nor deeply motivated.

It should be noted that all of these conditions, excepting the third, may be expected to enhance the accuracy of the report in the experimental situation, and to yield far less distortion and projection than in real-life rumor-spreading.

In spite of the fact that our experiment does not completely reproduce the normal conditions for rumor, still we believe that all essential changes and distortions are represented in our results. "Indoor" rumors may not be as lively, as emotionally toned, or as extreme as "outdoor" rumors, and yet the same basic phenomena are demonstrable in both.

What happens in both real-life and laboratory rumors is a complex course of distortion in which three interrelated tendencies are clearly distinguishable.

LEVELING

As rumor travels, it tends to grow shorter, more concise, more easily grasped and told. In successive versions, fewer words are used and fewer details are mentioned.

The number of details *retained* declines most sharply at the beginning of the series of reproductions. The number continues to decline, more slowly, throughout the experiment. Figure 1 shows the percentage of the details initially given which are retained in each successive reproduction.

The number of items enumerated in the description from the screen constitutes the 100 percent level, and all subsequent percentages are calculated from that base. The curve, based on 11 experiments, shows that about 70 percent of the details are eliminated in the course of five or six mouth-to-mouth transmissions, even when virtually no time lapse intervenes.

The curve is like the famous Ebbinghaus curve for decline in individual retention, though in his experiments the interval between initial learning and successive reproductions was not as short as under the conditions of our experiment. Comparing the present curve with Ebbinghaus's, we conclude that *social memory accomplishes as much leveling within a few minutes as individual memory accomplishes in weeks of time.*

Leveling (in our experiments) never proceeds to the point of total obliteration. The stabilization of the last part of the curve is a finding of some consequence. It indicates (1) that a short concise statement is likely to be faithfully reproduced; (2) that when the report has become short and concise, the subject has very little detail to select from and the possibilities of further distortion grow fewer; (3) that the assignment becomes so easy that a virtually rote memory serves to hold the material in mind. In all cases, the terminal and the ante-terminal reports are more similar than any two preceding reports.

The reliance on rote is probably more conspicuous in our experiments than in ordinary rumor-spreading where accuracy is not the

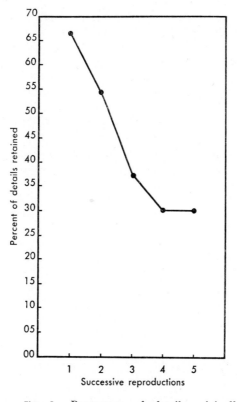

Fig. 1. Percentage of details originally given which are retained in each successive reproduction.

aim, where time interval interferes with rote retention, and where strong interests prevent literal memory. There are, however, conditions where rote memory plays a part in ordinary rumor-spreading. If the individual is motivated by no stronger desire than to make conversation, he may find himself idly repeating what he has recently heard in the form in which he heard it. If a rumor has become so crisp and brief, so sloganized, that it requires no effort to retain it in the literal form in which it was heard, rote memory seems to be involved. For example:

The Jews are evading the draft;
The CIO is communist controlled;
The Russians are nationalizing their women.

We conclude that whenever verbal material is transmitted among a group of people, whether as rumor, legend, or history, change will be in the direction of greater brevity and conciseness. Leveling, however, is not a random phenomenon. Our protocols show again and again that items which are of particular interest to the subjects, facts which confirm their expectations and help them to structure the story, are the last to be leveled out and often are retained to the final reproduction.

SHARPENING

We may define sharpening as the selective perception, retention, and reporting of a limited number of details from a larger context. Sharpening is inevitably the reciprocal of leveling. The one cannot exist without the other, for what little remains to a rumor after leveling has taken place is by contrast unavoidably featured.

Although sharpening occurs in every protocol, the same items are not always emphasized. Sometimes, a trifling detail such as a subway advertising card becomes the focus of attention and report. Around it the whole rumor becomes structured. But, in most experiments, this same detail drops out promptly, and is never heard of after the first reproduction.

One way in which sharpening seems to be determined is through the retention of odd, or attention-getting words which, having appeared early in the series, catch the attention of each successive listener and are often passed on in preference to other details intrinsically more important to the story. An instance of this effect is seen in a series of protocols where the statement, "there is a boy stealing and a man remonstrating with him" is transmitted throughout the entire series. The unusual word "remonstrate" somehow caught the attention of each successive listener and was passed on without change.

Sharpening may also take a *numerical* turn, as in the experiments where emphasized items become reduplicated in the telling. For example, in reports of a picture containing the figure of a Negro, whose size and unusual appearance invite emphasis, we find that the number of Negroes reported in the picture jumps from one to "four" or "several."

There is also *temporal* sharpening manifested in the tendency to describe events as occurring in the immediate present. What happens *here* and *now* is of greatest interest and importance to the perceiver. In most instances, to be sure, the story is started in the present tense, but even when the initial description is couched in the past tense, immediate reversal occurs and the scene is contemporized by the listener. Obviously, this effect cannot occur in rumors which deal specifically with some alleged past (or future) event. One cannot contemporize the rumor that "the *Queen Mary* sailed this morning (or will sail tomorrow) with 10,000 troops aboard." Yet it not infrequently happens that stories gain in sharpening by tying them to present conditions. For example, a statement that Mr. X bought a chicken in the black market last week and paid $1.50 a pound for it may be (and usually is) rendered, "I hear they *are* charging $1.50 a pound on the black market for chicken." People are more interested in today than in last week, and the temptation, therefore, is to adapt (assimilate) the time of occurrence, when possible, to this interest.

Sharpening often takes place when there is a clear implication of *movement*. The flying of airplanes and the bursting of bombs are frequently stressed in the telling. Similarly, the falling flower pot in one picture is often retained and accented. Indeed, the "falling motif" may be extended to other objects such as the cigar which a man in the picture is smoking. In one rumor, it is said to be falling (like the flower pot), though in reality it is quite securely held between his teeth.

Sometimes sharpening is achieved by ascribing movement to objects which are really stationary. Thus, a subway train, clearly at a standstill at a subway station, is frequently described as moving.

Relative size is also a primary determinant of attention. Objects that are prominent because of their size tend to be retained and sharpened. The first reporter calls attention to their prominence and each successive listener receives an impression of their largeness. He then proceeds to sharpen this impression in his memory. The large Negro may, in the telling, become "four Negroes," or may become "a gigantic statue of a Negro."

There are verbal as well as physical determinants of attention. Thus, there is a pronounced tendency for *labels* to persist, especially if they serve to set the stage for the story. One picture is usually introduced by some version of the statement, "This is a battle scene," and this label persists throughout the series of reproductions. Another story usually opens with the statement, "This is a picture of a race riot."

To explain this type of sharpening, we may invoke the desire of the subject to achieve some spatial and temporal schema for the story to come. Such orientation is essential in ordinary life and appears to constitute a strong need even when imaginal material is dealt with.

An additional factor making for preferential retention of spatial and temporal labels is the *primacy* effect. An item that comes first in a series is likely to be better remembered than subsequent items. Usually, the "label" indicating place and time comes at the beginning of a report and thus benefits by the primacy effect.

Sharpening also occurs in relation to familiar symbols. In one series of reports, a church and a cross are among the most frequently reported items, although they are relatively minor details in the original picture. These well-known symbols "pack" meaning and are familiar to all. The subject feels secure in reporting them because they have an accustomed concreteness that the other details in the picture lack. Retention of familiar symbols advances the process of conventionalization that is so prominent an aspect of rumor-embedding. In two of our pictures are a night stick, symbol of police authority, and a razor, stereotyped symbol of Negro violence. These symbols are always retained and sharpened.

Explanations added by the reporter to the description transmitted to him comprise a final form of sharpening. They represent a tendency to put "closure" upon a story which is felt to be otherwise incomplete. They illustrate the "effort after meaning" which customarily haunts the subject who finds himself in an unstructured situation. Such need for sharpening by explanation becomes especially strong when the story has been badly distorted and the report contains implausible and incompatible items. As an example, one subject who received a badly confused description of the subway scene inferred that there must have been "an accident." This explanation seemed plausible enough to successive listeners and so was not only accepted by them but sharpened in the telling.

In everyday rumors, sharpening through the introduction of specious explanations, is very apparent. Indeed, as we have said, one of the principal functions of a rumor is to explain personal tensions. To accept tales of Army waste or special privilege among OPA officials could "explain" food shortages and discomfort. Such stories, therefore, find wide credence.

Here, perhaps, is the place to take issue with the popular notion that rumors tend to expand like snowballs, become overelaborate, and verbose. Actually, the course of rumor is toward brevity, whether in the laboratory or in everyday life. Such exaggeration as exists is nearly always a sharpening of some feature resident in the original stimulus-situation. The distortion caused by sharpening is, of course, enormous in extent; but we do not find that we need the category of "elaboration" to account for the changes we observe.

ASSIMILATION

It is apparent that both leveling and sharpening are selective processes. But what is it that leads to the obliteration of some details and the pointing-up of others; and what accounts for all transpositions, importations, and other falsifications that mark the course of rumor? The answer is to be found in the process of *assimilation*, which has to do with the powerful attractive force exerted upon rumor by habits, interests, and sentiments existing in the listener's mind.

Assimilation to Principal Theme

It generally happens that items become sharpened or leveled to fit the leading motif of the story, and they become consistent with this motif in such a way as to make the resulting story more coherent, plausible, and well-rounded. Thus, in one series of rumors, the war theme is preserved and emphasized in all reports. In some experiments using the same picture, a chaplain is introduced, or people (in the plural) are reported as being killed; the ambulance becomes a Red Cross station; demolished buildings are multiplied in the telling; the extent of devastation is exaggerated. All these reports, false though they are, fit the principal theme — a battle incident. If the reported details were actually present in the picture, they would make a "better" *Gestalt*. Objects wholly extraneous to the theme are never introduced—no apple pies, no ballet dancers, no baseball players.

Besides importations, we find other falsifications in the interest of supporting the principal theme. The original picture shows that the Red Cross truck is loaded with explosives, but it is ordinarily reported as carrying medical supplies which is, of course, the way it "ought" to be.

The Negro in this same picture is nearly always described as a soldier, although his clothes might indicate that he is a civilian partisan. It is a "better" configuration to have a soldier in action on the battlefield than to have a civilian among regular soldiers.

Good Continuation

Other falsifications result from the attempt to complete incompleted pictures or to fill in gaps which exist in the stimulus field. The effort is again to make the resulting whole coherent, and meaningful. Thus, the sign, "Loew's Pa . . . ," over a moving picture theater is invariably read and reproduced as "Loew's Palace" and Gene *Antry* becomes Gene *Autry*. "Lucky Rakes" are reported as "Lucky Strikes."

All these, and many instances like them, are examples of what has been called, in *Gestalt* terms, "closures." Falsifications of perception and memory they are, but they occur in the interests of bringing about a more coherent, consistent mental configuration. Every detail is assimilated to the principal theme, and "good continuation" is sought, in order to round out meaning where it is lacking or incomplete.

Assimilation by Condensation

It sometimes seems as though memory tries to burden itself as little as possible. For instance, instead of remembering two items, it is more economical to fuse them into one. Instead of a series of subway cards, each of which has its own identity, reports sometimes refer only to "a billboard," or perhaps to a "lot of advertising." In another picture, it is more convenient to refer to "all kinds of fruit," rather than to enumerate all the different items on the vendor's cart. Again, the occupants of the car come to be described by some such summary phrase as "several people sitting and standing in the car." Their individuality is lost.

Assimilation to Expectation

Just as details are changed or imported to bear out the simplified theme that the listener has in mind, so also many items take a form that supports the agent's habits of thought. Things are perceived and remembered the way they *usually* are. Thus a drugstore, in one stimulus-picture, is situated in the middle of a block; but, in the telling, it moves up to the corner of the two streets and becomes the familiar "corner drugstore." A Red Cross ambulance is said to carry medical supplies rather than explosives, because it "ought" to be carrying medical supplies. The kilometers on the signposts are changed into miles, since Americans are accustomed to having distances indicated in miles.

The most spectacular of all our assimilative distortions is the finding that, in more than half of our experiments, a razor moves (in the telling) from a white man's hand to a Negro's hand. This result is a clear instance of assimilation to stereotyped expectancy. Black men are "supposed" to carry razors, white men not.

Assimilation to Linguistic Habits

Expectancy is often merely a matter of fitting perceived and remembered material to preexisting verbal clichés, which exert a powerful influence in the conventionalization of rumors. Words often arouse compelling familiar images in the listener's mind and fix for him the categories in which he must think of the event and the value that he must attach to it. A "zoot-suit sharpie" packs much more meaning and carries more affect than more objective words, such as, "a colored man with pegged trousers, wide-brimmed hat, etc." Rumors are commonly told in verbal stereotypes which imply prejudicial judgment, such as "draft dodger," "Japanese spy," "brass hat," "dumb Swede," "long-haired professor," and the like.

MORE HIGHLY MOTIVATED ASSIMILATION

Although the conditions of our experiment do not give full play to emotional tendencies underlying gossip, rumor, and scandal, such tendencies are so insistent that they express themselves even under laboratory conditions.

Assimilation to Interest

It sometimes happens that a picture containing women's dresses, as a trifling detail in the original scene, becomes, in the telling, a story exclusively about dresses. This sharpening occurs when the rumor is told by groups of women, but never when told by men.

A picture involving police was employed with a group of police officers as subjects. In the resulting protocol, the entire reproduction centered around the police officer (with whom the subjects undoubtedly felt keen sympathy or "identification"). Furthermore, the nightstick, a symbol of his power, is greatly sharpened and becomes the main object of the controversy. The tale as a whole is protective of, and partial to, the policeman.

Assimilation to Prejudice

Hard as it is in an experimental situation to obtain distortions that arise from hatred, yet we have in our material a certain opportunity to trace the hostile complex of racial attitudes.

We have spoken of the picture which contained a white man holding a razor while arguing with a Negro. In over half of the experiments with this picture, the final report indicated that the Negro (instead of the white man) held the razor in his hand, and several times he was reported as "brandishing it widely" or as "threatening" the white man with it.

Whether this ominous distortion reflects hatred and fear of Negroes we cannot definitely say. In some cases, these deeper emotions may be the assimilative factor at work. And yet the distortion may occur even in subjects who have no anti-Negro bias. It is an unthinking cultural stereotype that the Negro is hot tempered and addicted to the use of razors as weapons. The rumor, though mischievous, may reflect chiefly an assimilation of the story to verbal-clichés and conventional expectation. Distortion in this case may not mean assimilation to hostility. Much so-called prejudice is, of course, a mere matter of conforming to current folkways by accepting prevalent beliefs about an out-group.

Whether or not this razor-shift reflects deep hatred and fear on the part of white subjects, it is certain that the reports of our Negro subjects betray a motivated type of distortion. Because it was to their interest as members of the race to deemphasize the racial caricature, Negro subjects almost invariably avoided mention of color. One of them hearing a rumor containing the phrase, "a Negro zoot-suiter," reported, "There is a man wearing a zoot suit, *possibly* a Negro."

For one picture, a Negro reporter said that the colored man in the center of the picture "is being maltreated." Though this interpretation may be correct, it is likewise possible that he is a rioter about to be arrested by the police officer. White and Negro subjects are very likely to perceive, remember, and interpret this particular situation in quite opposite ways.

Thus, even under laboratory conditions, we find assimilation in terms of deep-lying emotional predispositions. Our rumors, like those of everyday life, tend to fit into, and support, the occupational interests, class or racial memberships, or personal prejudices of the reporter.

CONCLUSION: THE EMBEDDING PROCESS

Leveling, sharpening, and assimilation are not independent mechanisms. They function simultaneously, and reflect a singular subjectifying process that results in the autism and falsification which are so characteristic of rumor. If we were to attempt to summarize what happens in a few words we might say:

Whenever a stimulus field is of potential importance to an individual, but at the same time unclear, or susceptible of divergent interpretations, a subjective structuring process is started. Although the process is complex (involving, as it does, leveling, sharpening, and assimilation), its essential nature can be characterized as an effort to reduce the stimulus to a simple and meaningful structure that has adaptive significance for the individual in terms of his own interests and experience. The process begins at the moment the ambiguous situation is perceived, but the effects are greatest if memory intervenes. The longer the time that elapses after the stimulus is perceived the greater the threefold change is likely to be. Also, the more people involved in a serial report, the greater the change is likely to be, until the rumor has reached an aphoristic brevity, and is repeated by rote.

Now, this three-pronged process turns out to be characteristic not only of rumor but of the individual memory function as well. It has been uncovered and described in the experiments on individual retention conducted by Wulf, Gibson, Allport,[4] and, in Bartlett's memory experiments carried out both on individuals and on groups.[5]

Up to now, however, there has been no agreement on precisely the terminology to use, nor upon the adequacy of the three functions we here describe. We believe that our conceptualization of the three-fold course of change and decay is sufficient to account, not only for our own experimental findings and for the experiments of others in this area, but also for the distortions that everyday rumors undergo.

For lack of a better designation, we speak of the three-fold change as the *embedding* process. What seems to occur in all our experiments and in all related studies is that each subject finds the outer stimulus-world far too hard to grasp and retain in its objective character. For his own personal uses, it must be recast to fit not only his span of comprehension and his span of retention, but, likewise, his own personal needs and interests. What was outer becomes inner; what was objective becomes subjective. In telling a rumor, the kernel of objective information that he received has become so embedded into his own dynamic mental life that the product is chiefly one of projection. Into the rumor, he projects the deficiencies of his retentive processes, as well as his own effort to engender meaning upon an ambiguous field, and the product reveals much of his own emotional needs, including his anxieties, hates, and wishes. When several rumor-agents

[4] Conveniently summarized in K. Koffka, *Principles of Gestalt Psychology* (New York: Harcourt, Brace and Co., 1935).

[5] F. C. Bartlett, *Remembering* (Cambridge, England: Cambridge University Press, 1932).

have been involved in this embedding process, the net result of the serial reproduction reflects the lowest common denominator of cultural interest, of memory span, and of group sentiment and prejudice.

One may ask whether a rumor must always be false. We answer that, in virtually every case, the embedding process is so extensive that no credibility whatever should be ascribed to the product. If a report does turn out to be trustworthy, we usually find that secure standards of evidence have somehow been present to which successive agents could refer for purposes of validation. Perhaps the morning newspaper or the radio have held the rumor under control, but when such secure standards of verification are available, it is questionable whether we should speak of rumor at all.

There are, of course, border-line cases where we may not be able to say whether a given tidbit should or should not be called a rumor. But if we define rumor (and we herewith propose that we should), as *a proposition for belief of topical reference, without secure standards of evidence being present* — then it follows from the facts we have presented that rumor will suffer such serious distortion through the embedding process, that *it is never under any circumstances a valid guide for belief or conduct.*

Communicating

to

Another

Culture

International communication has the special problem of transferring meaning from one culture to another, which means from one "subjective world" to another. The first paper following illustrates how anthropologists and psychiatrists have approached this problem. Dr. Smith's paper takes up the more specific question of communicating with non-industrial countries, and Dr. White's paper the problem of overcoming resistance to "foreign" communication. Messrs. Buchanan and Cantril present data to show how different nations look at each other.

▲ ALEXANDER H. LEIGHTON

▲ MORRIS EDWARD OPLER

*P*sychiatry and Applied Anthropology

in Psychological Warfare Against Japan

During the war, the policy makers of our government were faced with a number of interesting and important questions that hinged on the nature of the Japanese as members of a society that carries a particular culture and as human beings with individual needs and motives.

One set of such questions concerned the high morale of the Japanese fighting forces. It seemed to many officials and to the general public that this morale was a solid and impregnable wall of uniform strength with every enemy soldier an ideal fighting machine — fearless, fanatic, obeying instantly without question and looking only for an opportunity to die for the Emperor. If this were so, then it would be necessary to prepare for a long war that would be extremely costly in American lives and resources. Every isolated Japanese garrison would have to be exterminated, no matter how hopeless its situation; and there would be the painful process of taking Japan foot by foot and of endless mopping up behind the lines wherever Japanese were left alive.

This may seem an exaggerated picture now, but during the first three years of the war it was seriously entertained as a grave and threatening possibility.

Policy makers in our government needed to know whether the morale of all the Japanese was uniformly high or whether it had weak spots that could deteriorate and spread their degenerative influence. Was the morale structure really entirely solid, or was the

▲ Trained in psychiatry and anthropology, these two authors headed the Foreign Morale Analysis Division of OWI during World War II, and thus were consulted on intercultural aspects of policy making. This article was published in the *American Journal of Psychoanalysis*, volume 6 (1946), and is reprinted here by permission of publisher and copyright holder. Dr. Leighton is a professor at Cornell, and Dr. Opler is now at the University of Lucknow, India.

Japanese soldier, in spite of his remarkable performance, caught in the ambivalence characteristic of other soldiers: the conflict between the will to resist and the will to exist?

Further, if there were weaknesses in morale, it would be vital to know what kinds of circumstances would cause their spread. Could we apply psychological warfare with any expectation of reducing the enemy's fighting efficiency? Might we even hope that by adding this element to military pressure significant numbers of Japanese troops could be induced to surrender?

And then there was the home front — Would the Japanese civilian population, in the face of the advance of the war on their homeland, show the same type of morale that had been repeatedly displayed by the soldiers in the field?

THE RESEARCH

During the last year and a half of the war, we participated in one of a number of efforts that were made to understand Japanese morale and to anticipate and describe its changes. The purpose of our particular unit was to provide a service for the policy makers in the State, War and Navy Departments, the Office of War Information, the Office of Strategic Services, and for various outposts in the Pacific and Asia. When the war was over, one of us (Leighton) had an opportunity of spending two and a half months in Japan with the U. S. Strategic Bombing Survey gathering additional data on wartime morale.

Our unit, known as the Foreign Morale Analysis Division,[1] was composed of about 30 persons (the number changed from time to time) and was sponsored by the Office of War Information with the support of the War Department. By agreement between the Office of War Information and the War Department, the Foreign Morale Analysis Division was able to collaborate closely with a War Department unit engaged in related work, to get assistance with personnel and office space and to secure basic research material.

The senior scientists in the unit were men and women trained in cultural anthropology, sociology, and psychiatry rather than as experts on Japan; but there were in the group also a number of people with knowledge of the Japanese language and culture, and consultant services were available from scholars who had specialized in Japan or the Far East.

The nucleus out of which this research unit grew was a team, composed largely of Japanese Americans, that had been previously developed in the Department of the Interior in order to study morale

[1] Leighton was Chief of the Division until he went to Japan, when Opler, who was Assistant Chief at the time, took his place.

and related matters in the Poston Relocation Center for persons of Japanese ancestry evacuated from the West Coast.[2]

The analysis of Japanese morale consisted of interpreting intelligence material in the light of a limited number of basic assumptions regarding the nature of man derived from psychiatry and cultural anthropology. Although the intelligence data were often rich and informative they were unavoidably fragmentary and incomplete for the requirements of systematic scientific study. Controlled observations were impossible and statistical methods could be used only to a very limited degree. It was therefore necessary to rely heavily on the assumed uniformities in human behavior, with the addition of major corrections for the influences of culture. At times we felt like paleontologists constructing dinosaurs from a few bits of jaw, ribs and tail bones.

Our approach to the problem had resemblances to medical practice. When a psychiatrist examines a patient he has in mind a set of general concepts regarding the way human beings function in good or poor health. He has to take what facts he can gather from the examination as hints and clues, and by evaluating them in the light of his basic concepts construct a diagnosis which is in essence an hypothesis concerning the patient's condition. The final judgment regarding the validity of the preliminary conclusions comes as a result of additional facts revealed by the course and outcome of the patient's illness and the way in which therapy succeeds or fails.

Similarly, in the analysis of Japanese morale, conclusions which in the beginning were largely hypothetical later became widely accepted as fact, due to the accumulation of enormous bodies of evidence from many sources.

GENERAL RESULTS

There is not space here to give all the findings regarding Japanese morale, but a few may be mentioned to afford an idea of range and nature before selecting one for more detailed scrutiny.

In regard to military morale, the analysts came to the conclusions that there was marked difference in its strength among individual Japanese soldiers, that it varied with circumstances, and that it would show decline when the Japanese were subject to prolonged military defeat.

Further, it was believed that some of the factors which contributed to and were symptomatic of high morale, were much more susceptible to deterioration than others. Thus, faith in the Emperor, faith in the rightness and justice of the war, and faith in the people of the Japanese nation were morale-producing attitudes that remained strong

[2] This work has been reported in part in *The Governing of Men,* by Alexander H. Leighton, Princeton University Press, 1945.

under adversity. On the other hand, confidence in victory, in weapons and industrial strength, confidence in lower ranking officers and determination not to be made a prisoner were susceptible to deterioration when battle conditions went against the Japanese.

It was concluded that these tendencies gave openings for psychological warfare and could be exploited by leaflets and loud-speaker broadcasts. Although little used in the beginning, such techniques against the Japanese were being fully employed toward the end of the war and contributed to the surrender of prisoners by the thousands. While more German troops surrendered in combat than did Japanese, it must be remembered that in the case of Japan, we eventually took the entire nation while it was still a functioning whole; and psychological warfare played its part in this.

In regard to home-front morale, it was believed by the analysts that at the beginning of 1945 a considerable decline was under way and that it took chiefly the form of apathy and of slackening in the war effort. Studies carried out in Japan since the end of the war by the U. S. Strategic Bombing Survey have amply documented this conclusion.[3]

A SPECIFIC ISSUE — THE EMPEROR

Let us turn now to a specific issue, examine it in some detail and outline not only the conclusions, but also how they were derived.

The subject selected is the significance of the Japanese Emperor to the Japanese people. This topic is of interest on a number of counts.

During the war, whether or not we should attack the Emperor in our propaganda directed at Japan was an important practical issue. It was hotly disputed with strong feelings on both sides of the question.

At present and in the future our policy in regard to the Emperor and the Imperial Institution remains of practical importance in our dealings with Japan. This was highlighted at the time of the surrender when the Japanese informed us they were prepared to accept the Potsdam Declaration, but wanted clarification regarding what would happen to the Emperor. This was the only question asked. It is therefore important for all of us as citizen critics of our Government's foreign policy to understand the cultural and psychological significance of the Emperor.

On a wider scale, the phenomenon of the Emperor illustrates the working out of some of those basic assumptions regarding human and cultural nature derived from psychiatry and anthropology which underlay our morale analysis.

[3] See Morale Division Report of U. S. Strategic Bombing Survey, Government Printing Office.

1. *Research Findings:* From our preliminary work in morale analysis, we concluded that the Japanese soldiers' attitudes toward the Emperor represented an exceedingly strong and enduring constellation of beliefs and feelings. As a consequence, it was thought not only useless and wasteful to attack this symbol, but actually dangerous, since such attacks could well serve to increase enemy resistance and determination. On the positive side, it seemed to us that resistance both in battle and on the home front could be lowered by a clear and repeated statement declaring that the fate of the Emperor and the Imperial Institution after an Allied victory would be up to the Japanese.

It was subsequently found that throughout the war no matter how their morale deteriorated in other respects, in this faith and belief the Japanese remained steadfast. After the end of hostilities, surveys in Japan[4] revealed that the overwhelming majority of the civilian population were strong in their devotion to the Emperor. In fact, next to the food question, the greatest fear of the Japanese seemed to be that the Allies might bring some harm to him. Even the Japanese communists, whose policy is to dispense with the Imperial Institution, recognized the strength of the popular feeling and at one time accepted the fact that they must compromise with it. Said one of them:

"If the majority of the people fervently demands the perpetuation of the Emperor, we must concede to them. Therefore we propose as a suggestion that the question of maintaining or disposing of the Emperor be decided after the war by plebiscite. Then, even if the outcome of the plebiscite is the perpetuation of the Emperor such an Emperor must be one who does not possess power."

A Japanese peer who is a member of the Social Democratic party told Leighton that he believed the Emperor should be outside of politics, but when the question of abolition was raised, said "No, it would be too lonely without him."

2. *The Nature of Human Beliefs:* To understand these attitudes, let us consider first the general nature of human belief and sentiment.

All people everywhere have systems of belief and among all people everywhere these beliefs show certain common characteristics.

For one thing, beliefs often have a *logical basis.* That is they have components based on and supported by observation combined with reasoning. This is true not only of scientific and scholarly thought, but of everyone's common daily experiences about the house, in the office, and at play. Nor it is true only of our culture, for the jungle native in his hunting and the Japanese peasant in his planting have hundreds of beliefs based on experience and reasoning.

[4] *Ibid.*

Beliefs also have a *social and cultural basis*. The individual maintains his ideas not only through reasoning, but from the precept and example of his fellows and from the pressure of their opinions. This involves the things which in any given society "everybody knows" without the need of proof or even demonstration, and he who questions them is made to feel either a fool or guilty. In actual fact, beliefs dominated by this characteristic may or may not be true and they may or may not be logical. Their chief quality is their social and cultural nature.

That the world is flat, that it is a crime against God to use anesthetics, that swine are unclean, that Holy Water has power, that corn pollen will make a man healthy and lucky, that vitamins are what we all need, that cannibalism is evil, that free competition will solve the world's economic difficulties — all these are examples of beliefs which exhibit a large element of the cultural component.

Still another support for belief lies in the *emotional balance within the individual, in his personal aspirations, anxieties and conflicts.* Beliefs primarily of this order may be socially shared and they may have a logical structure, but their main characteristic is their role as ideas which enable the individual to feel better about something which would otherwise produce an unpleasant or distressful state of emotions. Many of the neurotic convictions that are familiar to psychiatrists are of this type. However, they are by no means confined to neurotics, and are part of the equipment with which people of all types and nations make their way through life.

Beliefs, then, among all the various groups of people of the world show elements that are logical, cultural and tied to intrapersonal balance and sense of security. Any given belief will probably have all three elements inherent in it, but their relative proportions may vary greatly.

Beliefs also show varying degrees of strength. Those which have the *greatest tenacity and resistance to change are the fundamental assumptions regarding values, man's place in life, the nature of the world and the nature of the supernatural.* Although influenced and, within limits, modifiable by reason, they are profoundly *emotional rather than logical,* are felt with certainty rather than thought through and are largely *cultural and concerned with the intrapersonal balance.* They lie close to the roots of human motive, to the sense of protection in the storms of the world. They enable thousands, even millions of people to act together in common understanding and with a feeling of mutual belonging where otherwise there would be strife and confusion; they protect the conscious self from devastating doubts and uncertainties and provide a sense of compensation for such adverse influences in life as the inevitability of death and the loss sooner or later of all things held dear. The logical content of these beliefs does not matter nearly so much as their ability to fulfill these functions. In times of stress, human dependence on such beliefs has a tendency to become greater, at least for a time, and may be affirmed even at the price of life itself.

3. *Belief in the Emperor:* If these assumptions are true, it should be possible to estimate the strength of a system of belief by examining its cultural prevalence and its relationship to the sense of individual security (the intrapersonal balance).

As already noted, the greatest number of references to the Emperor from all Japanese sources during the war were expressions of faith, devotion, loyalty, and declarations concerning his importance. For example:

"From childhood on I was taught that the Emperor is of divine origin and that if capable I may become the premier of my nation, but never could I be Emperor."

"The Emperor is the father of the whole nation, a living god."

"I saw two Japanese soldiers worn out with wounds and hunger. One of them called to the section leader and asked to be killed, as he could not keep up with the retiring force. He asked that he be remembered to his family and said, 'Long live the Emperor!' ('Tenno Heika, banzai!'). The section leader then shot him through the head."

"A Japanese soldier stated that the morale in his unit was very high in spite of their hopeless situation. All the men were deeply instilled with the spirit of undying loyalty to the Emperor and were resigned to their fate."

"A good many people will unhesitatingly fight an invading army, even with nothing more than bamboo poles, if the Emperor so decrees. They would stop just as quickly if he so decreed."

In a diary was found this entry: "In order to do our best for the Emperor, we must deny ourselves and our families. One's faith then becomes a thing exalted in the world. We achieve immortality by casting aside our petty temporal lives and becoming a member of the Fraternity of the Spirits of Dead Heroes. Our spirits and bodies are not merely our own; they are rather for the gods who created the world to use and dispose of. We live by the grace of the Emperor. For people who live in this belief, life is worth while, living has a purpose."

A poem from a diary:

> "The shield of our Emperor's domain, this
> Iwo Jima,
> Upon our honor we hold this ground,
> We, the Defenders."

It should not be supposed from these quotations that every Japanese died willingly with "Long live the Emperor" on his lips. Our records revealed that many others called for their mothers or other loved ones instead. Nevertheless the number of references to the Emperor at a time of reverse, last effort or self-destruction indicates that he was one of the important supports in Japanese morale.

Why were loyalty to the Emperor and faith in him so strong? Can an explanation be found in terms of the concepts that have been outlined regarding the nature of strong belief?

In part the answers are already evident in the quotations given above.

To begin by summarizing, it may be said that for the Japanese the Emperor symbolizes the fundamental assumptions regarding values: the nature of the world, the nature of the supernatural and man's place — those things which among all peoples are strongly felt and extremely resistant to change because of their intimate connection with the sense of security, the sense of orientation and the hope of fulfilling aspirations.

The extent of the belief in the Emperor was found to be so wide as to constitute a nonlogical, cultural type of faith strongly reinforced in any one individual by the sheer pressure of the whole society. It would be impossible for one to reject it without stepping outside almost all the ideas and value systems that are Japanese; and since most Japanese are not members of any other society except their own, this would mean a kind of isolation that few human beings except psychotics and extreme mystics can endure.

However, the symbol also has wide latitude in the way it can be interpreted and this permits a strong personal indentification with the Emperor on the part of people who are very different from each other. A close scrutiny of Japanese comments on the Emperor and a checking of these against the point of view of the speaker in regard to other matters reveals that to the expansionists and militarists he was the strong war leader bent on liberating the East from Western domination; to those who were or became opposed to war, the Emperor was steadfastly a man of peace deceived by the warmakers in Japan; to the partisans of democracy, he was and still is a democrat at heart; to the simple and uneducated he wielded supernatural powers; to the sophisticated he symbolized the highest ideals of a way of life. Such flexibility in the interpretation of the Emperor's significance was made possible by the degree to which he was shielded by custom and etiquette from direct contact with public affairs and by the manner in which he was surrounded by subordinates who took responsibility for error. In this he resembles the "sacred chiefs" usually found in the Pacific Islands. In Samoa and Tonga, the sacred chief did not engage in the mundane but, occupying the highest position of prestige, left politics and administration to a secular chief.

The Emperor, then, is all ideal things to all men and the symbol of each individual's successful tussle with and relief from his insecurities. .

The structure of the Japanese family is another source of the faith in the Emperor displayed by adults. The rigid hierarchy and other restrictive aspects of the Japanese family have been described; less often stressed, though just as important, is the tremendous sense of security, and the strong feeling of belonging that also exists in this unit. The Japanese father is not so much the autocrat who demands, as he is the recipient of honors which others strive to give, feeling their worth in terms of their success and faithfulness in this giving. When failures occur, it is less often the father who chastises the offender than it is the other members of the group, and all feel the adverse opinion of the neighbors. The child who grows out of this setting into adult life and becomes aware of the larger society of the nation is ripe for a counterpart of the father in these adult relations. He finds it in the Emperor who is endlessly spoken of as the Father of his people. To him each can give and feel that this giving contributes a worth-while purpose to life.

Through all of this runs the religious aspect of the Emperor symbol. Here, as in the case of the Emperor's "real intentions," there is much room for interpretation so that he can fulfill the needs of very different sorts of persons, including Christians as well as Buddhists and those who belong to Shinto sects. However, the distinction between religion and everyday life so often formalized in Western thought, is much more fluid in the East, and this is true of the Japanese. Filial respect and devotion shade off into religious devotion to dead ancestors who are considered to be deities watching over their descendants. All men are potential deities to be revered after death, but the greater the man, the greater the god he will be. The Emperor with his line of ancestors stemming from the founders of the nation has the greatest potentiality of living men. Because of his frequent ceremonial communication with the departed imperial ancestors he is a symbolic bridge between the living and these mighty dead of the past. This parallels on a grander scale the ties between living and dead and the feeling of continued fellowship and intercourse that goes on in each Japanese household before its family shrines.

The Emperor symbol therefore plays a major role. It serves as a bond between the living members of Japanese society, it is a repository of national ideals, it links those alive and those departed, and it assures each Japanese a place in the afterlife.

Thus a man who might otherwise be lost in a chaotic universe and appalled by his littleness, helplessness, and temporariness finds meaning and security in believing he is a part of something far greater than himself that spans the natural and the supernatural world.

Such a system, like all such systems is full of logical contradictions. How, for example, can the Emperor be supremely divine and yet fooled by his advisers? These considerations are logical enough from an outsider's point of view, but are inconsequential in context, for the strength of the belief lies in its cultural force and in its meaning and service in the emotional life of man.

Although it is hard to find any exact parallel in our culture to the Japanese feeling for the Emperor, the difference is one of degree and combination rather than of kind. Almost all of us have symbols in which we believe with the same strength as that displayed by the Japanese toward the Emperor. With us, however, these beliefs are not so widely shared and differ more among various groups of people. Nor, as a rule, do we combine so many things in any one symbol. However, if we could imagine a symbol that represented together the flag, the constitution, a religious ideal and our feelings for the family we might get some insight into the Japanese attitude.

It is perhaps now clear why the analysts early came to the conclusion that it was not profitable to attack the Emperor in psychological warfare. At best, it seemed wasteful since dialectics in leaflets stood little chance of penetrating such a culturally and emotionally rooted non-logical system of belief. One cannot successfully attack with logic that which is not grounded in logic.

At worst, it seemed probable that attacks on the Emperor would remind the people of their allegiance and tighten their grip on their belief at a time when other aspects of morale might be giving away. There would be renewed determination and death would seem to them preferable to submission before an enemy who vilified the values that were at the foundation of existence. Better to lose one's life than to lose all hope.

Our view was frequently countered with the argument that the present form of Emperor belief was recent and to a large extent the product of militarist propaganda. Without raising the question of validity in this statement, it did not seem to us that either item was necessarily correlated with the strength or weakness of a belief system. It is not the "real" facts, but what a people *think* their history is that counts in matters of this sort. In this particular case, the Japanese thought of the Imperial System as having great antiquity. This was much more significant than whether or not it actually had such ancient history.

In regard to the use of the Emperor by militarists in their propaganda, ruling classes everywhere have commonly employed religious and other beliefs in this manner and such action cannot be assumed to signify weakness in the belief systems themselves.

CONCLUSIONS

It is our hope that the foregoing general description and the more specific illustration in the case of the psychological and cultural significance of the Emperor have given some understanding of the concepts and methods employed. It is these that we feel are important. Most of the issues with which we dealt during the war have disappeared or changed and wartime estimates in regard to them are no longer of much significance. Moreover, it is not likely that, in any future war, work such as ours will ever be used again. With atomic weapons, it is difficult to see how hostilities can last long enough to make it worth while.

However, even though the concepts and methods described in this paper have become obsolete in war, they remain pertinent to the problem of the relations between peoples during peace and to plans for maintaining that peace.

The present and future American policy in regard to Japan is a case in point and we may again use the attitudes about the Emperor as a more specific illustration of a general idea.

America no longer has to deal with the question of psychological warfare against Japan but there is the problem of developing a peaceful way of life in that nation and many think that the key is re-education. An understanding of the Emperor is necessarily important in this connection. He is still there, still functions as a symbol in the lives of the people, and is now credited by many of them with having saved Japan by stopping the war.

However, even though his influence is still strong and even though our analysis indicated that during the war there was nothing the Allies could do to shake this faith, it does not follow that the beliefs about the Emperor will continue changeless in the future or that we are powerless to influence the direction of change. On the contrary, as a result of emotional upheaval due to defeat, the impact of the American troops in Japan and conscious efforts on the part of American officials to influence Japanese thought through press, radio and movies, some alteration is exceedingly likely to occur. America's opportunity is on a scale and with a force that is far different from that which existed when we were outside Japan hurling in both leaflets and bombs.

This does not mean, however, that the change will necessarily be what America wishes or that a shift away from faith in the Emperor will make for peace. In this matter we are very likely to assume more than is warranted, and for an interesting reason.

The Emperor is a symbol to us as well as to the Japanese and we give to this symbol a measure of uncritical belief. Instead of representing security and high aspirations, however, the Emperor to us stands for oppression, cruelty, and a whole constellation of related evils. This is in part the result of war-time propaganda and in part the result of a cultural pattern that represents monarchs as a primary source of social evil. Its historical origin in successive generations of individuals and groups fleeing oppression in Europe is interesting, but not relevant here. The main point is that the pattern, while not undisputed, has been and is a prevalent one reaching far into the folklore of the mountains, the bottom lands and the prairies. As Huck Finn put it, "All kings is mostly rapscallions . . . Take 'em all around, they're a mighty ornery lot. It's the way they was raised."

Added to this, due to conflicts in our family and social life, we may have intrapersonal motives for wanting to crush and punish authoritarian symbols, motives related to our own struggles, insecurities, and aspirations.

It is therefore very easy for us to look on the Emperor as a kind of sore in the social body of Japan and to believe that if it is cut out everything will be satisfactory. Because he is called Emperor, we project into him attributes of tyrants. In a sense, this projection is similar to that exhibited by the Japanese, only in our case he symbolizes evil instead of good.

It is therefore worth while to be on guard against illusions and to ask ourselves what changes we want in the Emperor system and why, and to be sure that they are really related to peace and not merely serving personal emotional catharsis.

It is possible that belief symbols such as the Emperor can serve the welfare of men, self-government and good international relations just as well as they can serve home front oppression and overseas aggression. The Society of Friends and the Knights Templars both professed Christianity, and so did both the killers and the killed at St. Bartholomew. A Saracen at the time of the Crusades might have thought that the only way to stop these invasions was to eliminate Christianity. Now, however, we may wonder if he had his finger on the cause or only on a particular mode of expressing an aggression that came from other sources.

Belief systems, cultural patterns, and individual psychology are no doubt important in the development of aggression, but so are elementary biological causes of stress. Japan has a large population and small resources in food and other necessities. Although our aim is allegedly to bring Japan close to our way of thinking as a means of securing peace, it is not clear how any pattern which we possess would enable us to live peacefully within the standard of living that is available there. Emphasis only on reeducation is like a rich man advising a hungry one to behave better while ignoring the question of food and work.

Japan's war was in a large measure an unsuccessful attempt to solve this problem for herself. An earlier liberal period when soldiers were so unpopular that they hesitated to go out in the street in uniform was also an attempt at solution and it ended when matters got worse instead of better at the time of world-wide depression in the late twenties. At present Japan, without knowing just what it means, is looking to democracy for the formula. If this, too, fails, there will be a search for something else.

Other countries are worse off than Japan. None of them will be stable by any political or educational readjustment short of magic, as long as elemental stresses prevail.

The historic method of settling human problems of stress has been war. This has now become too costly and the need is to muster all possible information, insight, and understanding concerning the psychology and culture of other people and of ourselves in order to find a way of resolving stresses and hostilities through mutual adjustment.

If the task of the physical sciences in our national life is one of protection, preparedness, and the development of the more abundant life through material advances, the sciences that deal in human relations must work toward the prevention of wars and toward adequate understanding of how to utilize the material achievements for human benefit. If it was possible to take some steps forward in understanding the nationals of other countries when they were our enemies, it should be possible to turn these methods and concepts to account in preventing the eruption of animosities.

This may be a false hope, but it is the only one — and who can tell what it holds until science has been applied to the nature of man with some of the same zeal and intelligence with which it has been applied to the physical world.

Time is running out, however, and the stock pile of atomic bombs is growing. The alternative is a war which, as every one says and few realize, will exterminate the civilization we know and lead to a slave world run by an elite who have a secret, or a world for the most part empty of men, with Eskimos and jungle natives from remote valleys emerging to build again on the ashes.

▲ BRUCE L. SMITH

Communications Research on Non-Industrial Countries

The propaganda battle between the Soviet and non-Soviet forces for the allegiance of the peoples of the non-industrial world apparently is being "stepped up," as witness the Soviet germ-warfare charges, the nationalist developments in such places as Iran and Egypt, and the intensified efforts of the United States Government's International Information Administration in the Middle East and Asia. This brings to the fore the question of just what is known about the processes of communication among the peoples in countries of varying degrees of industrialization. Americans, as relative newcomers in the assumption of heavy international responsibilities, have rather often underestimated the profound differences in socio-political predisposition due to different amounts and sorts of exposure to industrialization. Consequently many of us probably are more baffled than we need to be by what seems to be the small effects of our official communications upon Chinese communism, Indian neutralism, Iranian and Egyptian intransigence, and the enclaves of communism and fascism in Latin America.

This paper is an effort to suggest lines of approach for communication research in this area, across perhaps the next decade. It takes for granted the general validity of the well-known "Who Says What to Whom" approach to communication analysis. For reasons of space, however, it is devoted almost wholly to one of the "To Whom" elements in the formula — namely, the predispositions of non-industrial audiences.

▲ Dr. Smith, formerly on the staff of the Foreign Service Institute, is now a member of the political science faculty of Michigan State College. This article was published in the *Public Opinion Quarterly,* in 1952, and is copyright by the Princeton University Press. It is reprinted here by permission of the author and the copyright holder.

"MOST OF THE WORLD" IS NON-INDUSTRIAL

The non-industrial areas of the world include two-thirds of the world's population — about a billion, for example, in and around China, India and Southeast Asia, some half billion in the Middle East, and other masses in Africa and Latin American.[1] Culturally diverse as these areas may be, they appear to possess certain similarities from the standpoint of communication policy. A good case may be made for considering their similarities.

What are the main characteristics of the non-industrial audiences of Asia, the Middle East, Africa, and Latin America? How do these characteristics affect the probability that communications by the Great Power nations will get the desired results?

THE THREE-CLASS SOCIAL SYSTEM

The general socio-political characteristics of these countries are well known. Leaving China aside for the moment, there is, in effect, throughout this vast area a three-class socio-political system.

The overwhelming majority of the population, from 80 to 95 per cent, are villagers. Only 5 to 15 per cent belong to the middle class, a class that numbers perhaps 30 per cent of the population of this United States and pretty much sets the tone of the country as a whole. Industrial labor, so prominent and respected in our society, where it numbers about 40 per cent of the population, is of course substantially non-existent in the areas we are discussing now. To mention India as an example, one authority estimates that "the total number of factory workers has never reached 1 per cent of the population."[2] Besides the villagers and the small middle class, there is only one more social stratum in these societies: the tiny group — perhaps 1 to 5 per cent —

[1] The best general social analysis of the non-industrial areas is Ralph Linton's *Most of the World,* New York: Columbia University Press, 1949. For elaborate statistics, see also *Report on the World Social Situation,* New York: United Nations Economic and Social Council, 1952 (E/CN. 5/267).

Inquiry into the characteristic differences between the citizen of the village, so to speak, and the citizen of our industrialized, urbanized, society is not exactly new to social science. As far back as 1887, the German sociologist Ferdinand Toennies brought out the first edition of his *Gemeinschaft und Gesellschaft.* Since the 1890's his works and those of many others have carried forward the systematic comparison of the relatively isolated peasant community on the one hand and the urban civilization on the other.

Today the scientific literature runs into scores of volumes. Much of this is not altogether satisfactory in quality, and there are a large number of significant gaps, particularly in the study of communication habits, but there is enough verified information and responsible conjecture to warrant some fairly concrete generalizations. For a general analysis of progress and of concepts used in recent literature, see Horace Miner, "The Folk-Urban Continuum," *American Sociological Review,* Vol. 17, October 1952, pp. 529-37.

[2] W. Norman Brown, ed., *India, Pakistan and Ceylon,* p. 25.

who belong to the class of landlords and moneylenders and (in a few cases such as Argentina and India) the owners of the very few big industries that exist there. This latter tiny group is, for all practical purposes, the ruling class, by virtue of its highly disproportionate economic power and its near-monopoly on secular and foreign education.

This handful of landowners and moneylenders and their industrialist allies occupies or controls most offices in the legislature, the judiciary, and of course the Foreign Office and the diplomatic service. In coalition with a small and seldom decisive group of urban professionals and businessmen, this group constitutes the National Assembly in almost any Latin American republic, the Majlis in Iran or Egypt, and to a considerable extent the Congress Party in India. They are challenged at times by movements expressing middle-class discontent, but, except in rare cases like the Turkey of Kemal Ataturk, thus far have not been overthrown.

When they are overthrown, it is typically members of the middle class who formulate the grievances of the masses, carry on propaganda and agitation, and lead the attack — sometimes in the name of vigorous nationalism as in Kemal's Turkey or Gandhi's India, sometimes in the name of socio-economic democracy as in Mao's China or Ho Chih-min's Indochina. Hence the tremendous significance of the middle classes of these areas for communications analysis.

The study of feudalism in the West can easily suggest some possible patterns of social evolution and public opinion in the non-industrial areas of today — provided always that we make allowance for considerable cultural differences, and especially for the fact that in a number of the non-industrial areas there are few of the natural resources that permitted the evolution from feudalism in the West.

THE COMMUNICATION NETWORK

Communications from the Great Power nations enter this three-class system at all three levels. In the course of dealings with Foreign Offices and other government agencies, and at international conferences such as the United Nations, the diplomats from the industrial nations negotiate day by day with members of landholder and moneylender families.[3]

In the course of efforts to push international trade and economic development, American diplomacy, especially through trade treaties

[3] The so-called "extended family" is characteristic of social organization throughout the area we are considering. Family considerations are usually very much more important in the mind of a Latin American, Middle Easterner or Asian than "merely" individual or national considerations. Often, indeed, these people regard *us* as immoral for failing to see the reasonableness of this intense attachment to the family as against a "mere abstraction" like a nation or an international agreement.

and through the ECA and Mutual Security Administrations, enters into contact not only with the landholder-moneylender class, but also, through them, with elements of the middle class.[4] And as we and the United Nations Organization develop our Point Four programs, our communications come into contact with the villagers — but again, it must be emphasized, through the intermediary of the landholder-moneylender class. For the latter, like Louis XIV, is the State.

Accordingly, an analysis of our communications problems vis-à-vis the non-industrial countries would include discussion of these three chains of communication:

(1) U.S. to Government (to landholder-moneylenders);
(2) U.S. through Government to middle class; and
(3) U.S. through Government to middle class and villagers.

Radio (e.g., the Voice of America, BBC, or Radio Moscow and its satellites) offers a direct channel to all three strata; but access to radio receivers is rather limited in the non-industrial areas.

EXTRA CHANNEL OPEN TO SOVIET UNION

For a full picture of existing communication patterns, it is important to bear in mind the additional communication channel open to those who control the Soviet Union. Being a government, they can of course use the three channels we have just mentioned, in any of the non-industrial countries where they have a diplomatic mission. Since Communists are members of a conspiratorial revolutionary party, they can use an additional channel:

Soviet Union to Communist Party (of the country concerned) to villagers and middle class — and even, in a few cases, to selected sympathizers in the landholder-moneylender class.

This extra channel gives the Soviet Union an immense advantage. It enables things to be said that would be extremely *non grata* if expressed through the other channels; and it has the added advantage of being confined primarily to face-to-face propaganda, which probably is far more effective among villager audiences.

CROSS-CULTURAL ANALYSIS OF "VALUE-CONSTELLATIONS"

A very great aid to policymaking in the international communication field would be a tracing-out of what knowledge we have as to the appeals that work or do not work in the channels at present open to the various Great Power nations. To plot the predispositions of the audiences, we could well start with a rigorously comparative catalogue of the value-profile (or "value-constellations," as I should prefer to

[4] See, e.g., Soedjatmoko, "Point Four and Southeast Asia," *Annals of Amer. Acad. of Polit. and Soc. Sci.*, 270: July 1950, 74-82. Also see Carleton S. Coon, "Point Four and the Middle East," *ibid.*, pp. 83-94.

call them) most highly prized by representatives of, say, the three strata just named, in the principal non-industrial areas of the world.[5]

These value-constellations could then be laid alongside comparable statements of the value-constellations currently being promoted by the Great Powers. Plotting the areas of congruence and divergence might lead to much better predictions than are now being made.

Particular attention should be paid to the value-constellations preferred by village audiences. We who are products of the industrial cultures are somewhat at home, probably, in fitting our communications to the value-constellations of diplomats, landholders, moneylenders, and middle-classes (who after all have received a large part of their education at Western hands). But in communicating with villagers there are certain things we are likely to underestimate or forget. Yet over the long term, as the case of China shows, both the moneylender-landholder class and the middle-class spokesmen of social reorganization have to work within the limits of the value-constellations of the villagers whom they "govern," or be ousted.

By way of indicating what this research might develop, the rest of this paper will comment on a few of the characteristics of villagers that seem to determine the ways their value-constellations can be affected by political communications from abroad.

THE "VALUE-CONSTELLATIONS" OF ILLITERATES

Many items in the value-constellations of the villager are due to the simple fact that he is illiterate. No doubt this is obvious. Everyone knows that from 70 to 95 per cent of the population in these areas are unable to read and write. Yet it may be almost impossible for people like ourselves to grasp the complete meaning of this for our problem of communication. First of all, it obviously means that we cannot use our own habitual media or modes of communication at all. The newspaper, the pamphlet, the book are simply of no avail except through intermediaries (school-teachers, town clerks, tavern keepers, itinerant storytellers . . .) who interpret them orally to the masses. Neither is our usual type of newsreel or radio newscast, for the content of these is based on the unspoken assumption that the audience already has a certain value-pattern derived from elementary reading, at least, in the public schools and the gum-chewers' magazines and the newspapers. Our newsreels and newscasts therefore assume a set of information and values that no villager of the Punjab or Iran or the Gold Coast or Brazil is likely to have.

[5] On methodological problems of placing such research on an acceptable quantitative basis, see especially Florence R. Kluckhohn, "Dominant and Substitute Profiles of Cultural Orientation," *Social Forces,* 28: 376-93 (May 1950). As an example, see the sensitive description of the value-profile of the Arab villager in Afif Tannous, "Extension Work among the Arab Fellahin," *Applied Anthropology,* April-June 1944, pp. 1-12.

Our usual media also assume a certain minimum of incentive for paying attention to those aspects of our communication content that *we* consider important. For example, one of our key values is "political freedom"; another is the military security of the "Free World." Are villagers really interested in what we have to say about the loss of personal freedom under Stalinism, or the importance of contributing one's personal iota to the total military defense of the Free World? A good bit of field research indicates that they are not.[6]

Interviews by psychologists may show that there is hardly anyone in a village where the illiteracy rate is 70 per cent or higher who possesses any concepts at all resembling what we mean by freedom, by Stalinism, by total military defense, or by the Free World. Yet it seems almost impossible for *us* to conceive of just what we want to tell these people if we do not want to tell them about these things. And so we have continued to pop in and out of their villages with our movies, jeeps and bookmobiles, extolling the Western way of life, in concepts that illiterate people cannot be expected to understand.[7] In so doing, we seem to have overlooked the apparent fact that the only visual or other sensory image our villager has of the Western way of life is derived from the most violent of Hollywood's motion pictures.

As believers in relatively unrestricted free enterprise, Americans can hardly complain if foreign exhibitors cash in on the discovery that the gangster and cowboy movies are almost the only exhibits of the Western way of life that are very interesting to audiences in the economically less-developed areas. But perhaps it is essential for our Government information programs, if they are to be politically effective, to learn to offset, not reinforce, the existing images of our own values. A great deal of concrete research on a continuous, recurring basis is essential to accomplish this.

SLOW TEMPO AS A CENTRAL VALUE

In part because of illiteracy, in part for other reasons, the non-industrial peoples move through life at a much slower tempo than we, or so it seems to *us*. Recently a member of one of our cultural missions in a Southeast Asian country complained that she found it very boring to go to the native theater or dances or movies. The tempo was too

[6] Much of the best of such research has been pioneered by the Program Evaluation Staff of the Voice of America, under the direction of Dr. Leo Lowenthal. See also the recent international research of Columbia University's Bureau of Applied Social Research, e.g., "Patterns of Communications in a Rural Greek Village," by J. Mayone Stycos, *Public Opinion Quarterly,* Vol. 16, No. 4 (Spring 1952), pp. 59-70. An admirable popular statement of some of the factors involved may be found in Arthur Goodfriend's *The Only War We Seek,* New York: Farrar, Strauss and Young, 1951.

[7] The U.S. International Information Administration has sought in recent months to correct this situation by having documentary motion pictures produced *in the countries concerned* and *about conditions in those countries.*

slow. The shows lasted for three or four hours, and they always seemed to deal with the same small set of situations or themes.

If conclusive evidence can be found that this slow tempo is a central value for representative people in these cultures, it might be accounted for in part by their greater dependence on the slow changes of the seasons, and their greater preoccupation with the slowly changing details of plant and animal life and of the family. Their satisfactions in life appear to come to a much greater extent from repetition, meditation, and relatively slow development. If this is true, it is full of implications for our information policy.

For example, it is possible that they experience a frustration-and-rejection reaction when they are exposed to the high and jerky tempo and short attention span of our usual motion pictures and public addresses, and especially to our newsreels and radio programs. The very much slower tempo of the BBC broadcasts as compared with the Voice of America may help to account for the fact that BBC is reported to be more popular with these audiences.

Considering this same factor of tempo, we might also want to ask ourselves about the psychological aspects of our Point Four and "productivity" campaigns among these populations. These are campaigns that demand speedy action on age-old problems. Does our handling of the human relations involved in this tend to reinforce the Russian propaganda which appeals to the predisposition of these people to believe that we are uncultured slave drivers who look down upon the way of life of the Asians, the Middle East and the Latin Americans?

POLITENESS AS A CENTRAL VALUE

A factor associated with the high valuation of slow tempo among these people is their high valuation of politeness. Cora DuBois recently asked some Southeast Asians and Chinese who have studied in the United States just what it is most important for Americans going to their countries to be told. A characteristic answer was:

Warn them that politeness is very important to us. . . . . It is not polite to rush bluntly into a discussion of the purpose of your visit. We like time to make the *sawasti,* to exchange polite remarks while we are getting used to strangers. In the East it is customary and courteous to derogate oneself and one's achievements and possessions. We feel one must be very modest. You must not boast or force yourself on people. If you are very modest and very quiet, then people want to do things for you. That is how to get things done.

Just how these friendly warnings tie in with the tempo, style and substance of our projection of America and American policy through informational and educational media is something that may be brought out by research.

These warnings may also indicate some difficulties that Soviet propaganda may possibly run into in these areas if it insists upon as rapid a rate of technological transformation and as blunt a manner of speaking as it does inside Russia. There is a chance, of course, that the Russian speed-up and bluntness will be softened by the fact that most of their external communication is mediated by Communist Party organizers who are themselves members of the foreign cultures concerned. It is also a fact that the tempo of some of their domestic as well as foreign radio programs has been slowed to what we Americans regard as a snail's pace, apparently to make allowance for illiteracy and for cultural differences in tempo, and also to permit listeners to take notes, or to enable the illiterate to commit a message to memory.

RELIGION AS THE CENTRAL VALUE OF LIFE

Most of these audiences are very much more religious than most of us. To the orthodox Moslem, Hindu or Buddhist in many a village, the only conceivable "way of life" is the Koran, the Vedas or the Eightfold Noble Path.

To say this is to call attention to the obvious. Since Toennies, and especially since Max Weber, it has been a commonplace of social science that the world of the illiterate is of necessity a world peopled by sacred beings and given richness and meaning primarily by sacred values. To him, his government, his social order and his political decisions are likely to appear as religious institutions, while our political efforts appear to be lacking in religious significance, or even to be grossly anti-religious. We often forget this, or we badly underestimate its importance.

In the world of the illiterate, the instrumental and manipulative attitude that we are accustomed to speak of as "scientific rationality," or "business is business," appears not only alien but anathema. Religion is merely an added satisfaction or a consolation to many of us; but its meaning obviously is far deeper to those who are confronted by the horrors of disease, famine, invasion, old age and death, and who have no scientific instruments except their bare hands, and no ways of diagnosis or cure except the lore of an illiterate village."[8]

[8] A recent study of villages in Egypt, conducted by the Rockefeller Foundation and reported in *The New York Times*, May 5, 1952, p. 4C, showed that: "all Egyptian villagers studied had amoebic dysentery; 90 per cent had bilharzia, a parasitic disease that undermines health and energy. Sixty-four per cent had intestinal worms. Five per cent had pellagra. . . . Six per cent had acute infections of the eyes, of the type leading to blindness, and 89 per cent had trachoma, an eye disease that can destroy sight, while 6.4 per cent were blind in one eye. . . . Fifty-six per cent lived on a diet of unleavened bread, skim milk and cheese, plus fresh vegetables approximately once a week. . . . (Another twelve per cent had no vegetables.) . . . Life expectancy at birth is 15 to 20 years of age."

Some of our Point Four experts are reported to be astounded and infuriated by the grip of ancient religions (or superstitions, as they sometimes call them) on the villagers in Latin America, in the Arab states and in India. Alert and sympathetic information officers have suggested a re-writing of some of the Point Four aims in terms of the Koran and the sacred writings of India. According to reports, a certain degree of success has already been realized in this. Here the relative tolerance of the Western world toward divergences of creed and eccentricities, together with our continually growing understanding of both social and individual psychology, may very well prove to be a great asset.

In regard to the religious question, the Communist movement has probably had more experience, much better channels of intelligence, and much better channels of communication than the United States. For one thing, it has had a generation of bitter but often successful experience in governing the hundred or more non-industrial culture groups inside the Soviet Union and in Communist China. For another, its main communication channel is the agitator who is himself a member of the non-industrial society.

More than one psychologist has remarked that Stalinism can be regarded as a secular religion to a much greater extent than can liberal capitalism. In spite of its emphatic demand for atheism the positive demands and practices of the movement contain many elements that are very close to the more authoritarian religions, such as Islam and Catholicism, and to the religiously sanctioned collectivism and anti-Westernism of the Hindu or Arab villager. Indeed, Communist practice in general contains many more elements of what Toennies called *Gemeinschaft* — the communal psychology of the villager — than does Westernism as practiced in these areas. Therefore, it may perhaps be substituted more rapidly for the traditional practices of the village. These factors may help to account for the relatively rapid spread of Stalinism in the non-industrial areas at the same time that Stalinism is spreading very slowly, or even retreating, in the more industrial West.

SOME HYPOTHESES

The foregoing notes have mentioned only a few of the points at which we have some research and need more. We could use much fuller information on the relative intensities and priorities with which the different strata in the various cultures concerned pursue such values as social mobility, physical courage, profit-taking, the sharing of wealth, self-government, the respective roles of the sexes, and the respect due older age-groups. Some research indicates that American behavior and communication in the latter two regards arouse profound antagonism in certain non-industrial cultures. It may be that we already know enough to frame some hypotheses on the relative roles of the United States (or "the West") and the Soviet Union in political communication with these peoples.

We know, for example, that many among the villagers, the middle classes and even the landholders and moneylenders are illiterate, poverty-stricken and ridden with illnesses. But many of them also are sophisticated representatives of ancient, well-rooted cultures whose meditations and accomplishments have enriched philosophy, literature, science and art for centuries. We know that many of their most central values — their races, their cultures, and their dignity as human beings — have for a long time been assaulted and insulted by "the West."[9] We know that a large percentage of the current political leaders of some of these countries have been jailed at one time or another for opposition to such "Western" ways as the wholesale removal of their natural resources. We know that the Communists, who have not yet been in a position to jail them or take away their resources, have a reputation for insisting emphatically upon their "liberation." We can infer that even if Communist propaganda today were highly incompetent — which it is not — it would have an easy time among peoples who have been so much offended.

What of America's role in conveying information and education to these people? It may be that whatever information we pass out must, for the time being, be based almost exclusively upon local reporting of concrete actions that we and the United Nations have taken in these areas to help them overcome their haunting tragedies of disease, famine, ignorance, and the loss of human dignity. It might be helpful for the United States and England, and other Powers if possible, to disassociate themselves openly from particular policies and value-symbols hitherto associated by these peoples with "the West," and to speak and act much more in concert with a majority of the United Nations. Gradually a redefinition of the philosophy of political freedom, economic security and human dignity as we *and the non-industrial peoples* understand it might then begin to seem real to them.

Admittedly it is hard to get material or psychological support in America for such a hard-headed communication program. There are many temptations to preach, to accuse, to over-emphasize "the West," and to try to buy friendship. Our country has entered upon its responsibilities in world politics so recently that we are not yet as a nation aware of the scale of the mistakes of this sort that have been made, or how late in the day it is. Yet some elements in the industrialized world are striving vigorously to make up for past mistakes and lost time. We have no choice but to hope that the day can be saved by ingenuity and energy and by a hitherto untapped capacity for investment, mass education, diplomacy — and communication research.

[9] See, e.g., F. S. C. Northrop, "Asian Mentality and United States Foreign Policy," *Annals of Amer. Acad. of Polit. and Soc. Sci.,* 276, July 1951, pp. 118-27 and Vera M. Dean, "How Asians View the United States," *ibid.,* 128-34.

▲ RALPH K. WHITE

*T*he New Resistance to International Propaganda

The world is more and more tired of "propaganda." This is the fundamental, all-embracing fact which every propagandist must face, and the implications of which he must recognize, if he is even to have an entree into the minds of those who are not already emotionally on his side. The psychological resistances of a skeptical, propaganda-weary world must be respected and intelligently taken into account; they cannot be simply battered down.

American propagandists have been from the beginning more aware of these resistances than their Communist opponents have been. Recent evidence, however, suggests that they should be given even more weight than they have been given in the past. There is accumulating evidence that the special antagonism felt by neutralists toward "propaganda" coming from either side in the present East-West conflict is the greatest single obstacle to our effectiveness, and that the greatest single factor in our being able to beat the Communists at their own propaganda game will be our ability to understand this neutralist skepticism and to see its practical implications.

Recent evidence, in other words, suggests that the following propositions are, if anything, more true today than ever before:

First, our Soviet opponents have lost more than most Americans realize by their almost continual use of the battering-ram technique. The idea prevailing in some quarters that we lose by being less crude, less repetitious, less "emotional" than the Russians is in the main a dangerous misconception. Second, the chief weakness of our own propaganda is not, as some Americans assume, that we are too gentle-manly to descend to Soviet tactics and "fight fire with fire." It is that

▲ Dr. White is a member of the research and evaluation staff of the United States Information Agency. His paper was published in the *Public Opinion Quarterly,* in 1952, and is copyright by the Princeton University Press. It is re-printed here by permission of author and copyright holder.

— at least in what we say to the non-Communist world — we too often give the impression of being "propagandistic." Third, the psychological resistances which the Communists fail to batter down by sheer crude repetition are equally incapable of being circumvented by subtlety or deviousness. The way into the heart of the skeptical neutralist lies not through artifice but through candor.

This does not mean that on the most essential points, such as the danger of Soviet aggression or the necessity of collective strength to deter Soviet aggression, we need to soft-pedal our own convictions. It does not mean that we need to have any sense of guilt or apology in our role as propagandists — in the better sense of that word, involving only a large-scale effort to persuade or convince. (Probably there are few listeners to the Voice of America who do not take it for granted that it is a propaganda arm of the American Government in this non-condemnatory sense of the word propaganda. Of course we are propagandists.)

It does mean two things. First, our *actions* must be in line with our words. The propaganda of the deed is more potent than the propaganda of the word, and the propaganda of the word is effective in direct proportion to the deeds which it is able to publicize. As Secretary Acheson has put it, "What is even more important than what we say to the world is how we conduct ourselves, at home and abroad. The force of example and action is the factor which finally determines what our influence is to be."

Second, it means that our words will be most effective — at least in what we say to the non-Communist world — when the *manner* of our effort to persuade and convince is modest, reasonable, discriminating, sensitive to the kinds of skepticism existing in the minds of any particular audience, and prepared to meet that skepticism candidly and factually, as neighbor might talk to neighbor. It means that we are most effective when we depart freely, wherever the facts warrant it, from a simple black-and-white picture of the world, when we avoid all of the stock ballyhoo techniques of the radio or television advertiser as well as the manners of the table-pounding orator and the finger-wagging schoolmarm, when, instead, we cultivate the highest standards of journalism.

FAILURES OF THE SOVIET BATTERING-RAM

There is a curiously widespread assumption in the United States that the cunning Communists are past masters at the propaganda game and that we innocent democrats are rank amateurs. Actually the reverse of this assumption would be at least as easy to defend. It is true that the Communists have had successes in China, in France, in Italy; but the Communist tide seems to have been receding for some years in France, at least. Even in these countries the successes can be attributed primarily to two great assets which they have had and we have not: the existence of widespread economic distress which their class ideology is inherently well calculated to capitalize upon, and their possession of a corps of dedicated, disciplined, face-to-face agitators within each of these countries. The United States has no fifth columns within France or Italy comparable with those which Russia has in the Italian and French Communist parties. Neither of these assets, however, has any necessary direct relationship to propaganda technique as such. When it comes to evaluating Communist propaganda techniques as illustrated in the Communist press and radio, the verdict of the typical reader or listener in either eastern or western Europe seems to be that they are boringly repetitious, obviously "propagandistic," and therefore *dull*. One Frenchman recently used a graphic gesture in describing Soviet propaganda — the gesture of an organ-grinder always grinding out the same mechanical tune.

Available figures on listenership tell the same story. For instance, in Western Germany 65 per cent of the radio listeners sampled by the Reactions Analysis Staff of HICOG said they had listened to the Voice of America, while the figure for the nearest Communist competitor of the Voice was 9 per cent. In Eastern Germany, where the Communists are in the saddle, the situation is remarkably similar; the most widely heard and respected station is not the Communist Radio Berlin but RIAS, the vigorously anti-Communist, American-directed, German-operated station in Western Berlin. Similarly, there is reason to think that the Western radios, BBC and the Voice of America, are much more listened to throughout the Satellite area than are Communist radios in Western Europe. As for America, how many Americans even know of the existence of Moscow's programs beamed to us in English?

It is also interesting to find that the Western European verdict on Communist dullness is shared to some extent by the Communists themselves. They are beginning to realize that methodical dogmatism does not draw listeners. In the spring of 1952 there was in the Communist press of East Berlin a campaign of "criticism and self-criticism" directed chiefly against Radio Berlin, and its chief charge, realistically enough, was that this station's output was dull. Several articles called for more humor, more conversation, more "sensitivity to what is alive" (Lebensgefühl), more "creative optimism," a less schematic approach, fewer catchwords (Schlagworte), and — this from a Communist! — less of a black-and-white picture (Schwarz-Weiss-Malerei). There was also some explicit recognition that the form or technique of Western propaganda is superior: "The content (of the Communist radio programs) triumphs over the form, which is too little paid attention to, in contrast with the West, where the form usually smothers the content." The writer of this statement was perhaps intentionally vague, but he seems to be obliquely accepting a proposition which in the minds of

most non-Communists in Western Europe is quite clear: the repe-.
titiousness and the propagandistic quality of Communist propaganda
make it relatively hard to listen to.

In a broader historical perspective, too, the success of the Communists' bludgeon type of propaganda is ambiguous, to say the least.
Probably the most effective single piece of international communication in the twentieth century was Wilson's list of Fourteen Points, and
it was not a bludgeon. The appeal lay rather in its adopting a broad
statesmanlike approach, above the battle and free from vindictiveness.
Hitler's propaganda bludgeon worked with the Germans, but few non-
Germans were impressed, and the more winsome eloquence of Roosevelt and Churchill helped to rally a world to defeat Hitler. The Soviet
bludgeon has been wielded on a large scale for thirty-five years; it has
perhaps worked well with the Russians (though even this is questioned
in some quarters), but world revolutionary propaganda has led to successful revolution only in the case of China. That is, it is only in China
that a Communist government has attained power without the help,
direct or indirect, of the Soviet Red Army, and even there the Chinese
Red Army, aided by the Kremlin, had a good deal to do with it. We
are free, then, to follow the present-day evidence in the direction in
which it leads. We are not compelled to assume that where our
methods differ from those of the Russians they are necessarily right and
we are necessarily wrong.

THE REAL PROBLEMS OF AMERICAN PROPAGANDA

The chief weakness of our own propaganda is not, as some Americans assume, that we are too gentlemanly to descend to Soviet tactics
and "fight fire with fire." We use plenty of fire (of a sort quite different
from that used by the Communists) in what we say to the peoples behind the Iron Curtain, and there is much reason to believe that it is
effective. The great difficulty lies in what we say to the non-Communist world; the danger here is that we may appear to be too
"propagandistic."

To appreciate the problem that our information program is up
against, it is necessary first to distinguish very sharply between the
psychological situation that confronts us on this side of the Curtain
and that which confronts us on the other side. On the other side, official
Communist propaganda is omnipresent, and the picture of the world
that it presents is of course grossly distorted. While usually avoiding
outright lying, it systematically omits any fact or idea that might
modify its all-black picture of us and its all-white picture of the
Kremlin. It continually and flagrantly stacks the cards. Against this
flood of selected data the listener must struggle as best he can, and our
information and "propaganda" are rightly designed to help him in the
struggle. Necessarily, we must spend most of our time setting the

record straight; and this means not only correcting the grossest lies but also taking the offensive and hitting the Kremlin hard on those vulnerable spots which the Soviet propagandist systematically covers up and glosses over. Necessarily, we must select our facts too, presenting primarily the kinds of facts that will to some extent redress the balance. We can and must "fight fire with fire" in this sense, and also in the sense that what we say must often have an emotional impact. Neither selectivity nor the occasional expression of strong emotion will impress this audience as "too propagandistic." On the contrary, a very hard-hitting anti-Stalin political message seems to be just what most of our listeners there want. Those who are already strongly anti-Stalin (and most of those who listen apparently are anti-Stalin) usually do not seem to judge our message in terms of its judiciousness and careful discrimination. Their emotional needs are for vicarious expression of their own smouldering hatred of the Stalinist tyranny, for evidence that the strongest nation beyond the reach of Stalin's power is on their side, and for hope that, with this and other allies in the West, their day of liberation will some day come. This is what they want, and this is what they are getting. Unquestionably, too, millions listen. It would be very rash to say "millions" in Russia, but the conclusion that there are millions in East Germany and the Satellite area who listen is no longer open to serious question.

In Western Europe and other parts of the non-Communist world the psychological situation is radically different. In contrast to our listeners behind the Curtain, who are starved for straight news and for a source of hope and emotional support, our listeners throughout the free world are not starved for either news or hope. As a rule their own press and radio give them plenty of news and comment, and as a rule a good deal of it is, like what they get from America, anti-Communist. If they turn their dials to the Voice of America, they do so not as starving men but as men who have just finished a Thanksgiving dinner, and they are in a choosy mood. In addition, we cannot take it for granted that these people are favorably disposed toward America and Americans. Finally, and most important, those who incline toward neutralism are hypersensitive to what they call "propaganda" coming from *either* side. It is imperative, therefore, that we study and take into account what they mean by "propaganda."

One thing we are fairly sure of: most of those who call both us and Russians "propagandistic" do not mean that we indulge in lying as the Russians do. If this were what they meant the prospect of improvement would be dark indeed, since, platitudinous as it may sound, we are already making every effort to be scrupulously accurate on all matters of tangible fact. Occasional errors creep in, in spite of all our effort, but no major improvement is to be expected from an intensified effort to be less like the Russians in this respect.

What these critics do mean is not by any means fully clear, especially since it varies from country to country. It would seem, though, that when a Belgian or an Egyptian or an Indonesian angrily twists his radio dial in order not to hear what he calls the "propaganda" of Moscow or of the Voice of America, the chances are that in the back of his mind there is a blending of several evil images. The first is of two crudely simple black-and-white pictures of the world, each of which he believes to be a gross distortion of the complexity of reality, even when it does not contain outright lies. Then there are two giant nations struggling for world power, each looking upon the listener's own country as a pawn or tool in that struggle and each using words in a calculated effort to subject his will to its own. The last image is of the gathering storm clouds of atomic war, in which the thunder of mutual denunciation is an omen of unthinkable things to come. Calculated distortion, domination and death — these, then, are some of the connotations of "propaganda" in its present historical context. It is no wonder that "Count me out" — i.e., neutralism — is a typical reaction.

Corresponding to these three evil images, three remedies suggest themselves. Each of them is already being applied to a considerable extent, and the extent to which any one of them *should* be applied is a matter of judgment and of balancing pros and cons. It is this writer's judgment, however, that what we say to the free world would gain even more in impact if we demonstrated more candor, more respect for the listener, and a more "positive" approach.

Less Selectivity

No one on our side questions the statement made at the beginning of this article: "The way into the heart of the skeptical neutralist lies not through artifice but through candor." No one doubts that our information program is and should be conspicuously superior to that of the Communists in candor — defining candor, provisionally, as a readiness to depart from the black-and-white picture when the available facts warrant such a departure. Yet even in the free world our task includes the countering of vicious Communist propaganda, and an awakening of those who are not yet aware of the nature and extent of the Soviet danger. There is a real problem, then: at what point should we draw the line between the kind of selectivity that the strengthening of the free world seems to require and the sort of nonselectivity that would demonstrate our candor and objectivity? To what extent is the selectivity which is clearly needed in our message to the Communist world also necessary or desirable in what we say to our friends and potential friends on this side of the Curtain? *How much* white or grey can we afford to admit on the "black" side of our own black-white picture, and how much black or grey on the "white" side?

The line would probably be drawn at one point by most of the professional American propagandists (e.g., desk chiefs, script-writers in the Voice of America) and at a somewhat different point by many in Congress and the general public. The professionals are likely to favor a lower degree of selectivity — that is, they are likely to put relatively more emphasis on the advantages of obvious candor and objectivity. While granting that we do not need to wash all of our dirty linen in public, they would usually feel that we should wash at least enough of it in public so that our audience could not possibly fail to notice what we are doing. Yet a fear exists — perhaps a misguided fear — that Congress and the public would see something "subversive" and insufficiently anti-Communist in the procedure if our propaganda were as candid as the professionals think it ought to be. In the interest of mutual understanding, therefore, it seems worth while to present in this paper the reasons why, in one person's opinion, the American information program to the non-Communist world should actually be *less* selective than it now is.

An anecdote will illustrate one of the ways in which too much selectivity could do harm. In the early days of World War II Goebbels did his best to discredit the BBC with phrases such as "the Ministry of Lies." He failed, and perhaps the most crucial single incident bringing about his failure was a news report by the BBC asserting that after a certain mission to the continent seven British planes had failed to return. The German radio had just described the same incident, stating that *five* planes had failed to return. In other words, the BBC was describing the British fortunes of battle as actually blacker than they were being described by the enemy. In this case it happens that the British were merely accurate; two planes which the Germans had seen leaving the continent were already crippled and failed to get to England when the others did. The psychological effect, however, was far greater than mere apparent accuracy would ever have achieved. It would have been worth while for the British to invent those two additional non-returning planes, even if they had not existed, in order to achieve a dramatic demonstration of British capacity to go beyond what was necessary in the direction of candor. Selectivity in the form of, let us say, reporting that seven British planes left the Continent (which was true, but not the whole truth) would have been a psychological mistake.

One generalization which this example illustrates is that, *where the audience has other sources of news,* comparisons are likely to be made. Applying this to our present problem, it implies that if we should soft-pedal anything that is emphasized by other news sources, Communist or non-Communist, we would not only fail to keep it from our listeners' ears but would also lose some of that credibility which is our most precious asset. This is especially true if the fact which is ignored or soft-pedaled is unfavorable to ourselves. As far as news is concerned, the soundest rule would seem to be to let *news value* — the newspaperman's conception of the inherent importance or reader-interest of an event — be almost the only criterion of what should be included or emphasized.

The experience of the British Broadcasting Corporation supports this view. The Voice of America is definitely more hard-hitting, more outspokenly anti-Communist, than the BBC, and this policy has reaped dividends in our broadcasts to Iron Curtain countries where the audiences crave hope and vicarious expression of their own hostility to the Stalinist tyranny. There the Voice of America is usually preferred just because it is in a sense more "propagandistic." On the other hand, the BBC is usually regarded as more objective than the Voice of America in the non-Communist countries where sensitivity to "propaganda" is greatest; and a major factor in its reputation is, probably, the great emphasis which it places on inclusiveness or non-selectivity in the news.

As for commentaries, selectivity has disadvantages there too. There are many topics on which an American preparing a pamphlet or a radio broadcast may hesitate to say anything at all: the Negro in America, slums in America, unemployment, corruption, our attitude toward British socialism, shifts in our policies toward Germany and Japan, MacArthur's advance to the Yalu, Franco, Chiang Kai-shek, Indochina, North Africa, the Arab refugees, our disarmament in 1945, American "imperialism" in Latin America, the perils of an arms race. On some of these topics we have a much sounder case than most of our critics realize, yet one often hesitates even to broach such a topic, knowing that any really honest treatment of it would involve certain "admissions," and knowing that every "admission" carries a certain danger.

The objection to admissions does have some factual support. There is reason to think that some listeners who are hostile enough to be looking for things to pounce on may react to an admission only by thinking "It must be true, since they admit it themselves." Because of this danger, candor is certainly not always self-evidently the best policy. But the available evidence does suggest that we should reconsider the matter; perhaps we have been too sensitive to the danger of making admissions and too insensitive to the opposite danger of losing both listeners and respect by seeming to gloss over problems which are very much present in our listeners' minds.

The evidence in favor of a need for even greater candor is impressionistic and, tentatively, experimental. The impressionistic evidence comes chiefly from the kinds of criticism of American propaganda that occur most often in the non-Communist world. With no statistics on the matter, this writer's impression is that those who criticize (and they appear to be in the minority) most often describe the Voice of America as *propagandistic* (with variants such as "table-pounding"), as *patronizing* (with variants such as "boastful," "condescending," "teaching," "didactic," and "educating"), and as simply *dull*. While there are persons who have made the very different criticism that its programs to the Free World are not "hard-hitting" enough, it is significant that this type of criticism is not frequent among our listeners in the non-Communist world. They do not often say, as some Americans do, that we are "too gentlemanly," that we should "fight fire with fire," or that we should "hit harder." What they do say, and say very often, is that we "pound the table" too hard and too much. Or they say that we are "getting to be too much like the Communists," or that the Communists are "even worse" than we are. The similarity in the pattern of adjectives is also striking. While the Communists are apparently not called "patronizing," the other two counts against us, "propagandistic" and "dull," are exactly the same as the two charges which are by all odds the most frequent in describing Communist propaganda. (Again — this is to some extent a natural reaction against the two great powers regardless of propaganda approach.)

Curiously enough, listeners do not often say in so many words that our programs are not candid enough. Yet if they were more analytical they probably would, since, in their minds, a lack of sufficient candor presumably underlies and partly accounts for each of the three defects that are most often mentioned. Greater candor would of course counteract the idea of "propaganda" in the sense of calculated distortion; similarly, more real humility (and candor about ourselves implies occasional humility) might go far toward counteracting the impression among critics that our programs are "patronizing"; and any variation from a black-white picture would be to them a welcome relief from boredom. When Anthony Eden recently spoke of the "magnificent" performance of the Red Army at Stalingrad — in a way which if anything added to the force of his later anti-Kremlin remarks — he probably accomplished three things simultaneously: he gained a little added prestige as a man who could rise above "propaganda"; he minimized any tendency of the Russians to think that he felt superior to them as Russians; and he gave a little refreshment to ears long jaded wtih "four legs good, two legs bad."

As far as it goes, then, the impressionistic evidence which has come to the attention of the writer supports the thesis that, in view of the changing climate of opinion in the Free World, diminished selectivity would add to the size of our audience, to our own prestige, and to the believability of everything else that we say. As for experimental evidence, preliminary results of an experiment done in Germany, with matched listening groups and controlled conditions, have turned out in favor of candor. An approach which was less selective than is now typical of the American information program appeared to be better both from the standpoint of preference for these particular programs and from the standpoint of general attitude toward the source from which these programs come.

More Respect for the Listener

It is hard for many Americans to appreciate the full extent of the fear of American domination that exists abroad, even among our non-Communist allies. Knowing the live-and-let-live spirit of the American people, it seems ridiculous to us that anyone should take charges of American "domination" or "imperialism" seriously. But such charges are taken seriously, and fear of our desire to use other countries as pawns in a power struggle colors much of the listening to our words. It behooves us, then, to see to it that the words themselves do not suggest any sense of superiority to the listener or any lack of understanding and appreciation of his nation and his culture. This is the least we can do to counteract the notion that we think he is, or could become, a pawn or tool.

In addition, there can be more of a person-to-person approach, with a focus on the idea of "we're all in this thing together," and without any explicit attention either to the fact that the speaker is an American or to the particular nationality of the listener. Even this, however, can be done best if the ideas and the forms of expression that are used show an intimate, easy familiarity with the listener's ways of thought.

And even this kind of thing calls for intimate *knowledge* of the listener's life and way of thought. Here we Americans are greatly handicapped by our geographical distance from our audiences. Although most of the script-writers in the Voice of America are natives of or have long lived in the country to which they are broadcasting, too often their knowledge is not up to date. Often the writer has not seen his audience for several years. An urgent need, therefore, is a greatly expanded program of rotation of personnel, to enable at least all of the creative writers of the Voice to spend two or three months refreshing their understanding of the minds, the current problems and the emotional preoccupations of the people they are talking to.

A More "Positive" Approach

The psychological association between denunciation of Communism and our audience's fear that we may drag them into an unnecessary war seems to be spreading in some parts of the free world. The more we denounce, the more "belligerent" they think we are, and the more they fear us. From this standpoint denunciation is the worst possible approach if we really want allies in a possible war of defense against Communist aggression. But it is not so easy to see what to do about it. If a certain people (let us say the people of India, or of Egypt) is not even really aware that the Soviet danger exists, how can we *not* talk to them about the Soviet danger? How can we justify our own policy of alliances, rearmament and fighting in Korea except against a background of Soviet aggression and the danger to all freedom which is involved if that aggression is not stopped?

The dilemma will remain regardless of all our efforts to resolve it. That is, there will necessarily be some neutralists who are so allergic to any anti-Soviet talk by us that they will always refuse to listen and always consider it further evidence of our "belligerence." But at least three things can be done to minimize the frequency of this reaction while maximizing the number of those who hear the most important elements in our anti-Soviet collective-security message:

(1) To make our actions as well as our words scrupulously non-aggressive and non-provocative; to emphasize and reemphasize the official American policy of opposition to a "preventive war" or a "war of liberation," and to avoid action which would make these words sound insincere.

(2) To state our accusations soberly and factually, without any of the sweeping unsupported statements which are the stock-in-trade of Soviet propaganda against us.

(3) To keep down the proportion of direct and indirect denunciation of the Kremlin to that amount which is empirically found to be reasonably acceptable to a given audience, and to fill the remainder of our time with "positive" material which is not even indirectly related to the East-West conflict. Since most of our present output to the free world is at least indirectly related to the East-West conflict (e.g., reports of the increasing defensive strength and unity of Europe) this limitation would probably cut down considerably on the present amount of direct and indirect denunciation. If we did this the chances are that we would both reassure those who now think we are "belligerent" and considerably increase the chance that they would listen to our sober and factual (but, let us hope, powerful) presentation of the essentials in the case for collective security, including the nature and dimensions of the Soviet danger.

▲ WILLIAM BUCHANAN

▲ HADLEY CANTRIL

$\mathcal{N}$ational Stereotypes

A central question in the matter of national attitude and belief is the way the members of any given nation perceive the members of another. Generally, the people of one nation — and the United States is no exception — harbor stereotyped images of other nations, starkly simple and exceedingly inaccurate. . . .

The nature of the various types of images . . . their comparison with reality, and the identification of causal factors are attackable problems. Until some headway is made, international relations must always be in danger of decisions based on fantasy.[1]

The Unesco questionnaire utilized a technique to attack this problem that had been used by social psychologists since early in the 1930's to investigate stereotypes of both races and nationalities, so there exists a body of previous research using comparable methods. However, aside from some surveys by the Office of Public Opinion Research during the war, it had not been frequently combined with the polling technique of gathering cases.

The Unesco question read:

Q.13: *From the list of words on this card, which seems to you to describe the American people best? Select as many as you wish and call off the letters and the words that go with them. If you have no particular feelings one way or the other, just say so.* The words listed were: HARD-WORKING, INTELLIGENT, PRACTICAL, CONCEITED, GENEROUS, CRUEL, BACKWARD, BRAVE, SELF-CONTROLLED, DOMINEERING, PROGRESSIVE, PEACE-LOVING, IMPOSSIBLE TO CHARACTERIZE.

[1] Alexander H. Leighton, *Human Relations in a Changing World* (New York: Dutton, 1949), 102-103.

▲ Based on international survey data gathered under the auspices of UNESCO, this paper appeared as a chapter in *How Nations See Each Other,* published and copyright by the University of Illinois Press (Urbana, 1953). It is reprinted here by permission of copyright holder.

TABLE 5

Summary of Q.13 Results (Percentage of respondents in each country selecting each adjective)

Country in Which Survey Was Made	AUSTRALIA			BRITAIN					GERMANY						FRANCE		
People Described Adjective	U.S.	Russ.	Self	U.S.	Russ.	Self	Fr.	Chin.	U.S.	Russ.	Self	Brit.	Fr.	Chin.	U.S.	Russ.	Self
Hardworking	33%	52%	43%	32%	53%	57%	24%	40%	19%	12%	90%	13%	4%	18%	37%	51%	46%
Intelligent	46	16	53	38	12	52	32	17	34	4	64	34	22	6	37	15	79
Practical	49	19	49	38	21	47	20	11	45	8	53	20	5	3	81	11	17
Conceited	42	14	17	52	13	11	29	2	15	3	15	23	20	—	24	14	30
Generous	40	4	63	52	3	48	14	7	46	2	11	14	5	1	34	7	62
Cruel	2	37	—	3	39	1	5	18	2	48	1	3	10	6	4	41	—
Backward	3	28	9	4	36	6	9	37	1	41	2	3	10	12	2	56	4
Brave	21	26	57	19	31	59	14	21	6	11	63	8	7	6	26	42	56
Self-controlled	18	15	26	10	9	44	3	15	11	3	12	24	5	5	34	9	12
Domineering	23	57	4	37	42	6	11	2	10	12	10	21	12	1	46	49	4
Progressive	77	25	39	58	21	31	14	8	58	2	39	17	7	1	75	19	34
Peace-loving	42	7	71	39	6	77	21	22	23	5	37	15	12	5	26	10	69
Impossible to characterize	a	a	a	8	18	5	30	32	17	34	5	34	49	71	4	12	3
Average no.: Positive adj.	3.3	1.6	4.0	3.0	1.6	4.1	1.4	1.4	2.4	.5	3.7	1.4	.6	.4	3.5	1.6	3.7
Neg. adj.	.7	1.3	.3	1.0	1.3	.2	.5	.6	.3	1.0	.3	.5	.5	.2	.8	1.6	.4

a Not tabulated.

Country in Which Survey Was Made	Italy			Netherlands						Norway			United States		
People Described	U.S.	Russ.	Self	U.S.	Russ.	Self	Brit.	Fr.	Chin.	U.S.	Russ.	Self	Russ.	Brit.	Self
Adjective															
Hardworking	39%	22%	67%	49%	36%	62%	23%	6%	12%	56%	36%	43%	49%	43%	68%
Intelligent	34	13	80	33	8	49	22	8	7	31	6	32	12	49	72
Practical	59	5	24	61	6	36	24	5	3	54	9	22	13	32	53
Conceited	22	12	24	15	10	14	24	10	2	11	7	19	28	38	22
Generous	60	5	41	40	3	23	7	16	2	39	5	31	3	13	76
Cruel	3	55	3	2	53	—	3	2	12	1	19	1	50	3	2
Backward	2	58	7	1	43	1	2	8	20	1	25	7	40	11	2
Brave	18	22	45	25	21	37	20	20	9	16	20	42	28	43	66
Self-controlled	16	4	5	16	3	36	34	3	9	15	5	21	14	35	37
Domineering	11	45	8	16	50	5	21	5	2	10	51	3	49	33	9
Progressive	32	13	17	57	15	43	17	10	4	42	7	27	15	25	70
Peace-loving	29	6	27	40	6	68	26	15	9	35	7	69	7	42	82
Impossible to characterize	9	20	7	10	13	8	22	46	54	13	31	8	17	15	3
Average no.:															
Positive adj.	2.9	.9	3.1	3.2	1.0	3.6	1.7	.8	.5	2.9	.9	2.9	1.4	2.8	5.2
Neg. adj.	.4	1.7	.4	.3	1.6	.2	.5	.3	.4	.2	.8	.3	1.7	.9	.4

This procedure was repeated for "the Russian people," then with reference to the people of the country in which the survey was being made. In certain surveys respondents were also asked to describe in the same manner the British, French, and Chinese peoples. Results of the Mexican survey were not cross-tabulated, so they are omitted from the following analysis.

DIFFICULTIES IN THE WORD-LIST METHOD

Several qualifications should be made concerning generalizations from results of a survey using this technique:

1. The wording on the question to some degree implies that a "people" may be described in one or a few words, and so may evoke from the compliant respondent an answer that can be classified as a stereotype, although the respondent is well aware that he has been forced into fallacious thinking. Eysenck and Crown found that 136 of 204 English middle-class subjects in a similar experiment gave some indication that they were aware of this. A majority indicated that "they did not know any representatives of the races concerned, and had quite unanimously to fall back in most cases on what they had heard or read about the unknown nationalities, or seen at the cinema, or picked up in casual conversation. They were recording stereotyped opinions, certainly, but in a high proportion of cases were fully conscious that their ideas were based on meager evidence."[2]

By including the "impossible to characterize" category, and in the last sentence of the question, the Unesco survey drafters provided two possible escape routes for those sophisticated respondents who felt strongly that the test was unfair.

2. The limited choice of twelve words may not give the respondent enough material to reproduce with any accuracy his mental image of one or several of the peoples to be described. Therefore, this survey is more useful in comparing stereotypes held among different groups of describers than in exploring the content of stereotypes. Free answer techniques are better adapted for the latter purpose.

3. The variations in familiarity between one word and another — some being in everyday, colloquial use, others met with more rarely — make it dangerous to assume that departures from chance expectations are due solely to stereotyping. In earlier studies using somewhat the same method, Schoenfeld[3] found that a control group picked from the Katz-Braly[4] word list certain adjectives which they would use more frequently to describe *any* race or nationality.

[2] H. J. Eysenck and S. Crown, "National Stereotypes: An Experimental and Methodological Study," *International Journal of Opinion and Attitude Research* (spring, 1948), pp. 26-39.

[3] N. Schoenfeld, "An Experimental Study of Some Problems Relating to Stereotypes," *Archives of Psychology*, No. 270 (1942).

This difficulty is aggravated in an international survey because it may be impossible to find a familiar word with even the approximate connotation of the term in the English-French text. Hence one should be slow to attribute a deviation from the international norm to a propensity on the part of a particular "describer nation" to stereotype a certain people in terms of one adjective; on the other hand, the existence of such a norm (i.e., the tendency of a large proportion of respondents in eight countries, speaking six languages, to apply the same term to one people and not to another) is indicative either of a stereotype or the sextuple coincidence of a canceling-out effect in the translating process.

4. There is no proof that certain of these words cannot be objectively shown to be more applicable to certain peoples than to others. A comparison, for example, of the average work week and rate of production might show one people as more "hardworking." This "kernel of truth" hypothesis is discussed by Schoenfeld and Klineberg.[5] Mace[6] sees a stereotype as the possible result of both "cognitive" and "emotional" factors.

In view of the public unavailability of such information, if it ever has been compiled, the word "stereotype" is used consistently herein because it conforms to the definition of stereotype as a view that is "not well thought out" even though it may not be provably "deceptive."

5. All the figures in Table 5 are no more than percentages of a sample which selected certain words. This fact, as well as the use of the term "describer nation," imputes a collective character to what is actually the sum of a common aspect of a number of individual stereotypes. It is necessary occasionally to remind oneself that, for example, the use of the values 25% in Australia and 13% in Italy in conjunction with the word "progressive" as applied to the Russians does not mean that Australians think of Russians as twice as progressive as Italians do, or that the penchant for thinking of Russians as progressive is twice as strong in a given Australian, or an average Australian, as in an Italian. The use of the term "describer nation" is an example of that compulsion to economy in thought and word which Lippmann originally advanced as the motive which underlies the stereotyping process!

[4] D. Katz and K. W. Braly, "Verbal Stereotypes and Racial Prejudice," in T. M. Newcomb and E. L. Hartley, *Readings in Social Psychology* (New York: Henry Holt & Co., 1947), pp. 204-10. This summarizes two experiments conducted in 1932, which led to wide use of the word-list technique in American studies of stereotypes.

[5] Klineberg, *op. cit.*, pp. 118-23.

[6] C. A. Mace, "National Stereotypes — Their Nature and Function," *Sociological Review,* January-April, 1943.

THE EXISTENCE OF STEREOTYPES

Table 5 brings together the percentages choosing each adjective for every country except Mexico, where this information was not tabulated. Many of the differences are "significant." However, vertical differences (i.e., between two adjectives applied to the same people) may be due to a variation in the familiarity of the words or to their place on the list; and horizontal differences (i.e., between the same adjective as applied to different peoples) may be due to the relative familiarity of the population with the peoples described, as evidenced by variations in the "impossible to characterize" category. If these factors could be held constant, the residue might fairly be labeled a pure "stereotype." Since they cannot, it must be cautioned that the characteristics which are to be analyzed contain an unspecified amount of impurities and that the indices computed are to be considered as qualitative rather than rigorously accurate.

It has been noted that respondents were given adequate opportunity to avoid responding with a stereotype. Were all those who fell in the "impossible to characterize" cell (ranging from 71% of Germans asked to describe the Chinese down to 3% of French and Americans asked to describe themselves) respondents who avoided the choice of adjectives on rational grounds? There is evidence that they were not. Four surveys (Germany, Netherlands, Norway, and the United States) were cross-tabulated by educational groups, and in all of them this category, "impossible to characterize," attracted a higher percentage of uneducated than educated respondents. This is in line with an almost universal tendency in opinion polling for the less advantaged group to prefer the "no opinion" and "no answer" boxes.

So it must be supposed that this category contains a mixture of sophisticated respondents, respondents who may have had stereotypes not describable in the adjectives on the list, respondents unfamiliar with the peoples asked about, and along with them a sprinkling of the taciturn, illiterate, and totally uncomprehending.

STANDARDIZATION OF STEREOTYPES

Each respondent was given a choice of twelve adjectives. In all, five peoples were described: the Russians by eight other nations, the Americans by themselves and seven others, the British and French by themselves and three others, and the Chinese by three others. All eight described their own countrymen. Table 6 gives the adjectives selected by the three highest percentages in each country, and the total in each cell represents the number of countries in which that adjective was among the three most popular. Table 7 gives the rank order of the six adjectives most frequently used.

The picture of the Russians is quite consistent from country to country, that of the Americans somewhat less so. There is an indication that the British, French, and Chinese are even less consistently pictured, but the lower percentages of respondents who found any adjectives applicable and the fact that these peoples were described in only three surveys make comparisons difficult.

TABLE 6

Number of Countries in Which an Adjective Was One of the Three Most Frequently Chosen to Describe Their Own Countrymen or Another Country; (e.g., "Hardworking" was among the three adjectives most often used to describe Americans in 3 out of the 7 countries describing them)[a]

People Described and Number of Countries Describing Them	Russians (8)	Americans (U. S.) (7)	British (3)	French (3)	Chinese (3)	Own Countrymen (8)
Adjective						
Hardworking	5½	3	1	1	3	5
Intelligent		1	2	2	⅓	5
Practical		6	½			
Conceited		1	1½	2		
Generous		3		1		3
Cruel	6				1⅓	
Backward	5				3	
Brave			1	1	⅓	5
Self-controlled			2			
Domineering	7½	1		½		
Progressive		6				
Peace-loving			1	1½	1	6
Total	24	21	9	9	9	24

[a] Fractions represent ties for third place.

These consistencies, which surmount the translation barrier, suggest that *stereotyped views of certain peoples are common property of the Western culture rather than the effect of bilateral national outlooks that differ from one country to another.* The consistency of the Russian and American stereotypes might also be counted an effect of the so-called "Bi-Polar World."

THE STEREOTYPE AS EXTENSION OF EGO

The last column in Table 6 gives the adjectives picked by the three highest percentages in each nation to describe their fellow countrymen. There is evident a universal tendency to appropriate the complimentary adjectives for one's own countrymen and, by reflection of

TABLE 7

The Six Adjectives Most Frequently Used to Describe Five Nations (Brackets indicate tie in percentages.)

Description of Russians by

Australians	*British*	*French*	*Germans*
Domineering	Hardworking	Backward	Cruel
Hardworking	Domineering	Hardworking	Backward
Cruel	Cruel	Domineering	⌠Hardworking
Backward	Backward	Brave	⌡Domineering
Brave	Brave	Cruel	Brave
Progressive	⌠Practical	Progressive	Practical
	⌡Progressive		

Italians	*Dutch*	*Norwegians*	*Americans (U. S.)*
Backward	Cruel	Hardworking	Cruel
Cruel	Domineering	Domineering	⌠Hardworking
Domineering	Backward	Backward	⌡Domineering
⌠Hardworking	Hardworking	Brave	Backward
⌡Brave	Brave	Cruel	⌠Conceited
⌠Intelligent	Progressive	Practical	⌡Brave
⌡Progressive			

Description of Americans (U.S.) by

Australians	*British*	*French*	*Germans*
Progressive	Progressive	Practical	Progressive
Practical	⌠Conceited	Progressive	Generous
Intelligent	⌡Generous	Domineering	Practical
Conceited	Peace-loving	⌠Hardworking	Intelligent
Peace-loving	⌠Intelligent	⌡Intelligent	Peace-loving
Generous	⌡Practical	⌠Generous	Hardworking
		⌡Self-controlled	

Italians	*Dutch*	*Norwegians*	
Generous	Practical	Hardworking	
Practical	Progressive	Practical	
Hardworking	Hardworking	Progressive	
Intelligent	⌠Generous	Generous	
Progressive	⌡Peace-loving	Peace-loving	
Peace-loving	Intelligent	Intelligent	

Description of British by

Germans	*Dutch*	*Americans (U. S.)*
Intelligent	Self-controlled	Intelligent
Self-controlled	Peace-loving	⌠Hardworking
Conceited	⌠Practical	⌡Brave
Domineering	⌡Conceited	Peace-loving
Practical	Hardworking	Conceited
Progressive	Intelligent	Self-controlled

Description of French by

British	Germans	Dutch
Intelligent	Intelligent	Brave
Conceited	Conceited	Generous
Hardworking	⎰Domineering	Peace-loving
Peace-loving	⎱Peace-loving	⎰Conceited
Practical	⎰Cruel	⎱Progressive
⎰Generous	⎱Backward	⎰Intelligent
⎨Brave		⎱Backward
⎩Progressive		

Description of Chinese by

British	Germans	Dutch
Hardworking	Hardworking	Backward
Backward	Backward	⎰Hardworking
Peace-loving	⎰Intelligent	⎱Cruel
Brave	⎨Cruel	⎰Brave
Cruel	⎩Brave	⎨Self-controlled
Intelligent	⎰Self-controlled	⎩Peace-loving
	⎱Peace-loving	

Description of Own Countrymen by

Australians	British	French	Germans
Peace-loving	Peace-loving	Intelligent	Hardworking
Generous	Brave	Peace-loving	Intelligent
Brave	Hardworking	Generous	Brave
Intelligent	Intelligent	Brave	Practical
Practical	Generous	Hardworking	Progressive
Hardworking	Practical	Progressive	Peace-loving

Italians	Dutch	Norwegians	Americans (U. S.)
Intelligent	Peace-loving	Peace-loving	Peace-loving
Hardworking	Hardworking	Hardworking	Generous
Brave	Intelligent	Brave	Intelligent
Generous	Progressive	Intelligent	Progressive
Peace-loving	Brave	Generous	Hardworking
⎰Practical	⎰Practical	Progressive	Brave
⎱Conceited	⎱Self-controlled		

virtue, for oneself. Lippmann said: "A pattern of stereotypes is not neutral. . . . It is not merely a short cut. . . . It is a guarantee of our self respect; it is a projection upon the world of our own value, our own position, and our own rights. . . . They are the fortress of our own tradition and behind its defenses we can continue to feel ourselves safe in the position we occupy."[7]

[7] Walter Lippmann, *Public Opinion* (New York: Harcourt, Brace & Co., 1922), p. 96.

STEREOTYPE DIRECTION AND TENSIONS

The drafters of the questionnaire designated four of the adjectives — conceited, cruel, backward, and domineering — as negative in connotation, and eight — hardworking, intelligent, practical, generous, brave, self-controlled, progressive, and peace-loving — as positive. This is a rough measure, since it makes no allowance for varying degrees of attractiveness or repugnance of the qualities concerned; but in view of the variations in connotation, familiarity, and forcefulness of the adjectives when translated into six different languages, no more precise index was practicable. The correctness of this division was

TABLE 8
"Stereotype" and "Friendliness Scores"

			"Stereotype Score"[a]	"Friendliness Score"[b]
Dutch	toward	Americans	2.6	26%
Norwegians	"	Americans	2.5	21
Italians	"	Americans	2.1	50
Australians	"	Americans	1.9	60
French	"	Americans	1.9	11
Germans	"	Americans	1.8	24
Americans	"	British	1.0	31
British	"	Americans	1.0	26
Dutch	"	British	0.7	8
British	"	French	0.4	9
Germans	"	British	0.4	9
Mexicans	"	Americans	0.3	18
Dutch	"	French	0.2	4
British	"	Chinese	0.2	0
Mexicans	"	French	0.1	0
Germans	"	Chinese	0	0
Mexicans	"	British	0	0
Dutch	"	Chinese	−0.3	0
Germans	"	French	−0.4	−2
Mexicans	"	Chinese	−0.6	−10
Norwegians	"	Russians	−0.7	−26
Mexicans	"	Russians	−0.8	−24
Australians	"	Russians	−1.0	−34
British	"	Russians	−1.0	−37
Germans	"	Russians	−1.5	−56
French	"	Russians	−1.6	−22
Americans	"	Russians	−2.0	−51
Dutch	"	Russians	−2.2	−36
Italians	"	Russians	−2.5	−39

[a] "Stereotype Score" — average number of positive adjectives applied to a people, minus twice the number of negative adjectives.

[b] "Friendliness Score" — percentage designating themselves "most friendly" toward a people, minus percentage designating themselves "least friendly."

demonstrated when the least popular positive adjective was found to have been chosen by a greater proportion of respondents than the most popular negative adjective in describing their countrymen, with the single exception of "conceited" in three of the nine countries.

The average number of mentions of the positive terms and of the negative terms (i.e., the total of the times each such term was applied to a particular people divided by the number of respondents in the sample) is given at the bottom of Table 5.

To get a "stereotype score" which evaluates the "direction" or tone of the stereotype, the average number of negative words used to describe a people was doubled (to adjust for the two-to-one ratio of positive to negative terms) and subtracted from the positive average. This provides an index which could vary from +8.0 (if every respondent had selected all positive but no negative adjectives) to −8.0 (if everyone had selected all negative but no positive adjectives). This "stereotype score" was computed for the 29 instances in which one nation described the people of another and is given in Column 1 of Table 8.

For each of the "stereotype scores," the percentage of respondents designating that country as the one which they felt "least friendly" toward on Q.12 was subtracted from the percentage designating it as the one they were "most friendly" toward on Q.11 in order to get a "friendliness score." (Less than 1% was counted as zero.) This could range between +100 (if 100% of respondents had been friendly toward the same country and none unfriendly) and −100 (if 100% had been unfriendly and none friendly). It may be worth reiterating that this represents friendly respondents minus unfriendly ones, rather

TABLE 9

Relationship of "Stereotype" and "Friendliness Scores" in Table 8

"Friendliness Score"	"Stereotype Score"										
	−2.1 and over	−1.6 to −2.0	−1.1 to −1.5	−.6 to −1.0	−.1 to −.5	0	.1 to .5	.6 to 1.0	1.1 to 1.5	1.6 to 2.0	2.1 and over
40% and over										1	1
31 to 49%								1			
21 to 30%								1		1	2
11 to 20%							1			1	
1 to 10%							3	1			
0					1	2	2				
−1 to −10%				1	1						
−11 to −20%											
−21 to −30%		1		2							
−31 to −40%	2			2							
−40 and over		1	1								

than the degree of friendliness shown by any or all the people; whereas the "stereotype score" summarizes over a group of people positive and negative tendencies which may be exhibited by the same individuals. The "friendliness score" is given in the last column of Table 8. Table 9 shows the relationship of the two scores. This bears out on an international level the conclusion, which Katz and Braly drew from a survey of 100 Princeton students, that "there is a marked similarity between the relative ranking on the basis of preference for group names and the average scores representing an evaluation of typical traits."

CHANGES IN STEREOTYPES

In 1942 the Office of Public Opinion Research asked a sample of 1,200 Americans to select those adjectives from a list of 25 which best described the Russians.[8] Seven of these adjectives were also used on the Unesco survey. The results are as follows:

	1942	1948
HARDWORKING	61%	49%
INTELLIGENT	16	12
PRACTICAL	18	13
CONCEITED	3	28
CRUEL	9	50
BRAVE	48	28
PROGRESSIVE	24	15

A "stereotype score" was computed for these percentages in the manner outlined above, except that the negative average was multiplied by 2.5 rather than 2 to adjust for the different ratio of positive to negative adjectives. For 1942 the score is +1.4; for 1948 it is −0.8. (For all twelve adjectives it is −2.0 in 1948. This is indicative of the effect that the alteration of only a few words can have.)

Allowing for the difference between the length and content of the two word lists, it still seems obvious that some other factor is at work, and it is most reasonable to believe that this is the deterioration in Russian-American relations. In this case, stereotypes may be more flexible than is often assumed.[9] In 1950 G. M. Gilbert repeated the Katz-Braly experiment on the same small segment of Americans — Princeton University undergraduates — a generation after the original study. He found those students more aware of the fallacy of describing a people in a few words, and much less addicted to the old popular stereotypes.

[8] Hadley Cantril and Mildred Strunk, *Public Opinion 1935-1946* (Princeton, N. J.: Princeton University Press, 1951), p. 502.

[9] Mace, *op. cit.*, "Current usage tends to restrict the term to ideas that are fixed when fixity is inappropriate, or appropriate on other than intellectual grounds. It implies most frequently fixity of ideas or invariability of responses in circumstances which call for plasticity or adaptability."

He also found that World War II had radically altered the picture of the Germans and Japanese.[10]

This alteration over a period of time suggests that *stereotypes are less likely to govern the likes and dislikes between nations than to adapt themselves to the positive or negative relationship based on matters unrelated to images of the people concerned.* Rather than summing up the characteristics of a people as "pictured in his head" and deciding whether this is a portrait of a "nice" or a "bad" person (a subjective method which would be somewhat analagous to the compilation of the "stereotype score" above), it seems that the individual is first brought to a feeling of like or dislike, after which he refocuses his mental image to correspond.

Schoenfeld, in comparing the content of the stereotypes he found just after Pearl Harbor with those found by Katz and Braly in the early 1930's, concludes that "the influence of historical events has changed somewhat the quality of the German, Italian, and especially the Japanese stereotypes. Many of the old qualities have been retained, but to them have been added new ones, such as 'arrogant,' 'conceited,' 'cowardly,' 'deceitful.' In addition, some former qualities of a pejorative nature have increased in frequency of assignment. To the traditional stereotypes of those nations with which we are allies, there have also been added new qualities, but these are generally of a likeable kind, while former complimentary qualities have in some instances increased in frequency of assignment — apparently it is possible for a nationality stereotype to undergo marked changes of direction or intensity without correspondingly great changes in quality.[11]

Further light on this process is obtained if the 1942 and 1948 stereotypes above are divided into two patterns — a positive and a negative. The rank order and the rough proportions of the percentages are the same for both periods within each pattern. In both, more respondents think the Russians cruel than think them conceited; in both, more think them hardworking than brave, brave than progressive, progressive than practical, practical than intelligent. But in the interim all the bad qualities have come to the fore and the good ones receded.

These isolated findings are, of course, indicative rather than conclusive; but repetition of word-list studies over a period of time long enough to relate national stereotypes to events of international significance may shed further light on their swiftness of change and susceptibility to events. Additional material on the choice of adjectives from the word list by different educational and socio-economic groups in the Dutch population is given on p. 80 [in Buchanan and Cantril].

[10] G. M. Gilbert, "Stereotype Persistence and Change Among College Students," *Journal of Abnormal and Social Psychology*, 46, No. 2 (April, 1951), 245-54.

[11] Schoenfeld, *op. cit.*

SUMMARY

The results on the stereotype question indicate: *(1) that there exists in all eight countries surveyed a tendency to ascribe certain characteristics to certain people; (2) that there is a uniform tendency of respondents of all countries, taken as a whole, to describe the Russians in the same terms, and somewhat less agreement on the Americans; (3) that stereotypes of one's own countrymen are invariably in flattering terms; and (4) that the prevalence of complimentary over derogatory terms in a national stereotype is a good index of friendliness between nations.*

There is limited evidence that national stereotypes are flexible over a period of years; and thus that they may follow and rationalize, rather than precede and determine, reaction to a certain nation.

The tenor of the findings as a whole is in the direction of minimizing the causative effect of either favorable or unfavorable stereotypes in relations between nations, and suggests that stereotypes may not exist until objective events demand their creation. Perhaps their important function is the wartime one of providing a rationale within which men are able to kill, deceive, and perform other acts not sanctioned by the usual moral code.

Evidence in Chapter 4 strongly suggests that friendliness or unfriendliness to another people may be attributed to relationships between their governments: whether they were in the allied or enemy camp in the past war or in the present "cold" war, whether one can understand the language they speak, and whether they are traditionally neutral. Yet here friendliness and unfriendliness are found to be related to the predominant stereotypes held in the various countries. This is, once again, evidence that *stereotypes should not be thought of as causative, but as symptomatic.* "These people threaten us, they have fought against us, they are just across our border, we cannot understand what they say, hence they *must be* cruel, conceited, domineering, etc."

POSSIBILITIES FOR FURTHER RESEARCH

This material was analyzed almost entirely for evidence of stereotypes as related to international tensions. It is obvious that there remains to be done a great deal of research toward describing and accounting for stereotypes. Unsummarized results of this type, in the form of punch cards, might reveal more about the extent to which stereotypes are phenomena of individual personality or class outlook; certainly these findings suggest that differences within a nation might be more extreme than those between nations.

Stereotypes of only five foreign peoples were delineated — too few to be fitted into the categorization scheme in Chapter 4. An investigation designed to show what characteristics are assigned to near-by peoples, to peoples speaking one's language, and to allies or former allies might produce useful information.

Graham recently found that a sample of British respondents reacted to individual Americans on the basis of immediate personal contacts but formed their impression of the American "type" on the basis of

. . . superficial contact or observation or on consistent portrayal over a long period of time in books, the press, or the films. . . . The trend from the individual to the "type" is from the specific to the more general, and from the strongly favourable to the moderately favourable. These trends continue as the still more general concept of the "American people" comes into consideration. Here, much greater reliance is placed on second-hand information such as press and literary accounts; personal attributes become more blurred, generalizations become more sweeping, considerations of American national and international policy begin to affect some respondents' replies, and the circle from the individual American friend to the U.S.A. as a dominant world power is closed.[12]

It is unquestionably one of the less personal, more generalized contexts which the word-list technique used in the Unesco survey taps. This is the context in which "peoples" and governments merge; it is the least favorable one in the British-American study, but this should not necessarily be true in every case.

There is a great need for more study of the processes of perception by individuals of acts of foreign governments and the intent behind these acts. Media of communication obviously must bear some responsibility for the stereotypes held by members of their audience. So must the leaders of the people who are the subject of the stereotype, since their acts, perceived at second hand through these media, are the events which form and change the stereotypes. The popular assumption that personal contacts between people will improve relationships between them is not necessarily true. The absurdity of a stereotype of a people as a whole does not apparently discourage individuals from holding it, even though they may recognize it as a stereotype and even though they may have a first-hand acquaintance with individual representatives of the people.[13] The stereotype seems to serve to explain acts of a distant entity (seen either as a government or as a "people") which would otherwise be inexplicable to the perceiver.

Leighton says of stereotypes that "these images are the basis upon which people feel for or against other nations, interpret their behavior as villainous or good, judge their actions, and judge what *they themselves as a nation should do in relation to others*. It follows, of course,

---

[12] Milton D. Graham, "An Experiment in International Attitudes Research," *International Social Science Bulletin*, III, No. 3 (autumn, 1951), 538-39.

[13] "Some of my best friends are Jews."

that if the images are false, the resulting action can hardly ever be adequate."[14]

The Unesco survey indicates that stereotypes are less effective in producing a positive or negative reaction than Leighton's appraisal implies. The danger lies, instead, in the inadequate action we may take on the basis of false notions of the intentions of other governments, notions which result from attributing a particular set of characteristics to the peoples which these governments represent.

We must know accurately at least two things to get on amicably with another nation: (1) what the purposes of these people are, and (2) how they see our purposes. Otherwise, both parties, traveling by different "maps," are likely to collide inadvertently.

[14] Leighton, op. cit. Italics are supplied by the authors of this study.

Modifying Attitudes and Opinions

Introductory Note

THE NATURE AND BEHAVIOR OF ATTITUDES

By attitudes we mean inferred states of readiness to react in an evaluative way, in support of or against a given stimulus situation. We say "inferred" states of readiness because there is no way to observe an attitude directly. Attitudes are one class of intervening variables, the existence of which we assume in order to explain how the human nervous system converts a given stimulus into a given response. We say "states of *readiness*" because we envisage attitudes operating as predispositions to action; if we know the nature of attitude an individual holds towards a given object or situation, we can predict that the individual, stimulated by the object or situation and free to act, will act in the direction of the attitude. We say "react in an *evaluative* way" because we envisage attitudes as being concerned with the relative values of life situations; they represent positions on a scale from favorable to unfavorable, for to against. And finally, these states of readiness to react in an evaluative way to a given stimulus are learned, and so, under appropriate conditions, presumably reinforced, generalized, and forgotten.

Therefore, what we really need to know about attitudes is how they are *learned*. Our knowledge of various parts of this problem ranges from folklore to experiment, and there are many gaps where the process is not clearly understood. The papers in this section, however, are representative of the better literature on the subject, and in the following pages we shall try to summarize briefly some of the conclusions about attitude change *through mass communication* to which the research evidence seems to point.

1. *Attitudes can be changed by mass communication.* This is no longer in question. More than one hundred papers have now presented quantitative evidence that such change occurs, and that it can occur as the result of messages translated by any of the mass media or combination of them, or by a combination of mass and interpersonal communication.

2. *To accomplish attitude change, a suggestion for change must first be received and accepted.* As intelligence is the critical factor in the learning of factual material, so it appears that the critical factor in learning attitudes is "acceptance." The import of the research evidence on this point is that persons will tend to avoid communications unsympathetic to their existing attitudes, or forget the unsympathetic communications once received, or recast them to fit the existing frame of reference. As Bartlett said, as soon as the message arrives at the nervous system, "what was objective becomes subjective." Thus the prejudiced persons who saw the anti-prejudice Mr. Biggott cartoons actually interpreted the cartoons as an endorsement of their prejudiced attitudes.

Investigating experimentally the process of building this resistance to change, Janis, Lumsdaine, and Gladstone found that it was possible by means of a preparatory communication to cushion a person or a population against later contrary messages. Apparently once a belief is modified by communication, the newly acquired opinion responses will tend to interfere with later acquisition of any incompatible responses. This helps to explain why the attitude structure of children seems to be more flexible than that of adults, and why opinion formation in a critical situation tends to rely so largely, where possible, on the activation of previous experiences and attitudes.

All experience leads us to believe that some areas of attitudes in an individual, at some times, will be more strongly defended than others. The question, then, is, what makes for acceptance of a suggestion?

3. *The suggestion will be more likely to be accepted if it meets existing personality needs and drives.* The evidence here is largely derivative from the well-demonstrated proposition that persons tend to respond in the direction of reducing drives. These drives are both biogenic and sociogenic. When the chips are down, the biogenic ones are likely to win over the sociogenic, a fact which missionaries have long recognized by meeting the hunger needs of people before trying to convert them, and which the Communists have turned to their own advantage by playing on the hunger and security needs of the people of Asia. However, we do not have to go to Asia for examples. All around us we have evidence of advertisers trying to connect the sex drive with any number of products, and trying to take advantage of the hunger drive to build favorable attitudes toward the purchase of a given food product. All of us have seen anger and fear drives open doors for attitude change, or, to put it another way, make a person "suggestible."

We can think of any target for attitude change thus as a spectrum of personality drives or needs, some of which are stronger in one individual than another, some of which are stronger at one time than another (for example, a hungry man is more likely to accept a food-related suggestion; sex-hungry front line troops are more likely to accept a sex-related suggestion). There is no evidence that intelligence is correlated with susceptibility except in the special case where more intelligent audiences seem to be *more* influenced by logical arguments, less influenced by slogans, unsupported generalities, etc. A considerable amount of clinical data supports the belief that persons who feel socially inadequate, frustrated, or depressed, are more "suggestible." Hovland sums this up by suggesting the hypothesis that persons with "low self-esteem" are more suggestible. This seems to agree with the age-old experience of propagandists who make their easiest converts among the people who feel hurt, mistreated, and inadequate to the situation in which they find themselves.

4. *The suggestion will be more likely to be accepted if it is in harmony with valued group norms and loyalties.* A number of experiments have now demonstrated the importance of group relationships to individual attitude change. Students coming into a new reference group tend to shift their attitudes in the direction of the group norms. When majority opinion has been made known, group members' attitudes have tended to move toward it. Group belongingness seems to affect voting behavior. When group norms are in conflict with expert opinion, they may win out, unless the matter is very technical or the expert unusually prestigeful or the matter relatively unrelated to the group norms. And members of a group will be more likely to reject standards opposed to the group norms than those opposed to their own individual norms. This and much other evidence is continuing to pile up on the importance of groups to attitude change.

The conclusion from this evidence is that, as Krech and Crutchfield said (1948), if a suggestion can be phrased "so as to be congruent with the need of people to identify with or be in harmony with other people . . . (it) . . . will be more readily accepted than one that does not draw upon such social support." Every successful propaganda campaign illustrates this proposition. The attention devoted by the Nazis to group organization is a case in point. So is the propaganda strategy of the Communists who make every effort, by such names as The *People's* Government and The *People's* Army, to let the individual identity with artificially implanted group norms, and who are careful to supplement their use of mass media with a carefully organized system of group membership.

Another way to put it is that the target's reference groups must always be kept in mind when designing a message intended to change attitudes. If the suggestion is favorable to the norms of one of the available reference groups, the message should by all means call attention to this relationship. If the suggestion is highly unfavorable to the norms of one reference group, that group should, if possible, be kept out of the field of the message. The more salient the group is, the more important this advice would seem to be, because small minority groups or highly salient groups tend to hold strongly to their group norms.

5. *The suggestion is more likely to be accepted if the source is perceived as trustworthy or expert.* In general, the research evidence indicates that associating a suggestion with a prestige source will make the suggestion more acceptable. Osgood and Tannenbaum, and Hovland and Weiss, whose papers are reproduced in this volume, have recently presented new material to add to the considerable literature on importance of source. Osgood and Tannenbaum make the point that an individual tends to handle a suggestion in such a way as to make the source and concept *congruent* — that is, favorable sources associated positively with favorable concepts, etc. Hovland and Weiss, in this and other work, have advanced evidence to the effect that persons are as likely to learn material from a source perceived as untrustworthy as from one perceived as trustworthy (if they will listen to the message at all), but that the perceived trustworthiness of the source has a powerful effect on the amount of attitude change. In a few weeks, with the process of forgetting, one tends to disassociate source and concept. It sometimes happens, therefore, that after some weeks there is no more attitude change from the "trustworthy" than from the "untrustworthy" source. If at any time, however, the individual is reminded of the source, then the influence of the source reasserts itself on his attitudes. This has important implications for propaganda.

6. *The suggestion is more likely to be accepted if the message follows certain rules of "rhetoric" for attitude-changing communication.*

These are some of the points that emerge from the literature:

a. *There is often an advantage in stating the desired conclusion specifically and positively.* The import of the research evidence is that "letting the facts speak for themselves" is usually not enough, and it is not safe to let the audience draw the conclusion for itself, except in the case of a highly intelligent audience. There is also some evidence that a concept is more likely to be learned when stated positively (what it is) than negatively (what it is not).

b. *Sometimes it is better to state both sides of an issue; other times, to state only one side.* This is not a simple choice, and the literature is to some degree conflicting. The simplest conclusion to draw from the evidence is that one can almost always accomplish more *immediate* attitude change with a one-sided presentation, and this should be used when one does not have to worry about his audience hearing later conflicting arguments, and especially when the audience is already favorable to the point of view one is advocating. But if one has reason to expect that the audience will later hear competing arguments, then he will be wise to use a two-sided presentation. By so doing, he will accomplish less at first, but probably more in the long run; because he will be cushioning the audience against the later opposition.

c. *Repeat with variation.* Throughout the research on learning from mass communication, the implication has been that more examples make for more learning, always with the provision that repetition shall not be so unvaried as

to become boresome, and with the understanding that there is some satura-
tion point beyond which the amount of learning no longer increases.

d. *Use simplifying labels and slogans where appropriate.* Both research
and practice present evidence of the importance of simplifying and using
slogans and labels, but it should be remembered that more intelligent audiences may be repelled by slogan repetition and similar devices.

e. *Make use, where possible, of audience participation.* Quite remarkable results in learning from mass communication have been obtained by
such a simple device as getting the audience to pronounce a word they are
seeing on the screen and trying to learn. Participation will work whether
overt or covert (mental practice, for example, is covert participation). It is
believed that if a subject can be made to participate to the extent of making
an effort to receive the information — that is, paying for it, going some
distance for it, risking something for it (as clandestine radio listeners sometimes risked their lives) — then learning and attitude change are very likely
to result. If a subject can be given a channel by which to express the desired
attitude, — something to do about it, write a letter, join a club, march in a
parade — then the attitude will probably be more likely to stick. Still more
important, if the subject can be put in a position of stating the arguments in
his own words — that is, playing the role of a propagandist advocating the
desired position — then he will be more likely to find the appeals which are
closest to him, and in effect convince himself.

f. *Fit the strength of the emotional appeal to the desired result.* Experiments with fear appeals suggest that a strong emotional appeal is likely to
result in a greater immediate effect, but that it may be dangerous if it does
not adequately reassure the subject and relieve the tension. That is apparently
why strong emotional appeals often result in complete rejection of the message or the idea. If an immediate reaction is desired, therefore, a strong emotional appeal may be justified. If a long-range or continued response is the
goal, then a milder appeal may be better. A recent study indicates that when
a strong appeal is used, the audience is more likely to remember the threat;
when a milder one is used, the audience is more likely to remember the
source and *explanations* of the threat.

g. *Organize the message to take advantage of primacy and recency.* Should
one begin with his best point or build up to it? Here the evidence seems to
be conflicting, Hovland, Janis, and Kelley have suggested two apparently
sound and useful propositions, however. Where the audience is familiar with
the subject, and deep concern is felt over it, then, they suggest, there seems
to be good reason for climax order — that is, for leading up to the main
point at the end. On the other hand, if the audience is unfamiliar with the
subject, or uninterested, there may be good reason to introduce the main
point first. By so doing, the communicator will be most likely to gain the
audience's attention and interest.

7. *A suggestion carried by mass media plus face-to-face reinforcement is more likely to be accepted than a suggestion carried by either
alone, other things being equal.* Both research and propaganda practice support the power of this combination. However, it makes some
difference how the two channels are combined. This is seen in experiments with illustrating printed material. Experiment indicates that

greater learning results from this combination only under certain conditions. Simply "illustrating" the text, or putting pictures in contiguity to the comparable text, will not do it. The pictures must be made a part, along with the text, of the learning process through which the reader goes, and apparently the two channels must be combined so that the reader has *additional* learning experience, beyond what he gets from either one alone. The same thing may be said of mass media plus face-to-face.

8. *Change in attitude is more likely to occur if the suggestion is accompanied by change in other factors underlying belief and attitude.* This very general proposition is hard to tie down in an experiment, and yet it has much practical and some research backing. The only way we have to change attitudes, in a mass communication situation, is by manipulating a man's environment. We can do that by manipulating messages or events. It stands to reason that the more completely we can make the environment support the desired change, the more likelihood there is of the change taking place.

In general, (a) if we can make our messages appeal to individual needs and wants, (b) if we can provide or point out social support for the desired attitudes, (c) if we can introduce our messages at such a time as will let them be reinforced by related events, (d) if we can point out or provide a channel for action along the line of the desired attitude, and if we can eliminate so far as possible or point out ways of surmounting the barriers to such action — then we can be as confident as possible, within the limits stated earlier, of accomplishing what we want to accomplish with our suggestion.

The following papers represent several different approaches to the study of attitudes and opinions. The general treatment by the Hartleys and Hart is followed by an attempt to find a general pattern by which to predict attitude change (Osgood and Tannenbaum). Then come two experimental papers, one from the War Department I & E researches, the other from the Yale program of communication study under Carl Hovland, both endeavoring to illuminate aspects of opinion change from the starting point of learning theory. Dr. Klapper's important memorandum is a summary of the evidence on persuasion by means of mass communication, as the evidence stood in 1949. The two final papers are specifically on public opinion. After paying his respects to attempts to state "laws" of public opinion, Professor Doob develops a few principles of his own. Dr. Berelson discusses public opinion in terms of the familiar pattern of communication analysis.

▲ EUGENE L. HARTLEY

▲ RUTH E. HARTLEY

▲ CLYDE HART

*A*ttitudes and Opinions

Previous chapters have discussed psychological phenomena as types or phases, not of purely individual action, but of interaction — characteristically symbolic interaction — among individuals in a dynamic setting. Perceiving, feeling, thinking, learning, doing, although dependent on neuro-muscular systems, can be understood only in the contexts of interactive social systems.

Interaction, however, implies both interacting units and a medium through which an exchange of influences is accomplished. It is individuals who interact. But individuals are highly complex entities who engage from moment to moment in a wide variety of specialized activities, each of which involves — in any direct way, at least — only segments of the entire complement of needs, wishes, and skills of the individuals. Interactions must be stated and analyzed in terms of these more specific factors or units; for the direction, intensity, and outcome of any given instance of interaction will vary with them. To the extent that they can be discovered and their modes of operation generalized, prediction of behavior under known conditions becomes, in some degree, possible.

At this point in our discussion, therefore, let us turn to the interacting units and examine what they are, how they come to be, how they affect and are affected by interactions of various kinds at various levels. In our earlier discussions, emphasis has been placed on the person as a whole in interaction with others. Here we shall focus on "parts" of a person, especially those relatively stable patterns of reac-

▲ This appeared as a chapter in the Hartley and Hartley book, *Fundamentals of Social Psychology,* published and copyright by Alfred A. Knopf (New York, 1952). It is reprinted here by permission of the copyright holder. Dr. Hartley is a member of the psychology faculty of Brooklyn College. Mrs. Hartley has taught psychology at the City College of New York and Brooklyn College. Dr. Hart is director of the National Opinion Research Center of the University of Chicago.

tion which, though developed through experience, characterize individuals and groups — the "parts" of the person now commonly referred to as attitudes. We shall have to examine carefully the nature of social attitudes. In this chapter, we shall review the general character of attitudes, and in the following two chapters, we shall systematically organize the research related to ethnic attitudes. In this way, we can integrate generalizations with findings. In reviewing social "attitudes" we shall first consider the meaning of the word and the ways in which it is used; then we shall proceed to an examination of the major dimensions of attitudes, and, finally, though briefly, to their development and operation. Because this chapter deals with social attitudes in general, it will be relatively abstract. The succeeding discussion of ethnic attitudes, having more specific focus, will be much more concrete.

CONSISTENCIES IN HUMAN BEHAVIOR

Scientific knowledge of any kind of behavior is possible only on the assumption that there are elements of consistency in behavior. In chemistry and other physical sciences, this assumption is made without difficulty, but its tenability in the realm of human action may seem doubtful. Yet, there are remarkable consistencies in people's reactions to social objects and social situations. Samuel A. Stouffer has put the point simply:

I suppose the main reason why anybody thinks there is or can be a social science is that all around us in our everyday behavior we see not only how necessary prediction is, but also how successful it is. True, we take most of the successful predictions for granted. Our very living from hour to hour is based on it. . . . While we drive a car down the street only a few blocks we may make a score of predictions about what other drivers will do — and we are hardly conscious of any of these predictions until one of them fails and we have a smashup or near miss. Indeed, all human living is possible only because a large part of our daily activities permit us to make successful predictions. . . .

Of course, nobody dreams of a science of human behavior which seeks to predict each private thought any more than one dreams of a science of hydraulics which would predict the location and duration of each little eddy in a Mississippi River flood. But a science of human nature or of social relations must be based on the solid fact that there are regularities in man's behavior which do admit of actuarial prediction. [*13, pp. 11–13*][1]

This consistency in human behavior is not a matter of rigid, automatic repetition of the same response, as in a conditioned response or a mechanical habit; it is consistency in the sense of social meaning. There is flexibility enough to adapt to a wide variety of situations and circumstances, but the reactions will tend to be in a consistent direction. Conceptually, the consistency is of the order of goal-oriented be-

---

[1] Bracketed citations refer to bibliography at end of chapter.

havior. The individual seems to have some patterned expectancies or wishes or hopes and desires, and he develops response patterns in specific situations that seem likely to help him achieve his goal.

Illustrative of the consistency found in attitude study, is the wartime research by the Army's Information and Education Division Research Branch. The following question was asked of soldiers: "Do you agree or disagree with the statement: 'Even if all the other countries agree not to have large armies, the United States should still draft all young men for military training.' " The answers provided a basis for dividing respondents into three groups for each of which reasonably accurate predictions could be made of how the men would answer such questions as the following:

After the war, do you think the United States could or could not have an Army sufficient for the country's needs by taking volunteers only?

If you had a son, would you want him to have a certain amount of Army training during peacetime, after this war, or not?

Do you agree or disagree with the statement — "The best way to protect the United States against another war is to make her so strong militarily that no one would dare attack her"? [23, p. 135]

Obviously, we do not find, nor would we expect to find, perfect consistency in an individual's behavior in varied situations, even though the situations might seem related to an observer. Nevertheless, there is sufficient *continuity* of reaction tendency, sufficient *consistency* in varying situations, to make us feel that there is *something stable in the individual*. The continuity and consistency and the consequent predictability of responses seem to inhere in the mental organization of the individual, in tendencies toward a general mode of response to objects that have previously entered into his experience. These inferred tendencies to respond in relatively stable and consistent ways are called *attitudes*.

ATTITUDE AND OPINION

In 1935, Gordon W. Allport, after an exhaustive review of the social psychological literature, wrote:

The concept of attitude is probably the most distinctive and indispensable concept in contemporary American social psychology. No other term appears more frequently in experimental and theoretical literature. . . . This useful . . . concept has been so widely adopted that it has virtually established itself as the keystone in the edifice of American social psychology.

Allport defined the concept as "a mental and neural state of readiness, organized through experience, exerting a directive or dynamic influence upon the individual's response to all objects and situations with which it is related [15, p. 798]."

Several features of this definition should be noted. First, an attitude is a "state of readiness" of the individual to deal with an object or type of objects — a book, an automobile, a dollar bill, a clock, a shoe, a dog, a symphony, a parent, a teacher, a Negro, a church, a word, an act, an attitude of another individual, or anyone of literally hundreds of thousands of other objects that have, in some way or another, previously entered into the individual's experience.[2] It is a mater of common observation that, in the course of an ordinary day, any individual seeks and utilizes, or avoids and rejects, objects of many kinds in fulfilling his needs and satisfying his wishes; he is "prepared" to deal with these objects as they are encountered, often without "stopping to think." He "knows" how to use them, how to relate them to himself in order to make them contribute to, or to keep them from interfering with, the carrying on of whatever activity he may from moment to moment be engaged in.

Secondly, Allport's definition embodies the general conclusion of students of behavior that, aside from a very few non-discriminating incipient reflexes (sucking, for example), perception of objects and readiness to respond to them in an organized manner develops through experience; furthermore, even though states of readiness, when once organized, tend to become stable and thus to impose patterns of consistency on the behavior of the individual through time, any state of readiness to respond in a certain way to an object does or may undergo modification in the course of each successive actual response. Thus, the attitude is a product of experience, but it enters into subsequent experience as a directive factor.

A third element in Allport's definition is anticipated in what has just been said — the attitude "exerts a directive or dynamic influence upon the individual's response" to an object or situation. The conception of an attitude as a preparation or readiness for response may imply that it is a passive entity which comes into play only when its object is actually present. But there is ample evidence that attitudes are dynamic, that they can lead the individual to seek the objects about which they are organized. As Allport suggests, an attitude is an organizing principle operative continuously throughout an act from its beginning to its consummation; it may become active because of tensions arising within the individual in the physical absence of the objects to which it relates and thus it initiates an act. In any case, it may seek, select, and reject objects or stimuli that are appropriate to the act's completion and evaluate, or provide a referential basis for evaluating, the progress of the act in terms of its prospective success or failure and, hence, lead to modification of the act while it is in progress. This dynamic role of attitudes is stated in somewhat more concrete terms in the following excerpt from George Mead:

[2] "There seems literally to be no end till we have exhausted the resources of the language to the catalogue of possible attitudes." E. B. Titchener: *A Textbook of Psychology* (New York: Macmillan, 1916), p. 506.

The central nervous system is only partly explored. Present results, however, suggest the organization of the act in terms of attitudes. There is an organization of the various parts of the nervous system that are going to be responsible for acts, an organization which represents not only that which is immediately taking place, but also the later stages that are to take place. If one approaches a distant object he approaches it with reference to what he is going to do when he arrives there. If one is approaching a hammer he is muscularly all ready to seize the handle of the hammer. The later stages of the act are present in the early stages — not simply in the sense that they are all ready to go off, but in the sense that they serve to control the process itself. They determine how we are going to approach the object, and the steps in our early manipulation of it. . . .

We can also recognize in such a general attitude toward an object an attitude that represents alternative responses, such as are involved when we talk about our ideas of an object. A person who is familiar with a horse approaches it as one who is going to ride it. He moves toward the proper side and is ready to swing himself into the saddle. His approach determines the success of the whole process. But the horse is not simply something that must be ridden. It is an animal that must eat, that belongs to somebody. It has certain economic values. The individual is ready to do a whole series of things with reference to the horse, and that readiness is involved in any one of the many phases of the various acts. . . .

. . . These possible actions have their effect on the way in which we do act. . . . [They] determine the immediate action itself and particularly the later stages of the act, so that the temporal organization of the act may be present in the immediate process. [*12, pp. 11–13*]

This excerpt from Mead echoes our earlier discussion of the reciprocal relationship of action and perception. In Chapter IX we discussed how percepts derive from the interaction between the individual and the external world. Since the percept derives from the interaction, it contains within itself the potentials for action. In other words, the individual perceives the objects he approaches in terms of what he can do to them or what they can do to him as well as in terms of their physical structure. This approach stems from his actual experience with the objects — directly or in symbolic form (for example, learning that a radiator is hot may be through direct interaction with the object; learning that certain kinds of people are not nice or that violating a social tabu brings dire consequences may represent experience with symbols rather than more direct participation). Moreover, since experience leads to expectation, percepts also include assumptions that objects, physical or social, animate or inanimate, will behave in certain ways. Such readiness for action as is involved in perceptions and expectations concerning the nature of the perceived object and the way it might affect the perceiving individual are also important components of attitudes. Thus we find attitude and perception inextricably linked.

Obviously, since percepts with which attitudes are connected grow out of contact with the perceived object, attitudes have a cognitive base. However, because the individual does not easily separate that which he cognizes, experiences or perceives from the effect such experiences have on him, the cognitive aspects of attitudes are integrated with the individual's emotional responses to the objects of his attitudes.

Attitudes Are Inferred

Attitudes are not themselves directly observable; only overt behavior is observable. Attitudes are *the inferred bases for observed consistencies in the behavior of individuals.* Inferences may be based on observations of either verbal or non-verbal behavior. Attitudes express themselves in what people do or abstain from doing and in the manner in which they do things, as well as in what people say. In ordinary social intercourse, how an individual feels, what he thinks, and what he is attempting to do for what purpose are surmised by other people involved in the same situation from his facial expression, his tone of voice, his bodily stance and movements, and his verbal statements. Not infrequently, inferences from verbal statements are based not only on the direct meaning of the words used but on slips of the tongue, the choice of words, and other subtle elements.

Frequently people try to describe their own attitudes either spontaneously or in response to questioning or other provocation. Under these circumstances, it is verbal behavior from which the attitudes are inferred. Verbal response *is* behavior; it involves the musculature in the same literal sense as does raising the hand to strike a blow or walking down the street to see a friend. The statement that applications for a particular job will not be accepted from certain minority group members, if the person talking is in a position of power, is discrimination even though the overt behavior is verbal. The statement that Richard Roe is an excellent, qualified candidate for a public office may influence the votes of others and consequently have social significance, even though the originator of the statement may himself abstain from voting or even vote for Roe's opponent. When W. S. Gilbert wrote the following of "a British Tar" in *H.M.S. Pinafore* he was describing not an attitude but a posture from which an attitude might be inferred:

> His foot should stomp, and his throat should growl,
> His hair should twirl, and his face should scowl,
> His eyes should flash, and his breast protrude,
> And this should be his customary attitude.

On a less practical, more scientific, level, we can say that all these manifold ways in which attitudes are revealed are utilized in an effort to get at the processes of attitude formation and the bearing of attitudes on individual and group conduct.

The statement that attitudes are the inferred bases for the consistency of the individual's response requires some qualification lest the term "consistency" be taken too literally. As we have already indicated, attitudes are not necessarily rigid or inflexible. They may, in fact, vary from highly tentative, more or less ephemeral, tendencies to fixed and persistent ones [4].

Problem Situations Evoke Opinions

Attitudes are commonly differentiated from opinions, although they are equally commonly confused with opinions. It scarcely seems helpful to consider opinion as merely the "verbalization of an attitude." Opinion is a fact of a different psychological order; it differs in its functional relation to behavior. It comes into being just when, and to the extent that, attitudes are not adequate to enable the individual or the group to cope with a situation. Many situations are problematical in that they involve new and strange objects or new combinations or arrangements of familiar objects, as in the old illustration of the cow in the parlor. These problem situations require that participants "take thought," that they try to find out what the situation portends, what will happen if this or that course of action is followed. In this process of assessing the situation, participants draw upon past experience, bringing to bear attitudes that seem to be relevant; but they cannot rely, except tentatively, upon these attitudes to carry them through the situation. With a greater or lesser degree of rationality, a definition of the situation, a conception of the kind of action appropriate to it, will be worked out; it is just such a definition that seems to be referred to, on both the practical and the scholarly level, as *opinion*. It involves, or is based in part upon, attitudes; but it is not, therefore, synonymous with attitude. It is always concerned with doubtful elements in the situation, with conflicts and uncertainties, with problems or "issues," and is, therefore, a more rational construct.

Of the situations that engage our active attention, few of them are sufficiently simple that one attitude will serve as an exclusive precondition and guiding principle. They are generally complex in that they involve many objects that call out divergent or conflicting tendencies, and frequently they contain new and puzzling elements. Many attitudes are, therefore, directly or indirectly involved in all but the very simplest acts. There is interaction among these attitudes in the course of developing the act. It is in this "conversation" of attitudes, which takes place within an individual or among individuals participating in the situation, that opinion arises as a mediating factor. Opinion, in this sense, is reflective and projective and is tentative until it has been proved through action. It pertains not to a single attitude but to an attitude-complex corresponding to the object-complex comprising the extra-individual aspect of the situation. It adapts attitudes to one another and to the circumstances in which action must go on.

Opinions may be used as a means of access to attitudes, but only with discrimination. They cannot be taken as direct exhibitions or descriptions of attitudes. People sometimes do attempt to express their attitudes in words, either spontaneously or when asked about them. An individual may announce or admit that he doesn't like young children, that he avoids them whenever he can and is annoyed by them when they cannot be avoided. This description of his attitude may be accurate, but it is not an expression of opinion as such. On the other hand, this same individual may oppose the opening of the dining-room of his club to families when a proposal to do so is being discussed; he may explain his opposition by claiming that the dining-room is already overcrowded and that it cannot expand without interfering with other essential uses of the club rooms. Here he is expressing an opinion and it may be the reasons he gives in support of it are objectively defensible; yet it may well be that his attitude toward children is the most weighty factor involved in his statements, even though its relevance is not perceived by the individual himself and would be denied by him if called to his attention.

Every opinion is, in large degree, an expression of one or several attitudes, but usually the attitudes are not immediately and obviously apparent. It takes skillful observation and extended probing, often by professionally trained analysts, to ferret them out. The question, *why* an individual takes this or that position, holds this or that opinion, is not an easy one for even the individual whose position it is to answer accurately; and it is a still harder question for even the most knowledgeable observer to answer validly. The perfection of methods for making correct inferences about the attitudes underlying objectively ascertainable opinions is one of the centrally important problems to which social psychologists are currently giving a great deal of attention.

Such study requires first dependable methods for presenting to people the precise problematical situation to which the opinion relates, so that the observer or experimenter can be sure about the referents of the opinion (that what is expressed is an opinion about just that situation and not about something else). It requires, further, dependable methods for bringing into view the "determinants" of this opinion, especially the attitudinal factors that lead the individual to define the situation as he does. To accomplish this, we must penetrate the inner or covert aspects of the individual's behavior. We need, therefore, varying degrees of active co-operation of the individual being studied with the one who is studying him. In the psychiatric interview, an extremely high degree is required; but even in the interviews of a sample survey, if the aim is to get at attitudes underlying opinions, a major requirement is the establishment of *rapport* between interviewer and interviewee.

DEGREES OF GENERALIZATION

In the early years of empirical study of the nature of attitudes, much interest was focused on the question "Are attitudes general or specific?" This question reflected, in part, the everyday usage which considers opinions relatively specific responses and attitudes relatively general ones. It also stemmed in part from the relatively static "trait theories" of personality, and in part from controversies over the nature of the learning process. At the present time, it is generally recognized that the problem was artificial, that we cannot establish a dichotomy between "specific" and "general," and that attitudes can be studied at different levels or degrees of generalization.

The search for primary social attitudes by Leonard W. Ferguson provides a good illustration of a conception of attitudes as varying in degree of generality from very specific to very general [7, 8]. In this study, 185 Stanford University students completed questionnaires designed to measure their attitudes toward war, the reality of God, patriotism, the treatment of criminals, capital punishment, censorship, evolution, birth control, law, and communism. The tests had been constructed by the method of equal-appearing intervals developed by L. L. Thurstone of the University of Chicago. (This method of scale construction is described below, on page 232.) Two forms, each having about twenty items, were used in the measurement of each of the ten attitudes. To each of the forty items for each of the ten attitude variables, the students responded by putting a check mark if they agreed with the statement, or a cross mark if they disagreed. Attitude scores could then be assigned on the basis of the previously determined "value" or social meaning of the statements with which each subject agreed.

The task confronting the students was to express agreement or disagreement with such statements as the following:

[From the Scale of Attitude Toward War]
Peace and war are both essential to progress.
If war is necessary to maintain national interests, every individual opinion must yield.
Because right may be more improtant than peace, war may be the lesser of two evils.
If a man's country enters a war which he does not consider justified, he should nevertheless serve at the front or wherever he is needed. [5]

[From the Scale of Attitude Toward the Treatment of Criminals]
We need punishment to defend society.
Failure to punish the criminal encourages crime.
Occasional offenders should be reformed.
One way to deter men from crime is to make them suffer. [28]

Each response, whether of agreement or of disagreement, was a relatively specific expression of opinion on a particular proposition. From twenty such expressions, an attitude score was assigned. Such a score provided from the specific reactions a single, more general, index of the individual's attitude, not to any one proposition but to the general subject under review — war, censorship, communism.

Ferguson's research went even farther. The attitude scores on each test were correlated with the scores on every other test. The full set of intercorrelations was then subjected to the procedure known as "factor analysis," a statistical analysis which attempts to discover the smallest number of independent variables that have to be postulated in order to account for a given set of intercorrelations. In spite of the fact that each of the ten tests used had separate names, was relatively reliable (that is, scores were stable), and had reasonable validity (there is evidence that the tests measured what they are supposed to measure), it was found that if one assumed that there were only three different factors, distributed in varying proportions in the different tests, essentially the same set of intercorrelations could be expected. Factors so isolated are, of course, mathematical abstractions which are useful in suggesting possible basic underlying components that might be otherwise obscured by the variety of ways in which behavior is sampled. Sometimes it is difficult to describe them except as Factors I or II, which may be represented in Test A with this weighting and in Test B with that weighting.

In Ferguson's analysis, Factor I was found predominantly in the belief in the reality of God and in the attitudes toward evolution and birth control. This first factor he called "Religionism." The second factor, called "Humanitarianism," was found particularly in the attitudes toward capital punishment, the treatment of criminals, and war. The third factor, "Nationalism," was located chiefly in the scales for the measurement of attitudes toward law, censorship, patriotism, and communism. The three factors, isolated in this way, could then be considered to represent social attitudes at an even greater level of generalization than the scores on the particular attitude tests which were used as the point of departure for the study.

In the next chapter we shall examine in detail recent developments in attitude study that have succeeded in relating social attitudes to the functional dynamics of the individual's personality. To the extent that attitudes are analyzed as expressions of personality, we would seem to be describing an even higher level of generalization.

There is a tendency to think of attitudes and opinions as being differentiated in terms of degree of specificity-generality. Opinions, as we have stated, are commonly thought of as relatively specific, attitudes as relatively general. We must be cautious in using such a distinction, however, since opinion-eliciting questions may relate to very general propositions. Questions asked in opinion surveys by the National Opinion Research Center (in April, 1948) have included such general queries as this:

1. How do you feel about our dealings with Russia — Do you think the United States should be more willing to compromise with Russia, or is our present policy about right, or should we be even firmer than we are are today?

More specific are the following questions:

2. Would you approve or disapprove of President Truman going to Europe to talk with Stalin, to try to settle the differences between the United States and Russia?
3. As you know, the Russians want our occupation officials and troops to get out of Berlin, and have been making things difficult for them there. Do you think we should avoid trouble by pulling our troops and officials out of Berlin, or should we stay there anyhow? [18]

The tendency to think of opinions as specific and attitudes as general is, therefore, not valid. In making inferences about attitudes, we may find ourselves dealing at any point in what may be considered a specificity-generality continuum.

PERCEPTUAL AND MOTIVATIONAL COMPONENTS

In analyzing opinions and attitudes, it is helpful to recognize the difference between their perceptual and motivational components. Acknowledgedly, perception and motivation are interrelated. Motives modify perceptions and perceptions define the available incentives and goals. Nevertheless, the functioning of the individual may be better understood if we attempt to separate out these two aspects of his behavior, inasmuch as interrelation does not necessarily imply identity.

Social attitudes are often thought of as a frame of reference structuring the social field. The reader will remember that we use the term frame of reference "to denote the functionally related factors (both present and past) which operate at the moment to determine the particular properties of a psychological phenomenon (perception, judgment, affectivity, etc.) [21, p. 309]." This general definition, originally offered by Sherif and Cantril, has been modified through loose usage in the field of attitude study so that "frame of reference" has largely come to be identified with the general structuring that the individual tends to impose on a social field.

The "frame of reference" is used, therefore, on the one hand to refer to an orientation of the individual, to those tendencies which cause him to structure his perceptions of a situation in a particular way; and on the other hand, it is also used to describe his general structuring of a situation, the context he provides for a particular observation. This dual use of the term represents its application in both attitude and opinion study. The attitudinal frame of reference is inferred from the expressed frames of reference.

Illustrations of the study of frames of reference can be found in the research conducted by the Survey Research Center of the University of Michigan as part of an analysis of "Public Reaction to the Atomic Bomb and World Affairs [1]." Interviews began with several questions which "provided information about the individual's general outlook on world affairs." The first six questions were the following:

1. Now that the war is over, how do you feel about the way the countries of the world are getting along together these days?
2. How satisfied are you with the way the United States has been getting along with other countries since the war ended?
3. Do you think the United States has made any mistakes in dealing with other countries since the end of the war?
   3a. (If yes) What?
4. What do you think is the best thing that the United States could do to help keep peace in the world? Why?
5. Some people would like to see Government keep to itself and not have anything to do with the rest of the world. How do you feel about that?
6. Some people say we should use our Army and Navy to make other countries do what we think they should. How do you feel about that? [*1, p. 221*]

In June, 1946, when the questions were asked, in response to the first query, 16 per cent of the respondents expressed themselves as satisfied, 9 per cent were undecided or "didn't know," and 64 per cent were dissatisfied. (For 11 per cent, the attitudes were not ascertained.) Answers like the following were obtained:

Well, I'm not very well satisfied. Surely they haven't come to anything definite about anything. There's too much suspicion and bickering between countries. Everyone is trying to grab what it wants. There's no unity.

The war *isn't* over! They're worse off now than they were before. How are you going to have any peace when they are fighting among themselves? They just agreed to disagree, as far as I can figure out.

I don't honestly feel very good about (the way the countries are getting along). I think Russia is trying to bulldoze the world. Unless she's "called" by this country or by the UN, there's going to be trouble. I think we've got the balance of power in the bomb. If the trouble with Russia is eliminated, I think everything will finally adjust itself. All the other countries seem to be agreeable and want peace in every way. The only disturbing element is Russia. [*1, p. 119*]

To the second question, there were answers like the following:

I think the United States is doing everything possible to get along with other countries. The only one we are having any difficulty with is Russia. They seem to want their own way all of the time and will make few if any concessions. I feel quite satisfied, however, the United States will make every effort to iron out all difficulties which may arise with other countries.

I don't think we're tough enough, to tell you the truth. You can call any American a sucker.

We are too soft. With Russia our attitude has been more appeasement than anything else. We should have taken a different stand at the very beginning. [*1, p. 150*]

To this same second question, 60 per cent of the respondents indicated that they were satisfied or mainly satisfied, 26 per cent dissatisfied or mainly dissatisfied, 9 per cent were undecided or "didn't know," and for 5 per cent opinions were not ascertained.

Note, however, the difference between describing the qualitative details of the opinions as quoted, and summarizing the net implications: "not satisfied" for the first question, 64 per cent; for the second question, 26 per cent. In the quotations the respondents indicated more

Reasons People Give for Their Attitudes Toward the United States' Conduct in World Affairs.

"How satisfied are you with the way the United States has been getting along with other countries?"

	Of those who are:	
	Satisfied, or mainly satisfied	Dissatisfied, or mainly dissatisfied
The U. S. is trying to get along on a peaceful basis with other countries........................	34%	1%
Is helping other countries with food, clothing, and other material aid........................	12	*
Is taking part in the UN and other international organizations.............................	1	—
Is taking a position of leadership in the world......	1	—
Is handling its part of the occupation of defeated countries well............................	1	—
Has been too lenient:		
With Russia.................................	2	11
With other countries (in general)..............	2	14
In its occupation policy.......................	*	2
Is sending too much food, clothing, etc. to:		
Other countries (in general)..................	3	16
England....................................	1	5
Russia.....................................	*	1
Is not getting along with Russia.................	7	10
Has not handled its foreign policy adequately......	1	10
Has no adequate foreign policy..................	—	5
Has interfered too much in internal affairs of other countries.................................	*	5
Has not followed a consistent policy:		
Toward Argentina............................	*	2
Toward Spain...............................	*	1
Has been too friendly with England..............	*	2
Has failed to take a position of leadership.........	—	2
Is not sending enough food, clothing, etc. to other countries.................................	*	1
Miscellaneous reasons.........................	3	12
Reasons not given............................	40	16
	**	**
Number of cases.............................	709	306

* Less than one per cent.
** Column adds to more than 100 per cent as some people gave more than one reason.

than just the affective component of their attitudes. (It should be noted in passing that these questions were of the "open ended" type designed to provide the fuller context of opinions rather than the "closed" questions which offer a fixed series of alternatives among which the respondents select.) The respondents described what the situation looked like to them, the perceptual structuring of the complex social stimulus of international relations. The satisfied-dissatisfied classification provides a statement of the affective component of the attitudes, the proportion of the people who endorse or approve the foreign policy and presumably would support it and want it continued, and the proportion who oppose or disapprove of it, would want the policy changed, and would probably take steps to change it or support its opponents. Such statements relate attitudes by way of emotional reactions, to motivation. The analysis of the frame of reference, illustrated in the answers quoted above and given in detail for Question 2 of the series (see p. 228) provides a description of the way in which foreign policy is seen, and hence relates attitudes to perception.

The interrelation of the two aspects of social attitudes, motivation and perception, noted above, may be seen clearly in these data. The person who is satisfied with our relations with other countries may see with approval that the United States is helping other countries with food, clothing, and material aid. The person who is dissatisfied may perceive the same data on shipments in a different way, that is, the United States is sending too much food and clothing to other countries. Conversely, a person who sees the United States as having been "too lenient" with other countries will be dissatisfied, while another individual may perceive comparable reports to mean that the United States is taking a position of leadership in the world and be satisfied. The basic problems of causal relations between perception and motivation need not concern us here. In this discussion it will be sufficient to note the relation of the two processes and to recognize that a social attitude of an individual, frequently treated as a single unit, has at least two psychologically different aspects.

DIMENSIONS OF ATTITUDES

Attitude research analyzes an abstraction. It cannot, therefore, provide a concrete, substantive picture of people's attitudes. Opinions can be so presented, but not attitudes. Even though we recognize an attitudinal frame of reference and emphasize that attitudes have motivational and perceptual significance, a full qualitative picture cannot be drawn. The best the student of attitudes can hope to do is to analyze the processes and describe the dynamics of attitude function. He may attempt to account for variation in attitudes or to describe how variations in attitudes account for other phenomena, but no static summary of people's attitudes can have much meaning. In undertaking such studies, research workers have found it helpful to analyze attitudes with respect to four major dimensions: direction, degree, intensity, and salience. Each of these dimensions represents a manner of describing the attitudes of individuals quantitatively in order that a large amount of data may be conveniently summarized and comparisons and analyses can be made, using statistical techniques. Each of the dimensions can be studied separately, or in combination. The more of the dimensions one studies, the more complete will be the understanding of the attitude.

We do not want to imply that these four dimensions are necessarily the only dimensions for attitude study. With further study other dimensions may be identified. For example, certainty may be clearly different from intensity as an aspect of social attitudes. In addition, for a systematic theoretical analysis, "degree" does not seem to be a dimension of the same order as the other three. For each dimension, direction, intensity, and salience, differences among individuals are sought in measurable form so that variations in degree are literally sought in each. What is here discussed as the degree dimension should ultimately be subsumed under direction. However, because of the current attention to this phase of attitude study, we are conforming to prevailing norms in this presentation in spite of such theoretical reservations.

Direction

The first and simplest attitude dimension which may be assessed is that of direction. In studying this aspect of attitude, we first ask whether a person is for or against a given social stimulus, person, group, activity, process, or institution. Are the affective connotations positive or negative? Does he like it or dislike it? Are his motivations such that he will behave in a manner to support or continue or endorse the stimulus, or will he tend to oppose or obstruct or condemn it? The direction of an attitude refers to this sort of gross appraisal of the individual's adjustments.

When we say that direction is the simplest dimension to assess, we do not mean that it is simple in an absolute sense. Everyone is "for virtue and against sin," but people differ greatly in what they define as virtue and what they consider sin. Almost everyone is against wars of aggression, but is any particular war unequivocally a war of aggression to all people? A man may be considered anti-feminist if he thinks women should not be admitted to jobs and professional occupations. (This stems from an "equal rights" value system, from which perspective he seems to be against granting women equal rights; therefore, he is against women.) His point of view, however, may be that women are biologically different, not necessarily inferior to men; quite the contrary, they may be superior in many respects. He would safeguard women from the need to work for a living and from the coarsening effects of commerce. From his perspective, he is definitely not aganist, but for, women.

The student of attitudes must consider whether the evaluation of direction is based on a set of personal values or is an objective representation of the dynamics of the individual's affective system. For many purposes, defining attitude direction by particular social values is of considerable use. However, the failure to make the precise orientation clear often leads to confusion of the psychological characteristics involved.

Degree

In addition to identifying the general direction of an individual's attitude, we need to assess variations in degree. Two people may hold negative, hostile attitudes toward a social stimulus (that is, they may hold attitudes of the same direction) ; but one may be strongly antagonistic and the other only mildly opposed. Variation in both direction and degree can often be studied in a single question. For example, soldiers were asked:

Do you think when you are discharged you will go back to civilian life with a favorable or unfavorable attitude toward the Army?

_____ Very favorable
_____ Fairly favorable
_____ About 50-50
_____ Fairly unfavorable
_____ Very unfavorable [23, p. 17]

At other times, degree can be studied by evaluating differences in the statements of opinion. For example, an individual who indicates agreement with the statement "My church is the primary guiding influence in my life" clearly is much more favorable to the church than a person who would endorse the statement "I believe in the ideals of my church, but I am tired of its denominationalism [25]."

The combination of the two dimensions, direction and degree, has represented the major concern of attitude studies in recent years. To proceed in investigations which require the analysis of a large amount of empirical attitude data, research workers have devised a number of methods for transmitting qualitative expressions of attitudes into quantitative terms. These methods are primarily concerned with establishing variations in attitude along a linear continuum.

Four methods have been developed for the construction of attitude scales: L. L. Thurstone has developed the method of equal-appearing intervals; R. Likert, the method of summated ratings; L. Guttman, the method of scale analysis; and A. L. Edwards and F. P. Kilpatrick have described the scale discrimination method for measuring social attitudes [24, 11, 23, 6]. The first two of these methods have been widely used for two decades; the third was put into use in World War II in the Army research program. The fourth is a still more recent proposal which combines the first two methods in an effort to derive results comparable to those secured from the third. In the next few pages, we shall outline briefly some of the major features of each of these methods in order to call attention to the fact that procedures have been developed to provide a basis for translating the qualitative data of attitude and opinion research into expressions of quantitative variation in degree. These methods transcend simple intuitive judgment and contribute greatly to the gathering of scientific data in the field of attitude and opinion study.

The Method of Equal-Appearing Intervals

The investigator employing this method collects a large number of opinion statements about a particular social stimulus. He tries to cover the full range of opinion and to obtain all the significant shades of feeling. Each statement is typed on a separate slip of paper. Judges are then asked to sort these opinions into eleven piles. Each pile represents a point on a subjective scale from "most favorable" through "neutral," which is the midpoint, to "most unfavorable." The judges are instructed to try to keep the subjective estimate of the difference between the piles about equal. If one hundred judges are used, each opinion statement will have one hundred assigned positions. The median of the assigned position for a given statement will be its scale position, and an index of the variability of the judgments for each statement (Q, the semi-interquartile range) is computed. Items can then be selected for the final scale to provide statements spaced evenly along the opinion continuum. Only those items on which there was highest agreement among the judges are used. The person taking the attitude test then merely reads through the final selection of items, checking those which come closest to his own opinion. Since the scale position of each item is known to the investigator, it is simple to translate the checked items into an attitude score for the subject.

The Method of Summated Ratings

The investigator selects a series of statements referring to the attitude being studied and phrases them in such a way that a reader can respond by checking one of five positions for each: strongly approve, approve, undecided, disapprove, or strongly disapprove. Weights from 1 to 5 assigned to each of the positions so that the high score always represents the extreme for the same attitude direction. The statements "All men who have the opportunity should enlist in the Citizens' Military Training Camps" and "In the interest of permanent peace, we should be willing to arbitrate absolutely all differences with other nations which we cannot readily settle by diplomacy" are examples of the kind of statements used [*16, p. 35*]. For the first of these statements, the "Strongly Approve" answer was given a weight of 1 and the "Strongly Disapprove" was weighted 5. For the second, however, the weighting was reversed: "Strongly Approve" received 5 and "Strongly Disapprove," 1. In this way, the higher weights are assigned to the more internationalist responses.

The series of statements is given to a number of subjects who express, individually, the degree of their approval or disapproval. The weights are then assigned to each individual's responses. These weights are summated so that there is a single numerical score representing each individual's ratings. When these total scores for a large number of subjects are available, the responses of those scoring extremely "high" and of those scoring extremely "low" are selected for further study. Each item is evaluated by determining whether the "high" scorers on the total test respond to the particular item with a higher score than do those who are "low" scorers on the total test. If there is (internal) consistency among the questions, each question should be answered differently by those whose total scores are at the opposing extremes of the distribution. Those items that differentiate the extreme groups most satisfactorily are retained for the scale. The scale may then be used with the items selected in this manner, and with scores for respondents equal to the sum of the weights assigned to their reactions to these items.

While the method of equal-appearing intervals relies on judges, the method of summated ratings depends on internal consistency criteria.

The Method of Scale Analysis

Scale analysis was developed from Guttman's conception of an attitude as a delimited totality of behavior with respect to something. With respect to any given social stimulus, all the possible behaviors comprise an "attitude universe" and the responses on a questionnaire concerning the social stimulus, a subuniverse of behavior. The questions posed for the research worker are the following: Can such a subuniverse of behavior be studied to discover if it represents a linear scale? Can a zero-point be located on the scale by objective means so that measurements can have a truly meaningful origin? To both of these questions, scale analysis provides an affirmative answer. Here we shall consider only the first (the second question is discussed under the intensity dimension). Scale analysis starts with questions selected *a priori* and proceeds to examine them to discover empirically whether they constitute a scalable subuniverse. Several different methods of "scalogram" analysis and the detailed procedures of this approach have been described, but all produce essentially the same results since they are all derived from the same basic theory.

Some of the implications of the idea of scalability can be seen in the following questions about height:

1. Are you over 6 feet tall?	_____Yes	_____No
2. Are you over 5 feet 9 inches tall?	_____Yes	_____No
3. Are you over 5 feet 6 inches tall?	_____Yes	_____No
4. Are you over 5 feet 3 inches tall?	_____Yes	_____No
5. Are you over 5 feet tall?	_____Yes	_____No

People under 5 feet in height would answer "No" to all five questions. People over 6 feet would answer "Yes" to all. People between 5 and 6 feet in height would shift from "No" to "Yes" at some point in the series. The items have a certain cumulative form which would not be present if the questions were of the following order: "Are you between 5 feet 3 inches and 5 feet 6 inches?" "Are you between 5 feet 6 inches and 5 feet 9 inches?" A scale can be detected in the cumulative questions when we use the scale analysis, but not when we employ the other types of questions. If we use a properly scaled set of questions, knowledge of the point at which the individual changed his responses from "no" to "yes" would provide us with knowledge of his height.

We do not have an external criterion for defining the linear scale of attitude and opinion data. Scalogram analysis, however, can determine whether responses to questions have the property of a linear scale. In dealing with height by means of a questionnaire, we know that if individuals were ranked on the basis of their height, all the people who answered question 2 in the affirmative would have higher ranks than those who answered in the negative. Those who answer question 1 affirmatively would answer all five affirmatively; and those who answer "no" to question 3 would also answer "no" to questions 1 and 2. Scalogram analysis provides a means of seeing to what extent the responses on a questionnaire meet with, or deviate from, what would be expected if a true linear scale were to exist and be reflected in the questions. Basically, "the scalogram hypothesis is that the items have an order such that, ideally, *persons who answer a given question favorably all have higher ranks on the scale than persons who answer the same question unfavorably.* From a respondent's rank or scale score we know exactly which items he endorsed. Thus, ideally, scales derived from scalogram analysis have the property that the responses to the individual items are reproducible from the scale scores [*23, p. 9*]." Practically, of course, this ideal is not attained. A special statistic, a coefficient of reproducibility, has been devised to measure the extent of deviation from the ideal that is found in an actual set of questions and their answers. This provides a partial test of whether the questions should, or should not be, considered a scale. If they are a scale, the study can proceed. If not, then either the universe is not scalable or those questions may pertain to more than one universe. Actually, reproducibility is not the only test of scalability in this method, but it is the most important one.

This method is similar to the method of summated ratings in that it depends on the interrelationships of answers to a set of discrete questions. It has, however, the advantage of an objective statistical procedure for evaluating the extent to which it conforms to the theoretical model it postulates.

The Scale Discrimination Method

This method has been proposed to overcome some of the objections to each of the foregoing procedures and to take advantage of the contributions of each. It represents a synthesis of all three. Opinion statements are first collected, then judged, then evaluated for scale position and variability as in Thurstone's Method of Equal-appearing Intervals. This serves to provide the original questions or a set of propositions on the basis of empirical data, something the other two methods do not. The selected statements are then put into form for response in accordance with the Likert Method of Summated Ratings, given to a group of subjects, and then evaluated for their discriminating power between the "high's" and the "low's." This procedure provides a basis for item evaluation through internal consistency. The items that pass this second screening are then tested for reliability and for reproducibility in accordance with Guttman's method of scale analysis.

This method supplements the Guttman technique by providing a basis for selecting among the original, subjectively selected items on an objective basis prior to testing for scalability by the Guttman criteria. It profits from Likert's contribution of testing the discriminating power of the items but adds the refinement of Guttman's improved testing for linearity in the scale.

Intensity

There has been a growing awareness in recent years of the importance of the intensity dimension in the analysis of opinions and attitudes. Intensity is the degree of conviction with which an attitude is held by an individual. Intensity is related to the dimension of degree of an attitude, but it is not identical with degree. Two individuals may hold the same opinion but may do so with different intensities. Similarly, two people may hold their opinions with the same intensity but the opinions they hold may be very different. The dimension of intensity, as distinct and separate from degree, is an important clue to determining whether an individual is more or less likely to shift his attitude, be frustrated if channels of expression are blocked, or be strongly instigated to action. Despite theoretical difficulties in conceptualizing the intensity dimension, Daniel Katz was able to devise and compare several different methods for gauging intensity. In his studies, two methods were found to be relatively satisfactory. One was an individual rating on sureness of opinion: "How sure are you that your opinion is right? — not sure; — fairly sure; — very sure [2, p. 59]." Another method was a graphic self-rating device illustrated in the following figure.

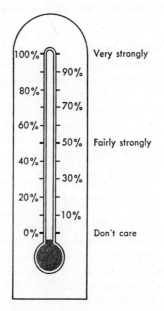

GRAPHIC SELF-RATING DEVICE FOR STUDYING INTENSITY OF OPINION

In addition to expressing opinions, respondents checked how strongly they felt in the matter, using the barometer illustrated [2].

In 1946, Cantril reported on the relation between attitude degree and intensity, using as the intensity indication the verbal self-rating response to the question "How strongly do you hold this opinion—very strongly, fairly strongly, or don't you care much one way or the other?" A general cross section of the population was sampled in a poll of attitudes toward Negroes and toward government control of business. For both scales the results showed that "the more extreme an attitude is in its direction, the more intensely it is likely to be held [3, p. 132]." The figure below illustrates this relationship; the vertical ordinate represents the variation in intensity, the baseline the direction and degree of the attitude toward government control. The scale value of the attitude statements, as indicated on the baseline, stems from the average scale placement by 80 judges who rated the statements on an eleven-place continuum. In this chart the responses of 1,081 cases are summarized.

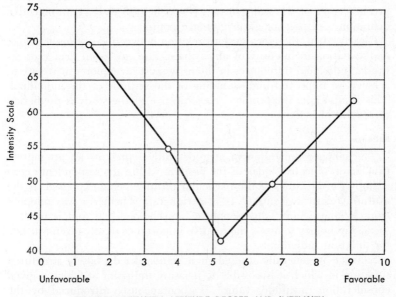

RELATION BETWEEN ATTITUDE DEGREE AND INTENSITY

Results of an opinion survey in which respondents gave their opinions on a public issue and also indicated how strongly they held the opinion. Note the minimal intensity at the neutral point of the attitude scale and the increase in intensity with the approach to the more extreme attitudes [3].

The attitude studies in the Army during World War II, in connection with which the scale analysis method was extensively used, also contributed to our knowledge of intensity. Questions of opinion were frequently followed by further questions:

How strongly do you feel about this?

_____ Not at all strongly
_____ Not so strongly
_____ Fairly strongly
_____ Very strongly
_____ No answer [23, *see p. 225 as an example*]

As in Cantril's study, intensity varied consistently with degree. The more extreme the opinion, in either direction, the more strongly, on the average, individuals felt about their position. So consistent was this finding that the lowest point on the intensity scale was used to define the zero point of the content scale. In the Army studies, the scales of attitudes or opinions gave linear continuums, and the cutting point for interpreting a change in the direction of the responses, from favorable to unfavorable, for example, was taken as that point on the content scale which had the lowest intensity. This was not always the precise center of the scale, so that it was helpful to have an objective definition of a psychological reference point.

Clearly, then, there is a general relation between variation in degree and variation in intensity of an attitude. For any given degree of attitude, individual differences in intensity must be explored if we are to achieve an improved understanding of the attitude of the individual. This is especially important if the objective of the study is prediction or control of behavior.

Salience

The salience dimension in attitude study represents an attempt to provide an objective index of the position within the respondent's constellation of attitudes of the particular attitude being expressed. Is the attitude relatively central? Is it peripheral? The term was adopted from William Stern's "personalistic" psychology [22] and is used in social psychology to assess the relative importance of any given attitude for different individuals.

Salience is generally studied in a standardized, loosely structured situation in which it is possible to measure the point at which a given consideration (attitude, value) is spontaneously introduced by the subject. For example, one of the devices used by Eugene Hartley in exploring the salience of ethnic attitudes was a series of portraits taken from a college senior class book. The portraits were separately mounted on index cards, and the subjects were asked to sort the pictures into different categories or different piles, on whatever basis the subjects might choose to use. After sorting, the investigator noted the arrangement of the pictures and secured from the subject a statement concerning the nature of the categories he had used. The pictures were then shuffled and the subject asked to sort them again on some other basis. This procedure was continued until the subjects ran out of categories. It was possible to analyze these data and discover for each subject at what point in the series, if any, nationality attributes served as the basis for classifying the pictured people. For some respondents, classifications were based on nationality very early in the series; for others, very late; for still others, nationality was not used as a principle for classification at all [9]. This variation was taken as a clue to the importance for the responding individuals of the national group memberships of others. In Hartley's study, a number of similar methods of salience measurement were used. No significant relationship was found between ethnic salience and tolerance, but a significant relationship was reported between ethnic salience and the "sociality" of the individual. Subjects for whom ethnic factors were not very salient were significantly more expansive in their social judgments of peers than were the respondents with high ethnic salience. They felt that more people were likable and, from a page of pictures, picked a larger number with whom they thought they might be able to develop a close friendship than did the high-salience subjects.

Salience is measured differently from intensity. To measure salience a situation is framed and the tendency of the subject spontaneously to introduce the attitude variable is noted; to measure intensity, the issue to which the subject responds is raised and then the subject indicates the degree of conviction with which he holds his opinion. In pre-Hitler Germany there was much anti-Semitism. Serious question may be raised whether the Nazi regime increased the amount of anti-Semitism, but there can be no question that it increased the salience of this attitude for the Germans. Pro-tolerance agitation in the United States in recent years may not have changed people's thinking about different ethnic groups, but it has raised the salience of those democratic ideals that are incompatible with discrimination. Direction represents the "pro" or "con" nature of an attitude, degree indicates the extent, and intensity indicates the strength of feeling with which the individual holds the opinion of a given direction and degree. Salience reflects the importance of the attitude within the individual.

VARIATION IN ATTITUDE

Attitudes Stem from the Group

Our discussion up to this point has been based on a conception of social attitudes as group norms which an individual acquires as a result of his relationship to his group. The vast amount of research on social attitudes reviewed by Gardner Murphy, Lois B. Murphy and Theodore M. Newcomb has led to the following conclusion:

Attitudes are rarely individual affairs, but are largely borrowed from groups to which we owe our strongest allegiance. Individual variations such as age, sex and various personality characteristics have much to do with the nature of the groups with which one becomes affiliated, and with the degree and permanence of such affiliations. Individual experiences, whether of accidental or occasional nature, on the one hand, or those occasioned by family membership or residential community, are also instrumental in determining group membership. This is by no means to deny the importance of purely psychological factors. But such experimental evidence as is available has led us to the conclusion that the latter are effective largely through their power to select this rather than that group affiliation, to react to it with greater or less intensity and, to some extent, perhaps, to modify it. The social psychology of attitudes is the sociology of attitudes illuminated by an understanding of the psychological factors which determine individual susceptibility to group influences. [*17, pp. 1045-6*]

In a recent survey of the literature on political behavior and voting in the American community David Truman has reported:

Evidence from a variety of sources indicates that voting is a group experience. Much of the ideology of a democratic system, of course, asserts or assumes that the individual voter is an independent unit exercising a completely free choice among all the alternatives presented. Recent evidence, notably from the studies of Lazarsfeld and his associates, indicates, however, that individuals tend to vote in conformity with the preferences dominant in the social groups with which they are most closely identified. [*14, pp. 226-7*]

This emphasis on the group as the point of departure for understanding attitudes may be difficult to accept. Human beings like to feel that their attitudes are their own. We prefer to associate with people whose attitudes are similar to ours and therefore the group will be observed to have similar attitudes. The similarity of attitudes in a group from this point of view represents a common rather than a collective phenomenon; that is, it is a result of each individual independently developing similar attitudes, not of interaction among individuals in the group. But even the attitude that leads an individual to associate with a group is most likely an emergent from previous group contacts and relationships. Allport, for example, in surveying the genesis of attitude, described four conditions for their formation: (1) through integration of a series of specific experiences of a similar type; (2) through differentiation (individuation or segregation) from more general mass responses to certain general situations, a process which is the reverse of integration; (3) through dramatic, emotional experience or trauma; and (4) through adopting ready-made attitudes from the models set by parents, teachers, or playmates [*15, pp. 810-11*]. Only the fourth of these conditions seems clearly to support the group-devised emphasis of this discussion, although integration, differentiation, and trauma may occur within social situations. Reflection, however, will make it clear that the results of pre-existing social pressures and learnings define for the individual what shall be perceived as similar, so that with the integration and differentiation of experience, a coherent unit, the attitude, can develop. Emotional, traumatic experiences are observed throughout the life span; yet not all are generalized to establish a social attitude. Moreover, the social learning of the individual provides those frames of reference within which the processes of integration, differentiation, and trauma may work to define his unique attitudes. The basic direction of the attitude, its contexts, its very existence as a discrete unit in the individual's organization, stems from his group identifications; and individual differences in experience will account for the variations within the group.

The studies by the Morale Division of the United States Strategic Bombing Survey may help clarify some of the problems involved in this discussion. These studies attempted to evaluate the effects of strategic bombing on the civilian populations of enemy countries during World War II. Large-scale sampling surveys were undertaken in Germany, during June and July of 1945. When responses were analyzed, city by city, it was found that there was a reliable and striking correlation between a drop in morale, as represented by acknowledging a willingness to accept unconditional surrender, and bomb damage to public utilities. The results based on data from 18 bombed cities showed correlations between willingness to surrender and disruption of transportation .81, of electricity .43, of gas .32, of water .30. Clearly the reality experiences influenced the thinking of the populace:

The higher degree of relationship between transportation and morale is probably due to the fact that transportation is more vital to everyday urban living than any other single utility. When transportation breaks down, people find difficulty in getting to work, in shopping for food, in reaching the drug store for medicine, etc. If electric service is knocked out, people can fall back upon substitutes for light and power. Water mains for a whole city were generally not destroyed, and relief was usually forthcoming in German towns through hydrants and water wagons. [*27, p. 3*]

When we turn, however, to a more analytical study of individuals, the importance of pre-existing sets can be very readily seen. Though the bombs fell on Nazi and non-Nazi alike, their reactions were very different. On each of a series of measures of morale used in the survey, Nazis showed consistently less impairment of morale than did the non-Nazi. When we turn from the general attitude of morale to a more specific attitude, we find that the difference remains. For example, Helen Peak reports the distribution of reactions to the bombing in terms of the blame assigned to the Allies for the raids. Among the Nazis, 68 per cent blamed the Allies and 16 per cent assigned no blame to them. Among the non-Nazis, however, only 26 per cent blamed the Allies and 59 per cent did not [*19*].

The findings of the Bombing Survey help to establish some of the principles of attitude functioning previously described. The falling bombs, the threat, and the ensuing damage were certainly traumatic for all. Nevertheless, the pro-Nazis maintained much higher war morale than did the non-Nazis. The former blamed the Allies for the air raids; the latter did not. Group identifications and prior value systems established frames of references within which specific experiences had different meanings. Within groups, however, all members were not exposed to identical experiences. From city to city, the damage inflicted by the raids varied, and morale was found to vary, for example, with the extent of the disruption of transportation facilities. City by city, the difference between Nazi and non-Nazi was found, but within each group, those individuals experiencing greater disruptive effects had lower morale than those less affected. Differences in experience contributed to individual differences in attitude within the framework provided by the over-all group norms.

When we turn to the question of whether like-minded people form groups or whether groups create like-mindedness, we must refer to our earlier discussion in Chapters XIII and XIV. Throughout childhood, and often long past adolescence, the individual is thrust into social groups with little opportunity for choice. His family, neighborhood playmates, school, and church are all assigned with practically no individual options. As he starts developing independent mobility and seems capable of exercising "free" choice, his range of potential groups is rather drastically limited by his prior group memberships, by the values they have standardized, and by the aspirations they encourage or tolerate. As we examine adult "independent" joining, for example, in clubs on a college campus, we find a tendency for like-minded individuals to seek one another. However, the area of common interests often tends to be much smaller than the total social area influenced by the given group membership. A man may join a chess club in order to meet and play with others who also have interest in chess. He will find, however, that attitudes about other forms of recreation may be influenced, as well as attitudes toward other subjects. The individual who joins a fraternity or sorority because of social interests which coincide with those of a given "house," may find that norms emerge which relate to many activities remote from eating, lounging, and dancing. Once the individual is in a group, he is subject to its influence, often without any awareness of the range of changes being induced. In short, while people of similar interests and attitudes do get together, it is also true that groups develop homogeneity among their members with respect to other interests and attitudes and that the originally similar interests and attitudes were products of prior group experiences.

Attitudes and Multiple Group Membership

In studying attitudes, we must take cognizance of the individual's multiple group memberships. Not all of his reference groups will endorse the same norm, and the individual will often seem to be holding conflicting attitudes. These need not represent conflict within the individual if the situations to which he is responding are unambiguous in evoking one or another reference group as regnant. For example, a college professor who was a teetotaller and who endorsed legal prohibition of the sale of liquor, nevertheless served guests at his home with potent drinks. As "host," serving drinks was a norm in the circle in which he moved. He would even pour himself one, and play with the glass throughout the evening — but he would not drink from it. When he was a "guest" in a friend's house, the norms permitted him politely to refuse a drink. His attitude toward alcohol varied with the roles he played. It may be suggested that his attitude was consistent, that he opposed the use of intoxicating beverages but was tolerant of the views of others. We need not quarrel as to whether the professor was being consistent or inconsistent, for the discussion would proceed at two different levels in the generalization-specificity analysis of the individual's attitude. At the more general level of analysis, he was consistent: he opposed the use of alcohol, but he was tolerant. At the more specific levels, he was inconsistent: he favored legal prohibition which would apply to all residents of the community whether they agreed or disagreed with him; he himself was opposed to the use of intoxicants, yet he served such beverages in his home. Since we do not as yet have any objective way of describing the precise level of generality at which we are making an analysis, research and theory concerning problems of consistency-inconsistency in behavior have tended to lag, and pursuing further such a discussion in this context would be fruitless. Another way of putting the problem would be to emphasize that the negative attitude toward liquor was consistent; but in different contexts, in combination with different constellations of other attitudes, it might or might not be a dominant factor in defining the behavior. To pursue the analysis along these lines, to consider the nature of opinion formation, would require a complete review of the psychology of thinking and problem solving, a review which would take us too far afield from the focus of our present discussion.

The problems of multiple group membership have been examined earlier. Here one study may relate the previous discussion to the present context. To test the effects of the social status of interviewers in opinion polling, Daniel Katz set up a controlled study. Two separate interviewing staffs, one composed of white-collar workers such as are customarily employed in polls, and one drawn from working-class backgrounds, were sent into the same low-rental areas in Pittsburgh with the same instructions and the same questionnaire. Both teams worked for the first two weeks of March, 1941, during which time about 600 interviews were collected by each team. When the responses obtained by the two groups were compared, striking differences appeared:

Middle-class or white-collar interviewers, such as the public-opinion polls employ, find a greater incidence of conservative attitudes among lower income groups than do interviewers recruited from the working class.

The more liberal and radical findings of working-class interviewers are more pronounced on labor issues.

The difference in the answers reported by white-collar as against working-class interviewers increases when union members, or their relatives are interviewed. [*10, p. 267*]

Comparable studies have been done with ethnic membership rather than socio-economic group identification as the variable. The findings of such studies may be interpreted somewhat as follows: The dominant group membership character of the interviewer, through interaction with the respondent, evokes a particular reference group for the latter, in the light of which answers are given to the questions asked. If interviewers on the same survey have (or appear to have) different membership groups they may evoke significantly different reference groups in comparable respondents, and to the extent that these different reference groups have differing norms with respect to the issue in question, different opinions will be expressed and different attitudes will be reflected. The respondents will speak as representatives of one, rather than another, of all their possible reference groups in response to the group represented by the interviewer.

Attitudes and Social Reality

In the dynamic times in which we live, group norms may be observed to accommodate to social realities. Some groups, some norms, show marked stability; others vary markedly with "the times." The relation of opinions and attitudes to the general conditions of life is illustrated in an analysis by Elmo Roper, in 1949, of labor's demands on management.

There was a time along about the turn of the century, when workers in this country offered their labor on the marketplace where it was bought and sold for a given wage — and many days not even bought at all. In those days, when the American Federation of Labor was just getting started under Samuel Gompers' leadership, wages and hours were the new basis of economic unionism. In fact, for a number of years, wages and hours were almost the only two issues over which management and labor bargained.

We are not very far from those days, either. It would not be a very wrong guess that one of the chief appeals of unions even today is the promise of bringing higher wages to workingmen.

But something has happened, perhaps both to the men who work on the assembly lines and in the plants and mills and mines of this land and to the men who hire and direct them and to the men who represent them in bargaining. Other values in labor relations are taking on added meaning and importance.

In a word, workingmen today want something more than better pay and shorter hours.

We have learned this in the many studies we have made over the past 15 years. In that time, we have interviewed thousands of employees in almost every part of the country, sometimes as part of a national cross section, sometimes in what we term employee attitude studies.

These latter studies attempt to measure worker reaction to his job, his company, and his daily work routine. They attempt to find out the degree of job satisfaction in a given plant or a given company. They attempt to find out what the individual employee thinks about not only pay and hours of work, but the chance of advancing, job security, communications between him and his bosses, the physical working conditions in his plant, the benefit plans his employers offer him, the methods of organization, and the efficiency with which he is put to work. In fact, we try in these surveys to find out what is on the worker's mind about his job and his work, how he thinks things could be improved and whether or not he is getting what he conceives to be a fair share. In other studies, broader in scope, we have tried to learn the aims and aspirations of people — what they want out of life as best they are able to tell us.

And out of these many studies we have conducted, there are certain broad conclusions which emerge. Conclusions which help to explain — in the workers' own terms — just what American labor wants out of the job today.

Broadly speaking, there are four chief things which American workers want, and the order in which I mention them is somewhat interchangeable. But these four things stand out as the major sources of worker satisfaction.

First of all, the American workingman wants a sense of security. I don't mean security handed to him on a silver platter by his government. Probably the closest description of what security means is the opportunity to work continuously at reasonably good wages. Home ownership, possession of a savings account, and life insurance are other forms of desired security. This desire for security extends to a better education for themselves and their children and, in recent years, the desire for old age security has become particularly important.

Second, American workers want a chance for advancement, to get ahead on the job. Particular stress is laid on ability and reward for capable work. The vast majority of workers resent politics or short-cuts in advancement and prefer advancement on merit as a criterion. The Horatio Alger tradition may be dimming a little, but the chance to keep climbing up the ladder of success is still a strong American tradition.

Next is the vague but important outgrowth of our mass production system — the desire to be treated like a human being. Workers do not want to be handled as automatons, as the mechanical men portrayed so many years ago by Charlie Chaplin. They want to be considered by their bosses as human beings, and they feel that somehow modern production methods must be geared to their needs as individuals.

They want friendly foremen, sympathetic management, and congenial fellow employees. They do not want to be treated as mere numbers on a pay roll.

And finally, American workingmen want to feel that they are doing significant work. There is nothing more discouraging to the worker than to feel he is considered unimportant, a dispensable cog in a vast industrial machine. In his small way, the worker wants to feel that he is contributing to the success of the world he lives in, that the work he is doing will advance all of his fellow human beings in some way. I think some professionals call this the desire for social significance.

People want these four things in different degrees. Some will gladly give up some of their security for a better chance to advance. Almost all would give up part of their security and part of their chance for advancement in order to be treated as human beings, in order to feel that they belong.

Perhaps at first glance you might wonder where these desires for security, advancement, a sense of significance, and desire to be treated as a human being — where do they all fit into the bargaining process between unions and management? Well, actually, there is hardly an issue which has divided labor and management and which means much to the rank-and-file of labor — which doesn't fit into one of these four major desires of American workers. And the truth of the matter seems to be that more and more the scope of industrial management and of union leaders is growing broader to include almost every one of the four as the direct concern of those who run modern business.

What it boils down to is this. Increasingly, a human emphasis is being put on the problems of American industry. Some of the results of our employee attitude studies form a curious pattern. In these studies we find a kind of progression of worries and complaints on the part of people who work. The most dissatisfied of the people who work in factories and mills are those who find fault with their pay and their physical working conditions. The most satisfied are those whose concern is directed more toward old age security, a better community life, better housing, a better education for themselves and their children. The more satisfied a worker is about his pay, the more concerned you will find him with welfare and health plans. He wants medical and hospital care for himself and his family. He wants the company to institute a pay roll savings plan. As the more elementary needs are satisfied, the worker continues to look to his job for greater satisfaction as a human being. In our kind of a society he must look either to his job or to his government for these human satisfactions.

Thus it is that greater and greater emphasis has been placed on the *needs* of the individual who is working on the assembly line or in the mill.

It has been found that a satisfied worker will generally be the most productive worker. A worker who has a sense of security and significance about his work, who believes he is getting ahead in the world and who feels he gets a square deal from his boss, this kind of a worker is the backbone of our industrial system.

It is a long way we have come from the 12-hour day and the sweat shop.

A good deal of this change has been attributed by the workers to the rise of unions, which have directly improved their working conditions and pay. Part of it they credit to federal legislation which has written floors under conditions of work and reward for work. But part of it is also credited to a more alert management in scientifically spotting and understanding the needs and aspirations of workingmen.

This human emphasis in industry is not accidental. It is a reflection of the things which workers have said they want. It is a reflection as well of our relative economic well-being as a nation. Our major industries on the whole pay well above subsistence wages. The standard of living of our American workers is far above that of any other workmen in the world.

To a large part of American labor, the primary needs of survival, for food, clothing, and shelter have been satisfied at least on a minimum basis.

This doesn't mean, of course, that there aren't many workers who still live in slums, who barely manage to feed and clothe their children during a layoff. But it does mean that we have at least set if not fully attained a minimum standard of satisfying the primary needs of industrial workers today. And our energies are now being directed more toward the broader problems of satisfaction in living. [20]

The way in which the social reality situation is related to attitudes may also be seen in the political sphere. In Germany, since the surrender in 1945, the shifts in political thinking have been marked. The policies of the occupying powers have not always appeared clear to the Germans, and their experience had taught them that supporting the "wrong" political program may prove dangerous. Opinions of West Germans have been systematically studied since the beginning of military government, and these studies have continued under the civilian High Commissioner for Germany. In his report for the period of January 1 to March 31, 1950, the United States High Commissioner, Mr. John J. McCloy, called attention to the determination of German attitudes by developments in two major problem areas:

In the first quarter of 1950 a crystallization of German attitudes was taking place, rather than the development of any basically new trends in public opinion. The year 1949 had witnessed a rapid series of events which set the framework for this process: the climax of the airlift and the raising of the Berlin blockade; the working out of the Bonn Basic Law and the Occupation Statute; the dramatic failure of the quadripartite Paris Conference of the Council of Foreign Ministers of May-June 1949 to reach a solution of the German problem; the elections for the Federal Parliament and the subsequent formation and consolidation of the Federal Government; and the creation by the Soviets of the so-called "German Democratic Republic" in Eastern Germany.

On analysis, German attitudes on these events could be seen crystallizing about two main complexes of problems: The East-West conflict and the future political-economic system in Germany. The second complex was probably more constantly in German consciousness, particularly the more immediate effects of Federal economic policy. Over all other considerations hung the shadow of the East-West split. [*26, p. 42*]

Here, too, specific issues are responded to in the light of frames of reference defined in part by the basic orientations provided by group identifications and in part by the related general reality situations as perceived by the individual.

There is widespread agreement that opinions and attitudes, to be understood, must be seen in the light of such fundamental matrices as have been described here for American labor demands and German opinions on political and economic issues. Nevertheless, little empirical testing has as yet been made of such hypotheses as have been advanced. For the present, we must rest with the vague generalization that there is such a background out of which opinions emerge as crystallizations of specific situations or issues, and we must await further study to describe the matrix and nexus more satisfactorily. To the extent that there is consistency in conditions as well as within the person, attitudes may be expected to remain stable. Changes in either can be expected to result in shifts of both attitudes and opinions.

Attitudes and Personality

The relation of variation in attitudes to variation in personality must be considered in the light of the foregoing discussion. Personality variables will be important factors in establishing the adjustment of an individual to a group and will decide to what extent he accepts or rejects the group influence. If he rejects the group, either by his own choice or in defense, on being rejected by the group, he will seek more congenial group identifications and derive his attitudes from his prevailing reference groups as he perceives their norms. The ability to accept the norms of a group will, of course, depend in large part on the personality of the individual. Hence we can expect a correlation between attitudes and personality.

In the next chapter, the relation of personality variables to a particular complex of attitudes, namely, the attitudes toward ethnic groups, will be considered at length. Personality and attitude relationships will vary with the attitudes being considered and the reference groups involved. The generalization we can make must, therefore, be confined to the description of the process by which personality factors contribute both to the selection of group affiliations and to adjustment to the group norms. The group norms interiorized by the individual represent his social attitudes. There is in consequence a correlation between personality and attitude mediated by group identifications.

SUMMARY

In this chapter we have considered the nature of opinions and attitudes. The term "attitude" is an abstraction used to refer to an individual's inferred characteristics that account for such consistency in his behavior and expressions as he may manifest, characteristics that are not prescribed by situational imperatives. Opinions are the integrations of attitudes in concrete situations when problems arise, when accustomed patterns of response do not seem adequate. Opinions and attitudes vary in degree of generality from quite specific to very general. They have both perceptual and affective-motivational aspects, the former identified with the term "frame of reference," the latter more customarily identified with attitudes. The major dimensions of attitudes are currently thought of as a series of four linear parameters: direction, degree, intensity, salience.

Social attitudes are group norms acquired by the individual as a function of his identification with the group. The role being played by an individual determines his regnant reference group and hence his group's norm at a particular moment. Attitudes of the individual vary when the objective circumstances of the group's functioning lead to the emergence of new adjustments. Attitudes are related to personality variables in that the latter are important in determining the individual's adjustment to a group and his selection, when choice is possible, of new reference groups.

BIBLIOGRAPHY

1. Campbell, A., S. Eberhart, and P. Woodward: "Findings of the Intensive Surveys," in *Public Reaction to the Atomic Bomb and World Affairs* (Ithaca, N. Y.: Cornell University Press, April, 1947).
2. Cantril, H. (Ed.): *Gauging Public Opinion* (Princeton, Princeton University Press, 1944).

3. Cantril, H.: "The Intensity of an Attitude," *Journal of Abnormal and Social Psychology*, Vol. 41 (1946), pp. 129-35. Reprinted by permission of *Journal of Abnormal and Social Psychology* and the American Psychological Association.

4. Chein, I., M. Deutsch, H. Hyman, and M. Jahoda (Special Eds.): "Consistency and Inconsistency in Intergroup Relations," *Journal of Social Issues*, Vol. 5, No. 3 (1949).

5. Droba, D. D.: "Attitude toward War." Scale No. 2 in "The Measurement of Social Attitudes" series, L. L. Thurstone (Ed.) (Chicago: University of Chicago Press, 1930).

6. Edwards, A. L. and F. P. Kilpatrick: "A Technique for the Construction of Attitude Scales," *Journal of Applied Psychology*, Vol. 32 (1948), pp. 374-84.

7. Ferguson, L. W.: "The Isolation and Measurement of Nationalism," *Journal of Social Psychology*, Vol. 16 (1942), pp. 215-28.

8. Ferguson, L. W.: "Primary Social Attitudes," *Journal of Psychology*, Vol. 8 (1939), pp. 217-23.

9. Hartley, E. L.: *Problems in Prejudice* (New York: King's Crown Press, 1946).

10. Katz, D.: "Do Interviewers Bias Poll Results?" *Public Opinion Quarterly*, Vol.26 (1942), pp. 248-68.

11. Likert, R.: "A Technique for the Measurement of Attitudes," *Archives of Psychology*, No. 140 (1932).

12. Mead, G. H.: *Mind, Self and Society* (Chicago: University of Chicago Press, 1934).

13. Meier, N. C. and H. W. Saunders (Eds.): *The Polls and Public Opinion*, "Basic Social Science Research," by S. A. Stouffer, (New York: Henry Holt & Company, Inc., 1949).

14. Mosteller, F., H. Hyman, P. J. McCarthy, E. S. Marks, and D. B. Truman: *The Pre-Election Polls of 1948. Report to the Committee on Analysis of Pre-Election Polls and Forecasts.* (Bulletin 60) (New York: Social Science Research Council, 1949).

15. Murchison, C. (Ed.): *A Handbook of Social Psychology*, "Attitudes," by G. W. Allport, (Worcester, Mass.: Clark University Press, 1935).

16. Murphy, G. and R. Likert: *Public Opinion and the Individual* (New York: Harper & Brothers, 1938).

17. Murphy, G., L. B. Murphy, and T. M. Newcomb: *Experimental Social Psychology* (Rev. ed.) (New York: Harper & Brothers, 1937).

18. National Opinion Research Center (Chicago: University of Chicago, Survey 157, April 22, 1948).

19. Peak, H.: "Observations on the Characteristics and Distribution of German Nazis," *Psychological Monographs*, Vol. 59 (1945), No. 6, whole No. 276.

20. Roper, E.:"Where the People Stand," Columbia Broadcasting System, Sunday, June 5, 1949.

21. Sherif, M. and H. Cantril: "The Psychology of 'Attitudes' Part I," *Psychological Review*, Vol. 52 (1945), pp. 295-319.

22. Stern, W.: *General Psychology from the Personalistic Standpoint* (New York: The Macmillan Company, 1938).

23. Stouffer, S. A., L. Guttman, E. A. Suchman, P. F. Lazarsfeld, S. A. Star, and J. A. Clausner: *Measurement and Prediction* (Princeton: Princeton University Press, 1950).

24. Thurstone, L. L. and E. J. Chave: *The Measurement of Attitude* (Chicago: University of Chicago Press, 1929).

25. Thurstone, L. L. and E. J. Chave: *Scale of Attitude toward the Church* (Chicago: University of Chicago Press, 1930).

26. U. S. High Commissioner for Germany: *Second Quarterly Report on Germany* (Washington: U. S. Government Printing Office, 1950).

27. United States Strategic Bombing Survey: *The Effects of Strategic Bombing on German Morale,* Morale Division, Washington (1946), Vol. II.

28. Wang, C. K. A. and L. L. Thurstone: "Attitude toward the Treatment of Criminals." Scale No. 9 in "The Measurement of Social Attitudes" series, L. L. Thurstone (Ed.) (Chicago: University of Chicago Press, 1931).

▲ CHARLES E. OSGOOD

▲ PERCY H. TANNENBAUM

Attitude Change and the Principle of Congruity

Despite the voluminous outpouring of research on attitude change during the past two or three decades, no principles of sufficient generality or precision to render predictions about the effects of communications have appeared. The theoretical model presented in this paper, while not pretending to take account of all relevant variables, does attempt to cover those variables believed to be most significant with respect to the *direction* of attitude change to be expected in any given situation. These variables are (1) existing attitude toward the source of a message, (2) existing attitude toward the concept evaluated by the source, and (3) the nature of the evaluative assertion which relates source and concept in the message. Predictions generated by the theory about the directions and relative amounts of attitude change apply to both sources and the concepts they evaluate. The principles described are assumed to be more general in application than to the particular communication situation in which a source evaluates a concept, and they are phrased and illustrated with this in mind.

Our work on attitude theory and measurement is an outgrowth of continuing research on experimental semantics, particularly development of objective methods for measuring meaning. From this viewpoint, the *meaning* of a concept is its location in a multidimensional space defined by a set of empirically derived factors; the *attitude* toward that concept is its location, or projection, onto one of these dimensions, that is defined as "evaluative." In the factor analytic work we have done so far, the first factor to appear in analysis, and the most

▲ This is based on a paper in the *Psychological Review*, and is published here by permission of the authors. Dr. Osgood is a professor in psychology and in the Institute of Communications Research at the University of Illinois, where Dr. Tannenbaum is a research assistant professor in the Institute. This selection omits the experimental data these authors advance in support of their propositions.

heavily loaded, is always one clearly identifiable as evaluative by the labels of the scales it represents — e.g., *good-bad, fair-unfair, valuable-worthless, pleasant-unpleasant,* and the like. This conception of attitude as a dimension or factor in total meaning has many implications, including those explored in the present paper. It implies, for example, that people having the same attitude toward a concept, such as NEGRO, may be sharply differentiated in terms of other dimensions of the semantic space (e.g., some perceiving NEGRO as *powerful* and *active,* others as *weak* and *passive*).

As will become evident in the following analysis, any application of the principle of congruity to prediction of attitude change requires the use of a *generalized attitude scale.* Attitudes toward the various objects of judgment associated in messages must be measured in the same units if comparative statements about attitude change are to be made. There have been several attempts to devise generalized attitude scales in the history of this field; if one is to judge by the criterion of acceptance and use, none of these has been outstandingly successful. In applying the *semantic differential* (a label that has been given to our measuring instrument), various objects of judgment, sources and concepts, are rated against a standard set of descriptive scales, their allocations to scales having large and exclusive loadings on the evaluative factor constituting the index of attitude. To the extent that location on the evaluative dimension of the semantic differential is a reliable and valid index of attitude (as determined by correlation with other criteria), it is then necessarily a generalized attitude scale. We have some evidence for validity and more is being obtained; reliability of the differential, particularly the evaluative dimension, is reasonably high, running in the .80's and .90's in available data.

THE PRINCIPLE OF CONGRUITY

To claim sufficiency, any theory of attitude change must include statements about at least the following: (1) the *direction,* favorable or unfavorable, of the change to be expected; (2) the *magnitude* of the change to be expected, in at least "more-or-less-than" terms; and (3) the *locus* of the change or changes to be expected, e.g., in which of the objects of judgment associated in a message.

The principle of congruity is one of several general notions about the nature of cognitive processes on which we have been working. The first of these concerns the function of an *evaluative frame of reference.* All objects of judgment, regardless of their localization with respect to the total dimensionality of the semantic space, have a projection onto the evaluative dimension. Given the pervasiveness and availability in language of judgmental scales reflect the evaluative dimension of meaning, certain objects of judgment and verbal qualifications (e.g., *good* and *bad*) early acquire stable positions along this dimension and then serve as focal points for the organization of later experiences. In other words, these already localized concepts provide a "scale" of reference in terms of which to judge new material. Even such relatively nonevaluative concepts as BOOKS and ALASKA have some position on the evaluative dimension and may be shifted along this dimension by association with evaluatively focal concepts (e.g., BOOKS with RADICALISM or ALASKA with AMERICA).

Another underlying notion about human thinking is that *judgmental frames of reference tend toward maximal simplicity*. Since extreme, "all-or-nothing" judgments are simpler than finely discriminated judgments of degree, this implies a continuing pressure toward *polarization* along the evaluative dimension (e.g., movement of concepts toward either entirely *good* or entirely *bad* allocations). We have evidence that extreme judgments have shorter latencies than more discriminative judgments and that extreme judgments are characteristic of less intelligent, less mature, less well educated, or more emotionally oriented individuals. Furthermore, since assumption of identities is a simpler process than maintenance of distinctions, this also implies a continuing pressure toward *elimination of differences* among concepts which are localized in the same direction of the evaluative framework. We have evidence that in the judgment of emotionally polarized concepts all scales of judgment tend to rotate toward the evaluative, e.g., their correlations with *good-bad* tend to increase and therefore the relative loading on the evaluative factor tends to increase.

The most "simple-minded" evaluative frame of reference is therefore one in which a tight cluster of highly polarized and undifferentiated *good* concepts is diametrically opposed in meaning to an equally tight and polarized cluster of undifferentiated *bad* concepts. The same underlying pressure toward simplicity requires that any new or neutral concept must be shifted in one way or the other. Thus the tendency in American thinking about which Pandit Nehru complains, requiring that INDIA be either "for us or agin' us." This is, of course, the state of mind referred to by Korzybski as a "two-valued orientation," and it is unfortunately characteristic of lay thinking in any period of conflict and emotional stress. The more sophisticated thinker, according to this view, should show less tendency to polarize, more differentiation among concepts, and thus greater relative use of factors other than the evaluative.

The principle of congruity in human thinking can be stated quite succinctly: *changes in evaluation are always in the direction of increased congruity with the existing frame of reference*. To make any use of this principle in specific situations, however, it is necessary to elaborate along the following lines: When does the issue of congruity arise? What directions of attitude change are congruent? How much stress is generated by incongruity and how is it distributed among the objects of judgment?

(1) *The issue of congruity.* Each individual has potential attitudes toward a near infinity of objects. The typical American college student, for example, has favorable attitudes toward HOME, MY COUNTRY, LOGICAL THINKING, DEMOCRACY, CLEANLINESS, etc., relatively neutral attitudes toward STATE RIGHTS, MATHEMATICS, FOREIGNERS, IRAN, etc., and unfavorable attitudes toward things like STEALING, COMMUNISM, SLUMS, MC CARTHYISM, and so on ad infinitum. It is possible to have such varying attitudes toward these diverse things without any felt incongruity or any pressure toward attitude change — as long as no association among these objects of judgment is made. As anthropologists well know, members of a culture may entertain logically incompatible attitudes toward objects in their culture (e.g., ancestor worship and fear of the dead) without any stress, as long as the incompatibles are not brought into association. *The issue of congruity arises whenever a message is received which relates two or more objects of judgment via an assertion.*

The most simple assertion is merely a *descriptive statement:* "Chinese cooking is good," "Jefferson was right," "This neurotic modern art." To the extent that the evaluative location of a particular qualifier differs from that of the thing qualified, there is generated some pressure toward congruity. Similar pressure is generated by ordinary *statements of classification:* "Senator McCarthy is a Catholic," "Tom is an ex-con," "Cigarettes contain nicotine." To the extent that the evaluative locations of instance and class are different, some degree of incongruity exists. A more complex situation is that in which *a source makes an assertion about a concept:* "University President Bans Research on Krebiozen," "Communists like strong labor unions." This is the most commonly studied situation, and one for which we have some empirical data against which to test our hypotheses. There are more complicated assertions, of course — for example, where one source states that another has such and such an attitude toward something, "McCarthy Accuses Atom Scientist of Communist Sympathy." We have not yet attempted to extend our principles to this level of complexity; it seems likely, however, that favorableness of attitude toward McCarthy would influence credulity for the core assertion, "Atom Scientist Sympathizes with Communism."

The source of an assertion may be *explicit,* as in the examples above, or *implicit,* as in the following: "Farmers said to make unfair demands for profits." The source may be *internal* to the message, as in "Truman praises labor movement," or *external* to the message per se, as happens whenever a palpably present individual makes an assertion about something (e.g., if I tell a student that such and such a course is valuable). Similarly, the assertion itself may be an explicit, linguistic statement of evaluation or an implicit (behavioral or situational) statement.

A newsphoto of Mrs. Roosevelt smiling and shaking hands with a little colored boy may be just as effective in setting up pressures toward congruity as an explicit linguistic statement on her part. Implicit positive assertions of relation between two objects of judgment are embodied in such *actions* as cooperating, helping, saving, smiling at, giving, supporting and the like and in such *situations* as coming or being together, showing common direction, being given the classification and the like — to have Russia support India on some U.N. issue, or to have it said that Russians and Indians are both Asiatic peoples, is as much a positive assertion as an outright verbal statement by Russia (source) in favor of India (concept). Implicit negative assertions are embodied in such actions as competing, hindering, frowning upon, taking from, resisting, and the like and in such situations as moving or being apart, showing opposed directions, being given different classifications and the like — to say that our State Department "views with concern" certain actions of the French Government, or to point out that England is a democracy while Spain is totalitarian, are negative assertions of relationship.

(2) *Directions of congruence and incongruence.* To predict the direction of attitude change from this general principle it is necessary to take into account simultaneously the existing attitudes toward each of the objects of judgment prior to reception of the message and the nature of the assertion which is embodied in the message. Attitudes and assertions both can be specified as positive $(+)$, neutral (0), and negative $(-)$. In indicating congruence relations, we may use the following general paradigm: *if* an individual holds such and such attitudes toward two associated objects of judgment, *then* such an assertion of relation is either congruent or incongruent. The following table summarizes the possible congruity relations that may exist when one object of judgment as a *source* makes an assertion about another object of judgment as a *concept,* this being the situation for which we already have experimental data:

TABLE 1

If Existing Attitude toward			A CONGRUENT		AN INCONGRUENT
		then		*and*	
SOURCE (*and*) CONCEPT			ASSERTION		ASSERTION
is: $+$	$+$	is:	$+$	is:	$-$
$+$	$-$		$-$		$+$
$-$	$+$		$-$		$+$
$-$	$-$		$+$		$-$

FOR EISENHOWER $(+)$ *to come out in favor of* FREEDOM OF THE PRESS $(+)$ is, of course, congruent with the existing frame of reference of most people in this country, but for THE DAILY WORKER (−) to *speak in favor of* FREEDOM OF THE PRESS — which it has — is attitudinally incongruent, since a bad source should not be capable of favoring something we consider good. On the other hand, THE DAILY WORKER (−) could *sponsor* FREE LOVE (−) and be congruent, while for EISENHOWER (+) to even suggest that he *favored* FREE LOVE (−) would be most uncongruent. In other words, in this simplest of states in which human thinking operates, sources we like should always sponsor ideas we like and denounce ideas we're against, and vice versa.

The situations described in Table 1 are extreme, in that all of the attitudes involved are polar, and as such they indicate the directions that *are* congruent. Now, when the existing attitude toward one of the objects of judgment is neutral and the other polar, we must speak of what directions *would be* congruent. If, for example, a favorable source like EISENHOWER were to make a favorable assertion about the MINISTER FROM SIAM (a neutral notion to most of us), it *would be congruent if* the latter were also favorable — and hence pressure is generated toward attitude change in this direction. In the situations shown in Table 2, given the known polar evaluation of one object of

TABLE 2

If the Existing Attitude toward ONE OBJECT OF JUDGMENT (source or concept)	*and* the ASSERTION	*then* the situation would be congruent *if* THE OTHER OBJECT OF JUDGMENT (source or concept)
is: +	is: +	were: +
+	−	−
−	+	−
−	−	+

judgment and the nature of the assertion, the direction of congruence for the other (neutral) object of judgment is completely determined, and pressure toward attitude change must be in this direction. If PRAVDA (−) *sponsors* GRADUAL DISARMAMENT (0), the pressure is such as to make the relatively neutral notion of disarmament *less* favorable; similarly, if a PROFESSOR (0) as a source *favors* PREMARITAL SEXUAL RELATIONS (−) as making for better marriages, it is the PROFESSOR that becomes less favorable. Conversely, for our neutral PROFESSOR (0) to *speak out against* MORAL DEPRAVITY (−) must have the effect of raising his esteem (this is the familiar "I am against sin" technique).

When *both* objects of judgment are neutral, there is no question of congruence between them, and movement is determined solely by the nature of the assertion, e.g., this becomes a case of simple qualification or classification. If MR. JONES *denounces* MR. SMITH, neither of whom is known, there is presumably some negative pressure on MR. SMITH by virtue of the sheer devaluation of "being denounced." Since the evaluation applies to the concept and not the source, the effect should be chiefly upon the concept. We shall find evidence for such an "assertion factor" in the available data.

The directions of congruence when both objects of judgment are polar (Table 1), when one is polar and the other neutral (Table 2), and when both are neutral have been stated and illustrated. We may now make a general statement governing the direction of congruence which will hold for any object of judgment, source or concept, and any type of assertion.

I. *Whenever one object of judgment is associated with another by an assertion, its congruent position along the evaluative dimension is always that equal in degree of polarization (p) to the other object of judgment and in either the same (positive assertion) or opposite (negative assertion) evaluative direction.*

Figure 1 provides some graphic illustrations of this and the following principles. Since the measuring instrument which has been used in our quantitative work so far (the semantic differential) treats the evaluative dimension as a 7-step scale with "4" defined as the neutral point, we have three degrees of polarization in each direction, e.g., + 3, + 2, + 1, 0, − 1, − 2, − 3. In example (1), we have a positive assertion (indicated by the + on the bar connecting source and concept) associating two equally favorable objects of judgments; in this situation maximum congruence already exists. Maximum congruence also exists in example (8), where equally polarized concepts in opposite directions are related by a negative assertion. In all of the other illustrations given, the existing positions are not those of maximum congruence, and those positions which would be maximally congruent for each object of judgment are shown by dashed circles. In situation (5), for example, a congruent source would be at − 2 or a congruent concept would be at − 3, given the favorable assertion between two negative items. Note that this initial operation in predicting attitude change implies measurement or inference of the existing attitudes toward the related objects of judgment at the time the message is received.

(3) *Magnitude and distribution of pressure toward congruity.* About the only principle available relating to the magnitude of attitude change is to the effect that susceptibility to change varies inversely with existing strength of attitude. This appears as an impirical generalization, unsupported by any general theory, but it is substantiated by a considerable number of experiments. However, as we shall see, this law runs into several difficulties — it does not take into account relations between objects of judgment, it fails to differentiate between movements in the direction of increased polarization and movements in the direction of decreased polarization, and so on. On the basis of two

principles — one of which specifies the *amount* of pressure toward congruity available and the other of which specifies its *distribution* — we shall try to derive detailed predictions as to amount and direction of attitude change under all possible conditions of object evaluation and assertion.

Knowing the existing locations of objects of judgment along the evaluative dimension as well as the locations of maximum congruence under the given conditions (by applying Principle I), it becomes possible to state the amount and direction of application of total pressure toward congruity.

II. *The total pressure toward congruity (P) for a given object of judgment associated with another by an assertion is equal to the difference, in attitude scale units, between its existing location and its location of maximum congruence along the evaluative dimension, the sign of this pressure being positive (+) when the location of congruence is more favorable than the existing location and being negative (−) when the location of congruence is less favorable than the existing location.*

For example (3) in Figure 1, the total pressure toward congruity available for the source is − 2 units and for the concept is + 2 units. As can be seen by inspection of these examples, the total pressures toward

Fig. 1.

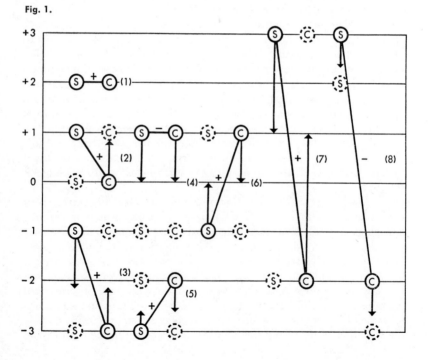

congruity for both objects associated by an assertion *are always equal in magnitude,* although they may be the same or different in sign. The upper figures in each cell of Tables 4 (SOURCES) and 5 (CONCEPTS) give the total pressures and directions of application for all possible relations among sources and concepts and both types of assertions. These computations are based upon the assumption of a 7-step scale with three degrees of polarization possible in each evaluative direction; they may be treated as general index numbers.

The third principle with which we shall operate incorporates the common notion that intense attitudes are more resistant to change, but does so in a way which generates more detailed predictions.

III. *The total pressure toward congruity (P) is distributed between the objects of judgment associated by an assertion in inverse proportion to their separate degrees of polarization* (p_1, p_2).

In other words, relatively less polarized objects of judgment, when associated with relatively more polarized objects of judgment, absorb proportionately greater amounts of the pressure toward congruity. In example (1) in Figure 1 (e.g., ENGLAND + 2 *favors* FREE TRADE + 2), there is no incongruity and hence no pressure toward attitude change. In example (2), all of the pressure is exerted upon the neutral concept (e.g., FRANCE + 1 *favors* ESPERANTO 0), but the total positive pressure is only one unit. Solid arrows indicate the direction and magnitude of predicted change. In example (3), the source must absorb twice as much pressure as the concept, and in a negative rather than positive direction (e.g., BULGARIA −1 *favors* THOUGHT CONTROL −3). The unexpected prediction here, that the even more unfavorable concept, THOUGHT-CONTROL, actually becomes a little *less* unfavorable under these conditions derives directly from the theoretical model and will be discussed later. In example (4), the negative assertion between two equally and slightly favorable objects produces equal negative pressure toward congruity (e.g., FRANCE + 1 *is against* UNIFICATION OF EUROPE + 1), and both objects decrease somewhat in favor. The small amount of pressure toward congruity in example (5) is exerted more toward further lowering a somewhat unfavorable concept and only slightly toward making the extremely unfavorable source less unfavorable (e.g., RUSSIANS − 3 *plan* SOUTH AMERICAN REVOLUTIONS − 2). In example (6) the favorable assertion associating two equally polarized, but oppositely evaluated, objects of judgment has the net effect of neutralizing them (e.g., BULGARIA − 1 *favors* UNIFICATION OF EUROPE + 1. A similar neutralizing effect is predicted for situation (7), but the pressure is greater on the less polarized concept than on the more polarized source (e.g., EISENHOWER + 3 *praises* SOUTH AMERICAN REVOLUTIONS − 2). In the final example, the negative assertion is largely congruent with existing attitudes, and hence there is only a slight change predicted, again greater in magnitude on the less polarized (e.g., EISENHOWER $+3$ *denounces* EGYPTIAN CONTROL OF SUEZ -2). Again note the predicted slight devaluation of the highly favorable object of judgment; it is as if EISENHOWER loses a little prestige by coming out against something that is not bad enough.

Given a generalized measuring instrument which provides quantitative units of attitude for any object of judgment, it becomes possible to determine (a) existing evaluative locations, (b) locations of maximal congruity, and hence (c) the total pressure toward congruity available with respect to each object of judgment.

Up to this point, we have been talking as though we could assume *complete credulity* of the message on the part of the receiver, a condition that exists only rarely, in all probability, for incongruous messages. Certainly, when presented with the incongruous message, EISENHOWER *sponsors* COMMUNISM, in an experimental situation, very few subjects are going to give it full credulence. If we are going to make predictions, it is apparent that the variable of credulity must be taken into account.

IV. *The amount of incredulity produced when one object of judgment is associated with another by an assertion is a positively accelerated function of the amount of incongruity which exists and operates to decrease attitude change, completely eliminating change when maximal.*

Incongruity only exists when similarly evaluated concepts are associated by negative assertions or when oppositely evaluated concepts are associated by positive assertions. Within these situations, the *amount* of this correction is assumed to increase with the degree of incongruousness, e.g., with the total pressure toward congruity available. It is assumed that no incongruity, and hence no incredulity, can exist where one of the objects of judgment is neutral, e.g., EISENHOWER may come out either for or against a neutral concept like ST. LAWRENCE WATERWAY without the issue of incredulity arising.

But incredulity, to the extent it is present, will not only operate to damp changes in attitude but should also appear in expressions of disbelief and rationalization.

[The authors here derive specific predictive formulae and introduce experimental data on these propositions.]

▲ CARL I. HOVLAND

▲ ARTHUR A. LUMSDAINE

▲ FRED D. SHEFFIELD

The Effect of Presenting "One Side" versus

"Both Sides" in Changing Opinions

on a Controversial Subject

THE PROBLEM

In designing Army orientation programs, an issue which was frequently debated by the producers was: When the weight of evidence supports the main thesis being presented, is it more effective to present only the materials supporting the point being made, or is it better to introduce also the arguments of those opposed to the point being made?

The procedure of presenting only the arguments supporting the thesis is often employed on the grounds that when the preponderance of the arguments supports the point being made, presenting opposing arguments or misconceptions merely raises doubts in the minds of the audience. On the other hand, the procedure of presenting the arguments for "both sides" may be supported on grounds of fairness — the right of the members of the audience to have access to all relevant materials in making up their minds. Furthermore, there is reason to expect that audience members already opposed to the point of view being presented may be "rehearsing" their own arguments while the topic is being presented and in any case will be distracted and antagonized by the omission of the arguments on their side. Thus, according to proponents of the two-sided arguments, presentation of the *audi-*

▲ Based on research by the Research Branch of the War Department's Information and Education Division, this selection appeared in the authors' volume, *Experiments on Mass Communication,* published and copyright by Princeton University Press (Princeton, 1949). It is here reprinted by permission of the copyright holders. The conclusions in this article should be supplemented by later data discussed in Hovland, Janis, and Kelley, *Communication and Persuasion* (New Haven: Yale University Press, 1953). Dr. Hovland and Dr. Sheffield are members of the psychology faculty at Yale. Dr. Lumsdaine is director of the Chanute laboratory of the Human Resources Research Center, United States Air Force.

ence's arguments at the outset possibly would be expected to produce better reception of the arguments which it is desired to convey.

The present experiment was set up to provide information on the relative effectiveness of these two alternative types of program content, in relation to the variable of men's initial position for or against the position advocated in the program.

METHOD OF STUDY

The Two Programs Used

At the time the experiment was being planned (early in 1945) it was reported that Army morale was being adversely affected by over-optimism about an early end to the war. A directive was issued by the Army to impress upon troops a conception of the magnitude of the job remaining to be done in defeating the Axis. This furnished a topic on which arguments were available on both sides but where the majority of military experts believed the preponderance of evidence supported one side. It was therefore chosen for experiment.

Radio transcriptions were used to present the two programs, primarily because of the simplicity with which they could be prepared in alternative forms. The basic outline of the programs' content was prepared by the Experimental Section of the Research Branch. All materials used were official releases from the Office of War Information and the War Department. The final writing and production of the programs were carried out by the Armed Forces Radio Service.

Both of the two programs compared here were in the form of a commentator's analysis of the Pacific war. The commentator's conclusion was that the job of finishing the war would be tough and that it would take at least two years after V-E Day.

"One Side." The major topics included in the program which presented *only* the arguments indicating that the war would be long (hereafter labeled *Program A*) were: distance problems and other logistical difficulties in the Pacific; the resources and stock piles in the Japanese Empire; the size and quality of the main bulk of the Japanese army that we had not yet met in battle; and the determination of the Japanese people. This program ran for about fifteen minutes.

"Both Sides." The other program (*Program B*) ran for about nineteen minutes and presented all of these same difficulties in exactly the same way. The additional four minutes in this latter program were devoted to considering arguments for the other side of the picture — U. S. advantages and Japanese weaknesses such as: our naval victories and superiority; our previous progress despite a two-front war; our ability to concentrate all our forces on Japan after V-E Day; Japan's shipping losses; Japan's manufacturing inferiority; and the future damage to be expected from our expanding air war. These additional points were woven into the context of the rest of the program, each point being discussed where it was relevant.

It should be pointed out that while Program B gave facts on *both sides* of the question, it did not give equal space to both sides, nor did it attempt to compare the case for thinking it would be a long war with the *strongest possible case* for believing it would be an easy victory and a short war. It took exactly the same stand as that taken by Program A — namely, that the war would be difficult and would require at least two years. The difference was that Program B mentioned the opposite arguments (e.g., U. S. advantages) whenever they were relevant. In effect it argued that the job would be difficult, even taking into account our advantages and the Japanese weaknesses.

Design for the Experiment

The general plan of the experiment was to give a preliminary "opinion survey" to determine the men's initial opinions about the Pacific war and then to remeasure their opinions at a later time, after the transcriptions had been played to them in the course of their orientation meetings. In this way the *changes* in their opinions from "before" to "after" could be determined. A control group, which heard *no* transcription, was also surveyed as a means of determining any changes in response that might occur during the time interval due to causes other than the transcriptions — such as the impact of war news from the Pacific.

a. Anonymity of response and avoiding suspicion of "guinea-pigging." It was considered necessary to obtain opinions *anonymously*, and also to measure the effects of the program without awareness on the part of the men that an experiment was in progress. These precautions were dictated by the type of effect being studied — it was felt that if the men either thought their responses were identified by name or if they knew they were being "tested," some men might give "proper" or otherwise distorted answers rather than answers expressing their true opinions in the matter. In the experiment reported here, the methods of achieving this lack of awareness and assurance of anonymity were inherent partly in the measuring instrument and partly in the design and administration of the experiment and will be mentioned as these subjects are discussed. These precautions were taken mainly on *a priori* grounds and they do not indicate that evidence for any tendency to be suspicious was actually found.

b. The measuring instrument. The questionnaire used in the preliminary "survey" (before hearing the transcription) consisted mainly of check-list questions plus a few questions in which men were asked to write in their own answers. The content of questions that formed the measuring instrument *per se* will be indicated later in presenting the results of the study. In addition, the preliminary "survey" contained *background* items for obtaining information about the individual's education, age, etc., and what might be called "camouflage" items — questions dealing with opinions not related to the orientation topic. The latter were not necessary for the experimental measurements *per se* but were used to give scope to the "survey" and prevent a concentration of items dealing with material to be covered in the transcriptions. This was done partly to help make the survey seem realistic to the men but mainly to avoid "sensitizing" them to the topic of the subsequently presented orientation material through placing too much emphasis on it in the survey.

c. "Pretesting." One of the important steps in preparing the items used in questionnaires was what may be termed *"qualitative pretesting"* of the wording and meaning of the questionnaire items. This consisted of face-to-face interviewing of soldiers, with the questions asked orally by the interviewer in some cases or read by the respondent in others. In this way, misinterpretations of the questions and misunderstood words were uncovered and at the same time natural wording and natural categories of response were revealed. In addition to its value in improving the wording of questions, this pretest also served as an important method of helping to determine the men's opinions on the relevant topics so that the arguments and appeals to be used in the programs could be geared to the men's opinions and information. To provide more extensive data for this purpose the interviewing was followed up by the administration of a preliminary questionnaire using a sample of about 200 soldiers. Liberal use of "free-answer" questions was made in this questionnaire in order to get detailed information concerning men's reasons for expecting a long or a short war.

d. Administration of the experiment. For proper administration of the experiments there were three major requirements: presentation of the transcriptions under realistic conditions, preventing the men in the sample from realizing that the experiment was in progress, and getting honest answers in the questionnaires. For realism in presentation, the transcriptions for the experimental groups were incorporated into the training program and scheduled as part of the weekly orientation hour. This not only insured realistic presentation but also helped to avoid indicating that effects of the transcriptions were being tested.

The preliminary "survey" had been presented as being part of a War Department survey "to find out how a cross section of soldiers felt about various subjects connected with the war," with examples being given of previous Research Branch surveys and how they were used. Questionnaires were administered to all the men in a company at once, the men being assembled in mess halls and other convenient buildings for the purpose. The questionnaires were administered by "class leaders" selected and trained for the job from among the enlisted personnel working at the camp. In an introductory explanation of the survey the class leader stressed the importance of the survey and the anonymity of the answers. No camp officers were present at these meetings and the men were assured that the surveys went directly to

Washington and that no one at the camp would get a chance to see what they had written.

e. Problems in the administration of the second questionnaire. To prevent suspicion of an "experiment" arising from the administration of two surveys within a short space of time, the second questionnaire differed from the first one both in its form and its announced purpose. Thus the first questionnaire was given as a general War Department "survey," while the second one was given during the orientation meetings to "find out what men thought of the transcriptions" (or, in the control group, "what they thought of their orientation meetings").

The preliminary "survey" was administered during the first week of April, 1945, to eight quartermaster training companies. During the following week eight platoons, one chosen at random from each of the eight companies, heard Program A (which presented only one side) during their individual orientation meetings. Another group of eight platoons, similarly chosen, heard Program B (which presented both arguments). Immediately after the program the men filled out the second questionnaire, ostensibly for the purpose of letting the people who made the programs know what the men thought of it. Included in this second questionnaire, with appropriate transitional questions, were some of the same questions that had been included in the earlier survey, asking the men how they personally sized up the Pacific war. A third group of eight platoons served as the control with no program. They filled out a similar questionnaire during their orientation meeting, which, in addition to asking the same questions on the Pacific war, asked what they thought of their orientation meetings and what they would like in future orientation meetings. For the control group, the latter questions — in lieu of the questions about the transcriptions — were represented to the men as the main "purpose" of the questionnaire.

While 24 platoons were used for this experiment, the units reported at only about 70 percent strength at the preliminary survey and at the orientation meetings. The "shrinkage" was therefore quite large as to number of men present *both* times, and the sample available for "before-after" analysis was consequently small (a total of 625 men, with 214 in each experimental group and the remaining 197 men in the control group). In view of the rapidly changing picture in the Pacific, however, it was considered inadvisable to repeat the experiment at another camp.

RESULTS

The following results are based on an analysis of the responses of men whose initial survey could be matched with their questionnaire given in the orientation meetings. While all of the questionnaires were anonymous, the "before" and "after" questionnaires of the same individuals could be matched on the basis of answers to such background questions as years of schooling, date of birth, etc.

Effects on Opinions of Men Who Initially Estimated a Long War and on Those Who Initially Estimated a Short War

The main question used to evaluate the effectiveness of the two presentation methods was one asking the men for their best guess as to the probable length of the Pacific war after V-E Day. The results of this question were tabulated in terms of changes in estimate of the probable duration of the Pacific war. A change was defined as a difference of one-half year or more between the man's estimate in the earlier survey as compared with his estimate after hearing the program.

The results are analyzed in terms of *"net effect."* Some men changed to a longer estimate and some changed to a shorter estimate; the "net change" for a group is the proportion changing to a longer estimate minus the number changing to a shorter estimate. However, some changes in each direction also occurred among the men in the control group who heard no program. The latter changes are attributable to the imperfect reliability of the question and also to the fact that, during the one week period between the before and after tests, war news and varying interpretations of this news probably affected the men's opinions to some extent. Therefore, in order to get *net effect* of the program on a given group, the net change among the program men had to be corrected by subtracting from it the net change that occurred among men in the control group.

As was mentioned earlier, one of the arguments against presenting only one side of an issue rests on the anticipated adverse effect upon the individuals opposed to the point being presented. Therefore, the results were analyzed separately for men who were initially "favorable" and those initially "unfavorable" to the stand taken by the programs. The basis for distinguishing these two groups was whether their initial estimate of the length of the war was less than two years, or was two years or more. A two-year estimate was taken as the criterion primarily because this was the minimum estimate given by the commentator in the transcriptions, and thus served to distinguish between those who favored and those who disagreed with his point of view.

The net effects of the two ways of presenting the orientation material are shown below for these two subgroups of men: those initially estimating a war of *two or more years* (the "favorable" group) and those initially estimating a war of less than two years (the "unfavorable" group).

The following chart shows that the *net effects* were different for the two ways of presenting the orientation material depending on the initial stand of the listener. The program giving only one side was more effective for men initially favoring the stand, that is, for the men who agreed with the point of view of the program that the war would take at least two years. On the other hand, the program giving some of the U. S. advantages in addition to the difficulties was more effective for men initially opposed, that is, for men who expected a war of less than two years. In the present sample there happened to be about

Net Effectiveness of Program A and Program B for Men with Initially Unfavorable and Men with Initially Favorable Attitudes

Among men whose initial estimate was *"Unfavorable"*
(Estimated a short war)

	Net percent of men changing to a longer estimate
PROGRAM A (one side only)	36%
PROGRAM B (both sides)	48%
Difference: (B−A)	12%

Among men whose initial estimate was *"Favorable"*
(Estimated a long war)

	Net percent of men changing to a longer estimate
PROGRAM A (one side only)	52%
PROGRAM B (both sides)	23%
Difference: (B−A)	−29%

three men with an initially unfavorable attitude to every man with an initially favorable attitude, so that the over-all net effect on the *total* group was almost exactly the same for the two programs.

Effects on Opinions of Men with Different Years of Schooling

When the results were broken down according to years of schooling it was found that the program which presented both sides was more effective with better educated men and the program which presented

Net Effectiveness of Program A and Program B for Men of Different Educational Backgrounds

Among men who did not graduate from high school

	Net percent of men changing to a longer estimate
PROGRAM A (one side only)	46%
PROGRAM B (both sides)	31%
Difference: (B−A)	−15%

Among men who graduated from high school

	Net percent of men changing to a longer estimate
PROGRAM A (one side only)	35%
PROGRAM B (both sides)	49%
Difference: (B−A)	14%

one side was more effective with less educated men. The results are shown below comparing the effects on men who did not graduate from high school with the effects on high school graduates.[1] This breakdown by education divides the sample into approximately equal halves.

The results show that the program giving both sides was *less* effective with the nongraduates but *more* effective with the high school graduates.

Effects When Both Education and Initial Estimates Are Considered

The differential effects shown above are for the educational subgroups as a whole, without regard to the differences between men initially favoring and initially opposing the stand taken by the programs within the educational subgroups. An analysis was made of the effects for these further subgroupings within the educational groups. However, this further break divides the total group of men into eight subgroups, some of which are very small and are consequently subject to large sampling errors. This fact should be kept in mind in interpreting the net effects in the table on the next page.

It can be seen that a greater net effect was obtained for the program covering both sides in all of the subgroups except that of the nongraduates who initially expected a war of two or more years. As mentioned above, the results are very unstable because of the small samples in the subgroups. This is particularly true of the subgroups with an initial estimate of two or more years since only about one man in four guessed a war of two or more years in the preliminary survey. However, the difference between the results from the two kinds of program is so large for the nongraduates initially expecting a war of two or more years that even though the number of cases is very small it is very unlikely that a difference this large would be obtained due to sampling error. (The statistical probability based on comparison of percentages for samples of the size used is less than one chance in 100.)

Conclusions Suggested Thus Far

The conclusions suggested by the results presented so far in this report may be summarized as follows: Giving the strong points for the "other side" can make an argument more effective at getting across its message, particularly for the better educated men and for the men who are already opposed to the stand taken. This difference in effectiveness, however, is likely to be reversed for the less educated men, and in the extreme case the material giving both sides may have a negative effect on poorly educated men already convinced of the stand

---

[1] The "Did Not Graduate" group included those whose schooling was limited to grammar school plus those who entered high school but did not finish. The "Graduated from High School" group included all high school graduates, regardless of whether they went on to college or not.

taken by a program. (This would seem especially likely if the strong points for the other side had not previously been known to, or considered by, this latter group of men.) From these results it would be expected that the total effect of either kind of program on the group *as a whole* would depend on the group's educational composition and on the initial division of opinion in the group.

Men's Evaluation of the Factual Coverage

One factor that should tend to make a presentation that takes into account both sides of an issue more effective than a presentation covering only one side is that the men would believe the former treatment more impartial and authoritative.

In the present study, however, the men as a whole did not consider the factual coverage more complete in the program giving our advantages in addition to the difficulties we face.

Net Effectiveness of Program A and Program B for Men with Initially Unfavorable and Men with Initially Favorable Attitudes, Shown Separately for Men with Different Educational Backgrounds

A. Effects among Men Who Did Not Graduate from High School

Among men whose initial estimate was *"Unfavorable"*
(Estimated a short war)

	Net percent of men changing to a longer estimate
PROGRAM A (one side only)	44%
PROGRAM B (both sides)	51%
Difference: (B−A)	7%

Among men whose initial estimate was *"Favorable"*
(Estimated a long war)

	Net percent of men changing to a longer estimate
PROGRAM A (one side only)	64%
PROGRAM B (both sides)	−3%
Difference: (B−A)	−67%

B. Effects among High School Graduates

Among men whose initial estimate was *"Unfavorable"*
(Estimated a short war)

	Net percent of men changing to a longer estimate
PROGRAM A (one side only)	30%
PROGRAM B (both sides)	44%
Difference: (B−A)	14%

Among men whose initial estimate was *"Favorable"*
(Estimated a long war)

Net percent of men
changing to a longer estimate

PROGRAM A (one side only) 39%
PROGRAM B (both sides) 54%
Difference: (B−A) 15%

Evaluation of Factual Coverage by Men Hearing Program A and Program B

Net percent of men saying
that the program did a good
job of giving the facts on
the Pacific War

Among those hearing

PROGRAM A (one side only) 61%
PROGRAM B (both sides) 54%

Net percent of men saying
that the program took all
of the important facts into
account

Among those hearing

PROGRAM A (one side only) 48%
PROGRAM B (both sides) 42%

It can be seen above that the factual coverage was not considered better in the program giving our advantages as well as the difficulties. If anything the difference was in the opposite direction.

The explanation of this unexpected result apparently lies in the fact that *both* programs omitted any mention of Russia as a factor in the Pacific war, and *this omission seemed more glaring in the presentation that committed itself to covering both sides of the question.* At the time that the Pacific war was chosen as the orientation subject for the experiment it was recognized that a weakness of this topic was that no stand could be taken on the help to be expected from Russia. Thus the difference between the two presentations was necessarily reduced because they *both* failed to mention an important argument on the "other side," namely that Russia might come in. It was not anticipated, however, that this omission would be more noticeable in the program that otherwise covered both sides. But that this happened is suggested by the evidence below:

Included in the program questionnaire was the following "write-in" question:

"What facts or topics that you think are important to the war with Japan are not mentioned in the program?"

The percentages writing in that aid or possible aid from Russia was not mentioned in the program was 23 for the program giving both sides and only 13 for the program giving just one side. This difference was *even more pronounced among groups that would be expected to be especially sensitive to this omission,* such as men who were initially optimistic about length of the war, men with better education, and men who had expected a great deal of help from Russia in the job against Japan.

Separate Analysis of Data for Men Most Likely to Note Omission of Russian Aid

Evidence that omitting to mention help from Russia detracted more from the program giving both sides than from the one-sided program was obtained from a separate analysis of (*a*) the evaluations of the factual coverage, and (*b*) the effects of the program on opinions, *among the men who would seem to be most likely to note the omission of possible aid.* These were the men who, in the preliminary survey, counted on a great deal of help from Russia and also expected a war of less than two years.[2] The results for the two programs on these men are shown below. For comparison, the results are also shown for the men who expected a war of less than two years but did not count on a great deal of help from Russia.

Evaluation of Factual Coverage for Men with Initially Unfavorable Opinions (i.e., optimistic about length of war)

A. Proportion of men who *say the program did a good job of giving the facts on the Pacific War*

Among men who *counted* on a great deal of Russian help[a]

Among those hearing	Percent saying it did a good job of giving the facts
PROGRAM A (one side only)	53%
PROGRAM B (both sides)	37%
Difference: (B−A)	−16%

Among men who *did not count* on a great deal of Russian help[b]

Among those hearing	Percent saying it did a good job of giving the facts
PROGRAM A (one side only)	56%
PROGRAM B (both sides)	61%
Difference: (B−A)	5%

[2] The breakdown according to expected help from Russia was based on a question asking the men how much help against Japan they expected from our allies and asking those checking "a great deal" to write in the names of the allies from which they expected a great deal of help. In the present sample, 41 percent of the men checked "a great deal" and wrote in "Russia" as one of the allies from which a great deal of help was expected.

B. Proportion of men who *say the program took all of the important facts into account*

Among men who *counted* on a great deal of Russian help[a]

Among those hearing	Percent saying it took all important facts into account
PROGRAM A (one side only)	46%
PROGRAM B (both sides)	28%
Difference: (B−A)	−18%

Among men who *did not count* on a great deal of Russian help[b]

Among those hearing	Percent saying it took all important facts into account
PROGRAM A (one side only)	44%
PROGRAM B (both sides)	46%
Difference: (B−A)	2%

[a] N's: 68 for Program A; 71 for Program B.
[b] N's: 91 for Program A; 80 for Program B.

a. Differences in evaluation of factual coverage (among men most likely to note omission of Russian aid). The implication of these results is that the authenticity of Program B (which presented both sides) suffered from the omission of the subject of Russia.

The above results suggest that if the program covering both sides had dealt with the subject of Russia, it might have been considered more complete in its factual coverage by the men as a whole. This implication received corroboration from the fact that in a fairly large-scale pretest of the two programs, conducted at a time when possible aid from Russia was a less important news topic, *the program covering both sides was considered more complete in its factual coverage.* This pretest was conducted on 347 infantry reinforcements in March, 1945, and practically no difference was obtained between the two programs in the percentages of men noting the omission of Russian aid. In the present study the programs were played during the second week of April, less than a week after the Russians announced that they would not renew their nonaggression pact with Japan.

b. Differences in effect on estimates of length of war (among men most likely to note omission of Russian aid). Not only did the omission of Russia affect men's evaluation of the factual coverage in Program B, but it also appeared to reduce the effect of the program on the men's estimates of the length of the war. Evidence on the latter point comes from an analysis of the *net effects* of the programs on opinions of men in the same subgroups as in the preceding chart. The results of this analysis are shown below:

Net Effectiveness of Program A and Program B for Men with Initially Unfavorable Opinions
(i.e., optimistic about length of war)

Among men who *counted* on a great deal of Russian help[a]

Among those hearing	Percent of men changing to a longer estimate
PROGRAM A (one side only)	36%
PROGRAM B (both sides)	43%
Difference: (B—A)	7%

Among men who *did not count* on a great deal of Russian help[b]

Among those hearing	Percent of men changing to a longer estimate
PROGRAM A (one side only)	36%
PROGRAM B (both sides)	52%
Difference: (B—A)	16%

[a] N's: 66 for Program A; 71 for Program B.
[b] N's: 86 for Program A; 79 for Program B.

These results indicate that among the men for whom the presentation with both sides is most effective (i.e., the men initially holding unfavorable opinions) the advantage of the "both sides" presentation was less among those counting on a great deal of help from Russia than among those not expecting much help. These findings strongly suggest that the effects of the program giving some of the "other side" would have been even greater on those opposed to the stand taken if *all* of the other side could have been covered.

All of the results in this section seem to support one important conclusion, namely, that if a presentation supporting a particular conclusion attempts to take both sides of the issue into account, it must include *all* of the important negative arguments or the presentation may "boomerang" by failing to live up to the expectation of impartiality and completeness. Apparently a one-sided presentation in which the conclusion is stated in advance and the reasons for this conclusion are then given will be accepted as the argument for a given point of view without much loss of authenticity resulting from failure to cover the other side. However, if a presentation commits itself to taking everything into account, either by announcing this in advance or by actually covering parts of each side of the issue, it will seem less authentic than a single-sided presentation if any important facts known to the audience are not included in the discussion, and its effectiveness at changing opinions will be reduced *among those who are most aware of the point omitted.*

SUMMARY

1. Presenting the arguments on both sides of an issue was found to be more effective than giving only the arguments supporting the point being made, in the case of individuals who were *initially opposed* to the point of view being presented.

2. For men who were *already convinced* of the point of view being presented, however, the inclusion of arguments on both sides was less effective for the group as a whole than presenting only the arguments favoring the general position being advocated.

3. Better-educated men were more favorably affected by presentation of both sides; poorly educated men were more affected by the communication which used only supporting arguments.

4. The group for which the presentation giving both sides was *least* effective was the group of poorly educated men who were already convinced of the point of view being advocated.

5. An important incidental finding was that omission of a relevant argument was more noticeable and detracted more from effectiveness in the presentation using arguments on both sides than in the presentation in which only one side was discussed.

▲ CARL I. HOVLAND

▲ WALTER WEISS

$\mathcal{T}$he Influence of Source Credibility

on Communication Effectiveness

An important but little-studied factor in the effectiveness of communication is the attitude of the audience toward the communicator. Indirect data on this problem come from studies of "prestige" in which subjects are asked to indicate their agreement or disagreement with statements which are attributed to different individuals.[1] The extent of agreement is usually higher when the statements are attributed to "high prestige" sources. There are few studies in which an identical communication is presented by different communicators and the relative effects on opinion subsequently measured without explicit reference to the position taken by the communicator. Yet the latter research setting may be a closer approximation of the real-life situation to which the results of research are to be applied.

In one of the studies reported by Hovland, Lumsdaine and Sheffield, the effects of a communication were studied without reference to the source of the items comprising the opinion questionnaire. They found that opinion changes following the showing of an Army orientation film were smaller among the members of the audience who believe the purpose of the film was "propagandistic" than among those who believed its purpose "informational."[2] But such a study does not

[1] See e.g. Sherif, M., "An Experimental Study of Stereotypes," *Journal of Abnormal and Social Psychology,* Vol. 29 (1935), pp. 371-375; Lewis, H. B., "Studies in the Principles of Judgments and Attitudes": IV. The Operation of "Prestige Suggestion." *Journal of Social Psychology,* Vol. 14 (1941), pp. 229-256; Asch, S. E., "The Doctrine of Suggestion, Prestige, and Imitation in Social Psychology." *Psychological Review,* Vol. 55 (1948), pp. 250-276.

[2] Hovland, C. I., A. A. Lumsdaine and F. D. Sheffield, *Experiments on Mass Communication.* Princeton: Princeton University Press, 1949, pp. 101f.

▲ This paper appeared in 1951 in the *Public Opinion Quarterly,* published and copyright by the Princeton University Press, and is reprinted here by permission of the copyright holders. Dr. Hovland is a professor of psychology at Yale. Dr. Weiss is a member of the research staff of Boston University.

rule out the possibility that the results could be explained by general predispositional factors; that is, individuals who are "suspicious" of mass-media sources may be generally less responsive to such communications. The present study was designed to minimize the aforementioned methodological difficulties by experimentally controlling the source and by checking the effects of the source in a situation in which the subject's own opinion was obtained without reference to the source.

A second objective of the present study was to investigate the extent to which opinions derived from high and low credibility sources are maintained over a period of time. Hovland, Lumsdaine and Sheffield showed that some opinion changes in the direction of the communicator's position are larger after a lapse of time than immediately after the communication. This they refer to as the "sleeper effect." One hypothesis which they advance for their results is that individuals may be suspicious of the motives of the communicator and initially discount his position, and thus may evidence little or no immediate change in opinion. With the passage of time, however, they may remember and accept *what* was communicated but not remember *who* communicated it. As a result, they may then be more inclined to agree with the position which had been presented by the communicator. In the study referred to, only a single source was used, so no test was available of the differential effects when the source was suspected of having a propagandistic motive and when it was not. The present experiment was designed to test differences in the retention, as well as the acquisition, of identical communications when presented by "trustworthy" and by "untrustworthy" sources.

PROCEDURE

The over-all design of the study was to present an identical communication to two groups, one in which a communicator of a generally "trustworthy" character was used, and the other in which the communicator was generally regarded as "untrustworthy." Opinion questionnaires were administered before the communication, immediately after the communication, and a month after the communication.

Because of the possibility of specific factors affecting the relationship between communicator and content on a single topic, four different topics (with eight different communicators) were used. On each topic two alternative versions were prepared, one presenting the "affirmative" and one the "negative" position on the issue. For each version one "trustworthy" and one "untrustworthy" source were used. The topics chosen were of current interest and of a controversial type so that a fairly even division of opinion among members of the audience was obtained.

The four topics and the communicators chosen to represent "high credibility" and "low credibility" sources were as follows:

	"High Credibility" Source	"Low Credibility" Source
A. *Anti-Histamine Drugs:* Should the anti-histamine drugs continue to be sold without a doctor's prescription?	*New England Journal of Biology and Medicine*	Magazine A* [A mass circulation monthly pictorial magazine]
B. *Atomic Submarines:* Can a practicable atomic-powered submarine be built at the present time?	Robert J. Oppenheimer	*Pravda*
C. *The Steel Shortage:* Is the steel industry to blame for the current shortage of steel?	*Bulletin of National Resources Planning Board*	Writer A* [A widely syndicated anti-labor, anti-New Deal, "rightist" newspaper columnist]
D. *The Future of Movie Theaters:* As a result of TV, will there be a decrease in the number of movie theaters in operation by 1955?	*Fortune* magazine	Writer B* [An extensively syndicated woman movie-gossip columnist]

* The names of one of the magazines and two of the writers used in the study have to be withheld to avoid any possible embarrassment to them. These sources will be referred to hereafter only by the letter designations given.

In some cases the sources were individual writers and in others periodical publications, and some were fictitious (but plausible) and others actual authors or publications.

The "affirmative" and "negative" versions of each article presented an equal number of facts on the topic and made use of essentially the same material. They differed in the emphasis given the material and in the conclusion drawn from the facts. Since there were two versions for each topic and these were prepared in such a way that either of the sources might have written either version, four possible combinations of content and source were available on each topic.

The communication consisted of a booklet containing one article on each of the four different topics, with the name of the author or periodical given at the end of each article. The order of the topics within the booklets was kept constant. Two trustworthy and two untrustworthy sources were included in each booklet. Twenty-four different booklets covered the various combinations used. An example of one such booklet-combination would be:

Topic	Version	Source
The Future of Movie Theaters	Affirmative	*Fortune*
Atomic Submarines	Negative	*Pravda*
The Steel Shortage	Affirmative	*Writer A*
Anti-Histamine Drugs	Negative	*New England Journal of Biology and Medicine*

The questionnaires were designed to obtain data on the amount of factual information acquired from the communication and the extent to which opinion was changed in the direction of the position advocated by the communicator. Information was also obtained on the subject's evaluation of the general trustworthiness of each source, and, in the after-questionnaires, on the recall of the author of each article.

The subjects were college students in an advanced undergraduate course in History at Yale University. The first questionnaire, given five days before the communication, was represented to the students as a general opinion survey being conducted by a "National Opinion Survey Council." The key opinion questions bearing on the topics selected for the communication were scattered through many other unrelated ones. There were also questions asking for the subjects' evaluations of the general trustworthiness of a long list of sources, which included the critical ones used in the communications. This evaluation was based on a 5-point scale ranging from "very trustworthy" to "very untrustworthy."

Since it was desired that the subjects not associate the experiment with the "before" questionnaire, the following arrangement was devised: The senior experimenter was invited to give a guest lecture to the class during the absence of the regular instuctor, five days after the initial questionnaire. His remarks constituted the instructions for the experiment:

Several weeks ago Professor [the regular instructor] asked me to meet with you this morning to discuss some phase of Contemporary Problems. He suggested that one interesting topic would be The Psychology of Communications. This is certainly an important problem, since so many of our attitudes and opinions are based not on direct experience but on what we hear over the radio or read in the newspaper. I finally agreed to take this topic but on the condition that I have some interesting live data on which to base my comments. We therefore agreed to use this period to make a survey of the role of newspaper and magazine reading as a vehicle of communication and then to report on the results and discuss their implications at a later session.

Today, therefore, I am asking you to read a number of excerpts from recent magazine and newspaper articles on controversial topics. The authors have attempted to summarize the best information available, duly taking into account the various sides of the issues. I have chosen up-to-date issues which are currently being widely discussed and ones which are being studied by Gallup, Roper and others interested in public opinion.

Will you please read each article carefully the way you would if you were reading it in your favorite newspaper and magazine. When you finish each article write your name in the lower right hand corner to indicate that you have read it through and then go on to the next. When you finish there will be a short quiz on your reaction to the readings.

Any questions before we begin?

The second questionnaire, handed out immediately after the booklets were collected, differed completely in format from the earlier one.

It contained a series of general questions on the subjects' reactions to the articles, gradually moving toward opinion questions bearing on the content discussed in the articles. At the end of the questionnaire there was a series of fact-quiz items. Sixteen multiple choice questions, four on each content area, were used together with a question calling for the recall of the author of each of the articles.

An identical questionnaire was administered four weeks after the communication. At no prior time had the subjects been forewarned that they would be given this second post-test questionnaire.

A total of 223 subjects provided information which was used in some phase of the analysis. Attendance in the history course was not mandatory and there was considerable shrinkage in the number of students present at all three time periods. For the portions of the analysis requiring before-and-after information, the data derived from 61 students who were present on all three occasions were used. Thus for the main analysis a sample of 244 communications (four for each student) was available. Since different analyses permitted the use of differing numbers of cases, the exact number of instances used in each phase of the analysis is given in each table.

RESULTS

Before proceeding to the main analyses it is important to state the extent to which the sources selected on *a priori* grounds by the experimenters as being of differing credibility were actually reacted to in this manner by the subjects. One item on the questionnaire given before the communication asked the subjects to rate the trustworthiness of each of a series of authors and publications. Figure 1 gives the percentages of subjects who rated each of the sources "trustworthy."

TOPIC	SOURCE	N	PERCENT RATING SOURCE AS TRUSTWORTHY
ANTI-HISTAMINES	NEW ENGL. J. BIOL. & MED.	208	94.7%
	MAGAZINE A	222	5.9%
ATOMIC SUBMARINES	OPPENHEIMER	221	93.7%
	PRAVDA	223	1.3%
STEEL SHORTAGE	BULL. NAT. RES. PLAN. BD.	220	80.9%
	WRITER A	223	17.%
FUTURE OF MOVIES	FORTUNE	222	89.2%
	WRITER B	222	21.2%

Fig. 1. Credibility of sources.

The first source named under each topic had been picked by the experimenters as being of high credibility and the second of low. It will be observed that there is a clear differentiation of the credibility in the direction of the initial selection by the experimenters. The differences between members of each pair are all highly significant (*t's* range from 13 to 20). The results in Figure 1 are based on all of the subjects present when the preliminary questionnaire was administered. The percentages for the smaller sample of subjects present at all three sessions do not differ significantly from those for the group as a whole.

Differences in perception of communication of various audience sub-groups. Following the communication, subjects were asked their opinion about the fairness of the presentation of each topic and the extent to which each communicator was justified in his conclusion. Although the communications being judged were *identical,* there was a marked difference in the way the subjects responded to the "high credibility" and "low credibility" sources. Their evaluations were also affected by their personal opinions on the topic before the communication was ever presented. Audience evaluations of the four communications are presented in Table 1. In 14 of the 16 possible comparisons the "low-credibility" sources are considered less fair or less justified than the corresponding high credibility sources. The differences for the low credibility sources for the individuals initially holding an opinion different from that advocated by the communicator and those for the high credibility sources for individuals who initially held the same position as that advocated by the communicator are significant at less than the .004 level.[3]

EFFECT OF CREDIBILITY OF SOURCE ON ACQUISITION OF INFORMATION AND ON CHANGE IN OPINION

Information. There is no significant difference in the amount of factual information acquired by the subjects when the material is attributed to a high credibility source as compared to the amount learned when the same material is attributed to a low credibility source. Table 2 shows the mean number of items correct on the information quiz when material is presented by "high credibility" and "low credibility" sources.

[3] The probability values given in the table, while adequately significant, are calculated conservatively. The two-tailed test of significance is used throughout, even though in the case of some of the tables it could be contended that the direction of the differences is in line with theoretical predictions, and hence might justify the use of the one-tail test. When analysis is made of *changes,* the significance test takes into account the internal correlation (Hovland, Sheffield and Lumsdaine, *op. cit.,* pp. 318ff.), but the analyses of cases of post-communication agreement and disagreement are calculated on the conservative assumption of independence of the separate communications.

TABLE 1

Evaluation of "Fairness" and "Justifiability" of Identical Communications When Presented by "High Credibility" and "Low Credibility" Sources Among Individuals Who Initially Agreed and Individuals Who Initially Disagreed With Position Advocated by Communicator

A. PER CENT CONSIDERING AUTHOR "FAIR" IN HIS PRESENTATION*

Topic	High Credibility Source		Low Credibility Source	
		Initially		Initially
	Initially Agree	Disagree (or Don't Know)	Initially Agree	Disagree (or Don't Know)
Anti-Histamines	76.5%	50.0%	64.3%	62.5%
Atomic Submarines	100.0	93.7	75.0	66.7
Steel Shortage	44.4	15.4	12.5	22.2
Future of Movies	90.9	90.0	77.8	52.4
Mean	78.3%	57.9%	60.5%	51.9%
N =	46	76	43	79

B. PER CENT CONSIDERING AUTHOR'S CONCLUSION "JUSTIFIED" BY THE FACTS**

Topic	High Credibility Source		Low Credibility Source	
		Initially		Initially
	Initially Agree	Disagree (or Don't Know)	Initially Agree	Disagree (or Don't Know)
Anti-Histamines	82.4%	57.1%	57.1%	50.0%
Atomic Submarines	77.8	81.2	50.0	41.2
Steel Shortage	55.6	23.1	37.5	22.2
Future of Movies	63.6	55.0	55.6	33.3
Mean	71.7%	50.0%	51.2%	36.7%
N =	46	76	43	79

* Question: Do you think that the author of each article was fair in his presentation of the facts on both sides of the question or did he write a one-sided report?

** Question: Do you think that the opinion expressed by the author in his conclusion *was* justified by the facts he presented or do you think his opinion *was not* justified by the facts?

Opinion. Significant differences were obtained in the extent to which opinion on an issue was changed by the attribution of the material to different sources. These results are presented in Table 3. Subjects changed their opinion in the direction advocated by the communicator in a significantly greater number of cases when the material was attributed to a "high credibility" source than when attributed to a "low credibility" source. The difference is significant at less than the .01 level.

From Figure 1 it will be recalled that less than 100 per cent of the subjects were in agreement with the group consensus concerning the trustworthiness of each source. The results presented in Table 3 were

TABLE 2

Mean Number of Items Correct on Four-Item Information Quizzes on Each of Four Topics When Presented by "High Credibility" and "Low Credibility" Sources (Test Immediately After Communication)

Topic	*Mean Number of Items Correct*			
	High Credibility Source		*Low Credibility Source*	
Anti-Histamines	(N = 31)	3.42	(N = 30)	3.17
Atomic Submarines	(N = 25)	3.48	(N = 36)	3.72
Steel Shortage	(N = 35)	3.34	(N = 26)	2.73
Future of Movies	(N = 31)	3.23	(N = 30)	3.27
Average	(N = 122)	3.36	(N = 122)	3.26
Per cent of items correct		84.0		81.5
$p$diff. M.			.35	

TABLE 3

Net Changes of Opinion in Direction of Communication for Sources Classified by Experimenters as "High Credibility" or "Low Credibility" Sources*

Topic	*Net percentage of cases in which subjects changed opinion in direction of communication*			
	High Credibility Sources		*Low Credibility Sources*	
Anti-Histamines	(N = 31)	22.6%	(N = 30)	13.3%
Atomic Submarines	(N = 25)	36.0	(N = 36)	0.0
Steel Shortage	(N = 35)	22.9	(N = 26)	−3.8
Future of Movies	(N = 31)	12.9	(N = 30)	16.7
Average	(N = 122)	23.0%	(N = 122)	6.6%
Diff.		16.4%		
$p$diff.		< .01		

* Net changes = positive changes *minus* negative changes.

reanalyzed using the individual subject's own evaluation of the source as the independent variable. The effects on opinion were studied for those instances where the source was rated as "very trustworthy" or "moderately trustworthy" and for those where it was rated as "untrustworthy" or "inconsistently trustworthy." Results from this analysis are given in Table 4. The results, using the subject's own evaluation of the trustworthiness of the source, are substantially the same as those obtained when analyzed in terms of the experimenters' *a priori* classification (presented in Table 3). Only minor shifts were obtained. It appears that while the variable is made somewhat "purer" with this analysis this advantage is offset by possible increased variability attributable to unreliability in making individual judgments of the trustworthiness of the source.

TABLE 4

Net Changes of Opinion in Direction of Communication for Sources Judged "Trustworthy" or "Untrustworthy" by Individual Subjects

Topic	*Net percentage of cases in which subjects changed opinion in direction of communication*			
	"Trustworthy" Sources		*"Untrustworthy" Sources*	
Anti-Histamines	(N=31)	25.5%	(N=27)	11.1%
Atomic Submarines	(N=25)	36.0	(N=36)	0.0
Steel Shortage	(N=33)	18.2	(N=27)	7.4
Future of Movies	(N=31)	12.9	(N=29)	17.2
Average	(N=120)	22.5%	(N=119)	8.4%
Diff.		14.1%		
Pdiff.		<.03		

TABLE 5

Mean Number of Items Correct on Four-Item Information Quizzes on Each of Four Topics When Presented by "High Credibility" and "Low Credibility" Sources (Recall Four Weeks After Communication)

Topic	*Mean Number of Items Correct*			
	High Credibility	*Source*	*Low Credibility*	*Source*
Anti-Histamines	(N=31)	2.32	(N=30)	2.90
Atomic Submarines	(N=25)	3.08	(N=36)	3.06
Steel Shortage	(N=35)	2.51	(N=26)	2.27
Future of Movies	(N=31)	2.52	(N=30)	2.33
Average	(N=122)	2.58	(N=122)	2.67
Per cent of items correct		64.5		66.7
Pdiff.		.46		

RETENTION OF INFORMATION AND OPINION IN RELATION TO SOURCE

Information. As was the case with the immediate post-communication results (Table 2), there is no difference between the retention of factual information after four weeks when presented by high credibility sources and low credibility sources. Results in Table 5 show the mean retention scores for each of the four topics four weeks after the communication.

Opinion. Extremely interesting results were obtained for the retention of opinion changes. Table 6 shows the changes in opinion from immediately after the communication to those obtained after the four-week interval. It will be seen that compared with the changes immediately after the communication, there is a *decrease* in the extent of agreement with the high credibility source, but an *increase* in the case of the low credibility source. This result, then, is similar to the "sleeper effect" found by Hovland, Lumsdaine and Sheffield. The results derived from Tables 3 and 6 are compared in Figure 2, which

TABLE 6

Net Changes of Opinion From Immediately After Communication to Four Weeks Later in Direction of "High Credibility" and "Low Credibility" Sources

Topic	High Credibility Source (A)		Low Credibility Source (B)		Difference (B-A)
Anti-Histamines	(N=31)	−6.5%	(N=30)	+6.7%	+13.2%
Atomic Submarines	(N=25)	−16.0	(N=36)	+13.9	+29.9
Steel Shortage	(N=35)	−11.4	(N=26)	+15.4	+26.8
Future of Movies	(N=31)	−9.7	(N=30)	−6.7	+3.0
Average	(N=122)	−10.7%	(N=122)	+7.4%	+18.1%
Pdiff.					.001

TABLE 7

Recall of Source Immediately After Communication and After Four Weeks

Recall	Trustworthy Source		Untrustworthy Source	
	Individuals initially holding position advocated by communicator	Individuals not initially holding position advocated by communicator	Individuals initially holding position advocated by communicator	Individuals not initially holding position advocated by communicator
Immediately after communication	93.0% (N=43)	85.7% (N=77)	93.0% (N=43)	93.4% (N=76)
Four weeks after communication	60.5 (N=43)	63.6 (N=77)	76.7 (N=43)	55.3 (N=76)

shows the changes in opinion from before the communication to immediately afterwards and from before to four weeks afterwards.

The loss with the "trustworthy" source and the gain with the "untrustworthy" source are clearly indicated. A parallel analysis using the individual's own evaluation of the source credibility (similar to the method of Table 4) showed substantially the same results.

Retention of name of source. One hypothesis advanced for the "sleeper effect" involved the assumption that forgetting of the source would be more rapid than that of the content. This is a most difficult point to test experimentally because it is almost impossible to equate retention tests for source and for content. It is, however, possible to make a comparison of the retention of the name of the source where the subjects initially agreed with the source's position and considered the communicator a "trustworthy" source, and those where they disagreed and considered the source "untrustworthy." Data on this point are presented in Table 7.

No clear differences are obtained immediately after the communication, indicating comparable initial learning of the names of the different sources. At the time of the delayed test, however, there appears

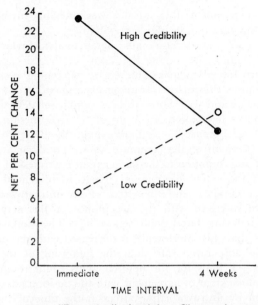

Fig. 2. "Retention" of opinion. Changes in extent of agreement with position advocated by "high credibility" and "low credibility" sources.

to be a clear difference in the retention of the names of "untrustworthy" sources for the group initially agreeing with the communicator's position as compared with that for the group disagreeing with the communicator's position ($p = .02$). Since the "sleeper effect" occurs among the group which initially disagrees with an unreliable source (but subsequently comes to agree with it), it is interesting to note that among this group the retention of the source name is poorest of all. Too few subjects were available to check whether retention was poorer among the very subjects who showed the "sleeper effect," but no clear-cut difference could be seen from the analysis of the small sample.

DISCUSSION

Under the conditions of this experiment, neither the acquisition nor the retention of factual information appears to be affected by the trustworthiness of the source. But changes in opinion are significantly related to the trustworthiness of the source used in the communication. This difference is in line with the results of Hovland, Lumsdaine and Sheffield, who found a clear distinction between the effects of films on information and opinion. In the case of factual information they found that differences in acquisition and retention were primarily related to differences in learning ability. But in the case of opinion, the most important factor was the degree of "acceptance" of the material.

In the present experiment, this variable was probably involved as a consequent of the variation in source credibility.

The present results add considerable detail to the Hovland-Lumsdaine-Sheffield findings concerning the nature of the "sleeper effect." While they were forced to make inferences concerning possible suspicion of the source, this factor was under experimental control in the present experiment and was shown to be a significant determinant of subsequent changes in opinion. In terms of their distinction between "learning" and "acceptance," one could explain the present results by saying that the content of the communication (premises, arguments, etc.) is learned and forgotten to the same extent regardless of the communicator. But the extent of opinion change is influenced by both learning and acceptance, and the effect of an untrustworthy communicator is to interfere with the acceptance of the material ("I know what he is saying, but I don't believe it"). The aforementioned authors suggest that this interference is decreased with the passage of time, and at a more rapid rate than the forgetting of the content which provides the basis for the opinion. This could result in substantially the same extent of agreement with the position advocated by trustworthy and by untrustworthy sources at the time of the second post-test questionnaire. In the case of the trustworthy source, the forgetting of the content would be the main factor in the decrease in the extent of opinion change. But with an untrustworthy source the reduction due to forgetting would be more than offset by the removal of the interference associated with "nonacceptance." The net effect would be an increase in the extent of agreement with the position advocated by the source at the time of the second post-communication questionnaire. The present results are in complete agreement with this hypothesis; there is a large difference in extent of agreement with trustworthy and untrustworthy sources immediately after the communication, but the extent of agreement with the two types of source is almost identical four weeks later.

The Hovland-Lumsdaine-Sheffield formulation makes forgetting of the source a critical condition for the "sleeper" phenomenon. In the present analysis the critical requirement is a decreased tendency over time to reject the material presented by an untrustworthy source.[4] This may or may not require that the source be forgotten. But the individual must be less likely with the passage of time to associate spontaneously the content with the source. Thus the passage of time serves

---

[4] In the present analysis the difference in effects of trustworthy and untrustworthy sources is attributed primarily to the *negative* effects of rejection of the untrustworthy source. On the other hand, in prestige studies the effects are usually attributed to the *positive* enhancement of effects by a high prestige source. In both types of study only a difference in effect of the two kinds of influence is obtained. Future research must establish an effective "neutral" baseline to answer the question as to the absolute direction of the effects.

to remove recall of the source as a mediating cue that leads to rejection.[5]

It is in this connection that the methodological distinction mentioned earlier between the procedure used in this experiment and that customarily employed in "prestige" studies becomes of signficance. In the present analysis, the untrustworthy source is regarded as a cue which is reacted to by rejection. When an individual is asked for his opinion at the later time he may not spontaneously remember the position held by the source. Hence the source does not then constitute a cue producing rejection of his position. In the usual "prestige" technique, the attachment of the name of the source to the statement would serve to reinstate the source as a cue; consequently the differential effects obtained with the present design would not be expected to obtain. An experiment is now under way to determine whether the "sleeper effect" disappears when the source cue is reinstated by the experimenter at the time of the delayed test of opinion change.

Finally, the question of the generalizability of the results should be discussed briefly. In the present study the subjects were all college students. Other groups of subjects varying in age and in education will be needed in future research. Four topics and eight different sources were used to increase the generality of the "source" variable. No attempt, however, was made to analyze the differences in effects for different topics. Throughout, the effects of the "Atomic Submarine" and "Steel Shortage" communications were larger and more closely related to the trustworthiness of source variable than those of the "Future of Movies" topic. An analysis of the factors responsible for the differential effects constitutes an interesting problem for future research. A repetition of the study with a single after-test for each time interval rather than double testing after the communication would be desirable, although this variation is probably much less significant with opinion than with information questions. The generality of the present results is limited to the situation where individuals are experimentally exposed to the communication; i.e., a "captive audience" situation. An interesting further research problem would be a repetition of the experiment under naturalistic conditions where the individual himself controls his exposure to communications. Finally for the present study it was important to use sources which could plausibly advocate either side of an issue. There are other combinations of position and source where the communicator and his stand are so intimately associated that one spontaneously recalls the source when he thinks about the

---

[5] In rare instances there may also occur a change with time in the attitude toward the source, such that one remembers the source but no longer has such a strong tendency to discount and reject the material. No evidence for the operation of this factor in the present experiment was obtained; our data indicate no significant changes in the evaluation of the trustworthiness of the sources from before to after the communication.

issue. Under these conditions, the forgetting of the source may not occur and consequently no "sleeper effect" would be obtained.

SUMMARY

1. The effects of credibility of source on acquisition and retention of communication material were studied by presenting identical content but attributing the material to sources considered by the audience to be of "high trustworthiness" or of "low trustworthiness." The effects of source on factual information and on opinion were measured by the use of questionnaires administered before, immediately after, and four weeks after the communication.

2. The immediate reaction to the "fairness" of the presentation and the "justifiability" of the conclusions drawn by the communication is significantly affected by both the subject's initial position on the issue and by his evaluation of the trustworthiness of the source. Identical communications were regarded as being "justified" in their conclusions in 71.7 per cent of the cases when presented by a high credibility source to subjects who initially held the same opinion as advocated by the communicator, but were considered "justified" in only 36.7 per cent of the cases when presented by a low credibility source to subjects who initially held an opinion at variance with that advocated by the communicator.

3. No difference was found in the amount of factual information learned from the "high credibility" and "low credibility" sources, and none in the amount retained over a four week period.

4. Opinions were changed immediately after the communication in the direction advocated by the communicator to a significantly greater degree when the material was presented by a trustworthy source than when presented by an untrustworthy source.

5. There was a *decrease* after a time interval in the extent to which subjects agreed with the position advocated by the communication when the material was presented by trustworthy sources, but an *increase* when it was presented by untrustworthy sources.

6. Forgetting the name of the source is less rapid among individuals who initially agreed with the untrustworthy source than among those who disagreed with it.

7. Theoretical implications of the results are discussed. The data on post-communication changes in opinion (the "sleeper effect") can be explained by assuming equal *learning* of the content whether presented by a trustworthy or an untrustworthy source but an initial resistance to the *acceptance* of the material presented by an untrustworthy source. If this resistance to acceptance diminishes with time while the content which itself provides the basis for the opinion is forgotten more slowly, there will be an increase after the communication in the extent of agreement with an untrustworthy source.

▲ JOSEPH T. KLAPPER

Mass Media and Persuasion

THE FACT AND NATURE OF PERSUASION BY ALL MEDIA

Thousands of experiments have established beyond reasonable doubt that persuasion can be achieved by the planned, or even unplanned presentation of appropriate content through mass media.

The experiments of Wilke and Knower, cited in the memorandum on comparative effectiveness of media, indicate that attitudes on controversial subjects (e.g., war, birth control, religion, etc.) can be modified by appropriate content transmitted by face-to-face discourse, by wired speakers, or by print. Many other experiments on propaganda impact not only confirm the Wilke and Knower studies in this regard but suggest the wide variety of topics in regard to which content presented through any media may be persuasively effective. We will here cite only a few widely different examples.

That face-to-face discourse can be effective has been demonstrated by Chen, who, during the Sino-Japanese War exposed one group of American university students to oral propaganda favoring the Chinese cause and another group to similar propaganda favoring the Japanese cause; significant attitude modifications in the direction intended by the propaganda occurred in both groups.

Print has been effectively used particularly often, and in varied forms. Thus Annis and Meier working with a deliberately peculiar

▲ This memorandum, prepared for the Public Library Inquiry, was reproduced and copyright by the Columbia University Bureau of Applied Social Research (New York, 1949), and is here reprinted by permission of author and copyright holder. Dr. Klapper is a member of the research and evaluation staff of the United States Information Agency. In the interests of space and simplicity of presentation, many of the footnotes and all the references have been removed from this article. Readers who turn to the original publication of this memorandum (entitled *The Effects of Mass Media*) will find reference for each quotation, and a very large bibliography summarizing most of the relevant research up to 1949.

topic, modified American students' opinions of the Prime Minister of Australia by use of propaganda content planted in editorials of college newspapers. Britt and Menefee shifted the attitudes of students towards various persons by exposing the students to ordinary newspaper reports of Dies Committee hearings in which these persons figured. Effective results were obtained with specialized printed material by Bateman and Remmers in reference to attitude towards labor unions, by Sims in regard to attitudes toward TVA, and by a host of other experimenters.

That regular commercial films, let alone documentaries, can modify opinion has been demonstrated by Thurstone and Peterson who observed statistically significant shifts in the attitudes of adolescents toward capital punishment, race relations, and Nazism after exposure to ordinary commercial films dealing with these subjects. Persuasive successes of certain specific types were also observed by Hovland, Lumsdaine, and Sheffield to follow semi-documentary films presented by the army in an attempt to influence the opinions of American soldiers.

The persuasive effectiveness of radio has been attested by various social scientists, including Cantril and Allport. More recently Merton has published an elaborate analysis of the devices, techniques, and conditions which helped Kate Smith obtain "thirty-nine million dollars of [war] bond pledges in the course" of an eighteen hour broadcast.

A list of all pertinent studies would be endless. Suffice it to say that propaganda, whether presented by personal address, print, radio or film, has been frequently observed to shift group attitudes in the intended direction.

Certain characteristics of the attitude changes induced by the various media have been observed in numerous experiments, and have rarely, if ever, been questioned by any contrary evidence. Such general agreement is found in regard to two points in particular.

(1) *In regard to some attitude changes, incomplete regression often follows termination of exposure*

It has hitherto been believed that after exposure to propaganda is terminated, such individual (and, in sum, group) attitudes as have been changed tend to regress *toward* their original direction and intensity. That the induced changes are quite persistent and are likely to be in some degree permanent, has been frequently noted. Waples, Berelson and Bradshaw, for example, report, after reviewing the appropriate literature, that "even small amounts (fifteen minutes) of reading can produce an attitude change which will be measurable at the end of eight months."

That such regression does *not* occur in regard to all attitude changes and that some such changes, in fact, become more extensive during the years following termination of exposure, have been recently demonstrated in the series of experiments reported by Hovland, Lumsdaine, and Sheffield. Their analysis of this newly discovered phenomenon of "sleeper effect" in attitude change is discussed at some length below.

(2) *Individual attitude shifts more frequently consist of modification or innovation than they do of conversion*

Persons who are originally neutral in regard to the issue at hand tend to develop an attitude in the direction intended by the propaganda; for those already holding opinions, however, the propaganda usually acts merely as an intensifying or weakening agent, rather than accomplishing complete conversion.

Sims, for example, subjected a group of persons opposed to the TVA to propaganda favoring that project; the intensity of opposition was reduced far more frequently than conversion was effected. Sims also observed that among persons who already hold intense opinions, sympathetic propaganda occasionally produces a quantitative, though not qualitative boomerang. After exposure to sympathetic propaganda such persons are sometimes found to hold *less* intense, but not contrary opinions.

Each of the media, then, has been observed to be effective in laboratory and social situations, and certain characteristics of propaganda-induced attitude changes seem fairly well established. On the other hand, each of the media has often been observed to fail in attempts at mass persuasion, and contradictory findings have been offered regarding other characteristics of attitude changes induced by propaganda.

In reference to print, for example, Mott analyzed the partisan contents of newspapers in presidential elections from 1792 to 1940. He concluded that "there seems to be no correlation, positive or negative, between the support of a majority of newspapers during a campaign and success at the polls." Lundberg, after conducting a controlled experiment with 940 residents of Seattle, concluded that the modern newspaper had little influence on the opinions of its readers.

Cartoons designed to influence their audience toward racial tolerance were observed by Kendall and Wolff and by Cooper and Jahoda to be successful for some of the audience, to have no effects on others, and frequently to "boomerang," i.e., to produce effects diametrically opposite from those intended.

In the Thurstone-Peterson study cited above, the screen was observed to be unpersuasive just as frequently as it was persuasive. Of thirteen films used in the study, six produced statistically significant attitude changes in the intended direction, six failed to produce such a shift, and one boomeranged. Hovland, Lumsdaine, and Sheffield likewise report that army orientation films failed in many instances to produce the attitude changes envisaged by the film makers.

Intense boomerang effects of a radio program designed to convince the audience to have chest X-rays were observed by Lazarsfeld and Kendall.

Studies indicating the persuasiveness of the mass media can thus be paralleled by studies citing instances of mass media's failure to persuade.

Disagreement also exists regarding the relation between exposure and effect. Some investigators found that extremely brief or very few exposures were sufficient to accomplish the intended shift of attitude. Chen, for example, found a few minutes of oral propaganda sufficient to achieve attitude modifications, while Annis and Meier found exposure to seven editorials *precisely as effective as* exposure to fifteen. Hovland, Lumsdaine, and Sheffield found that exposure to two army orientation films produced no consistently greater results than exposure to single (but different) films in the same series. Thurstone and Peterson, however, found that the effect of cumulative or prolonged exposure to be in all respects greater than the effect of single exposure, and the findings of these investigators are in part substantiated by Lazarsfeld, Berelson, and Gaudet and by Merton. However, Hovland, Lumsdaine, and Sheffield found exposure to two supposedly persuasive films to be no more effective than exposure to one related film.

In sum, then, the pertinent literature indicates that material presented over any medium may be persuasively effective, but on the other hand, that it may not be effective. It is generally agreed that attitude changes consist more often of modifications than of conversions, and that although some of these modifications wane after propaganda exposure is terminated, they are to some degree highly persistent. One series of experiments indicates that some attitude changes become intensified during the weeks following exposure. Some experimenters find brief exposure exactly as effective as cumulative exposure, while others find cumulative exposure far more effective.

Put another and more general way, it appears that the mere fact of propaganda communication by any medium is not the sole criterion of propaganda effect. Other conditions apparently determine whether or not the persuasion will be successful. The remainder of this memorandum will be devoted to the evidence and conjecture which identifies, with various degrees of certainty, the conditions and devices which render persuasion most likely to be successful.

THE "I AND E" RESEARCHES

An impressive collection of data on the fact and nature of persuasion by mass communication has recently emerged from the extensive research pursued during World War II by the Experimental Section of the Research Branch of the Information and Education Division of the War Department. Some of the findings of those studies have been mentioned in Memorandum II, in connection with the pedagogical effectiveness of the various media, and certain highly specific findings have been mentioned in the preceding pages of the present memorandum. Certain other findings and certain hypotheses of these studies bear so immediately and importantly upon the fact and nature of persuasion by mass communication that it seems desirable that they be here presented in some detail. Accordingly, we will consider in turn the area of research, major findings, certain hypotheses offered in partial explanation of the major findings, and additional findings.

(1) *The area of research*

The Research Branch of the Information and Education Division was charged with the broad task of collecting and analyzing "data on soldiers' attitudes and opinions." In order to provide data for "policy-makers . . . responsible for planning the information, education, and orientation programs," the Experimental Section of the Research Branch undertook a series of "studies dealing with the effectiveness of films and other mass-communication devices" used in the orientation program. Several of these studies "thought to be of general interest to persons concerned with the use of mass-communication methods" have been reported in detail by Hovland, Sheffield, and Lumsdaine.

During the several years of research, the investigators attempted to assess the effects of various special films, radio programs, and miscellaneous communicational devices. Experimental and control groups typically numbered between 500 and 1,500 soldiers, so selected as to comprise reliably random and representative samples of the army population.

The communicational products and devices studied were designed for either or both of two purposes. Some of the films, film strips, and techniques were intended to impart certain facts and skills — to teach the military, for example, how to read maps, or how to use the phonetic alphabet. Other products, such as a series of films entitled "Why We Fight," were designed to serve more persuasive and more complex ends. Hovland, Lumsdaine, and Sheffield describe the intended function of these orientation films as involving three steps: (1) the communication of certain facts about the background of the war, which was intended (2) to induce in the soldiers more favorable opinions and attitudes relative to American participation, which opinions and attitudes, in turn, were intended (3) to increase the soldiers' motivation and willingness to serve. A realization of the distinction between the communicational goals of imparting factual knowledge on the one hand, and of modifying opinion or motivation on the other hand, is basic to an appreciation of the findings.

(2) *Findings*

In brief, all media products and all devices investigated were found to be highly effective in communicating information and imparting skills. All were, however, found to be very much less effective, and at times wholly ineffective, in modifying opinions or in increasing motivation.

Literally all of the products and devices were highly successful in imparting factual information. As noted in the memorandum on comparative media effectiveness, a film and a film strip were both highly effective, although to differing degrees, in teaching map reading; similarly significant, if unequal, pedagogical successes followed films with and without supplementary face-to-face instruction, as well as film strips presented with and without occasion for audience participation. The products designed to impart factual knowledge were, in brief, all highly successful.

Products designed to affect opinion and motivation also succeeded in imparting the *facts* which, it was hoped, would stimulate the formation of the desired attitudes. The film "The Battle of Britain," for example, indicated among other things that German lack of success in bombing ground-parked British planes was due to a scattered parking procedure used by the British. A question designed to determine knowledge of this military fact was answered correctly by only 21% of a group of soldiers who had not seen the film, but by 78% of a group which had seen the film. Similar, if less phenomenal, successes in imparting other military facts were achieved by the "Battle of Britain" and the three other orientation films.

In addition to such successful communication of facts, the

films also had some marked effect on opinions where they [the films] specifically covered the factors involved in a particular interpretation, that is, where the opinion test item was prepared on the basis of film-content analysis. . . . Such opinion changes were, however, less frequent and, in general, less marked than changes in factual knowledge.

Thus percentage differences as high as 27 were observed by the control and experimental groups in regard to such opinions as that "there was an actual 'Battle of Britain' " in which "heroic British resistance" was manifest, and was aided by the great "contribution of the Royal Air Force." A notable portion of men were convinced by the picture that "British resistance gave the United States time to prepare." The other three orientation films achieved roughly similar successes in inducing opinion or interpretation for which *the necessary grounds were specifically covered by film content.*

The more general opinions, which the basic facts and specific interpretations were presumably to induce were not, however, found to have been actually induced in any notable portion of the audience.

Since one of the principal intended effects of "The Battle of Britain" was to establish a feeling of confidence in the integrity and fighting ability of one of our allies, a number of [test] items were included which were less specifically related to the film content, but concerned general attitudes to the British. In contrast to the large effects afforded above, where the items were tied to specific phases of the British war effort covered in the film, the effects were small or unreliable *on the more general questions dealing with confidence in the British effort.*

Differences of only 3%, for example, were found between the control group and those who had seen the film as regarded the proportion who disagreed with the view that Britain was "largely to blame for our being in this war," or who believed that "we ought to send food to England, even if it means . . . more rationing here." Practically none of the observed effects on these general opinion items were statistically significant, which is to say that even the small noted effects could not be confidently attributed to the experience of seeing the picture, but might very well have been due to chance variations in the samples of men observed.

Effects of the films upon the men's motivation were even smaller and statistically less reliable than effects upon general opinions. No statistically significant effect was observed in regard to test items related to the men's "willingness to serve," "agreement with the unconditional surrender policy," or "resentment against the enemy."

The observed effects of "The Battle of Britain" were in general similar to the effects of the other orientation films, as well as to the effects of cumulative exposure to two of the other films. The authors' summary of findings notes that

The "Why We Fight" films had marked effects on the men's knowledge of factual material concerning events leading up to the war. [It appears] . . . that highly effective presentation methods are possible with this type of film.

The films also had some marked effects on opinions where the films specifically covered the factors involved in the particular interpretation. . . . Such opinion changes were, however, less frequent and in general less marked than changes in factual knowledge.

The films had only a very few effects on opinion items of a more general nature that had been prepared independently of film-content, but which were considered the criteria for determining the effectiveness of the films at achieving their orientation objectives.

The films had no effects on the items prepared for the purpose of measuring effects on the men's motivation to serve as soldiers, which was considered the ultimate objective of the orientation program.

(3) *Hypotheses concerning lack of effects on orientation objectives*

Hovland, Lumsdaine, and Sheffield note that

The question arises as to the explanation for the pattern of results summarized above. It is not possible to answer this question, but a number of possible contributory factors may be suggested.

Several of these hypotheses are more or less obvious — as, for example, that exposure to the films was too brief to affect opinions and that exposure to several films might provide a different result. Three hypotheses seem, however, less obvious and particularly significant for purposes of the present report.

(a) *Resistance of the deviant minority.* Hovland, Lumsdaine, and Sheffield suggest that previous indoctrination may have already induced the desired opinions in all members of the audience who were susceptible of holding such opinions. Most of these opinions were held at the time by the large majority of Americans, and the deviant might be so resistant to change that all normal attempts at attiude modificaion were a priori doomed to failure.

To persons concerned with "persuasion with regard to important civic attitudes" the implications of this hypothesis are obvious and somewhat discouraging. Many important civic attitudes are already held by the majority of the community. The task of persuading the deviant minority becomes, if this hypothesis be true, progressively harder as the minority decreases.

(b) *Lack of transfer in the absence of specific coverage.* Hovland, Lumsdaine, and Sheffield suggest that

the lack of effects may be due simply to the fact that the attitudes and motivations investigated in these studies cannot be appreciably effected by an information program which relies primarily upon "letting the facts speak for themselves." It may be that such a program will prove effective with only a small segment of the population whose attitudes are primarily determined by rational considerations. For most other individuals, motivations and attitudes may generally be acquired through non-rational channels and may be highly resistant to rational considerations.

The implications which, in the opinion of Hovland, Lumsdaine, and Sheffield, are cast by this hypothesis upon the basic assumptions of the army orientation program, are cast with equal force upon all programs of persuasion which involve the same assumptions. It is clear that the successful communication of appropriate facts will not automatically entail the changes of opinion in the interests of which such facts have been presented. For persons engaged in persuasion for important civic attitudes, the conclusions to be drawn are comparatively obvious: if the persuasion is to be successful, the attitudes in question must be specifically formulated and the facts presented in their support must be sufficiently specific to require the absolute minimum of inference on the part of the audience.

(c) *Possible "need for a 'sinking in' period."* Tests to determine the effectiveness of the training films were ordinarily presented to the audience a week after they had been exposed to the film. Suspecting that certain "sleeper" effects might occur over a long period of time, the investigators tested certain audience groups after a period of not one, but nine weeks.

As might have been predicted on the basis of previous experimental findings, factual information imparted by the films was found to have suffered approximately a 50% loss of retention during the nine week interval. Surprisingly enough, however, responses to test items bearing on attitudes and opinions revealed no such regular decrement of effect. Some short-time opinion changes did indeed appear to have been nullified by time. Others, however, were found to have attained large increments. Both opinions presumably sought by the film-makers and opinions presumably alien to the goals of the orientation program were found to have become far more common after a nine week lapse. In regard to some opinions, the increment was eleven times the size of the short-term effect.

For this sleeper effect, which is wholly unique among the findings of communications research, the investigators are unable fully to account. Four hypotheses are suggested, but the available data are confessedly inadequate to confirm strongly any of the four. Concerned essentially with the technicalities of psychological processes of attitude formation, the hypotheses themselves are not greatly relevant to the purposes of the present paper. For persons concerned with persuasion in regard to civic attitudes, the salient points are

(1) that incremental attitude modification does occur over comparatively long periods following exposure to persuasive films. The mere demonstration of the occurrence of incremental effect suggests that much of the persuasion previously thought, on the basis of immediate tests, to be effectless may have come to wield potent but undiscovered influence. Innumerable additional questions about incremental effect spring at once to mind, but cannot as yet be answered. Nothing is as yet known, for example, as to when the increments first appear, for how long they accrue, or whether and under what circumstances, the ultimate end of the process is a permanent change of attitude.

(2) that such incremental effect apparently is greater in regard to such opinions and among such persons as were originally so predisposed at the time of exposure but who, for one reason or another, were unaware of the latent belief, or unwilling to express it.

(3) that such incremental effect is most likely to occur in regard to opinions and interpretations which are *not* specifically stated in the original vehicle of persuasion, but must rather be inferred by the audience members.

(4) *Additional findings*

Various additional findings regarding the persuasive effects of film and radio accrued to the investigators in the course of their extended research. Practical limitations prohibit the detailed report of all such findings. Of those which are most relevant to the purpose of the present memorandum, some have been cited in earlier sections, and some have been set forth in detail immediately above. Three other findings, of particular interest to persons engaged in persuasion for civic attitudes, should be briefly noted.

(a) A "documentary" type radio program, containing montages, dramatic interludes, and the like, was found to be neither significantly more nor less effective in modifying attitudes and opinions than a simple "commentator" type program of similar thermatic content.

(b) Modification of opinion, where present, tended to follow the predispositions of the audience as manifested by persons on various educational levels. The investigators found, for example, that opinions which were more frequently induced among more-educated men than among less-educated men were precisely those opinions which were most characteristic of the more-educated persons who had not seen the films. Similarly, opinions characteristic of "uninformed" persons who had not seen the film were more frequently induced among the less-educated audience members than among their more-educated companions.

(c) Comparisons were made of the effectiveness of presenting one side as against both sides of controversial issues. The significant differences of effect which were observed are noted in the discussion of specific devices of successful persuasion.

(5) *Summary*

The Research Branch of the Information and Education Division of the War Department carried out extensive investigations of the effectiveness of films and other media in imparting information to large military audiences and in modifying the attitudes of the audience members. All media products and techniques tested were found to be extremely effective in imparting factual information, but only slightly effective in modifying opinions and attitudes. In general, the less specifically the desired interpretation is presented, the more unlikely is that interpretation to be communicated to any significant number of the audience.

There is some reason to believe that the greater the majority which holds a given opinion to begin with, the less is any persuasive attempt likely to succeed in converting the deviant minority; the fewer the non-believers, the greater is their apparent resistance.

Opinion and attitude change, where present, seemed to follow patterns of audience predisposition as determined by educational levels. Opinions widely acceptable to more-educated men, for example, can apparently be more easily induced in more-educated men not already holding such opinions than they can among less-educated men not already holding such opinions.

A "documentary" type radio program was found to be neither more nor less effective in attitude persuasion than a "commentator" type program of similar thematic content.

Tests of film effects nine weeks after exposure revealed that although factual material had been forgotten by about 50% of the men who had presumably learned it, attitude modification had been in some instances greatly magnified. Such increments tended to follow the patterns of audience predisposition as determined by educational level. Incremental effects furthermore seem likely to be greatest in regard to inferences which are *not* specifically made in the original persuasive material.

Certain additional findings regarding the comparative effectiveness of presenting one side as against both sides of a controversial issue are described later.

CONDITIONS OF MAXIMUM LIKELIHOOD OF EFFECT

(1) *Monopoly propaganda and reinforcement of sanctioned views*

Research indicates that of the various conditions which make persuasion likely to be successful, one of the most, if not *the* most powerful is a monopoly propaganda position.

The term "monopoly propaganda," or "monopolization" is used to refer to propaganda which is for one or another reason unopposed, i.e., which is faced with no competing counter-propaganda.

Monopoly propaganda has characterized almost all the very highly successful campaigns of persuasion and, to the present author's best knowledge, has never wholly failed of its goals. While monopoly propaganda is not a necessary condition of successful persuasion, research[1] indicates that it is nevertheless sufficient. The occasions of its actual or possible use are quite varied, but are also distinctly limited.

The effectiveness as well as some of the instances of monopoly propaganda are emphasized by Lazarsfeld and Merton, who point out that such monopolization

is, of course, indigenous to the political structure of authoritarian society, where access to the media of communication is wholly closed to those who oppose the official ideology. The evidence suggests that this monopoly played some part in enabling the Nazis to maintain their control of the German people. But this same situation is approximated in other social systems. During the war, for example, our government utilized the radio, with some success, to promote and to maintain identification with the war effort. The effectiveness of these morale building efforts was in large measure due to the virtually complete absence of counter propaganda.

Similar situations arise in the world of commercialized propaganda. The mass media create popular idols. The public images of the radio performer,

---

[1] The "research" on this topic has included no controlled experiments in which the effects of monopoly propaganda were compared with the effects of competing propandas on the same topic. If monopolization exists, such comparisons are ipso-facto impossible. The research is therefore limited to noting situations in which monopoly propaganda exists, and noting that such propaganda is vastly more effective than propaganda which is opposed.

Kate Smith, for example, picture her as a woman with unaparalleled understanding of other American women, deeply sympathetic with ordinary men and women, a spiritual guide and mentor, a patriot whose views on public affairs should be taken seriously. Linked with the cardinal American virtues, the public images of Kate Smith are at no point subject to a counter propaganda. Not that she has no competitors in the market of radio advertising. But there are none who set themselves systematically to question what she has said. In consequence, an unmarried radio entertainer with an annual income in six figures may be visualized by millions of American women as a hard working mother who knows the recipe for managing life on fifteen hundred a year.

This image of a popular idol would have far less currency were it subjected to counter propaganda. Such neutralization occurs, for example, as a result of preelection campaigns for Republicans and Democrats. By and large, as a recent study has shown, the propaganda issued by each of these parties neutralizes the effect of the other's propaganda. Were both parties to forego their campaigning through the mass media entirely, it is altogether likely that the net effect would be to reproduce the present distribution of votes.[2]

No research has been directed to identifying the specific psychological bases of the extreme effectiveness of monopoly propaganda. Such bases, are, in fact so conspicuous, that empirical demonstration is perhaps unnecessary. It is patently obvious, for example, that monopoly propaganda results in the audience being exposed to an undiluted influence in one direction. The advantages of acting or believing in a given way are continually pointed out and are never questioned. Alternate lines of conduct or belief are either shown to be disadvantageous or are not even mentioned. The nail is, as it were, steadily pounded. It either sinks, or, less frequently, remains where it is. That monopoly propaganda also natively possesses certain other advantages for persuasion (e.g., a sympathetic audience, the capability of offering real rewards, the task of canalizing rather than converting, extreme prestige, varied appeal) will be shown both in the succeeding discussion of monopolization and the later discussion of incidental devices of effective persuasion.

Monopoly, or very nearly monopoly propaganda, is exercised in the United States not only in favor of such national interests as a war effort, but also in regard to those social attitudes which govern the audience's daily life and social interaction — upon those attitudes which, depending upon the observer's own values, may be called civically desirable or undesirable. The major source of this monopoly propaganda is the entertainment content of mass media; its goal and

---

[2] The remarks on the public image of Kate Smith are based upon Merton's elaborate analysis of her successful marathon broadcast in the interest of war bond sales. References to political campaigns are based on the Lazarsfeld, Berelson, and Gaudet study of the 1940 presidential campaign, which is discussed in greater detail at several other points in these memoranda.

main effect seems to be the maintenance and reaffirmation of the status quo.[3]

The American radio, screen, and the larger part of its press is controlled almost exclusively by commercial agencies whose frankly primary concern is profit. In the interests of such profit, they are devoted to the status quo for two reasons. In the first place the commercial agencies are giants indigenous to a social system which they have no desire to change. In the second place they are intent upon reaching and continually pleasing the largest possible audience.

Both informal and formal analyses of the content of radio, screen, and mass press suggest that the commercial interests rarely undertake a deliberate outright glorification of the existing social system. Very little time or space is in fact devoted by the mass media to anything which can reasonably be called deliberate propaganda. But the desire to please everyone necessarily involves displeasing no one. Accordingly, the content of commercial mass media is forced to conform to the attitudes already sanctioned by the vast majority of the audience. The businessman who wishes to hold the largest possible audience through an hour or page of entertainment, either to lead them to a commercial or simply to insure further admission fees, must see to it that the script or story expresses no attitudes with which any substantial number may disagree. The width of the requisite sanction depends directly on the degree of majority sought. Mass media, through which big business units aim at unanimous good will, face and meet the simple demands of a nationally common denominator of attitudes. The more completely mass media content reasserts the existent social mores, the more efficiently does it serve its commercial purposes. To depart from the properly sanctioned path is to invite economic disaster.

That the media products do actually devote themselves almost exclusively to this end has been noted by both informal observers and rigidly scientific investigators. The general reaffirmation pattern has been pointed out by Lazarsfeld and Merton in various papers. Berelson and Salter found that popular magazine stories, while overtly accepting the ideology of religious and racial equality, actually perpetuate stereotypes of minority groups, applaud the maintenance of caste lines, and picture a world where the highest income is reserved for white, American-born gentiles who practice the Protestant ethic. Lowenthal has shown that biographies in popular magazines are essentially dem-

[3] The next five paragraphs are adopted and in part directly quoted from a previous article by the present author. Permission to use this material has been graciously given by the editors of *The American Scholar*.

The opinions presented in that article and so in these paragraphs are substantiated by objective data only to the degree specifically noted. Otherwise, these opinions are the considered conjectures of the author. The general argument is supported in whole or in part by such writers as Lazarsfeld, Lazarsfeld and Merton, Berelson, and Slesinger.

onstrations that the current hero has been since birth an embodiment of popularly sanctioned values. In less scientific but equally acute key, James Farrell has remarked that the usual American magazine story tells of a young man who questions some established value, eventually sees the error of his ways, and is rewarded by being permitted to marry a pure American girl and reside in a cottage furnished with all the commodities advertised in the surrounding pages of the same magazine. Arnheim has shown that soap opera pictures a world devoid of working class persons, where almost all problems derive from complex personal relations, and where everything will turn out all right if one follows socially accepted patterns of behavior. The bare and frightening bones of the formula were recently exhibited before Congressional representatives by a witness who branded a picture as un-American because it suggested that there were poor people who were unhappy.

The actual effect upon the audience of such monopoly propaganda for the status quo has not, and perhaps cannot be objectively determined. It would seem altogether likely, however, that the major effect is to widen and intensify the sanction for already accepted views. If this is indeed the case, then such propaganda comes fully around a vicious, albeit not wholly preplanned circle: it further reduces the possibility of articulate opposition and so reinforces its own monopoly position.

It is this last point which is particularly significant for our present inquiry and bears most closely upon persuasion for important civic attitudes. If such persuasion can avail itself of a monopoly propaganda position, its success is almost certainly assured. Monopoly position can be enjoyed in the United States only by propaganda in favor of attitudes already highly sanctioned by the great majority of the audience. Persuaders for important civic attitudes will thus be either capable or incapable of achieving mass media or monopolistic voice, depending on the specific attitude involved. If it is the desire of the persuader to stimulate an already universally accepted attitude, or to elicit behavioral manifestations of such an attitude, their success depends only on making proper arrangements with mass media management. Persuasion toward observance of flag-day, registering to vote, protection of the family, vaccination, clean streets, or contributing to the community fund will be aided by mass media, will be unopposed, and will very probably be largely successful. Persuasion toward any attitude opposed by a substantial part of the audience will probably not be undertaken by mass media,[4] or, if by some chance aired or

[4] Apparent exceptions turn out, upon closer inspection, to prove the rule. Thus, either side of controversial issues will be espoused in mass media content provided that the difference in opinion is itself generally recognized as permissible and either alternative is socially acceptable. Campaign disputes between the major political parties are a case in point.

printed, the propaganda will be heavily opposed, possibly dropped, and probably quite ineffective. Mass media normally will aid only so long as no one is annoyed. But persuasion in regard to civic attitudes which are not universally considered civic can look neither for mass media aid nor the incomparable advantages of monopoly position.

(2) *Difficulties of conversion and conditions of likely success*

Persuasion toward attitudes to which a substantial portion of the populace is opposed is not only denied monopoly position and significant mass media aid, but is also rendered difficult by psychological processes of the individual reader or listener.

The processes of self-selection, previously noted in regard to taste, are also operative in regard to material which espouses a given view. Numerous researches, some conducted in the laboratory and some in normal social situations, indicate that by and large people perceive only what they wish to perceive, that they read or listen to only such material as espouses or can be misinterpreted to espouse their existing views, and in general use controversial material to reinforce the opinions they already possess.

That persons will deliberately or unconsciously avoid material which they know questions their existing opinions has been so clearly demonstrated as to be now axiomatic in the literature on communication. The most exhaustive and perhaps the classic demonstration of this tendency is provided by Lazarsfeld, Berelson, and Gaudet in their study of how the voters of Erie County, Ohio, made up their minds in their presidential election of 1940. As regards exposure to partisanship propaganda, the investigators found that

actual exposure does *not* parallel availability. Availability *plus* predispositions determine exposure — and predispositions lead people to select communications which are congenial, which support their previous position. More Republicans than Democrats listened to Willkie and more Democrats than Republicans listened to Roosevelt. The universe of campaign communications — political speeches, newspaper stories, newscasts, editorials, columns, magazine articles — was open to virtually everyone. But exposure was consistently partisan. . . .

By and large about two-thirds of the constant partisans — the people who were either Republican or Democratic from May right through to Election Day — managed to see and hear more of their own side's propaganda than the opposition's. About one-fifth of them happened to expose more frequently to the other side, and the rest were neutral in their exposure. But — and this is important — the more strongly partisan the person, the more likely he is to insulate himself from contrary ponits of view. The constants with great interest and with most concern in the election of their own candidate were *more* partisan in exposure than the constants with less interest and less concern. Such partisan exposure can only serve to reinforce the partisan's previous attitudes. In short, the most partisan people protect themselves from the disturbing experience presented by opposition arguments by paying little attention to them. Instead, they turn to that propaganda which re-affirms the validity and wisdom of their original decision — which is then reinforced.

One of the assumptions of a two-party democratic system is that consider-able inter-communication goes on between the supporters of the opposing sides. This evidence indicates that such intercommunication may go on in public — in the media of communication — without reaching very far into the ranks of the strongly partisan, on either side. In recent years, there has been a good deal of talk by men of good will about the desirability and necessity of guaranteeing the free exchange of ideas in the market-place of public opinion. Such talk has centered upon the problem of keeping free the channels of expression and communication. Now we find that the con-sumers of ideas, if they have made a decision on the issue, themselves erect high tariff walls against alien notions.

Such selective attendance upon sympathetic propaganda obtains, of course, only where a choice exists. But even if choice does not exist, even if exposure to unsympathetic material is accidental or forced, persons either do not perceive it, or, having perceived it, either tend to forget it or actually distort it to fit their existing views.

A host of laboratory experiments have established that perception of moving lights, relative size of coins, relative position of lines and the like is in part or whole determined by what persons want to perceive, have habitually perceived, or expect some form of social or physical reward for perceiving. Various devices have been successfully used to elicit apparently wholly sincere reports of perception quite out of accord with fact.

Similar findings have resulted from experiments using communica-tional material. Levine and Murphy found that pro-Soviet material was better learned and retained by pro-Communists than by anti-Communists, and that anti-Soviet material met the appropriately op-posite fate. Similar findings in reference to material on controversial issues are reported by Seeleman, Clark, and Watson and Herman. The typical conclusion is that "material which support(s) the subject's attitudinal frame . . . [is] retained better than material which oppose(s) it."

That communicational material on a controversial subject is actu-ally recast to fit the existent attitudes or frames of reference of the perceiver has been demonstrated both in the laboratory and in obser-vations of more normal social situations. Bartlett notes that material which cannot conveniently fit an existing predisposition is at once modified by the perceiver.

. . . recast to fit not only his span of comprehension and his span of reten-tion, but likewise his own personal needs and interests. What was outer becomes inner; what was objective becomes subjective.

Allport and Postman note a similar process of modification in rumors. That many cases of propaganda boomerang are merely results of this unconscious distortion of material to fit pre-existing attitudes is indicated by two studies, the one by Kendall and Wolf, the other by Cooper and Jahoda; in both cases the investigators found that cartoons ridiculing racial and religious prejudice were variously misunderstood by prejudiced persons as celebrating pure American lineage, as devices invented by Jews to stir up religious strife, and the like.

The importance of this data for our present inquiry lies in its clear indication of the potent obstacles immediately confronting would be attitude converters, whether working in the service of important civic attitudes or any other areas of opinion. Persons uninterested in or hostile to the persuader's case will deliberately avoid the communicated material, or, if they cannot avoid it, will tend to forget it or recast it to fit their already existing attitudes.[5] It is hardly surprising, when all these tendencies are noted, that Lazarsfeld, Berelson, and Gaudet found that seven months of campaign propaganda had reinforced the original intentions of 53% of the respondents and was *definitely known to have converted only 5%*.[6]

None of this, however, is to deny the possibilities of conversion,

---

[5] We have chosen to exclude discussion of "ego-involved" attitudes, which would add nothing to the present memorandum but a distinction in degrees of attitude persistence. In general, the massive literature on ego-involvements demonstrates that some attitudes are more important, basic, and affective to the individual than are others. These more "ego-involved" attitudes are the more resistant to change. As any attitude may be highly ego-involved for one individual and less ego-involved for another, extended discussion would in no way alter the conclusions of the present memorandum. It may be remarked, however, that attitudes regarding race or religion, both of which are civic attitudes, are generally believed to be highly ego-involved for most individuals.

[6] The present author regards as reinforced those whose stated vote intentions in October were the same as they were in May; as definitely converted those whose stated vote intentions in October were opposite to their stated May intentions.

Lazarsfeld, Berelson, and Gaudet emphasize "predisposition" more strongly than stated vote intention. The investigators discovered that voters could be classified as Republican-predisposed or Democratic-predisposed on the basis of certain socio-economic characteristics, and that even though the voters might be unaware of this predisposition, the classification could be used to predict final vote intention with approximately 67% accuracy. To the three investigators, therefore, persons who were at first undecided and then made a decision contrary to their predispositions are also convertees; those who had vote intentions in May but were undecided in October have undergone "partial conversion;" and those whose May intention was contrary to predispositions as have undergone "*re*conversion." "Reinforcement" is used by Lazarsfeld, Berelson, and Gaudet as we use it here. An additional 14% who were undecided in May but who finally decided in accord with predisposition are regarded as having undergone "activation." Using all these classifications, the three investigators report the effects of the campaign as follows:

Reinforcement, or activation of predispositions: 67%
Conversion, partial conversion, or reconversion: 17%
No effect: 16%

Total   100%

whether in regard to important civic attitudes or other beliefs. After all, 5% of the Erie County respondents are known to have been converted, and an additional 12% may have been converted. Instances of conversion are seen in everyday life.

Thus conversion is possible, although difficult and comparatively rare. The data already adduced not only indicate the obstacles to conversion, but suggest several conditions and techniques making for its greater likelihood. The point most strongly suggested by the existing literature is the futility of direct destructive attack on existing opinion and the greater desirability of building up the opposite belief.

Direct attack on an existing opinion[7] may be compared to asking a person to surrender a belief or way of life in which, for some reason, he places trust, i.e., from which he has obtained or expects to obtain some real or "psychic income." Such a direct attack is an attempt to convince the person that he will be disappointed, that he will not receive what he expects. Against such an attack the individual is strongly resistant. The attack thus meets the obstacles of selective perception in head-on collision. A positive appeal in favor of the opposite view, while often capable of eliciting resistance, seems however to be the less reluctantly received. This may well be due to the fact that such an appeal suggests positive rewards, rather than denying expected income.

Research suggests, in any case, that successful conversion more often follows the constructive appeal than the destructive attack. The process involved seems to consist in a slow building up of opposing opinion in regard to specific things, until the new view comes to override the older more general opinion. Thus Lowell remarks, without presenting confirming evidence, that

opinion changes by making exceptions to general rules until the rule itself is broken down . . . opinions have this in common with intrenchments that they offer an obstinate resistance to a frontal attack, but not to a turning movement.

Waples, Berelson, and Bradshaw, after a review of the literature on on conversions attributed to reading, find that

the change generally results from the reinforcement of an associated but subordinate attitude, which causes it to dominate the matrix of conflicting attitudes and interests . . . conversion is most likely to occur either when the counterappeal is made in terms which promise the reader the satisfaction of his personal interests (if nothing more tangible, simply the prestige of being converted) or when it elevates a previously subordinate attitude to a superordinate position (usually by supporting one loyalty or one part of the conscience against another.

[7] This paragraph is a purely personal attempt by the present author to explain in terms of simple reward psychology the fact that direct attack on existing opinion is less frequently successful than constructive appeal to the opposing view. The explanation is purely conjectural.

These quotations suggest that conversion begins with a birth of new opinion, rather than a questioning of the older view. It will also be remembered that laboratory experiments indicated that propaganda is much more effective among persons originally having no opinion than among those originally opposed. These observations seem to the present author to go far in explaining the observed effectiveness of another, or subsidiary device characteristic of conversions, viz. the introduction of new issues, about which the individual has as yet no opinion. Lazarsfeld, Berelson, and Gaudet observed, for example, that insofar as mass media led to conversion at all, it was through a redefinition of the issues . . . issues about which people had previously thought very little or had been little concerned, took on a new importance as they were accented by campaign propaganda.

These new issues may give birth to the new opinion, which, if properly fed, may slowly rise until it is in position to question the older view. It is noteworthy that many laboratory experimenters, working with extremely specific material (e.g., attitudes about conservation issues), note increased perplexity among persons otherwise unaffected by the propaganda. That such perplexity may be the first step in a process of conversion which could be completed by further exposure is suggested by a generalization of Waples, Berelson and Bradshaw.

Conversions may range from a minor alteration of attitude to a sweeping change in sympathies, knowledge, and behavior. The larger changes can seldom be ascribed to a single reading experience. Typical case studies of conversion to communism, for example, have the following steps in common: first, the reader chances on a liberal publication, which slightly increases his tolerance for that type of writing and his interest in reading more of it; second, the reader begins an eager search for publications which will meet his more serious objections to the doctrine; third, the readers say, "after much reading, I gradually came to see the wisdom of communism." The case study evidence supports the conclusions of group studies in explaining the predispositions favorable to such conversions. The explanation is that a change of attitude in the direction of the reading is facilitated by a sharp conflict of attitudes. The reading offers relief from the emotional disturbances caused by the conflict.

The fact that conversion, especially as it is the more extensive, may entail changes in daily living militates against such an effect occurring among those who can ill afford such changes. Lazarsfeld, Berelson, and Gaudet found that most of the very few persons

who tried more or less conscientiously to resolve their doubts, one way or the other during the campaign . . . [possessed] social position . . . such that they could "afford" conversion through thought.

In similar vein, Waples, Berelson, and Bradshaw note that

for any group conversions by reading, we must postulate a social environment which tolerates departures from the prevailing stereotypes. For this reason, the literary conversions are largely confined to the more liberal professions — to writers, teachers, artists, scientists, and philosophers.

(3) Summary

Of all conditions making for maximum likelihood of effective persuasion, the most potent seems to be the ability to achieve a monopoly propaganda position. Because American mass media are controlled by commercial interests who are concerned with maintaining the status quo, monopoly propaganda in America is and can be directed only upon the reinforcement or activation of attitudes already almost universally sanctioned. Persuasion for already sanctioned civic attitudes can avail itself of the aid of mass media and monopoly position.

Persuasion for civic or other attitudes to which there is substantial opposition cannot avail itself of such aid and furthermore encounters resistance in the psychological processes of the individual reader or listener. Selective perception and selective attention result in communicational material being largely unnoticed, forgotten, or distorted by those originally opposed to the view it espouses. Attitude conversions are thus comparatively rare.

Studies of accomplished conversions indicate that likelihood of conversion is increased if a destructive attack is avoided and an attempt is made instead to build up the opposing view. Such building is accomplished the more easily by introducing new issues. Conversion is, however, likely to occur only among those who can afford the risk of changing their opinions and possibly their social allegiances.

ADDITIONAL DEVICES OF SUCCESSFUL PERSUASION

While no exhaustive listing of propaganda techniques is either possible or relevant in the present memorandum, we will nevertheless attempt to cite some of the more general principles and practices which have been frequently observed as characterizing the more successful campaigns of persuasion. Except as specifically noted, the effectiveness of the devices is not dependent upon the nature of the goal of persuasion nor upon the climate of opinion at the start of the campaign. We have noted at some length that conversion is always more difficult than reinforcement or activation, and that working against the popular view is more difficult than working in league with generally sanctioned opinion. Existing opinion is a basic criterion of both the ease of the job and the likelihood of its success. Except as noted the devices discussed here merely serve to reduce somewhat the basic difficulty of the persuasive task, and thus to increase somewhat the likelihood of its successful effect.

(1) "Canalization"

Social scientists, public relations experts, and the like have commonly observed that persons are far more amenable to having their existing needs implemented than they are to developing entirely new needs. The efficacy of advertising is believed by some observers to be largely due to its almost exclusive concern with such "canalization." Lazarsfeld and Merton, for example, note that

advertising is typically directed toward the canalizing of preexisting behavior patterns or attitudes. It seldom seeks to instil new attitudes or to create significantly new behavior patterns. "Advertising pays" because it generally deals with a simple psychological situation. For Americans who have been socialized in the use of a toothbrush, it makes relatively little difference which brand of toothbrush they use. Once the gross pattern of behavior or the generic attitude has been established, it can be canalized in one direction or another. Resistance is slight.

The same authors caution, however, that

the leap from efficacy of advertising to the assumed efficacy of propaganda is as unwarranted as it is dangerous. . . . Mass propaganda typically meets a more complex situation. It may seek objectives which are at odds with deep-lying attitudes. It may seek to reshape rather than to canalize current systems of values.

Nevertheless, various successful propaganda campaigns have wittingly or unwittingly assumed for a time the cloak of canalizers. Some of the success of Kate Smith's marathon broadcast in the interest of war bond sales[8] was due, Merton believes, to her providing implementive aids for those just about ready to buy anyway. To elicit pledges from some persons

Smith had merely to canalize their intention to purchase the bonds then and there. . . . Her drive was perceived [by such persons] as an immediate and convenient opportunity for removing any lingering doubts. "I had planned to buy one anyway, but Kate Smith gave me a push." It enabled some to convert an intention into a commitment: "I decided to call even though I did not have the money in the house, so that I would have it in. I wanted to be sure I had it ordered, that's why I called." Similarly, others recognized that as long as they deferred the actual purchase, their good intentions were subject to the attrition of competing claims and expenditures. As one housewife put it, "the money would have been harder to part with the longer I waited." For these, the Smith drive afforded a ready occasion for resolving a conflict.

Various comparatively successful agitators have attempted to give their activity a similarly directive or canalizing aspect. The now established axiom of social psychology that many persons join a movement because of its promise of providing for an existing need suggests a positive response to what is essentially a canalizing appeal.[9]

[8] This particular case of mass persuasion is perhaps more akin to advertising than to engendering attitudes. Smith's marathon might more precisely be regarded as advertising in the civic interest.

[9] Whether such provision more properly falls under the head of "canalization" or "offering real rewards" is a moot question and one which seems to the author not particularly important to the present inquiry. The classificational imprecision is, however, duly acknowledged.

Persuasion in the interests of civic attitudes would seem as a rule unable to employ canalizing appeals. Occasionally, however, such persuasion may be able to offer a new channel for an existing behavior pattern or for the satisfaction of some need, however abstract. An outlet for patriotic feeling, a method of "belonging," or the like can probably be offered with good effect by certain campaigns of persuasion in the civic interest.

(2) Offering real rewards

The more objective literature on communication has taken only the most occasional and incidental note of the relation between the success of propaganda and the fact, nature, or certainty of the rewards it offers or appears to offer. That such expectation of reward is highly instrumental in any attitude change is, however, accepted as an established fact by a host of social psychologists, and is accorded extreme and at times even primary importance by such writers as Thorndike, Skinner, Hull, Levine, Dollard, and Hovland — in short by psychologists subscribing in whole or in part to Thorndike's "law of effect" or the various later related formulations.

It seems at the very least a reasonable conjecture that persons are the more likely to be persuaded as they envisage or experience a tangible or psychic reward from being persuaded.

The possible types of reward which might be effective in such a connection are perhaps infinite. Aside from such obvious desiderata as bonus checks, reduced taxes, and the like, any reduction in tension, any increase in status, any partial provision for any need might be sufficiently attractive to elicit a more widespread consent for the persuasion.

Such psychic income has been exploited either consciously or unconsciously by various successful persuaders. The more commonly offered psychic rewards include (a) agreement with social norms or majority opinion, (b) various types of in-group membership or "belongingness," and (c) release from tension.

The prospect of agreement with majority or respected opinions has been shown capable of altering individual belief by a plethora of experiments and investigations. The classic study by Sherif and its refinement by Asch deal with judgments about the movement of a light and are thus irrelevant to the present paper except for their classic demonstration of the general proposition. Newcomb's elaborate studies of attitudes among college students bear on numerous phases of personal opinion and the interpretation of various kinds of communicated material; in general he demonstrates that students moved from originally neutral positions on controversial issues to attitudes approximating those of their positive "reference groups," i.e., attitudes held by groups which they desired to join. Wheeler and Jordan modified student opinion on campus issues by making the majority view known. Sorokin and Baldyreff played two identical records of a symphony to a group of listeners previously informed that one record was "unanimously judged" by a group of music critics to be the better; 96% of the subjects thought one superior to the other, and 59% agreed with the "choice" of experts. Only 4% recognized the fact of identicality.

That agreement with majority opinion is regarded as an "end in itself" is at least implied by all these experiments and has been explicitly stated by Asch. Lazarsfeld, Berelson, and Gaudet likewise found numerous persons in Erie County whose vote decision was based entirely on the desire to be on the bandwagon. One respondent reported, for example, that

Just before the election it looked like Roosevelt would win so I went with the crowd. Didn't make any difference to me who won, but I wanted to vote for the winner.

The efficacy of psychic rewards in at least one successful campaign of radio persuasion is revealed in Merton's study of Kate Smith's war bond marathon. Smith not only offered rewards, but further insured their success by building up the need for them in her audience.

Smith continually reminded her listeners of the sacrifices being made by the servicemen, by other purchasers, and by herself, so eliciting in them a feeling of guilt in their own lesser sacrifices, a tension from which relief could now be attained. Thus, one respondent reported:

I was moved when she described a boy dying on the battlefield. She was telling about him from childhood up and telling how a bond could maybe save him. Of course, I thought of my own boy. That was the most impressive. Also the story of the legless man.[10] That was a beautiful sacrifice. I'd have been heartbroken with all the pleading and knowing Kate was sacrificing her time if I hadn't bought the bond.

By couching her "appeal . . . in terms of "we," "our," and "us" . . . Smith

brought her listeners in as co-workers. . . . The Smith war bond drive provided an occasion for joining in something specific, immediate and dramatic. It provided surcease from individuated, self-centered activity and from the sense that the war is too big for the individual's effort to count.

Thus one successfully persuaded respondent reported:

We felt that others had been impressed and bought a bond. And the fact that so many people felt the same way made me feel right — that I was in the right channel.

Merton notes that for such persons the purchase

represented not merely a stake in the war, but a stake in the communal undertaking directed by Smith. And, in many instances, once having bought

[10] Smith had previously told of a legless man who had saved for years to buy new limbs but had used the money for bonds instead.

a bond, people continued to listen to the radio drive, thus obtaining vicarious satisfaction from what others were doing in the same enterprise . . . [a] flow of gratification stemming from the success of a joint endeavor in which one was participating.

Smith's emphasis on the role of bonds in bringing back the boys permitted purchasers an additional and more personal reward.

I said to my daughter — "buy it off Kate Smith. Maybe that'll be the bond that will bring your brother home."

The veritable idolatry with which she is regarded by many of her audience permitted Smith to offer yet an additional reward — the joy of helping her personally both in her endeavor to amass pledges and in bringing her own drawn-out effort to a successful close. Some such purchasers looked upon telephoning their pledge as a gratifyingly close contact with Smith.

I felt that she was talking to me. . . . The thing that really made me pick up the phone [to order a bond] was when she said, "You're probably sick of listening to me, and I'm sick of talking about it, too, but I can't stop." I bought it then.

I really thought Kate would answer the phone. I just had the feeling she would; but I guess it was impossible. I could hear how busy the switchboard was . . .

At least one girl felt that "Smith's song was a response to her purchase," and another woman reported that

My daughter was wildly excited after she had made the phone call, and when some of her friends came in afterwards, she ran about the room from one to the other crying, "I bought a bond from Kate Smith."

All in all, it would seem that Smith's offered rewards of release from guilt, majority group membership, helping to bring back the boys, and personal contact contributed significantly to the success of her persuasion.

Vague in-group membership is apparently regarded as a reward by those who, after being persuaded by an agitator, consider themselves "in the know." A very concrete in-group membership was provided by Father Coughlin, whose followers actually met at scheduled times in organized local groups. For the socially insecure this cabalistic participation probably answered a real need, in addition to providing face-to-face contact which supplemented the mass media propaganda. Coughlin's local-group technique is considered by several social scientists, among them Lazarsfeld and Merton, to have contributed in various ways to his significant propaganda successes.

It would thus appear that persuasion is the more likely to be effective if tangible or psychic rewards are believed by the audience to follow upon consent. Specific application of this principle to persuasion for important civic attitudes is considered below.

(3) *Exploiting the prestige of media and spokesmen*

The proposition that persons are more susceptible to persuasion as they attach more prestige to the persuader is perhaps beyond the need of demonstration. That the actual speaker, writer, or attestor is not, however, the only possible effective prestige agent is revealed by various studies of propaganda success. The media themselves, an existent in-group, and majority opinion have all been found to be additional potent loci of prestige.

The mass media are themselves invested with an aura of prestige by a large portion of their audience. While the process of such investment can no longer be traced in detail, two stimulating agents would seem to be the frequent provision by the media of useful or needed information, and, perhaps more importantly, the very ubiquity of the mass media.

(a) The ubiquity of the media is noted by many social scientists and propaganda experts as the source of a prestige halo sufficiently great as to cast its light over the speakers and content presented through the media. Lazarsfeld and Merton are particularly emphatic and particularly cogent in remarking upon this process of "status conferral."

The mass media confer status on public issues, persons, organizations and social movements.

Common experience as well as research testifies that the social standing of persons or social policies is raised when these command favorable attention in the mass media. In many quarters, for example, the support of a political candidate or a public policy by *The Times* is taken as significant, and this support is regarded as a distinct asset for the candidate or the policy. Why?

For some, the editorial views of *The Times* represent the considered judgment of a group of experts, thus calling for the respect of laymen. But this is only one element in the status conferral function of the mass media, for enhanced status accrues to those who merely receive attention in the media, quite apart from any editorial support.

The mass media bestow prestige and enhance the authority of individuals and groups by legitimizing their status. Recognition by the press or radio or magazines or newsreels testifies that one has arrived, that one is important enough to have been singled out from the large anonymous masses, that one's behavior and opinions are significant enough to require public notice. The operation of this status conferral function may be witnessed most vividly in the advertising pattern of testimonials to a product by "prominent people." Within wide circles of population (though not within certain selected social strata), such testimonials not only enhance the prestige of the product but also reflect prestige on the person who provides the testimonials. They give public notice that the large and powerful world of commerce regards him as possessing sufficiently high status for his opinion to count with many people. In a word, his testimonial is a testimonial to his own status.

The ideal, if homely, embodiment of this circular prestige-pattern is to be found in the Lord Calvert series of advertisements centered on "Man of Distinction." The commercial firm and the commercialized witness to the merit of the product engage in an unending series of reciprocal pats on the back. In effect, a distinguished man congratulates a distinguished whiskey which, through the manufacturer, congratulates the man of distinction on his being so distinguished as to be sought out for a testimonial to the distinction of the product. The workings of this mutual admiration society may be as non-logical as they are effective. The audiences of mass media apparently subscribe to the circular belief: "If you really matter, you will be at the focus of mass attention and, if you are at the focus of mass attention, then surely you must really matter."

This status conferral function thus enters into organized social action by legitimizing selected policies, persons and groups which receive the support of mass media.

The mass media in fact possess sufficient prestige to invest a person deliberately with a powerful prestige of his own. Merton has shown that Kate Smith's phenomenal success in selling war bonds was due in no small measure to her having been variously built up as a "symbol of security and truth" and a person "competent in public affairs." Many persons purchased bonds simply because Kate Smith advised it. Respondents reported, for example, that

"She talk how the mother talk to the children."
"If everyone would follow her with their hearts,
    everything would be all right."
"You know what she says is true. Next to God
    she comes when she tells it to you."

(b) In addition to "legitimizing policies, persons, and groups" by casting upon them the prestige born of ubiquity, the mass media enjoy the peculiar trust of a large portion of their audience. Whether again because of their ubiquity, or because they have frequently provided necessary or useful information, the mass media are widely regarded sources of reliable advice and founts of truth. Hughes believes, on the basis of little or no objective evidence, that the human interest story accustomed readers "to regard the daily as an omnicompetent proxy for individual inquiry into matters they were idly curious about." Actual case studies reveal to Waples, Berelson, and Bradshaw that

when appropriate factual articles are not available . . . readers concerned about their own health . . . will seek answers to their problems in nonfactual reading, even in the bible.

That this prestige aura and the general trust in mass media contribute to effective persuasion is attested by numerous observers. Waples, Berelson, and Bradshaw find evidence that by and large people "tend to accept arguments they see [or hear] in the public communications" and that "an attitude frequently changes from a subordinate to a dominant position when it is justified by the authority of print," celluloid, or wireless.

Majority, or even special in-group or "in the know" opinion, has already been shown to possess sufficient prestige to render persuasion more effective. Indeed, the prestige attached to such opinion is so great that mere agreement with the majority or special group is apparently widely regarded as an end to be sought in itself.

The exploitation of prestige sources by persuasion in the service of important civic attitudes is briefly considered below.

(4) *Use of appropriate media*

That all media can be used for effective persuasion has been indicated in the early sections of this memorandum. That there is, however, some differential in their persuasive efficiency has also been noted, at some length, in the memorandum on comparative media effectiveness.

It seems to the present author that such differential effectiveness might be exploited by would be persuaders. The specific persuasive task could be analyzed for aspects suggesting that one medium might be preferable to another. An attempt to place any material before the more poorly cultured of the community, for example, would almost unquestionably reach more of its target group over the air than it would in print. Persuasion involving complex issues or instructions, on the other hand, would seem more likely of success if distributed in print. There seems little question, furthermore, that the use of multiple media would always contribute to the likelihood of persuasive success.

Supplementing mass media appeal by face-to-face contact has characterized several highly successful persuasive campaigns. Both the Nazis and the Soviets supplemented their domestic mass media campaigns by local discussion groups. The singular persuasive successes of Father Coughlin in this country likewise followed upon his simultaneous use of newspapers, pamphlets, radio, and local discussion groups.

Such combined media usage not only places the propaganda before the somewhat different audiences of the various media, but may also possess certain distinct advantages in intensity of appeal, in offering real and immediate rewards, and in conferring peculiarly high status upon both the media spokesman and his audience.

Intensity and reinforcement of appeal is probably provided by the local discussions following upon the media presentation. "Such mutual confirmation," Lazarsfeld and Merton believe, "produces a 'clinching effect.'"

Real and immediate reward accrues to the persuaded in the form of membership in a cabalistic "in-group." Social and status needs are immediately provided for.

More importantly, as Lazarsfeld and Merton point out,

the appearance of a representative of the movement on a nationwide network, or his mention in the national press, serves to symbolize the legitimacy and significance of the movement. It is no powerless, inconsequential enterprise. The mass media, as we have seen, confer status. And the status of the national movement reflects back on the status of the local cells, thus consolidating the tentative decisions of its members. In this interlocking arrangement, the local organizer ensures an audience for the national speaker and the national speaker validates the status of the local organizer.

In sum, whatever the reasons and processes of its effectiveness, the use of mass media supplemented by face-to-face contact seems a peculiarly effective persuasive device. The possible use of such a technique in persuading for civic attitudes is briefly discussed below.

(5) *Repetition and variation*

Belief that repetition in itself helps to make persuasion successful is manifested by current advertising techniques and asserted by public opinion experts. Analyses of the more successful campaigns of persuasion suggest, however, that although repetition is of some value, sheer parrot-like reiteration may begin to irritate the audience. Repetition with variations, on the other hand, serves both to remind the listener or reader constantly of the goal of the persuasion, and simultaneously to appeal to his several needs and drives. Thus Bartlett believes that it is not sheer repetition that is influential, but repetition with variations . . . so . . . that some new welcoming tendency stands a chance of being brought into play.

Repetition with variation is believed by Merton to have contributed heavily to the success of Kate Smith's war-bond marathon. Merton identified some sixty appeals, each to some degree distinct from any of its fellows, and all aimed at the same goal: the creation and reinforcement of the desire to buy a war bond and the intensification of that desire to the point of overt response. "Each new entreaty sought out a new *vulnerability* in some listeners," and the repeated exposure to these variant appeals reinforced the growing response-tendency in individual listeners. Lazarsfeld, Berelson and Gaudet not only found that varying appeals were peculiarly successful in campaign propaganda, but also that a certain degree of ambiguity apparently increased the effectiveness of appeals by rendering them susceptible of various interpretations.

(6) *Partial impartiality* ("One side versus both sides.")

Several rather elaborate experiments and observations have recently thrown additional light on the old question of whether persuasion is the more effective when only one side of the issue is presented, or when both sides are presented. In general, impartiality has been found to be the *less* effective technique except under certain specific conditions.

Actually opposing propagandas apparently tend to nullify each other's effects. In a controlled experiment, for example, Schank and Goodman found that persons exposed to propaganda on both sides of an issue showed no significant effects, except when "the issue was close to the life of the individuals, so that the details can be checked against private experiences"; in this specific case the subjects exhibited perplexity, but showed no immediate attitude change. Lazarsfeld, Berelson and Gaudet, observing a more normal social situation, found that opposing political propagandas had very litle effect upon the proportionate distribution of partisan vote intentions.

During the war years, the Information and Education Division of the War Department conducted extensive experiments comparing the "effects of presenting 'one side' versus 'both sides' in changing opinions on a controversial subject" (48-Ch.8). It is to be noted that while the Schank and Goodman experiment and the Lazarsfeld, Berelson and Gaudet survey were concerned with actual opposing propagandas, the two types of propaganda used by the War Department experimenters consistently favored the same view, differing only in the degree to which opposing arguments were recognized.

The War Department investigators found that presentation of "both sides" was more effective as a *converting* agent for the highly educated but that one-sidedness was more effective for the poorly educated. One-sidedness also proved more effective among men originally favoring the advocated view.

Presenting both sides in apparent by illusory impartiality was also found to be likely to boomerang for either of two reasons. If the pretense to impartiality is in any way suspect, the two-sidedness becomes peculiarly ineffective: omission "of one relevant argument against the stand taken by the programs was more noticeable in the presentation in which only one side was discussed." On the other hand, if the impartiality is too nearly complete, the propaganda may become a truly balanced presentation, in which case it will tend to be without effect. "When . . . readers are confronted with arguments both for and against an issue, the effects tend to cancel out."

SUMMARY

Persuasion for civic attitudes is subject to the same conditions as any other persuasion. With reference to persuasion in general, experiments and less formal observations indicate that the following generalizations can be made with reasonable confidence.

1. All mass media can and have been effectively used in persuasion. Investigators are generally agreed that attitude changes more often consist of modification than of conversion, and that the effects of successful persuasion wane but never entirely disappear. Cumulative exposure has been variously found to increase effects in some instances, to provide no incremental effect in others.

2. All mass media have also been observed to *fail* in attempted persuasion. Conditions other than the mere fact of propagandistic communication are apparently at work.

3. The condition believed to render persuasion most effective is

monopoly propaganda position. In the United States, such a position can be achieved only by persuasion for attitudes which already enjoy almost universal sanction.

4. Persuasion for attitudes toward which there is even mild community opposition is not only precluded from exercising monopoly propaganda, but furthermore encounters the resistance of the audience's selective perception and selective attention. Persons opposed to the espoused view tend to ignore or forget the material presented, or to distort it to fit their own views.

5. The difficulties of conversion seem to be somewhat reduced if the propaganda avoids destructive attack on existing opinion and attempts instead to build opposing opinion. Such building is facilitated by the introduction of new issues. Conversion is, however, likely to occur only among those who can afford to risk changing their opinions and possibly their social allegiances.

6. Certain additional devices and techniques have been observed to characterize successful propaganda campaigns. These include:

a. "Canalization," i.e., offering a new way to implement existing needs, as opposed to attempting to create the needs themselves.

b. Offering real rewards, which may be of a psychic nature, such as agreement with majority opinion, membership in an in-group, or release from some kind of tension.

c. Exploiting the prestige attendant upon mass media or particular persons, by using the media and such persons as transmitters or attestors of the propaganda.

d. Use of technically preferable media, and, in particular, supplementing mass media appeal by direct face-to-face contact.

e. The use of repetition, especially "repetition with variations."

f. The use of one-sided rather than illusorily impartial propaganda, *except* when appeal is made to more highly cultured persons known to be opposed to the view espoused.

SPECULATIONS REGARDING PERSUASION FOR CIVIC ATTITUDES

We have previously remarked that the conditions of likely success for persuasion in regard to important civic attitudes are no different from the conditions for likely success of any other persuasion.

It seems to the present author, however, that the general nature of persuasion for civic attitudes is sufficiently homogeneous that a few specific remarks and cautions might properly follow the general discussion of persuasion. The observations which therefore follow are, however, largely speculative, and are presented by the present author as merely personal conjectural offerings.

A distinction must first be made between civic attitudes which enjoy the *active* sanction of the community, and those which enjoy merely *verbal* sanction.

By active sanction we mean that community members commonly practice behavior in accordance with the attitude. All civic attitudes are likely to enjoy verbal sanction, but not all enjoy such active sanction. Thus, attitudes of political awareness and participation by voting enjoy both verbal and active sanction; people vote and encourage others to vote also. The concepts of racial tolerance and racial equality, on the other hand, enjoy verbal sanction in the North, but their active sanction is not so widespread. Quite aside from outright liars, many a white person who honestly believes himself in favor of racial equality will not in practice admit Negroes to his table, and prefers that they be kept out of his office except in a menial capacity. To the concept of racial equality he thus offers verbal, but not active sanction.

Persuasion in favor of civic attitudes which enjoy the *active* sanction of the community can take advantage of many of the conditions and devices cited in this memorandum. Persuasion to get out and vote, to take part in town meetings, and the like, can in fact avail itself of almost every device and condition mentioned. Such persuasion is likely to be unopposed, and thus to enjoy monopoly position; mass media will have no objection to taking part in the campaign, and will probably do so unless such participation involves too heavy a financial imposition. Insofar as some drive toward the espoused response-behavior already exists in the community, persuasion can offer a means of satisfaction of the drive and thus of release from tension. Additional rewards of majority membership and "belonging" can be honestly offered. Because the community approves, persons of prestige will be willing to take part in the campaign.

Persuasion in regard to civic attitudes which are *verbally* sanctioned, but which are denied *active* sanction by any significant portion of the community, starts out with a heavy handicap. Monopoly position may be possible to obtain, in the sense that the propaganda will not be verbally opposed by mass media, but neither will it be sympathetically regarded by media directors. The mass media will probably hesitate to carry the propaganda, and may even refuse to do so or may render the propaganda inoffensive by emasculation.[11]

[11] Note, for example, the activity by mass media and commercial advertising in apparent persuasion for racial tolerance. Slogans such as "Let's keep prejudice out of our town," or "We need all races to make our city run," may not even be recognized by the opposition as an attack. The verbally tolerant but actively intolerant do not consider themselves prejudiced; they merely believe that Negroes should serve in menial capacity, and since someone must serve in this way they agree that "we need all races to make our city run." *Crossfire,* one of mass media's touted attacks on anti-Semitism, also avoided offending the opposition. Anti-Semitism was portrayed as a homicidal drive. The great majority of anti-Semites in the audience were probably not murderously inclined to begin with, and the picture may well have made them feel that their own mild discriminatory practices were not, after all, "real" anti-Semitism.

Prestige spokesmen will be less easy to acquire. If the climate of opinion in the community is generally inimical, no reward of belonging to a majority group can be honestly held out, since social ostracism might follow conversion. A man, for example, who, like all his friends and business associates, discriminates against Negroes in employment, faces an actual loss of social position if he changes his practice. Above all other obstacles, propaganda against the *actively* sanctioned attitude will crash head on against the barriers of selective perception and selective attendance. The opposition will simply not hear, and, if by chance they do, will distort.

Yet such propaganda is not foredoomed to utter failure. In the first place, organized *verbal* opposition is unlikely. In the second place, it should be possible to obtain public endorsement by at least a few persons of prestige. Although the audience will consist largely of persons already sympathetic to the espoused view, some persons without strong opinions one way or the other will also make themselves accessible. Psychic rewards can be offered in the form of belonging to an in-group, if not a majority. Face-to-face contact and local group discussion can be planned to supplement more impersonal appeals.[12] The propaganda itself can be carefully designed to include such devices as repetition with variation, "partial impartiality," and the like.

Such propaganda, however, if it is to have any chance of success, *must* be carefully and deliberately planned. The exhibition of occasional posters, the repetition of mild slogans, are wastes of time, money, and posters which will avail literally nothing. The righteously civic minded must realize that the mere statement of the allegedly better way is useless. Conversion, to be successful, must be recognized as a difficult and aggressive operation, and must be planned accordingly.

[12] In the absence of local groups, some other possibility of active participation should be offered. Propaganda often succeeds in capturing its audience, and then lays down the gauntlet by providing no means of releasing tension. A good example is the current series of car cards which present a picture of a truly horrifying demon clothed in red, over the simple caption "Stop Fires and Save Lives." Many people who see this card are probably convinced, but being unsure of what methods to take they do nothing and shortly forget about the matter. Similar frustration in regard to propaganda for racial tolerance is amusingly noted by Dr. Louis Wirth: "I recall an experience I had a few months ago, riding in a streetcar in Chicago. There were three placards in front of me. One was a red, white, and blue placard, with a picture of George Washington, which said, 'Brotherhood Week — Be a Brother.' The next one read, 'No Prejudice in Our Town,' and it showed a group of children, white and Negroes, and a dog. And the third one said, 'Joe Doakes, Candidate for Alderman from the Fifth Ward — Vote for Joe next Tuesday.' I knew what to do about Joe, but I did not know what to do about the rest."

▲ LEONARD DOOB

$\mathcal{T}$he Behavior of Public Opinion

Public opinion has been defined and its relation to culture has been indicated. The next problem is to examine the characteristics of attitudes which people share. How does public opinion behave? The answer to this question may be a literary description of people in a social setting or an analysis growing out of their behavior as individuals.

Cantril's approach can serve as the serious prototype of the literary or loosely impressionistic description.[1] After observing the findings of public opinion polls in the United States from 1939 to 1941, he has formulated what he calls seventeen "laws of public opinion." Even as they stand, these "laws" do not reveal anything startling and many of them are vague and ambiguous. Most are applicable only to the period and the kind of opinion he studied. At least two are not "laws" in any sense but represent uncritical praise of public opinion and a gratuitous bit of sensible advice to democratic leaders. Cantril's "laws" are both tempting and vulnerable targets, tempting because they are superior to less systematic attempts and vulnerable because they are so glibly stated and so confused.

The first "law" states: "Opinion is highly sensitive to important events." Certainly such sensitivity is not always revealed. Many American experts, for example, consider a project like the Tennessee Valley Authority an important event, but there is little evidence to show that Americans by and large have concerned themselves intimately with the inception, development, notable achievements, and political ad-

[1] Hadley Cantril and associates, *Gauging Public Opinion* (Princeton University Press, 1944), pp. 226-30.

▲ This is a chapter from Professor Doob's *Public Opinion and Propaganda*, published and copyright by Henry Holt and Company (New York, 1948). It is reprinted here by permission of the copyright holder. Professor Doob is a member of the psychology faculty at Yale.

versities of that regional plan. What, moreover, is "important" and who is to make the judgment? In the fall of 1946, it seemed to many observers that the criticism of American foreign policy by Henry Wallace and his consequent resignation from the President's cabinet were important events. A Gallup poll on October 13 of that year, nevertheless, revealed that only 42 percent of a representative sample of Americans paid attention to the controversy, a figure scarcely indicating high sensitivity. The "law," consequently, must mean that people react to those events to which they have already reacted by considering them important — they react when they react.

The third "law" is: "Opinion is generally determined more by events than by words — unless those words are themselves interpreted as an 'event.' " This is a generalization derived directly from the war situation when battles speak louder than words. Or else the qualification of words being interpreted as an "event" means that people react to stimuli, which is certainly true. The gossip in a small community that rips apart an individual's reputation in the eyes of public opinion seems to be a series of phrases and sentences communicated in a provoking manner, as is an advertisement for a mouth wash. If gossip and advertisements be called "events," then every stimulus is an event.

The ninth "law": "When self-interest is involved, public opinion in a democracy is likely to be ahead of official policy." Here Cantril refers to evidence indicating that prior to Pearl Harbor "a majority of the public" in the United States favored measures which helped Great Britain in her war against Germany and Italy "on an average of four months before legislation was passed." There is a definite value-judgment involved in the simple word "ahead": the implication is that, under the specified condition, public opinion somehow grasps the wiser policy before its representatives do and that public opinion, therefore, is wiser or more far-sighted than its representatives. The fact that people think something before their representatives act may simply demonstrate that leaders are affected by followers and that what eventually occurs is no sign of the leaders' wisdom but a reflection of public opinion. Cantril's own data based on polls between September 1939 and December 1941, moreover, can be turned against this "law" if the answers to other polling questions are made the units of measurement. Presumably, for example, the same "self-interest" of the American people was involved in March of 1940 before the German invasion of Norway; yet only 1 percent believed then that this country "should declare war on Germany." In July of the same year after the fall of France the figure rose a mere 2 percent. In May 1941 after the sweep of the Germans through the Balkans and Greece it reached a high of 10 percent. Why did not "self-interest" function during those critical days? One month before Pearl Harbor only about one-quarter of a polling sample thought the United States "should enter the war." A week or so before the Japanese attacked, less than one-third stated that they "would vote to go to war against Germany if a national vote were taken." Public opinion apparently needed some Japanese bombs before it could catch up with itself. If the United States had not entered World War II, Cantril could have then employed these data — rather than the ones he misleadingly chose — to pay tribute to the wisdom of public opinion.

The seventeenth and final "law" proclaims: "By and large if people in a democracy are provided educational opportunities and ready access to information, public opinion reveals a hard-headed common sense. . . ." This is a direct and no doubt laudable plea for public enlightenment. But it is not a characterization of public opinion because every man has his own meaning of "hard-headed common sense." In addition, the statement seems merely to suggest that the more information people are given; the better informed they will be — with the weasel provision — "by and large."

These "laws" of Cantril, it can be seen, reveal the pitfalls confronting anyone attempting to generalize about the behavior of public opinion on the basis of a loose conception of public opinion. Cantril has admitted that his statements apply only "with respect to public opinion in a democracy." As a matter of fact, they are informally derived from the crudest type of pubic opinion measurement (the poll) which was applied to a particular group of people (Americans) on an unusual set of issues (mostly war) at a specific time (1939-1941) when the United States was organized or disorganized in a more or less unique fashion and when the media of communication were expressing a series of heterogeneous viewpoints.

The specificity of Cantril's type of approach to public opinion can be avoided — as he himself avoids it in three of his "laws" which will be mentioned in the course of this chapter — only by first considering the general characteristics exhibited by people in their thinking and behavior. Public opinion has the characteristics about to be enumerated and analyzed because people possess them. People possess them because they are learned during socialization and reinforced thereafter.

CONSISTENCY

It is a notorious fact that people are inconsistent. One day they like a painting, and the next day they are repelled by it. One week they are in love, and the next they avoid the person without whom, they have been saying, life would be unendurable. One month they like warm weather, and the next they seek the cold. One year they are enthusiastic about their occupation, and the next they make every effort to find a new position. In addition, the same individual may possess two or more beliefs which an outsider considers inconsistent, a view with which he himself might agree if he could be made to concentrate upon their strictly logical consequences. He may distrust or sneer at the judgments of the masses but also be in favor of "democracy"; or he may like and dislike the same individual simultaneously.

To call behavior inconsistent at a given moment or over a period of time is frequently misleading because, as Allport has shown in his analysis of personality, apparently inconsistent actions may be consistent with a broader principle or set of attitudes within the individual. The man who distrusts the masses but who favors "democracy" may be quite consistent from his own viewpoint: as a social critic he is convinced that people have faults but that in the long run a system which takes their fumblings into account is "better" than the alternatives at hand. Socially and perhaps logically he is inconsistent; psychologically he is consistent.

The criterion of consistency is usually applied by an outsider; the individual himself may or may not appreciate the consistency or inconsistency of his own behavior. That outsider expects two responses to be aroused and to lead to a state of conflict. The conflict, however, may not occur. In the first place, one of the two internal responses which might produce the conflict is not evoked because past experience has not placed the present stimulus along its generalization gradient. To the stimulus "government-ownership-of-railroads" most Americans respond with something like "socialism-and-I-don't-like-it"; whereas to "government-ownership-of-mail" they do not respond "socialism-but-I-like-it" but "necessary-and-I-like-it." Here there is no conflict and hence no inconsistency because the different stimuli give rise to compatible responses. Approximately the same stimulus, moreover, can arouse different responses which may be labelled inconsistent or fickle by the outsider when he neglects to observe that the individual concerned has changed in the interim. In our society the young boy's contempt for girls almost completely disappears as he matures and is replaced by a positive attraction toward them. The explanation is fairly obvious: the initial reaction to girls has proved after a while to be more punishing than rewarding; hence it has been extinguished and has been replaced by a more satisfactory one. The question of inconsistency merely calls attention to the changed behavior over a period of time.

The conflict between two internal and "inconsistent" responses, in addition, can be quickly resolved when the drive strength of one is stronger than the other. The American who consistently demands ice with his highball may "inconsistently" consume a lukewarm whiskey-and-soda in England because there, unless he is willing to accept a drink without ice, he may not drink at all. Hartshorne and May have shown that American school children in the twenties tended to be neither consistently honest nor dishonest: they cheated in one situation like the school and not in another like the home. The complex stimulus of the school elicited a drive to achieve a high grade and cheating became an instrumental act toward that end, in comparison with which any response involving "honesty-is-the-best-policy" apparently was much weaker. In the home, on the other hand, that latter response was stronger and the equivalent of the former was weaker as a result of punishments received for being dishonest. If a child is to be consistently honest in all situations, then he must learn that every situation falls along the gradient which evokes a strong drive in connection with honesty.

As Cantril indicates in his sixteenth "law," inconsistency or fickleness of public opinion may be similarly viewed. Many people possess incompatible beliefs concerning the issues of the day without being in a state of conflict. The responses which could give rise to conflict may not exist, may be evoked at different times, or may be of different strength. The hero of yesterday, for example, becomes the villain of today or is forgotten altogether not because people are downright superficial or perversely whimsical but because their attitudes in the meantime have been altered as a result of the experiences they have had. Charles A. Lindberg was not the same stimulus in 1927 after he had flown alone to Paris as he was in 1939 after he had expressed political and social views at variance with those to which many Americans were subscribing.

In short, the problem of the consistency of public opinion cannot be posed or settled for all time. What must be examined is not the end products as revealed by a poll or by other behavior but either the entire organization of attitudes and habits within people or their reasons for changing — or both. People may continually disapprove of murder, they may change their style of clothing once every fourteen months, or they may grow to love a leader only after he is dead. They may be seduced into smoking one brand of cigarettes rather than another as a result of a high-pressure advertising campaign, they may refuse to use lemon juice to cure hangovers in spite of another vociferous campaign, or they may more or less spontaneously adopt zootsuits. Such descriptions — revealing inconsistency or consistency — require deeper probing before the reasons for the stability or the instability can be ascertained.

RATIONALIZATION

Life for most people, as the platitude would have it, seldom runs smoothly. Drives are evoked and the goal responses which would reduce their tension and bring satisfaction cannot be made. There is scarcity, whether natural or artificially created, in any society. Human relations produce friction. Socialization is not pleasant, for the neophyte is required to renounce many of his goals and modes of behavior and to learn to conform to society's demands. Crises continually occur in the life of the individual and his country. Frustration, conflict, and anxiety are always present.

Few people, however, accept frustrations and anxieties without seeking to make themselves feel less dissatisfied and more comfortable, nor do they tolerate conflicts without striving to resolve them. The avoidance or the reduction of frustration, anxiety, and conflict, therefore, is a constant problem. Public opinion can be understood in large part as a collection of responses to adversity.

Rationalization occurs when the pain resulting from one response sets up a stronger response which thereby reduces or almost eliminates that pain. "Sour-grapes" is the traditional way of describing what rationalization involves. The individual who fails to achieve an objective then explains to himself or others that he really preferred to fail because the attained objective would have been unsatisfactory. The rejected suitor sighs with relief when his lady love says "no," consciously because he manages to convince himself that married life with her would have been intolerable and unconsciously because he may have been afraid of marriage and the sexual, social, and economic responsibilities it entails. Sometimes a conflict is resolved by eliminating one of the conflicting responses through a response which in turn conflicts with it: the citizen who cannot decide whether to vote or play golf on election day weakens the first tendency by deciding that his one vote would be unimportant anyhow.

The ability to find an appropriate if misleading justification for behavior may have beneficial consequences. The individual can protect himself from the distress which conflict, anxiety, or failure produces. It is comforting to think that the grapes would have been sour since then the failure to obtain them becomes not a disappointment, but a piece of good luck. Dodging reality thus can diminsh dissatisfaction. The soldier in combat who is afraid, bored, or disgusted feels happier and is probably more efficient if he can tell himself or be told that it is better to be in the armed forces during wartime than to remain a civilian and if he can also find other good reasons for seeming to prefer his present occupation. Middle-class people who actually envy the upper class find solace in pointing out that they themselves are more moral, respectable, or useful than their envied contemporaries.

Rationalizations, however, can also lead to difficulties. The anxiety, the frustration, or the conflict may be only superficially assuaged, and its pain can continue to affect the individual in ways which his rationalization prevents him from consciously detecting. He may feel vaguely discontent without knowing precisely why. He may dream about sweet grapes. He may forget about fruit or failure and displace his anger upon some innocent and irrelevant object. Or he may remain simply muddled or neurotic.

Many people exhibit more or less similar rationalizations when they are uncomfortable for more or less similar reasons. Under such circumstances it can be said that public opinion is rationalizing because the attitudes regarding the issue have resulted from the unsolved problems at hand. In spite of concentration camps, death marches, and other instances of "man's inhumanity to man," for example, it is not always easy for one group of people to exploit or be cruel to another group. There may be ethical principles in the society which oppose exploitation or cruelty, or individuals who are taught to be cooperative and kind in the family cannot automatically behave differently in relation to outsiders. Race prejudice, therefore, is almost always accompanied by theories which justify current practices and thus help to rid the dominant group of some of its guilt:

"They are lazy."
"They are biologically inferior."
"They are like animals."
"They are just children."
"They are immoral."
"They love to be bossed."
"They have no one but themselves to blame."
"They are all alike."

Rationalizations like these may also be accepted in part by the subordinated group and thus serve to allay some of its frustration. Similarly, "good excuses" are offered whenever people feel guilty about aspects of their society, such as poverty, unemployment, imperialism, war, and the dropping of atomic bombs.

Rationalizations of groups appear to have at least three origins. In the first place, there are the traditional, ready-made explanations which are part of the culture and which are inevitably transmitted during socialization. Justification of race prejudice, through a commonly accepted theory about the subordinated group, is part of the dominant group's heritage which is accepted by each generation not merely because it is promulgated at home, in the school, and in the media of communication but also because each individual feels within himself — consciously or unconsciously — the need for such a theory as a result of the guilt he experiences after contact with the out-group. Then, secondly, there are rationalizations of new situations which are provided by leaders and propagandists. During a war men and women frequently must be told why they are fighting, since fighting is an activity in which relatively few of them are willing to engage until they are given good reasons for doing so. One of the most important techniques in propaganda is to offer hesitant people the effective rationalizations they require to alter their behavior in a manner that helps the propagandist achieve his objective. There are, finally, other rationalizations which seem to arise spontaneously among many people without previous provision by the culture or by leaders. Cantril points out in connection with one of his "laws" that "there was invariably a rise of around ten percent" in the number of people favorable to measures which aided Great Britain before the United States entered the last war (like Lend-Lease) immediately after those measures became law. People changed no doubt because the measures were publicized as Congress was debating them, but they could not conceivably have experienced at the time any direct effects from the new regulations. At least in part they must have been rationalizing an accomplished fact.

Be it noted, in passing, that rationalization always raises a question of fact. The grapes may actually be sour, a condition which the individual can perceive by looking at them. The group against which discrimination is expressed may be "really just children" in some juvenile sense (though, of course, the reason for their childish characteristics is not their physiological structure but the subordination they have had to suffer). To accuse an individual or group of rationalizing, consequently, presupposes knowledge of their real psychological states or of the relevant factors in the external environment that are being perceived.

DISPLACEMENT

When confronted with frustration, anxiety, or conflict, the individual may seek not only to rationalize the adversity but also to do something else which will bring him satisfaction. That something else is a substitute goal response evoked in large part by the pain which thus acts as a drive. One of the commonest forms of substitute activity is the partial reduction of the pain through responses involving destruction or the expression of hostility.

A drive to destroy or be hostile is one of the consequences of frustration and in this sense frustration is the failure to reduce a drive, to eliminate anxiety, or to resolve a conflict. It appears as though the initial impulse is to express aggression toward the person, persons, or object that is thought to have brought on the frustration in the first place. The child strikes the chair into which he has bumped or hits the playmate who has been teasing him. Frequently, however, this initial impulse is inhibited because the individual knows that such behavior will bring him only additional grief. In this situation, a substitute target is consciously or unconsciously sought. The expression of aggression against such a substitute is called displacement. Instead of hitting his older and stronger playmate, the child hits a younger and hence less dangerous associate or he may even strike himself.

One of the important psychological functions of society is to provide its members who suffer from various frustrations with targets onto which aggression can be displaced. A favorite target seems to be another group which actually is, or which is considered to be, different from the individual's own. The ancient Hebrews sought each year to escape from the guilt generated by their sins and dispatched into the wilderness a goat that was supposed to bear these sins away. Usually, however, the scapegoat is less symbolic: it is much easier to hate and feel aggressive toward other human beings.

Germans were in a state of readiness to respond to the Nazis' anti-Semitism because, in addition to historical and cultural precedents for this form of persecution, they were eager to affix responsibility upon someone or something for the frustrations they endured or thought they endured during the period after World War I and especially during the depression of the early thirties. It seemed to many allied observers during the last war that Propaganda Minister Goebbels launched an attack upon the Jews whenever Germans had experienced or were about to experience another military reverse or a cut in the food ration. Thus the Jews were used as scapegoats onto whom the bitterness and disappointment of many Germans could be displaced.

Frequently individuals in their more rational moments hesitate to displace aggression. The tired businessman tries valiantly to control his temper when he returns home after a miserable day at work. He knows that his wife and children are not the source of his annoyance and he inhibits himself, if he can, from considering them to be annoying. He presumably loves his family, moreover, and wishes to cause them no additional unpleasantness. The advantage of displacing aggression upon outsiders becomes apparent when it is realized that the individuals specified as the target by society or by leaders usually are those toward whom no or little affection has been previously felt. Shortly after the last war, some Germans inside Germany admitted to the writer — without guile, he believes — that they did not object to Hitler's anti-Semitic maneuvers until they themselves knew particular Jews who had been persecuted or until they came to learn in detail exactly what persecution entailed.

The presence of other people frequently facilitates displacement since individuals by themselves hesitate to inflict pain or injury upon a scapegoat. As members of a group, however, they may find the courage to do so because they feel that the involvement of the others legitimatizes their own actions or renders them less liable to punishment. Rationalization of displacement can also occur when people feel that others who cannot be immediately perceived but whose existence is suggested by the media of communication are similarly behaving. During a war the displacement of aggression upon the enemy is effectively promoted by propaganda among people who are widely separated.

COMPENSATION

Aggression, whether displaced or not, is only one of the consequences of frustration. Another form of substitute goal response called compensation consists of reducing a different drive which has not been involved in the original frustration. Sometimes compensation is thought to be the healthy or sensible thing to do rather than to rationalize the pain or to be aggressive. The girl who cannot attract boys because she is not sufficiently beautiful may find in intellectual pursuits a form of compensation which brings its own rewards. Those rewards and the drives they satisfy, it must be quickly added, are probably not quite so satisfactory as the ones originally sought. For this reason the young lady may over-compensate by expending extra energy in achieving the substitute goal — and still remain unsatisfied.

Compensation is frequently necessary when there is no other way to reduce the blocked drive. Wishful thinking and day-dreaming, for example, represent innocuous forms of compensation to which the individual resorts because thoughts and dreams cannot be easily inhibited by environmental pressures. Much of the activity associated with the arts is compensatory: people escape from well-known harsh realities into a region of fantasy where life is pleasant and where problems are either solved or, if unsolved, can be gloatingly disassociated from the normal personality.

There are, in addition, social institutions which serve the psychological function of relieving misery and pain in a compensatory manner. Besides the arts, established forms of entertainment and games, festivals and holidays, and religious and other associations enable people to withdraw, temporarily at least, from their ordinary obligations and restraints. Each society has its own kind of circus and, after the performance has ended, the spectators are less reluctant to return to their customary way of life.

People demand compensatory activity especially when they are experiencing some kind of crisis. Forms of indulgence like drinking and sexual promiscuity are popular, for example, during a war. This drink-and-be-merry behavior seeks not only to drown the sorrows of the moment but also to diminish anxiety concerning the anticipated fate of tomorrow.

Public opinion in small and powerless countries tends to be both actual and intense regarding issues like national greatness of sovereignty. Such attitudes result in part from the ease with which group spirit can be established when the group is smaller and also from the need to cooperate which is produced by a somewhat hostile outside world. In addition they are compensatory reactions to feelings of inferiority: the country may be tiny, its inhabitants say and are told, but its water and milk are pure and its history is most ancient and honorable.

PROJECTION

To understand another person is usually difficult. For the external behavior which he is exhibiting can be variously interpreted and the drives, attitudes, and knowledge which have produced the behavior also cannot be immediately deciphered. When faced with the problem of understanding someone else, therefore, the individual can adopt one of two shortcuts: he can believe that the other person is like himself or that he himself is like the other person. The first process is called projection and the second identification.

Among psychiatrists and laymen the classical illustration of projection which provokes both pity and mirth is the old maid who reports to the police that a man has designs on her. Consciously or unconsciously, the explanation goes, she wishes to be raped (or at least to experience some of the preliminaries thereto) ; she dares not acknowledge such feelings to herself; she protects herself, therefore, by ascribing her own drive to the hapless male; and the hostility she displays toward him is in fact a reflection of the shock which her own impulses have created within her. Ordinarily projection is neither so dramatic nor clearcut. The individual may have had a series of painful experiences with strangers or with people in general. He is afraid that social contact will bring additional punishment. He avoids people or becomes generally hostile toward them, though he still wishes to be sociable. He then rationalizes his own avoidance tendency and he smothers his desire to be with them by concluding that they are seeking to hurt him. He thus projects onto them his own hostility, while complaining that nobody is really interested in his welfare. If he is neurotic, he may never discover that he is the victim of his own delusions.

Projection, however, need not be motivated by repression or hostility. "We are all human after all" is a sentence which frequently introduces projection: the other people whose behavior is being called human are thought to be like the individual who utters the cliché. For each individual feels that to a certain extent he understands his own behavior. If others are felt to be similarly motivated, then their actions become clear — or at least clearer. Projection on a large scale usually permeates most of the institutions of a society. In the field of religion, for example, men make gods in their own images and project upon them their own foibles and virtues.

The attitudes at the base of public opinion exhibit projection for a variety of reasons. People have a tendency to rationalize some of their own displacements by concluding that others are similarly displacing. In-group solidarity, for example, is promoted by the presence of an out-group as Sumner and others have pointed out: internal aggression is displaced upon members of the out-group and it is claimed that they and not one's own group is aggressive. Hitler employed this technique again and again to rationalize Nazi penetration of a foreign country.

Then socialization occurs primarily in the family, the one social group in which the members closely resemble one another. In this situation projection is more likely to be accurate, as it is whenever people are subjected to similar cultural stimuli and possess rather similar personalities from the outset. The habit of projecting, consequently, is reinforced and is later generalized to situations outside the family.

In addition, the leaders of a society frequently attempt to encourage projection. He who hesitates to leap on a bandwagon, for example, is told by a politician that the people already astride the vehicle are like himself: they want the same things, they are "plain folks" too. The citizen is supposed to ascribe to them all of his own feelings and hence to vote as they do.

IDENTIFICATION

Projection in reverse is identification: instead of ascribing his own behavior to other people and saying "They are like me," the individual feels that he is acting like them or tries consciously or unconsciously to do so. "I am like them," he maintains. Impulses may be projected upon other people who are loved or hated, but identification occurs only when the individual already possesses a favorable attitude toward the people with whom he identifies. A mother is torn with mental pain when she perceives that her child is undergoing physical suffering. Naturally her pain is not the same as the child's, but its drive strength is such that she becomes more attentive, perhaps over-attentive, and seeks means to reduce the suffering. Identification between an individual and a real or imaginary villain indicates that this villain or some of his traits are not thoroughly detested.

Projection and identification, though opposite in nature, may occur in the same situation and serve to complement each other. The follower, for example, projects his own reactions to a crisis onto a leader whom he respects. If he feels weary or ill-at-ease, he imagines that the leader is experiencing similar misery and, after making the assumption, he then identifies himself with the man and hence experiences what he believes would be his own responses in that position. The target of his projection and identification of course may be blasé and unmoved by the crisis, or he may be responding to it quite differently.

Many of the subtler forms of communication which occur between people involve identification. As poets have frequently observed and as every man in his own manner at some time in his life perceives with cosmic sorrow, each of us is dreadfully alone in the world. Every human experience is unique for the individual who has the experience. The unspeakable remains unspeakable or at least is never adequately expressed. People can break through the solipsistic crust which envelops them only by contact with other people. The contact consists of observation or the exchange of experience through language. Language is an imperfect means of communication because words, in the terminology of modern semantics, are only signs or symbols for the experience of the speaker or for the objects or situations to which they refer. By making every effort to place oneself in the psychological mood of the other person — the lover does this in reference to his beloved and the attentive reader in regard to the poetry before him — the individual is thus better equipped to understand someone beside himself and perhaps to be understood.

The earliest form of identification is that between the child and his parents and later perhaps between the child and his older or younger brother or sister. Gradually the individual learns to identify with more and more people as he matures until the good patriot believes that he himself experiences about the same emotions and feelings of all his countrymen. Psychologically, therefore, identification is one of the mainsprings of social or group life. Copious but not completely convincing evidence has been gathered which indicates that the success of a group leader is in part a function of his ability to act as a substitute for the person, usually the parent, with whom the individual first learned to identify. Certainly it is no coincidence that modern leaders occasionally employ family terms like "my children" and "my son" and that the Deity is referred to as Father. Such symbolic metaphors suggest, as Freud in particular has pointed out, the original foundation for in-group loyalty.

Public opinion involves identification with leaders or with fellow members of the same group. Esprit de corps, for example, consists of the awareness not only of a common goal and of group traditions, but also of the members of the group who are striving for that goal. The individual is willing to make sacrifices and conform regardless of his own attitudes when he is convinced that others are enduring similar privations. People are moved by pity and hence the leader who can elicit this response and direct it toward himself has increased his chances of being effective.

CONFORMITY

One of the characteristics of group life which almost always requires rationalization is the pressure to conform to the will of the majority. On the one hand, people know that conformity usually brings safety and security. They know this because the advantages of conforming have been stressed from earliest infancy: children in our society who do not conform to their parents' wishes are generally punished. As part of the socialization process they are quickly indoctrinated with a sense of family solidarity, for they can easily observe that their own welfare and rewards are dependent upon the ways they conduct themselves in relation to those who immediately engulf them. When they mature, they learn the immediate and ultimate value to themselves of esprit de corps or school or community spirit, phrases which automatically suggest that the group is more important than the individual. People are educated to be sensitive to the responses of others. They are reared to become parts of publics whose opinions they possess, reflect, and affect.

On the other hand, conformity can be frustrating. Individuals have their distinctive personalities and, more often than is usually imagined, they react unfavorably to the procrustean demands of their group. Sometimes conformity is then rationalized; at other times society is defied.

The very existence of public opinion on a given issue is an indication of conformity. For public opinion means that people agree to the extent that they have rather similar attitudes. The conformity may be more or less complete. If there is real conformity, the range of verbal or non-verbal responses may be represented graphically by a curve which, as Floyd H. Allport and his students have shown, has the shape of an inverted J. Along the horizontal line or abscissa are plotted the various responses to the issues and along the vertical line or ordinate the number of individuals displaying the responses indicated on the abscissa. The curve connecting the points starts high up on the ordinate since many individuals make almost identical responses. Then it slopes down steeply since few people exhibit the other or non-conforming responses. If responses were distributed by chance — and what chance would be is by no means clear since social responses tend always to be affected by conformity-producing institutions or situations — the so-called normal or Gaussian curve that resembles the shape of a bell would appear. Under these circumstances few individuals display extreme responses and hence both ends of the curve slope downwards (resembling the edges of the bell's profile); but many individuals are in a middle position and hence the curve has a hump in the center (resembling the top of the bell). Research has shown a marked tendency for external public opinion on a given issue to be J-shaped and for internal public opinion on the same issue to be normally distributed. The discrepancy between what some people openly say they believe and what they really believe indicates the pressure of conformity.

Whether the distribution of external public opinion itself is J- or bell-shaped on a given issue is a very important fact to know. The more the curve — hypothetical or actual — approximates the shape of the inverted J, the more conformity there is in respect to the response being observed. The external public opinion of a well-unified group on a variety of issues is J-shaped; the size of the tail of the J or the tendency of the curve to approach the form of a bell is a measure of the group's disunity. The shape of the curve, however, is a function of the group whose responses are being considered. The responses of an entire country on an issue like taxation may be normally distributed: a few people believe that taxes are much too high and approximately an equal number that they are much too low; the majority cluster around the position that taxes are about right or perhaps a trifle too high. The possibility must be recognized that public opinion on the issue may be stratified along social or economic class lines. The distribution of lower-class public opinion and that of upper-class opinion may be J-shaped, with the majority of the former believing taxes are much too low and the majority of the latter maintaining that they are much too high. The distribution curve for the entire country may thus be masking the real class-determined conformity which exists.

The opponents of democracy are fond of saying that people are like sheep: they conform to the wishes of their leader. This statement contains a grain of truth if its poorly concealed sneer is eliminated. It does require courage or a neurosis or both not to conform to public opinion, and few people have these qualifications. Many of the heroes of present-day American society, including historical characters like George Washington as well as products of folklore like Paul Bunyan, are now portrayed and praised as men who defied the convention of their times. A radical in any field who is still alive and exhibiting his nonconformity, however, is likely to be persecuted or shunned. In retrospect a man's motivation is not always considered as important as his social accomplishments, whereas at the moment all phases of him are judged and evaluated. Fortunately or unfortunately, there are always some individuals in any society whose constitutions and experiences are sufficiently peculiar or different so that they become nonconformers. It is they, the true leaders of a generation, who sense latent public opinion even while recognizing that actual public opinion is opposed to their efforts.

To be unconventional or to defy the culture is usually a punishing experience, and therefore individuality is freely and willingly sacrificed to achieve other gratifications or, at the very least, to avoid the penalties of being an out-grouper. The bandwagon of culture remains attractive because it is carrying other people and because so many human gratifications come from people. The conventionally dressed male in our society sometimes dreams of being able to toss aside his collar and to have his neck feel perpetually comfortable. He rarely gives expression to this impulse, except in the privacy of his home and in other situations where society is more tolerant. This is indeed a sacrifice which he makes because discarding collars on all occasions would produce inconveniences not worth the revolutionary gesture. William James's famous phrase describing habit as "the enormous flywheel of society, its most precious conservative agent" dramatically calls attention to the mechanism producing social conformity. Such habits are continually reinforced because they lead to satisfaction. This is true in any society: men cannot or will not live alone.

SIMPLIFICATION

It is a truism that nothing is simple. Or at least anything can become complicated when the essence of its nature is contemplated. "$1 + 1 = 2$" is not simple if it is recalled that this elementary equation requires at least a knowledge of language and a tacit agreement to abstract the characteristics of numbers from the concrete objects to which they more often are applied. It is simple to turn on an electric light, but the act involves an extremely complicated neuromuscular coordination as well as the electricity itself, both of which are by no means thoroughly understood. Even the spelling of "c-a-t" can be thought of as far from simple; for example, why is the first letter of the word *c* and not *k* or why is that same letter pronounced like *s* when it is followed by the vowel *e* as in the word "cent"? Naturally the equation is completed, the light is turned on, and the word is spelled without raising the questions hastily mentioned here. No one could do anything unless he were to make certain assumptions, forget certain problems, or simplify the problem at hand. Abstraction is inevitable.

One common form of simplification occurs when only part of a stimulus is perceived and the rest is disregarded. Such a partial response ensues because the individual is incapable of making the complete response or because a prior drive prevents him from perceiving the remainder of the stimulus. Both the absence of the complete response and the presence of the restricting drive in many instances are due to previous cultural influences which have affected the individual who, therefore, is heir to the simplifications of the past. In the United States, for example, a favorite device of demagogy is to brand an opponent with the label of "communist." For that word elicits an unfavorable response among most Americans. An unpleasant way of life or type of individual is associated with the word as a result of many factors: the historical belief of Americans that "free enterprise" represents a set of valuable institutions worth preserving; the ways in which the country's media of communication portrayed the Bolshevik revolution in Russia and the activities of the Soviet regime from its inception; the hysterical red-baiting of the early 1920's and the late 1940's; the hostility aroused or engineered by the strategy and tactics of the American Communist party; etc. The transition from these past associations to the present is accomplished by means of the stimulus "communist." The precise pronunciation by the political demagogue at the moment may be different from the way in which the individual has heard it spoken in the past, but the general form of the vocal vibration is sufficiently similar to evoke the pre-existing responses.

To call an opponent a "communist" is to simplify a complicated situation in the interest of discrediting him. Disregarded are all the nuances of his personality and individuality; all the ways in which he differs from communists in the Soviet Union, in China, in Bulgaria, and in the United States; and all of his particular beliefs and ideologies. Instead only the hostile reaction is sought: he is a blinkety-blank communist and nothing more. Admittedly it is easier to think of him in such simple terms, and for this very reason demagogy has psychological advantages over rationality.

Most simplification consists of more than selective perception. The perceptual response may be a rather accurate reflection of the stimulus but what is learned and retained undergoes changes as time passes. The changes which occur are not haphazard, though they may be quite unconscious. They depend upon what has been originally perceived as well as upon prior habits which the individual already possesses and whatever other drives are active within him. Many of the metamorphoses through which handed-down reports and rumors go, for example, have been described in terms of the levelling and sharpening of the original stimuli, both of which are forms of simplification. In an experiment one person looked at an ambiguous drawing of some people in what might have been a New York subway car; he reported what he had seen to a second person; that second person reported to a third what he had heard from the first; and so on down the line, as in a well-known parlor game. One of the figures in the original drawing was a Negro. Chains of white and colored reporters had different attitudes toward the same drawing and hence they introduced quite different simplifications and distortions.

According to Bartlett, some chiefs from an African tribe once visited London and later recalled most vividly the English policemen directing traffic whose uplifted hands resembled the greeting they were accustomed to employ at home. London for them had been simplified: as a result of previous training, they perceived it as a city in which certain persons followed one of their tribal practices. Naturally they observed other stimuli, but the one which impressed them was in accord with their habit systems. In like manner, the novice sees and remembers an abstract painting only as a confused blur which, from the viewpoint of the artist, is a libelous simplification.

People who react to an event and find that their internal responses have no appropriate or satisfying outlet are sorely tempted to assign an explanation which has proven successful or satisfying in the past. This is especially true when the correct or more adequate explanation is difficult or when the event appears to defy rational analysis. Many superstitions, for example, are associated with events over which the individual has no control. In our society, gamblers are especially prone to be superstitious: they cannot regulate their winnings and therefore seek refuge in actions which from the scientific viewpoint have no relevance to success or failure. The card player must have a particular ring on his index finger and he feels vaguely that this symbolic act in some way or other influences the cards he is dealt. Such a belief may be founded on a single, fortuitous reinforcement in the past: on this occasion he was successful when he happened to wear the ring on that finger. Thereafter he sees a causal connection between the ring and success. Even heavy losses may never extinguish the habit. He can always assert that he might have lost more if he had not performed the ritual.

The simplified explanations which generally have proven most successful or satisfying are those which the individual has been accustomed to apply to himself and which he then projects upon events outside himself. He is really using a metaphor without realizing what he is doing. Anthropomorphism, for example, is the ascription of human characteristics to animals or deities. The master believes that his dog is devoted to him and may maintain that the animal has the same subtle feelings of attachment which one human being has for another; the dog prefers him to all other men "because" of his devotion. When the qualities of the human spirit are projected upon the inanimate object or upon the universe in general, the projector is said to be behaving animistically. Sailors even from "advanced" countries are traditionally animistic in regard to the sea which they say has moods, seeks revenge, lures them, etc. Sometimes, too, abstract words are made concrete by being considered persons or objects, a process labelled reification. The kind of preferred relationship among men known as "justice" is not always easy to grasp, and hence there is a tendency to reify the concept by thinking of a blindfolded woman with scales in her hand or of a physical restraint controlling human action.

Any metaphor tends to oversimplify the phenomenon it describes and thus to imply an explanation which at best is only partially correct. The ocean does have moods in the sense that it fluctuates like people, but these alternations are due to causes quite different from those which produce, for example, a manic-depressive psychosis in a patient. The use of the word "moody" to describe both calls attention only to superficial similarities and ignores significant differences.

Another method of simplification, as logicians and semanticists take delight in indicating, is the confounding of an object with the arbitrary name assigned it. If one individual is told that an ambiguous drawing of two slightly irregular circles joined by a straight line is a pair of "eyeglasses" and another that it is some "dumbbells," each is then corrupted by the verbal label and each subsequently tends to remember and draw a different version of the original drawing. The one with the word "eyeglasses" in his head retains the two circles but connects them not with a straight but a curved line. The other who had been told that the figure "resembles" dumbbells changes the width of the connecting line and makes it merge into the two circles.

To say that "this fruit is an orange" is to make a necessary but still a simplified statement; for the object referred to has many more attributes than the one suggested by calling it "an orange." Besides being an object which most men and some animals like to eat, it can also be considered to be a collection of seeds surrounded by a particular kind of substance; a weight which is heavier than a man's tooth; a weapon to throw at a spider or a motorist; a streak of color; etc. For practical purposes the designation "orange" is usually sufficient and it is the one which has been most heavily reinforced. It must be recognized, though, that the choice of a particular word, convenient as this is, masks other conceivable attributes. The individual who requires an object to heave at a tarantula would be a victim of his own language if he were unable to perceive that the piece of fruit could serve this function as well as the usual one of being eaten.

Language also encourages simplification by enabling individuals to designate an object, person, or situation as black or white and thus to forget the gradations of hues that separate the two extremes. According to Korzybski and his followers, this tendency in our society results from the influence of Aristotle who maintained that anything could be either A or B but not both A and B at the same time. These semanticists tend to overlook the logical justification for such simplified abstractions as they pounce upon what they call traditional logic.

Psychologically, however, they are on sounder ground when they call attention to the fact that there is an inclination to forget that abstraction has occurred after its purpose has been served. It is tempting to label people good or bad, honest or dishonest, moral or immoral, whereas in fact few if any of them are ever complete saints or devils. It is usually more difficult to choose a moderate hue or to add a qualifying adjective since moderation or qualification requires refined observation and cogitation. In addition, *if's* and *but's* suggest indecision, and hesitating individuals can resolve their conflicts and doubts more readily when they are confronted with apparently clear-cut alternatives. The black-white label assigned the issue then helps determine its appraisal.

The widespread quest for simple explanations and short-cuts suggests in large part why people are willing to accept simplifications offered them by someone else. Cantril for example, has observed in his fourth "law" of public opinion that "verbal statements and outlines of courses of action have maximum importance when opinion is unstructured, when people are suggestible and seek some interpretation from a reliable source." An event that affects people adversely is puzzling. They are ready to rationalize what has happened, to displace

their insecurity, to engage in compensatory activity, to project themselves into the situation, or even to identify with what has happened —
or they await an explanation of why the event has occurred and what
its consequences for them are likely to be. The leader or propagandist
with prestige then has the opportunity to give his version. For example,
people ordinarily show little concern for public-health agencies until
an epidemic breaks out. The disease arouses public opinion, and
authorities are immediately consulted and heeded. The explanation of
the epidemic which they give is as scientific as knowledge permits.
In an earlier age the disease might have been blamed on a demon or
on man's immorality.

Not all of the issues of public opinion need to be simplified in order
to be grasped. Each issue falls along a kind of path, at one extreme of
which the individual simply knows or states that he has a favorable or
unfavorable attitude and at the other he tortures himself with all of
the problems he believes to be involved. In this sense a well-informed
public opinion is one whose decision rests not on simple acceptance or
rejection, nor on tons of scholarship or soul-raking, but on a consideration of as many of the relevant factors as possible.

PRINCIPLES OF PUBLIC OPINION

The principal characteristics of attitudes and hence of public opinion have now been specified. It has been shown that public opinion
may be consistent or inconsistent, may be based on rationalization,
may represent displacement, may be functioning as a compensatory
mechanism, may involve projection, may produce or reveal conformity,
and very likely is a simplification of the issues. Some of the interrelationships of these characteristics have been described. Can principles
be derived from the characteristics?

It is evident that the characteristics themselves are not principles.
They are mere descriptions of what occurs or what may occur. In
addition, their relation to social behavior in general has been suggested. But do they give rise to principles?

This question of principles cannot be dodged. More concretely
stated, it is an inquiry concerning the conditions under which one or
more of the characteristics will be demonstrated. The inquiry, in turn,
is really much more general, for what is true of public opinion must
be equally true of the behavior of individuals whether or not that
behavior involves public opinion.

It is, in fact, premature to hazard a set of principles or "laws." Not
enough is known concerning the behavior of the individual and still
less concerning the simultaneous behavior of individuals. As a most
tentative guess, however, the following principles may be stated:

1. Public opinion remains latent until an issue arises for the group;
an issue arises when there is conflict, anxiety, or frustration.

2. Actual public opinion, therefore, is an attempt to diminish conflict, anxiety, and frustration:

a. When these punishing circumstances cannot be avoided, there is rationalization.

b. When they cannot be avoided but when aggressive activity is rewarding, there is displacement.

c. When they cannot be avoided, when aggression is punished, but when substitute activity is rewarding, there is compensation.

3. Public opinion requires conformity:

a. When this conformity can be achieved by having some people attribute their own attitudes and knowledge to others, there is projection.

b. When it can be achieved by having some people assume that they possess the attitudes and knowledge of others, there is identification.

c. When it can be achieved by having people share almost identical knowledge, there is simplification.

4. Internal public opinion becomes external public opinion when:

a. The drive strength of the attitude is great.

b. Knowledge exists that the expression of attitude in action will be rewarding rather than punishing.

Crude principles like these, it is immediately admitted, merely state the kinds of problems which better principles must face. In connection with each one, there are questions involving the conditions under which a set of circumstances may be said to exist:

1. When and for what reasons do individuals experience "conflict, anxiety, or frustration?"

2. When and for what reasons can these "punishing circumstances" not "be avoided" and when is "aggressive" or "substitute" activity "rewarding?"

3. When and for what reasons can conformity be "achieved" in the identical ways?

4. Just how "great" does the drive strength of the attitude have to be before action occurs; when and how do people know that they will be rewarded rather than punished; and how "great" must drive strength be before it can overcome a fear of punishment?

The answers to each of these questions in turn requires a set of elaborate sub-principles pertaining to the individual as well as to the stimuli in his society. And then each of the sub-principles demands some sub-sub-principles until — well, until all of social science and human knowledge are codified and systematized. Before the arrival of this great day at the time of the millennium, all that principles can accomplish is to call attention to the complexity of the problem and to caution as forcefully as possible against premature generalizations and glibness.

▲ BERNARD BERELSON

Communication and Public Opinion

Of the importance of this topic it is hardly necessary to speak. If the defenses of peace and prosperity, not to mention other desirable political conditions, are to be constructed in men's minds, then the critical position of communication and public opinion for that defense is evident. What is not so evident, perhaps, is why social scientists have given so little systematic attention to problems of the formation of public opinion with special reference to the role of the media of communication in that process. It was not evident to a "classical" writer on public opinion twenty-five years ago,[1] and it may be even less so today.

In any case, the field of interest is now developing and the line of development is reasonably clear. The political scientist's concern with political parties was generalized to a concern with the role of pressure groups in political life. The concern with pressure groups led directly into concern with propaganda, and that into concern with public opinion and the effect of propaganda upon it. At about this time, technicians began to develop scientific instruments by which to measure public opinion; a new medium of communication with great potentialities for popular influence came vigorously upon the scene; in a series of presidential elections people voted strongly for one candidate while their newspapers voted strongly for his opponent; and a World War made more visible as well as more urgent the battle for men's minds. Thus the background of academic interest was prepared just when dramatic events highlighted the urgency of the problem and

[1] Walter Lippmann, *Public Opinion*, Harcourt Brace, 1922, p. 243.

▲ This paper first appeared in *Communications in Modern Society*, edited by Wilbur Schramm, published and copyright by the University of Illinois Press (Urbana, 1948). It is reprinted here by permission of author and copyright holder. Dr. Berelson is director of the behavioral sciences division of the Ford Foundation.

when technical developments provided means for at least some solutions. As a result, interest in communication and public opinion is now at an all-time high.

The purpose of this paper is to discuss the relationship between communication and public opinion. "Discuss" here means to report on some (illustrative) research findings in the area and to propose relevant (and again illustrative) hypotheses for investigation. By communication is meant the transmission of symbols via the major media of mass communication — radio, newspaper, film, magazine, book — and the major medium of private communication — personal conversation. By public opinion is meant people's response (that is, approval, disapproval, or indifference) to controversial political and social issues of general attention, such as international relations, domestic policy, election candidates, ethnic relations.

The paper is organized into two parts because the relationship between communication and public opinion is twofold. The first section deals with the effect of public opinion upon communication and the second with the effect of communication upon public opinion. The second section is traditional, and there is more to say about it; the first is usually neglected.

EFFECT OF PUBLIC OPINION UPON COMMUNICATION

This problem is usually neglected in analyses of the relationship because it is not so obvious as the other and perhaps because it is more difficult to study. The problem deals with the extent to which, and the ways in which, communication content is determined to harmonize with the actual or presumed opinions of the actual or potential audience. It is clear that one factor, among others, that conditions what the media of communications say on social and political issues is the desire or expectation of the readers-listeners-seers to be told certain things and not others. The reporter or commentator or editor or producer may know or may think he knows "what his public wants" on a given issue, and to the extent that such knowledge affects what he communicates, to that extent public opinion becomes a determinant of communications. This aspect of the relationship between communication and public opinion is not always admitted, or even recognized, because of the immorality of suggesting that anything but "truth" or "justice" contributes to the character of communication content.[2] However, everyone knows that communication channels of various kinds tell people what they want to hear. In such cases, public opinion sets limits upon the nature of what is typically communicated.

---

[2] However, some circles frankly acknowledge the power of the public to participate thus indirectly in the construction of communication content. This position is usually rationalized in terms of the presumed democratic ethic in which "the public is entitled to what it wants."

This determination (or really, partial determination, since this is of course not the only factor responsible for communication content any more than communication content is the only factor responsible for public opinion) can operate in two ways, once the communication channel (newspaper, magazine, political writer, radio commentator, and so forth) has attracted to itself a distinguishable audience. The two ways are themselves interrelated and can coexist. First, it can operate through conscious and deliberate and calculated manipulation of the content in order to coincide with the dominant audience opinion. Sometimes this operates by rule of thumb, as when someone on the production line in the communication process decides that "our public won't take this, or won't like it." Sometimes it operates through elaborate machinery organized precisely for the purpose, as when thousands of research dollars and hours are spent in finding out what kinds of people the audience is composed of and what kinds of opinions they hold on controversial issues. Whether the decision to conform to audience predispositions is taken on the front line or in the front office is for the moment immaterial; so is the question of why it happens, e.g., the desire or need for constant and large audiences for economic reasons. The important point is that overt consideration of audience opinion does (help to) shape the social and political content of the mass media. Everyone recalls the story of the foreign correspondent who cabled a thoroughgoing analysis of a relatively obscure Hungarian crisis to the home office only to be told: "We do not think it advisable to print it because it does not reflect Midwestern opinion on this point."[3]

The other method by which public opinion can affect communications is implicit, through the sincere and more or less nonconscious correspondence of ideology between producers and consumers. The two groups often see the world through the same colored glasses. The correspondence is achieved through a two-way process: the audience selects the communications which it finds most congenial and the producers select people with "the right viewpoint" to prepare communications for other people with "the right viewpoint." Although this latter process also occurs through deliberate decision,[4] it also happens through the most laudable and honest motives that people of the same general persuasion as their audience are found in influential positions in particular communication agencies. This is all the more true in specialized enterprises like trade papers or magazines like *Fortune* or *The Nation*. In such cases, producers react to new issues and events like the modal members of their audience; and their communications fit audience predispositions, not through a process of tailoring, but through correspondence in outlook. "The daily re-elec-

[3] Leo Rosten, *The Washington Correspondents*, Harcourt Brace, 1937, p. 231.
[4] See Rosten, *op. cit.*, for examples.

tion of the editor" serves to make the editor quite sensitive to the wishes of the electors. Here again the economic necessity to hold an audience and the political desire to do so are relevant factors, as well as the "correctness" of outlook. The point is that the nature of one's audience places certain limits upon what one can say to it — and still have an audience. The need of the audience is not only to be informed but also to be satisfied, and the latter is sometimes evaluated more highly than the former.

It is important to take account of this direction in the flow of influence between communication and public opinion in order to appreciate the reciprocal nature of that influence, i.e., to recognize that it is not all a one-way process. It is also important to note that the total effect of this reciprocal process is probably to stabilize and "conservatize" opinion since ideologies are constantly in process of reinforcement thereby. The over-all picture, then, is that of like begetting like begetting like.

THE EFFECT OF COMMUNICATION ON PUBLIC OPINION

But the effect of communication on public opinion needs to be examined much more closely and directly than that. To speak roughly, in the 1920's propaganda was considered all-powerful — "it got us into the war" — and thus communication was thought to determine public opinion practically by itself. In the 1930's the Roosevelt campaigns "proved" that the newspaper had lost its influence and that a "golden voice" on the radio could sway men in almost any direction. Now, in the 1940's, a body of empirical research is accumulating which provides some refined knowledge about the effect of communication on public opinion and promises to provide a good deal more in the next years.

What has such research contributed to the problem? By and large, do communications influence public opinion? By and large, of course, the answer is yes. But by-and-large questions and answers are not sufficient for a scientific theory of communication and public opinion. The proper answer to the general question, the answer which constitutes a useful formulation for research purposes, is this:

> Some kinds of *communication* on some kinds of *issues,*
> brought to the attention of some kinds of *people* under
> some kinds of *conditions,* have some kinds of *effects.*

This formulation identifies five central factors (or rather groups of factors) which are involved in the process, and it is the interrelationship of these variables which represents the subject matter of theory in this field. At present, students can fill out only part of the total picture — a small part — but the development of major variables and the formulation of hypotheses and generalizations concerning them are steps in the right direction. Theoretical integration in any full sense is not as yet possible, but descriptions of some ways in which these factors operate can be usefully made. Each set of factors will be discussed illustratively (*not* completely) in an effort to demonstrate how each of them conditions the total effect of communication on public opinion and thus contributes to the formulation of a general theory.

KINDS OF COMMUNICATION: The effectiveness of communications as an influence upon public opinion varies with the nature of the communication.

First let us deal with the effect of certain media characteristics. The more personal the media, the more effective it is in converting opinions. This means (other things being equal) that personal conversation is more effective than a radio speech, and that a radio speech is more effective than a newspaper account of it. The greater the amount of "personalism" the communication act contains, the more effective it presumably is. Recent analyses have confirmed the critical importance in opinion formation of personal contact between the individual and his fellows. The individual's opinions are formed in the context of his formal and informal group associations. College students become more liberal in political opinion over the period of their college attendance largely through the influence of the liberality of the college community, that is, the older students and the instructional staff.[5] Intensive case studies of current opinion toward the USSR held by adult men reveal the powerful influence of personal contacts: "The need to conform in one's opinion to the opinions of one's associates and of members of favored groups is an important motivational factor."[6] This effect operated in two ways: directly through the process of conformity as such and indirectly through the sharing of common values and information. The formation of political opinion during a presidential campaign was dependent upon personal influence to a large extent; the political homogeneity of social groups was strikingly high. "In comparison with the formal media of communication, personal relationships are potentially more influential for two reasons: their coverage is greater and they have certain psychological advantages over the formal media."[7] Personal contacts are more casual and nonpurposive than the formal media, they are more flexible in countering resistance, they can provide more desirable rewards for compliance, they offer

[5] Theodore M. Newcomb, *Personality and Social Change: Attitude Formation in a Student Community*, Dryden Press, 1943.

[6] Mahlon Brewster Smith, *Functional and Descriptive Analysis of Public Opinion*. Doctoral dissertation, Harvard University, 1947, p. 500.

[7] Paul Lazarsfeld, Bernard Berelson, and Hazel Gaudet, *The People's Choice: How the Voter Makes up His Mind in a Presidential Campaign*, Duell, Sloan and Pearce, New York, 1944, p. 150.

reliance and trust in an intimate source, and they can persuade without convincing.[8]

The greater effectiveness of radio over newspapers derives to some extent from its greater "personalism." The radio speaks "to you" more than the newspaper does; it more closely approximates a personal conversation and can thus be more persuasive. The listener can "get a feel" of the speaker's personality, and this is often more effective a factor making for conversion of opinion than the content of the argument itself. The dominant characteristic which enabled Kate Smith to sell nearly $40,000,000 worth of war bonds in one day was the listener's image and evaluation of her personality established over a period of time.[9] In other areas, too, the (radio) personality of such influencers of public opinion as Raymond Gram Swing or Gabriel Heatter or Franklin Delano Roosevelt contributes to their influence.

This discussion of the role of personal contact in opinion formation would not be complete without mention of the relationship between personal conversation and the formal media of communication. This relationship introduces the notion of the "opinion leader" or "opinion transmitter" who takes material from the formal media and passes it on, with or without distortion or affect, to associates who do not use the formal media so frequently in the particular area of concern. There are such people in all social groups and for all social topics, from politics to sports and fashions. This "two-step flow of communication" has been identified and is currently being studied intensively.[10] The concept is of central importance for the formation of a general theory of communication and public opinion.

Within a medium of communication, the particular channels specialized to the subject's predispositions are more effective in converting his opinion than the generalized channels. "The specialized magazine already has a foot in the door, so to speak, because it is accepted by the reader as a reliable spokesman for some cause or group in which he is greatly interested and with which he identifies himself. The general magazine tries to speak to everyone at once and as a result is less able to aim its shots directly at a particular target. . . . In Erie County in 1940, *The Farm Journal* was mentioned as a concrete influence upon changes in vote intention as frequently as *Colliers*, despite their great difference in circulation, and the Townsend publication as frequently as *Life* or *The Saturday Evening Post.*"[11] Similarly

---

[8] For a full discussion of these factors, see chapter 16 of *The People's Choice*.

[9] Robert K. Merton with the assistance of Marjorie Fiske and Alberta Curtis, *Mass Persuasion; the Social Psychology of a War Bond Drive*. Harper & Brothers, New York, 1946.

[10] See *The People's Choice*, pp. 49-51 and pp. 151-52; and the forthcoming study of the flow of influence among women in a midwestern community by Paul Lazarsfeld and C. Wright Mills.

[11] Lazarsfeld, Berelson, and Gaudet, *The People's Choice*, pp. 135-36.

farm programs on the air are probably more effective in influencing farmers' opinions than general radio programs dealing with the same issues.[12] Although there is little direct evidence on this point, it is at least a plausible hypothesis that the specialized communication, per unit of exposure, is more effective in promoting opinion changes than the generalized communication. In a sense, then, this is an obstacle to the homogenizing influence of the mass channels in the mass media.

These are a few ways in which distinctions among the media themselves are involved in the effect of communication upon opinion. What about communication content? Obviously it has a central position in this process. Perhaps the primary distinction in communication content as a factor affecting public opinion is the most primitive, namely, the distinction between the reportorial content and the editorial or interpretive content. Too often discussions of the general problem of the effect of communications upon public opinion is restricted to the latter kind of content. Yet the former is probably more effective in converting opinion. The events reported through the media presumably change more minds — or solidify more — than the comments of editorial writers, columnists, and commentators. "It was Sherman and Sheridan, and not Greeley and Raymond, who had elected him (Lincoln in 1864)."[13] And again, "Opinion is generally determined more by events than by words — unless those words are themselves interpreted as an 'event.' "[14] In addition events tend to solidify opinion changes produced by words, changes which otherwise would be short-lived; and the *fait accompli* event crystallizes opinion in favor of the event even though words had not previously been able to do so.[15] Thus the reportorial content of the media is probably more influential than the interpretive.

However, it is necessary to make two remarks here. First, the distinction between "events" and "words" is not easy to make. Is a major speech by the President of the United States an "event" or just "propaganda"? Or a report issued by a pressure group? Or an investigation by a Congressional committee? Or a tour of inspection? What about "propaganda of the deed"? Although the distinction is useful, the borderline is not always crystal-clear. And secondly, many events exercise influence not in and of themselves, but with active assistance from "words." Thus, for example, the relatively sharp changes in

[12] Some indirect evidence for this is available in William S. Robinson, "Radio Comes to the Farmer" in Lazarsfeld and Stanton, editors, *Radio Research, 1941*, Duell, Sloan and Pearce, New York, 1941, pp. 224-94.

[13] Frank Luther Mott, "Newspapers in Presidential Campaigns," *Public Opinion Quarterly*, Vol. VIII, 1944, p. 354.

[14] Hadley Cantril, "The Use of Trends," in Cantril, editor, *Gauging Public Opinion*, Princeton, 1944, p. 226.

[15] See Cantril, *op. cit.*, pp. 227-28, for examples.

opinion on the interventionist-isolationist issue which occurred at the time of the fall of France in June, 1940, are often attributed to the event itself. However, it must be recognized that this event was strongly interpreted in one way (i.e., pro-interventionism) by most newspapers and radio commentators and by the pronouncements of the national administration. What if most communication channels and the official administration had taken another view of the event? At the least one might suppose that the effect of "the event" would have been different. More recently, the event represented by people's experience in the meat crisis in the fall of 1946 was sometimes credited with the Republican congressional victory at that time. Yet it must be remembered that the communication media gave that event a dominant interpretation (i.e., anti-administration) even though another was possible. In short, the interrelationship of "events" and "words" must be recognized in this connection. The fact is that the communication media are most effective when their reportorial and interpretive contents are in congruence.

Finally, to illustrate this aspect of the process, there is the hypothesis that emotional content of the media is more effective in converting opinions than rational content. There is some evidence for this. Votes for a Socialist candidate were increased more by "emotional" leaflets than by "rational" ones.[16] The highly effective bond broadcasts by Kate Smith even omitted two "rational" themes in favor of emphasis upon various "emotional" ones.[17] In the case of this distinction, of course, the need is not so much to test the finding as to refine it, especially for different population groups.

KINDS OF ISSUES: The effectiveness of communications as an influence upon public opinion varies with the nature of the issue.

Communication content is more effective in influencing public opinion on new or unstructured issues, i.e., those not particularly correlated with existing attitude clusters. The closer the opinion situation is to the *tabula resa,* the easier it is for the communication media to write their own ticket. "Verbal statements and outlines of courses of action have maximum importance when opinion is unstructured. . . ."[18] Again, with reference to opinion toward the USSR: "The object of the attitude is remote, the facts are ambiguous, and a person may fashion his own picture of Russia or fall in with the

[16] George W. Hartmann, "A Field Experiment on the Comparative Effectiveness of 'Emotional' and 'Rational' Political Leaflets in Determining Election Results," *Journal of Abnormal and Social Psychology,* Vol. XXXI, 1936, pp. 99-114.

[17] See Merton, *op. cit.,* Chapter III: "The Bond Appeals: A Thematic Analysis," pp. 45-69.

[18] Cantril, "The Use of Trends," in Cantril, editor, *Gauging Public Opinion,* p. 226.

prevailing stereotypes"[19] — which are provided predominantly by the formal media.

Communication content is more effective in influencing opinion on peripheral issues than on crucial issues. That is, it is easier for the media to shape opinion on what to do about local courts than what to do about organized labor; and it is probably easier for them to shape opinion toward organized labor than on ethnic relations. The "relevance-quotient" or "intensity-quotient" of the issue is inversely correlated with the capacity of communication content to change minds.

Finally, communications are probably more effective in influencing opinion on "personalities" than on "issues." In the first place, Americans are an individualistic people. They like to have heroes; and the communications media do their best to supply heroes of various kinds to various groups in the population.[20] Secondly, Americans do not like to believe that there are deep-cutting political issues which have the potentiality of "class-ifying" the public so that they tend to resist the acceptance or even the recognition of some basic issues. As a result, the media probably can sway more people with "personality" arguments than with "issue" arguments.[21]

KINDS OF PEOPLE: The effectiveness of communications as an influence upon public opinion varies with the nature of the people.

In the first place, varying proportions of people simply do not read or see or listen to the different media. So far as direct effect of the media is concerned (and omitting considerations of indirect effects through such a process as opinion leadership), two-thirds of the adult population is not influenced by books, about one-half is not influenced by motion pictures, and so on. Direct effects of the media upon public opinion can be exercised only upon that part of the public which attends to the different media (and to different parts of them) — and that rules out distinguishable groups at the outset.

On one side of the coin is the distinction between peripheral and central issues; on the other side is the distinction between strong and weak predispositions. The stronger predispositions are on the issue, the more difficult it is for the media to convert opinions. Strong predispositions "compel" an opinion which the media only helps to rationalize and reinforce; in recent presidential elections very few people of high income, rural residence, and Protestant religion were *converted* to a Republican vote by the media of communication. Strong predispositions make for greater interest in the issue, an earlier decision on it,

---

[19] Smith, *op. cit.*, p. 195.

[20] For an example see Leo Lowenthal, "Biographies in Popular Magazines," pp. 507-48, in Lazarsfeld and Stanton, editors, *Radio Research, 1942-1943,* Duell, Sloan and Pearce, New York, 1944.

[21] For a specific instance in which this was the case, see Bernard Berelson, "The Effects of Print upon Public Opinion," in Waples, editor, *Print, Radio and Film in a Democracy,* University of Chicago Press, 1942, pp. 55-56.

and fewer changes afterwards. All this is clear enough. What may or may not be so clear, however, is that the strongly predisposed on an issue actually manage not only to avoid contrary communication material, so that it just does not come to their attention, but also that they manage to misunderstand the material (which objectively is straightforward) when confronted by it. This has been particularly demonstrated in connection with communication material on ethnic relations, a topic on which predispositions run strong. Prejudiced people find several ways in which to evade the message of pro-tolerance propaganda: they avoid the intended identifications, they invalidate the message, they change the frame of reference, they "just don't get it."[22]

The less informed people are on an issue, the more susceptible they are to opinion conversion through the influence of the communication media. This means that the less informed are more mercurial in their opinions; the base of data upon which stable opinion is more securely founded[23] is simply absent for them, and the media (or more frequently, personal contacts) can more readily move them in different directions. "The compulsion of (media-supplied and other) stereotypes is great, particularly for persons with meager informational backgrounds."[24]

KINDS OF CONDITIONS: The effectiveness of communications as an influence upon public opinion varies with the nature of the conditions.

Many mass communications on controversial issues in this country have to make their way in a competitive situation, i.e., under conditions in which alternative proposals are also available in the media. In some areas, such as the desirability of professing religious beliefs, this is not true: there is a virtual pro-religious monopoly on communications available to large audiences in America today. But it is the case in most areas of political and social concern, although here too various minority groups, e.g., the Communists, feel that their point of view is not given fair or proper attention in the mass media. It is necessary to recognize that the effect of communications upon public opinion must usually be exercised in this context of competing communication content and not in a context of monopoly. This is of central importance: communication has effects upon converting opinion under conditions of monopoly which are much greater than its effects under conditions of competition (even though that competition might be quite uneven). However, the effectiveness of formal communications is not unlimited; there are suggestions that the virtual monopoly exer-

---

[22] Eunice Cooper and Marie Jahoda, "The Evasion of Propaganda: How Prejudiced People Respond to Anti-prejudice Propaganda," *Journal of Psychology*, Vol. XXIII, 1947, pp. 15-25.

[23] Cantril, "The Use of Trends," *op. cit.*, p. 229.

[24] Smith, *op. cit.*, p. 195. In this connection, see also Herbert Hyman and Paul Sheatsley, "Some Reasons Why Information Campaigns Fail," *Public Opinion Quarterly*, Vol. XI, 1947, pp. 412-23.

cised by the Nazis over communication content did not succeed in converting some large groups of Germans to their political philosophy.

That is one point — the greater but not absolute effectiveness of communication monopoly. Another deals with the problem of "balance" within competition. What does "balance" mean in the mass media? Does it mean a fifty-fifty division between pro and anti content? What is a "fair" distribution of attention to the different sides on a public controversy? One approach to this matter is to consider what might be called "functional balance" in the media, i.e., the proportionate distribution of content which enables partisans on an issue to read or see or listen to their own side with reasonably equal facility. This does not necessitate an automatic fifty-fifty division of the content. In one presidential campaign, for example, the Republicans and Democrats in a community read and heard their own side about equally, even though there was about a two-to-one disproportion of content favoring the Republicans.[25] In any case, the effect of the communication media upon public opinion is a function of the degree of competition on the issue within the media.

Another condition of communication exposure which affects opinion conversions is the purposiveness or non-purposiveness of the exposure. There is some slight evidence to suggest that non-purposive (or accidental) reading and listening is more effective in changing opinions than purposive (or deliberate).[26] In the first place, people see and hear more congenial material through deliberate communication exposure, and accidental reading and listening is more likely to bring diverse viewpoints to their attention. Secondly, in such exposure defenses against new ideas are presumably weaker because preconceptions are not so pervasively present. Finally, there may be other psychological advantages centering around the gratification of "overhearing" something "not meant for you," a consideration that also weakens the resistance to "propaganda" (since "it would not be propaganda if it wasn't intended for you"). This factor of accidental-and-deliberate communication exposure corresponds to the factor of indirect-and-direct communication content, and the same hypothesis probably holds.[27] Direct content attacks the issue head-on (e.g., an article urging fairer treatment of the Negroes). Indirect content takes the round-about approach (e.g., a story about Negro children without

[25] Lazarsfeld, Berelson, and Gaudet, *The People's Choice,* Chapters XIII and XIV, pp. 110-36.

[26] Based upon an unpublished manuscript by Paul F. Lazarsfeld.

[27] For recent discussions of other conditions affecting this relationship, see Samuel Flowerman, "Mass Propaganda in the War Against Bigotry," *Journal of Abnormal and Social Psychology,* Vol. XLII, 1947, pp. 429-39; and Ernst Kris and Nathan Leites, "Trends in 20th Century Propaganda," in *Psychoanalysis and the Social Sciences,* International University Press, 1947, pp. 393-409.

direct reference to the problem of race relations). The indirect content is more effective in converting opinions for much the same reasons which apply to accidental exposure.

KINDS OF EFFECTS: Finally, the media of communication have different kinds of effects upon public opinion.

First, a distinction should be made between the effect of the media upon the holding of certain opinions rather than others and their effect upon the holding of political opinions at all. Most attention has been given to the former problem, but the latter — the problem of the creation and maintenance of political interest or political apathy — is of considerable importance. The media have a major influence in producing an interest in public affairs by constantly bringing them to people's attention in a context of presumed citizenly concern. The more the media stress a political issue, the less indecision there is on the issue among the general public.[28] At the same time, however, the communication media may also be promoting in actuality, but without intention, a sense of political apathy among some of its audience. This can occur in at least two ways.

In the first place, it is at least a plausible hypothesis that the attractive substance and easy accessibility of the entertainment or recreational or diversionary content of the mass media operate to minimize political interest for some groups in the population. Comedians, dramatic sketches, and popular music on the air; light fiction of the adventure, mystery, or romantic variety in magazines and books; comics and comic strips; feature films of "straight entertainment" — such "non-serious" content of the media may well serve to divert attention from political affairs directly and also to re-create the audience so that it is under less compulsion to "face up" to the general political problems which confront it and which shape its life. This is said with complete recognition of the psychological relief provided by such communication materials for many people; at the same time, their effect in lowering political interest and attention seems equally clear.

Secondly, the media may increase political apathy simply through presentation of the magnitude, the diversity, and the complexity of the political issues on which the responsible citizen is supposed to be informed. Some readers and listeners, conscious of their inability to become informed other than superficially on more than a few public problems, retreat from the whole area. How can one know what should be done about the Palestine partition, about inflation, about the Greek guerrillas and the Chinese communists, about race relations in the United States, about the cold war with the USSR, about labor-management relations generally or the latest strike specifically, about "free enterprise" or "planning," about the atom — all at the same

[28] Berelson, *op. cit.*, p. 53.

time? The media atmosphere of public responsibility for public actions may thus become a boomerang: the more the public is enjoined to exercise its duty to become an "informed citizenry," the less it feels able to do so. And, overwhelmed by the presentation of issues and problems of a public nature, part of the audience may withdraw into the relative security of their private problems and their private lives.

In any discussion of the effect of the media upon the *kinds* of political opinions held by people, an initial distinction should be made between long-run and short-run effects. The importance of the former is inversely related to the research attention which has been given them. The fact that it is easier to study short-run changes in attitudes produced by the communication media — not that that is easy! — should not divert attention from the pervasive, subtle, and durable effects of the media over long periods of time. For example, motion pictures undoubtedly affect the political attention of their audiences over the long run by strengthening certain "basic" values in terms of which political issues are later decided. The influence is remote and indirect, but it is nonetheless present and active. Or again, the communication media affect public opinion over the long run by providing a set of definitions for key political terms (of an affective nature) which come to be accepted through lack of adequate challenge. Thus, "freedom" in this country has mainly been defined in the media in terms of the absence of governmental intervention; and when the value of "freedom" is invoked in a political argument, it usually carries this meaning into the attitudinal battle. Other definitions are possible, but not so current. When it is suggested that "freedom of the press" be defined in terms of the ability of various population groups to secure the kind of communication they want (or someone thinks they should have) rather than in terms of governmental control, the proposal is confronted by the established definition — established through repetition over a long period of time.

Now for the short-run effects of the media upon opinion. Most is known about this area of the general problem, but not much is known. At the least, distinctions should be made among the various kinds of effects which the communication media can have upon public opinion. Usually the term "effect" includes only the conversion of opinions (i.e., changes away from a predispositional position or prior attitudes), but the (more frequent) reinforcement and activation effects should not be overlooked. The media are extremely effective in providing partisans with the deference and the rationalizations needed to maintain their position (i.e., reinforcement): "If the press follows a tenacious policy during an economic crisis, it may be able to retard or prevent shifts from one major party to another."[29] And they are

[29] Harold F. Gosnell, *Machine Politics: Chicago Model,* University of Chicago Press, 1937, p. 181.

also effective in bringing to visibility people's latent attitudes (i.e., activation).[30]

More than that, the media are effective in structuring political issues for their audiences. For example, there is a tendency for partisans on each side of a controversial matter to agree with their own side's argument in the order in which those arguments are emphasized in mass communications. Thus, the media set the political stage, so to speak, for the ensuing debate. In addition, there is some evidence that private discussions of political matters take their cue from the media's presentation of the issues; people talk politics along the lines laid down in the media.[31]

Finally, one thing must be made quite clear in this discussion of the effects of the media upon public opinion. That is that effects upon the audience do not follow directly from and in correspondence with the intent of the communicator or the content of the communication. The predispositions of the reader or listener are deeply involved in the situation, and may operate to block or modify the intended effect or even to set up a boomerang effect. This has been found time and again in studies of the effectiveness of materials promoting tolerance toward ethnic groups, on which topic predisposition runs strong.[32] In another context — and under relatively favorable conditions — Communist propaganda provided a catharsis for its subjects, inefficiently for its own objectives, because its themes directly countered strong feelings of individualism and nationalism held by the audience.[33]

CONCLUSION

This brief discussion of communication and public opinion has indicated the reciprocal effects of the two major factors upon one another, and has presented a categorization in terms of which the effects of communication upon public opinion can usefully be investigated. In this latter analysis, five sets of variables were identified: communications, issues, people, conditions, effects.

The interrelationships of these variables constitute the subject-matter of a scientific theory in this field. For example, illustrative hypothesis can be suggested which deal with these interrelationships:

The more specialized the media (communication), the greater reinforcement (effect).

The greater the competition in a communication system (conditions), the greater reinforcement (effect).

[30] For a fuller description of these effects, see Lazarsfeld, Berelson, and Gaudet, *The People's Choice*, Chapters VIII-X.

[31] For documentation of these points, see Berelson, *op. cit.*

[32] For example, see Cooper and Jahoda, *op. cit.*

[33] Harold D. Lasswell and Dorothy Blumenstock, *World Revolutionary Propaganda: A Chicago Study*, Knopf, 1939. Section V: "The Influence of Propaganda," pp. 247-358.

The "deeper" the predispositional affect toward the issue (people), the more effective the indirect content (communication) in converting opinion (effect).

And so on, within the formulation: some kinds of communication on some kinds of issues, brought to the attention of some kinds of people under some kinds of conditions, have some kinds of effects.

It is hypotheses of this sort that should be systematically explored as the next step in research in this field. Whatever the method of investigation (and some of these are better than others) — historical (Mott), trend analysis (Cantril), statistical correlation of ecological and voting data (Gosnell), case study (Smith), opinion survey and analysis (Cottrell),[34] experimental (I. and E. Division),[35] panel (Lazarsfeld, Berelson, and Gaudet) — this sort of propositional organization should be considered as the framework of study. In this way, a scientific theory of communications and public opinion can be developed for the enrichment not only of the field of communications research generally, but for social science as well.

[34] Leonard Cottrell, *American Opinion on World Affairs in the Atomic Age,* Princeton University Press, 1948.

[35] Information and Education Division, U. S. War Department, "The Effects of Presenting 'One Side' vs. 'Both Sides' in Changing Opinions on a Controversial Subject," in Theodore Newcomb and Eugene Hartley, eds., *Readings in Social Psychology,* Holt, 1947, pp. 566-79.

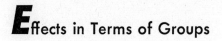

Effects in Terms of Groups

Introductory Note

THE IMPORTANCE OF THE GROUP

IN THE COMMUNICATION CHAIN

"Each in his time plays many parts," said Shakespeare. We play these parts, or roles, because they help us systematize life. They are responsible for many of the enduring satisfactions of life (as, for example, the role of a good father or mother). The kind of roles we play and the values and attitudes we build around them are largely determined by the groups we belong to. Each in his time, to paraphrase the preceding quotation, belongs to many groups. He belongs to a number of groups at the same time, and these overlapping memberships sometimes cause role conflicts or value conflicts. But nevertheless, one's group relationships provide the setting for most of the communicating one does during his life, and determine what use is made of mass communication. Therefore, the group structure of a society is one of the most important pieces of information for a mass communicator to know.

There are many kinds of groups. The usual way to divide them is in terms of *statistical* and *functional* groups. Statistical groups are those by which an outside observer chiefly describes and enumerates a society — age, sex, education, geographical, and class groups, for instance. We may or may not be aware of our membership in these groups, and we may or may not have any contact with other members of the groups. But members of the same statistical group tend to respond in about the same way to certain communication stimuli (for example, better educated persons tend to read more "serious" material), and thus it helps a communicator to know how his audience is divided into these classifications.

Functional groups are those which assemble to work together for some purpose. The most influential of all these is the primary group, of which the family is an example. Other functional groups are assembled with varying degrees of permanency. The crowd, for example, may be a group for only a few minutes. A football team may be a

group for only one season. A working group may be a group only as
long as the job lasts. A fraternal order or a church congregation may
be a group for many years, but its members may have much or little
contact outside the formal meetings. In any case, assembled as they
are to meet some kind of common purpose, providing repeated contacts of the same persons, and furnishing a variety of roles and jobs
within them, they are extremely important in the communication
chain.

How do functional groups enter into mass communication? One
obvious thing to say is that the communication organization — the
newspaper staff, the publishing house, the radio, TV, or film staff —
is itself a functional group. But leaving those out of the picture, it is
easy to see that the functional group is the chief place where mass
communication is discussed and evaluated, where members of the
audience firm up their opinion of the idea they have received through
mass communication, and in many cases where resultant action, if any,
has to be taken. How often have you heard a functional group discuss
last night's editorial, or an article in one of the big magazines, or what
someone said on the air? How often have you heard a member of a
functional group advise the others to select something out of mass
communication — a particular motion picture, for example? Even
when there is no overt discussion of mass communication and its
ideas in the group, still the group provides a set of norms and
standards which a member accepts, to greater or less degree, by joining the group, and which help determine how he individually evaluates
the suggestions he receives from mass communication.

A mass communicator should always remember that only in the
most elementary sense is he communicating to a *mass*. He may be
offering his message to a mass, but the statistical and functional group
memberships of members of the mass will help to determine which
members select the message. And every member which does select it
will also belong to certain groups whose norms, standards, and relationships will help determine how he responds to the message.

There is now a considerable amount of literature on group processes
— on leadership, for example, morale, productivity, role, and status.
We can't summarize all this literature here, but it may be helpful to
set down certain tentative principles of attitude change in groups. In
so doing we are going to paraphrase some of the principles stated by
Dorwin Cartwright.

1. If a group is to be used to bring about attitude change, it is
important that the persons who are to be changed and those who are
to exert influence for change should have a strong sense of belonging
to the same group. In other words, change can be brought about more
easily from the inside than the outside. You have seen this operate.

For example, have you ever resisted when someone on the outside told you how to run your business or your family?

2. A group exerts more influence on attitudes, values, or behaviors which are close to the reason for the group's existence. For example, a business group would be expected to influence a member's business values more than his religious or his family values. In the case of overlapping membership, a propagandist who wanted to change a man's religious values would probably try to approach him as a member of a religious group rather than as a member of a business group.

3. The more a group means to its members, the more influence it can exert on their attitudes, values, and behavior. One's family, for example, can exert more influence than a casual crowd which one joins to watch a sidewalk excavation or a traffic accident. The more one needs a group (to take care of his feelings of loneliness or social inadequacy, for instance) the more likely he is to conform to its standards.

4. The higher the prestige of a member in the eyes of his fellow members, the more influence he can exert on the group. There are many different roles and jobs within a group, and often a complex pattern of influence. But if one can get the most highly respected members of the group to advocate the change he wants made, it is more likely to get group approval.

5. The more clearly all members of a group can be made to feel the need for change, the more likely change is to occur. Likewise, it is important that information about a change be shared by all members of the group. The more nearly, that is, a group can operate like a team with all members participating in important decisions, the more likely change is to be accomplished without serious tension.

6. The nature of a group is such as to resist deviance on the part of a minority. If an outsider tries to change the attitudes or behavior of a few members of a group in such a way as to make them go counter to group norms, he is likely to encounter severe resistance — both from the individuals, who value these norms they have accepted, and from the other group members who may punish the deviants by loss of status or exclusion from the group.

7. Change in any part of a group is likely to introduce strain and unbalance in the group as a whole. The only smooth change is accomplished by bringing the group along together. For the propagandist, of course, this is a two-edged sword. He may sometimes wish to introduce disequilibrium into a group, and he can accomplish this by making a few members of the group dissatisfied or rebellious. The strength of a group lies in its unity and its ability to reinforce the values and actions of its individual members. The Shils-Janowitz article in this volume shows the importance of the small military group in this

respect. Regardless of military reverses and propaganda, not until the primary military unit was actually broken up, did the morale of the World War II German army crumble.

The group spectrum which a mass communicator perceives in a society is, therefore, a combination of statistical groupings which help him estimate response in a general way; and of functional groupings, which may be relatively permanent like the primary group, or temporary and spectacular like the acting crowd, or temporary and casual like the football audience, but which, depending on their nature and how much they mean to the individual member, enter into almost every change accomplished through mass communication.

The following selections are all concerned in one way or another with the group as a part of the communication process. Dr. Blumer outlines the functional differences between the crowd, the public, and the mass. Dr. Freidson takes a hard look at the mass as a target of "mass" communication. The Rileys' paper explores the hypothesis that an individual's opinion is a product of his group affiliation. The USIA selection is a simple and clear statement of what is known about personal influence and opinion leaders in the process of opinion change. Dr. Cantril's selection is a summary of his book which analyzed the panic effect of the Orson Welles broadcast describing an imaginary invasion from Mars. Finally, Dr. Merton states some of the implications of his analysis of the Kate Smith war bond broadcasts.

▲ HERBERT BLUMER

$\mathcal{T}$he Crowd, the Public, and the Mass

THE ACTING CROWD

Much of the initial interest of sociologists in the field of collective behavior has centered on the study of the crowd. This interest was lively particularly towards the end of the last century, especially among French scholars. It gained its most vivid expression in the classical work, *The Crowd*, by Gustave Le Bon. This work and others have provided us with much insight into the nature and behavior of the crowd, although much still remains unknown.

Types of Crowds

It is convenient to identify four types of crowds. The first can be called a *casual* crowd, as in the instance of a street crowd watching a performer in a store window. The casual crowd usually has a momentary existence; more important, it has a very loose organization and scarcely any unity. Its members come and go, giving but temporary attention to the object which has awakened the interest of the crowd, and entering into only feeble association with one another. While the chief mechanisms of crowd formation are present in the casual crowd, they are so reduced in scope and weak in operation, that we need not concern ourselves further with this type of crowd. A second type may be designated as the *conventionalized* crowd, such as the spectators at an exciting baseball game. Their behavior is essentially like that of casual crowds, except that it is expressed in established and regularized ways. It is this regularized activity that marks off the conventional crowd as a distinct type. The third type of crowd is the *acting*, aggressive crowd, best represented by a revolutionary crowd or a lynching

▲ This is a section from *New Outline of the Principles of Sociology*, edited by Alfred M. Lee, Jr., published and copyright by Barnes and Noble, Inc. (New York, 1946). It is reprinted here by permission of publisher and copyright holder. Dr. Blumer is professor of sociology at the University of Chicago.

mob. The outstanding mark of this type of crowd is the presence of an aim or objective toward which the activity of the crowd is directed. It is this type of crowd which is the object of concern in practically all studies of the crowd. The remaining type is the *expressive* or "dancing" crowd, such as is so common in the origin of religious sects. Its distinguishing trait is that excitement is expressed in physical movement merely as a form of release instead of being directed toward some objective. In this chapter, we shall consider the acting crowd, and in the following chapter, the dancing crowd.

Formation of Crowds

The essential steps in the formation of a crowd seem to be quite clear. First is the occurrence of some exciting event which catches the attention and arouses the interest of people. In becoming preoccupied with this event and stirred by its excitatory character, an individual is already likely to lose some of his ordinary self-control and to be dominated by the exciting object. Further, this kind of experience, by arousing impulses and feelings, establishes a condition of tension which, in turn, presses the individual on to action. Thus, a number of people stimulated by the same exciting event are disposed by that very fact to behave like a crowd.

This becomes clear in the second step — the beginning of the milling process. The tension of individuals who are aroused by some stimulating event, leads them to move around and to talk to one another; in this milling the incipient excitement becomes greater. The excitement of each is conveyed to others, and, as we have indicated above, in being reflected back to each, intensifies his own excited condition. The most obvious effect of this milling is to disseminate a common mood, feeling, or emotional impulse, and also to increase its intensity. This really leads to a state of marked rapport wherein individuals become very sensitive and responsive to one another and where, consequently, all are more disposed to act together as a collective unit.

Another important result may come from the milling process, and may be regarded as the third important step in the formation of the acting crowd. This step is the emergence of a common object of attention on which the impulses, feelings, and imagery of the people become focused. Usually the common object is the exciting event which has aroused the people; much more frequently, however, it is an image which has been built up and fixed through the talking and acting of people as they mill. This image, or object, like the excitement, is common and shared. Its importance is that it gives a common orientation to the people, and so provides a common objective to their activity. With such a common objective, the crowd is in a position to act with unity, purpose, and consistency.

The last step may be thought of as the stimulation and fostering of the impulses that correspond to the crowd objective, up to the point where the members are ready to act on them. This nurturing and crystallizing of impulses is a result of the interstimulation that takes place in milling and in response to leadership. It occurs primarily as a result of images that are aroused through the process of suggestion and imitation, and reinforced through mutual acceptance. When the members of a crowd have a common impulse oriented toward a fixed image and supported by an intense collective feeling, they are ready to act in the aggressive fashion typical of the acting crowd.

Characteristics of the Acting Crowd

Now we may characterize the nature of the acting crowd, or as some writers also term it, the psychological crowd. It should be noted, first, that such a group is spontaneous and lives in the momentary present. As such it is not a society or a cultural group. It has no heritage or accumulation of tradition to guide its activity; it has no conventions, established expectations, or rules. It lacks other important marks of a society such as an established social organization, an established division of labor, a structure of established roles, a recognized leadership, a set of norms, a set of moral regulations, an awareness of its own identity, or a recognized "we-consciousness." Instead of acting, then, on the basis of established rule, it acts on the basis of aroused impulse. Just as it is, in this sense, a noncultural group, so likewise is it a nonmoral group. In the light of this fact it is not difficult to understand that crowd actions may be strange, forbidding, and at times atrocious. Not having a body of definitions or rules to guide its behavior and, instead, acting on the basis of impulse, the crowd is fickle, suggestible, and irresponsible.

This character of the crowd can be appreciated better by understanding the condition of the typical member. Such an individual loses ordinary critical understanding and self-control as he enters into rapport with other crowd members and becomes infused by the collective excitement which dominates them. He responds immediately and directly to the remarks and actions of others instead of interpreting these gestures, as he would do in ordinary conduct. His inability to survey the actions of others before responding to them carries over to his own tendencies to act. Consequently, the impulses aroused in him by his sympathetic sharing of the collective excitement are likely to gain immediate expression instead of being submitted to his own judgment. It is just this condition which is the mark of suggestibility; it explains why the role of suggestion is so pronounced in the crowd. It should be noted, however, that this suggestibility exists only along the line of the aroused impulses; suggestions made contrary to them are ignored. This limiting of the area of suggestibility, but with an intensification of the suggestibility inside of these limits, is a point which is frequently overlooked by students of crowd behavior.

The loss of customary critical interpretation and the arousing of impulses and excited feelings explain the queer, vehement, and surprising behavior so frequent among members of a genuine crowd. Impulses which ordinarily would be subject to a severe check by the individual's judgment and control of himself now have a free passage to expression. That many of these impulses should have an atavistic character is not strange, nor, consequently, is it surprising that much of the actual behavior should be violent, cruel, and destructive. Further, the release of impulses and feelings which encounter no restraint, which come to possess the individual, and which acquire a quasi-sanction through the support of other people, gives the individual a sense of power, of ego-expansion, and of rectitude. Thus, he is likely to experience a sense of invincibility and of conviction in his actions.

The behavior of the crowd can be understood better with a realization of these aspects of the individual member: his loss of self-concern and critical judgment, the surging forth of impulses and feelings, many of which are usually suppressed, his sense of expansion and greatness, and his suggestibility to his fellows. It should be borne in mind that this state of the members of the crowd is due to their extreme rapport and mutual excitement; and, in turn, that this rapport in the acting crowd has become organized around a common objective of activity. Common focusing of attention, rapport, and individual submergence — these exist as different phases of one another, and explain the unity of the crowd and the general character of its behavior.

To prevent the formation of a mob or to break up a mob it is necessary to redirect the attention so that it is not focused collectively on one object. This is the theoretical principle underlying crowd control. Insofar as the attention of the members is directed toward different objects, they form an aggregation of individuals instead of a crowd united by intimate rapport. Thus, to throw people into a state of panic, or to get them interested in other objects, or to get them engaged in discussion or argumentation represents different ways in which a crowd can be broken up.

Our discussion of the crowd has presented the psychological bond of the crowd, or the spirit, that may be called "crowd-mindedness" to use a felicitous phrase of E. A. Ross. If we think in terms of crowd-mindedness, it is clear that many groups may take on the character of a crowd without having to be as small in size as in the instance of a lynching mob. Under certain conditions, a nation may come to be like a crowd. If the people become preoccupied with the same stirring event or object, if they develop a high state of mutual excitement marked by no disagreement, and if they have strong impulses to act toward the object with which they are preoccupied, their action will be like that of the crowd. We are familiar with such behavior on a huge scale in the case of social contagion, like that of patriotic hysteria.

THE EXPRESSIVE CROWD

The Dominant Mark of the Expressive Crowd

The distinguishing feature of the acting crowd, as we have seen, is the direction of the attention toward some common objective or goal; the action of the crowd is the behavior gone through to reach that objective. As opposed to this characteristic, the dominant mark of the expressive crowd is that it is introverted. It has no goal or objective — its impulses and feelings are spent in mere expressive actions, usually in unrestrained physical movements, which give release to tension without having any other purpose. We see such behavior in a marked form in the saturnalia, the carnival, and the dancing crowds of primitive sects.

Comparisons with the Acting Crowd

In explaining the nature of the expressive crowd we should note that in formation and fundamental character it is very much like the acting crowd. It consists of people who are excited, who mill, and who in doing so, spread and intensify the excitement. There develops among them the same condition of rapport marked by quick and unwitting mutual responsiveness. Individuals lose awareness of themselves. Impulses and feelings are aroused, and are no longer subject to the constraint and control which an individual usually exercises over them. In these respects the expressive crowd is essentially like the acting crowd.

The fundamental difference is that the expressive crowd does not develop any image of a goal or objective, and, consequently, suggestion does not operate to build up a plan of action. Without having an objective toward which it might act, the crowd can release its aroused tension and excitement only in physical movement. Stated tersely, the crowd has to act, but it has nothing toward which it can act, and so it merely engages in excited movements. The excitement of the crowd stimulates further excitement which does not, however, become organized around some purposive act which the crowd seeks to carry out. In such a situation the expression of excited feeling becomes an end in itself; the behavior, therefore, may take the form of laughing, weeping, shouting, leaping, and dancing. In its more extreme expression, it may be in the form of uttering gibberish or having violent physical spasms.

Rhythmic Expression

Perhaps the most interesting feature of this expressive behavior, as it is carried on collectively, is that it tends to become rhythmical;

so that with sufficient repetition and with the existence of sufficient rapport, it takes on the form of people's acting with unison. It is easy to see that it may come to be like a collective dance; it is this aspect that leads one to designate the expressive crowd as a dancing crowd. It may be said that just as an acting crowd develops its unity through the formation of a common objective, the expressive crowd forms its unity through the rhythmical expression of its tension.

This feature is of outstanding significance, for it throws considerable light on the interesting association between "dancing" behavior and primitive religious sentiment. To illustrate this point, let us consider the experience of the individual in the dancing crowd.

The Individual in the Expressive Crowd

The stimulation that the individual receives from those with whom he is in rapport lessens his ordinary self-control and evokes and incites impulsive feelings which take possession of him. He feels carried away by a spirit whose source is unknown, but whose effect is acutely appreciated. There are two conditions which are likely to make this experience one of ecstasy and exaltation, and to seal it with a sacred or divine stamp. The first is that the experience is cathartic in nature. The individual who has been in a state of tension, discomfort, and perhaps anxiety, suddenly gains full release and experiences the joy and fullness that come with such relief. This organic satisfaction unquestionably yields a pleasure and exhilaration that makes the experience momentous. The fact that this mood has such complete and unobstructed control over the individual easily leads him to feel that he is possessed or pervaded by a kind of transcendental spirit. The other condition which gives the experience a religious character is the approval and sanction implied in the support coming from those with whom he is in rapport. The fact that others are sharing the same experience rids it of suspicion and enables its unqualified acceptance. When an experience gives complete and full satisfaction, when it is socially stimulated, approved, and sustained, and when it comes in the form of a mysterious possession from the outside, it easily acquires a religious character.

The Development of Collective Ecstasy

When an expressive crowd reaches the height of such collective ecstasy, the tendency is for this feeling to be projected upon objects which are sensed as having some intimate connection with it. Thereupon such objects become sacred to the members of the crowd. These objects may vary; they may include persons (such as a religious prophet), the dance, a song, or physical objects which are felt to be linked with the ecstatic experience. The appearance of such sacred objects lays the basis for the formation of a cult, sect, or primitive religion.

Not all expressive crowds attain this stage of development. Most of them do not pass beyond the early milling or excited stage. But implicitly, they have the potentiality of doing so, and they have most of the characteristic features, even though they be in a subdued form.

Like the acting crowd, the expressive crowd need not be confined to a small compact group whose members are in immediate physical proximity of one another. The behavior which is characteristic of it may be found on occasion in a large group, such as the nation-wide public.

Evaluation

A brief evaluation of the acting crowd and the expressive crowd can be made here. Both of them are spontaneous groupings. Both of them represent elementary collectivities. Their form and structure are not traceable to any body of culture or set of rules; instead, such structures as they have, arise indigenously out of the milling of excited individuals. The acting crowd focuses its tension on an objective and so becomes organized around a plan of action; the expressive crowd merely releases its tension in expressive movement which tends to become rhythmical and establishes unity in this fashion. In both crowds the individual is stripped of much of his conscious, ordinary behavior, and is rendered malleable by the crucible of collective excitement. With the breakdown of his previous personal organization, he is in a position to develop new forms of conduct and to crystallize a new personal organization along new and different lines. In this sense, crowd behavior is a means by which the breakup of the social organization and personal structure is brought about, and at the same time is a potential device for the emergence of new forms of conduct and personality. The acting crowd presents one of the alternative lines for such reorganization — the development of aggressive behavior in the direction of purposive social change. We shall view this line of reorganization as giving rise to a political order. The expressive crowd stands for the other alternative — the release of inner tension in conduct which tends to become sacred and marked by deep sentiment. This might be regarded as giving rise to a religious order of behavior.

THE MASS

We are selecting the term *mass* to denote another elementary and spontaneous collective grouping which, in many respects, is like the crowd but is fundamentally different from it in other ways. The mass is represented by people who participate in mass behavior, such as those who are excited by some national event, those who share in a land boom, those who are interested in a murder trial which is reported in the press, or those who participate in some large migration.

Distinguishable Features of the Mass

So conceived, the mass has a number of distinguishable features. *First,* its membership may come from all walks of life, and from all distinguishable social strata; it may include people of different class position, of different vocation, of different cultural attainment, and of different wealth. One can recognize this in the case of the mass of people who follow a murder trial. *Second,* the mass is an anonymous group, or more exactly, is composed of anonymous individuals. *Third,* there exists little interaction or exchange of experience between the members of the mass. They are usually physically separated from one another, and, being anonymous, do not have the opportunity to mill as do the members of the crowd. *Fourth,* the mass is very loosely organized and is not able to act with the concertedness or unity that marks the crowd.

The Role of Individuals in the Mass

The fact that the mass consists of individuals belonging to a wide variety of local groups and cultures is important. For it signifies that the object of interest which gains the attention of those who form the mass is something which lies on the outside of the local cultures and groups; and therefore, that this object of interest is not defined or explained in terms of the understandings or rules of these local groups. The object of mass interest can be thought of as attracting the attention of people away from their local cultures and spheres of life and turning it toward a wider universe, toward areas which are not defined or covered by rules, regulations, or expectations. In this sense the mass can be viewed as constituted by detached and alienated individuals who face objects or areas of life which are interesting, but which are also puzzling and not easy to understand and order. Consequently, before such objects, the members of the mass are likely to be confused and uncertain in their actions. Further, in not being able to communicate with one another, except in limited and imperfect ways, the members of the mass are forced to act separately, as individuals.

Society and the Mass

From this brief characterization it can be seen that the mass is devoid of the features of a society or a community. It has no social organization, no body of custom and tradition, no established set of rules or rituals, no organized group of sentiments, no structure of status roles, and no established leadership. It merely consists of an aggregation of individuals who are separate, detached, anonymous, and thus, homogeneous as far as mass behavior is concerned. It can be seen, further, that the behavior of the mass, just because it is not made by pre-established rule or expectation, is spontaneous, indigenous, and elementary. In these respects, the mass is a great deal like the crowd.

In other respects, there is an important difference. It has already been noted that the mass does not mill or interact as the crowd does. Instead, the individuals are separated from one another and unknown to one another. This fact means that the individual in the mass, instead of being stripped of his self-awareness is, on the other hand, apt to be rather acutely self-conscious. Instead of acting in response to the suggestions and excited stimulation of those with whom he is in rapport, he acts in response to the object that has gained his attention and on the basis of the impulses that are aroused by it.

Nature and Mass Behavior

This raises the question as to how the mass behaves. The answer is in terms of each individual's seeking to answer his own needs. The form of mass behavior, paradoxically, is laid down by individual lines of activity and not by concerted action. These individual activities are primarily in the form of selections — such as the selection of a new dentifrice, a book, a play, a party platform, a new fashion, a philosophy, or a gospel — selections which are made in response to the vague impulses and feelings which are awakened by the object of mass interest. Mass behavior, even though a congeries of individual lines of action, may become of momentous significance. If these lines converge, the influence of the mass may be enormous, as is shown by the far-reaching effects on institutions ensuing from shifts in the selective interest of the mass. A political party may be disorganized or a commercial institution wrecked by such shifts in interest or taste.

When mass behavior becomes organized, as into a movement, it ceases to be mass behavior, but becomes societal in nature. Its whole nature changes in acquiring a structure, a program, a defining culture, traditions, prescribed rules, an in-group attitude, and a we-consciousness. It is for this reason that we have appropriately limited it to the forms of behavior which have been described.

Increasing Importance of Mass Behavior

Under conditions of modern urban and industrial life, mass behavior has emerged in increasing magnitude and importance. This is due primarily to the operation of factors which have detached people from their local cultures and local group settings. Migration, changes of residence, newspapers, motion pictures, the radio, education — all have operated to detach individuals from customary moorings and thrust them into a new and wider world. In the face of this world, individuals have had to make adjustments on the basis of largely unaided selections. The convergence of their selections has made the mass a potent influence. At times, its behavior comes to approximate that of a crowd, especially under conditions of excitement. At such times it is likely to be influenced by excited appeals as these appear

in the press or over the radio — appeals that play upon primitive
impulses, antipathies, and traditional hatreds. This should not obscure
the fact that the mass may behave without such crowdlike frenzy. It
may be much more influenced by an artist or a writer who happens
to sense the vague feelings of the mass and to give expression and
articulation to them.

Instances of Mass Behavior

In order to make clearer the nature of the mass and of mass behavior, a brief consideration can be given to a few instances. Gold
rushes and land rushes illustrate many of the features of mass behavior.
The people who participate in them usually come from a wide variety
of backgrounds; together they constitute a heterogeneous assemblage.
Thus, those who engaged in the Klondike Rush or the Oklahoma
Land Boom came from different localities and areas. In the rush, each
individual (or at best, family) had its own goal or objective, so that
between the participants there was a minimum of cooperation and very
little feeling of allegiance or loyalty. Each was trying to get ahead of
the other, and each had to take care of himself. Once the rush is
under way, there is little discipline, and no organization to enforce
order. Under such conditions it is easy to see how a rush turns into a
stampede or a panic.

Mass Advertising

Some further appreciation of the nature of mass behavior is yielded
by a brief treatment of mass advertising. In such advertising, the
appeal has to be addressed to the anonymous individual. The relation
between the advertisement and the prospective purchaser is a direct
one — there is no organization or leadership which can deliver, so to
speak, the body of purchasers to the seller. Instead, each individual
acts upon the basis of his own selection. The purchasers are a heterogeneous group coming from many communities and walks of life; as
members of the mass, however, because of their anonymity, they are
homogeneous or essentially alike.

Proletarian Masses

What are sometimes spoken of as the proletarian masses illustrate
other features of the mass. They represent a large population with
little organization or effective communication. Such people usually
have been wrested loose from a stable group life. They are usually
disturbed, even though it be only in the form of vague hopes or new
tastes and interests. Consequently, there is a lot of groping in their
behavior — an uncertain process of selection among objects and ideas
that come to their attention.

THE PUBLIC

Nature of the Public

We shall consider the public as the remaining elementary collective grouping. The term *public* is used to refer to a group of people (*a*) who are confronted by an issue, (*b*) who are divided in their ideas as to how to meet the issue, and (*c*) who engage in discussion over the issue. As such, it is to be distinguished from a public in the sense of a national people, as when one speaks of the public of the United States, and also from a *following*, as in the instance of the "public" of a motion-picture star. The presence of an issue, of discussion, and of a collective opinion is the mark of the public.

The Public as a Group

We refer to the public as an elementary and spontaneous collective grouping because it comes into existence not as a result of design, but as a natural response to a certain kind of situation. That the public does not exist as an established group and that its behavior is not prescribed by traditions or cultural patterns is indicated by the very fact that its existence centers on the presence of an issue. As issues vary, so do the corresponding publics. And the fact that an issue exists signifies the presence of a situation which cannot be met on the basis of a cultural rule but which must be met by a collective decision arrived at through a process of discussion. In this sense, the public is a grouping that is spontaneous and not pre-established.

Characteristic Features of the Public

This elementary and spontaneous character of the public can be better appreciated by noticing that the public, like the crowd and the mass, is lacking in the characteristic features of a society. The existence of an issue means that the group has to act; yet there are no understandings, definitions, or rules prescribing what that action should be. If there were, there would be, of course, no issue. It is in this sense that we can speak of the public as having no culture — no traditions to dictate what its action shall be. Further, since a public comes into existence only with an issue it does not have the form or organization of a society. In it, people do not have fixed status roles. Nor does the public have any we-feeling or consciousness of its identity. Instead, the public is a kind of amorphous group whose size and membership varies with the issue; instead of having its activity prescribed, it is engaged in an effort to arrive at an act, and therefore forced to *create* its action.

The peculiarity of the public is that it is marked by disagreement and hence by *discussion* as to what should be done. This fact has a number of implications. For one thing, it indicates that the interaction that occurs in the public is markedly different from that which takes place in the crowd. A crowd mills, develops rapport, and reaches a unanimity unmarred by disagreement. The public interacts on the basis of interpretation, enters into dispute, and consequently is characterized by conflict relations. Correspondingly, individuals in the public are likely to have their self-consciousness intensified and their critical powers heightened instead of losing self-awareness and critical ability as occurs in the crowd. In the public, arguments are advanced, are criticized, and are met by counterarguments. The interaction, therefore, makes for opposition instead of the mutual support and unanimity that mark the crowd.

Another point of interest is that this discussion, which is based on difference, places some premium on facts and makes for rational consideration. While, as we shall see, the interaction may fall short by far of realizing these characteristics, the tendency is in their direction. The crowd means that rumor and spectacular suggestion predominate; but the presence of opposition and disagreement in the public means that contentions are challenged and become subject to criticism. In the face of attack that threatens to undermine their character, such contentions have to be bolstered or revised in the face of criticisms that cannot be ignored. Since facts can maintain their validity, they come to be valued; and since the discussion is argumentative, rational considerations come to occupy a role of some importance.

Behavior Patterns of the Public

Now we can consider the question as to how a public acts. This question is interesting particularly because the public does not act like a society, a crowd, or the mass. A society manages to act by following a prescribed rule or consensus; a crowd, by developing rapport; and the mass, by the convergence of individual selections. But the public faces, in a sense, the dilemma of how to become a unit when it is actually divided, of how to act concertedly when there is a disagreement as to what the action should be. The public acquires its particular type of unity and manages to act by arriving at a collective decision or by developing a collective opinion. It becomes necessary to consider now the nature of public opinion and the manner of its formation.

PUBLIC OPINION

Public opinion should be viewed as a collective product. As such, it is not a unanimous opinion with which everyone in the public agrees, nor is it necessarily the opinion of a majority. Being a collective opinion it may be (and usually is) different from the opinion of any of the groups in the public. It can be thought of, perhaps, as a composite opinion formed out of the several opinions that are held in the public; or better, as the central tendency set by the striving among these separate opinions and, consequently, as being shaped by the relative strength and play of opposition among them. In this process, the opinion of some minority group may exert a much greater influence in the shaping of the collective opinion than does the view of a majority group. Being a collective product, public opinion does represent the entire public as it is being mobilized to act on the issue, and as such, does enable concerted action which is not necessarily based on consensus, rapport, or chance alignment of individual choices. Public opinion is always moving toward a decision even though it never is unanimous.

The Universe of Discourse

The formation of public opinion occurs through the give and take of discussion. Argument and counterargument become the means by which it is shaped. For this process of discussion to go on, it is essential for the public to have what has been called a "universe of discourse" — the possession of a common language or the ability to agree on the meaning of fundamental terms. Unless they can understand one another, discussion and argumentation are not only fruitless, but impossible. Public discussion today, particularly on certain national issues, is likely to be hampered by the absence of a universe of discourse. Further, if the groups or parties in the public adopt dogmatic and sectarian positions, public discussion comes to a standstill; for such sectarian attitudes are tantamount to a refusal to adopt the point of view of one another and to alter one's own position in the face of attack or criticism. The formation of public opinion implies that people share one another's experience and are willing to make compromises and concessions. It is only in this way that the public, divided as it is, can come to act as a unit.

Interest Groups

The public, ordinarily, is made up of interest groups and a more detached and disinterested spectator-like body. The issue which creates the public is usually set by contesting interest groups. These interest groups have an immediate private concern in the way the issue is met and, therefore, they endeavor to win to their position the support and allegiance of the outside disinterested group. This puts the disinterested group, as Lippmann has pointed out, in the position of arbiter and judge. It is their alignment which determines, usually, which of the competing schemes is likely to enter most freely into the final action. This strategic and decisive place held by those not identified with the immediate interest groups means that public discussion is carried on primarily among them. The interest groups endeavor to shape and set the opinions of these relatively disinterested people.

Viewed in this way, one can understand the varying quality of public opinion, and also the use of means of influence such as propaganda, which subvert intelligent public discussion. A given public opinion is likely to be anywhere between a highly emotional and prejudiced point of view and a highly intelligent and thoughtful opinion. In other words, public discussion may be carried on different levels, with different degrees of thoroughness and limitation. The efforts made by interest groups to shape public opinion may be primarily attempts to arouse or set emotional attitudes and to provide misinformation. It is this feature which has led many students of public opinion to deny its rational character and to emphasize instead, its emotional and unreasoned nature. One must recognize, however, that the very process of controversial discussion forces a certain amount of rational consideration and that, consequently, the resulting collective opinion has a certain rational character. The fact that contentions have to be defended and justified and opposing contentions criticized and shown to be untenable, involves evaluation, weighing, and judgment. Perhaps it would be accurate to say that public opinion is rational, but need not be intelligent.

The Role of Public Discussion

It is clear that the quality of public opinion depends to a large extent on the effectiveness of public discussion. In turn, this effectiveness depends on the availability and flexibility of the agencies of public communication, such as the press, the radio, and public meetings. Basic to their effective use is the possibility of free discussion. If certain of the contending views are barred from gaining presentation to the disinterested public or suffer some discrimination as to the possibility of being argued before them, then, correspondingly, there is interference with effective public discussion.

As mentioned above, the concerns of interest groups readily lead them to efforts to manipulate public opinion. This is particularly true today, when public issues are many and the opportunities for thorough discussion are limited. This setting has been conducive to the employment, in increasing degree, of "propaganda"; today most students of public opinion find that their chief concern is the study of propaganda.

PROPAGANDA

Propaganda can be thought of as a deliberately evoked and guided campaign to induce people to accept a given view, sentiment, or value. Its peculiarity is that in seeking to attain this end it does not give fair consideration to opposing views. The end is dominant and the means are subservient to this end. Hence, we find that a primary characteristic of propaganda is the effort to gain the acceptance of a view not on the basis of the merits of that view but, instead, by appealing to other motives. It is this feature that has made propaganda suspect. In the area of public discussion and public consideration, propaganda operates to mold opinions and judgments not on the basis of the merits of an issue, but chiefly by playing upon emotional attitudes and feelings. Its aim is to implant an attitude or value which comes to be felt by people as natural, true, and proper, and, therefore, as one which expresses itself spontaneously and without coercion.

Collective Action Through Propaganda

It is important to realize that propaganda seeks to bring about collective action rather than mere individual action. In this sense it should be distinguished from advertising, since advertising tries to influence individual action. In propaganda, by contrast, there is the effort to create a conviction and to get action in accordance with this conviction. Those who share a conviction are most easily disposed to act together and to give one another support. From this point of view, everyone who preaches a doctrine or who seeks to propagate a faith is a propagandist, for his ultimate purpose is not to discuss the merits of an issue, but instead to implant a given conviction. With this character, it is clear that propaganda operates to end discussion and reflection.

Practical Rules of Propaganda

There are a few simple rules which are generally recognized to apply to propaganda. *First,* of course, to implant a desired view or attitude, it is necessary to attract the attention of people. *Next,* the object in which it is desired that they become interested should be given a favorable and appealing setting, as in the instance of advertising. *Third,* the images which are used to influence them should be simple and clean-cut. *Fourth,* there should be continuous repetition of the slogans or catchwords or of the presented images. *Fifth,* it is best never to argue, but simply to persist in assertion and reassertion. Such simple techniques are held to be particularly effective in the case of the bulk of people whose attention is ordinarily easily diverted and whose interest is easily flagged.

The Chief Procedures of Propaganda

The chief lines along which propaganda may operate, however, are broader and deserve more thorough consideration. We can distinguish three primary ways by which propaganda is likely to achieve its ends. The first is by simply misrepresenting facts and by providing false information. Judgments and opinions of people are obviously shaped by such data as are available to them. By manipulating the facts, concealing some and misrepresenting others, the propagandist can do much to induce the formation of a given attitude.

Another favorite means of propaganda is to make use of in-group–out-group attitudes. It is well known by sociologists that when two groups develop a keen sense of opposition, strong and unreasonable feelings are released. Each group tends to foster attitudes of loyalty and altruism among the members and to inculcate bitter feelings of hatred and enmity toward the outsiders. The ability to use this in-group–out-group pattern is a primary desideratum to the propagandist. He endeavors to get people to identify his views with their in-group feelings, and opposing views with out-group attitudes. It is the presence of this in-group–out-group setting that explains the extreme effectiveness of propaganda during times of war.

Perhaps the outstanding method of the propagandist is to utilize the emotional attitudes and prejudices which people already have. His purpose here is to build up an association between them and his propagandistic message. Thus, if he can link his views to certain favorable attitudes which people already have, these views will gain acceptance. Also, if opposing views can be associated with unfavorable attitudes, they are likely to be rejected. We see a great deal of this device in current discussions. Efforts are made to identify contentions with such beneficently toned stereotypes as "democracy," "save the Constitution," and "individual liberty," and opposing contentions with such stereotypes as "communism" and "anti-American." It is by playing upon the feelings and prejudices which people already have, that propaganda primarily operates.

The Ingenuity of Propagandists

While it is possible to indicate the simple rules which propaganda follows and the psychological mechanisms which it employs, it is important to realize that it depends primarily upon ingenuity. Each situation has to be met in terms of its peculiarities; a device which may be very successful in one situation may be of no value in another. In this sense, propaganda is like persuasion in face-to-face situations; much depends on intuitive impression and artful ingenuity.

Conflicting Propagandas

Without doubt, there is an increasing use of propaganda at the present time in the public arena, and undoubtedly, this factor has influenced both the nature of public opinion and the manner of its information. This consequence has led to despair on the part of many as to the serviceability of democratic machinery. However, it is important to realize that the presence of propaganda and counter-propaganda sets, again, an issue and ushers in the discussional process which we have spoken of above. For when there are conflicting and opposing propagandas at work, the stage is set for a logical duel, where facts have a premium and rational considerations enter. From this point of view one may understand the remark that propaganda is harmful and dangerous only when there is *one* propaganda.

THE PUBLIC, THE CROWD, AND THE MASS

Before concluding the discussion of the public, it should be pointed out that under certain conditions the public may be changed into a crowd. Most propaganda tends to do this, anyway. When the people in the public are aroused by an appeal to a sentiment which is common to them, they begin to mill and to develop rapport. Then, their expression is in the form of public sentiment and not public opinion. In modern life, however, there seems to be less tendency for the public to become the crowd than for it to be displaced by the mass. The increasing detachment of people from local life, the multiplication of public issues, the expansion of agencies of mass communication, together with other factors, have led people to act increasingly by individual selection rather than by participating in public discussion. So true is this, that in many ways the public and the mass are likely to exist intermingled with one another. This fact adds confusion to the scene of contemporary collective behavior and renders analysis by the student difficult.

COLLECTIVE GROUPINGS AND SOCIAL CHANGE

In the discussion of elementary collective groupings we have considered the acting crowd, the expressive crowd, the mass, and the public. There are other primitive groupings which we can mention here only briefly, such as the panic, the stampede, the strike, the riot, the "popular justice" vigilante committee, the procession, the cult, the mutiny, and the revolt. Most of these groupings represent variations of the crowd; each of them operates through the primitive mechanisms of collective behavior which we have described. Like the four major types which we have considered, they are not societies, but operate outside of a governing framework of rules and culture. They are elementary, natural, and spontaneous, arising under certain fit circumstances.

The appearance of elementary collective groupings is indicative of a process of social change. They have the dual character of implying the disintegration of the old and the appearance of the new. They play an important part in the development of new collective behavior and of new forms of social life. More accurately, the typical mechanisms of primitive association which they show have a significant role in the formation of a new social order.

▲ ELIOT FREIDSON

*C*ommunications Research

and the Concept of the Mass

The study of mass communications has not interested many sociologists until quite recently. Sociologists who are now working in the field find themselves confronted by a rather large body of research literature created over the past twenty years by such diverse workers as educators, psychologists, librarians, professional consultants to business or government, and the like. Each of the workers has been interested in a special problem, and on the whole those problems have been practical, requiring what is immediately useful for action rather than what is or will be useful for basic knowledge.

That practical orientation has not only been responsible for the diversity of research but also for a notable lack of the systematic point of view that a theory of mass communication would give. Such a theory could illuminate the area of research better than mere common sense, and by doing so make the application of specific research techniques more appropriate and more accurate.

Such a theory must begin with some definition of the area of concern. While the sociologist is perhaps not the most qualified to deal with the nature of communication itself, he is at least qualified to deal with the nature of human groups. He can participate in the creation of a theory of mass communication by defining the character of the social enterprises that organize, produce and maintain mass communications and their media, and by defining the character of the human groups called audiences, or collectively, "the audience." In this paper the sociological concept of the mass will be examined to see if it may be used to define the character of the audience of mass communications.

▲ This paper was first published in the *American Sociological Review*, in 1953, and was copyright by the American Sociological Society. It is reprinted here by permission of copyright holder and author. Dr. Freidson is a Ford Fellow at the University of Illinois.

THE CONCEPT OF THE MASS

In the dictionary the mass is defined as the great body of the people
of a nation, as contrasted to some special body like a particular social
class.[1] Lazarsfeld and Kendall use such a definition when they write,
"The term 'mass,' then, is truly applicable to the medium of radio,
for it more than the other media, reaches all groups of the population
uniformly."[2] This notion of the mass merely implies that a mass communication may be distinguished from other kinds of communication
by the fact that it is addressed to a large cross-section of a population
rather than only one or a few individuals or a special part of the population. It also makes the implicit assumption of some technical means
of transmitting the communication in order that the communication
may reach at the same time all the people forming the cross-section
of the population.

This is a conception that is not incorrect, but rather inadequate. It
does not exploit its own implications about the nature of the behavior
we may expect from members of the mass or about the characteristic
features of the mass that set it apart from other groups. By its lack
of specific system or following-out of implications it neither encourages
nor requires specific research to contradict or elaborate it.

A second notion of the mass and its behavior is systematic, logical
and specific enough to provide testable hypotheses about the characteristics of the audience of mass communications and the determinants
of its behavior. As such, it is eminently suited to be worked into a
larger theory of mass communication. In this conception[3] the mass is
said to have four distinctive features. First, it is heterogeneous in
composition, its members coming from all groups of a society. Second,
it is composed of individuals who do not know each other. Third,
the members of the mass are spatially separated from one another and
in that sense, at least, cannot interact with one another or exchange
experience. Fourth, the mass has no definite leadership and has a very
loose organization if any at all. These features are all implied by the
common sense notion and are logically compatible with each other.

The members of the mass are characteristically concerned with
ideas, events and things that lie outside their local experience. Because
those ideas, events and things lie outside the local experience of the
members of the mass, they are not defined or explained "in terms of
the understanding or rules of (the) local groups" to which the mem-

[1] *Webster's Collegiate Dictionary,* Springfield, Mass.: G. and C. Merriam
Co., 1941, p. 615.
[2] P. F. Lazarsfeld and P. L. Kendall, "The Communications Behavior of the
Average American," in W. Schramm (editor), *Mass Communications,* Urbana:
University of Illinois Press, 1949, p. 399.
[3] Herbert Blumer, "Collective Behavior," in A. M. Lee (editor), *New Outline
of the Principles of Sociology,* New York: Barnes and Noble, Inc., 1946, pp.
167-222. Blumer's work rests upon the earlier formulations of Robert E. Park.

bers of the mass belong.[4] These therefore turn the attention of the members of the mass away from their "local cultures and spheres of life" and towards areas not structured by "rules, regulations or expectations." In this sense, the mass

has no social organization, no body of custom and tradition, no established set of rules or rituals, no organized group of sentiments, no structure of status roles, and no established leadership. It merely consists of an aggregation of individuals who are separate, detached, anonymous.[5]

Since the mass has no societal character, the form of its behavior is not to be found in organized, concerted group activity but rather in the behavior of the separate individuals who make up the mass. Each individual seeks to gratify his own needs by selecting certain extra-local ideas, events or things in preference to others.

In another paper Blumer states that the audience of at least one mass medium, the movies, is a mass. In attending to movies, members of the audience are anonymous, heterogeneous, unorganized and spatially separated, and the content of the movies is concerned with something that lies outside the local lives of the spectators.[6] According to his notion, then, the audience of such mass communications as we find in movies may be distinguished from other social groups or aggregates by the specific, generic characteristics of the mass.

It is clear that this concept of the mass is sufficiently logical and articulated that if we use it to characterize the audience of mass communications, as Blumer suggests we do, it could well serve as an important source of fruitful hypotheses, and in turn become part of some systematic theory of mass communication. The problem remains, however, whether what we already know about the audience is compatible with the concept of the mass, and in this sense whether or not it would be *accurate* to characterize the audience as a mass. It is to this problem that we must turn now.

THE CHARACTER OF AUDIENCE EXPERIENCE

The major methodological implication of Blumer's conception of the mass is that it is appropriately studied by using a "sample in the form of an aggregation of disparate individuals having equal weight."[7]

[4] *Ibid.*, p. 186.
[5] *Ibid.*, p. 186.
[6] Herbert Blumer, "The Moulding of Mass Behavior Through the Motion Picture," *Publications of the American Sociological Society,* Vol. XXIX (1936), pp. 115-127.
[7] Herbert Blumer, "Public Opinion and Public Opinion Polling," *American Sociological Review,* Vol. XII (1948), p. 548. In this article he specifically describes "going to motion picture shows, and reading newspapers" as "mass actions of individuals in contrast to organized actions of groups," and attacks public opinion pollers for applying to the study of the public and public opinion methods of sampling that are appropriate only to the study of the mass or other aggregates.

The method of study appropriate to the concept thus gives equal weight to individuals by classifying them according to such essentially demographic attributes as age, sex, socio-economic status and education: the subjects are treated as solitary individuals who have certain traits in common but who do not interact with each other and who do not share certain socially-derived expectations about the communication.

Blumer has indicated that the characteristic behavior of the members of the mass takes the form of *selection*. In this sense, if it is accurate to consider members of the audience to be members of the mass, then their characteristic behavior lies in their selections of particular movies, programs and newspapers. These selections become the important thing to explain. If it is accurate to consider the audience to be a mass, then according to the concept of the mass those selections are to be explained by factors that are not an essential part of the primary or local group experience of the audience. The factors that reduce the individual to a member of the mass are such things as age, sex, years of education, socio-economic status, and "personality," attributes that he shares with thousands who are unknown to him and who have no immediate influence on him.

Such attributes must explain audience selections or we are justified in concluding that the audience is not a mass. Of late there has been some feeling that such data are not sufficient to explain audience selections. Riley and Flowerman advance the opinion that

any given person in the audience reacts not merely as an isolated personality but also as a member of the various groups to which he belongs and with which he communicates.[8]

To support this they offer some preliminary data that cannot be ignored, even though they refer only to an audience of children.

There are in fact other grounds for concluding that the audience is only inaccurately termed a mass. We are told that the mass consists of individual members. When we look at a particular individual member of the audience we find that his actual experience is of a decidedly different quality than might be expected if he were a solitary member of the mass. We find that most individuals go to the movies in the company of another person[9] and that family rather than solitary listening and watching tend to be characteristic of radio[10] and tele-

[8] M. W. Riley and S. H. Flowerman, "Group Relations as a Variable in Communications Research," *American Sociological Review*, Vol. XVI (1951), p. 171. See also M. W. Riley and J. W. Riley, Jr., "A Sociological Approach to Communications Research," *Public Opinion Quarterly*, Vol. XV (1951), pp. 445-460.

[9] L. A. Handel, *Hollywood Looks at its Audience*, Urbana: University of Illinois Press, 1950, pp. 113-114.

[10] A. L. Eisenberg, *Children and Radio Programs*, New York: Columbia University Press, 1936, p. 194.

vision[11] audiences. The individual seems to experience those media frequently in an immediately sociable setting[12] that cannot be characterized as anonymous or heterogeneous, with no interaction with other spectators, and no organized relationships among them.

The fact of the existence of a characteristically interpersonal setting of the spectator's contact with some of the mass media would lead us to suspect and seek the existence of other characteristically social features of his experience. When we learn that the most effective mode of stimulating members of the audience to make one selection rather than another (i.e., the most effective mode of advertising) lies in what is called word-of-mouth advertising[13] (i.e., the transmission of opinions about movies from one person to another), it seems certain that there is some lively interchange between any individual and other members of the audience. From this datum we are able to infer among the members of an audience the existence and continuous re-creation of shared understandings, common selections and concerted social activity. Further, since we are told that such a thing as an "opinion leader" exists,[14] we may conclude there to be some sort of well-developed web of organized social relationships that exists among members of the audience and that influences their behavior.

This material implies that the member of the audience selects his mass communications content under a good deal of pressure and guidance from his experience as a member of social groups, that in fact his mass communications behavior is part of his social behavior, and that *mass communications have been absorbed into the social life of the local groups.* The act of "selection" itself seems to have become a habitual type of social act that frequently is no longer even self-conscious. Handel indicated that only about 21 per cent of the movie audience shows any great effort consciously to select a particular movie to see[15] (rather than go to the Rialto on Saturday nights because that's what one always does on Saturday nights).

[11] E. E. Maccoby, "Television: Its Impact on School Children," *Public Opinion Quarterly,* Vol. XV (1951), p. 425.

[12] Herbert Blumer, *Movies and Conduct,* New York: The Macmillan Co., 1933, *passim,* is particularly rich in personal documents that indicate the quality and significance of that immediately sociable setting of movie-going.

[13] Handel, *op. cit.,* p. 69.

[14] *Ibid.,* pp. 88-90. See also the discussion provoked by the "discovery" of the opinion leader, R. K. Merton, "Patterns of Influence," in P. F. Lazarsfeld and F. N. Stanton, *Communications Research,* New York: Harper & Brothers, 1949, pp. 180-219.

[15] Handel, *op. cit.,* pp. 151-154. We may also note Berelson's finding in "What 'Missing the Newspaper' Means," in Lazarsfeld and Stanton, *op. cit.,* pp. 122-123, that "reading (the newspaper) itself, rather than *what* is read, provides an important gratification for the respondents." Radio research, too, has found such habitual rather than consciously selective audience behavior.

In many ways the ordinary member of an audience can be equated with the normal, unself-conscious member of a long-established church congregation,

Much audience behavior, then, takes place in a complex network of local social activity. Certain times of day, certain days, certain seasons, are the socially appropriate times for engaging in particular activities connected with the various mass media. The individual is frequently accompanied by others of his social group when he is engaged in those activities. The individual participates in an interpersonal grid of spectators who discuss the meaning of past experience with mass communications and the anticipated significance of future experience. Certain theaters, programs and newspapers tend to form focal points for his activity on specific occasions no matter what the content might actually be.

The behavior of the members of the mass is said not to be "integral to the routine of local group behavior,"[16] but the communications behavior of the members of the audience, on the other hand, *does* seem to be integrated into the routine of local group life. The mass media are institutions that are organized around providing services to a clientele. The services of the local theater, television station and newspaper are absorbed into the pattern of local life, becoming only some of a number of focal points around which leisure activities have been organized by the members of the group.

It is this point about the social nature of the experience of the members of the audience that has been somewhat obscurely made by past research when the "predispositions" of the individual are referred to in order to explain the failure to find strong and consistent correlations between content and specific types of reactions to it. It is this point that is being referred to by the recent thorough review of the literature on the effects of mass media that concluded at one point that a substantial number of careful objective studies indicate that cultural milieu is one of the most important, if not the single most important determiner of an individual's pattern of communications behavior. . . . The individual apparently adopts, or develops, patterns of communications behavior characteristic of persons in his own cultural level. . . . Should he come into contact with a new medium of communication, his behavior in relation thereto is governed *by* the pattern. The new medium is in short not so likely to change the pattern of his behavior as rather to be absorbed."[17]

On the basis of this material on the experience and behavior of members of the audience, it is possible to conclude that the audience, from the point of view of its members, at least, is *not* anonymous, heterogeneous, unorganized and spatially separated. The individual

while the fan can be equated with the devoted member of a tightly-organized, militant cult. The former shows habitual social behavior while the latter shows ritual social behavior.

[16] Blumer, "Moulding of Mass Behavior," p. 116.

[17] J. T. Klapper, "The Effects of Mass Media," (mimeographed) New York: Bureau of Applied Social Research, Columbia University, 1949, Section I-15, p. 6.

member of the audience frequently does not manifest the selective activity characteristic of the mass, and when such selection has been observed to occur it appeared to arise out of the stimulation of organized social processes rather than merely the individual's personal interests. Given this, it is possible to conclude that the concept of the mass is not accurately applicable to the audience.

METHODOLOGICAL IMPLICATIONS

If this conclusion is correct, what are its implications for communications, and particularly audience, research?

The bulk of past students of the audience of mass communications will no doubt be surprised to be told that their method and their underlying assumptions about the nature of the audience presuppose reliance on the concept of the mass that has been described here. There is no justification for studying the audience as an aggregation of discrete individuals whose social experience is equalized and cancelled out by means of allowing only the attributes of age, sex, socioeconomic status, and the like, to represent them except by subscribing to the assertion that the audience is a mass.

Further, the popular procedure of studying audience behavior solely in relation to content also relies on equating the audience with the mass. Assuming the audience to be a mass, the implicit reasoning of such research is as follows: Since the mass attends to areas which are not conventionally defined (and which are in some way conveyed by content), and since members of the mass do not behave according to the conventions, expectations and values of their local groups and do not interact with each other, it follows that the two really important variables in mass communication are individual traits of the members of the audience and the content itself. Content is then studied as a set of stimuli from which members of the audience *as individuals* create "objects" in terms of their individual interests. There is only interaction between content and personal interests. When the audience is viewed as a social group rather than a mass, then content and personal interests are seen to be only some of the elements of the over-all social process determining responses.

To the extent that past research has studied the audience as if it were composed of discrete individuals, and has sought the significant determinants of audience taste and behavior only in the relation between content and the personal interests implied by the attributes of the individual spectator, past research has considered the audience to be a mass. If the concept of the mass is only inaccurately applied to the audience, the past research that owes its justification to such application has rested on an inaccurate foundation and suffers because of it.

THE USE OF THE CONCEPT OF THE MASS IN COMMUNICATIONS RESEARCH

In order to create a more adequate notion of the audience, it must be recognized that there is an essential ambiguity[18] involved, an ambiguity that becomes sharply focused when we realize that one can speak of the audience in two major senses. On the one hand we can speak of the *national audience* and on the other of the *local audiences* that make up the national audience.

The national audience is more or less a mass in Blumer's sense provided that we speak of members of one local audience not in relation to each other but to those of other local audiences. Members of one local audience are anonymous, heterogeneous, spatially separate and unorganized in relation to those of another local audience. There is no well-organized bond between different local audiences, and in this sense the type of social experience presupposed by such a bond need not be taken into account when one deals with the sum of the local audiences — the national audience. Thus, so long as one treats the national audience as an aggregate body, the concept of the mass is not inaccurately applied.

However, while one can *describe* such an aggregate without reference to the organized groups that compose it, one cannot *explain* the behavior of its members except by reference to the local audiences to which they belong. It is their experience as members of local audiences that determines how they act, not the fact that there happen to be members of other local audiences whom they do not not know, who are not necessarily similar to them, do not interact with them and do not have well-organized relationships with them. The existence of those other local audiences has no necessary relation to their own experience. If we are to consider the actual experience of members of the audience to determine their responses, then the concept of the mass has little relevance to that experience and is not appropriately used as the basis for explaining audience behavior. Research concerned with the problem of explaining why members of the audience behave as they do should avoid using the concept at the risk of using inappropriate methods of study and obscuring pertinent facts. This conclusion in no way questions the usefulness of the concept of the mass for other areas of research.

[18] Some of the ambiguity of the problem of defining the audience lies in the fact that the audience changes as we change our perspective. To the stubbornly pragmatic producer of movies who relies only on box office receipts for his conception of the audience, it is typically a mass. To the television producer who is strongly affected by a tiny but extremely vocal group of parents who do not want violence portrayed on the screen, the audience is typically a public and his decisions are made on the basis of "public opinion." Our major point here, however, is that if we assume the perspective of the members of the audience as they themselves experience mass media, the audience is a distinctly social, local group that neither typically makes selections nor discusses an issue.

The behavior of members of the audience, in sum, does not seem to conform to the criteria of collective behavior in general; rather, it seems to be distinctly social. Thus, an adequate concept of the audience must include some idea of its social character, some idea that being a member of a local audience is a social activity in which interaction with others before, during and after any single occasion of spectatorship has created definite shared expectations and predisposing definitions. These in turn have a determinate effect, in conjunction with the institutionalized character of the activity, on what members of the audience select or do not select, and how they react or do not react. Such a concept requires research that is not satisfied with studying only such things as the age, sex or personality of the spectators in conjunction with the content of the communication, but that would go on to study the local audience itself as a social group composed of individuals who have absorbed mass communications into their relatively settled ways of behaving and who, in the real or vicarious company of their fellows, behave towards mass communications in an organized, social manner.

▲ MATILDA WHITE RILEY

▲ JOHN W. RILEY, JR.

A Sociological Approach to Communications Research

This is a brief progress report on some research that has been under-way at Rutgers during the past two years.[1] But in a more immediate sense it represents a continuation of one of the sessions sponsored by the American Association of Public Opinion Research in June 1950. This was the session entitled "Processes of Opinion Formation," chaired by William Albig, with principal papers by Eugene Hartley and Burton Fisher.[2]

It will be recalled that the burden of this symposium was to call attention to the relationship between opinions and attitudes, on the one hand, and the social structure in which they exist, on the other. Thus Hartley, for example, asserted that "the opinion of an individual is a function of his group affiliations" and Fisher went on to observe that "even the simplest definition of public opinion implies a study of the social structure and process in which opinions occur," and both the main speakers and the discussants who followed agreed in effect that among the most critically needed developments in communications research is an approach which can begin to handle in operational terms some of the obvious but long neglected social factors in the process of opinion formation.

[1] Paper delivered at the Princeton convention of the American Association of Public Opinion Research, June, 1951.

[2] "Process of Opinion Formation: A Symposium." *Public Opinion Quarterly,* Vol. 14, No. 4, pp. 367-386.

RELEVANCE OF MANNHEIM'S HYPOTHESIS TO PUBLIC OPINION RESEARCH

But this, of course, is neither a new point of view to sociological theory nor a new hypothesis for communications research.

In the most basic sociological sense, the theoretical orientation for this point of view is closely related to the work of Karl Mannheim and that branch of sociology which has come to be known to the English speaking world as the sociology of knowledge. Grossly oversimplified, what Mannheim has attempted to set forth is a relationship between social structure, on the one hand, and knowledge on the other. Or, to use his own terms, "a description and structural analysis of the ways in which social relationships, in fact, influence thought.[3]

While it is scarcely within the compass of this report to attempt to trace the implications of Mannheim's work to the theory of communications, at least two of his specific hypotheses would seem to have special relevance to the problems of public opinion and communications research, and hence to any body of generalized theory which may emerge.

The first may be called the *interest hypothesis*. Here the emphasis is placed upon vested interests, whether they are political, economic, or religious. Thus, for example, economically well-to-do respondents in a survey may well express a different attitude toward a proposal to expand social security benefits as compared with the economically less privileged. An established relationship of this sort is a commonplace finding in public opinion research.

A second hypothesis of special relevance is Mannheim's *focus of attention hypothesis,* according to which "perspective is limited in order to deal with a particular problem . . . awareness of which may in turn be attributed to the social position of the subject."[4] Here, certainly, is an insight of tremendous significance to the sociology of knowledge and to any general theory of communications. Yet it squarely presents the empirical challenge as to whether operationally adequate techniques can be devised to effectively and accurately measure the relationship between the social position of the recipient of a communicated message and his awareness, rejection, acceptance, or distortion of the message itself.

CURRENT FOCUS ON THE GROUP IN OPINION RESEARCH

This brief excursion into one branch of sociological theory, however, is in no sense intended to indicate that the general hypothesis is new, or that current research has been completely negligent in bringing data to bear. Much attention has, for example, been focussed on the "leader," who may be surveyed as he epitomizes the attitudes of

---

[3] *Ideology and Utopia,* p. 277, quoted in Merton, *Social Theory and Social Structure,* Glencoe, Ill., Free Press, 1949, p. 250.

[4] Merton, *op. cit.,* p. 252.

his group. The importance of the group is often implicit in the effort of market research to observe consumer demand "under normal conditions": a new food product, for instance, is tested, not on the housewife alone as an individual, but in actual home use where the final judgment of the product can reflect the views of the whole family; a hit tune is gauged by the reaction of the whole gang of teenagers at the juke box; etc.

Furthermore, the field has not been devoid of some real pioneers who have broken new ground. Thus Hyman, Newcomb, Lazarsfeld, Berelson, Gaudet and others have all demonstrated in one fashion or another the relevance of this type of relationship. But such studies have been all too rare and their most basic contributions all too frequently overlooked.

One of the neatest cases of the relevance of this kind of approach is to be found in Merton's stimulating analysis of opinion leaders.[5] The original problem was to identify, for a national news magazine, the opinion leaders in a test community, and to determine how this news magazine was used within the patterns of interpersonal influence and general communications behavior in the local community. The more conventional indices of "leadership," — e.g., occupational status, income level, organizational affiliations, etc., were considered at the outset to be inadequate for dealing with the problem and an elaborate classification in terms of the different stages in the life cycle of the leader was set up.

Yet even this vastly more sophisticated classification, going as it did far beyond those objective characteristics which are typically found on the so-called "fact sheets" of questionnaires, resulted at first in a welter of meaningless relationships and apparently unrelated discrete impressions. For example, about half of the opinion leaders, so located and classified, read news magazines of the type under study, but the data could give no clues whatsoever as to why the other half did not.

It was only on the basis of an incidental observation that a crucial key was finally discovered. In response to the same set of questions, it was observed that some of the leaders were prone to talk largely in terms of the local community situation, whereas others frequently tended to incorporate into their answers considerations which went far outside the immediate social setting. It was at this point that the investigators were able to divide their leaders into two types: the "local" and the "cosmopolitan." What this accomplished, of course, was a classification in terms of the opinion leaders' orientation to two different types of social structures: on the one hand, the local community, on the other hand, the larger social structure of the cosmopolitan society. "Only then," as Merton reports, "did data, not

---

[5] "Patterns of Influence" in Lazarsfeld and Stanton, *Communications Research 1948-49*, New York, Harper & Brothers, 1949, pp. 180 ff.

previously assimilable by our interpretive scheme, 'fall into place.' With the recasting of the data in terms of the new concepts, there emerged a set of suggested uniformities in place of the previously untidy aggregations of facts."[6]

One cannot help but suspect in connection with the rather substantial amount of research which has gone into daytime serials on the radio that the surprisingly few differences which are discoverable between the 50 per cent of the women who listen and the other half who do not might be further illuminated through some such approach as this. In fact, Herta Herzog, in her brilliant report on daytime serial listeners, indirectly hints at such a possibility when she writes:

. . . the evidence suggests that the gratifications which women derive from daytime serials are so complex and so often unanticipated that we have no guide to fruitful observations unless we study in detail the actual experiences of women listening to these programs.[7]

In similar fashion, the various studies in film effectiveness conducted under Army auspices during the war and reported in *Experiments on Mass Communication*[8] indicate clearly that such objective demographic characteristics as age, marital status, rank, length of service, religious affiliation, region of birth, etc., are almost uniformly unrelated to the effects of the films. Here, too, it would seem to be a most reasonable suggestion that, were the complex of social relations to be translated into an operational variable, significant differences might be expected. In fact, the senior researcher in these investigations, Carl Hovland, has made precisely this suggestion in another paper. In commenting upon the importance of psychological theory, he says,

Equally important is the development of sociological theories concerning communications. The way in which communication is transmitted in various types of social structure is an obvious example where the individual and the group are interdependent.[9]

With this background in mind, what the Rutgers research has attempted to do has been to take some steps, however faltering they may be, toward finding variables which will help to explain complex social relations in operational terms. To be sure, we have been working with school children, and with very small samples.[10] Our conceptualization

[6] *Ibid.*, pp. 183 ff.

[7] Lazarsfeld and Stanton, *Radio Research 1942-43*, New York, Duell, Sloan and Pearce, 1944, p. 23.

[8] Hovland, Lumsdaine and Sheffield, Princeton University Press, 1949.

[9] Berelson and Janowitz, *Reader in Public Opinion and Communication*, Glencoe, Illinois, Free Press, 1951, p. 189.

[10] Research operations have been largely financed by Rutgers University and the American Jewish Committee, and have been made possible through the cooperation of the New Lincoln School of New York City and the Public Schools of Metuchen, N. J. Continuation of the research will be financed by grants from the Rockefeller Foundation and the Human Resource Research Institute of the U. S. Air Force.

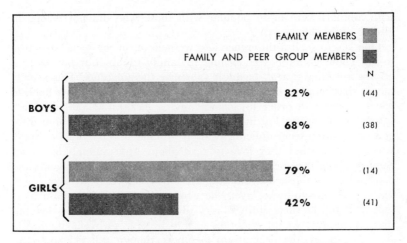

FAMILY MEMBERS

FAMILY AND PEER GROUP MEMBERS

N

BOYS
82% (44)
68% (38)

GIRLS
79% (14)
42% (41)

Chart 1. Percentage of younger children liking little animal comics.

is only now developing, and our findings to date are entirely tentative. Nevertheless, we have taken seriously Harry Alpert's comment made at the 1950 AAPOR meetings that there is a "widening gap between our theoretical conceptions of the nature of public opinion and the methodological techniques which are most frequently employed to measure and record that opinion." The evidence which follows represents our small contribution toward narrowing the gap.

PEER GROUP MEMBERSHIP AS A VARIABLE

A sociological approach to the attitudes of the adolescent and pre-adolescent must take into account at least two important social groups: his parents and his friends or peers.[11] Practically all children belong to family groups. Only certain children belong to peer groups, however, so that we have concerned ourselves with an analysis of children as either members, or non-members, roughly speaking, of peer groups.

Our first experiments indicated, as the theory led us to expect, that there might indeed be many and far-reaching differences between members and non-members of peer groups.[12] Chart 1 shows that among younger (5th and 7th grade) children, comic books dealing

[11] Cf. David Riesman's penetrating analysis of peer orientation in *The Lonely Crowd*, Princeton, N. J.: Princeton University Press, 1950.

[12] Cf. Matilda White Riley and Samuel H. Flowerman, "Group Relations as a Variable in Communications Research," *American Sociological Review*, April, 1951. Members and non-members of peer groups are there referred to as "high" and "low" communicators, with verbal interaction used as an index of group integration.

with animals were more popular with those who did not belong in groups of friends.

One key to such a difference lies, we believe, in the social structure itself. Those children who belong in family groups but not in peer groups are offered a set of adult values by their parents. This usually means that they are expected to help at home, to do well in school, to learn to strive in order to achieve, and in general to prepare for a future life as adults. For many ten- and twelve-year-old children these goals may often seem difficult, or even completely unattainable. Small wonder, then, that they love to read about little animals like Bugs Bunny, whom they perceive as the complete negation of the goals and conventions established by adults. "He's a rascal," they say about him, "lazy," "happy-go-lucky," yet "he gets away with it." Because he is only a rabbit, he successfully evades adult standards, much as the children themselves would doubtless like to be able to evade them. On the other hand, the peer group members, though still tickled by his humor, are less engrossed by Bugs Bunny (75 per cent as compared with 92 per cent). This is perhaps because they have less need to defy parent values, since they, as members of two groups, have a choice between two sets of values — those of their parents and those of their peers. Peer values are usually far less discouraging, having to do with being just like the group (not too poor but also not too good at anything), and involving certain routines of keeping up with baseball and with the latest tunes, hanging around with the gang, and seeing the funny side of things. Thus the child who belongs in the peer groups is offered a relatively easy set of peer goals, and is also in a better position to accept his parents' goals voluntarily only when they seem fair or legitimate to him. This appears to throw some light on his differing media selection.

Chart 2 suggests another form in which this frustration with parent values may be expressed in media selection. This deals with another category of radio and television programs which proved outstandingly popular among the 400 children interviewed — programs characterized by violence, action, and aggression, and including westerns, mysteries, crime, horror, and other such adventure themes. Now when we use traditional analytical breakdowns, it becomes quite clear that this type of program, like little animal comics, is more popular with boys than girls, and considerably more popular with the younger as compared with the older children surveyed. Education and economic breakdowns are not useful in this case, since all the children attended the same school and came from a fairly homogeneous home background. Over and beyond this, analysis by peer group membership as shown in Chart 2, with age and sex held constant, appears to throw further light on program selection. Again it is the non-members of peer groups among the younger children who tend to report the

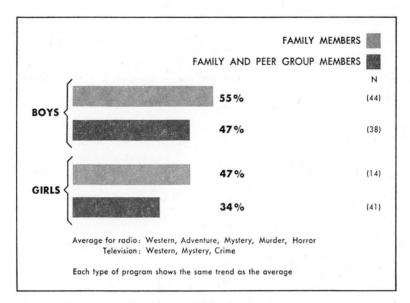

FAMILY MEMBERS

FAMILY AND PEER GROUP MEMBERS

		N
BOYS	55%	(44)
	47%	(38)
GIRLS	47%	(14)
	34%	(41)

Average for radio: Western, Adventure, Mystery, Murder, Horror
Television: Western, Mystery, Crime

Each type of program shows the same trend as the average

Chart 2. Percentage of younger children liking programs of action and violence.

greatest liking for programs of action and violence, and who presumably are in a social position which is most likely to provoke feelings of hostility and aggression.

In an effort to understand more clearly such possible sociological differences, we made a further subdivision of the non-members of peer groups according to their predominant *reference groups*.[13] In effect, we attempted to find out from the children themselves (using only the approximately 200 older children in the sample) whether they regarded their own values as being closer to the values of their parents, or closer to the values of the other children in the school class. This allowed us to classify children roughly into those who were more apt to use parents as a reference group (that is, to share parent values), or to use peers as a reference group (that is, to espouse peer values as they perceived them).

Chart 3 shows this breakdown of older children as related to programs of action and violence. (It should be pointed out that favorable reports from older children on the four types of action-violence radio and television programs seem to form a Guttman scale with 90 per

[13] In line with reference group theory as developed in Newcomb, *Social Psychology*, New York, the Dryden Press, 1950, and Merton and Kitt, "Contributions to the Theory of Reference Group Behavior," in Merton and Lazarsfeld, *Continuities in Social Research: Studies in the Scope and Method of the "American Soldier,"* Glencoe, Ill., The Free Press, 1950.

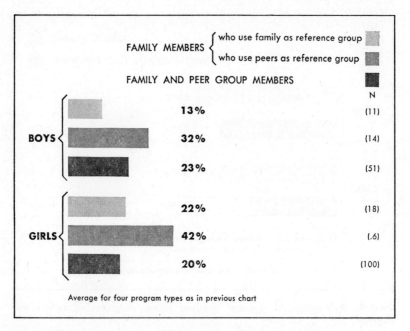

Chart 3. Percentage of older children liking programs of action and violence.

cent reproducibility; but that comic books, which seemed to us similar in content, did not fit the scale. This suggests that action comics may fill a different need or reach a different category of children as compared with the apparently similar radio-television programs.) This chart indicates that among older children, who ordinarily have lost a good deal of the earlier interest in programs of action and violence, the interest remains strongest among those non-members of peer groups who nevertheless use peers as a reference group. While the number of cases is far too small to demonstrate such a finding, the sociological theory would lead us to expect fantasies of aggression and power among children so placed in the social structure. These are, by definition, the children who are most frustrated relative to the peer group: they do not belong, yet give clear evidence of wanting to belong. Even if they do conform to peer norms, they stand little chance of recognition and reward from the peer group, since they are outside it. Relative to their parents, they are also under the greatest strain since, by definition, they tend to support the values not of their parents but of an envied group of peers.

Chart 4 suggests one possible index of such strain relative to parents, using the same subdivision of non-members of the peer group into those who use parents and those who use peers as a reference group. This shows the per cent of children who perceive themselves

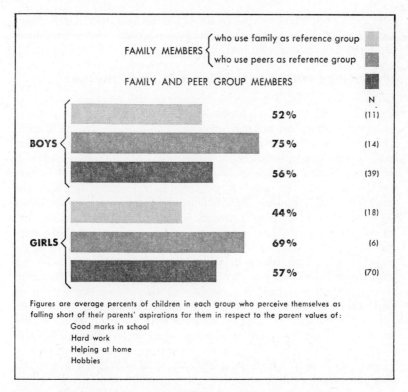

FAMILY MEMBERS
{ who use family as reference group
{ who use peers as reference group

FAMILY AND PEER GROUP MEMBERS

		N
BOYS	52%	(11)
	75%	(14)
	56%	(39)
GIRLS	44%	(18)
	69%	(6)
	57%	(70)

Figures are average percents of children in each group who perceive themselves as falling short of their parents' aspirations for them in respect to the parent values of:
Good marks in school
Hard work
Helping at home
Hobbies

Chart 4. Index of strain in older children's relations with parents.

as falling short of their parents' aspirations for them in regard to adult values of good marks, hard work, helping at home, and hobbies. Strain appears to be greatest among the non-members who use peers as a reference group. According to the recently developed theory of Talcott Parsons,[14] *strain* springs from a failure of one group member to meet the group's expectations of him. In this case, those children who believe they are failing to meet parent expectations may well be the most likely to feel insecure and inadequate. Insofar as they perceive this failure correctly, they may also be most apt to be punished by parents for their failure, which in turn produces feelings of hostility toward the parents. When the social structure imposes undue strain upon the individual in such ways as this, we should expect him to be highly productive of fantasies, and therefore to select a kind of media material, such as little animals or violent action, which would foster such fantasies.

Sociological analysis of this sort may well help us to discover why,

[14] Parsons Talcott, *The Social System,* The Free Press, 1951, Chapter VII and *passim.*

among children who are alike in respect to age, sex, social and educational background, certain individuals like action-violence programs, while other individuals do not.

INTERPRETATION AFFECTED BY RELATIONSHIP TO SOCIAL STRUCTURE

There was, moreover, some indication in the two-hour interviews conducted with the 400 children that the child's relation to the social structure might affect not only *what* he liked but also *why* he liked it. The same media materials appear to be interpreted and used differently by children in different social positions. For the non-member of the group, funny animals and wild west heroes may form a fantasy world into which he may escape from a real world in which the standards seem impossibly high. The peer group member, on the other hand, often likes such media themes, when he does like them, because he can convert the stories into every day play activity in his group. Among younger children, 69 per cent of the peer group members reported liking Lone Ranger, for instance, as compared with 85 per cent of the non-members. While the non-members often described him in subjective terms as "scarey," "creepy," "hard to get out of your mind when you go to sleep," the peer group members were more apt to couple their reading of westerns with "playing guns" in the woods afterward. Thus the peer group members, oriented as they are to the need for getting along in the group, appear to judge media in terms of a criterion which we might call *social utility*, to select media materials which will in some way be immediately useful for group living.

Such a tendency is apparent among older boys, for example. Thus, continuing with the adventure programs, the members of peer groups appear to like them for reasons which may be thought of as related in a more or less immediate sense to their every day lives or for apparently larger utilitarian reasons. This seems to manifest itself in the way they describe the heroes of these programs. Thus:

I sorta like Mr. North. . . . I admire the way he gets out of jams. He's just an ordinary sporting guy — just a regular average man.

Jack Webb — the police sergeant in Dragnet. I like him because they tell true stories about the functioning of the police department.

They picture the Lone Ranger as fearless and brave. They say he's on the part of the law . . . but I don't care if he's an outlaw or anything. . . . It sometimes brings in the history of the U. S.

In marked contrast, the heroes of these same programs seem to be interpreted in a very different way by the non-members of peer groups. Typically they are endowed with invincible or even super-human qualities. For example:

. . . He can get right out of a grave — he's a spirit like. . . . (Suspense)
He always turns into the Shadow and catches the crook.

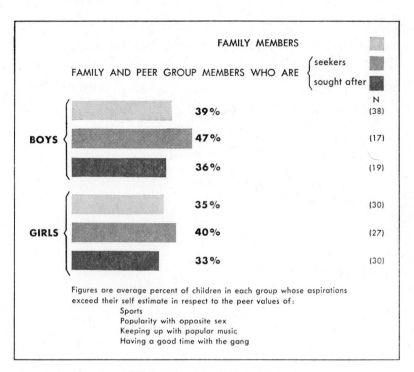

Chart 5. Index of socialized drive toward peer values.

He never loses his head — he always knows what to do in a tough spot. (Lone Ranger)

The program comes just before I go to bed and it gives me something good to dream about.

For these boys, the adventure type program appears to be sheer escape — bearing little or no relationship to everyday life or immediate reality.

We should expect such a criterion of social utility to operate particularly in situations where the process of becoming adjusted to a group is at its height, that is, where the need for socially useful media materials is strongest. In order to investigate this, we subdivided the peer group members for analysis according to the degree of their integration into the group, into "seekers" and "sought after."[15] Chart 5 uses this breakdown in experimenting with a possible index of drive toward integration in the group. This index of *socialized drive*[16] repre-

[15] Future analysis will also provide for study of the reciprocally related peer group members.

[16] This term is used to refer to strong motivation to learn the values of the group and to adjust to them. It is related to Allison Davis' concept of the

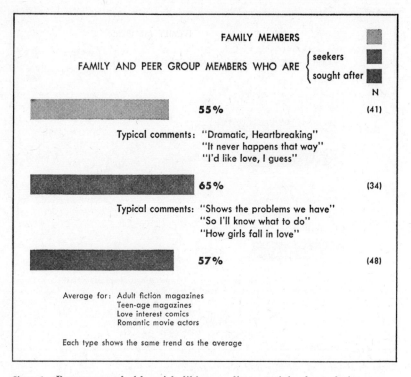

Chart 6. Percentage of older girls liking media materials about dating, opposite sex, and romance.

sents the per cent of children whose aspirations exceed their self-estimate in respect to the peer values of sports, popularity with opposite sex, keeping up with popular music, and having a good time with the gang. This index is somewhat higher for the "seekers," although we should expect a sharper instrument of measurement to show considerably greater differences.

If, therefore, the seekers are making the strongest effort to become integrated into the peer group, we should expect that they would tend to select media materials with the highest peer group utility. As Chart 6 shows, for example, materials about dating, romance, and the opposite sex tend to be more popular with the seekers among older girls who are the audience for such themes. A distinction must be drawn here between conventional association with the opposite sex, a desideratum of the peer group, and glamor and romance on the

middle-class use of anxiety-building pressures in the process of socialization of the child. See Davis, Allison, "Socialization and Adolescent Personality," in Newcomb, Hartley, et al., *Readings in Social Psychology,* New York, Henry Holt & Co., 1947, p. 148.

level of fantasy or forms of sex behavior unacceptable to the peer group. Media themes apparently have social utility only if they deal with the former (daytime serials, for instance, describing love at the adult level, do not follow the pattern of this chart, but are acceptable only to non-members of peer groups). There is obviously a vast difference in the interpretation placed, for instance, on the so-called love comics by a practical minded seeker when she reports:

They're all about girls falling in love — and in a lot of them it teaches you how to act when you go out with fellows on dates . . . what to do and when to do it. . . .

and the non-member of a peer group who says:

I just enjoy them — I just do — there isn't anything that helps me or anything. It's just the way people act when they get in love and all that stuff.

THE NEED FOR NEW RESEARCH TECHNIQUES

Our research experiments have gone only far enough to suggest the possible usefulness for communications research of such sociological concepts as "group membership," "reference group," and "strain." The concept of the "social utility" of mass media, depending as it does on the individual's group relationships may, we believe, be used to go far beyond the traditional approach in explaining communications behavior. It is our conviction that sociological theory is now far enough developed to throw a great deal of light on the selection of media and programs, the interpretation of media messages, and the nature and extent of media influence. At the same time, however, operational techniques have lagged far behind this theoretical development. Our own operations, as we have just shown, are far from demonstrating the theory as sharply as we believe they should. Moreover, the techniques which we have used were adapted to the school class, and we are not yet sure whether or how they can be modified for application to the adult world. Our measures of peer group membership, for instance, depend upon asking every child about his associations with every other child in the class, in order to distinguish between the isolates and those who are members of very small as well as the larger peer groups; and we do not yet know how to achieve the same objective using a population sample. Our materials on values and reference groups were obtained from rather lengthy self-administered questionnaires, a process which is vastly facilitated by the discipline of the school situation.

Nevertheless, we are about to embark at Rutgers upon a next step which will attempt to formulate such a sociological approach to communications research within the Armed Forces. Here we shall be operating in a situation intermediate between the child's classroom and the normal world of adults. It is our hope that these attempts may stimulate much larger efforts toward a practical sociological approach.

▲ PREPARED BY STANLEY K. BIGMAN

FOR UNITED STATES INFORMATION AGENCY

Prestige, Personal Influence, and Opinion

Prestige and Personal Influence

There are two kinds of influence upon opinion, attitudes, and behavior. The one, which may be called *prestige,* is the prerogative of those who occupy positions of power and prominence in society. It is the kind of influence of which the advertiser makes use when he publishes testimonials to his product's worth from movie stars or other "celebrities." There is also *personal influence,* the exclusive possession of no group in society, found at all levels. This is the sort of influence exerted every time A tells his neighbor or fellow worker B his ideas on how to vote, what brand of shoes he thinks is a good buy, or his opinion of the film playing down the street.

Prestige is wielded in the modern world through control over or access to the formal channels of mass communication — press, radio, film, and, in another respect, church and school. Those with such access tend to be the formal leaders of society — officials of government, business and labor leaders, journalists, educators, and clergymen; in short, the "elite" of the educated, the wealthy, and the respected.

Personal influence, on the other hand, is largely a matter of face-to-face contact. B asks A, over a glass of beer, what he thinks of the candidates in the forthcoming election. Mrs. C tells Miss D, when they meet at the marketplace, about the wonderful American movie she saw last night. Now probably most people express some such opinions on *some* topic to *some* person at *some* time. We are concerned here with the *opinion leaders* who exert such personal influence upon those around them rather steadily with regard to decisions in at least one area of life (e.g., public affairs, food purchases). By opinion leaders we refer to the people who, within the circle of their acquaintances

▲ This is a section from the USIA book *Are We Hitting the Target?,* copyright by USIA and reproduced for use within the agency in 1952. It is reprinted here by permission of the agency.

and friends, are looked upon as sources of sound advice, whose opinions are sought out and copied.

It is often assumed that these opinion leaders are identical with the powerful, the wielders of prestige. This chapter is intended to show that such an assumption may be quite remote from the facts. Reference will be made to research studies that corroborate what "common sense" observation might reveal — that the personally influential opinion leaders are found not only among the formal leaders but among the "unknown" and inconspicuous as well. Persons of high prestige may have great personal influence among those with whom they come into personal contact — or they may have little such influence despite their prestige.

This chapter is concerned with personal influence and the opinon leaders who exercise such influence. These are discussed under the following headings:

The importance of personal influence and its relation to the mass media

The nature of personal influence — its informality and the specialization of opinion leaders

A picture of opinion leaders on public affairs

How to identify opinion leaders

The Importance of Personal Influence

The spectacular growth of the newer mass media in the Western industrial countries during recent decades has sometimes made it appear that they are the sole important means of exchanging and influencing opinions. Both those concerned with influencing public opinion and those interested in its study have generally belittled the importance of personal influence. It is indeed with this in mind that the present discussion appears at the beginning of this manual. Much of what appears in the succeeding chapters will have little reference to personal influence but will concentrate on testing the effectiveness of materials disseminated via the mass media. It is essential to bear in mind that *popular* evaluations of such materials are constantly being made in informal discussion.

Even in the United States, the country par excellence of mass media, the role of personal influence is of great significance. The reader may recall the notorious "whispering campaign" directed against Al Smith in the United States presidential campaign of 1928. Conducted without benefit of support by the mass media, this campaign was generally credited with a major part in Smith's defeat. In a more recent presidential campaign, according to a study made in one Ohio city in 1940:

On any average day, at least 10% more people participated in discussions about the election — either actively or passively — than listened to a major speech or read campaign items in a newspaper. . . . In comparison with the formal media of communication, personal relationships are potentially more influential.

In countries where the mass media are less widely diffused, the communication of ideas by personal contact may play an even more important role. In the villages of one Near Eastern country, according to interviews gathered by the Bureau of Applied Social Research, there is usually only one copy of a newspaper to be found, generally at the coffeehouse. News comes largely by word of mouth, from the village official, teacher, or Moslem priest, from the postman and others whose work brings them into frequent contact with people in different places. The news, passed from person to person at such places as the mosque or the barber shop, is usually discussed later on at the coffeehouse.

Similarly, a U.S. Army poll among Japanese civilians on Saipan reported that in reply to the question: "How did you learn the news before we came to Saipan?" the following proportions of respondents mentioned the sources indicated:

Never heard any news	5%
Moving pictures	6
Magazines	26
Radio	31
Newspapers	53
Word of mouth	63

That is, personal contacts provided the chief source for the transmission of ideas.

Opinion Leaders and the Mass Media

Transmission of ideas and opinions by personal contact or "word of mouth" is, then, of major importance. But where do those people get the news who pass it on to others? What is the source of *their* ideas on the significance of news? The answer to such questions may vary with the country. In the United States, at least, it is somewhat as follows.

The distribution of information and opinion is accomplished like that of most commodities — through a network of large wholesale and smaller retail distributors. The mass media act as the wholesale distributors; the opinion leaders play the role of retail purveyors of ideas. The opinion leaders form a vital middle link in what has been referred to as a "two step flow of communication . . . from radio and print to the opinion leaders, and from them to the less active part of the population."

The mass media gather together and serve to their readers or listeners a vast assortment of material — more, taken together, than any reader or listener has the time or interest to absorb. The opinion leaders, each in the field of his special interests, sift and digest and evaluate the content of the media. Reading, thinking, talking more than the average about the subject that interests him, the opinion leader becomes a minor specialist whose ideas are really worth consulting. It is from the opinion leaders, to a great extent, that the rest of the people learn what is "really" happening and what opinions one should adopt.

THE NATURE OF PERSONAL INFLUENCE

The personal influence exerted by the opinion leaders has two note-worthy characteristics: it is *informal,* independent of prestige, and lines of authority; and it is *specialized,* for the same persons do not usually influence opinions on brands of breakfast cereals and opinions on politics.

The Informal Nature of Personal Influence

By "informal" we wish to imply several things. In the first place, personal influence is not prescribed by any rules or customs or authority. Prestige is inherent in certain positions in society; any holder of such a position, e.g., a business executive, a government official, a college professor, commands a certain prestige regardless of his *personal* traits. Personal influence, on the other hand, represents a definite achievement by the individual; it is based on the free and spontaneous consensus of those with whom he comes in contact that "he knows what he's talking about."

The use of the term "informal" is meant to indicate also that personal influence is not organized. There is no chief opinion leader who passes the word along through the ranks, although in the Soviet Union opinion leaders are indeed trained and organized into the official propaganda system. What does exist is an informal and unorganized network of personal relations. Opinion leaders usually know more other persons who are also opinion leaders than does the average person. In the informal give and take of unplanned conversations and discussions, ideas are exchanged and passed along among opinion leaders, as well as from them to those whose opinions they "lead."

"Informal," finally, is meant to refer to the dissimilarity that may exist between popular opinion, i.e., that of the opinion leaders, and the formal, visible, prestige-wielding leaders of society. If we consider as the latter the wealthy and prominent, it is evident that their opinion is not what leads working men to join trade-unions. If we think of the press as leading society, it cannot be said that the press leads opinion in the United States and some other countries for the newspapers increasingly oppose the candidates for office whom the people elect.

The discrepancy between the opinions of those of high prestige and the opinions of the bulk of the people might be interpreted to mean that different segments of the population have different individuals as their opinion leaders. This is indeed the case, as several United States researchers have shown. The authors of the first such

study pointed out that "The opinion leaders are not identical with
the socially prominent people of the community, or the richest people,
or the civic leaders. They are found in all occupational groups."
Among the opinion leaders are young and old, men and women,
persons of all religious groups.

Yet it is not the formal leaders of the various occupational or religious groups that necessarily exert the decisive influence upon the
members' opinions. For example, a USIE evaluation report contains
this interesting information:

> Though many moving pictures have been shown to labor groups, attend-
> ance has always been poor. The enthusiasm of the officials in requesting
> pictures always seems to exceed the interest of the audiences themselves.

The trade-union officials referred to are evidently not the opinion
leaders of the rank-and-file members, at least as regards which motion
picture is worth seeing.

Such findings are only to be expected. It is quite obvious that whom
a person consults for an opinion on a book exhibit, the relative merits
of two brands of fertilizer, or the significance of yesterday's parliamentary debate may have anything, or *nothing*, to do with relative
position in an organized structure of power, authority, or prestige.
Indeed the lines of personal influence within such hierarchies as those
of business and industrial or political organizations may cut squarely
across the lines of authority. Influence among office holders in a
business bureaucracy does not necessarily follow the pattern of authority laid down in an organization chart. The most influential person
in a factory or shop, when the subject of discussion is public affairs,
may as often be an articulate and politically interested "rank-and-filer"
as a foreman or union-shop steward. In a government bureaucracy
the most influential person may be holding a minor job under the
candidate he put into office; the former has the personal influence,
the latter the prestige.

In each of the instances cited, the opinion leaders in the group,
those whose personal influence on opinions and behavior in various
spheres is greatest, are to be found as often as not well below the
positions of top leadership in the formal organization. Indeed, a study
of leadership and influence in an American town, which compared
a list of persons holding office in community organizations with a
list of the "top influential" persons, found less than half of the latter
group among the formal leaders.

The Specialized Nature of Personal Influence

The instance cited of divergence in opinion between the formal
leaders and the members of a labor group points also to the specialization among opinion leaders. The union members probably accept

their leaders' opinions on job-related matters — as the members define them. They can presumably follow their leaders with respect to what constitute desirable working conditions, while rejecting their notions of what constitutes a desirable film. The followers apparently look else-where, to informal opinion leaders, for sound advice on matters which they define as outside the special sphere of their official leaders. This impression again is borne out by the findings of research studies. These show what should be obvious — that opinion leaders on political affairs may be considered to have no ideas worth hearing on such matters as the choice of a movie or a style of clothing. On the other hand the housewife who can discourse with eloquence and authority on the relative merits of a dozen brands of coffee may be consulted about just such matters. Thus it is possible to identify "marketing opinion leaders," who are consulted for shopping advice; "movie opinion leaders;" "sports opinion leaders;" and no doubt numerous other specialized types.

THE OPINION LEADER ON PUBLIC AFFAIRS

Our concern is less with opinion leaders in general than with the opinion leaders whose influence is felt on thinking and action on pub-lic affairs. A fairly detailed account of such opinion leaders can be drawn from studies made in the United States. How applicable this description may be to opinion leaders in other countries it is hard to say. We may begin with a brief description of what we have called opinion leaders, although the writer quoted does not use the term, in Croatia of the early twentieth century, among the peasants who constituted 90 percent of the country's population. The opinion lead-ers, he writes, were:

. . . mostly literate peasants of a middle economic status in the village. . . . Because of their literacy, and because they were not unsuccessful in their own small peasant economies, they enjoyed a certain authority over the rest of the peasants, who were mostly illiterate. Owning little property, with two to eight hectares, they also had more time at their disposal to dedicate to political activities. Being literate, they showed more knowledge and were relatively more talkative than the others. Such peasants were also inde-pendent in relation to the clergy and the authorities, which was not always the case with more well-to-do peasants, who behaved like "gospoda" [gentlemen].

The extent to which the above details coincide with the following description from United States studies suggests that the public-affairs opinion leaders of other countries may not be too unlike those of this country.

The opinion leader is more interested in public affairs than those around him. If he is a political party member, he is more strongly attached to his party. Fewer opinion leaders fail to vote in elections. If he is a trade-union member, he is more strongly devoted to his union than are his fellows.

The opinion leader's interest in public affairs is manifest in his reading and listening habits. He reads more books, more magazines, and more different kinds of magazines than others do. Within the magazines he tends to read more "information-oriented" items, e.g., news features, biographies. Though he may not read more newspapers, he is more apt to take a metropolitan paper than is the non-opinion leader. When he turns on his radio he is more apt than the average person to listen to forum and discussion programs.

In sum, the opinion leaders tend to read and hear all of the same publications and programs as the persons in their own segment of society — and more besides. If one considers only the slightly educated group, the contrast in reading and listening habits between the opinion leaders and their fellows is particularly marked. It is not surprising to find that opinion leaders indicate a greater reliance on the mass media — press and radio — as a source of information and opinions than do other people. The latter more often refer to personal contacts as their chief source of ideas on public affairs.

The public-affairs opinion leader, however, is no quiet homebody, dividing his time between reading and radio listening. On the contrary, he is much more in contact with other people than the average person. He is active in more clubs and organizations. He has more friends, knows more of his neighbors. Among the circle of his acquaintances he counts more persons to whom *he* can turn for advice on public issues and more active workers or members of the party he supports. His ideas come not only from the mass media but also from "inside dope." Probably, too, he "gets around" more than others he knows: he has traveled and seen something of the larger world, or regularly travels in the course of his work. As a consequence probably of his greater interest in public affairs and his greater contact with sources of ideas, the public-affairs opinion leader is better informed, in his field of interest, than is the average non-opinion leader.

Finally, the opinion leaders are active beyond the average person in spreading their ideas in discussions with other persons. Along with their greater-than-average range of contacts, interest, and store of information concerning public affairs, the opinion leaders are also more sure of their views. They are more often involved in discussions, especially with persons outside of their families. It is usually other people who initiate the discussions in which they are involved, but once in the discussion the opinion leaders take an active rather than a passive part. The opinion leader then is not an agitator, anxious to arouse discussions; rather, others urge him to share his sound judgments with them.

HOW TO IDENTIFY OPINION LEADERS

Probably the easiest way to single out opinion leaders is to interview people, asking them to whom they turn for advice on current issues. If the whole population of an area could be interviewed, as in one past research study, the opinion leaders might be listed as those persons most often mentioned as sources of advice.

Interviewing all the inhabitants of a country for such a purpose is, however, hardly a reasonable task. Ordinarily a sample is chosen for interviewing, by procedures outlined in the following chapter. But it is quite improbable that in any sample chosen any individual would be named by enough others to warrant listing him among the "top influentials" or opinion leaders of significant influence. This is especially true because, as pointed out above, each segment of the population has its own opinion leaders.

If interviewing a sample will not reveal the individual identity of opinion leaders, it can perhaps indicate where in the social structure they may be found. It is, for example, possible that certain occupations provide both opportunities to obtain information and frequent informal face-to-face contacts with large numbers of persons. Such occupations may contain large numbers of opinion leaders. Available information suggests this is true *in some countries* of barbers, innkeepers, mail carriers. Therefore, in addition to asking interview respondents whether there is any person from whom they seek advice, one would ask also for the occupation of such a person. Analysis of the answers might show concentration in a few occupations of persons identified as advice-givers.

If, however, such questions are broached too abruptly, the interviewee may suspect the motives of the questioner. It is therefore necessary to lead up to these questions in some such manner as the following:

How do people living around here obtain information on what is going on in this country and abroad? By reading newspapers? By reading magazines? By seeing newsreels? By listening to the radio? By conversations with friends and neighbors? By talking with persons who are respected and considered well-informed? By using other sources?

Note that this group of questions concerns "people living around here"; the respondent is not asked *at first* to put his own behavior on record. Only after he has described the pattern of communications as he sees it, which tends in any case to be pretty much a reflection of his own behavior, is he asked:

How do *you* get *your* information? By reading newspapers? Etc. Do you know anyone around here whom you consider particularly well-informed about current affairs? Anyone to whom you can turn for a sound opinion on current issues? What is his occupation?

Thus the respondent is not made to feel that he is being asked to reveal confidential matters to police agents or the equivalent.

SUMMARY

An important distinction may be made between two kinds of influence — *prestige* and *personal influence*. The former, prestige, is the kind of influence that comes with occupation of key positions of power or prominence in society; personal influence is exercised by persons at all levels. While prestige is exerted through access to the mass media, especially press, radio, and films, personal influence is largely a matter of face-to-face contacts. The most influential in personal contacts are called *opinion leaders*. Such opinion leaders may likewise be persons of prestige, but are as often not; for prestige and personal influence may each be exerted independently of the other.

Even in countries like the United States, with maximum development of the mass media, person-to-person communication of ideas retains great importance. The opinion leaders, who make such interpersonal contacts, act as conveyors of ideas from the mass media to the bulk of the people, modifying the ideas in the process of transmission.

Personal influence is marked by two characteristics of note: it is *informal* and it is *specialized*. The term "informal" refers to the following facts:

1. Personal influence is not due to any rules or authority but comes about through the recognition of his everyday acquaintances of the opinion leader's "sound judgment."

2. Personal influence is not organized.

3. Personal influence is not localized in the formal leaders of hierarchial groups but cuts across formal lines of authority. The formal leaders may not share the popular views as do the opinion leaders.

Personal influence is specialized in that opinion leaders usually wield such influence only in regard to one field of interest, whether sports or marketing or public affairs. It is the opinion leader in the latter area who is of most significance here, and a detailed picture of some of his characteristics, as revealed by United States studies, is presented.

Opinion leaders may be identified by conducting interviews and asking respondents questions concerning their sources of information. Examples of the kind of questions useful in this connection are offered.

▲ HADLEY CANTRIL

*T*he Invasion from Mars

On the evening of October 30, 1938, thousands of Americans became panic-stricken by a broadcast purported to describe an invasion
of Martians which threatened our whole civilization. Probably never
before have so many people in all walks of life and in all parts of the
country become so suddenly and so intensely disturbed as they did on
this night.

Such rare occurrences provide opportunities for the social scientist
to study mass behavior. They must be exploited when they come.
Although the social scientist unfortunately cannot usually predict such
situations and have his tools of investigation ready to analyze the
phenomenon while it is still on the wing, he can begin his work before
the effects of the crisis are over and memories are blurred. The situation created by the broadcast was one which shows us how the common man reacts in a time of stress and strain. It gives us insights into
his intelligence, his anxieties, and his needs, which we could never get
by tests or strictly experimental studies. The panic situation we have
investigated had all the flavor of everyday life and, at the same time,
provided a semi-experimental condition for research. In spite of the
unique conditions giving rise to this particular panic, the writer has
attempted to indicate throughout the study the pattern of the circumstances which, from a psychological point of view, might make this
the prototype of any panic.

The fact that this panic was created as a result of a radio broadcast

▲ This is a summary by Dr. Cantril of part of the volume entitled *The Invasion
from Mars,* by Hadley Cantril, Hazel Gaudet, and Herta Herzog, published
and copyright by the Princeton University Press (Princeton, 1940). This
summary appeared first in Newcomb, Hartley, and others, *Readings in Social
Psychology,* published and copyright by Henry Holt & Company (New York,
1947) and is here reprinted by permission of author and copyright holder.
Dr. Cantril is professor of psychology at Princeton.

is today no mere circumstance. The importance of radio's role in current national and international affairs is too well known to be recounted here. By its very nature radio is the medium *par excellence* for informing all segments of a population of current happenings, for arousing in them a common sense of fear or joy, and for exciting them to similar reactions directed toward a single objective.

Because the social phenomenon in question was so complex, several methods were employed to seek out different answers and to compare results obtained by one method with those obtained by another. Much of our information was derived from detailed interviews of 135 persons. Over 100 of these persons were selected because they were known to have been upset by the broadcast.

Long before the broadcast had ended, people all over the United States were praying, crying, fleeing frantically to escape death from the Martians. Some ran to rescue loved ones. Others telephoned farewells or warnings, hurried to inform neighbors, sought information from newspapers or radio stations, summoned ambulances and police cars. At least six million people heard the broadcast. At least a million of them were frightened or disturbed.

For weeks after the broadcast, newspapers carried human-interest stories relating the shock and terror of local citizens. Men and women throughout the country could have described their feelings and reactions on that fateful evening. Our own interviewers and correspondents gathered hundreds of accounts. A few of these selected almost at random will give us a glimpse of the excitement. Let the people speak for themselves.

"I knew it was something terrible and I was frightened," said Mrs. Ferguson, a northern New Jersey housewife, to the inquiring interviewer. "But I didn't know just what it was. I couldn't make myself believe it was the end of the world. I've always heard that when the world would come to an end, it would come so fast nobody would know — so why should God get in touch with this announcer? When they told us what road to take and get up over the hills and the children began to cry, the family decided to go out. We took blankets and my granddaughter wanted to take the cat and the canary. We were outside the garage when the neighbor's boy came back and told us it was a play."

From a small midwestern town came Joseph Hendley's report. "That Hallowe'en Boo sure had our family on its knees before the program was half over. God knows how we prayed to Him last Sunday. It was a lesson in more than one thing to us. My mother went out and looked for Mars. Dad was hard to convince or skeptical or sumpin', but he even got to believing it. Brother Joe, as usual, got more excited than he could show. Brother George wasn't home. Aunt Grace, a good Catholic, began to pray with Uncle Henry. Lily got sick to her stomach. I don't know what I did exactly but I know I prayed harder and more earnestly than ever before. Just as soon as we were convinced that this thing was real, how pretty all things on earth seemed; how soon we put our trust in God."

Archie Burbank, a filling-station operator in Newark, described his reactions. "My girl friend and I stayed in the car for a while, just driving around. Then we followed the lead of a friend. All of us ran into a grocery store and asked the man if we could go into his cellar. He said, 'What's the matter? Are you trying to ruin my business?' So he chased us out. A crowd collected. We rushed to an apartment house and asked the man in the apartment to let us in his cellar. He said, 'I don't have any cellar! Get away!' Then people started to rush out of the apartment house all undressed. We got into the car and listened some more. Suddenly, the announcer was gassed, the station went dead so we tried another station but nothing would come on. Then we went to a gas station and filled up our tank in preparation for just riding as far as we could. The gas station man didn't know anything about it. Then one friend, male, decided he would call up the *Newark Evening News*. He found out it was a play. We listened to the rest of the play and then went dancing."

Mrs. Joslin, who lives in a poor section of a large eastern city and whose husband is a day laborer, said, "I was terribly frightened. I wanted to pack and take my child in my arms, gather up my friends, and get in the car and just go north as far as we could. But what I did was just set by one window, prayin', listenin', and scared stiff and my husband by the other snifflin' and lookin' out to see if people were runnin'. Then when the announcer said 'evacuate the city,' I ran and called my boarder and started with my child to rush down the stairs, not waitin' to ketch my hat or anything. When I got to the foot of the stairs I just couldn't get out, I don't know why. Meantime my husband he tried other stations and found them still runnin'. He couldn't smell any gas or see people runnin', so he called me back and told me it was just a play. So I set down, still ready to go at any minute till I heard Orson Welles say, 'Folks, I hope we ain't alarmed you. This is just a play!' Then, I just set!"

If we are to explain the reaction, then, we must answer two basic questions: Why did this broadcast frighten some people when other fantastic broadcasts do not? And why did this broadcast frighten some people but not others? An answer to the first question must be sought in the characteristics of this particular program which aroused false standards of judgment in so many listeners.

No one reading the script can deny that the broadcast was so realistic for the first few minutes that it was almost credible to even relatively sophisticated and well-informed listeners. The sheer dramatic excellence of the broadcast must not be overlooked. This unusual

realism of the performance may be attributed to the fact that the early
parts of the broadcast fell within the existing standards of judgment
of the listeners.

A large proportion of listeners, particularly those in the lower income and educational brackets, have grown to rely more on the radio
than on the newspapers for their news. Almost all of the listeners, who
had been frightened and who were interviewed, mentioned somewhere
during the course of their retrospections the confidence they had in
radio and their expectation that it would be used for such important
announcements. A few of their comments indicate their attitudes:

"We have so much *faith in broadcasting.* In a crisis it has to reach
all people. That's what radio is here for."

"The announcer would not say if it was not true. *They always quote
if something is a play.*"

As in many situations where events and ideas are so complicated or
far removed from one's own immediate everyday experience that only
the expert can really understand them, here, too, the layman was
forced to rely on the expert for his interpretation.

The logical "expert" in this instance was the astronomer. Those
mentioned (all fictitious) were Professor Farrell of the Mount Jen-
nings Observatory of Chicago, Professor Pierson of the Princeton Observatory, Professor Morse of MacMillan University in Toronto,
Professor Indellkoffer of the California Astronomical Society and
"astronomers and scientific bodies" in England, France, and Germany.
Professor Richard Pierson (Orson Welles) was the chief character in
the drama.

When the situation called for organized defense and action the
expert was once more brought in. General Montgomery Smith, commander of the State Militia at Trenton, Mr. Harry McDonald, vice-
president of the Red Cross, Captain Lansing of the Signal Corps, and
finally the Secretary of the Interior described the situation, gave
orders for evacuation and attack, or urged every man to do his duty.

This dramatic technique had its effect.

"I believed the broadcast *as soon as I heard the professor from
Princeton* and the officials in Washington."

"I knew it was an awfully dangerous situation *when all those military men were there and the Secretary of State spoke.*"

The realistic nature of the broadcast was further enhanced by descriptions of particular occurrences that listeners could readily imagine.
Liberal use was made of the colloquial expressions to be expected on
such an occasion. The gas was "a sort of yellowish-green"; the cop
warned, "One side, there. Keep back, I tell you"; a voice shouts,
"The darn thing's unscrewing." An example of the specificity of detail
is the announcement of Brigadier General Montgomery Smith: "I
have been requested by the Governor of New Jersey to place the

counties of Mercer and Middlesex as far west as Princeton, and east to Jamesburg, under martial law. No one will be permitted to enter this area except by special pass issued by state or military authorities. Four companies of State Militia are proceeding from Trenton to Grovers Mill and will aid in the evacuation of homes within the range of military operations."

The events reported proceeded from the relatively credible to the highly incredible. The first announcements were more or less believable, although unusual to be sure. First there is an "atmospheric disturbance," then "explosions of incandescent gas." A scientist then reports that his seismograph has registered a shock of earthquake intensity. This is followed by the discovery of a meteorite that has splintered nearby trees in its fall. So far so good.

But as the less credible bits of the story begin to enter, the clever dramatist also indicates that he, too, has difficulty in believing what he sees. When we learn that the object is no meteorite but a metal casing, we are also told that the whole picture is "a strange scene like something out of a modern Arabian Nights," "fantastic," that the "more daring souls are venturing near." Before we are informed that the end of the casing is beginning to unscrew, we experience the announcer's own astonishment: "Ladies and gentlemen, this is terrific!" When the top is off he says, "This is the most terrifying thing I have ever witnessed. . . . This is the most extraordinary experience. I can't find words. . . ."

The bewilderment of the listener is shared by the eye-witness. When the scientist is himself puzzled, the layman recognizes the extraordinary intelligence of the strange creatures. No explanation of the event can be provided. The resignation and hopelessness of the Secretary of the Interior, counseling us to "place our faith in God," provides no effective guide for action.

In spite of the realism of the broadcast, it would seem highly unlikely that any listener would take it seriously had he heard the announcements that were clearly made at the beginning of the hour. He might then have been excited, even frightened. But it would be an excitement based on the dramatic realism of the program. There would not be the intense feeling of personal involvement. He would know that the events were happening "out there" in the studio, not "right here" in his own state or his own county. In one instance a "correct" (esthetically detached or dramatic) standard of judgment would be used by the listener to interpret events, in another instance a "false" (realistic or news) standard of judgment would be employed. Tuning in late was a very essential condition for the arousal of a false standard of judgment. To be sure, many people recognized the broadcast as a play even though they tuned in late. It is important to raise and to answer the question of how anyone who tuned in at the beginning could have mistaken the clearly introduced play for a news broadcast. Analysis of these cases reveals two main reasons why such a misinterpretation arose. In the first place, many people who tuned in to hear a play by the Mercury Theatre thought the regular dramatic program had been interrupted to give special news bulletins. The technique was not a new one after their experience with radio reporting of the war crisis in September 1938. The other major reason for the misunderstanding is the widespread habit of not paying attention to the first announcements of a program. Some people do not listen attentively to their radios until they are aware that something of particular interest is being broadcast.

Tuning in late was very decisive in determining whether or not the listener would follow the program as a play or as a news report. For the story of the Martian invasion was so realistic that misinterpretation was apt to arise without proper warning signals.

In spite of the fact that many persons tuned in late to hear this very realistic broadcast, by no means all of them believed it was news. And not all of those who thought the invasion was upon them behaved the same way in the face of danger. Before we can understand the reasons for the varying behavior, the reactions must be arranged in some significant grouping. Otherwise no fruitful conceptualization is possible.

CLASSIFYING THE LISTENERS

1. Those Who Checked the Internal Evidence of the Broadcast

The persons in this category were those who did not remain frightened throughout the whole broadcast because they were able to discern that the program was fictitious. Some realized that the reports must be false because they sounded so much like certain fiction literature they were accustomed to.

"At first I was very interested in the fall of the meteor. It isn't often that they find a big one just when it falls. But *when it started to unscrew and monsters came out, I said to myself, 'They've taken one of those Amazing Stories and are acting it out.'* It just couldn't be real. It was just like some of the stories I read in *Amazing Stories* but it was even more exciting."

2. Those Who Checked the Broadcast Against Other Information and Learned That It Was a Play

These listeners tried to orient themselve for the same reasons as those in the first group — they were suspicious of the "news" they were getting. Some simply thought the reports were too fantastic to believe; others detected the incredible speeds revealed; while a few listeners checked the program just because it seemed the reasonable thing to do. Their method of verifying their hunches was to compare the news on the program to some other information.

"I tuned in and heard that a meteor had fallen. Then when they talked about monsters, I thought something was wrong. *So I looked in the newspaper to see what program was supposed to be on and discovered it was only a play.*"

3. Those Who Tried to Check the Program Against Other Information but Who, for Various Reasons, Continued to Believe the Broadcast Was an Authentic News Report

Two characteristic differences separated the people in this group from those who made successful checks. In the first place, it was difficult to determine from the interviews just why these people wanted to check anyway. They did not seem to be seeking evidence to test the authenticity of the reports. They appeared, rather, to be frightened souls trying to find out whether or not they were yet in any personal danger. In the second place, the type of checking behavior they used was singularly ineffective and unreliable. The most frequent method employed by almost two-thirds of this group was to look out the window or go outdoors. Several of them telephoned their friends or ran to consult their neighbors.

There are several reasons why the checks made by these persons were ineffectual. For some of them, the new information obtained only verified the interpretation which their already fixed standard of judgment provided.

"I looked out of the window and everything looked the same as usual *so I thought it hadn't reached our section yet.*"

"We looked out of the window and Wyoming Avenue was black with cars. *People were rushing away, I figured.*"

"No cars came down my street. *'Traffic is jammed on account of the roads being destroyed,' I thought.*"

4. Those Who Made No Attempt to Check the Broadcast or the Event

It is usually more difficult to discover why a person did *not* do something than why he did. Consequently it is more difficult for us to explain why people in this group did not attempt to verify the news or look for signs of the Martians in their vicinity than it was to determine why those who attempted unsuccessful checks displayed their aimless behavior. Over half of the people in this group were so frightened that they either stopped listening, ran around in a frenzy, or exhibited behavior that can only be described as paralyzed.

Some of them reported that they were so frightened they never thought of checking.

"We were so intent upon listening that we didn't have enough sense to try other hook-ups — *we were just so frightened.*"

Others adopted an attitude of complete resignation. For them any attempt to check up, like any other behavior, appeared senseless.

"I was writing a history theme. The girl from upstairs came and made me go up to her place. Everybody was so excited I felt as if I was going crazy and kept on saying, 'what can we do, *what difference does it make* whether we die sooner or later?' We were holding each other. Everything seemed unimportant in the face of death. I was afraid to die, just kept on listening."

Some felt that in view of the crisis situation, action was demanded. A few prepared immediately for their escape or for death.

"I couldn't stand it so I turned it off. I don't remember when, but everything was coming closer. My husband wanted to put it back on but I told him *we'd better do something instead of just listen,* so we started to pack."

Some listeners interpreted the situation in such a way that they were not interested in making a check-up. In a few instances the individual tuned in so late that he missed the most incredible parts of the program and was only aware of the fact that some kind of conflict was being waged.

"I was in my drugstore and my brother phoned and said, 'Turn the radio on, a meteor has just fallen.' We did and heard gas was coming up South Street. There were a few customers and *we all began wondering where it could come from.* I was worried about the gas, it was spreading so rapidly but I was puzzled as to what was actually happening, when I heard airplanes I thought another country was attacking us."

WHY THE PANIC?

A variety of influences and conditions are related to the panic resulting from this particular broadcast. We have found no single observable variable consistently related to the reaction, although a lack of critical ability seemed particularly conducive to fear in a large proportion of the population. Personality characteristics made some people especially susceptible to belief and fright; the influence of others in the immediate environment caused a few listeners to react inappropriately. The psychological pattern revealed by these and other influences must be shown if we are to understand the situation as a whole and not have to resort exclusively to the understanding of single, isolated cases.

WHY THE SUGGESTION WAS OR WAS NOT BELIEVED

What is most inconceivable and therefore especially interesting psychologically is why so many people did not do something to verify the information they were receiving from their loudspeakers. The failure to do this accounts for the persistence of the fright. To understand any panic — whether the cause is a legitimate one or not — it is necessary to see precisely what happens to an individual's mental processes that prevents him from making an adequate check-up.

The persons who were frightened by the broadcast were, for this occasion at least, highly suggestible, that is, they believed what they heard without making sufficient checks to prove to themselves that the broadcast was only a story. Those who were not frightened and those who believed the broadcast for only a short time were not suggestible — they were able to display what psychologists once called a "critical faculty." The problem is, then, to determine why some people are suggestible, or to state the problem differently, why some people lack critical ability.

There are essentially four psychological conditions that create in an individual the particular state of mind we know as suggestibility. All these may be described in terms of the concept of standard of judgment.

In the first place, individuals may refer a given stimulus to a standard or to several standards of judgment which they think are relevant for interpretation. The mental context into which the stimulus enters in this case is of such a character that it is welcomed as thoroughly consistent and without contradiction. A person with standards of judgment that enable him to "place" or "give meaning to" a stimulus in an almost automatic way finds nothing incongruous about such acceptance; his standards have led him to "expect" the possibility of such an occurrence.

We have found that many of the persons who did not even try to check the broadcast had preexisting mental sets that made the stimulus so understandable to them that they immediately accepted it as true. Highly religious people who believed that God willed and controlled the destinies of man were already furnished with a particular standard of judgment that would make an invasion of our planet and a destruction of its members merely an "act of God." This was particularly true if the religious frame of reference was of the eschatological variety providing the individual with definite attitudes or beliefs regarding the end of the world. Other people we found had been so influenced by the recent war scare that they believed an attack by a foreign power was imminent and an invasion — whether it was due to the Japanese, Hitler, or Martians — was not unlikely. Some persons had built up such fanciful notions of the possibilities of science that they could easily believe the powers of strange superscientists were being turned against them, perhaps merely for experimental purposes.

Whatever the cause for the genesis of the standards of judgment providing ready acceptance of the event, the fact remains that many persons already possessed a context within which they immediately placed the stimulus. None of their other existing standards of judgment was sufficiently relevant to engender disbelief. We found this to be particularly true of persons whose lack of opportunities or abilities to acquire information or training had insufficiently fortified them with pertinent standards of judgment that would make the inter-

pretation of the broadcast as a play seem plausible. More highly educated people, we found, were better able to relate a given event to a
standard of judgment they *knew* was an *appropriate* referent. In such
instances, the knowledge itself was used as a standard of judgment to
discount the information received in the broadcast. These listeners,
then, had the ability to refer to relevant standards of judgment which
they could rely on for checking purposes and therefore had no need
of further orientation.

A second condition of suggestibility exists when an individual is
not sure of the interpretation he should place on a given stimulus
and when he lacks adequate standards of judgment to make a reliable
check on his interpretation. In this situation the individual attempts
to check on his information but fails for one of three reasons: (1) He
may check his original information against unreliable data which may
themselves be affected by the situation he is checking. We found that
persons who checked unsuccessfully tended to check against information obtained from friends or neighbors. Obviously, such people were
apt themselves to be tinged with doubt and hesitation which would
only confirm early suspicions. (2) A person may rationalize his checking information according to the original hypothesis he is checking
and which he thinks he has only tentatively accepted. Many listeners
made hasty mental or behavioral checks but the false standard of judgment they had already accepted was so pervasive that their check-ups
were rationalized as confirmatory evidence. For example, one woman
said that the announcer's charred body was found too quickly but
she "figured the announcer was excited and had made a mistake." A
man noticed the incredible speeds but thought "they were relaying
reports or something." Others turned to different stations but thought
the broadcasters were deliberately trying to calm the people. A woman
looked out of her window and saw a greenish eerie light which she
thought was from the Martians. (3) In contrast to those who believe
almost any check they make are the people who earnestly try to verify
their information but do not have sufficiently well-grounded standards
of judgment to determine whether or not their new sources of information are reliable.

A third and perhaps more general condition of suggestibility exists
when an individual is confronted with a stimulus which he must interpret or which he would like to interpret and when *none* of his
existing standards of judgment is adequate to the task. On such occasions the individual's mental context is unstructured, the stimulus does
not fit any of his established categories and he seeks a standard that
will suffice him. The less well structured is his mental context, the
fewer meanings he is able to call forth, the less able will he be to
understand the relationship between himself and the stimulus, and the
greater will become his anxiety. And the more desperate his need for

interpretation, the more likely will he be to accept the first interpretation given him. Many conditions existed to create in the individuals who listened to the invasion from Mars a chaotic mental universe that contained no stable standards of judgment by means of which the strange event reported could be evaluated. A lack of information and formal educational training had left many persons without any generalized standards of judgment applicable to this novel situation. And even if they did have a few such standards these were vague and tenuously held because they had not proved sufficient in the past to interpret other phenomena. This was especially true of those persons who had been most adversely affected by the conditions of the times.

The prolonged economic unrest and the consequent insecurity felt by many of the listeners was another cause for bewilderment. The depression had already lasted nearly ten years. People were still out of work. Why didn't somebody do something about it? Why didn't the experts find a solution? What was the cause of it anyway? Again, what would happen, no one could tell. Again, a mysterious invasion fitted the pattern of the mysterious events of the decade. The lack of a sophisticated, relatively stable economic or political frame of reference created in many persons a psychological disequilibrium which made them seek a standard of judgment for this particular event. It was another phenomenon in the outside world beyond their control and comprehension. Other people possessed certain economic security and social status but wondered how long this would last with "things in such a turmoil." They, too, sought a stable interpretation, one that would at least give this new occurrence meaning. The war scare had left many persons in a state of complete bewilderment. They did not know what the trouble was all about or why the United States should be so concerned. The complex ideological, class, and national antagonisms responsible for the crises were by no means fully comprehended. The situation was painfully serious and distressingly confused. What would happen, nobody could foresee. The Martian invasion was just another event reported over the radio. It was even more personally dangerous and no more enigmatic. No existing standards were available to judge its meaning or significance. But there was quick need for judgment and it was provided by the announcers, scientists, and authorities.

Persons with higher education, on the other hand, we found had acquired more generalized standards of judgment which they could put their faith in. The result was that many of them "knew" that the phenomenal speeds with which the announcers and soldiers moved was impossible even in this day and age. The greater the possibility of checking against a variety of reliable standards of judgment, the less suggestible will a person be. We found that some persons who in more normal circumstances might have had critical ability were so overwhelmed by their particular listening situation that their better judgment was suspended. This indicates that a highly consistent structuration of the external stimulus world may, at times, be experienced with sufficient intensity because of its personal implications to inhibit the operation of usually applicable internal structurations or standards of judgment. Other persons who may normally have exhibited critical ability were unable to do so in this situation because their own emotional insecurities and anxieties made them susceptible to suggestion when confronted with a personally dangerous circumstance. In such instances, the behavioral consequence is the same as for a person who has no standards of judgment to begin with, but the psychological processes underlying the behavior are different.

A fourth condition of suggestibility results when an individual not only lacks standards of judgment by means of which he may orient himself, but lacks even the realization that any interpretations are possible other than the one originally presented. He accepts as truth whatever he hears or reads without even thinking to compare it to other information.

WHY SUCH EXTREME BEHAVIOR?

Granted that some people believed the broadcast to be true, why did they become so hysterical? Why did they pray, telephone relatives, drive at dangerous speeds, cry, awaken sleeping children, and flee? Of all the possible modes of reaction they may have followed, why did these particular patterns emerge? The obvious answer is that this was a serious affair. As in all other panics, the individual believed his well-being, his safety, or his life was at stake. The situation was a real threat to him. Just what constitutes a personal threat to an individual must be briefly examined.

When an individual believes that a situation threatens him he means that it threatens not only his physical self but all of those things and people which he somehow regards as a part of him. This Ego of an individual is essentially composed of the many social and personal values *he* has accepted. *He* feels threatened if his investments are threatened, *he* feels insulted if his children or parents are insulted, *he* feels elated if his alma mater wins the sectional football cup. The particular pattern of values that have been introcepted by an individual will give him, then, a particular Ego. For some individuals this is expanded to include broad ideals and ambitions. *They* will be disturbed if a particular race is persecuted in a distant country because that persecution runs counter to their ideal of human justice and democracy; *they* will be flattered if someone admires an idea of theirs or a painting they have completed.

A panic occurs when some highly cherished, rather commonly accepted value is threatened and when no certain elimination of the threat is in sight. The individual feels that he will be ruined, physically, financially, or socially. The invasion of the Martians was a direct threat to life, to other lives that one loved, as well as to all other cherished values. The Martians were destroying practically everything. The situation was, then, indeed a serious affair. Frustration resulted when no directed behavior seemed possible. One was faced with the alternative of resigning oneself and all of one's values to complete annihilation or of making a desperate effort to escape from the field of danger, or of appealing to some higher power or stronger person whom one vaguely thought could destroy the oncoming enemy.

If one assumed that destruction was inevitable, then certain limited behavior was possible: one could cry, make peace with one's Maker, gather one's loved ones around and perish. If one attempted escape, one could run to the house of friends, speed away in a car or train, or hide in some gas-proof, bomb-proof, out-of-the-way shelter. If one still believed that something or someone might repulse the enemy, one could appeal to God or seek protection from those who had protected one in the past. Objectively none of these modes of behavior was a direct attack on the problem at hand, nothing was done to remove the cause of the crisis. The behavior in a panic is characteristically undirected and, from the point of view of the situation at hand, functionally useless.

In short, the extreme behavior evoked by the broadcast was due to the enormous felt ego-involvement the situation created and to the complete inability of the individual to alleviate or control the consequences of the invasion. The coming of the Martians did not present a situation where the individual could preserve one value if he sacrificed another. It was not a matter of saving one's country by giving one's life, of helping to usher in a new religion by self-denial, of risking the thief's bullet to save the family silver. In this situation the individual stood to lose *all* his values at once. Nothing could be done to save *any* of them. Panic was inescapable. The false standard of judgment used by the individual to interpret the broadcast was not itself the motivational cause of the behavior but it was absolutely essential in arousing the needs and values which may be regarded as the sources of the actions exhibited. A false standard of judgment aroused by the broadcast and causing the individual to be disturbed had its roots in values which were a part of the Ego.

▲ ROBERT K. MERTON

*M*ass Persuasion: The Moral Dimension

Our primary concern with the social psychology of mass persuasion should not obscure its moral dimension. The technician or practitioner in mass opinion and his academic counterpart, the student of social psychology, cannot escape the moral issues which permeate propaganda as a means of social control. The character of these moral issues differs somewhat for the practitioner and the investigator, but in both cases the issues themselves are inescapable.

The practitioner in propaganda is at once confronted by a dilemma: he must either forego the use of certain techniques of persuasion which will help him obtain the immediate end-in-view or violate prevailing moral codes. He must choose between being a less than fully effective technician and a scrupulous human being or an effective technician and a less than scrupulous human being. The pressure of the immediate objective tends to push him toward the first of these alternatives.[1] For when effective mass persuasion is sought, and when "effectiveness" is measured solely by the number of people who can be brought to the desired action or the desired frame of mind, then the choice of techniques of persuasion will be governed by a narrowly technical and amoral criterion. And this criterion exacts a price of the prevailing morality, for it expresses a manipulative attitude toward man and society. It inevitably pushes toward the use of whatsoever techniques "work."

[1] R. K. Merton, "Social Structure and Anomie," *Amer. Soc. Review,* 1938, 3, 672-82.

▲ This is the concluding chapter of Dr. Merton's book, *Mass Persuasion,* which is an analysis of the effect of Kate Smith's marathon broadcasts to sell war bonds during World War II. The book was published and copyright by Harper & Brothers (New York, 1946), and is reprinted here by permission of the copyright holder. Dr. Merton is a professor of sociology at Columbia.

The sense of power that accrues to manipulators of mass opinion, it would appear, does not always compensate for the correlative sense of guilt. The conflict may lead them to a flight into cynicism. Or it may lead to uneasy efforts to exonerate themselves from moral responsibility for the use of manipulative techniques by helplessly declaring, to themselves and to all who will listen, that "unfortunately, that's the way the world is. People are moved by emotions, by fear and hope and anxiety, and not by information or knowledge." It may be pointed out that complex situations must be simplified for mass publics and, in the course of simplification, much that is relevant must be omitted. Or, to take the concrete case we have been examining, it may be argued that the definition of war bonds as a device for curbing inflation is too cold and too remote and too difficult a conception to be effective in mass persuasion. It is preferable to focus on the sacred and sentimental aspects of war bonds, for this "copy slant" brings "results."

Like most half-truths, the notion that leaders of mass opinion must traffic in sentiment has a specious cogency. Values *are* rooted in sentiment and values *are* ineluctably linked with action. But the wholetruth extends beyond this observation. Appeals to sentiment within the context of relevant information and knowledge are basically different from appeals to sentiment which blur and obscure this knowledge. Mass persuasion is not manipulative when it provides access to the pertinent facts; it is manipulative when the appeal to sentiment is used to the exclusion of pertinent information.

The technician, then, must decide whether or not to use certain techniques which though possibly "effective" violate his own sentiments and moral codes. He must decide whether or not he should devise techniques for exploiting mass anxieties, for using sentimental appeals in place of information, for masking private purpose in the guise of common purpose.[2] He faces the moral problem of choosing not only among social ends but also among propaganda means.

[2] During the war, imagination triumphed over conscience among advertisers who "ingeniously" related their products to the war effort. Radio commercials were not immune from this technique. A commercial dentist, for example, suggests that a victory smile helps boost morale and that we can have that smile by purchasing our dentures from him. So, too, a clothing manufacturer reminds listeners that morale is a precious asset in time of war and that smart clothes, more particularly Selfridge Lane Clothes, give a man confidence and courage. Even ice cream becomes essential to the war effort. "Expecting your boys back from an army camp? Give them JL Ice Cream. They get good food in the army and it's your job to give them the same at home." And a manufacturer of cosmetics becomes solicitous about the imbalance in the sex ratio resulting from the war. "Fewer men around because of the war? Competition keen? Keep your skin smooth. Keep attractive for the boys in the service when they come marching home." Office of Radio Research, *Broadcasting the War,* Bur. Intelligence, OWI, 1943, p. 37.

Although less conspicuous and less commonly admitted, a comparable problem confronts the social scientist investigating mass opinion. He may adopt the standpoint of the positivist, proclaim the ethical neutrality of science, insist upon his exclusive concern with the advancement of knowledge, explain that science deals only with the discovery of uniformities and not with ends and assert that in his role as a detached and dispassionate scientist, he has no traffic with values. He may, in short, affirm an occupational philosophy which appears to absolve him of any responsibility for the use to which his discoveries in methods of mass persuasion may be put. With its specious and delusory distinction between "ends" and "means" and its insistence that the intrusion of social values into the work of scientists makes for special pleading, this philosophy fails to note that the investigator's social values do influence his choice and definition of problems. The investigator may naïvely suppose that he is engaged in the value-free activity of research, whereas in fact he may simply have so defined his research problems that the results will be of use to one group in the society, and not to others. His very choice and definition of a problem reflects his tacit values.

To illustrate: the "value-free" investigator of propaganda proceeds to the well-established mode of scientific formulations, and states his findings: "*If* these techniques of persuasion are used, *then* there will be (with a stated degree of probability) a given proportion of people persuaded to take the desired action." Here, then, is a formulation in the honored and successful tradition of science — apparently free of values. The investigator takes no moral stand. He merely reports his findings, and these, if they are valid, can be used by any interested group, liberal or reactionary, democratic or fascistic, idealistic or power-hungry. But this comfortable solution of a moral problem by the abdication of moral responsibility happens to be no solution at all, for it overlooks the crux of the problem: the initial formulation of the scientific investigation has been conditioned by the implied values of the scientist.

Thus, had the investigator been oriented toward such democratic values as respect for the dignity of the individual, he would have framed his scientific problem differently. He would not only have asked which techniques of persuasion produce the *immediate result* of moving a given proportion of people to action, but also, what are the *further, more remote* but not necessarily less significant, *effects* of these techniques upon the individual personality and the society? He would be, in short, sensitized to certain questions stemming from his democratic values which would otherwise be readily overlooked. For example he would ask, Does the unelaborated appeal to sentiment which displaces the information pertinent to assessing this sentiment blunt the critical capacities of listeners? What are the effects upon the personality of being subjected to virtual terrorization by advertisements which threaten the individual with social ostracism unless he uses the advertised defense against halitosis or B.O.? Or, more relevantly, what are the effects, in addition to increasing the sale of bonds, of terrorizing the parents of boys in military service by the threat that only through their purchase of war bonds can they ensure the safety of their sons and their ultimate return home? Do certain types of war bond drives by celebrities do more to pyramid their reputations as patriots than to further the sale of bonds which would otherwise not have been purchased? No single advertising or propaganda campaign may significantly affect the psychological stability of those subjected to it. But a society subjected ceaselessly to a flow of "effective" half-truths and the exploitation of mass anxieties may all the sooner lose that mutuality of confidence and reciprocal trust so essential to a stable social structure. A "morally neutral" investigation of propaganda will be less likely than an inquiry stemming from democratic values to address itelf to such questions.

The issue has been drawn in its most general terms by John Dewey: "Certainly nothing can justify or condemn means except ends, results. But we have to include consequences impartially. . . . It is wilful folly to fasten upon some single end or consequence which is liked, and permit the view of that to blot from perception all other undesired and undesirable consequences."[3] If this study has one major implication for the understanding of mass persuasion, it consists in this recognition of the intimate interrelation of technique and morality.

[3] John Dewey, *Human Nature and Conduct* (New York: Henry Holt & Co., 1922), pp. 228-229. *Cf.* R. K. Merton, "The Unanticipated Consequences of Purposive Social Action," *American Sociological Review*, 1936, 1, 894-904.

Special Problems of Achieving an Effect
with International Communications

Introductory Note

THE DIMENSIONS OF THE PROBLEM

So far, practically everything in this volume has been *generally* applicable to the understanding of communication. At this point, therefore, we could turn to any of the great social laboratories in which the effects of communication may be studied on a large scale. We could turn, for example, to advertising or domestic political campaigns or adult education or health information campaigns or campaigns aimed at better social relations or any one of a number of others. By design and intention, however, the book turns now to one of the most complex and currently important laboratories of all: international communications.

Mutual understanding among nations, on the one hand, or the manipulation of events and messages by one nation so as to influence the policy of another nation on the other hand, have been human concerns for thousands of years. Only in the last few decades, however, have the methods and constructs of social science been applied to those problems. The problems, therefore, are far from solved. Indeed, even the sociometry of international communication is not well known; we do not know how much communication passes over borders, to whom and from whom, and in what form, and what happens to it in the process, and what effect it has. We know something about what image one nation holds of another, but we know only incompletely how that image is formed. So far as international political communication, or psychological warfare, is concerned, we must admit that it is still more art than science, although it is certainly a field which is accessible to science, and considerable progress has been made in the last fifteen years or so in applying social science methodology to it.

Considering the important theoretical and outline papers in the pages following, there is no need here to define political or psychological warfare, or to try to summarize the theory or data bearing on it. We have already pointed out, earlier in this volume, some of the difficulties in the way of effective use of international communication: the difference in communication availability and patterns of communication use in different countries; the problems in communicating meaning from one "subjective world" of culture to another; the existence of national stereotypes and resistance to propaganda; the complexity of trying to predict communication effects at all, and especially in a strange and distant culture — these among others. Consistently effective practice of international political communication calls for clearest possible understanding of the target culture, for adequate tools and skills of communication and a clear understanding of the use and capabilities of these tools, for a working relationship between the communicators and the sources of policy, and for constantly updated intelligence not only on the opinions and situation of the target audience but also on the effects of communication on them. Science-wise, it calls for an approach combining all the behavioral sciences and some other disciplines. Policy-wise, it calls for an understanding of many of these things on a very high level within government.

As Davison and George say, therefore, we are hardly ready as yet for a systematic study of international political communication, but we are prepared to illuminate certain aspects of the process. The Davison and George "Outline," in the following pages, is a good start in that direction. Hans Speier's "Psychological Warfare Reconsidered" is already a kind of classic in this area of communication theory. Dr. Glock points out some of the problems that urgently need attention if we are to understand the influence of international communication channels on opinion. Dr. Lerner takes up the difficult problem of evaluating the effectiveness of propaganda. Kris and Leites summarize some trends in twentieth century propaganda. Shils and Janowitz examine the social and communication factors involved in the long cohesion and the final disintegration of Wehrmacht morale in World War II. Leonard Doob discusses Goebbels' theory of propaganda, and Harold Lasswell outlines the Soviet theory. Finally, Philip Selznick considers the problem of counteroffensive against international Communism.

▲ W. PHILLIPS DAVISON

▲ ALEXANDER L. GEORGE

*A*n Outline for the Study of International

Political Communication

By "international political communication" we refer to the use by national states of communications to influence the politically relevant behavior of people in other national states. Thus we include the propaganda and information activities of most government agencies — especially the State and Defense Departments — and certain aspects of diplomatic communication, but we exclude the activities of the press associations and bodies which are interested principally in international education or in religious missionary activities. By "communication" we refer to the transfer of meaning, whether by written, spoken or pictorial symbols, or by various types of action. "International political communication" is thus a summary term which includes many of the activities subsumed under the terms "negotiation," "propaganda," "political warfare," and "psychological warfare."

SOME SPECIAL DIFFICULTIES

Efforts to systematize the study of international political communication have, in our opinion, been unsuccessful to date. Some of the reasons why this has been the case are the following:

1. The study of international political communication cuts across the established boundaries of academic disciplines. All the social sciences, and some other disciplines, can contribute something to it; none has the complete answer. Theoretically, therefore, an expert in international political communication should have mastered all existing data bearing on human behavior.[1]

[1] Cf. Marjorie Fiske and Leo Lowenthal, "Some Problems in the Administration of International Communications Research," *Public Opinion Quarterly*, Vol. 16, No. 2 (Summer 1952), p. 149. The authors report an effort to define the scope of international communications research which ended by including "practically the whole sphere of human knowledge."

▲ This paper originally appeared in the *Public Opinion Quarterly*, in 1952, and has been revised for this volume. In its first appearance it was copyright by the Princeton University Press, and is reprinted by permission of copyright holder and authors. Dr. Davison and Dr. George are members of the social science staff of the RAND Corporation, Washington, D.C.

2. A related reason for slow progress in this field is that the communication process is extremely complex. The variables involved in communication have been summarized in the following formula:

Who says *what* to *whom* through what *medium* for what *purpose* under what *circumstances* and with what *effects?*

This is a convenient way of describing the chief elements of the communication process, but the variables in question are intricately related and most efforts to study and state their interrelationships have been seriously over-simplified. What we know about communication — i.e., the principles or propositions which express a relationship between two or more of these variables — is usually of only modest utility for purposes of solving a particular communication problem at a given time and place. In an operational situation we can apply our general knowledge about communication only if we supplement it with a careful "taking into account" of many of the specific components in the given situation. This means keeping many factors in the communication process in mind at once in order to get the insight we need into the concrete communication problem at hand.

The study of communication is sufficiently complicated if we confine it to the domestic scene. When we turn our attention to international political communication, where the "who" is a complicated propaganda apparatus in one culture, the "whom" is often an amorphous audience in another culture, and the purposes and circumstances are bound up with all the intricacies of international relations, then it is clear that we are not yet qualified to undertake a *systematic* study of international political communication. All we can hope to do is to illuminate certain aspects of the process, and perhaps help to pave the way for more systematic study at a later date.

3. The pay-off in international communication, and in the last analysis the reason we study it, is its effect. Social scientists have had considerable success in studying audience responses to certain types of domestic communications. But, as noted above, these communication situations are usually simpler than those encountered in trying to communicate for political purposes across national boundaries.

In the laboratory, for example, social psychologists are able to measure the "learning" which takes place after selected subjects are exposed to certain carefully defined communications. And in testing the effect of certain advertising upon consumer purchases the market researcher deals with a relatively uncomplicated matter. He is able to define what he means by effectiveness — whether or not the audience likes or buys the product — and he is sometimes able to measure at least a part of the behavior which occurs as a result of his communication. The researcher's problem in studying and evaluating the effects of international communication, on the other hand, is more complicated for several reasons: (a) the researcher is faced with the fact that the communicator frequently has only a vague notion of exactly what it is that he is trying to achieve; (b) the communicator often pursues many goals with many audiences simultaneously; (c) the communication itself cannot be neatly structured in order to facilitate the researcher's job of evaluation; (d) the foreign audience is often inaccessible for direct observation and measurement; and (e) clear-cut, simple criteria of effectiveness are wanting.

As a result, while we know quite a bit about the effects of different types of domestic communications, we know only in a general way that some international communications achieve the effect that was intended, some achieve effects which were not intended, and some result in no effects at all.

4. Another difficulty is that political communication is usually — although not always — an auxiliary instrument of policy. It is used in conjunction with decisions or actions which may fall in the diplomatic, economic or military sphere. If we try to study a communication without reference to the decision or action of which it is an auxiliary, we may be in the position of examining a meaningless abstraction. Thus, study of the content of specific communications may lead us into consideration of the North Atlantic Treaty Organization, the Marshall Plan, or the tactical situation in some military theatre where surrender propaganda was successfully or unsuccessfully employed.

5. Finally, a strictly scientific approach to evaluation of international communication is often difficult to maintain because of the political and administrative conditions under which it is undertaken. International communication programs — at least in this country and in some nations abroad — do not command firm political support at home and are dependent upon the vagaries of annual budgets. As a result, agencies charged with producing international communications programs are sometimes forced to combine evaluation tasks with the need for domestic public relations. In order to justify program and budget requests before those who control the purse strings, the communication agency is tempted to play up in its self-evaluation the more striking examples of its success. This is bad from a scientific viewpoint insofar as it distorts the task, already difficult to begin with, of setting up adequate criteria of effectiveness; it may lead to the adoption of invalid, oversimplified or ambiguous criteria for this purpose. We may note that this problem is faced not only by international communications agencies but by domestic commercial agencies as well. Certainly one of the chief tasks of the student of communications is to develop methods of auditing communication programs which are both scientifically respectable and reasonably comprehensible.

APPROACHES TO THE STUDY OF INTERNATIONAL POLITICAL COMMUNICATION

In spite of the fact that systematic study of political communication is at present so difficult as to be almost impossible, international information, propaganda and psychological warfare today constitute a field of endeavor in which thousands of highly-trained individuals are employed and which promises to become more rather than less significant in the years ahead. Furthermore, international political communication has an impressive past. It played a considerable role during both world wars and — on a smaller scale — can be traced back through history to the earliest stages of international struggles for power. The subject, then, is one which the social scientist is obligated to treat if he is not to ignore a major field of human activity.

Under these circumstances, we believe that there are several directions which the study of international political communication can take. First, even if we do not know very many of the correct answers about the effects of political communication, we know some things that are *not* true. A debunking role at this stage of the game can be of considerable utility, especially if it enables the student to reject some of the nonsense about propaganda and psychological warfare which is unfortunately widespread today. One such common misconception, for instance, is that a nation which has an effective propaganda program can afford to cut down expenditures for its armed forces. But the more we study political communication the more we see that propaganda which is not backed up by power is unlikely to achieve its goals. Propaganda is not a substitute for armed forces or other instruments of power; it merely complements them.

Second, we can refer to a few propositions about international communication which have been established with a fair degree of certainty. For instance, we know that an indirect approach to audiences which are in conflict with the propaganda-using nation is more likely to succeed than a direct approach. That is, one is more likely to elicit the desired type of behavior by hiding the fact that one desires it than by advertising it. Propositions such as these unfortunately do not link together to form a chain of systematic theory — they are more like isolated islands in a large sea of ignorance — but we hope that they are the beginnings of an emerging continent, and we can use them to take our bearings from time to time.

Third, one can observe that political communication campaigns in the past have been waged with a measure of success by those who have had a certain "feel" for them. These successful operators have usually been those who because of their wide experience knew what was the right thing to do, even if they did not know exactly why. Some of them have been professional propagandists and psychological warfare experts, but most have been politicians or statesmen with a rare sense of how to use the media of communication. One can group together here such strange bedfellows as Napoleon Bonaparte, Joseph Goebbels, Winston Churchill and George Creel. A study of the experience of these practitioners can contribute something toward developing a similar "feel" for the role of communication in political affairs.

NATIONAL POLICY AND DOMESTIC PRESSURES

As mentioned above, there is no standardized map that can be used in exploring the territory of international political communication — no periodic table of elements as in chemistry, or even an ongoing sequence of events as in history. Nevertheless, we must have *some* framework to hold together the relevant observations on the subject. Therefore we have constructed a diagram which may be useful for this purpose. Like most such aids in social science it does not in itself represent any basic relationships or truths. It merely serves as a reminder that the international political communication process involves relationships among a number of complicated and diverse factors.

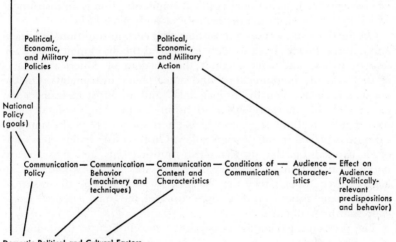

International Political Situation

FACTORS ENTERING INTO THE INTERNATIONAL COMMUNICATION PROCESS

One of the most important of these relationships is between communication policy and national policy. In the absence of a clear national policy on any given issue the communicator is in the position of a swimmer treading water just to keep from going under; he is unable to strike out in any direction. Successful propaganda presupposes a clear and explicit national policy — long term as well as short term. Consequently, to understand the behavior of propagandists the student must be able to relate this behavior to the policy of the nation they represent.

National policy, in turn, derives in part from the international political situation, and in part from domestic political and cultural forces. Aspects of both these determinants of national policy affect the activities of international communication specialists directly and indirectly. Therefore, we must also consider carefully certain facets of the international and domestic scenes.

For instance, the distribution of power and the alignment of values in the international arena following World War II have contributed to a bi-polarization of world politics. The leaders of each of the two rival blocs are faced with two principal tasks: (1) the "internal" problem: to consolidate their own bloc of nations and peoples in order to maximize power capabilities and minimize vulnerability to outer or inner disintegrating pressures; (2) the "external" problem: to devise policies and means of dealing with the rival power bloc, e.g., developing strategies for weakening the rival power bloc, neutralizing its threat to the self, and/or for arriving at an acceptable *modus vivendi* with it. International political communication is an instrument which may be used in the furtherance of both these tasks.

On the domestic scene we must note that certain traditional political and cultural factors have strongly influenced the development of U. S. foreign policy, and tend to limit the freedom of American leaders in their use of communication and other policy instruments. On the one hand, an aversion to "propaganda" and an effort to transfer the moral code of interpersonal relationships to the international plane have tended to limit the role which international political communication has played in our foreign policy. On the other hand, pressure is often exerted on the propagandist to orient his activities toward national aspirations — those goals which the nation would like to achieve even though they may be seen as lying outside the realm of present capabilities — rather than toward the more limited goals expressed by national policy.

The problem of domestic constraints is not limited to the democracies. The influence of domestic codes and practices on the foreign policy of totalitarian nations is just as strong, or even stronger. The leaders of the Soviet Union, for example, are bound by a self-imposed code which often makes it impossible for them to comprehend the motives behind the behavior of other peoples, and it is probable that many of them take their own propaganda image of the "capitalist" enemy seriously.

COMMUNICATION POLICY

Communication policy — i.e., decisions as to what we want to achieve through the use of communications — is derived in part from national policy and the constraints which help to shape national policy, but also from an evaluation of the other factors in the communication process: available media and techniques of communication, audience characteristics, and the conditions under which the communication is received. That is, communication policy as well as being in accord with national policy must prescribe goals which the propagandist regards as feasible in the light of what he knows about the capabilities of the total communication process. For example, it would be unrealistic to set up as a goal for communications the achievement of behavior in our audience which we knew to be manifestly impossible. At the outset of World War II, some Allied propagandists called on the Germans to revolt and overthrow Hitler. This was poor propaganda policy, since the victorious Germans were in no mood or position to revolt, and it was soon revised.

The line in our diagram connecting "political, economic, and military policies" with "communication policy" is intended to indicate that communication is merely one tool with which we try to achieve national goals. Other tools are usually used simultaneously with it. Although the propagandist cannot expect to play a major role in formulating political, economic and military policies, his position in the governmental structure sometimes enables him to advise that they be shaped in a way which will produce a desirable effect on foreign audiences. For instance, certain procedures for labeling and packaging goods sent abroad under the Marshall Plan were adopted in order to make the purposes of the program clearer to recipients abroad. In some cases policies may be formed and actions taken primarily in order to serve as non-verbal communications, or "propaganda of the deed." Military demonstrations are a case in point. Thus the propagandist, in addition to forming his own communication policy, has a staff function with respect to the formation of other types of policy.

COMMUNICATION BEHAVIOR AND CONTENT

Once communication policy is decided, specialists in the use of international communications take this policy and transform it into action: a broadcast, a leaflet, a diplomatic note, and so on. This transformation process we refer to as "communication behavior." Study of communication behavior includes consideration of the machinery by which communication policy is transformed into communication content, and also study of the personnel who operate this machinery and the media and techniques which they use. Thus, in concrete terms, the student of international political communication should know something about the structure, techniques and personnel of the U. S. foreign information program, the British foreign information program, the Soviet Agitprop, the diplomatic services of the major powers, and so on. Included here also are organizations designed to conduct psychological warfare in time of war.

Communication behavior results in the preparation of communication content — the only part of the communication process which ordinarily is perceived by the audience. Content is nearly always produced as the result of a compromise between conflicting pressures from the two ends of the communication process. On the one hand, the propagandist is expected to adhere to national policy and communication policy, and he may be exposed to domestic pressures of considerable intensity. On the other hand, he tries to shape his content according to what he knows about the probable responses of his audience and about the conditions under which the communication will be received.

THE PROBLEM OF EFFECT

The effectiveness of communications in influencing behavior depends in large measure on the *conditions* under which they are received. We use the term "conditions" here very broadly to include all stimuli from sources external to the audience which may affect response to the propaganda message. The conditions of any given communication include such matters as its "timeliness," whether it is forced to compete with rival communications or enjoys a monopoly position, whether events tend to support or contradict the message, whether the originator of the communication is winning a war or losing it, whether or not the tactical situation favors the communicator, and so on.

One of the major problems of communication policy and technique is to find ways of controlling the interpretation which an audience will place upon events and actions. People are swayed not merely or even primarily by what is said. More important is what is done and what happens. Actions and events, however, can be interpreted in a variety of ways by both individual and group audiences. Communication specialists cannot be certain that events and actions will always speak for themselves in the desired manner. There are two ways of meeting this problem by means of communication: (1) The specific action or event in question can be presented by the communicator in such a way as to further the type of interpretation which is desired — that is, the propagandist "plays up" the story in a certain way, or gives it an "angle." (2) The communicator may aim at shaping the broader perspective or frame of reference of the audience in such a way that members of the audience will themselves see events and actions in the desired manner — that is, the propagandist tries to give the reader a special pair of glasses through which he is to see what takes place.

To the extent that the propagandist is able to shape the actions taken by his own nation he may be able to exercise some control over the conditions under which his communication takes place. For example, the combat psychological warfare operator may be able to synchronize his surrender appeals with the activities of his own artillery or air force. It has been found that the most fruitful time to make a surrender appeal is when an exposed enemy unit has just undergone one bombardment and is threatened with another. Conversely, when an enemy unit is in a secure position and artillery or air power is lacking surrender appeals are likely to have little effect.

Equally important to the effectiveness of a communication are *audience characteristics*. These vary, of course, with each audience, and it is therefore difficult to make general statements which apply to more than a few of the audiences which are exposed to international political communications. Nevertheless, we can call attention to various *types* of audience characteristics which are of crucial importance. We are interested here in such questions as the audience's listening, reading, or "exposure" situation, the motivations of the person who receives the communication, and the extent to which the actual listener or reader relays what he hears to others.

For our purposes, however, perhaps the most important characteristic of those who constitute the audience is their position in the political structure of the nation to which they belong. This means that an important part of our audience or "target" analysis must be to assess in detail the political structure and dynamic political processes in the country to which our communications are addressed. How is power and influence distributed? What are the contributions which different groups make to national morale and to the power potential of the state? In totalitarian societies the courses of political action open to individuals are very few; one cannot expect to influence their voting behavior, for instance, because they never have a chance to vote — or if they do it is usually a meaningless formality. Certain groups of leaders, however, may have a wider range of political choices open to them. Similarly, the way the society in question is organized, its social constraints, popular beliefs and customs, and so on, exercises an important influence on the way communications are received and the effect they have. And finally, the members of any given group tend to react as individuals in certain patterns, and the communicator must be familiar with these patterns.

The principal difficulty in the study of audience characteristics is that almost everything about the audience appears to be relevant in one way or another to the communication process. As a result, the student always runs the risk of becoming mired in an enormous mass of descriptive detail. This danger can be partially averted if an audience is studied with reference to the specific behavioral or attitudinal effects which the propagandist desires to achieve. For instance, if he wishes to gain acceptance on the part of another nation of a given trade policy, then his primary focus of interest will be on the history of that country's trade policies, on the individuals and groups who have the most influence in determining trade policy, and on the means of reaching these individuals and groups. In general, the more specific the effects which are envisaged by communication policy, the easier will be the task of the propagandist in studying relevant audience characteristics.

If the communications content is adequate, and geared in with other types of action, if the conditions of communication are favorable and audience characteristics are taken adequately into account, a communication may have certain effects on one or more members of the audience which receives it. But what do we mean by "effects"? They may be changes in attention or attitudes, reinforcement of existing attitudes or behavioral responses. The student is interested in all these, but he is particularly concerned with actions or predispositions to actions which have political significance, since the influencing of politically-relevant behavior is the goal of international political communication. He will observe, moreover, that some of the effects which were achieved were intended and some (including the category of no effect) were unintended. The task of the propagandist is to study effects as thoroughly as he can and then to reshape his propaganda in such a way as to maximize those effects which were intended and to minimize those which were not.

Evaluation of the effect of international communications is thus more than a post-mortem, or audit of success or failure. It is, or should be, an on-going intelligence process. Since the effect of communication stimuli on human behavior can rarely be predicted with a high degree of certainty, the propagandist's policy and techniques must be continually corrected by observation of effect.

THE COMPLICATING ROLE OF THE PAST

A further caution should be given regarding the description of the communication process which has been sketched in above. It may be misleading in that it fails to indicate that each element in the process has a history. We cannot understand national policy, the conditions of communication, communication behavior, or any of the other elements unless we examine what they have been in the past as well as what they are in the present. This consideration serves as a final blow to efforts to simplify study of the subject.

This outline does not begin to cover all aspects of interest in the international communication process; it does not even provide for the inclusion of all the relevant information which is currently available. But it does, we hope, stress the relationship — even if it is a highly involved one — between national policy and the politically relevant behavioral effects of communication. With that in mind we are in a position to study and evaluate with somewhat more clearness of focus the various elements in the international political communication process.

▲ HANS SPEIER

*P*sychological Warfare Reconsidered

INADEQUACIES OF THE TERM "PSYCHOLOGICAL WARFARE"

The term psychological warfare has gained wide currency in popular and scientific discussions, but its meaning is not clear. For three reasons the term is debated among those who use it freely.

First, warfare cannot readily be expected to be waged in times of peace or, for that matter, against the populations of neutral and allied countries in wartime, unless it is felt that by virtue of being "psychological" this kind of warfare is not "real" warfare. During the Second World War, psychological warfare was indeed regarded primarily as a responsibility of the military who fought the enemy, whereas the civilian Office of War Information never officially professed before the Congress and the public its concern with it. Soon after the end of the war the relationship between the Soviet Union and the Western powers began to be characterized as a state of cold war — incidentally no less ambiguous a term than "psychological warfare" — but while according to many observers of the international scene the traditional distinction between war and peace cannot be applied in the postwar period, no government involved in the cold war has as yet stated that it is engaged in psychological warfare against other nations. Rather, there is talk of "international information" and, reluctantly, of propaganda.

Second, the terms "psychological warfare" and "political warfare" (as the British prefer to call their activities in this field) are misleading if they designate exclusively propaganda to enemy countries in times of war. Wars are waged against enemies in order to defeat them; yet

▲ This article appeared in *The Policy Sciences,* edited by Daniel Lerner and Harold D. Lasswell, published by the Stanford University Press and copyright by the Board of Trustees of Leland Stanford Junior University. It is reprinted here by permission of the copyright holder. Dr. Speier is head of the social science staff of the RAND Corporation, Washington, D.C.

during a war, psychological warfare comprises not only ancillary activities to the same end by certain non-lethal means but also actions which attempt to reach and make friends in the enemy camp.

For yet a third reason, the term psychological warfare is easily misunderstood. When it is used as a synonym for combat propaganda and related activities in wartime, it seems to be implied that other forms of warfare have no psychological effects, but only physical consequences, and are conducted without regard for the mind of the enemy and the moral forces at his command. In this context, then, psychological warfare emerges as a specialized activity which injects into the "unpsychological" wars of the machine age the recollection and rediscovery of man as the agent of aggression, the object of suffering, the human element in bureaucratized strategy and industrialized battles.[1]

The ambiguities of meaning from which the term psychological warfare suffers stems from the lack of a more basic agreement on the nature of war. It is inadvisable as well as tedious to begin this reconsideration of psychological warfare with a proposal of new definitions. The following discussion will cover activities which the reader should feel free to include or exclude from the field of psychological warfare as he delimits it. Fortunately it will be possible to engage in this inquiry without using the word "psychological" at all.

THE ABILITY AND THE WILL TO FIGHT

Military writers are in the habit of distinguishing between the ability and the will to fight. An enemy can be defeated by destroying his capability of resistance, but failing this he will also succumb when his will to fight is broken. These two elements of war are not independent of one another. The will to fight is likely to be stronger if the ability to fight, compared with that of the enemy, promises a chance of success. Capability counts for nothing, however, if resolution to use it is wanting, and within certain limits strong will can offset the disadvantage of inferior capability, particularly when the opponent's resolution and perseverance do not match his superiority of force.

Incapacitation of the enemy by destruction, conquest of territory, capture or denial of men and material, blockade, etc., and incapacitation by demoralizing the enemy are two roads to victory. To assume that only destruction wins wars is tantamount to denying the intellectual and moral elements in war. It is obvious that demoralization, i.e., breaking the will to resist, may in turn be achieved by physical destruction, but statesmen and generals throughout the ages have also used less crude and more ingenious means to win wars. The amount

---

[1] I once was asked by an officer, "Does psychological warfare include warfare psychologically waged?"

and kind of destruction necessary for victory varies not only with the state of technology but also with the political conduct of the war.

The distinction between capability and will can be profitably applied to the analysis of international relations in times of peace, since in peace as well as in war the status of nations depends upon their ability and their will to change or maintain the prevailing distribution of power. Organized violence by means of military power is not brought to bear upon other nations in times of peace. For the citizen life is safer and more comfortable than it is in wartime. His risk of suffering violent death is low and so are, relatively speaking, his deprivations. The potential use of organized violence, however, bears on the policies which are pursued in peacetime. The same holds true of scientific and technological developments which affect the protective and striking power of arms; of threats, warnings, denunciations of their possible use; of demonstrations that they exist and are efficient; of re-organizations and re-dispositions of the available forces; and of partial mobilizations. Nor are the other instruments of international policy invariably and exclusively reserved for either wartime or peacetime use: diplomacy, espionage, counter-intelligence, economic measures, organizational activities ("fifth columns"), propaganda — all these means are used in the pursuit of international policy in peace as well as in war. The erroneous opinion that the employment of any of these instruments is confined to wartime breeds illusions about the nature of peace, impairs the pursuit of foreign policy goals in peacetime and may render wars, when they come, more ferocious. It is quite possible that the recent popularity of the term "cold war" indicates not only the precarious nature of the postwar relations among the great powers allied during part of World War II but also the unjustified demand that peacetime relations ought not to reflect a struggle for power.

There are, of course, secular trends in the use and function of the instruments of policy. Military force has been applied with fewer political and moral restrictions in the wars of the twentieth century than in the conflicts of the two preceding centuries. Correspondingly, the function of diplomacy in eighteenth century international affairs was more continuous, i.e., less subject to modification and disruption by war, than has been true in the twentieth century. The effort of all great nations during the last four decades in using propaganda as an instrument of foreign policy in peace as well as in wartime has been more formidable that the effort these nations made in this field during the preceding four decades.

Regardless of secular trends in the use of foreign policy instruments and regardless of the different modes of their employment in war and peace, war is not a state of affairs in which military force replaces all other means of policy. Nor is the state of international affairs in periods of peace independent of the balance of national war potentials.

The national ability to attain or defend positions of international power, which is put to a test in war, influences the state of peace. So does the will to resist or commit aggression. But it now is necessary to determine more closely what "will" means in this context.

THE WILL TO FIGHT RECONSIDERED

Unless we ascertain *whose will* we have in mind when speaking of "the will to fight" we are in danger of committing an anthropomorphic fallacy: clearly, not everybody in a nation at war is really fighting. Unless we ascertain further what is being done and "willed" by those who are not fighting as the nation pursues a given course of action, we miss the various *aims* of "the will" that matter: evidently, not only "the will to *fight*" is necessary for victory. Finally, if we are satisfied with the simple justaposition of "capability" and "will," we neglect the intellectual functions in warfare and peacetime foreign affairs: there must be knowledge and thought if a will is to use means for a purpose. The following discussion will attempt to clarify these three issues.

If wars were still waged by armed forces alone and if their leaders could count on blind obedience to command, the only will to fight that would count would be that of the officers — a situation which was approximated in the European wars of the eighteenth century prior to the French Revolution. Soldiers then were disciplined, unhappy and more afraid of their own superiors than of the enemy. Nor did they depend at that time on a continuous flow of freshly-produced supplies to replenish and improve their arms and ammunitions while the war lasted.

Today, war efforts can no longer be sustained from arsenals or loans with which to buy foreign manpower and available weapons. The physical resources of the country must be exploited and the human resources of the whole nation be mobilized in order to insure survival in large-scale war. A large part of the non-combatant population must be put to work in order to equip and re-equip, arm and re-arm the fighting forces of the nation. The industrialization of the economy has changed both the standard of living and the standard of dying. The functional role of the non-combatants in the war effort is buttressed by widespread emotional participation and intellectual interest in the war, which rarely existed prior to the modern nationalistic, literate, age. Finally, civilians as well as the armed forces are exposed to the danger of violent death, since the modern means of destruction permit attacks on the enemy's sources of armament, the urban centers of his industrial war production.

The will to fight is essentially a *will to work* on the part of the civilians in a nation at war. Moreover, while both combatants and non-combatants must be ready to die and suffer deprivation (regard-

less of any attractions and profits war may offer to some of them),
the latter do not need to have a will to kill; the former do. They are
victims rather than executioners of violent death. These differences
have an important bearing on any intelligent enemy effort to break
the national will to resist, and require differentiated warfare.

The large non-combatant part of the population comprises at least
four general classes of persons, which are of importance to this analysis.

There are, first, those who hold political power — the political elite.
Assuming that they, rather than the rulers of the military hierarchy,
determine the policy of the nation as a whole, their "will to fight" is
of supreme importance at the outbreak of war, for the conduct of the
war and for its conclusion. Similarly, they are responsible in times of
peace for the international policy which the nation "as a whole" pursues. But this elite cannot be said to have a will to fight (or not to
fight) in the same sense in which such will is asserted in combat. It is
more appropriate to speak of the elite's function to decide what is to
be done by the nation. Here we are primarily concerned with elite
decisions in the field of foreign policy; but the relative stability of the
domestic regime bears upon the process in which these decisions are
made and its outcome. The conduct of foreign affairs requires, of
course, elite decisions which affect the domestic conditions of life, so
that the stability of the regime necessarily narrows or widens the scope
of choices which confronts the decision-making elite. Instead of
ascribing to the political elite a will to fight (or not to fight) we shall
therefore speak of its *ability to govern* (at home) — taking it for
granted that they have a will to do so if they can — and its *deciding*
of *foreign policy*.

Those who hold power govern by means of staffs and control personnel; this personnel will be considered here as part of the elite. The
function of this auxiliary personnel is to render it possible for the
elite to avoid foolish decisions[2] and to see to it that decisions, whether
foolish or not, are acted upon, once they are made. Among other things,
the elite relies on foreign intelligence about capabilities and intentions
of other powers, domestic intelligence on the stability of the regime
and the capabilities of the country, advice in estimating the consequences of alternative foreign and domestic policies, control and sup-
pression of domestic opposition (however defined), and communication
with other groups holding less power. Note that the disruption of any
of these functions impairs the elite's ability to govern and to make
sound decisions, possibly with repercussions on the political elite
itself, and particularly in times of war, on the nation as a whole.

[2] Cf. Harold D. Lasswell's and Abraham Kaplan's proposition, "Upper elites
tend to be skilled in the practices of inter-personal relations rather than of the
area in which decisions are to be made." (*Power and Society*, Yale University
Press, New Haven, 1950, p. 203.)

The second and largest group of the non-combatants will be considered here as a unit and be called the working population. Its function in modern war has been mentioned. It must have "the will to work." In addition, the working population is required to obey the laws of the country. To the extent that the political elite has authority, instead of merely exercising its rule by means of sanctions, the working population may, therefore, be said to have also a *will to obey* (or not to obey) the law of the elite.

The will to obey meets the minimum requirements of efficiency and authority, but in a well functioning society the working population does in fact always perform "above and beyond the call of duty." If the performance is reduced to mere obedience to orders the control functions of the auxiliary elite personnel are inevitably overloaded.

The relation between the political elite and the working population varies, of course, with the formal and informal political structure of the state. The bearing which this fact has on attempts to break the will to work and the will to obey will be discussed in due course.

The working population comprises people of different skills. Persons of high skill are scarcer than persons of low skill. The loss of experts to the community through death, abduction, desertion or disloyalty, therefore, has grave consequences since they cannot be replaced easily. The top group of such "irreplaceable" skilled specialists within the working population, including selected scientists, administrators, business men, inventors, intelligence experts, engineers, etc., form the civilian key personnel. Like the working population to which they belong, the civilian key personnel must be willing to work and obey. Any successful enemy effort to weaken their will to work and obey, which is especially directed at this part of the community, is likely to have especially high returns not only because substitutes for key personnel are difficult to find but also because malfunctioning members in this group affect the operations of many others. Inefficiency of a charwoman is a nuisance, that of a top administrator a calamity. Moreover, many persons in key positions possess knowledge of high intelligence value. If they become talkative or disloyal, their value to the enemy as a source of information may exceed the value of their elimination.[3]

The non-combatants include a number of dependents, whose age or

[3] On the importance of secrecy among key scientific personnel *in peacetime,* see H. D. Smyth's *General Account of the Development of Methods of Using Atomic Energy for Military Purposes* (1945), chapt. III. The hypothesis of fission was announced and its experimental confirmation took place in January, 1939. "At that time," reports Smyth, "American born nuclear physicists were so unaccustomed to the idea of using their science for military purposes that they hardly realized what needed to be done. Consequently the early efforts at restricting publication . . . were stimulated largely by a small group of foreign born physicists. . . ."

state of health makes them worthless to the war effort. Their will does not matter. The graphic military term for describing such dependents under conditions of siege warfare will be be used: these non-combatants are useless mouths (*bouches inutiles*).[4] While useless, such mouths may cry or sing and thus affect the feelings and actions of those who care for them.

Corresponding to the distinction between political elite and working population, we shall speak of military elite and fighting population in the combatant sector of the nation. (There are no military useless mouths, unless one were to regard non-fatal casualties as such.)

It will be assumed that the military elite determines military strategy and tactics in accordance with foreign policy decided by the political elite.[5] Under this assumption, the military elite has a *will to obey* the political elite or must expect sanctions in case of disobedience. In this respect the military elite does not differ in principle from the working and fighting populations. As the military elite holds power over the latter, however, it must have *ability to command* (corresponding to the ability to govern of the political elite). Furthermore, since the military elite and its staffs plan and execute military operations, we shall speak of its *determination of military missions* to attain policy goals. Finally, it shares with the fighting population the *will to fight* (or not to fight), although it should be observed that a large part of this elite holds planning, administrative and other posts which in some ways resemble top positions in civilian life.

Strictly speaking, the *will to obey* military superiors and to act "above and beyond the call of duty" is of greater importance than the will to fight even in the fighting population, inasmuch as under mod-

---

[4] For an early recognition of this social stratum see Byzantine Anonymous, *Strategikos*, I, 4 ("The useless people who cannot do anything for the common good . . ."), II, 9 (". . . neglected by nature and fate . . ."), and III, 13.

[5] In practice, the functions of determining political and military strategies are neither easily distinguished nor always clearly separated. During the Second World War the supreme authority in both spheres of power was in fact held by the same person in the United States, the United Kingdom, China, the Soviet Union and Germany. (The situation differed during the First World War notably in the United Kingdom and Germany.) Concerning the place occupied by "psychological warfare" in the decisions of the political and military elites in World War II, see for the United States: Wallace Carroll, *Persuade Or Perish*, Boston, 1948; Ellis Zacharias, *Secret Missions*, New York, 1946; Charles A. H. Thomson, *Overseas Information Service of the United States Government*, Washington, D. C., 1948, Part I; Daniel Lerner, *Sykewar*, New York, 1949; for Great Britain: Bruce Lockhart, *Comes the Reckoning*, London, 1947; for Germany: Derrick Sington and Arthur Weidenfeld, *The Goebbels Experiment*, London, 1942 (American edition: New Haven, 1943); Rudolf Semmler, *Goebbels — The Man Next to Hitler*, London, 1947; *The Goebbels Diaries*, 1942-1943, ed. by Louis P. Lochner, New York, 1948. — For the first World War, see Harold D. Lasswell, *Propaganda Technique in the World War*, New York, 1927, and Hans Thimme, *Weltkrieg ohne Waffen*, Stuttgart, 1932.

ern conditions of warfare the majority of those "under arms" does not fight the enemy but supports combat troops which do.[6] This division of labor, or rather, of the broad combatant function is reflected in the differential casualty rates of various services and branches in the armed forces. Thus, the Infantry in the U. S. Army, "while constituting about 10 percent of the strength of the Army, accounted for 70 percent of all the battle casualties in World War II.[7] In planning combat propaganda this stratified distribution of risks, which is associated to a significant extent with differences in social recruitment and civilian background, merits close study but for present purposes the whole combatant part of the population will be held to possess a will to fight (or not to fight).[8]

There are of course rare and common skills in the fighting population as well as among non-combatants, and the existence of key military personnel, distinguished by high skill and highly specialized training, needs special attention. Tribute has often been paid to these experts, because their contributions to war efforts are great. The function of key combatant personnel in war seems to have increased with increasing industrialization of warfare. Illustrations abound: the German shock troops introduced at the end of the First World War after the collapse of linear infantry tactics, the fighter pilots who defended the British Isles in the battle of Britain in 1940, commandos, airborne contingents, etc. An extreme case has been related in Churchill's account of the Second World War. In March 1941 the British succeeded in sinking the German submarine U-47 commanded by "the redoubtable Prien" as well as U-99 and U-100 commanded by two other "tiptop" officers. "The elimination of these three able men," Churchill comments, "had a marked effect on the progress of the struggle."[9]

In summary, a glance at the broadest outline of the functional and political structure of the nation at war has led to a considerable refinement of the notion with which we started and which plays so important a role in psychological warfare. The general notion of "the will to fight" has been replaced by six factors. Consequently, there are six ways of weakening "the will to resist," namely interference with:

1. the deciding of foreign policy (by the political elite),

[6] On January 5, 1951, Senator Taft asked in the Senate, "Is it necessary for this country to provide from sixty to seventy thousand men in uniform and half as many more civilians in order to put a division of 18,000 men in the field?" (*Congressional Record,* Vol. 97, p. 64).

[7] Samuel A. Stouffer, et al, *The American Soldier,* Vol. I, Princeton, 1949 (Princeton University Press), p. 330.

[8] In times of peace, the will to fight should not be taken as a desire to break the peace.

[9] Winston Churchill, *The Grand Alliance, Boston,* 1950 (Houghton Mifflin Company), p. 127.

2. the determination of military missions (by the military elite),
3. the ability to govern (of the political elite),
4. the ability to command (of the military elite),
5. the will to obey (of the military elite, the working population and the fighting population),
6. the will to fight (of the military elite and the fighting population).

If the indispensable functions of the auxiliary personnel attached to the elites are borne in mind, it appears that hostile action against foreign political and military elites can be taken especially by interfering with:

a. intelligence on foreign capability and intention,
b. intelligence on domestic capabilities and obedience,
c. estimates of the consequences of alternative policies,
d. control of the working and fighting populations and of the military elite by the political elite,
e. communication with these groups.

Finally, we have found that combatant and non-combatant key personnel are crucial for the functioning of society in peace and war and thus a rewarding target in the international struggle for power. This is due to the fact that key personnel are difficult to replace and often possess information of high intelligence value.

THE DEMOCRATIC FALLACY IN MASS PROPAGANDA

The political influence which the mass of the population is constitutionally able to exert upon the elite, i.e., their recruitment and their decisions, determines in large part the structure of the political community. Account must be taken of this structure in the international struggle for power. When the political regime is despotic, the mass of the population has no chance to affect the recruitment of the elite, to fill vacant elite positions, and to pass public judgment on elite decisions. In modern despotism, i.e., in totalitarian regimes, the political elite disseminates its exotic opinion to the masses of the population. Moreover, the population is tightly organized and thus controlled. All deviant political opinions are either esoteric or are in any case kept secret, because of terroristic measures against those who are alleged to lean toward heresy.

An understanding, however false, of domestic and international events of the past and the future is offered through an official "ideology" — a phenomenon absent in older tyrannies. These ideologies also contain the political definition of friend and foe, law and moral standards. The ideology invests reality with meaning, however simplified, and provides the masses of the population with permitted language. Ideologies are therefore a comfort in a world which appears incomprehensible and menacing without them. As the political elite blankets the area it controls with approved opinions fitting into the official ideology.[10] it offers security, however costly, to the minds of all as it stabilizes the regime.

In view of these considerations it is folly to expect that the dissemination of another ideology by foreign propagandists can convert the masses of a population living under despotic rule to become adherents to a new ideology or to shake off the shackles of ideology altogether.

The political elite is on guard against the emergence of counter-elites, i.e., those aspirants to power who attempt to reach their goals against the will of the ruling elite. In despotic regimes counter-elites, like less consequential opposition, can operate only under-ground or abroad.

The subordinate military elite is regarded as a potential counter-elite by those who hold supreme power. It is, therefore, distrusted, infiltrated, controlled, and purged from time to time. In the Soviet Union so large a proportion of senior officers were liquidated before the outbreak of the Second World War that the efficiency of Soviet military power was considered in the West to be seriously impaired.[11] Similarly, the National Socialist leaders fought more relentlessly against the German military elite than the resistance of its members to Hitler's regime seemed to warrant.[12]

Since in modern societies the mass of the population cannot overthrow, or actively influence the policies of, despotic regimes without armed domestic or foreign support and without organized leadership, the population at large is no rewarding target of conversion propaganda from abroad. Any notion to the contrary may be called the fallacy of democratic propagandists who disregard the differences in political structure between the regimes under which they and their audiences live.

The will to obey and work or at least the inclination to perform "above and beyond the call of duty" will be weakened as satisfaction with the regime is lessened; but such demoralization is not likely to be furthered by conversion propaganda and may in fact be hindered by it. Dissatisfaction with the regime may result from experiencing deprivations which are unexpected and regarded as unnecessary, futile or unjust. Such experience is not likely to be sharpened by the promotion of strange beliefs, i.e., by ideological propaganda.

Ideological propaganda to the mass of the population living in despotic regimes is sometimes advocated because of the cumulative

[10] Alexander Inkeles, *Public Opinion in the Soviet Union*, Cambridge, 1950.

[11] Erich Wollenberg, *The Red Army*, London, 1938.

[12] During World War II, of 36 Lt. Generals 21 were dismissed by Hitler, 2 were expelled from the Army, and 3 were executed after July 20, 1944. Of 800 officers of the General Staff, 150 are said to have lost their lives as opponents to the regime. See Walter Görlitz, *Der Deutsche Generalstab*, Frankfurt, 1950.

effect it is alleged to have. As its effect increases over a period of time, it is presumed to lead to explosive action. Evidence for this proposition is lacking.[13] Politically relevant mass action presupposes the destruction or disorganization of controls by means other than propaganda, especially military force or subversion. It also requires leadership by a counter-elite. The control apparatus at the disposal of the elite may crumble in consequence of disruption from without and within, but hardly on account of attempts at converting those who are controlled.

Similar considerations apply to combat propaganda directed at the fighting population. Without prejudice to the need for propaganda directed at the combatant population in time of peace and during a war in stalemate and defeat situations, there can be little doubt that the wartime conditions favoring success of such propaganda are military superiority, victory, pursuit, and stalemate. A propagandist speaking for the side that retreats, has lost a battle, or is militarily weak, must fight uphill. Propaganda in war is an auxiliary weapon. Auxiliary weapons cannot turn the wheel of fortune if the main weapons are blunt, scarce, or lost.

DEVIANT POLITICAL BEHAVIOR AND ITS INDUCEMENT

In the conduct of psychological warfare sight must never be lost of the fact that a change in attitudes and private opinions amounts to little if it fails to result in deviant, politically relevant behavior.[14]

Generally speaking deviant, politically relevant behavior comprises all action which weakens the ability of the elites to govern and command. In war, those who fight may cease fighting, fight their own authorities and resist the enemy inefficiently. Those who work or fight may give information to the enemy, cooperate with him by fighting on his side once they are taken prisoner or have deserted. Members of the working population may slow down in their work, commit sabotage, spread rumors, organize those who are dissatisfied, or engage in illegal activities.

Like mutiny in the armed forces, revolution at home or secession under the leadership of a counter-elite are the most dramatic instances of disorder, weakening the regime or incapacitating it to pursue its foreign policy.

[13] But there is evidence for cumulative effects of propaganda on opinions and attitudes, particularly when propaganda is monopolistic. Cf. Joseph T. Klapper, *The Effects of Mass Media,* New York, 1949 (mimeographed by the Bureau of Applied Social Research of Columbia University). Cf. also the review article by Wilbur Schramm, "The Effects of Mass Communications," in *Journalism Quarterly,* December, 1949.

[14] Goebbels distinguished between *"Stimmung"* and *"Haltung,"* the former being politically irrelevant internalized responses (attitudes), the latter representing externalized responses (behavior) which matter. As long as the authorities can prevent the transition from *"Stimmung"* to *"Haltung,"* Goebbels was entirely right in deprecating concern about depressed *"Stimmung."*

The conditions of politically relevant actions taken by the working population and by those who fight differ significantly in one respect. The latter have, in favorable military circumstances, a chance, however small, to desert or surrender to the enemy if their will to fight is broken. By contrast, the working population has no such opportunities. There is no line its members can cross in order to get out of the war. Once an enemy soldier deserts or surrenders, he increases his chance of survival. If an enemy worker wants to disobey his authorities, he cannot avail himself of the protection of foreign powers; as a rule, not doing what his authorities expect and want him to do considerably decreases the margin of his safety and adds to his chance of violent death by enemy action the risk of losing his life through sanctions by the domestic police.

It is not certain that military personnel can desert more easily in times of peace than in wartime: its moves can be supervised and controlled more closely in garrisons. For example, while the defections of Soviet soldiers during World War II surpassed in magnitude those of any other belligerent nation, the Soviet armed forces stationed in occupied countries after the war live in so strictly enforced isolation from their foreign environment that desertions are rare.

Civilians can leave their country more easily in peacetime, despite emigration and immigration laws which restrict such movements particularly from and to countries with despotic regimes. The only groups with ample opportunities to defect are diplomatic and other personnel, including individuals belonging to the civilian key personnel, whose business takes them abroad.

Some of the deviant, politically relevant actions do not require joint efforts but can be taken individually, others cannot possibly succeed without organization. The power interested in breaking or weakening the will to obey must give thought to the *organizational requirements* of the deviant behavior it tries to induce, and to the magnitude of the *risks* incurred by such behavior.

Finally, intelligence estimates must be made of the *self-interests* of enemy non-combatants and combatants in deviant behavior, since these interests may be compatible with the interests pursued by the rival foreign power itself. Such compatability signifies what may be called the chance of alliance in non-combat warfare, and it is a matter of elementary statesmanship to assess the political worth of its exploitation.

Not much need be said here about the measures the rival power can take to help meet the *organizational requirements* of deviant behavior in an enemy regime. These measures range from the formation of counter-elites abroad (governments-in-exile) to their clandestine or overt support if they operate in the enemy country; from giving material aid and organizational assistance to the opposition in the enemy camp (such as arms and communications facilities) to assigning liaison personnel[15] or leadership to them;[16] from advice to bide time to strategic coordination of joint, foreign, and domestic moves against the regime.

Intelligent non-combat warfare attempting to induce deviant actions in the enemy camp must try to reduce the *risks* of such actions and show awareness of the irreducible risks even in its propaganda. Since in war some of these risks can be curtailed by foreign military action, coordination of the use to which the various instruments of policy are put is of great importance if good will, i.e., the will to disobey, in the enemy camp is not to be lost. Apart from military damage to the control apparatus, there are three principal ways of reducing the risks of deviant behavior.

(1) Psychological warfare can be careful to encourage only such actions which in view of the prevailing conditions are feasible without decimating the "resistance" in the enemy camp. If this care is not taken, the directors of the psychological warfare effort will appear either stupid or callous and lose whatever influence they are able to wield abroad.

(2) By the same token, psychological warfare can warn "allies" in the enemy camp of perils which threaten them. For example, RIAS (Radio in the American Sector of Berlin) broadcasts to the Soviet zone of Germany the names of informers so that anti-communists can be on guard against them. Moreover, specific advice can be given on how to minimize or avoid the hazards of deviant behavior. To cite a case of dubious value, during the last war soldiers were occasionally informed by the enemy how to produce undetectable symptoms of diseases which would put them on the sick roll.

(3) Instead of attempting to induce deviant behavior in the enemy population at large — a practice predicated on the absurd assumption that whole populations are imbued with the spirit of heroism and self sacrifice — psychological warfare can concentrate on selected groups whose self-interest, predispositions and organization are conducive to deviation. Work with and through existing cells of resistance and disaffected parts of the population is likely to be more effective and will boomerang less easily than indiscriminate agitation. Correspondingly, in foreign propaganda, attention must be paid to the fact that talking the way one talks to friends, even though their existence in the enemy camp may be unknown or doubtful, is preferable to a verbal combat with the enemy at large, since such talk is bound to reinforce the opinion of hostile foreign intentions which the enemy elite spreads assiduously in the area it controls. Foreign propaganda of this sort

[15] E.g. Fitzroy MacLean's airdrop in wartime Yugoslavia to work for the British with Tito.
[16] E.g. Lenin's famous journey in a sealed German train to Russia in 1917.

may strengthen rather than weaken the will to obey among the large mass of those who, in situations of stress, derive comfort and security from the support they give to their leaders.

The *self-interests* of groups and individuals in the enemy population which can be exploited for "alliances" through the non-combat warfare comprise a wide range of possibilities. Broadly speaking, there may be political interests of ethnic minorities in secession or liberation, a case skillfully utilized by the British against the Austro-Hungarian Empire in the First World War; there may be interests in the removal of controls which are felt to frustrate the aspirations of counter-elites and organized support of the will to disobey, as was the case among the European resistance movements in World War II during the period of German occupation; there may be dissatisfaction with social injustice, etc. Important opportunities for political warfare have arisen throughout history in wars of coalition, since combined national self-interests always are a somewhat brittle foundation for the pursuit of a common policy, particularly in successful offense. In World War II, Goebbels exploited adroitly the mass murder at Katyn to intensify discord between Poland and the Soviet Union, and until the very end of the war, Hitler and his lieutenants hoped for a split between the Western powers and the Soviet Union. Similarly, the Japanese astutely exploited political differences among the Filipinos when at the beginning of 1942 Tojo promised that independence of the Philippines be established at an early date.

Apart from these and other kinds of deviant political self-interest, which are of great value to judicious political warfare, there is elementary self-interest in survival which non-combat warfare can utilize. This is especially true when the employment or the threat of physical weapons intensifies the fear of violent death among the subjects of attack. As has been pointed out, civilians cannot surrender when their courage wanes or their will to obey is broken. They exhibit panic, become apathetic or die. Yet impelled by the need for self-preservation they may also take to flight. Flight in response to propaganda is obviously confined to wartime operations when the subjects of attack are warned that they may be killed unless they take precautionary action in order to survive. Since non-combatants are not expected to have a will to fight and are in some measures less reconciled than are combatants to the prospects of death through enemy action, they are perhaps more susceptible to warning than soldiers.

Warnings of impending attack differ from ultimata. An ultimatum tries to force one course of action upon the enemy by threatening severe reprisals if another course of action is followed. By contrast, warnings to non-combatants of attacks to come, which were often delivered during World War II, offer escape from the horrors of action which the warning power has resolved to take. Those who are thus warned are again treated as "allies" rather than as enemies. The political interest of the foreign propagandist in disabling the enemy elite to govern a well organized population is reconciled with the interest of the warned population in its own self-preservation. Instruction or advice to the target population as to what it should do in view of the warning is a more powerful non-combat warfare measure than mere warning which leaves to the resourcefulness of the target population and its government what kind of evasive action to take.

The latter type of pure warning may be illustrated from Admiral Halsey's memoirs. In January, 1943, at Bougainville, the following type of message was dropped in pidgin English on native villages.

A serious warning from the big white chief
to all natives of Buka Passage, Buin, and Kieta:
This is straight talk. You must listen.
The village of Sorum has been disloyal, has
taken orders from the Japs, and has helped the Japs.
We have now bombed them.
We have also bombed Pidia, Pok Pok, Toberoi, and
Sadi when they helped the Japs.
If any villages help the Japs, we will bomb
them and destroy them altogether.
We have many planes, many bombs, and many soldiers.
We will not hesitate to carry out this work.
Before long we will come with all the American
Soldiers to dislodge the Japs and kill them all and punish
all natives who helped them.
                    That is all.
                    You have been warned.[17]

It will have been noted that by having regard for organizational requirements, risk and self interest, those engaged in non-combat warfare play a role quite different from that which the conversion propagandist assumes. The latter is like a missionary, possessed of a faith which he deems superior to that of the heathen, but unlike the missionary he talks from a safe distance. The former identify themselves with the persons whose hazardous political conduct they try to guide; they talk or at least appear to talk to allies and friends. To the extent that their careful consideration of what is expedient from case to case is governed by a sense of responsibility, they are less likely to be tempted by the ruinous gratifications which all tasks of human manipulation offer. Political warfare requires many skills, but also certain moral qualities. Its directors must be able to move against the currents of popular passion and to forego adventurous showmanship. In addition, they must know the foreign policy objectives of their country.

[17] Halsey, W. F., and Bryan J., *"Admiral Halsey's Story,"* Whittlesey House, New York, 1947, pp. 150-151.

THE RANGE OF PLANNING AND THE SHAPING OF EXPECTATIONS

Decisions reflect varying degrees of foresight. Foreign policy decisions are reactive, when they are taken in response to *faits accomplis;* in this case other powers move according to *their* plans, and the reactive elite "muddles through." Decisions taken according to a plan are not strictly speaking predetermined by that plan but issue rather from a re-examination of a given plan in view of a new situation. In other words, all plans of action embody estimates of future countermoves, and each new decision to respond to a countermove enables the planners to re-examine the adequacy of their foresight as well as to bring their plan up to date. Since the pursuit of a foreign policy is affected not only by the ability to carry out intentions, but also by the execution of the opponent's policy, the foresight becomes dimmer the farther it penetrates the future. It would be irrational to predetermine in a political plan the exact decisions to be taken in the more distant future, because the intervening counter moves are matters of probability rather than fact, and unforeseeable events are matters of chance. Good plans of action are therefore based on the determination of attainable objectives, but since the estimates of what is feasible change with time, they allow for flexibility through a change of moves to reach these objectives. Good plans of action also reflect a preference for initial moves which do not irrevocably commit the decision maker to subsequent moves nor restrict his freedom to revise subsequent moves in view of unforeseen events. If planning ahead frees the political elite from the pressure of unconsidered countermoves, rational (i.e., flexible) planning may be paradoxically said to free it from the pressure of irrational (i.e., rigid) plans. This rationality of planning is well illustrated by a phrase which Churchill repeatedly used in setting forth possible courses of action to be taken against the Axis during World War II: after determining feasible objectives and certain suitable moves to attain them, he pointed out that the moves might have to be modified "as events serve us."

Military elites engage in planning as a matter of course, and in modern wars, at least, are able to state exactly how many days ahead or behind schedule a campaign has progressed. The dependence of modern warfare on the time consuming processes of mobilization, training, the development and production of new weapons as older models become obsolete, and on logistical requirements, renders such planning imperative and constitutes, in fact, a powerful stimulus toward planning the economy of the nation as a whole. Planning in the field of foreign policy is more difficult, chiefly because the control of the future embraced by the plan is shared with opposing elites. The time over which the considerations of political planners range, moreover, is longer than the time range of military plans.

Broadly speaking, it is a military short range objective in war to complete successfully a phase in a battle; winning a battle means reaching a medium range objective; and victory in a campaign attains a military long range objective. For the political elite in war, the victorious end of a military campaign is, as it were, tantamount to attaining a political short range objective; the winning of the war is a matter of medium range considerations, and the best utilization of the international distribution of power at the conclusion of hostilities is a long range matter. Any consideration to establish peace forever, i.e., to abolish foreign policy, may be said to be politically out of range or utopian.

There are probably historical and national differences in the extent of foresight which various political elites incorporate into their foreign policy plans and decisions. Given the lack of research on this intriguing subject all propositions concerning it must be hypothetical in nature.

1. Utopianism, including the belief that the international struggle for power can be replaced by a harmony of interests, is associated with a lack of articulateness in defining political objectives of any range.

2. Relative military weakness is associated with attempts to extend the time range of planning or with "reactive" moves.

3. Political elites that have risen to power from a state of persecution (when they were counter-elites) are more likely to plan far ahead than elites without such history.

4. Unless the staff of democratically constituted elites is powerful and has a slower replacement rate than the top elite itself, decisions are "reactive," short range or utopian; by contrast decisions by elites recruited from a political class (e.g., an aristocracy) are governed by considerations of medium and long range objectives.

5. Preoccupation of the political top elite with administrative staff functions is indicative of "reactive" decisions in foreign policy; with domestic intelligence: of short range aims; with foreign intelligence: of medium range objectives; with history: of long range goals.

Propaganda reflects in any case the time range prevalent in the decisions of the political elite. If the policy is reactive, propaganda is likely to be an uninspired news service, because it lacks any relation to policy objectives. In that case news has no political focus and the propagandist cannot establish the "meaning" of the events, although facts often do not speak for themselves and if they do, not the same way to all people.

If the political thinking of the elite is utopian, the propaganda effort will be missionary; against recalcitrant opponents who refuse to become converted it will turn fanatical. Only when the foreign policy objectives of the political elite are both articulate and "within range" can foreign propaganda perform a useful function. It does so, broadly speaking, by deriving the political meaning of events from policy objectives in order to influence the expectations of future events.

For it is the *expectations* of the enemy population on which psychological warfare can exert its most profound influence by disseminating "news." What has happened or what has been done, especially by another power, heightens or lowers expectations and changes their content.

In an intelligent psychological warfare program propaganda does not attempt to convert the foreign population to another ideology by claiming its superiority. Rather, the propagandist tries to *shape expectations* by interpreting events as tokens of the future. In doing so he creates an image of intentions. Moving from ideology to the concrete and specific concerns of the people he talks to, he descends, to use a phrase of Karl Marx, from language to life.

The propagandist can sometimes predict what the enemy elite will do in its domestic policy and what the masses he addresses will have to suffer in consequence. Such propaganda presupposes not only good intelligence about the prospective moves of the enemy elite (e.g., curtailment of food rations), but also reliable estimates that increased deprivations will be resented rather than accepted with patience or austere fervor.

More important, however, are the expectations of the population concerning the plans of the power for whom the propagandist speaks. Theoretically, the propagandist gains access more easily to his own elite than to the secrets of the enemy elite. In practice, however, the effort of the propagandist in influencing expectations depends on the extent to which his own elite permits him to share some of its secrets.

The members of the political elite and its staff concerned with decisions on what is to be done rather than on what is to be said have a natural desire for secrecy, because premature disclosures may enable the enemy to parry prospective moves. Even in Nazi Germany, ruled by an elite that attached great importance to international propaganda, the coordination of propaganda and policy was far from perfect. The propagandist is a professional talker. Who likes to confide secrets to professional talkers? The fallacy hidden in this question lies in the implication that the propagandist will divulge the secrets he learns. As every diplomat knows, it is possible to hide and betray secrets by both silence and talk. By the same token, the propagandist may conceal by talking or reveal by silence[18] what he is supposed not to disclose, but he cannot do either, unless he is informed about the secret. It should be noted, however, that the usual differences in

[18] For example, National Socialist propaganda directives (so-called *Sprachregelungen*) prohibited at a certain date during the last war any mention of heavy water in magazines. If *previous* references to heavy water had been noted from time to time, the abrupt silence about the matter would have been a disclosure.

social background and career of "policy makers" and propagandists increase the secretiveness of the former.

The propagandist does of course not need to know all secrets of his political elite. Yet, in order to influence expectations abroad and to be effective in the timing and direction of this effort, he must be able to derive propaganda policy from the foreign policy decisions of the elite. Otherwise he is thrown back to get his inspirations from news or ideology. More generally speaking, the *existence* of policy objectives — short, medium and long range — is a prerequisite of political warfare. The *communication* of these objectives to the directors of propaganda merely insures coordination in the use of policy instruments.

Who, precisely, in the opposing nation is the enemy? Is it the military elite as much as the political elite? Who, in the enemy camp, are potential or actual allies? Which groups should have more power, which less? Is it the foreign policy of the other nation that is to be modified or also its social institutions? Precisely which, if any, of the latter; and in what way? Are revolution and secession permissible, required, or not permissible (since they cannot possibly be a matter of indifference)? If required, precisely what means are to be applied to produce the desired state of affairs: incitement, infiltration, support? If support, what kind? What is the time scale of operations, i.e., the relation of short term to medium term objectives? In war, what are the political long range objectives, if victory is a medium range aim? In peacetime, what are the elements of a desirable relationship between the powers concerned? It is answers to questions of this kind which furnish the basis of political warfare, as distinguished from the gossip of news, the preaching of ideology, the performance of tricks and the projection of the self.

POLITICAL WARFARE AGAINST ELITES

According to the assumption made throughout this essay, the elites are hostile or at least have designs to maintain defensively or attain offensively positions of international power at the expense of other nations. Elite decisions to surrender, to disarm, to form an alliance, to yield or to compromise are goals of political warfare in the same sense in which mutiny in the fighting population, sabotage among the workers, the rise of strong counter-elites or the defection of key personnel may be such goals. Maintaining the assumption of "warfare" as the specific state of international affairs with which we are here concerned, the decisions of other elites, if taken *without interference,* are not only in the interest of the nations they govern but also disadvantageous to the power engaged in political warfare against them. Hence the special task of political warfare to influence enemy decisions in order to reduce the power gain which they are intended to bring about and to turn it possibly into a loss.

Decisions by the political elite concerning foreign policy and the determination of military missions by the subordinate military elite require cooperation among the elite members. It is also necessary that certain staff functions be performed and coordinated. Political warfare can therefore attack the cooperation among elite members or the performance of their staff functions.

Cooperation is dependent upon a modicum of mutual trust. In this respect despotic elites are more vulnerable than democratic elites. It has already been mentioned that the subordinate elite is easily suspected of treason and easily regarded as a potential counter-elite. A study of relations beween the political and military leaders in Germany during the Hitler period is especially revealing in this respect.[19] During World War II it was not fully appreciated how easily distrust can be created.[20] A systematic exploitation of these predispositions of a despotic political elite requires reliable intelligence on frictions within the enemy elite and need not be confined to the use of propaganda. It appears that subtler, less public means, such as studied diplomatic indiscretions in neutral countries or the sacrifice of intelligence for the purpose of compromising certain elite members in the eyes of others are more suitable means.

Desertions of elite members are rare and difficult to induce. If they occur, however, they provide great opportunities to political warfare. The sensational defection of Rudolf Hess, Hitler's deputy, was not exploited by the British, which characteristically aroused rather than allayed suspicion of the British on Stalin's part.

There is also evidence from the last war, particularly in the Goebbels Diaries, that propaganda directed at the masses may directly or indirectly through the monitoring services reach the political elite, which is subject to less censorship than the population at large, and thus have an unintended effect. It would therefore appear possible to use this channel of communication with the elite for specified purposes rather than by default. The same holds true of using mass communications for contacts with members of the military elite. Vir-

[19] Similarly rewarding is a study of military failures and misfortunes of German and Italian commanders during World War II compared with those of British and American generals.

[20] Liddell Hart quotes General Blumentritt, "Hitler knew that Field Marshal von Rundstedt was much respected by the army and by the enemy. Allied propaganda broadcasts often suggested that the views of the Field Marshal and his staff differed from those of Hitler. It was notable, too, our headquarters are never subjected to air attacks. Nor was the Field Marshal ever threatened by the French resistance movement — presumably, because it was known that he had always been in favor of good treatment for the French. All these things were brought to Hitler's notice, of course, in reports from his own agents. While he treated the Field Marshal with respect — more respect than he showed other soldiers — he kept him under careful watch." See *The German Generals Talk,* New York, 1948, pp. 260-261.

tually all memoirs of military leaders in the last war frequently cite
enemy propaganda statements, and there are a few instances in which
action was influenced by them.[21]

More important, however, than these relatively minor weapons in
the arsenal of non-combat warfare against enemy elites are the measures that can be taken to interfere with the performance of staff
functions. The following remarks are confined to the subject of interference with foreign intelligence and with advice on the consequences
of alternative decisions by means of deception.[22]

According to the saying which Plutarch ascribed to Lysander,
"Where the lion's skin will not reach, you must patch it out with the
fox's," deception has been used throughout history in order to confuse
the enemy. All deception is aimed at creating erroneous estimates of
enemy capabilities or intentions and thus at inducing counter-moves
which are wrong but appear to be right to the enemy.

Like successful secrecy, successful deception produces surprise and
helps put the opponent off guard. Secrecy attempts to keep intelligence
from the enemy whereas deception provides him with misinformation.
If secrecy about the next planned move were complete, the enemy
elite would still make the best possible estimate of this move and act
in accordance with this estimate. Deception is superior to secrecy in
that it attempts to *influence* the estimate; at the same time it aids in
obscuring real intent by disclosing a fake intent. Since deception is a
form of communication with the enemy elite which it expects to be
withheld, the disclosures instrumental to deception must appear either
unavoidable or as mishaps: in either case the disclosure may be mistaken by the enemy as the result of its own reconnaissance or intelligence activities. Seemingly unintentional disclosures are studied
indiscretions, planted misinformation, etc. Seemingly unavoidable disclosures result from staging a dummy reality in the hope that enemy
reconnaissance will spot and mistake it for an indication of genuine
capability or intent.

Many paradigmatic forms of deception occur in the animal world.
Friedrich Alverdes distinguishes between the following forms of
animal deception.[23]

1. *"Sympathese,"* i.e., sympathetic coloration and behavior in relation to the environment in order to deceive for aggressive or protective

[21] See for example the entry under 20 June 1944 in Lt. Gen. Lewis H.
Brereton, *The Brereton Diaries* (William Morrow & Co.) New York, 1946,
p. 289, "Owing to the enormous enemy propaganda on damage done by V-Is,
it was decided at commander's meeting to stage a strong air attack on Berlin
tomorrow to counteract it."

[22] Interference with the control and communication functions of the auxiliary
elite personnel have been touched upon when measures to reduce the ability to
govern and command were discussed.

[23] Friedrich Alverdes, "Täuschung und 'Lüge' im Tierreich," in *Die Lüge,*
ed. by Otto Lippmann and Paul Plaut, Leipzig, 1927, pp. 332-350.

purposes the sense of sight. Since *"Sympathese"* covers behavior as well as coloration, "playing possum" (*"Thatanose"*) is included under this heading. So are forms of protective coloration which give the impression that the body of the animal "dissolves" into the environment, e.g., the stripes of the zebra, (called by Alverdes *"Somatolyse"*). Finally there are forms of deception which create the impression that the persecuted, fast moving and vividly colored animal suddenly appears to change into one that is not moving and is protectively colored. Such *"Heteropsie"* may also be directed at the sense of hearing, as in the case of locusts whose whirring stops when they settle down.

2. *Mimesis* consisting in protective similarity with indifferent elements in the environment. Alverdes distinguishes between *"Allomimesis,"* i.e., imitation of inanimate things, *"Phytomimesis,"* i.e., imitation of plants or parts of plants and *"Zoomimesis,"* i.e., imitation of another species.

3. *Mimicry*. Alverdes uses "zoomimesis" to denote cases of deception producing failure to detect, whereas mimicry is deception producing avoidance by adaption of unprotected animals to the appearance of others which are protected by poison, smells, etc.

4. *"Phobese,"* i.e., means which defenseless animals use to ward off their enemies by terrifying colors or behavior.

5. *"Allekation,"* i.e., coloration or behavior which lures other animals into the vicinity of those which prey upon them.

It may be added that animals (especially birds) may simulate being wounded in their flight in order to divert the attention of the aggressor from their young. There are also cases in which animals actively use parts of their environment in order to mask themselves.

The obvious similarity between deception "techniques" in the animal world and those used in human warfare is evident, but should not be over-emphasized inasmuch as man can add to the deception of the senses the deception of the mind. There is then a premium on inventiveness in the field of human deception.

Military history abounds with attempts to mislead the enemy by deceiving his intelligence service through ruses.[24] Military deception

---

[24] See General Waldemar Erfurth, *Surprise* and the introduction to this book by Stefan T. Possony, Harrisburg, 1943 (Military Service Publishing Company), from which the following illustration is taken. During the first World War the British misled the Turks at Gaza to believe that the main blow of Gen. Allenby's forces would fall at the left flank.

"A whole month was spent in sending 'misleading messages by wireless telegraphy in a code which the Turks, by various ruses, had been taught how to solve, without realizing the situation.' In addition, a British staff officer on patrol ride let himself be surprised by a Turkish guard. He feigned to be wounded and ostensibly lost his haversack with an especially prepared notebook, including money, love letters and several purported orders and military documents. The haversack was picked up by the Turks. The next morning, a is used to mislead enemy intelligence concerning place and time, strength and objectives of offensive or defensive operations in order to induce the enemy either to overlook the imperative need for making a decision or to reach faulty decisions which increase his vulnerability. Major deception schemes to mask operations that involve a large number of combatants are often accompanied by self-deception, i.e., cover-schemes which conceal the purpose of preparing the real operation from those who are supposed to execute it.

It is doubtful that propaganda can effectively contribute to military deception, although some major efforts to that effect were made in World War II. U. S. propaganda after the invasion of Normandy kept calling attention to the possibility of additional landings elsewhere in France in order to tie down German reserves. These verbal efforts would probably have been of little avail, had it not been for the deception measures taken in Great Britain which strengthened German expectations of further landings. As has been pointed out, the effectiveness of communications with the intent to deceive is altogether dependent on the credible appearance of a mishap and on supporting evidence provided by "dummy reality." It is not sufficient to claim that a move is afoot if observable, deceiving preparations of this move are not actually made or if the preparations that are observed clearly deny the claim.

This simple principle of military deception was disregarded by Goebbels who thereby testified to both his ignorance of military matters and his ludicrous over-estimation of the power of cunning. Twice he attempted to deceive enemy intelligence about imminent German offensives. The first effort was directed in June 1941 at creating the impression that England rather than the Soviet Union was about to be invaded by German forces. The scheme involved self-deception at a confidential conference when the department heads of the Propa-

notice appeared in the paper that was issued to the Desert Mounted Corps, stating that a notebook had been lost by a staff officer on patrol and that the finder should return it at once to Allenby's headquarters. 'A small party was sent out to search the country for the pocketbook. . . . An officer was stupid enough to wrap his luncheon in a copy of these orders, and to drop it near the enemy.' These ruses were successful." (p. 10).

For a few illustrations from World War II, cf. Field Marshal The Viscount Montgomery of Alamein, *El Alamein to the River Sangro*, New York, 1949, p. 31 ff., 57, 78-80; Desmond Young, *Rommel, London,* 1950, pp. 173-4; Sir Giffard Martel, *An Outspoken Soldier,* London, 1949, p. 206; Brereton, *op. cit.,* pp. 273-4; Anthony B. Martienssen, *Hitler and His Admirals,* New York, 1949, p. 79, 101; George C. Kenney, *General Kenney Reports,* New York, 1949, pp. 268, 281-2, 330, 374, 384, 501; Admiral Halsey, *op. cit.,* p. 197, 207-8; Field Marshal Lord Wilson of Libya, *Eight Years Overseas,* London, 1948, p. 40; Sir Frederick Morgan, *Overture to Overlord,* New York, 1950; Sir Francis de Guingand, *Operation Victory,* New York 1947, pp. 108, 155-6. See also Jasper Maskelyne, *Magic-Top Secret,* London (no date).

ganda Ministry were told that operations planned in the East had been called off. Then Goebbels himself described in an article published in the *Völkischer Beobachter* the invasion of Crete as a rehearsal for a great airborne operation and implied that an invasion of the British Isles was imminent. On secret orders from Goebbels the article was immediately withdrawn, but not until foreign correspondents had cabled the contents of the article out of the country. As soon as it was known through tapping telephone wires that the order for confiscation had also been telephoned abroad, all foreign lines were closed.[25] It is not known what happened to British and Soviet Russian intelligence estimates in consequence of this ruse, but it is safe to assume that the massing of more than 100 divisions on the German-Russian border spoke louder than Goebbels' propaganda and censorship measures.[26]

A similar ruse was tried by Goebbels in the spring of 1942 in order to divert attention from the impending German summer offensive on the Southern front in the U.S.S.R.[27] It again involved an article by Goebbels and the dispatch of a German journalist first on a trip to the Eastern front, which was much publicized, and then to Lisbon where he was instructed to let it be known in a state of feigned drunkenness that the Germans would attack on the *central* front.

These cases illustrate the wasteful histrionics of zealous propagandists. They do not prove the futility of efforts to mislead enemy intelligence by appropriate means.

It is likely that deception of political elites is more easily accomplished than that of military elites, because in efforts directed at political intelligence relatively less attention need be paid to producing "dummy *capabilities*" or to camouflaging them and more reliance can be placed on the effectiveness of producing false notions of *intent*. A given capability can be used for various purposes and the intent to use it in any definite way cannot be safely derived from it, but the margin of error in deriving intent from capability grows in proportion to the scope of the enterprise under review. Whether or not a field commander is preparing for attack in times of war may be safely derived from the observation of certain unmistakable preparations for battle. Evidence of preparations for war itself may be less conclusive, simply because the political elite may decide to confine the "use" of national capabilities to rendering threats of war more effective. Deception in

[25] Rudolf Semmler, *op. cit.*, p. 39-42.

[26] I am indebted to Miss Jean Hungerford for an examination of the *New York Times,* the *London Times,* the *Daily Mail* and the *News Chronicle* from June 9 to June 22, 1941, for possible public effects of Goebbels' article. The incident was duly reported but was completely overshadowed by reports of the massing of troops on the Russian frontier, the possibility of war between Germany and the U.S.S.R., etc.

[27] See the *Goebbels Diaries, op. cit.,* pp. 162-227.

this case would be successful if the intent of war were conveyed in order to heighten the impact of the threat.

Furthermore, there are many political actions, e.g., the conclusion of treaties, which do not require observable physical capabilities. In these cases, again, induced mistakes in assessing the intent of foreign political elites suffice for deception.

Finally, to the extent that political elites are concerned with longer range objectives, deception bearing on these objectives may succeed without arranging elaborate "dummy capabilities." An illustration may be taken from Hitler's military conferences. On January 27, 1945, Hitler said to General Jodl,[28]

I have ordered that a report be played into their hands to the effect that the Russians are organizing 200,000 of our men, led by German officers and completely infected with Communism, who will then be marched into Germany. I have demanded that this report be played into English hands. I told the Foreign Minister to do that. That will make them feel as if someone had stuck a needle into them.

In conclusion, it should be stressed, however, that the use of deception in attempting to influence the expectations and intelligence of opposing political elites is not confined to actions perpetrated by ingenious specialists in trickery. The highest form of political deception consists rather in major political *actions* which lead the opposing elite to misjudge the political strategy it attempts to fathom. Like political warfare in general this kind of deception is no substitute for policy planning: it presupposes the determination of the objectives which deception can help attain, particularly by actions which mislead the opposing elite in assessing the nature of these objectives and their interrelation in time and space.

[28] *Hitler Directs His War*. The Secret Records of his Daily Military Conferences, selected and annotated by Felix Gilbert (Oxford University Press) New York, 1950, p. 118.

▲ CHARLES Y. GLOCK

*T*he Comparative Study of Communication

and Opinion Formation

It has only been within the last two decades that research on communications and opinion formation have been recognized and accepted as special disciplines within the fields of social psychology and
sociology. In that period, the focus of attention among American
scholars has been given to studying "who is saying what to whom
and with what effect" in the United States. A considerable body of
literature has appeared on the results of studies of the American
communications scene much of it of notable quality.[1] More recently,
under the impetus of needs deriving from the world political situation,
a mushroom growth in interest in the study of communications and
opinion formation on a world-wide basis has occurred. We now speak
of international communications research as we talked but a few
years ago of "domestic" communications research.

It is not at all clear that we are in agreement as to what the field
of international communications and opinion formation encompasses.[2]

[1] An excellent bibliography of these studies is contained in Bernard Berelson
and Morris Janowitz, Eds., *Reader in Public Opinion and Communication*.
Glencoe, Illinois: The Free Press, 1950.

[2] The writings of some scholars would suggest that it is limited to the study
of the transmission of news and opinions across national boundaries. They
would not include within its orbit a study of, let us say, the system of mass
communications in Iran. Others have suggested a much broader definition and
would include under international communications, research done anywhere on
the communications behavior of a people or the communications system of
a nation whether it refers to matters of national or international importance
or to matters of local gossip. While it is likely that this problem of definition
will continue to be explored for some time, it is not the intention of this paper
to undertake such needed exploration.

▲ This article first appeared in the *Public Opinion Quarterly*, in 1952. It was
copyright by the Princeton University Press, and is reprinted by permission of
the copyright holder and author. Dr. Glock is director of the Bureau of Applied Social Research, Columbia University.

For the purposes of the present paper, we have adopted a conception of international communications which includes the transmission and reception of news and opinion both within and between national boundaries. Our emphasis is on the comparative study of communications and opinion formation and we assume, therefore, that research done on the internal communications of a country or other political or geographical unit is international when it envisions comparison with the internal communications of another area.

The importance of the mass media as transmitters of news and opinion varies considerably, of course, in different parts of the world. In almost every area, however, some form of mass communication exists. The early part of this paper gives attention to the kinds of information most needed to clarify the role of the mass media as channels of communication under varying conditions.

There are, however, many ways in which the content of mass media is transmitted to people not directly exposed to them, and much of what is communicated is never channeled through the mass media. While assuming a different character, this is true in areas where the mass media are plentiful and easily accessible as well as in areas where there are no radios and where a majority of the population is illiterate. Knowledge of the functioning of the mass media, therefore, must be supplemented by an understanding of the role of informal communications channels in the communications process.

Cognizance also has to be taken of the fact that attitudes towards knowledge and opinions differ in different parts of the world. In the United States, for example, it is expected that every person will be informed about current affairs and will form opinions about them. In Islamic countries, however, it is not as obvious as with us that such knowledge is essential or that having an opinion is important. Knowledge of the variations in receptivity to information and ideas in different areas is needed to round out an understanding of the role of mass media and informal channels in communication.

The development of a comparative study of communications and opinion formation cannot be made the responsibility of any single discipline of the social sciences. By its very nature, it requires the application of a variety of skills and a basically inter-disciplinary effort. Because the problems needing attention should be of practical interest to the sociologist, the anthropologist, the area expert, and the public opinion specialist, it is to be hoped that such an inter-disciplinary effort will be forthcoming.

MASS MEDIA

The role of the mass media as disseminators of news and opinion will vary from country to country and, within a country, will vary for different groups in the population.[3] Furthermore, the role of one medium will differ from that of another and one segment of any one medium will perform somewhat different functions from another. It will be the long term objective of a comparative study of communication and opinion formation to clarify the role of the mass media at each of these levels of specificity. To lay the ground work for eventually satisfying such a long term objective, there are certain kinds of problems and data collecting which should be given first priority.

It is self-evident that the role of the mass media in an area will be highly influenced by what media are available and how widely they are distributed. Collecting more basic quantitative information on the availability and distribution of media will be a first task. Such fundamental questions as how many radio stations and newspapers there are in each of the countries of the world, how many and what kinds of books and motion pictures are produced and/or distributed, and how large an audience these various media reach are still largely unanswered. It can be assumed that many of these data are kept up to date by appropriate public and private agencies and need only to be systematically brought together.[4]

Having such information about the existence and distribution of the mass media in a country allows in itself some interpretation of their role as carriers of news. In Turkey, for example, radio ownership is restricted almost entirely to metropolitan areas. As a result radio ownership is frequent among the national minorities which are concentrated in these areas. However, in Turkey, the national minorities seem to be less influential in the political life of the country than the Moslem population. We have thus a situation where material transmitted via the radio is more likely to reach certain groups that have little political importance. Newspapers, on the other hand, are relatively less concentrated in the cities and it can be inferred that their influence among politically significant groups will be proportionately greater than radio.

It is unlikely, of course, that the data about the mass media which can be readily collected from already existing records is going to be as detailed or as complete as we should like. Such records will probably give us information as to the number of radio sets which have been sold or are in use and the circulation figures for newspapers, but they

[3] The examples reported in this and succeeding sections on communication and opinion formation in countries of the Near and Middle East are based on a study of these problems conducted by the Bureau of Applied Social Research, Columbia University, the results of which will be published in a forthcoming book.

[4] Some work in this area has already been undertaken by the United Nations Educational, Scientific and Cultural Organization. See particularly the four volumes "Press, Film, and Radio" released by UNESCO between 1948 and 1951.

normally will not provide important data on whom they reach in the
population and with what frequency. Here, there are several related
questions needing answers. How accessible are the media to different
segments of the population? What is the relationship between accessibility and actual exposure? What are the restrictions on accessibility
and what are the resistances to exposure? The relevancy of these questions will vary, of course, according to the country being studied. In
the United States, where most of the mass media are accessible to
everyone, the questions of exposure and resistances to exposure require
primary attention. In a country, such as Jordan, where the distribution
of the mass media is limited, accessibility and restrictions on accessibility are currently more crucial problems.

Restricted accessibility in various countries has led to innovations
in the distribution of the mass media which are relatively uncommon
in this country and which require special study. Several examples may
be mentioned. One is radio listening in public places like coffee houses
and village squares. Another is the mobile movie unit. A third is the
development of wired radio which was used by the Nazis and is now
frequently used in Russia and the satellite countries. A fourth example
is the practice of reading newspapers aloud to small groups. Such innovations make the media more widely accessible, but in certain instances
impose restrictions on the character of exposure. In some coffee houses
of the Middle East, for example, it was found that the proprietor
maintained authoritative control over the tuning of the radio set.
Whether or not Cairo, or Radio Moscow, or the Voice of America
was tuned in became a matter of his personal predilection. In the
satellite countries, the introduction of wired radio by the Russians has
meant greater accessibility to radio but limited exposure to varying
interpretations of world affairs.

Comparative studies of accessibility and exposure to the mass media
need to be supplemented by inquiries into the general attitudes which
people have toward the media. Such attitudes will influence the effectiveness of the media with regard to the formation of opinion. What
kind of images of the various media exist under varying cultural conditions? In Arabic countries, especially in those areas of orthodox
Islamic background, the secular use of radio violates for many their
interpretation of certain precepts of the Koran. Radio is imagined by
them to be the "voice of the devil." Its effectiveness among these
people, therefore, is likely to be seriously conditioned by this prevailing
image. In Western Europe, it is taken for granted that most newspapers are the organs of a political party. Because this orientation is
reflected in the news as well as the editorial columns, readers tend to
be cautious in their willingness to accept what they read. In the United
States, the political affiliation of a paper plays a minor role with
readers who are more willing to accept news reports as accurate and

unbiased. In Greece, radio has been found to enjoy considerably more prestige among the population than newspapers. Radio, which is government operated, is surprisingly considered to be less biased in its reporting than newspapers, which though privately operated, generally identify themselves with one of the many existing political points of view. A comparative study of the mass media can do much to codify the varying images of the media which exist, as exemplified by these illustrations.

This leads to the question of differences in media tastes between audiences in different areas. In Greece, where radio is regarded as an instrument of adult education and culture, quite different standards of programming prevail than in the United States. In this country, national magazines are proabbly the main reading material with which the masses of the population come in contact. In Germany, which is certainly a literate country, national magazines play a much smaller role. Variations in taste also influence audience receptivity to movies. It is only too well known that "Hollywood movies" are not an unmixed blessing when they are shown abroad. It will be important not only to record the variations in tastes which arise but to consider the cultural factors conditioning such variations.

The role of the mass media is also likely to be affected by the character of the control which is exercised over what information and ideas they may present. In some countries, such as Russia, the state exercises virtually complete control over what is said over the radio, in the newspapers, and in books and magazines. Some of the implications of such a development are self-evident, but, among other things, it is important to know in such situations how, if at all, conflicting ideas are introduced into the communications process. In other countries, governmental control of the media is negligible but private groups exert a strong influence over what is presented. In France, literary artistic circles have been influential in raising the cultural standard of French radio. We know that in this country religious groups exert a special influence over the character and content of motion pictures. It is also quite evident that in Moslem countries the religious authorities are considerably concerned with the content of the mass media. Aside from such manifest influences on what the mass media have to say, the more subtle effects of the economic or social system need to be studied. American radio is often said to have been guided by the general axioms of free enterprise thinking. In other countries certain basic ideas on the role of government might equally have influenced the organization of the mass media. Political preference for one rather than another of the Great Powers may lead to rather mechanical imitation of a system which cannot be easily integrated into local conditions. The general question of control is among those particularly in need of systematic inquiry.

INFORMAL CHANNELS OF COMMUNICATION

People extend the horizons of their knowledge and ideas by exposure to the mass media, by talking with other people, and by personal observation. The relative importance of each of these channels of communication is determined, in part, by their accessibility and, in part, by the content of the material which is being communicated. More specifically, news about the world as we ordinarily think of it is communicated to some through the mass media, to others by word of mouth, to some through both channels, and to others not at all. Personal observation is not likely to play more than a minor role in this connection. Our attention will now be directed toward suggesting some of the problems requiring study to clarify the role of word-of-mouth, or, as we shall call it, oral communication, in bringing news and opinions about events of local, national and international character to different peoples.

It is self-evident that the role of oral communication will vary according to the degree to which the mass media are also accessible. It will be important, therefore, to distinguish between those people who rely on both direct exposure to the mass media and oral channels to bring them news and those people for whom only oral communication is accessible.[5]

It is a first task to identify the carriers of news and opinion under varying conditions. In areas of the world where the mass media are in abundance, it is not at all clear how much people rely on the mass media relative to conversation to keep them informed. Recent American studies have highlighted the fact that in all strata, there are some people who expose themselves more to the mass media than do other members of their primary groups. These people, in turn, are more likely to communicate with others and to deliberately or unwittingly use their greater exposure to develop a leadership position in the general network of communication. Such opinion leadership may be exercised by persons of apparently low station as well as persons with acknowledged status in the community. Opinion leadership varies greatly from one society to another and requires careful description and analysis.

In many areas of the world where the mass media are not readily accessible, local populations nevertheless exhibit interest in and knowledge of what is going on outside of their own communities. Here, again a form of opinion leadership arises, though possibly differing in character from that found where the mass media are widely distributed. Special attention in this connection should be given to the role of

[5] Those people who are isolated from communication about anything but their local life will not be considered, though obviously, they cannot be altogether ignored in a comparative study of communication.

migratory persons as carriers of news. The grocer, in one Turkish village, was found to be the source of the information which the local population exhibited about current affairs. His occupation led him to make trips to Ankara from which he returned with news of the "big city." In certain pre-industrialized areas, where there are far flung autobus systems, the bus drivers may play the role of dissemination agents, as they in fact do in rural Syria. Soldiers and migratory workers, because they often spend part of their time in one environment, and then return to their regular places of abode, may also serve as carriers of news. In other areas, the one literate person in a community, often a teacher or priest, may function as the source of the community's touch with the outside world. Such persons, themselves exposed to one or more of the mass media, convey their content in the classroom and the church to large groups in a community.

It will not, of course, be sufficient that we identify who the carriers of news are in different parts of the world. Their role and function in a community must also be studied as must the content of the material which they communicate and its effect on those who are exposed to it. The news carrier in societies where the mass media are widely accessible performs a somewhat different function from the grocer or bus driver who is the sole or one of a few carriers of news into a rural community. In the former case, the information and ideas which he imparts interact with what people have seen or heard in the mass media and learn from other people. In such areas, the news carrier is not an information or opinion monopolist but may be an opinion leader. Within a system of oral communication, the news carrier plays a somewhat different role and his influence is likely to be somewhat differently felt. In one Lebanese village, the older residents were found to experience news from the outside world as a threat to their traditional ways of life. For younger members of the community, conversation with a traveler with news of urban life opened up new and attractive vistas, and contact with him was as much sought by the younger people as it was avoided by the older.

It is also likely that in areas which rely largely on oral transmission of news, different kinds of news material are likely to have higher currency than in areas well covered by the mass media. In the latter case, since the media quickly provide the population with most of the day's news, it is often knowing the "news behind the news" which gives one a privileged status. Within a system of oral communication, the situation seems to be quite different. Not even the daily news is easily accessible and many news topics, when they become known, are patently out of date. This may lead to certain types of information being assigned a more enduring value, so that they are regarded as still worth learning about even weeks after the event has occurred.

It may be, for example, that some aspects of the life of national leaders, or national catastrophes or events related to larger problems of war and peace, are probably more desired than what we call daily news.

Finally, it will be necessary to turn attention to the structure of the oral communication network. Until recently, it was a generally accepted stereotype that in the United States the communication of news and opinion is essentially a vertical process, i.e., that the ideas and opinions of the acknowledged leaders of a community filter "down" through the social structure and eventually reach the "poorest wage earner." More recent studies have shown that such a stereotype greatly oversimplifies and misrepresents the actual situation. On each level of the social structure, there are individuals who become, usually through the strength of their personalities rather than their status, leaders of opinion for other individuals on their own strata. While it is true that the communication process is, in part, vertical, its horizontal aspects cannot be overlooked. In many rural areas of the world, still relatively untouched by the mass media, it is often a person of relatively low station in the social structure who introduces news of the outside world to the local population. His monopoly on such news often places him in a leadership position in the local community in opposition to the local Sheik or Elder, the traditional moral and spiritual leader of the population. As more and more news of the outside world filters in, the traditional communication structure of such communities is likely to undergo a continuous change. The social processes involved in such change and their effect on the communications structure of the community need to be carefully scrutinized. It is in this area that the most difficult problems arise and where the combined efforts of scholars from several of the social sciences are most required.

OPINION, ITS NATURE AND ITS DETERMINATION BY NEWS

To gain an understanding of the ways in which opinions and attitudes on local, national, and international affairs are formed in different parts of the world, it is, of course, essential that we know how news is disseminated both by the mass media and informal channels. Answers to the kinds of questions which have thus far been raised will lay the groundwork for such understanding. However, it is evident that opinions are formed only in part on the basis of the form and content of communication. The way in which news is interpreted and the factors influencing interpretation have also to be considered.

To begin, the way in which "holding an opinion" is valued in a society is likely to influence whether or not the individual seeks out news, what news he seeks, and the way in which he interprets it. In this country, having opinions on public affairs is considered part of the "rights and duties" of a fully developed citizen. In countries which are closer to their own medieval past, opinions are likely to be much more a matter of loyalties. People may quite consciously accept the attitudes of their leaders or of the groups with which they live, as something they feel they should adhere to. Even in the United States, there are still many women who feel that holding opinions on public affairs is not becoming to a member of their sex. Among the Bedouins, opinions on matters outside the tribe are the concern of the tribal chieftain, and the opinion he forms on such matters has, until recently, been the basis for tribal consensus.

In some cases, the idea of holding opinions on public affairs as we think of them is a completely alien notion. Among orthodox Moslems a fatalistic viewpoint on life is still very strong. This is reflected in the narrow range of topics on which it is considered appropriate to have opinions. If there are many matters about which nothing can be done, it is not likely, so long as the traditional religious values hold, that the Western notion of opinion as a directive for action will develop. The Anatolian peasant, for example, traditionally has not been expected to have opinions, nor has he expected his opinions to make any difference, on very many issues and policies of public life. The changes brought about in this perspective, symbolized by the surprising election results of 1950, need to be investigated as part of the "communications revolution" initiated by Ataturk in 1924. In certain Far Eastern countries, inner directed contemplation plays a great role. A large number of daily events which are important to us might not seem deserving of any opinion as sharp caste differences exclude whole sectors of the population from an interest in public affairs.

When it comes to opinions on specifically international affairs, news, when it reaches people, is likely to be interpreted in terms of how they visualize the world outside of their own experience. Many people in pre-industrialized areas have great difficulty in understanding what they are told about the rest of the world. An illustrative case is the Turkish worker who lives in a one-room dwelling with two other families and suffers from the continuous quarrelling among them. He is horrified when he sees a movie of a New York skyscraper where a thousand families live. He visualizes all the fights and tragedies which develop among these families who have to "live together." There can be little doubt, too, that the Russian-American struggle is experienced in the most distorted form by millions of people all over the world. The concepts and phrases in which American writers and speakers discuss such matters might be most inappropriate in many places, because the typical images of the external world are different from those taken for granted among Americans.

One special aspect of this problem of the way people imagine life outside of their own is its effect on attitudes towards propaganda. There are indications that the countries which were defeated during the last war are very distrustful of all communications from abroad;

they have the kind of "propaganditis" which was prevalent in certain parts of this country as an aftermath of the First World War. On the other hand, the populations of countries which remained neutral, Sweden and Switzerland, for example, seem to look at international propaganda more as a source of useful information. They became accustomed, during the war, to get both sides of the news; and they have maintained the desire to continue to get both sides and to form their own picture of events. We would like to know to what extent the nationalistic awakening among former colonial peoples in the East has led to a general distrust of anything which comes from the "imperialist" West. In Egypt, there is some evidence to suggest that among intellectuals, news from America is viewed somewhat ambivalently. The traditional friendly viewpoint of America is tempered by the strong feelings of nationalism which have recently been given expression. This is reflected in a situation in which a desire to have news from America comes in conflict with a feeling that anything America has to say will threaten Egypt's nationalistic goals.

What needs to be studied, then, in the area of opinion formation is the different ways in which information about the world is absorbed into the lives of people living under varying social, political, and economic systems.

To systematically develop a comparative study of communications and opinion formation, such as we have postulated, an inter-disciplinary effort is essential. Anthropologists, sociologists, area experts, and public opinion specialists, among others, each have something to contribute to the fulfillment of such a program. In turn, however, a program of this kind is also likely to serve certain traditional interests of each of these disciplines.

Anthropologists concerned with acculturation have not systematically nor regularly included the character of the communications process in their methodological frame of reference. Herskovits and Hallowell, among others, have pointed out this deficiency and suggested the value of such inquiry towards developing an understanding of the process of acculturation. The program developed here may contribute to meeting this requirement if the interest of anthropologists in its development can be aroused.

Toennies' concept of "Gemeinschaft und Gessellschaft" formulated some 50 years ago continues to intrigue the sociologist and considerable intuitive thinking has gone into its development. Surprisingly little attention, however, has been given to tightening the concept through empirical research. Data drawn from a variety of societies on the process of opinion formation when properly analyzed, may help to fill this gap.

The function of comparative communications research for the area specialist is obvious and we need comment on it little here. The full comprehension of the life of peoples of another culture, to which end the area specialist is devoted, can scarcely be realized without appropriate attention being given to the process of communication and its influence on the patterning of values, modes of life, and ways of thinking.

Finally, for the public opinion specialist whose attention is increasingly being turned to the study of the role of the opinion leader in the process of opinion formation, data from other societies is essential for building a theoretical structure around which to formulate and test his hypotheses. At the same time, he will have much to contribute to the development of a methodology for studying this phenomenon under variable conditions.

▲ DANIEL LERNER

Effective Propaganda: Conditions and Evaluation

Goebbels once said: "Propaganda has no policy, it has a purpose." In this way the ingenious obscurantist emphasized that propaganda is the tool, not the master, of policy. A less cynical, more accurate way to make the point is this: Propaganda always has some policy. The policy probably will not be made by propagandists, and it probably will not remain forever the same. Since policy is the sequence of governing decisions in any body politic, it is likely to fluctuate through time as changing conditions alter issues and modify alternatives. Although its policy may shift, however, the purpose of propaganda remains constant: to serve that policy with maximum effectiveness.

The problem under discussion is how we can evaluate the effectiveness of propaganda activity in world politics. We state the view that reliable evaluation requires clarity on: (1) the nature of policy goals; (2) the function of propaganda, along with the other instruments of policy, in promoting these goals; (3) the conditions essential for effective propaganda; (4) the effects which propaganda can be designed to achieve; (5) the canons of evidence by which the actual achievement of these effects can be estimated. Under these five heads we review briefly some central problems in the evaluation of recent and current propaganda experience.

THE NATURE OF POLICY GOALS

Policy is a sequence of decisions governing the behavior of a person, group, nation, or world body politic. The policymakers of any community, however large or small, are those whose decisions enunciate

▲ This is a chapter from a volume edited by Dr. Lerner, *Propaganda in War and Crisis*. The book was published and copyright by George W. Stewart (New York, 1952), and is reprinted here by permission of the copyright holder. Dr. Lerner, formerly on the faculty of Stanford and Columbia Universities, is now a member of the staff of the international communication project at Massachusetts Institute of Technology.

the continuing goals, stakes, and rules-of-the-game which are observed by all members in good standing of the community. The scope of such decisions is conditioned by various characteristics of the particular body politic, notably the stability of its long-range goals; and by various characteristics of its environment, notably the threats and dangers to stability.

Long-range goals are affirmations of ultimate and mediate purposes of life in the body politic. As such, they are inevitably formulated in resonant symbols of ambiguous reference: liberty, equality, fraternity, peace, security, salvation, abundance, democracy, enlightenment, A World Commonwealth of Human Dignity. Ambiguity is inevitable because such words are historical in their origin and career. As the particular circumstances which generated them are modified through time, the contents of these symbols change. The task of policy is continually to respecify their operational meaning so that the vision of the future which these symbols embody may survive the changing needs and demands of present events. One policy function, then, is to maintain the stability of long-range goals by overcoming threats and dangers in the current environment.

Such threats and dangers may be internal to the community, e.g., the effort of a special group to seize disproportionate shares of the public power. Or it may be external, e.g., the attempt of a rival community to impose its own decisions by force. Faced with such threats and dangers, policymaking consists of choosing among the available alternatives those present actions most likely to enhance the long-range goals of the community.

THE PROPAGANDA FUNCTION

The actions among which policymakers must choose involve two different, but interrelated, kinds of activity: saying and doing. A fundamental fact which has been inadequately articulated is that talking *is* acting. Talking, indeed, is the way of acting which probably occupies the greatest part of our lives. Yet, "mere talk" is often deprecated by such phrases as "talk is cheap." In American society, particularly, "action" is equated with *doing* and is over-valued at the expense of talking. This preference, however, is more enlightening as part of the cultural folklore than as a description of typical American behavior. Here as elsewhere, the most effective action is that which integrates words and deeds to a common purpose.

In the arena of world politics, which directly concerns us here, policy uses four instruments to achieve its goals: propaganda, diplomacy, economics, war. These dominate, respectively, in strategies of persuasion, negotiation, bargaining, and coercion. Their respective vehicles are symbols, contracts, commodities, and violence.

Of the four, persuasion is undoubtedly the most pervasive mode of political intercourse. It is essential to the effective function of the others, in war as in peace. If the "party of the second part" is sufficiently persuaded by one's symbols, then the negotiation of diplomatic contracts becomes easier or unnecessary. Also, there is not much use applying economic sanctions unless you make clear why the other community is being deprived of commodities and what it can do to remove such semi-coercive measures. The same is true with even greater urgency when violence is employed, which explains why no war is fought without some declaration of "war aims" to clarify the conditions under which peaceful relations may be restored.

These remarks indicate the distinctive function of propaganda in the service of policy. The policy function, we have said, is to promote by present actions the attainment of goals in the future. War, economics, and even diplomacy serve this purpose by operations upon the material environment. The propaganda function is to advance policy goals by manipulating the symbolic environment. What people *believe* *about* the future shapes their responses to present events. And it is these beliefs about the future — the *structure of expectations* — which propaganda attempts to modify on behalf of policy goals.

SOME CONDITIONS OF EFFECTIVE PROPAGANDA

The manipulation of expectations is an instrument with powerful uses, but also with definite limits. The uses will be better served if the limits are clearly understood. The fundamental limitation is inherent in the instrument: its strategy is *persuasion* and its vehicle is *symbols*. Propaganda does not change *conditions* but only *beliefs about* conditions; it cannot force people to change their beliefs but can only persuade them to do so.

Under what conditions are people most likely to be persuaded by symbols to modify their expectations of the future, and consequently their behavior in the present? This question is in need of systematic investigation. Several main points are clear, however, from recent experience. We may summarize these lessons by stating four essential conditions of effective propaganda:

(1) The *attention* of the audience must be secured.

(2) The *credence* of the audience must be secured.

(3) The *predispositions* of the audience must include the modifications sought by propaganda as plausible alternatives to present expectations.

(4) The *environment* of the audience must permit the courses of action prescribed by the modified structure of expectations.

These conditions seem obvious upon statement. To persuade a man to do what you tell him, you must first get him to listen to you. Once you have his attention, you must get him to believe what you say if he is to take your message seriously. His credence gained, what you tell him to believe must be within the realm of his existing predispositional structure of expectations and aspirations. It is a waste of words to try to persuade a loyal citizen that he would rather see his nation lose a war than win it; no such alternative preference is possible within his predispositional set. But it may be quite possible to persuade the same man, once you have his attention and credence, to believe that the nation is going to lose a war.

Such a modification of expectations by propaganda may be facilitated by focussing attention on other existing aspirations in the audience, e.g., by pointing out that such long-range goals as world peace or national dignity will be better served by ending the war now in defeat than by prolonging it in vain efforts to achieve victory. On the other hand, policy may require propaganda to make no concessions to audience aspirations — e.g., unconditional surrender. Whether or not audience aspirations are invoked to help modify audience expectations constitutes a policy decision of great importance for the propagandist. What we wish to emphasize here, however, is that, whether audience aspirations are explicitly respected or implicitly rejected, predispositions define the limits within which audiences can be effectively persuaded to modify their expectations.

A fourth condition of effective propaganda is that the actions required of the audience by their modified expectations should be feasible in the environing circumstances which define for them the limits of meaningful behavior. It would make no sense, for example, to call on Soviet citizens in Vladivostok (even if we had persuaded them to believe that their present regime was headed for disaster and that their future happiness depended on its removal) to assassinate Stalin or imprison the Politburo. In the environment which limits their feasible alternatives of behavior, propaganda which called for such action would not be meaningful. Indeed, the impracticability of such action might lead to the utter rejection of our statements, otherwise plausible, because they impose obligations impossible to fulfill.

What types of action, then, *can* propaganda require of audiences whom it has persuaded?

TYPICAL AIMS OF PROPAGANDA

The aims of propaganda always include audience actions which alter the distribution of power in ways advantageous to the policy of the propagandist. Propaganda does aim, as most current writers claim, to "change attitudes" (modify expectations, in our terminology). But this is only the means by which propaganda gets to its ultimate aim of influencing behavior. It would be of small consequence, for example, that the Voice of America persuaded some Russians that Americans are peace-loving democracies rather than imperialistic warmongers, if this changed attitude (expectation about our future behavior) made no difference in the behavior of these Russians now or in the future.

It is important to recognize that the behavioral consequences of modified expectations need not appear immediately. Indeed some of the most important consequences of any attitude-alterations appear only in the longer-range future. Propaganda adjusts the timing of the behavioral consequences it seeks to the short-range or long-range aims of its policy goals.

What are some of these aims toward which propaganda is typically directed? Dr. Hans Speier has distinguished five "natural aims" of propaganda: (1) submission (2) subversion (3) cooperation (4) privatization (5) panic. His elaboration of these categories demonstrates their utility for clarifying the final aims of propaganda activity. They are valuable, too, for evaluating the effectiveness of a particular propaganda campaign when it is concluded.

For current evaluation of ongoing propaganda activity, other schema may be used. Take a simple example:

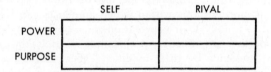

This fourfold table illustrates a usable framework for the evaluation of current propaganda, before sufficient time has elapsed for the types of overt action categorized by Dr. Speier to have occurred. Suppose the final aim is to secure the *submission* of certain groups within a rival power. Research has shown that there is no doubt of our power among this audience; what keeps them rivalrous is doubt of our purpose. The propaganda task is to persuade these groups that our purpose is virtuous *by their standards*. Evaluation of our propaganda must gauge the value of each item in terms of its effectiveness in strengthening this image of our moral purpose among the audience. This would call for continuous content analysis of both our propaganda output and of audience responses to that output, to indicate whether we are achieving the effects we desire. This is no substitute for the final payoff in action, but a way of continuously reminding ourselves of our goal and of checking whether our current activity is advancing us in the desired direction.

Conversely, suppose our final aim is to activate *subversion* against the rival regime among these groups within its population. The intelligence estimate is that expectations among the audience about *our* power and purpose are irrelevant to this aim. The relevant points are: that these groups are already persuaded that our rival's purpose is immoral, that their action is delayed only by their fears that the power of the rival regime is too great against their own means. (In such a situation, our policy may use other instruments besides propaganda, e.g., sanctions which deprive the rival regime of essential power-commodities while we increase the means of the subversive group.) The main propaganda aim in such a situation, however, would be to position the subversive group and the rival regime as Self: Other (removing the irrelevant propagandist power from the scene) ; and then to increase the confidence of the subversive group in its own power, relative to the regime, to the point where subversive action takes place. Such action, as Dr. Speier properly emphasizes, is the payoff in terms of which effectiveness must finally be evaluated. A campaign of this sort may take years, however, and some running measure of current effectiveness is needed during the long period before the payoff point is reached.

This simple schema can be refined and complicated as required to provide categories relevant to the content of our propaganda output and of audience effects. It is one among several that can be used to evaluate propaganda activity on a current basis. The point we wish to emphasize here is that evaluation of propaganda effects achieved requires, first, a framework which embodies a correct perspective on the effects desired. Next it requires rather strict canons of evidence by which to test the effects achieved. To illustrate the needs, we review briefly the methods used to evaluate on a current basis the effectiveness of Allied psychological warfare against the Germans in World War II (Sykewar).

TYPES OF EVIDENCE ON EFFECTS[1]

Four general types of evidence are usually adduced to show that propaganda has, or has not, been effective: (1) responsive action; (2) participant reports; (3) observer commentaries; (4) indirect indicators. All of these postulate, logically, that propaganda output and effects constitute a stimulus-response situation from which conclusions must be *inferred*. The four types of evidence named above are arranged, methodologically, in increasing remoteness from the concrete stimulus-response situation, i.e., in increasing length of the inference from propaganda stimulus to propaganda effect. Unfortunately, evidence usually grows more abundant as remoteness increases. This becomes clear as we briefly characterize each in turn.

(1) *Responsive action* is behavior which can more plausibly be attributed to propaganda stimuli than to any other stimuli in the environment. In the ideal case, a 1:1 ratio can be established: e.g.,

[1] This section is adapted from the author's book entitled *Sykewar: Psychological Warfare Against Germany, D-Day to VE-Day* (1949), pp. 289-301.

immediate surrender of German troops precisely as directed by a combat loudspeaker broadcast. More often, the inference from propaganda stimulus to audience response must cross a wider gap, but the crossing still can be made with confidence: e.g., Sykewar output directed Frankfurt citizens to hang white flags from their windows and thereafter American troops arrived to find many white flags hanging. Since these flags corresponded in detail with Sykewar instructions, and since no other source gave similar instructions, it could safely be inferred that this was direct responsive action.

Such evidence, though desirable, is rare. It requires, also, analysts trained to avoid two logical fallacies. We must avoid, first, the pitfall of assuming (*post hoc propter hoc*) that any action which conforms to the directive stimulus is a response, i.e., that an action is an effect simply because it happens after a stimulus. Second, the fallacy of displaced inference must be avoided: e.g., that Frankfurt residents hung out white flags as directed properly leads to an inference that *this particular response* was stimulated by a particular propaganda stimulus; it does not lead to any conclusion (except as one item in a distribution) that this or any other propaganda acts did or did not *change Frankfurt attitudes toward surrender*. There may have been *no* change in such attitudes — i.e., those who hung white flags in 1945 may have been ready to do so in 1940. Or, whatever change did occur may have been stimulated by other acts — i.e., bombing, rationing, news of a son's death on the eastern front. This second caution in evaluating the evidence of responsive action is particularly important because so much propaganda activity, especially of the sort called "strategic" (rather than "tactical"), aims at long-range behavioral effects attained by repetition, attrition, and the gradual modification of predispositions.

(2) *Participant reports* on propaganda effects by the persons stimulated constitute a less reliable kind of evidence than responsive action. No verbal report on one's own private responses can be quite as conclusive as observable action in the public domain. For, it is clear, a person's report on his internal behavior frequently — whether by mechanisms beyond his control or by design — misrepresents what actually went on inside. When such participant reports are treated as indexes they may be quite useful, as is shown by the study of trends in *Wehrmacht* morale.

The caution to be observed in handling such data, after their reliability has been established within reasonable limits of confidence, is that *indexes to* morale are *not identical with* morale. An inference is required, and the inference must account for relevant variables which determine whether a given "attitude" will in fact lead to a given "action." To illustrate with one index that was used by evaluators of both German and Japanese morale in the recent war: Diminished loyalty to the leader will be sufficient motivation for some soldiers to surrender; it will be necessary but not sufficient for others; for still others it will have little or no bearing on the readiness to surrender. The analyst must have the relevant variables isolated, and accounted for, when he undertakes to *infer* future actions (such as surrender) from present indexes (such as loyalty to the leader) in particular cases.

(3) *Observer commentaries,* though made by witnesses to the presumed stimulus-response situation, are notoriously treacherous. The stock illustration of danger inherent in such testimony is the case of the six witnesses to an automobile accident who, when asked to report what they had seen, gave six candid and circumstantial and confident — *and contrary* — versions of the event.

The tests applicable to data from observer commentaries are the reliability and heterogeneity of sources. Each source is tested separately for *reliability* — and approved when past information it supplied has regularly been accurate, disapproved when it has not. (Ideally in large intelligence operations, sources should be ranked on a calibrated scale of reliability, to enable all analysts to assign identical weightings and thus objectify "confidence.") All sources together are tested for *heterogeneity* — which is a function of their number, variety and independence. This test postulates that the probability of accuracy for any specific item reported increases with the *number* of *different* sources which *independently* report it as accurate.

(4) *Indirect indicators* are measures of effectiveness which are not at all involved in the particular stimulus-response situation being evaluated. Such a measure, for example, might be a high correlation between increasing size of audience to a propaganda source and increasing frequency of reference to this source among other audience channels of information. The analysis of audience communications is generally a fertile source of data on effectiveness, and particularly when such refined and precise techniques as Content Analysis are employed. Both the uses to be made of such data, and the cautions to be observed in gathering and analyzing them, are stated clearly in our study of German propaganda to France.

IN CONCLUSION

Propaganda is effective when it modifies audience behavior in ways advantageous to the policy it serves. Policy goals thus define one set of limits for propaganda activity — by postulating what is *desirable.* Another set of limits is defined by audience predispositions — which determine what is *possible.* Propaganda strategy manipulates the terrain bounded by these policy and audience considerations. The propagandist's maxim must be: Know thy goals: know thy conditions.

For the main conditions given the propagandist — i.e., that aspect of the current political situation with which he is most directly concerned

— are the predispositions of his audience. What we here call predispositions, psychologists at other times have called attitudes, instincts, motivations. The term used is less important than clarity about its operational meaning. Our point is that the propagandist works upon the identifications and expectations of the audience in order to modify their demands and deeds in desired directions. Whatever names one chooses, we must be clear that the propagandist is concerned with that part of man's psyche which controls his behavior.

The reason: to make a man *do* what he says, the propagandist must persuade that man to *believe* what he says. Belief is always, in some degree, a function of desire. Hence the propagandist is concerned with the desires of his audience and their possible modification. Effective propaganda consists in persuading the audience to *want to do* that which the propagandist wants them to do. For this, more than skilful chicanery is needed. Lincoln's aphorism is still relevant: you can't fool all of the people all of the time. Any long-run view of propaganda effectiveness postulates that audience desires must be understood and respected; often indeed, when they cannot be altered, these desires must be granted.

It is in such cases that the intelligence function serves policy. Properly conceived, intelligence is the continuous evaluation of the effectiveness with which our propaganda modifies conditions (including audience predispositions) in behalf of goals. Intelligence in this sense is indispensable to both policy and propaganda. Its findings should form the basis on which our formulation of goals and our propaganda strategy are continuously revised in the light of our knowledge of changing conditions. Not only audience predispositions, but also our own predispositions, are variables in the continuing process of world politics. Democratic wisdom begins with the recognition that policy can not do more — and should not do less — than the *most* of what is possible with the *least* sacrifice of what is desirable. Nothing less than this provides an adequate perspective for talking about propaganda effectiveness.

▲ ERNST KRIS

▲ NATHAN LEITES

Trends in Twentieth Century Propaganda

In speaking of propaganda, we refer to the political sphere and not to promotional activities in general. We define acts of propaganda, in agreement with H. D. Lasswell[1] as attempts to influence attitudes of large numbers of people on controversial issues of relevance to a group. Propaganda is thus distinguished from education which deals with non-controversial issues. Moreover, not all treatments of controversial issues of relevance to a group fall under the definition; they are not propaganda if they aim at the clarification of issues rather than at the changing of attitudes.

In the following, we deal mainly with propaganda by agents of government and exclusively with propaganda using the channels of mass communication, i.e., principally print, radio and film.

However, neither the potentialities of any one medium, nor the variety of promotional devices used by all will be discussed here. We are concerned with the place of propaganda in Western civilization. Our general hypothesis is that responses to political propaganda in the Western world have considerably changed during the last decades; and that these changes are related to trends in the sociopsychological conditions of life in the twentieth century.

We shall not be able to offer conclusive proof for the points we wish to make. We do not know of the existence of data comprehensive and reliable enough to demonstrate in quantitative terms broad hypotheses about changes in responses to propaganda. We start out from changes

[1] Lasswell, H. D. *Propaganda Techniques in the World War*, New York, Alfred A. Knopf, 1927. Smith, B. L., Lasswell, H. D. and Casey, R. D. *Propaganda, Communication, and Public Opinion*, Princeton Univ. Press, 1946.

▲ This paper appeared first in *Psychoanalysis and the Social Sciences*, volume I. It was published and copyright (New York, 1947) by the International Universities Press, by whose permission it is reprinted here.

in content and style of propaganda, assuming that they reflect the propagandist's expectation as to the response of his audience. The propagandist may be mistaken in his expectations, but finally he will be informed to some extent about his audiences' response, and adapt his output, within limit, to their predispositions.

We choose two situations in which propaganda was directed towards comparable objectives: the two World Wars.

Wartime propaganda is enacted in a situation with strictly limited goals. Under whatever conditions, the objective of propagandists in wartime is to maximize social participation among members of their own group and to minimize participation among members of the enemy group. Social participation is characterized by concern for the objectives of the group, the sharing of its activities, and the preparedness to accept deprivations on its behalf. High "participation" is therefore identical with high "morale." Its psychological dynamics are mutual identifications among group members, and identification of individual members with leaders or leading ideals of the group, strong cathexis of the goal set up by the group, and decreased cathexis of the self; processes that at least in part are preconscious and unconscious. Low participation may manifest itself in two ways: first, participation may be shifted partly or totally from one group to another. In this case, one may speak of a split in participation. Second, low participation may manifest itself as a withdrawal of individuals from the political sphere; in this case, we speak of privatization[2] (H. Speier and M. Otis).[3]

The psychological dynamics of a split in participation are obvious; one set of identifications and objectives has been replaced by another. The only dynamic change consists in the fact that, as a rule, the old group has not lost its cathexis, but has become the target of hostility.

The dynamics of privatization are more complex: withdrawal of cathexes from the group of its objectives leads to a process comparable to, but not identical with a narcissistic regression. Concern with the self becomes dominant. Since the striving for individual indulgence is maximized, the individual becomes exceedingly vulnerable to deprivation.

Modern warfare is distinguished from older types of warfare by the fact that it affects larger numbers of individuals. In total war "nations

[2] Two kinds of decreased participation in the direction of privatization can be distinguished: first, a decrease of active attitudes towards the political sphere, in favor of passive or merely adjusting attitudes; in this case, one must speak of a decrease of attitudinal participation; second, a decrease of the actual sharing in political action; in this case, one might speak of a decrease of behaviorial participation.

[3] Speier, H. and Otis, M. "German Radio Propaganda to France during the Battle of France," in *Radio Research,* 1942/43 eds. P. F. Lazarsfeld and F. N. Stanton, New York, Duell, Sloan & Pearce, 1944, pp. 208-247.

at arms" oppose each other with all their resources. Hence participation becomes increasingly important. To the extent that preparedness for war infringes upon life in peace, the problem continues to exist in peacetime.

Participation of whole nations was more essential during World War I than during any previous war; and yet it was somewhat less essential than during World War II; the first World War, especially at its onset, was "less total" than the second. On the other hand, the media of mass communication were less developed; radio and film had hardly been tested. Three areas of difference between the propagandas of the two wars seem particularly relevant in our context:

1. Propaganda during the second World War exhibited, on the whole, a higher degree of sobriety than propaganda during World War I; the incidence of highly emotionalized terms was probably lower.

2. Propaganda during the second World War was, on the whole, less moralistic than propaganda during the first World War; the incidence of preference statements as against fact statements was probably lower.

3. Propaganda during the second World War tended to put a moderate ceiling on grosser divergences from presently or subsequently ascertainable facts, divergences that were more frequent in propaganda during the first World War. Also, propaganda during the second World War tended to give fuller information about relevant events than propaganda during World War I.

In summarizing the psychological aspects of these differences, we might say that propaganda appeals were less frequently directed to id and superego, more prominently to the ego.

In this respect, these areas of difference are representative of others. At least two qualifications to the points mentioned above are essential: first, most of the differences we stress became ever clearer the longer the second World War lasted; second, they were more accentuated in the propaganda of the Western democracies than in that of Germany and Russia.[4]

The use of emotionalized language was, at the outset of World War II, almost completely absent in British propaganda. When, in the autumn of 1939, Mr. Churchill, then First Lord of the Admiralty, referred to the Nazis as "Huns," thus using the stereotype current during World War I, he was publicly rebuked. Basically, that attitude persisted throughout the war in Britain and the United States. "We don't want to be driven into hate" was the tenor of opinion. There were modifications of this attitude: in the United States in regard to Japan, in Britain after the severe onslaught of bombing. However, hate campaigns remained largely unacceptable. In Germany, a similar attitude persisted: attempts of German propaganda to brandish the bombing of German cities by British and later by American

---

[4] In the following, we shall in the main limit ourselves to examples from American, British and German propaganda, and some data on response; information on reactions of Russian and Japanese audiences is not accessible.

planes as barbarism, to speak of the crews of these planes as "night pirates" and of German raids against Britain as retaliatory largely failed to arouse indignant hate.

The waning power of *moral* argumentation in propaganda is best illustrated by the fact that one of the predominant themes of propaganda during World War I played no comparable part in World War II. The theme "Our cause is right; theirs is wrong" was secondary in the propaganda of the Western powers; its part in German propaganda was limited; only in Russian propaganda was its role presumably comparable to that it had played in World War I propaganda. In the democratic countries and in Germany, the moral argumentation was replaced by one in terms of indulgence and deprivation (profit or loss): "We are winning; they are losing"; and: "These will be the blessings of victory; these the calamities of defeat." There is evidence indicating that both in the democracies and in Germany this type of appeal was eminently successful. In other words: success of propaganda was dependent on the transformation of superego appeals into appeals to the ego.[5]

The third area of difference, the increased concern for some agreement between the content of propaganda and ascertainable facts, and the increased concern for detailed information was to some considerable extent related to technological change. Thus, during the first World War, the German people were never explicitly (and implicitly only much later) informed about the German defeat in the battle of the Marne in September 1914. A similar reticence during the second World War would not have proved expedient, since in spite of coercive measures, allied radio transmissions were widely listened to by Germans. However, technological progress was not the only reason for the change. The concern with credibility had increased, independently of the technology of communication. The tendency to check statements of one's own against those of enemy governments, existed both in Germany and in the democracies; while it was limited in Germany, it was widely spread in Britain and the United States.

The differences of propaganda during World Wars I and II are epitomized in the treatment of a theme related to all three areas discussed — enemy atrocities. As far as we know, only Russian propaganda on German atrocities, and German propaganda on Russian atrocities gave to this theme about the same importance in World War II that all propagandists had given it during World War I. But German reports on allied atrocities were rather timid, if compared to the inventiveness of German propaganda in other areas; and German propaganda about Soviet atrocities was largely designed to create fear and defensive combativeness rather than hate and indignation. In the democracies, however, the "playing down" of reports on enemy atrocities was a guiding principle of propaganda, at least until 1945. While during World War I, allied propagandists did not refrain from

[5] Masserman, J. H. *Principles of Dynamic Psychiatry*, Philadelphia, W. B. Saunders, 1946. He makes a similar point (p. 219). He speaks of "resonance with personal incentives."

exaggerating and even inventing atrocities, uncontestable evidence of enemy atrocities was, for a long time, withheld during World War II. It is needless to say that the atrocities to which this documentation referred and which, at the end of the war and after the war became manifest to the soldiers of armies traversing Europe, were of a kind totally different in horror from anything the world of the earlier twentieth century had known. The purposeful reticence of the democratic governments becomes thereby even more significant.

No adequate understanding of these propaganda trends is possible, unless we take two closely related trends in the predispositions of the public into account. Our thesis is that the differences between the propaganda styles during both World Wars are largely due to the rising tendencies towards *distrust* and *privatization* — tendencies that we believe to have existed in the Western democracies as well as in Germany.

Distrust is directed primarily against the propagandist and the authority he represents, secondarily also against the "suggestibility" of the "propagandee."[6]

The first mentioned manifestation of distrust can be traced back to the last war. Propaganda operated then on a new level of technological perfection; the latent possibilities of the mass communication media became suddenly manifest; in all belligerent countries, outbursts of enthusiasm for war occurred. Propagandists, like children playing with a new toy, charged their messages with many manufactured contents. After the war, they reported on their own achievements — sometimes exaggerating the extent to which they had distorted events. These reports helped to create the aura of secret power that ever since has surrounded propagandists. In Britain and the United States, some of this prestige was transferred from the propagandist to the public relations counsel; some of the men who had successfully worked in government agencies became pioneers of modern advertising. Beliefs in the power of propaganda led to a phobia of political persuasion: propaganda became "a bad name," an influence against which the common man had to guard himself.

The political and economic failures of the postwar era, the futility of the idealistic appeals which had helped to conclude the first World War, reinforced this distrust. Its spread and influence on the political scene, however, was sharply different in different areas. In Germany, the distrust of propaganda was manipulated by the nationalist, and later, the national-socialist movement. Propaganda was identified with those allied propaganda efforts that had accompanied German defeat.[7] While distrust was directed against one side, nationalist and national-socialist propaganda could operate more

[6] Kris, E. "The Danger of Propaganda," *American Imago*, 2, 1941, pp. 1-42. Kris, E. "Some Problems of War Propaganda." A Note on Propaganda, Old and New, *Psychoanalytic Quarterly*, 2, 1943, pp. 381-99.

[7] For the question of the actual contribution of propaganda to this defeat and generally for the question of the limited influence of propaganda on warfare, see Kris, E., Speier, H. and Associates, *German Radio Propaganda,* New York, Oxford Univ. Press, 1944.

freely under the guise of anti-propaganda. In the Western democracies, the propaganda phobia rose during the Great Depression. It became a lasting attitude both in the United States and possibly to a lesser degree, in the United Kingdom; and it took years of experience to discover a propaganda style that would at least not provoke distrust. While the disdain of propaganda had been initiated by the upper strata, it was during the second World War more intense with lower socio-economic groups.

At this point, it becomes essential to supplement our analysis of the distrust of propaganda by a discussion of contemporary privatization tendencies. Many motivations contribute to such tendencies. Some of them are not taken up here.[8]

Individuals in the mass societies of the twentieth century are to an ever increasing extent involved in public affairs; it becomes increasingly difficult to ignore them. But "ordinary" individuals have ever less the feeling that they can *understand* or *influence* the very events upon which their life and happiness is known to depend.[9] At the same time, leaders in both totalitarian and democratic societies claim that decisions ultimately rest upon the common man's consent, and that the information supplied to him fully enables him to evaluate the situation. The contrast between these claims and the common man's experience extends to many areas. Thus in economic life ever more depends upon state interference. But, on the other hand, people increasingly regard economic policy as a province in which the professional specialist is paramount and the common man incompetent. The increasing "statification" of economic life has been accompanied by a rising mass reputation of scientific economics as a specialty. The emotional charges of simple economic formulae such as "free enterprise" or "socialization of the means of production" seem to have decreased (one might speak, at least in certain areas, of the silent breakdown of "capitalism" and "socialism" as ideologies). While the economic specialist is to fulfill the most urgent demand of the common man, that for security of employment, the distance between him and his beneficiary grows; he becomes part of a powerful elite, upon which the common man looks with a distrust rooted in dependency.

This is but one instance of the experience of disparity — of insight as well as power — between the common man and the various political organizations into which he is integrated. That disparity counteracts the feeling of power which accompanies the manipulation of increasingly effective machinery, whether of production or destruction: the common man is usually acutely aware of the fact that the "button" he is "pushing" belongs to an apparatus far out of the reach of any unorganized individual.

This feeling of disparity greatly affects the common man's attitude to foreign policy. The potential proximity of total war produces situations that not only seem inherently incomprehensible, but that he, the common man, feels cannot be made comprehensible to him by his government. "Security

---

[8] For instance, we do not propose to discuss how privatization is related to changes in values.

[9] Mannheim, K. *Man and Society in an Age of Transition,* K. Paul, Trench, Trubner & Co., London, 1940. Kecskemeti, P. and Leites, N. *Some Psychological Hypotheses on Nazi Germany,* Washington, D.C. Library of Congress, 1945 (multigraphed).

considerations," he infers, are the reason why the "real dope" is kept away from him. Thus the distance between the common man and the policy maker has grown to such an extent that awe and distrust support each other. The common man feels impotent in a world where specialized skills control events that at any moment may transform his life. That feeling of impotence bestows upon political facts something of the solidity of natural events, like weather or hurricane, that come and go. Two attitudes result from this feeling: First, one does not inquire into the causation of the events thus viewed; second, one does not inquire into their morality.[10]

The feeling that politics as such is outside the reach of morals is an extreme form of this attitude. Probably moral indignation as a reaction to political events has been declining since the turn of the century. One may compare the intense reactions to injustice against individuals under comparatively stable social conditions — the Dreyfus affair, the cases of Ferrer, Nurse Cavell, Sacco and Vanzetti — with the limited reactions to Nazi terror and extermination practices as they gradually became notorious. In the case of the Nazis, public reaction went through a sequence of frank disbelief, reserved doubt, short lived shock and subsequent indifference.

The psychological dynamics operating the interplay of distrust and privatization can now be formulated more sharply. We here distinguish in the continuum of distrustful attitudes, two cases: One we call critical distrust; the other projective distrust.[11] In the child's development, the former arose not independently from the latter. Critical distrust facilitates adjustment to reality and independence; it is at the foundation of scientific thought, and is an essential incentive in the battle against what Freud called the prohibition of thinking in the individual. Critical distrust has gained a decisive importance in modern society, since technology has played havoc with many kinds of magic. Projective distrust, on the other hand, is derived ultimately from ambivalence; it is an expression of hostility, in which aggressive tendencies against others, frequently against authority, are perceived as tendencies of others, frequently as attitudes of authority.

We allude to these complex questions only in order to round off our argumentation: in the world of the twentieth century, the exercise of critical distrust by the common man meets with many obstacles; it is at the same time increasingly stimulated and increasingly frustrated. He therefore regressively turns to projective distrust: He fears, suspects and hates what he cannot understand and master.

Privatization is, amongst other things, a result of the hostility be-

[10] American soldiers during the second World War were frequently explicitly opposed to discussions of its causation: going into its pre-history was frequently regarded as futile and somewhat "out of this world."
[11] We do not propose here to discuss in detail their genetic interrelation, nor their pathological manifestations, especially in obsessional neuroses and paranoid syndromes. (See H. Deutsch's classical expositions. "Zur Psychologie des Misstrauens," *Imago*, 7, 1921, pp. 71-83.) A fuller treatment would also have to consider the question of retaliatory and self-punitive distrust.

tween the individual and the leadership of the group: We mentioned that it is comparable to what is known as a narcissistic regression. In order to maintain this attitude in which self-interest predominates over group interest — the self in this case may include "primary" groups such as the family — projective distrust is set into operation. Scepticism becomes the guarantor of privatization: scepticism here acts as a defense. If the individual, for instance, were to accept available evidence on atrocities, his emotional involvement in politics might rise; he might hate or experience enthusiasm. Thus privatization could not be maintained. The propagandist's concern in wartime is therefore to reduce such scepticism.

That concern, we said, was more clearly expressed in the democracies than in Germany or Russia. In order fully to understand this difference, we turn to a more detailed discussion of the relationship between propagandist and "propagandee." Every propaganda act occurs in such a relationship; in the case of propaganda by agents of governments, it is the relationship between the individual and his government.

We discuss this relationship in regard to two types of political organization: the totalitarian state with the charismatic leader and democracy. In both cases, the propagandists speak for the leaders, who are the chief propagandists. In both cases, propaganda presupposes, and attempts to strengthen identifications of the propagandees with the propagandists. These identifications, however, have a different characer under the two regimes.

In a totalitarian state these identifications concern, to a large extent, id and superego functions. These identifications facilitate the gratifying completion of impulses, as superego functions have been projected upon the propagandist, and as he is idealized in an archaic sense: omnipotence, ominscience and infallibility are attributed to him.

In democratic states, the corresponding identifications concern, to a large extent, ego functions which are delegated to the propagandist. Amongst these functions, the scrutiny of the existing situation and the anticipation of the future are of predominant importance. While the propagandee relies upon the propagandist for the fulfillment of these functions, he retains a critical attitude in relation to him.

Superego and ego identifications, of course, constantly interact. The distribution of their intensities, however, is clearly dependent upon the institutionalized relationship between propagandist and propagandee. In this sense, we may say that the one is typical of totalitarian, the other of democratic propaganda relations.

That difference is reflected in the devices of propaganda. Totalitarian propaganda tries to sway the audience into participation; its preferred setting is the visible leader talking to the masses; it is modeled after the relations between the hypnotist and his medium. Democratic propaganda gives weight to insight as basis for participation; it is to a greater extent modeled after the principles of guidance or education.

The nature of the two propaganda situations accounts for the fact that for each of the two kinds of propagandists different goals are difficult to reach. The totalitarian propagandist finds it arduous to stimulate initiative among his followers. When German propaganda was faced with the task of stimulating cooperative action "from below" among the citizens of bombed towns, that difficulty became apparent: the devices then adopted were plain imitations of the techniques of British propagandists in a similar situation. Democratic propagandists meet a comparable difficulty when faced with the task of manifestly denying information on reasons for government action, that is, of demanding implicit trust for a limited time. The impasse in which allied leadership found itself when faced with a public demand for the opening of a second front, especially in 1943, is an example.

The two types of propagandists react to the impact of distrust and privatization in different ways; these tendencies show a different incidence under the two political orders. In a totalitarian state, privatization grows with deprivation. Then the latent cleavage of the totalitarian state becomes manifest, the cleavage between the faithful, from whose ranks elite and sub-elite are recruited, and the indifferent, who are controlled by the faithful. Their mounting privatization renders this control more difficult. Superego identifications cease to function with ever more individuals, and finally they function only with the fanatics. When that situation crystallized in Germany with the approach of defeat, two devices were adopted: First, a gradual revision of propaganda policy. Appeals to superego identifications became less and less important and increased weight was given to the stimulation of fear; ego interests should now motivate continued allegiance. But this did not prevent further privatization. Thus the central method of all totalitarian social control was applied ever more consistently: violence. In its last phases, Nazi propaganda hardly fulfilled the purpose of gaining participation in the present; building the Nazi myth, it addressed its appeals to future generations.

Democratic propaganda is better equipped to deal with the tendency towards privatization, since it puts greater emphasis on the creation of insight. Its appeals are better in tune with a high level of distrust. In totalitarian regimes, there is a polarization between the politicized and the privatized, which is, however, difficult to perceive from the outside. In democratic states, tendencies towards privatization are clearly perceptible but their distribution within the society is less clear cut.

There are periods when this tendency decreases: in America after Pearl Harbor, in Britain after May 1940. While enthusiasm was kept at a low level, determination prevailed and sacrifice was willingly sustained.

What was the part of the propagandist in such situations? It may be illustrated by turning to one specific situation, in which democratic propaganda reached its greatest success.

We refer to Churchill's propaganda feat during the spring of 1940. The series of speeches he made in May, June and July of 1940 are remembered for the singular depth of feeling and the heroic quality of language. But these qualities were only accessories to the major political impact of these speeches. Their function was a threefold one — to warn Britain of the danger, to clarify its extent, and to indicate how everyone could help to meet it. In order to illustrate this point, we refer to one topic only: the announcement of the Battle of Britain.

The first intimation was made on May 12th, three days after Churchill's appointment, when the Battle of Flanders had not yet reached its climax. After having described the battles on all fronts, Churchill added that "many preparations had to be made at home." On May 19th, after the surrender of Holland, and during the climax of the Belgian battles, he devoted well over one-third of his speech to announcing "that after this . . . there will come the battle for our island." And after demanding full mobilization of production, he gave for the first time the "box score": he reported that the R.A.F. had been downing three to four enemy planes for each of their own. This, he inferred, was the basis of any hope. On June 4th, in his famous speech after Dunkirk, the theme was taken up anew and an elaborate account of the chances of the fighter force in a battle over the homeland was given. Churchill went into technical details; at a time when France seemed still vigorously to resist, he acquainted the British people with the chances of their survival. While the enemy had broken through the allied front with a few thousand armored vehicles, he forecast the future by saying: "May it not also be that the course of civilization itself will be defended by the skill and devotion of a few thousand airmen." And while he discussed the necessity of ever increasing production, he spoke at this time of imminent defeat of "the great British armies of the later years of war."

In the later speeches of that unforgettable spring, he elaborated on the subject. Every one could understand how his own behavior was related to the total situation, and how this situation was structured; how supplies were needed for the repair and construction of fighter planes, and how in this matter every detail, even the smallest one, could contribute to the final result. All this information was released well in advance of any German attack.

Thus Churchill had not only given the "warning signal" and mobilized "emergency reactions." His detailed analysis of the situation also contributed to the prevention of an inexpediently large and rapid increase in anxiety: unknown danger was transformed into a danger known in kind and extent. He fulfilled those functions of leadership that can be compared to those fulfilled in the life of the individual by the organization of the ego.[12] At the same time, Churchill offered his own courage as a model: "If you behave as I do, you will behave right." He not only spoke of Britain's "finest hour" but was careful to add that in this hour "every man and woman had their chance."

The propagandist thus seems to fulfill a double function: first that of structuring the situation so that it can be anticipated and understood, and second, that of offering himself as a model.

It is essential to understand the difference between the democratic leader who functions as a model and the charismatic leader.[13] The latter offers himself as an object that replaces superego functions in the individual. The model function of leadership implies that in identifying with the leader, the individual will best serve the ideals he shares with him. But the understanding of the situation is a precondition for such moral participation.

The general problem which we here finally approach concerns the relation between ego and superego functions. One might tentatively formulate the hypothesis that in a situation in which the ego functions smoothly, the tension between ego and superego is apt to be low. In fact, we find in the study of superego formation in the child some evidence in support of such a formulation.[14] However, other evidence is contradictory. Frequently, successful ego performance is accompanied by intense conflicts between ego and superego. We therefore reject this formulation and substitute another: unsuccessful ego functions endanger the positive relationship between ego and superego. They tend to encourage regressive trends. Individuals who feel impotent in the face of a world they do not understand, and are distrustful of those who should act as their guides, tend to revert to patterns of behavior known from childhood, in which an increase of hostility against the adults and many neurotic or delinquent mechanisms may develop. The incidence of such maladjustments may increase in a society in which privatization tendencies have become dominant.[15]

Little can be said here about what conclusions can be drawn for the

[12] Kris, E. "Danger and Morale," *American Journal of Orthopsychiatry*, 14, 1944, pp. 147-155.

[13] Redl, F. "Group Education and Leadership," *Psychiatry*, 5, 1942, pp. 573-596.

[14] Friedlander, K. "Formation of the Antisocial Character," *The Psycho-Analytic Study of the Child*, New York, International Universities Press, I, 1945, pp. 189-204.

[15] We here note that the traditional discussion of the applicability of "individual" psychological hypotheses to "social" events lacks substance, since events dealt with in the empirical analysis of human affairs, "psychological" or "sociological," occur in individuals. We deal with frequencies of incidence.

future of democratic propaganda from these considerations. They clearly point to the desirability of sharp and wide increases of insight into events in the world at large among the citizens. Briefly, the trend towards distrust and privatization among the audience of the propagandist should be turned into a trend towards increase of insight. That trend would find a parallel in changes of related techniques: psychotherapy and education, largely under the influence of psychoanalysis, have substituted or are substituting insight for pressure. If the appropriate education, on a vast enough scale and at a rapid enough rate is not provided for, the distrust and privatization of the masses may become a fertile soil for totalitarian management.

▲ EDWARD A. SHILS

▲ MORRIS JANOWITZ

Cohesion and Disintegration in the Wehrmacht

in World War II

Strategic Aspects of the War

For the mass of the German Army, the strategic phases of the war were viewed apathetically. The ignorance of the German troops about important military events, even on their own front, was partly a result of the poverty of information about the actual course of the war — itself a part of Nazi policy.[1] But the deliberate management of ignorance need not always result in such far-reaching indifference as the German soldiers showed. Deliberately maintained ignorance would have resulted in a flood of rumors, had the German soldiers been more eager to know about the strategic phases of the war. As it was, there were very few rumors on the subject — merely apathy. Three weeks after the fall of the city of Aachen, there were still many prisoners being taken in the adjoining area who did not know that the city had fallen. For at least a week after the beginning of von Rundstedt's counter-offensive, most of the troops on the northern hinge of the bulge did not know that the offensive was taking place and were not much interested when they were told after capture. Of 140 Ps/W taken between December 23-24, 1944, only 35 per cent had heard of the counter-offensive and only 7 per cent said that they thought it significant.[2]

[1] Nazi propagandists, with their hyperpolitical orientation, tended to overestimate the German soldier's responsiveness to politics.

[2] The fact that the High Command made no attempt to explain away the defeat of the counter-offensive may have been due, among other things, to its conviction of the irrelevance of strategic consideration in the morale of the ordinary soldier.

▲ This article first appeared in the *Public Opinion Quarterly*, in 1948. Copyright by the Princeton University Press, it is here reprinted by permission of the copyright holder. Dr. Shils is on the faculty of the University of Chicago, Dr. Janowitz on the faculty of the University of Michigan.

Some exception to this extensive strategic indifference existed with respect to the Eastern front. Although the German soldiers were extremely ignorant of the state of affairs on that front and made little attempt to reduce their ignorance, still the question of Russians was so emotionally charged, so much the source of anxiety, that it is quite likely that fear of the Russians did play a role in strengthening resistance. National Socialist propaganda had long worked on the traditional repugnance and fear of the German towards the Russian. The experience of the German soldiers in Russia in 1941 and 1942 increased this repugnance by direct perception of the primitive life of the Russian villager. But probably more important was the projection onto the Russians of the guilt feelings generated by the ruthless brutality of the Germans in Russia during the occupation period. The shudder of horror which frequently accompanied a German soldier's remarks about Russia was a result of all these factors. These attitudes influenced German resistance in the West through the shift of soldiers from East to West and the consequent diffusion of their attitudes among their comrades. They also took effect by making soldiers worry about what would happen to their families if the Russians entered Germany. Of course, it should also be mentioned that this fear of the Russians also made some German soldiers welcome a speedier collapse on the Western front in the hope that a larger part of Germany would fall under Anglo-American control.

Before the actual occupation, only a small minority expressed fear of the consequences of an Anglo-American occupation. The continuing monthly opinion poll conducted by the Psychological Warfare Branch, mentioned elsewhere, never showed more than 20 per cent of the prisoners answering "yes" to the question, "Do you believe that revenge will be taken against the population after the war?" Those who feared retribution were confirmed Nazis. Yet the general absence of fear of revenge did not cause a diminution of German resistance.

Neither did expectations about the outcome of the war play a great role in the integration or disintegration of the German Army. The statistics regarding German soldier opinion cited below show that pessimism as to final triumph was quite compatible with excellence in fighting behavior. The far greater effectiveness of considerations of self-preservation, and their vast preponderance over interest in the outcome of the war and the strategic situation, is shown by German prisoner recall of the contents of Allied propaganda leaflets (see Table I). In the last two months of 1944 and the first two months of 1945, not less than 59 per cent of the sample of prisoners taken each month recalled references to the preservation of the individual, and the figure rose to 76 per cent in February of 1945. On the other hand, the proportion of prisoners recalling references to the total strategic situation of the war and the prospect of the outcome of the war

TABLE I

Tabulation of Allied Leaflet Propaganda Themes Remembered by
German Ps/W

	Dec. 15-31 1944	*Jan. 1-15 1945*	*Jan. 15-31 1945*	*Feb. 1-15 1945*
Number of Ps/W	60	83	99	135
Themes and appeals remembered:				
a. Promise of good treatment as Ps/W and self-preservation through surrender	63%	65%	59%	76%
b. Military news	15	17	19	30
c. Strategical hopelessness of Germany's position	13	12	25	26
d. Hopelessness of a local tactical situation	3	1	7	7
e. Political attacks on German leaders	7	5	4	8
f. Bombing of German cities	2	8	6	...
g. Allied Military Government	7	3	..	...
h. Appeals to civilians	5	4	2	...

(The percentages add up to more than 100% since some Ps/W remembered
more than one topic. Only Ps/W remembering at least one theme were included in this tabulation.)

seldom amounted to more than 20 per cent, while references to political subjects seldom amounted to more than 10 per cent. The general tendency was not to think about the outcome of the war unless
forced to do so by direct interrogation. Even pessimism was counter-
balanced by the reassurances provided by identification with a strong
and benevolent Führer, by identification with good officers, and by
the psychological support of a closely integrated primary group.

The Ethics of War and Patriotism

Quite consistently, ethical aspects of the war did not trouble the
German soldier much. When pressed by Allied interrogators, Ps/W
said that Germany had been forced to fight for its life. There were
very few German soldiers who said that Germany had been morally
wrong to attack Poland, or Russia. Most of them thought that if anything had been wrong about the war, it was largely in the realm of
technical decisions. The decision to extirpate the Jews had been too
drastic not because of its immorality but because it united the world
against Germany. The declaration of war against the Soviet Union
was wrong only because it created a two-front war. But these were
all arguments which had to be forced from the Ps/W. Left to themselves, they seldom mentioned them.

The assumption underlying these arguments was that the strong national state is a good in itself. But it was not, in fact, the highest good for any but the "hard core." In September 1944, for example, only 5 per cent of a sample of 634 Ps/W said that they were worried about anything other than personal or familial problems, while in the very same survey, more than half of the Ps/W said they believed that Germany was losing the war or that they were at best uncertain of the war's outcome. In brief, fear for Germany's future as a nation does not seem to have been very important in the ordinary soldier's outlook and in motivating his combat behavior. As a matter of fact, as the war became more and more patently a threat to the persistence of the German national state, the narcissism of the German soldier increased correspondingly, so that the idea of national survival did not become an object of widespread preoccupation even when it might have been expected to become so.[3]

Ethical-religious scruples seem to have played an equally small role. Although there were a few interesting cases of Roman Catholic deserters, Roman Catholics (except Austrians, Czechs and Polish nationals) do not seem to have deserted disproportionately. Prisoners seldom expressed remorse for Nazi atrocities, and practically no case was noted of a desertion because of moral repugnance against Nazi atrocities.

Political Ideals

The significance of political ideals, of symbols of political systems, was rather pronounced in the case of the "hard core" minority of fervent Nazis in the German Army. Their desire for discipline under a strong leader made them enthusiasts for the totalitarian political system. Their passionate aggressiveness also promoted projective tendencies which facilitated their acceptance of the Nazi picture of an innocent and harmless Germany encircled by the dark, threatening cloud of Bolsheviks, Jews, Negroes, etc., and perpetually in danger from inner enemies as well. But for most of the German soldiers, the political system of National Socialism was of little interest.

The *system* was indeed of very slight concern to German civilians also, even though dissatisfaction increased to a high pitch towards the end of the war. Soldiers on the whole were out of touch with the operation of the Party on the home front. Hence the political system impinged little on their consciousness. Thus, for example, of 53 potential and actual deserters in the Mediterranean theater, only one

---

[3] The proposition often asserted during the war that the Allies' refusal to promise a "soft peace" to the Germans was prolonging the war, i.e., that German military resistance was motivated by fear of what the Allies would do to Germany in event of its defeat, scarcely finds support in the fact that in October 1944, when the German front was stiffening, 74 per cent of a sample of 345 Ps/W said they did not expect revenge to be taken against the German population after the war.

alleged political grounds for his action. The irrelevance of party politics to effective soldiering has already been treated above: here we need only repeat the statement of a German soldier, "Nazism begins ten miles behind the front line."

Nor did the soldiers react in any noticeable way to the various attempts to Nazify the army. When the Nazi Party salute was introduced in 1944, it was accepted as just one more army order, about equal in significance to an order requiring the carrying of gas masks. The introduction of the *National Socialistische Führungsoffiziere* (Guidance, or Indoctrination Officer), usually known as the NSFO, was regarded apathetically or as a joke. The contempt for the NSFO was derived not from his Nazi connection but from his status as an "outsider" who was not a real soldier. The especially Nazified Waffen SS divisions were never the object of hostility on the part of the ordinary soldier, even when the responsibility for atrocities was attributed to them. On the contrary, the Waffen SS was highly esteemed, not as a Nazi formation, but for its excellent fighting capacity. Wehrmacht soldiers always felt safer when there was a Waffen SS unit on their flank.

Devotion to Hitler

In contrast to the utterly apolitical attitude of the German infantry soldier towards almost all secondary symbols, an intense and personal devotion to Adolph Hitler was maintained in the German Army throughout the war. There could be little doubt that a high degree of identification with the Führer was an important factor in prolonging German resistance. Despite fluctuations in expectations as to the outcome of the war the trust in Hitler remained at a very high level even after the beginning of the serious reverses in France and Germany. In monthly opinion polls of German Ps/W opinion from D-Day until January 1945, in all but two samples over 60 per cent expressed confidence in Hitler,[4] and confidence in January was nearly as high as it was in the preceding June. During this same period considerably more than half of the German soldiers in seven out of eight polls said they believed that it was impossible for the German Army to defeat the Allies in France. Only when the German Army began to break up in the face of overwhelming Allied fire power and deep, communications-cutting penetrations, did confidence in Hitler fall to the unprecedentedly low level of 30 per cent. Even when defeatism was rising to the point at which only one-tenth of the prisoners taken as of March 1945 believed that the Germans had any chance of success, still a third retained confidence in Hitler.[5]

[4] See Gurfein, M. I., and Janowitz, Morris, "Trends in Wehrmacht Morale," *The Public Opinion Quarterly*, Vol. 10, No. 1 (1946), p. 78.

[5] Much of the reduction of trust in Hitler which occurred in this final period was simply a diminution in esteem for Hitler's technical skill as a strategist and as a diplomat.

Belief in the good intentions of the Führer, in his eminent moral qualities, in his devotion and contributions to the well-being of the German people, continued on an even higher level. This strong attachment grew in large part from the feeling of strength and protection which the German soldier got from his conception of the Führer personality.

For older men, who had lived through the unemployment of the closing years of the Weimar Republic and who experienced the joy of being reinstated in gainful employment by Nazi full-employment policies, Hitler was above all the man who had provided economic security. This attitude extended even to left wing soldiers of this generation, who denounced the National Socialist political system, but found occasion to say a good word for Hitler as a man who had restored order and work in Germany. For men of the generation between 22-35, who had first experienced Hitler's charisma in the struggles to establish their manliness during late adolescence, Hitler was the prototype of strength and masculinity. For the younger Nazi fanatics, he was a father substitute, providing the vigilant discipline and the repression of dangerous impulses both in the individual and in the social environment; for them he had the additional merit of legitimating revolt against the family and traditional restraints.

Prisoners spoke of Hitler with enthusiasm, and even those who expressed regret over the difficulties which his policies had brought on Germany by engendering a two-front war and by allowing the Jews to be persecuted so fiercely as to arouse world hatred — even these men retained their warm esteem for his good intentions. They found it necessary to exculpate him in some way by attributing his errors to dishonest advisors who kept the truth from him, or to certain technical difficulties in his strategic doctrines which did not in any way reflect on his fundamental moral greatness or nobility.

It was difficult for German soldiers, as long as they had this attitude toward Hitler, to rebel mentally against the war. Time after time, prisoners who were asked why Hitler continued the war when they themselves admitted it was so obviously lost, said he wouldn't continue the war and waste lives if he did not have a good, even though undisclosed, strategic reason for doing so, or if he didn't have the resources to realize his ends. Nazis as well as non-Nazis answered in this way. Or else they would say, "the Führer has never deceived us," or, "he must have a good reason for doing what he does."

There was obviously a fear of rendering an independent judgment of events among the German soldiers and a desire for some strong leader to assume the responsibility for determining their fate. American and British soldiers often complained that the complexity of the army organization and strategy was so great and their own particular part was so small that they could not see the role of their personal missions. Their failure to see the connection made them miserable because it reduced their sense of personal autonomy. In the German Army, on the other hand, there was no difficulty for soldiers who were used throughout their lives to having other persons determine their objectives for them.

It is also possible that the very high devotion to Hitler under conditions of great stress was in part a reaction formation growing from a hostility against lesser authorities, which emerged as the weakness of these authorities became more manifest. In the last year of the war, hostility and contempt on the part of the German soldiers toward Nazi Party functionaries and toward Nazi Party leaders below Hitler (particularly Goebbels and Goering) was increasing. After the *Putsch* of July 20, hostility toward senior Wehrmacht officers also increased somewhat, although it never reached the levels of hostility displayed by civilians against local civilian Party officials and leaders. It is possible, therefore, that guilt created in ambivalent personalities by giving expression, even though verbally, to hostility against subordinate agents of authority, had to be alleviated by reaffirmed belief in the central and highest authority.

Weakening of the Hitler Symbol

As the integral pattern of defense was broken down, however, and as danger to physical survival increased, devotion to Hitler deteriorated. The tendency to attribute virtue to the strong and immorality to the weak took hold increasingly, and while it did not lead to a complete rejection of Hitler, it reached a higher point than at any other stage in the history of National Socialism. The announcement of Hitler's death met an incapacity to respond on the part of many soldiers. There seemed to be no willingness to question the truth of the report, but the great upsurge of preoccupation with physical survival as a result of disintegration of the military primary group, the loss of contact with junior officers and the greatly intensified threat of destruction, caused a deadening of the power to respond to this event. For the vast horde of dishevelled, dirty, bewildered prisoners, who were being taken in the last weeks of the war, Hitler was of slight importance alongside the problem of their own biological survival and the welfare of their families. For the small minority who still had sufficient energy to occupy themselves with "larger problems," the news of Hitler's death released a sort of amorphous resentment against the fallen leader whose weakness and immorality had been proven by the failure of his strategy. But even here, the resentment was not expressed in explicit denunciations of Hitler's character or personality. The emphasis was all on technical deficiencies and weaknesses.

The explanation of the deterioration and final — though probably only temporary — hostility toward Hitler may in part be sought in the average German soldier's ambivalence toward the symbols of authority. This psychological mechanism, which also helps to explain the lack of a significant resistance movement inside Germany, enables us to understand the curve of Hitler's fame among the German people. Hitler, the father symbol, was loved for his power and his great accomplishments and hated for his oppressiveness, but the latter sentiment was repressed. While he remained strong it was psychologically expedient — as well as politically expedient — to identify with Hitler and to displace hostility on to weaker minority groups and foreigners. But once Hitler's authority had been undermined, the German soldiers rejected it and tended to express their hostility by projecting their own weakness on to him.

Thus the only important secondary symbol in motivating the behavior of the German soldiers during the recent war also lost its efficacy when the primary group relations of comradeliness, solidarity and subordination to junior officers broke down, and with it the superego of the individual, on which the effective functioning of the primary group depends.[6]

Propaganda Themes

The most striking aspect of Nazi indoctrination of their own men during combat was the employment of negative appeals and counter-propaganda, which attempted less to reply directly to the substance of our claims than to explain the reasons why the Allies were using propaganda.

The Nazis frankly believed that they could employ our propaganda efforts as a point of departure for strengthening the unpolitical resolve of their men. They had the legend of the effectiveness of Allied propaganda in World War I as a warning from which to "conclude" that if the Germans failed to be tricked by propaganda this time, success was assured. A typical instance of this attitude was contained in a captured order issued by the Officer in Command of the garrison of Boulogne on September 11, 1944, in which he appealed to his men not to be misled by Allied propaganda. The German order claimed that the propaganda attack in the form of leaflets was in itself an expression of the weakness of the Allied offensive, which was in desperate need of the port for communications. During the same period, an NSF (political officer) issued an elaborate statement in which he reminded the garrison at Le Havre that the "enemy resorts to propa-

---

[6] The mixture of apathy and resentment against Hitler persisted through the first part of the demobilization period following the end of the war, but as life began to reorganize and to take on new meaning and the attitudes toward authority, which sustain and are sustained by the routines of daily life, revived, esteem for Hitler also began to revive. It is likely to revive still further and to assume a prominent place in German life once more, if the new elite which is being created under the Allied occupation shows weakness and lack of decisiveness and self-confidence.

ganda as a weapon which he used in the last stages of the first world war," in order to point out that German victory depended on the determination of the German soldier to resist Allied propaganda.

In the fall and winter of 1944, the campaign to counteract Allied propaganda by "exposing" it was intensified and elaborated. (This method had the obvious advantage that direct refutations of Allied claims could largely be avoided.) *Mitteilung für die Truppe* (October 1944), a newspaper for officer indoctrination, reviewed the major weapons in the "poison offensive." They included: attacks against the Party and its predominant leaders ("this is not surprising as the enemy will, of course, attack those institutions which give us our greatest strength"); appeals to the Austrians to separate themselves from the Germans ("the time when we were split up in small states was the time of our greatest weakness"); sympathy with the poor German women who work in hellish factories ("the institution must be a good one, otherwise the enemy would not attack it").

Other themes "exposed" in leaflets were: the enemy attempts to separate the leaders from the people ("Just as the Kaiser was blamed in 1918, it now is Hitler who is supposed to be responsible"); the enemy admits his own losses in an exaggerated way in order to obtain the reputation of veracity and to lie all the more at the opportune moment.

Even earlier in the Western campaign, the Germans followed the policy of stamping Allied leaflets with the imprint, "Hostile Propaganda," and then allowing them to circulate in limited numbers. This was being carried out at the same time that mutually contradictory orders for the complete destruction of all enemy propaganda were being issued. The explanation, in part, is that the Nazis realized that it would be impossible to suppress the flood of Allied leaflets, and therefore sought to clearly label them as such and to employ them as a point of departure for counter-propaganda.

The procedure of overstamping Allied leaflets was linked with follow-up indoctrination talks. Such indoctrination lectures, which were conducted by the Nazi NSFO's, became towards the end of the war one of the main vehicles of Nazi indoctrination of their own troops. Ps/W claimed, although it was probably not entirely correct, that they usually slept through such sessions, or at least paid little attention, until the closing *Sieg Heil* was sounded. At this late date in the war, emphasis on oral propaganda was made necessary by the marked disruption of communications. Radio listening at the front was almost non-existent due to the lack of equipment; when in reserve, troops listened more frequently. Newspapers were distributed only with great difficulty. More important were the leaflets which were either dropped by air on their own troops or distributed through command channels.

"Strength Through Fear"

Major lines of the negative approach employed by these leaflets in indoctrination talks, in the rumors circulated by NSF officers, stressed "strength through fear," particularly fear of Russia and the general consequences of complete destruction that would follow defeat.

Because of the German soldier's concern about the welfare of his family living inside Germany, Nazi agencies were constantly issuing statements about the successful evacuation of German civilians to the east bank of the Rhine.

Equally stressed in the strength through fear theme were retaliation threats against the families of deserters, mistreatment of prisoners of war in Anglo-American prison camps, and the ultimate fate of prisoners. The phrase *Sieg oder Sibirien* (Victory or Siberia) was emphasized and much material was released to prove that the Anglo-Americans planned to turn over their prisoners to the Russians. When the U.S. Army stopped shipping German Ps/W to the United States, Nazi propaganda officers spread the rumor among German soldiers "that the way to Siberia is shorter from France than from the United States."

Statements by Ps/W revealed that shortly before the Rundstedt counter-attack, speeches by NSFO's were increased. One of the main subjects seems to have been weapons. In retrospect, the intent of the directives under which they were working was obvious. Attempts were made to explain the absence of the Luftwaffe, while the arrival in the near future of new and better weapons was guaranteed.

Psychological preparation for the December counter-offensive was built around the Rundstedt order of the day that "everything is at stake." Exhortations were backed up with exaggerated statements by unit commanders that large amounts of men and material were to be employed. Immediately thereafter, official statements were issued that significant penetrations had been achieved; special editions of troop papers were prepared announcing that 40,000 Americans had been killed.

Such announcements received little attention among the troops actually engaged in the counter-offensive because of the obvious difficulties in disseminating propaganda to fighting troops.

Nevertheless, after the failure of the counter-attack, the Nazis felt called upon to formulate a plausible line to explain the sum total result of that military effort, especially for those who felt that better military judgment would have resulted in a purely defensive strategy against Russia. On January 25, *Front und Heimat* announced that the December offensive had smashed the plan for a simultaneous onslaught: "The East can hold only if the West does too. . . . Every fighting man in the West knows that the Anglo-Americans are doing all they can, although belatedly, to start the assault on the Fortress

Germany. Our task in the West now is to postpone that time as long as possible and to guard the back of our Armies in the East."

Despite the obvious limitations on the efficacy of propaganda during March and April 1945, the Nazis continued to the very end to keep up their propaganda efforts. Due to the confusion within the ranks of the Wehrmacht and the resulting difficulties of dissemination, the task devolved almost wholly on the NSFO's who spent much of their time reading to the troops the most recent orders governing desertion. Leaflets called largely on the Landser's military spirit to carry on. One even demanded that he remain silent (*zu schweigen*). The Nazis taxed their fancy to create rumors as the last means of bolstering morale. Here a favorite technique for stimulating favorable rumors was for CO's to read to their men "classified" documents from official sources which contained promises of secret weapons or discussed the great losses being inflicted upon the Allies.

THE IMPACT OF ALLIED PROPAGANDA ON WEHRMACHT SOLIDARITY

The system of controls which the social structure of the Wehrmacht exercised over its individual members greatly reduced those areas in which symbolic appeals of the Allies could work. But the millions of leaflets which were dropped weekly and the "round-the-clock" broadcasts to the German troops certainly did not fail to produce some reactions.

The very first German Ps/W who were interrogated directly on their reactions to Allied propaganda soon revealed a stereotyped range of answers which could be predicted from their degree of Nazification. The fanatical Nazi claimed, "No German would believe anything the enemy has to say," while an extreme attitude of acceptance was typified by a confirmed anti-Nazi who pleaded with his captors: "Now is the moment to flood the troops with leaflets. You have no idea of the effect sober and effective leaflets have on retreating troops." But these extreme reactions of soldiers were of low frequency; Nazi soldiers might admit the truth of our leaflets but usually would not accept their conclusions and implications.

The fundamentally indifferent reaction to Allied propaganda was most interestingly shown in an intensive study of 150 Ps/W captured in October 1944 of whom 65 per cent had seen our leaflets and for the most part professed that they believed their contents. This was a group which had fought very obstinately, and the number of active deserters, if any, was extremely small. Some forty of these Ps/W offered extended comments as to what they meant when they said they believed the contents of Allied leaflets.

Five stated outright that they believed the messages and that the leaflets assisted them and their comrades to surrender.

Seven declared they believed the leaflets, but were powerless to do anything about appeals to surrender.

Eight stated that they believed the contents, but nevertheless as soldiers and decent individuals would never think of deserting.

Twenty-two declared that events justified belief in the leaflets, but they clearly implied that this had been of little importance in their battle experiences.

In Normandy, where the relatively small front was blanketed with printed material, up to 90 per cent of the Ps/W reported that they had read Allied leaflets, yet this period was characterized by very high German morale and stiff resistance.

Throughout the Western campaign, with the exception of periods of extremely bad weather or when the front was fluid, the cumulative percentage of exposure ranged between 60 and 80 per cent. (This cumulative percentage of exposure was based on statements by Ps/W that they had seen leaflets sometime while fighting on the Western front after D-Day. A few samples indicated that penetration during any single month covered about 20 per cent of the prisoners.) Radio listening among combat troops was confined to a minute fraction due to the lack of equipment; rear troops listened more frequently. In the case of both leaflets and radio it was found that there was widespread but desultory comment on the propaganda, much of which comment distorted the actual contents.

Not only was there wide penetration by Allied leaflets and newssheets, but German soldiers frequently circulated them extensively among their comrades. A readership study of *Nachrichten für die Truppe*, a daily newssheet published by the Allied Psychological Warfare Division, showed that each copy which was picked up had an average readership of between four and five soldiers — a figure which is extremely large in view of the conditions of combat life. Not only were leaflets widely circulated, but it became a widespread practice for soldiers to carry Allied leaflets on their person, especially the "safe conduct pass" leaflets which bore a statement by General Eisenhower guaranteeing the bearer swift and safe conduct through Allied lines and the protection of the Geneva convention. There is evidence that in certain sectors of the front, German soldiers even organized blackmarket trading in Allied propaganda materials.

It is relevant to discuss here the differences in effectiveness between tactical and strategic propaganda. By tactical propaganda, we refer to propaganda which seeks to promise immediate results in the tactical situation. The clearest example of this type of propaganda is afforded by "cross the lines" loudspeaker broadcasts, which sometimes facilitated immediate capture of the prisoners of war — not by propaganda in the ordinary sense, but by giving instructions on how to surrender safely, once the wish to surrender was present.

No sufficiently accurate estimate is available of the total number of prisoners captured by the use of such techniques, but signal successes involving hundreds of isolated troops in the Normandy campaign have been credited to psychological warfare combat teams. Even more successful were the loud-speaker-carrying tanks employed in the Rhine River offensive, when the first signs of weakening resistance were encountered. For example, the Fourth Armored Division reported that its psychological warfare unit captured over 500 prisoners in a four-day dash from Kyll River to the Rhine. Firsthand investigation of these loudspeaker missions, and interrogation of prisoners captured under such circumstances, establish that Allied propaganda was effective in describing the tactical situation to totally isolated and helpless soldiers and in arranging an Allied cease fire and thereby presenting an assurance to the German soldier of a safe surrender. The successful targets for such broadcasts were groups where solidarity and ability to function as a unit were largely destroyed. Leaflets especially written for specific sectors and dropped on pin point targets by fighter-bombs were used instead of loudspeakers where larger units were cut off. This method proved less successful, since the units to which they were addressed were usually better integrated and the necessary cease fire conditions could not be arranged.

Less spectacular, but more extensive, was strategic propaganda. Allied directives called for emphasis on four themes in this type of propaganda: (1) ideological attacks on the Nazi Party and Germany's war aims, (2) the strategical hopelessness of Germany's military and economic position, (3) the justness of the United Nations war aims and their unity and determination to carry them out (unconditional surrender, although made known to the troops, was never stressed), (4) promises of good treatment to prisoners of war, with appeals to self-preservation through surrender.

Although it is extremely difficult, especially in view of the lack of essential data, to assess the efficacy of these various themes, some tentative clues might be seen in the answers given to the key attitude questions in the monthly Psychological Warfare opinion poll of captured German soldiers.[7] Thus, there was no significant decline in attachment to Nazi ideology until February and March 1945. In other words, propaganda attacks on Nazi ideology seem to have been of little avail, and attachment to secondary symbols, e.g., Hitler, declined only when the smaller military units began to break up under very heavy pressure.

Since the German soldier was quite ignorant of military news on other fronts, it was believed that a great deal of printed material should contain factual reports of the military situation, stressing the strategical hopelessness of the German position. As a result, the third most frequently recalled items of our propaganda were the military

[7] Cf. Gurfein and Janowitz, *op. cit.*

news reports. It seems reasonable to believe that the emphasis on these subjects did contribute to the development of defeatist sentiment.

Despite the vast amount of space devoted to ideological attacks on German leaders, only about five per cent of the Ps/W mentioned this topic — a fact which supported the contention as to the general failure of ideological or secondary appeals. Finally, the presentation of the justness of our war aims was carried out in such a way as to avoid stressing the unconditional surrender aspects of our intentions, while emphasizing postwar peace intentions and organizational efforts; much was made of United Nations unity. All this fell on deaf ears, for of this material only a small minority of Ps/W (about 5 per cent) recalled specific statements about military government plans for the German occupation.

As has been pointed out previously, the themes which were most successful, at least in attracting attention and remaining fixed in the memory, were those promising good treatment as prisoners of war. In other words, propaganda referring to immediate concrete situations and problems seems to have been most effective in some respects.

The single leaflet most effective in communicating the promise of good treatment was the "safe conduct pass." Significantly, it was usually printed on the back of leaflets which contained no elaborate propaganda appeals except those of self-preservation. The rank and file tended to be favorably disposed to its official language and legal, document-like character. In one sector where General Eisenhower's signature was left off the leaflet, doubt was cast on its authenticity.

Belief in the veracity of this appeal was no doubt based on the attitude that the British and the Americans were respectable law-abiding soldiers who would treat their captives according to international law. As a result of this predisposition and the wide use of the safe conduct leaflets, as well as our actual practices in treating prisoners well, the German soldier came to have no fear of capture by British or American troops. The most that can be claimed for this lack of fear was that it may have decreased or undercut any tendency to fight to the death; it produced no active opposition to continued hostilities.

As an extension of the safe-conduct approach, leaflets were prepared instructing non-commissioned officers in detailed procedures by which their men could safely be removed from battle so as to avoid our fire and at the same time avoid evacuation by the German field police. If the Germans could not be induced to withdraw from combat actively, Allied propaganda appealed to them to hide in cellars. This in fact became a favorite technique of surrender, since it avoided the need of facing the conscience-twinging desertion problem.

As a result of psychological warfare research, a series of leaflets was prepared whose attack was aimed at primary group organization in the German Army, without recourse to ideological symbols. Group organization depended on the acceptance of immediate leadership and mutual trust. Therefore this series of leaflets sought to stimulate group discussion among the men and to bring into their focus of attention concerns which would loosen solidarity. One leaflet declared, "Do not take our (the Allies) word for it; ask your comrade; find out how he feels." Thereupon followed a series of questions on personal concerns, family problems, tactical consideration and supply problems. Discussion of these problems was expected to increase anxiety. It was assumed that to the degree that the soldier found that he was not isolated in his opinion, to that degree he would be strengthened in his resolve to end hostilities for himself at least.

CONCLUSION

At the beginning of the second world war, many publicists and specialists in propaganda attributed almost supreme importance to psychological warfare operations. The legendary success of Allied propaganda against the German Army at the end of the first world war and the tremendous expansion of the advertising and mass communications industries in the ensuing two decades had convinced many people that human behavior could be extensively manipulated by mass communications. They tended furthermore to stress that military morale was to a great extent a function of the belief in the rightness of the "larger" cause which was at issue in the war; good soldiers were therefore those who clearly understood the political and moral implications of what was at stake. They explained the striking successes of the German Army in the early phases of the war by the "ideological possession" of the German soldiers, and they accordingly thought that propaganda attacking doctrinal conceptions would be defeating this army.

Studies of the German Army's morale and fighting effectiveness made during the last three years of the war throw considerable doubt on these hypotheses. The solidarity of the German Army was discovered by these studies — which left much to be desired from the standpoint of scientific rigor — to be based only very indirectly and very partially on political convictions or broader ethical beliefs. Where conditions were such as to allow primary group life to function smoothly, and where the primary group developed a high degree of cohesion, morale was high and resistance effective or at least very determined, regardless in the main of the political attitudes of the soldiers. The conditions of primary group life were related to spatial proximity, the capacity for intimate communication, the provision of paternal protectiveness by NCO's and junior officers, and the gratification of certain personality needs, e.g., manliness, by the military organization and its activities. The larger structure of the army served to maintain morale through the provision of the framework in which

potentially individuating physical threats were kept at a minimum —
through the organization of supplies and through adequate strategic
dispositions.

The behavior of the German Army demonstrated that the focus of
attention and concern beyond one's immediate face-to-face social
circles might be slight indeed and still not interfere with the achievement of a high degree of military effectiveness. It also showed that
attempts to modify behavior by means of symbols referring to events
or values outside the focus of attention and concern would be given
an indifferent response by the vast majority of the German soldiers.
This was almost equally true under conditions of primary group integrity and under conditions of extreme primary group disintegration.
In the former, primary needs were met adequately through the
gratifications provided by the other members of the group; in the
latter, the individual had regressed to a narcissistic state in which
symbols referring to the outer world were irrelevant to his first concern — "saving his own skin."

At moments of primary group disintegration, a particular kind of
propaganda less hortatory or analytical, but addressing the intensified
desire to survive and describing the precise procedures by which physical survival could be achieved, was likely to facilitate further disintegration. Furthermore, in some cases aspects of the environment
towards which the soldier might hitherto have been emotionally
indifferent were defined for him by prolonged exposure to propaganda
under conditions of disintegration. Some of these wider aspects, e.g.,
particular strategic consideration, then tended to be taken into account in his motivation and he was more likely to implement his
defeatist mood by surrender than he would have been without
exposure to propaganda.

It seems necessary, therefore, to reconsider the potentialities of
propaganda in the context of all the other variables which influence
behavior. The erroneous views concerning the omnipotence of propaganda must be given up and their place must be taken by much more
differentiated views as to the possibilities of certain kinds of propaganda under different sets of conditions.

It must be recognized that on the moral plane most men are
members of the larger society by virtue of identifications which are
mediated through the human beings with whom they are in personal
relationships. Many are bound into the larger society only by primary
group identifications. Only a small proportion possessing special training or rather particular kinds of personalities are capable of giving a
preponderant share of their attention and concern to the symbols of
the larger world. The conditions under which these different groups
will respond to propaganda will differ, as will also the type of propaganda to which they will respond.

▲ LEONARD DOOB

Goebbels' Principles of Propaganda

Among the Nazi documents salvaged by American authorities in Berlin in 1945 are close to 6,800 pages of a manuscript ostensibly dictated by Propaganda Minister Goebbels as a diary which covers, with many gaps, the period from January 21, 1942 to December 9, 1943. The material was typed triple-spaced in large German-Gothic script and with wide margins upon heavy watermarked paper, with the result that the average page contained less than 100 words. About 30 per cent of this manuscript — the most interesting and generally the most important parts — has been very accurately and idiomatically translated by Louis P. Lochner.[1] The analysis in the present article is based upon careful examination of the entire document which is now in the Hoover Institute and Library on War, Peace, and Revolution at Stanford University.[2]

The material undoubtedly was dictated by Goebbels, but it is not necessarily an intimate or truthful account of his life as an individual or propagandist. He was too crafty to pour forth his soul to a secretary. What he said must have been motivated by whatever public audience he imagined would eventually see his words; or — as Speier has

[1] Lochner, Louis P. [Editor]. *The Goebbels Diaries*. New York: Doubleday & Company, 1948.

[2] The writer wishes to express his gratitude to Mr. Philip T. McLean of the Library for making arrangements to have the manuscript microfilmed; to the Yale Attitude Change Project for paying the costs of the microfilm; and to Professor Carl F. Schreiber of Yale University for aid in translating some of the more difficult words and phrases.

▲ After World War II, Goebbels' diary became available to scholars. Dr. Doob has derived from this diary a set of propaganda principles which Goebbels appears to have followed. This article was published in the *Public Opinion Quarterly*, in 1950. Copyright by the Princeton University Press, it is here reprinted by permission of the copyright holder. Dr. Doob is a professor of psychology at Yale.

pointed out[3] — the document may possibly represent parts of an authentic diary which were selected by him or someone else for some specific purpose. A section called "Yesterday — Military Situation," with which each day's entry began and which Lochner has sensibly omitted altogether, was definitely not written by Goebbels: the writing was most objective; often the same events mentioned therein were reported again and commented upon in other parts of the same day's entry; and infrequently a blank page appeared under the same heading with the notation "to be inserted later." In the manuscript we have, there are few personal details. Instead it appears that Goebbels wished to demonstrate an unswerving loyalty to Hitler; to expose the ineptitudes of the German military staffs; to boast about his own accomplishments, his respectability, and his devotion to the Nazi cause; and to place on the record criticisms of rival Nazis like Goering and Rosenberg.

The nature of the document would be a problem most germane to an examination of Goebbels' personality or the history of Nazidom, but these topics are not being discussed here. Attention has been focused only on the principles which appear to underlie the propaganda plans and decisions described in the manuscript. Spot checks suggest but do not prove that the words of the diary actually correspond to the activities of Goebbels' propaganda machine. One typical example of the correspondence must suffice. The entry in the diary for November 11, 1943, contained this observation: "There is no longer any talk in the English press of the possibility of a moral collapse of the Reich. On the contrary, we are credited with much greater military prowess than we enjoy at the moment. . . ." On the same day, the *Berliner Illustrierte Nachtausgabe* carried an editorial which asserted that the "jubilant illusions" of the British regarding a German collapse have "suddenly changed to deep pessimism; the enemy's strongest hopes are crushed." Two days later the headline of the leading article in the *Voelkischer Beobachter* was "War of Nerves Departs." On November 13 the diary stated that the English "have been imagining that exactly on this day [November 11] there would be in the Reich a morale breakdown which, however, has now been pushed by them into the invisible future." A day later a Nazi official spoke over the domestic radio: "The key-dates chosen by the enemy are now passed: our people have repulsed this general attack. . . ."

All that is being assumed, in short, is that the manuscript more or less faithfully reflects Goebbels' propaganda strategy and tactics: it is a convenient guide to his bulky propaganda materials. He always magnified the importance of his work, no doubt to indicate his own significance. The truth of what he dictated in this respect is also

[3] Speier, Hans. Review of Lochner, *op. cit., Public Opinion Quarterly,* Fall, 1948, pp. 500-505.

irrelevant, inasmuch as the effects of his efforts are not being scrutinized.

The analysis which follows, it must constantly be remembered, is based on a very limited period of Goebbels' stewardship, a period in which on the whole Germany was suffering military and political defeats such as the winter campaigns in Russia, the withdrawal from North Africa, and the capitulation of Italy. From time to time, nevertheless, events such as temporary military advances and the triumphs of Japan in Asia occurred; hence there are also suggestions as to how Goebbels functioned as a winner. The writer has checked primary and secondary sources from 1925 through 1941 and after 1943, and is therefore at least privately confident that the principles are not limited to the diary.

In this analysis a principle is adduced — in an admittedly but unavoidably subjective manner — from the diary when a minimum of six scattered references therein suggests that Goebbels would have had to believe, consciously or unconsciously, in that generalization before he could dictate or behave as he did. To save space, however, only a few illustrations are given under each principle. Whenever possible, an illustration has been selected from the portion published by Lochner: the reader has readier access to that volume than to the manuscript at Stanford. The same procedure has been employed regarding references. A quoted phrase or sentence is followed by the number of the page being cited, either from the Lochner book (in which case a simple number is given in parentheses), or from the Stanford manuscript (in which case the number is preceded by the letter "M," and represents the Library's pagination). The concluding sentence of each paragraph, moreover, contains the one reference considered to be either the best or the most typical for the entire paragraph, again preferably from the Lochner book. The writer will gladly honor written requests for additional references.

These principles purport to summarize what made Goebbels tick or fail to tick. They may be thought of as his intellectual legacy. Whether the legacy has been reliably deduced is a methodological question. Whether it is valid is a psychological matter. Whether or when parts of it should be utilized in a democratic society are profound and disturbing problems of a political and ethical nature.

PROPAGANDISTS MUST HAVE ACCESS TO INTELLIGENCE CONCERNING EVENTS AND PUBLIC OPINION

In theory, Goebbels maintained that he and his associates could plan and execute propaganda only by constantly referring to existing intelligence. Otherwise the communication would not be adapted either to the event or the audience. As Germany's situation worsened, he permitted fewer and fewer officials to have access to all relevant intelligence. By May of 1943 he persuaded Himmler to supply unex-purgated reports only to himself (373).

The basic intelligence during a war concerns military events. Each day's entry began with a separate description of the current military situation. There is every indication that Goebbels was kept acquainted with Germany's own military plans (162).

Information about Germans was obtained most frequently from the reports of the *Sicherheits-Dienst* (SD) of the secret police. In ad-dition, Goebbels depended upon his own Reich Propaganda Offices, German officials, and written or face-to-face contacts with individual German civilians or soldiers. As has been shown elsewhere,[4] little or none of this intelligence was ever gathered or analyzed systematically. Once Goebbels stated that the SD had conducted "a statistical investi-gation . . . in the manner of the Gallup Institute," but he said he did "not value such investigations because they are always undertaken with a deliberate purpose in mind" (M827). Goebbels, moreover, tended to trust his own common sense, intuition, or experience more than formal reports. He listened to his mother because, he said, "she knows the sentiments of the people better than most experts who judge from the ivory tower of scientific inquiry, as in her case the voice of people itself speaks" (56).

The SD as well as German officials supplied intelligence concerning occupied countries. Information about enemy, allied, and neutral nations was gathered from spies, monitored telephone conversations, and other classified sources; from the interrogation of prisoners as well as from the letters they received and sent; and from statements in or deductions from those nations' mass media of communication. Here, too, Goebbels often relied upon his own intuitive judgment, and he seldom hesitated to make far-reaching deductions from a thread of evidence. A direct reply by the enemy, for example, he unequivocally interpreted as a sign of his own effectiveness: "a wild attack on my last article" by the Russian news agency "shows that our anti-Bolshevik propaganda is slowly getting on Soviet nerves" (271).

PROPAGANDA MUST BE PLANNED AND EXECUTED BY ONLY ONE AUTHORITY

This principle was in line with the Nazi theory of centralizing authority and with Goebbels' own craving for power. In the diary he stressed the efficiency and consistency which could result from such a policy (M383). He felt that a single authority — himself — must per-form three functions:

a. *It must issue all the propaganda directives.* Every bit of propa-

[4] United States Strategic Bombing Survey. *The Effects of Bombing on Ger-man Morale.* Washington, D.C.: U.S. Government Printing Office, 1947. Vol. I, p. 42.

ganda had to implement policy, and policy was made clear in directives. These directives referred to all phases of the war and to all events occurring inside and outside of Germany. They indicated when specific propaganda campaigns should be begun, augmented, diminished, and terminated. They suggested how an item should be interpreted and featured, or whether it should be ignored completely. Goebbels willingly yielded his authority for issuing directives only to Hitler, whose approval on very important matters was always sought. Sometimes gratification was expressed concerning the ways in which directives were implemented; but often there were complaints concerning how Goebbels' own people or others were executing a campaign. The Nazi propaganda machine, therefore, was constantly being reorganized (341).

b. *It must explain propaganda directives to important officials and maintain their morale.* Unless these officials who either formally or informally implemented directives were provided with an explanation of propaganda policy, they could not be expected to function effectively and willingly. Through his organizational machinery and also through personal contact, Goebbels sought to reveal the rationale of his propaganda to these subordinates and to improve their morale by taking them, ostensibly, into his confidence. The groups he met varied in size from an intimate gathering in his home to what must have been a mass meeting in the Kroll Opera House in Berlin (484).

c. *It must oversee other agencies' activities which have propaganda consequences.* "I believe," Goebbels told Hitler, "that when a propaganda ministry is created, all matters affecting propaganda, news, and culture within the Reich and within the occupied areas must be subordinated to it." Although Hitler allegedly "agreed with me absolutely and unreservedly," this high degree of unification was not achieved (476). Conflicts over propaganda plans and materials were recorded with the following German agencies: Ribbentrop's Foreign Office and its representatives in various countries; Rosenberg's Ministry for the Eastern Occupied Areas; the German Army, even including the officers stationed at Hitler's G.H.Q.; the Ministry of Justice; and Ley's Economic Ministry. Goebbels considered himself and his ministry trouble-shooters: whenever and wherever German morale seemed poor — whether among submarine crews or the armies in the East — he attempted to provide the necessary propaganda boost (204).

Goebbels' failure to achieve the goal of this principle and its corollaries is noteworthy. Apparently his self-proclaimed competency was not universally recognized: people whom he considered amateurs believed they could execute propaganda as effectively as he. In addition, even a totalitarian regime could not wipe out personal rivalries and animosities in the interests of efficiency (M3945).

THE PROPAGANDA CONSEQUENCES OF AN ACTION MUST BE CONSIDERED IN PLANNING THAT ACTION

Goebbels demanded that he rather than the German Ministry of Justice be placed in charge of a trial in France so that "everything will be seized and executed correctly from a psychological viewpoint" (M1747). He persuaded Hitler, he wrote, to conduct "air warfare against England . . . according to psychological rather than military principles" (313). It was more important for a propagandist to help plan an event than to rationalize one that had occurred (209).

PROPAGANDA MUST AFFECT THE ENEMY'S POLICY AND ACTION

Propaganda was considered an arm of warfare, although Goebbels never employed the phrase "psychological warfare" or "political warfare." Besides damaging enemy morale, he believed that propaganda could affect the policies and actions of enemy leaders in four ways:

a. *By suppressing propagandistically desirable material which can provide the enemy with useful intelligence.* Often Goebbels claimed that he refused to deny or refute enemy claims concerning air damage: "it is better," he said in April of 1942, "for the English to think that they have had great successes in the air war than for them actually to have achieved such victories" (M2057). For similar reasons he regretfully censored items concerning the poor quality of Soviet weapons, Germany's plans to employ secret weapons, and even favorable military news (272).

b. *By openly disseminating propaganda whose content or tone causes the enemy to draw the desired conclusions.* "I am also convinced," Goebbels stated in the spring of 1943, "that a firm attitude on our part [in propaganda] will somewhat spoil the appetite of the English for an invasion" (302). As the Battle of Tunisia drew to a close, therefore, the resistance of German troops there was used as an illustration of what would happen if the European continent were invaded. Perhaps, Goebbels must have reasoned, General Eisenhower's plans might be thus directly affected; British or American public opinion might exert influence upon SHAEF; or the morale of the armies in training for the invasion might be crippled (M4638).

c. *By goading the enemy into revealing vital information about himself.* At the end of the Battle of the Coral Sea Goebbels believed that the Japanese had scored a complete victory. The silence of American and British authorities was then attacked "with very precise questions: they will not be able to avoid for any length of time the responsibility of answering these questions" (M2743).

d. *By making no reference to a desired enemy activity when any reference would discredit that activity.* Goebbels did not wish to bestow a "kiss of death" on matters which met his approval. No use was made of news indicating unfriendly relations between two or more of the countries opposing Germany because — in Goebbels' own favorite, trite, and oft repeated words — "controversy between the Allies is a small plant which thrives best when it is left to its own natural growth" (M941). Likewise the Nazi propaganda apparatus was kept aloof from the Chicago *Tribune,* from a coal strike in the United States, and from anti-Communist or pro-fascist groups in England. Quarrels between Germany's enemies, however, were fully exploited when — as in the case of British-American clashes over Darlan — the conflict was both strong and overt (225).

DECLASSIFIED, OPERATIONAL INFORMATION MUST BE AVAILABLE

A propaganda goal, regardless of its importance, required operational material that did not conflict with security regulations. The material could not be completely manufactured: it had to have some factual basis, no matter how slight. It was difficult to begin an anti-semitic campaign after the fall of Tunis because German journalists had been failing to collect anti-Jewish literature. Lack of material, however, never seems to have hindered a campaign for any length of time, since evidently some amount of digging could produce the necessary implementation. Journalists were dispatched to a crucial area to write feature stories; steps were taken to insure a supply of "authentic news from the United States" (92); a change in personnel was contemplated "to inject fresh blood into German journalism" and hence better writing (500); or, when necessary, the Protocols of Zions were resurrected (376).

Like any publicity agent, Goebbels also created "news" through action. To demonstrate Germany's friendship for Finland, for example, a group of ailing Finnish children was invited to Germany on a "health-restoring vacation" (M91). The funerals of prominent Nazis were made into news-worthy pageants; the same technique was applied to the French and Belgian victims of British air attacks. German and Nazi anniversaries were celebrated so routinely that the anniversary of the founding of the Three Power Pact was observed even after the downfall of the Italian member (M5859).

TO BE PERCEIVED, PROPAGANDA MUST EVOKE THE INTEREST OF AN AUDIENCE

Much energy was devoted to establishing and maintaining communications media. Motion picture theaters and newspapers were controlled or purchased in neutral and occupied countries. "It's a pity that we cannot reach the people of the Soviet Union by radio propaganda," Goebbels stated, since "the Kremlin has been clever enough to exclude the Russian people from receiving the great world broadcasts and to limit them to their local stations" (453). The schedule of

many German radio programs was adjusted when the British introduced "double summer time." A dilemma existed regarding receiving
sets in occupied countries: if they were confiscated, people would be
cut off from Nazi as well as enemy propaganda; if they were not, both
brands could be heard. Inside the Reich, machinery was created to
reopen motion picture theaters as quickly as possible after heavy air
raids (M5621).

Some kind of bait was devised to attract and hold an audience.
What Goebbels called "propaganda" over the radio, he believed,
tended after a while to repel an audience. By 1942 he concluded that
Germans wanted their radio to provide "not only instruction but also
entertainment and relaxation" (M383), and that likewise straight
news rather than "talks" were more effective with foreign audiences.
Like any propagandist in war time, he recognized that a radio program could draw enemy listeners by providing them with the names
of war prisoners. The best form of newspaper propaganda was not
"propaganda" (i.e., editorials and exhortation), but slanted news
which appeared to be straight (M4677).

Goebbels was especially attached to the motion picture. At least
three evenings a week he previewed a feature film or newsreel not only
to seek relaxation and the company of film people but also to offer
what he considered to be expert criticisms. Feature pictures, he stated,
should provide entertaining and absorbing plots which might evoke
and then resolve tension; simultaneously they should subtly affect the
attentive audience not through particular passages but by the general
atmosphere. Evidence for Goebbels' belief in the supreme importance
of newsreels comes from the fact that he immediately provided his
newsreel company with emergency headquarters after one of the
heaviest air raids Berlin experienced toward the end of 1943. "It costs
much trouble to assemble the newsreel correctly each week and to
make it into an effective propaganda weapon," he observed on
another occasion, "but the work is worthwhile: millions of people
draw from the newsreel their best insight into the war, its causes, and
its effects." He also believed that newsreels provided "proof" for many
of his major propaganda contentions: visual images — no matter how
he himself manipulated them before they were released — possessed
greater credibility than spoken or written words (M335).

Goebbels never stated explicitly whether or not in his opinion some
media were better suited to present particular propaganda themes than
others. Only stray observations were made, such as that leaflets were
ineffective when "opinions are too rigid and viewpoints too firm"
(M2065). His one basic assumption appears to have been that all
media must be employed simultaneously, since one never knew what
type of bait would catch the variety of fish who were Nazi targets
(M828).

CREDIBILITY ALONE MUST DETERMINE WHETHER PROPAGANDA OUTPUT SHOULD BE TRUE OR FALSE

Goebbels' moral position in the diary was straightforward: he told the truth, his enemies told lies. Actually the question for him was one of expediency and not morality. Truth, he thought, should be used as frequently as possible; otherwise the enemy or the facts themselves might expose falsehood, and the credibility of his own output would suffer. Germans, he also stated, had grown more sophisticated since 1914: they could "read between the lines" and hence could not be easily deceived (M1808).

Lies, consequently, were useful when they could not be disproved. To induce Italians to leave the areas occupied by English and American forces and then to shanghai them into Germany as workers, Goebbels broadcast the claim that "the English and Americans will compel all men of draft age to enlist" (462). Even truth, however, might damage credibility. In the first place, some apparently true statements could later turn out to be false, such as specific claims concerning the damage inflicted by planes against enemy targets. Then, secondly, truth itself might appear untrue. Goebbels was afraid to inform the Germans that General Rommel had not been in Africa during the closing days of the campaign there: "everybody thinks he is in Africa; if we now come out with the truth when the catastrophe is so near, nobody will believe us" (352).

Similarly, every feature and device had to maintain its own credibility. A special communique or bulletin was employed, for example, to announce important events. Goebbels was afraid to resort to this device too frequently, lest it lose its unusual character, and hence he released some significant news through routine channels (M5799).

FACTORS THAT DETERMINE WHETHER ENEMY PROPAGANDA SHOULD BE IGNORED OR REFUTED

Most of the time Goebbels seemed mortally afraid of enemy propaganda. Even though he had controlled all the mass media in Germany since 1933, he must have been convinced that Germans had not been completely converted to the Nazi cause, or at least that they might be corrupted by enemy efforts. He admitted in January of 1942 that "foreign broadcasts are again being listened to more extensively" even though death could be the penalty for doing so (44). Fourteen months later he noted with dismay that "the English and Americans have greatly expanded their radio broadcasts to the Axis countries and intend to step them up even more" (312).

Goebbels' first impulse was to reply to enemy propaganda. He wrote as though he were a member of a great International Debating Society and as if silence on his part would mean the loss of the argument and of his own prestige. Actually, however, he judiciously balanced a number of factors before he decided to ignore or refute enemy claims (M2593).

In the first place, he analyzed enemy propaganda. If it seemed that the goal of the propaganda was to elicit a reply, he was silent. "The English," he stated on February 6, 1942, "are now employing a new mode of propaganda: they commit General Rommel to objectives which at the moment he certainly cannot have, in order to be able to declare perhaps in eight or fourteen days that he has not reached these goals" (M423). A direct reply would have been equivalent to selling the German armies short. His practice was to expose such traps to his subordinates and then to have them maintain silence in the mass media (M4606).

On the other hand, a reply was made if it were felt that the enemy was transmitting blatant falsehoods. Since almost any enemy statement was considered false, Goebbels believed that only the blatant ones should be exposed. In this category he included claims that Germans had bombed Vatican City, that there had been "disturbances in Berlin" (M4664), that Stalin was adopting a more lenient policy toward religion, etc. (M4971).

Ineffective enemy claims required no reply, since a refutation would either give them more currency or else be a waste of propaganda energy. Enemy propaganda was very frequently branded as being ineffective, judgments which appear to have been either intuitive or rationalizations of an inability to reply. Effective enemy propaganda, however, demanded immediate action. The enemy, for example, was seldom permitted to acquire prestige; thus Goebbels attacked British boasts concerning a parachute landing at Le Havre, a raid on St. Nazaire, and the occupation of Madagascar. Sometimes it appears as though he instituted counter-proceedings not because the enemy was being successful but simply because he was able to do so. When the enemy was thought to be employing horoscopes and other occult propaganda against Germany, a reply in kind was immediately prepared. If the enemy seemed to be scoring an especially important propaganda triumph in its "war of nerves" — specifically at the beginning of the heavy British raids on German cities, after the downfall of Mussolini, or in the midst of strong pressure on Turkey by Britain in the late fall of 1943 — the only really adequate reply was considered to be a speech by Hitler himself (251).

Then, secondly, Goebbels examined his own propaganda arsenal before he assayed a reply. He kept silent if he believed that his case, in the absence of facts or arguments, would appear too weak. He was so afraid of the German National Committee which the Russians formed in Moscow that he carried on no counter-propaganda against this group. Sometimes an enemy claim was disregarded and a counter-claim advanced. As Germany was attacked for her treatment of Jews, the policy of "complete silence" seemed unwise: "it is best to seize the offensive and to say something about English cruelty in India or the Near East" (M3064) and also to "intensify . . . our anti-Bolshevik propaganda" (M3225).

Goebbels tried, too, to estimate in advance the effectiveness of a rebuttal. If his own case as well as the enemy's appeared strong but if the enemy's might look stronger because of his attempts to refute it, he withheld his fire. It always seemed better to concentrate on the dissemination of a Hitler speech rather than to reply to foreign critics. Often, however, he believed that an exposé could protect Germans or help immunize foreigners from an enemy campaign that was either about to be or actually had been launched. Peace appeals by the three allies were therefore anticipated, and his reply to the communique from the Teheran Conference was "biting and insolent; we empty buckets of irony and derision over the Conference" (545).

In the third place, Goebbels believed that his current propaganda had to be surveyed before enemy propaganda could be ignored or refuted. He attempted no reply when that reply might divert attention away from, or when it ran counter to more important propaganda themes. "There's no point in concerning oneself daily with new themes and rumors disseminated by the enemy," he stated, since it was essential to concentrate on the "central theme" of anti-Semitism (M4602). In March of 1943 he permitted "Bolshevik reports of victories . . . to go into the world unchallenged": he wanted Europe to "get the creeps," so that "all the sooner it will become sensible" and cooperate against the Russians (284).

FACTORS THAT DETERMINE WHETHER PROPAGANDA MATERIALS SHOULD BE CENSORED

Goebbels had no scruples whatsoever concerning the use of censorship. "News policy," he stated, "is a weapon of war; its purpose is to wage war and not to give out information" (210). His decision rested upon three pragmatic considerations (299).

Goebbels recognized, first, that often credibility might be impaired if an item were censored: "in excited and strained times the hunger for news must somehow be satisfied" (40). When the Foreign Office censored news which he considered important, he complained that "by that sort of policy we are fairly compelling the German public to listen to foreign and enemy broadcasts" (164). Again and again, therefore, he felt that he had to speak up, although he would have preferred to be silent. Toward the end of 1943, for example, he stated that the problem of evacuating people from the bombed areas "has become so serious that it must be discussed with the clarity it deserves" (M6435).

The usual policy was to suppress material which was deemed undesirable for German consumption, but simultaneously to employ it in foreign propaganda if it were suited thereto. Tales concerning alleged cannibalism by the Soviets were spread in foreign countries, but such material was banned inside Germany lest it terrify Germans whose relatives were fighting the Russians. Sometimes, however, undesirable material was not censored domestically in order to maintain its credibility abroad (M2699).

Censorship was invoked, in the second place, when intelligence concerning the outcome of a development was insufficient. Here Goebbels wished either to preserve credibility or to have more facts before formulating a directive. Military forecasts he considered especially risky, but he also avoided comments on political events outside the Reich until he could fairly definitely anticipate their effects upon Germany (M5036).

Then, finally, Goebbels estimated the possible effects of communicating the information. Censorship was pursued when it was thought that knowledge of the event would produce a reaction which was undesirable in itself or which, though desirable under some circumstances, was not in line with a current directive. Judged by the kind of news he suppressed, Goebbels was afraid that the following might damage German morale: discussions about religion; statements by officials in neutral or occupied countries that were hostile to Germany or by enemy officials that might evoke sympathy for them; enemy warnings that there would be raids before heavy ones began and — later — the extent of the damage inflicted by enemy planes; dangerous acts which included the assassination of officials, sabotage, and desertion; the unfortunate decisions or deeds of German officials; the belittling of German strength by an occurrence like the escape of General Giraud from a German prison; an unnecessarily large increase in Germans' anxiety; and hints that Germany did not approve completely of her Axis partners (249).

WHEN MATERIAL FROM ENEMY PROPAGANDA MAY BE UTILIZED

Although his basic attitude toward enemy propaganda was one of contempt, Goebbels combed enemy broadcasts, newspapers, and official statements for operational items. Here he was not motivated by the somewhat defensive desire to reply to the enemy, but by offensive considerations: words of the enemy (Cf. Principle 8) could help him reach his propaganda goals. "In the morning we published in the German press a collection of previous Churchill lies and featured ten points; this collection is making a deep impression on the neutral press and shows Churchill to be, as it were, the Admiral of Incapability" (M202). In particular the enemy provided a basis for Goebbels' "strength-through-fear" campaign as indicated below in Principle 16. "This fellow Vansittart is really worth his weight in gold to our propaganda" (342), he wrote, and likewise he felt that any discussion in England or Russia concerning reparations or boundary questions after Germany's defeat "contributes significantly to the maintenance and strengthening of morale" inside the Reich (M765).

BLACK RATHER THAN WHITE PROPAGANDA MUST BE EMPLOYED WHEN THE LATTER IS LESS CREDIBLE OR PRODUCES UNDESIRABLE EFFECTS

By "black" propaganda is meant material whose source is concealed from the audience. Goebbels disguised his identity when he was convinced that the association of a white medium with himself or his machine would damage its credibility. At one time, for example, he wanted to induce the English to stop bombing Berlin by convincing them that they were wasting their bombs. He claimed that he used rumor-mongers to spead the idea there that the city "for all practical purposes is no longer capable of supporting life, *i.e.*, no longer exists" (M6654). Presumably the tale had a better chance of being believed if German authorities were not connected with it. A most elaborate plan was concocted to try to deceive the Russians regarding the section of the front at which the Germans in the summer of 1942 had planned their offensive. A German journalist, who had first been sent deliberately to the Eastern front, was then dispatched to Lisbon where he was to commit, ostensibly under the influence of liquor, what would appear to be indiscretions but which actually were deceptions. In addition, it was planned to plant "a camouflaged article . . . through middlemen either in the Turkish or the Portuguese press" (226), and the *Frankfurter Zeitung* was made to print an "unauthorized" article which was later "officially suppressed and denounced in a press conference" (221). Goebbels sought to increase the number of Soviet deserters by improving the prisoner-of-war camps in which they would be kept — this ancient psychological warfare device rested on the hope that news of the improvement would reach Soviet soldiers through informal channels. Otherwise, except for a security-conscious hint from time to time, the diary made no reference to black operations inside enemy countries (M4235).

Goebbels also utilized black means to combat undesirable rumors inside the Reich. An official denial through a white medium, he thought, might only give currency to the rumors, whereas what he called "word-of-mouth" propaganda against them could achieve the desired effects. This method was employed to offset German fears that "in case more serious raids were to occur, the government would be the first to run away" from Berlin (421). At all times "citizens who are faithful to the state must be furnished with the necessary arguments for combating defeatism during discussions at their places of work and on the streets" (401). Sometimes, however, rumors were officially attacked when, in Goebbels' opinion, all the facts were completely and unequivocally on his side (518).

PROPAGANDA MAY BE FACILITATED BY LEADERS WITH PRESTIGE

Such a principle is to be expected from Goebbels, whose Nazi ideology stressed the importance of leadership. Germans, it was hoped, would feel submissive toward propaganda containing the name of a prestigeful leader. Ostensibly Goebbels always anticipated momentous results from a Hitler statement especially during a crisis; he noted routinely that the communication had been received by Germans with complete enthusiasm or that it "has simply amazed the enemy" (506).

Leaders were useful only when they had prestige. Goebbels utilized propaganda to make heroes out of men like Field Marshal Rommel. In the privacy of his diary he savagely attacked German leaders whose public behavior was not exemplary, since they thus disrupted propaganda which urged ordinary Germans to make greater sacrifices and to have unswerving faith in their government. An incompetent Nazi official was not openly dismissed from office, lest his incompetence reflect upon "the National Socialist regime"; instead it was announced that he had been temporarily replaced because of illness (224).

PROPAGANDA MUST BE CAREFULLY TIMED

Goebbels always faced the tactical problem of timing his propaganda most effectively. Agility and plasticity were necessary, he thought, and propagandists must possess at all times the faculty of "calculating psychological effects in advance" (204). Three principles seemed to be operating:

a. *The communication must reach the audience ahead of competing propaganda.* "Whoever speaks the first word to the world is always right," Goebbels stated flatly (183). He sought constantly to speed up the release of news by his own organization. The loss of Kiev was admitted as quickly as possible "so that we would not limp behind the enemy announcement" (M6061).

b. *A propaganda campaign must begin at the optimum moment.* Goebbels never indicated explicitly or implicitly how he reached the decision that the time to begin a campaign or make an announcement was either ripe or right. He made statements like this: "we have held back for a very long time" in using an Indian leader, who as a German puppet committed his country to a war against England, "for the simple reason that things had not advanced far enough as yet in India" (107). At one point he stated that counter-propaganda against enemy claims should not be too long delayed: "one should not let such lying reports sink in too deeply" (M2430).

c. *A propaganda theme must be repeated, but not beyond some point of diminishing effectiveness.* On the one hand, Goebbels believed that propaganda must be repeated until it was thoroughly learned and that thereafter more repetition was necessary to reinforce the learning. Such repetition took place over time — the same theme was mentioned day after day — as well as in the output of a single day. An anti-Semitic campaign, for example, continued for weeks, during which time "about 70 to 80 per cent of our broadcasts are devoted to it" (366). On the other hand, repetition could be unnecessary or even undesirable. It was unnecessary when "the material thus far published has completely convinced the public" (386). It was undesirable when the theme became boring or unimpressive, as occurred in connection with announcements concerning German submarine successes. Sometimes, moreover, booming guns at the start of a campaign, though desirable psychologically, could make the propaganda too "striking" and consequently result in a loss of credibility (M6343).

PROPAGANDA MUST LABEL EVENTS AND PEOPLE WITH DISTINCTIVE PHRASES OR SLOGANS

Again and again Goebbels placed great stress upon phrases and slogans to characterize events. At the beginning of 1942, for example, he began a campaign whose purpose was to indicate economic, social, and political unrest in England. He very quickly adopted the phrase *"schleichende Krise"* — creeping crisis — to describe this state of affairs and then employed it "as widely as possible in German propaganda" both domestically and abroad (M762). His thinking was dominated by word-hunts: privately — or semi-privately — in his diary he summarized his own or enemy propaganda with a verbal cliché, even when he did not intend to employ the phrase in his output. He admitted that the experiencing of an event was likely to be more effective than a verbal description of it, but he also recognized that words could stand between people and events, and that their reaction to the latter could be potently affected by the former (M1385). To achieve such effects, phrases and slogans should possess the following characteristics:

a. *They must evoke desired responses which the audience previously possesses.* If the words could elicit such responses, then Goebbels' propaganda task consisted simply of linking those words to the event which thereafter would acquire their flavor. When the British raid on St. Nazaire in March of 1942 aborted, Goebbels decided to claim that it had been made to appease the Russians who had been demanding that their ally engage in military action. The raid was dubbed the "Maisky Offensive," after the Soviet envoy in London. Sometimes news could speak for itself in the sense that it elicited desired responses without the addition of a verbal label. A military victory was not interpreted for Germans when Goebbels wished them to feel gratified. Most news, however, was not self-explanatory: Goebbels had to attach thereto the responses he desired through the use of verbal symbols. The most regulated news and commentary, nevertheless, could produce undesirable and unintended actions; even a speech by Hitler was misinterpreted (M4677).

b. *They must be capable of being easily learned.* "It must make use of painting in black-and-white, since otherwise it cannot be convincing to people," Goebbels stated with reference to a film he was criticizing (M271). This principle of simplification he applied to all media in order to facilitate learning. The masses were important, not the intellectuals. All enemy "lies" were not beaten down, rather it was better to confine the counter-attack to a single "school example" (M2084). Propaganda could be aided, moreover, by a will to learn. Cripps' appeal to European workers under German domination to slow down on the job, for example, was ignored: "it is difficult to pose a counter-slogan to such a slogan, for the slogan of 'go slow' is always much more effective than that of 'work fast' " (107).

c. *They must be utilized again and again, but only in appropriate situations.* Here Goebbels wished to exploit learning which had occurred: the reactions people learned to verbal symbols he wished to transfer easily and efficiently to new events. He criticized English propaganda because "its slogans are changed on every occasion and hence it lacks real punch" (M1812). The context in which people's reactions occurred was also important. "I forbid using the word *'Fuehrer'* in the German press when applied to Quisling," Goebbels declared. "I don't consider it right that the term *Fuehrer* be applied to any other person than the *Fuehrer* himself. There are certain terms that we must absolutely reserve for ourselves, among them also the word 'Reich' " (66).

d. *They must be boomerang-proof.* Goebbels became furious when he thought of the expression "Baedeker raids, which one of our people so stupidly coined during a foreign press conference" (M2435): it interfered with his own effort to call British raids wanton attacks on "cultural monuments and institutions of public welfare" (M2301). "There are certain words," he added, "from which we should shrink as the devil does from Holy Water; among these are, for instance, the words 'sabotage' and 'assassination' " (93).

PROPAGANDA TO THE HOME FRONT MUST PREVENT THE RAISING OF FALSE HOPES

It was clear to Goebbels that the anticipation of a German success along military or political lines could have certain immediate beneficial effects from his viewpoint. The confidence of Germans and the anxiety of the enemy could be increased. Such tactics, however, were much too risky: if the success turned out to be a failure, then Germans would feel deflated and the enemy elated. His own credibility, moreover, would suffer. For this reason he was wildly indignant when, after the German army withdrew, the enemy ascribed to him "premature reports of victories" at Salerno. Actually, he claimed, the announcements had come from German Generals (457).

Often the false hopes seemed to spring from the Germans themselves, a form of wishful thinking which occurred spontaneously as they contemplated the possibility of an offensive by the German armies, as they received news of a single victory, or as they imagined that the enemy could be defeated by political events. Goebbels, therefore, frequently issued warnings about "false illusions" and he prevented particular victories from being trumpeted too loudly. At other times enemy propaganda strategy was thought to be committing the German armies to military goals which they could not be expected to achieve (118).

PROPAGANDA TO THE HOME FRONT MUST CREATE AN OPTIMUM ANXIETY LEVEL

For Goebbels, anxiety was a double-edged sword: too much anxiety could produce panic and demoralization, too little could lead to complacency and inactivity. An attempt was constantly made, therefore, to achieve a balance between the two extremes. The strategy can be reduced to two principles (M6162).

a. *Propaganda must reinforce anxiety concerning the consequences of defeat.* Enemy war aims were the principal material employed to keep German anxiety at a high pitch. "The German people must remain convinced — as indeed the facts warrant — that this war strikes at their very lives and their national possibilities of development, and they must fight it with their entire strength" (147). Lest the campaign of "strength-through-fear" falter, no opportunity was missed to attack enemy peace terms which might appear mild. Anti-Bolshevik campaigns attempted not only to stiffen German resistance but also to enlist the cooperation of all neutral and occupied countries. On the one hand, Goebbels tried to convince himself in the diary that Germans would not be misled again — as they had been, according to his view, in World War I — by enemy peace terms: they "are quite accurately acquainted with their enemies and know what to expect if they were to give themselves up" (M6684). On the other hand, he felt very strongly that Germans were most vulnerable to peace propaganda. He feared, for example, that American propaganda might be directed "not . . . against the German people but against Nazism" (147) and "we can surely congratulate ourselves that our enemies have no Wilson Fourteen Points" (47).

Occasionally it became necessary to increase the anxiety level of Germans concerning a specific event. On February 24, 1942, after the first disastrous winter campaign in Russia, Goebbels "issued orders to the German press to handle the situation in the East favorably, but not too optimistically." He did not wish to raise false hopes but, perhaps more importantly, he did not want Germans to "cease to worry at all about the situation in the East" (99).

b. *Propaganda must diminish anxiety (other than that concerning the consequences of defeat) which is too high and which cannot be reduced by people themselves.* Air raids obviously raised German anxiety much too high, but they were a situation over which Goebbels could not exercise propaganda control. In other situations involving a demoralizing amount of anxiety he could be more active. "To see things in a realistic light" when the military situation in Tunisia became hopeless, German losses were portrayed as being "not of such a nature that as a result our chances for [ultimate] victory have been damaged" (M4542). In contrast, he attempted to use the same principle in reverse — the so-called "strategy of terror" — against his enemies. Leaflets were dropped on English cities "with pictures of the damage done by the English in Luebeck and Rostock, and under them the Fuehrer's announcement of his Reichstag speech that reprisal raids are coming" (193).

PROPAGANDA TO THE HOME FRONT MUST DIMINISH THE IMPACT OF FRUSTRATION

It was most important to prevent Germans from being frustrated, for example, by immunizing them against false hopes. If a frustration could not be avoided, Goebbels sought to diminish its impact by following two principles:

a. *Inevitable frustrations must be anticipated.* Goebbels' reasoning seems to have been that a frustration would be less frustrating if the element of surprise or shock were eliminated. A present loss was thus endured for the sake of a future gain. The German people were gradually given "some intimation that the end is in sight" as the fighting in Tunisia drew to a close (352). They likewise received advance hints whenever a reduction in food rations was contemplated; the actual announcement, nevertheless, always disturbed them (M1484).

b. *Inevitable frustrations must be placed in perspective.* Goebbels considered one of his principal functions to be that of giving the Germans what he called a *Kriegsüberblick,* a general survey of the war. Otherwise, he felt, they would lose confidence in their régime and in himself, and they would fail to appreciate why they were being compelled to make so many sacrifices (M4975).

PROPAGANDA MUST FACILITATE THE DISPLACEMENT OF AGGRESSION

Goebbels had few positive gratifications to offer Germans during the period of adversity covered by the diary. He featured enemy losses, quite naturally, whenever he could and whenever Germans were not over-confident. Only once did he praise Germans for withstanding the enemy as long as they had. By and large, the principal technique seems to have been that of displacing German aggression on to some out-group (M6220).

Favorite hate objects were "Bolsheviks" and Jews. Goebbels was disturbed by reports which indicated that "the fear of Bolshevism by the broad masses of European peoples has become somewhat weaker" (M4572) or that "certain groups of Germans, especially the intellec-tuals, express the idea that Bolshevism is not so bad as the Nazis represent it to be" (335). Anti-Semitic propaganda was usually combined with active measures against Jews in Germany or the occupied countries. German aggression was also directed against American and British pilots, but on the whole the United States and Great Britain did not stir Goebbels' wrath, at least in the diary (147).

In enemy countries Goebbels had a strong penchant to engage in "wedge-driving": he sought to foment suspicion, distrust, and hatred between his enemies and between groups within a particular country. He thus assumed that the foundation for hostility between nations or within a nation already existed for historical reasons or as a result of the frustrations of war. His task was to direct the aggression along disruptive channels (46).

PROPAGANDA CANNOT IMMEDIATELY AFFECT STRONG COUNTER-TENDENCIES; INSTEAD IT MUST OFFER SOME FORM OF ACTION OR DIVERSION, OR BOTH

In almost all of his thinking about propaganda strategy and ob-jectives, Goebbels adopted the distinction between what were called *Haltung* (bearing, conduct, observable behavior) and *Stimmung* (feel-ing, spirit, mood).[5] After a heavy raid on a German city, he generally claimed that the *Haltung* of the people was excellent but that their *Stimmung* was poor. He wished to have both of these components of morale as favorable as possible. *Stimmung* he considered much more volatile: it could easily be affected by propaganda and events; it might be improved simply by offering people some form of entertain-ment and relaxation. *Haltung* had to be maintained at all costs, for otherwise the Nazi régime would lose its support and people would be ready to surrender. Germans, in short, were compelled to preserve external appearances and to coöperate with the war effort, regardless of their internal feelings. As more and more defeats and raids were experienced, Goebbels became convinced that *Stimmung* had to be almost completely ignored (M6452).

Goebbels clearly recognized his own propaganda impotency in six situations. The basic drives of sex and hunger were not appreciably

[5] Lochner has ignored the distinction and has generally translated both as "morale," a term which Goebbels likewise occasionally employed in an equally ambiguous manner.

affected by propaganda. Air raids brought problems ranging from discomfort to death which could not be gainsaid. Propaganda could not significantly increase industrial production. The religious impulses of many Germans could not be altered, at least during the war. Overt opposition by individual Germans and by peoples in the occupied countries required forceful action, not clever words. Finally, Germany's unfavorable military situation became an undeniable fact. When propaganda and censorship could not be effective, Goebbels advocated action or, in one of his official positions (for example, as Gauleiter of Berlin), he himself produced the action. Diversionary propaganda he considered second-best (M3508).

Consider his propaganda with reference to military defeats. For a while he could describe them as "successful evacuations" (461). For a while he could even conceal their implications. Eventually, however, they were too apparent, especially after the heavy air raids began and the difficulties of fighting a two-front war increased. Then he was reduced not quite to silence but certainly to despair. At the end of the fighting in Tunisia he was forced to conclude that the following propaganda themes were not proving impressive: "our soldiers there have written a hymn of heroism that will be graven eternally on the pages of German history; they retarded developments for half a year, thereby enabling us to complete the construction of the Atlantic Wall and to prepare ourselves all over Europe so that an invasion is out of the question" (360). He tried to divert Germans through another anti-Bolshevik campaign, but this too was insufficient. What Germans really needed were "some victories in the East to publicize" (M4433). German losses in Russia, moreover, plagued Goebbels. Whenever possible, he tried to offset news of defeat in one section with reports of victories in others, but by 1943 he simply had no favorable news to employ as a distraction. *Stimmung* was doomed, and even *Haltung* worried him: "at the moment we cannot change very much through propaganda; we must once again gain a big victory somewhere" (M3253). Most fortunately, that victory and ultimate triumph never came.

▲ HAROLD D. LASSWELL

*T*he Strategy of Soviet Propaganda

It is no news to anyone that Soviet propaganda is full of inconsistencies whether you look at it through time or at the same time. At first there was fervent stress upon the themes of world revolution and the inevitable triumph of communism over capitalism. Suddenly at the Genoa Conference, Chicherin told us of "peaceful coöperation of two social systems during a given historical epoch." And the seesaw between coöperation and war to the death has been going on ever since. For years the Socialist and Liberal parties of the world were vilified by the Russian leaders as "Social Fascists," until suddenly a terrific threat appeared in Nazi Germany. And then the "united front against war and fascism" took top billing. But not for long. Came the Pact, and Stalin drank the health of the Führer. Came the German offensive, and slogans uncongenial to the West sank into the shadow, while Stalin made news by mentioning God in a favorable tone of voice. Came the end of hostilities, and the beginning of a new epoch of separatism and hatred. The United States now rises to the dignity of chief devil, taking the place occupied by the Nazis and the "Anglo-French plutocracies" in earlier times.

If there are differences, there are also consistencies in Russian propaganda. Many of the key symbols and slogans of the Marxist inheritance linger on.

Is there an interpretation capable of accounting for the zig-zags of Russian propaganda? I suggest that there is unity of strategic aim: *to maximize the power at home and abroad of the ruling individuals and groups of Russia.* Propaganda is an instrument of total policy, together with diplomacy, economic arrangements and armed forces.

▲ This article appeared in the *Proceedings* of the Academy of Political Science, Columbia University, in 1951. Copyright by the Academy, it is here reprinted by permission of the copyright holder. Dr. Lasswell is professor of political science in the Yale Law School.

Political propaganda is the management of mass communications for power purposes. In the long run the aim is to *economize the material cost of power*. Even more specifically: *the aim is to economize the material cost of world dominance*.

What will happen if this strategic goal is perfectly attained? There will be no general war. Indeed, it is doubtful that there will be local aggressions of the Korean type. Nation after nation will fall into the Russian orbit through complacency, division and intimidation. The United States will adopt policies that weaken its economic, political and social fabric; the United States will decline peacefully into a secondary place in world affairs. Perfect success by Russian propagandists will cut down the material costs that would be entailed by general war, or by a series of local aggressions, or by colossal preparations for war.

A fraction of the success just described can contribute mightily to the reduction of the material cost of Russian domination. Whatever shortens war, without compromising success, saves Russian resources.

Perhaps it is superfluous to point out that the use of propaganda as an instrument of power is no idiosyncrasy of the Russian ruling class. All ruling classes in large-scale communities resort to propaganda. There are, however, factors in the Russian case that set it somewhat apart. The contrast is particularly great when we think of the United States. The leaders of Russia are operating in a tight, supercentralized garrison-police state, while the leaders of the United States are still dispersed through government, business, education, and other relatively independent institutions. The elite of Russia is oriented toward power, and possesses a tradition of calculating power at home and abroad. In the United States the ruling elements are much less conscious of power as a predominating value, since they are more preoccupied with wealth, respect and other values.

The top rulers of Russia possess a doctrine and a tradition in which the use of propaganda plays a conspicuous part in the execution of total policy. No one is unmindful of the fact that the power seizure of 1917 was prepared by years of activity in which every member of the revolutionary party was supposed to devote most of his energies to propaganda.

It would be a mistake, however, to assume that the Russian elite emphasizes propaganda out of deference to the human mind, or to the rôle of ideas in history.[1] It is much closer to the mark to say that the tradition of the Russian ruling class is to discount both ideas and the human mind; for the strategy of Russian propaganda acts upon pessimistic assumptions about the capabilities of mankind for enlightenment by peaceful persuasion.

[1] The most important study of the perspectives of the Soviet elite is by Nathan Leites, *The Operational Code of the Politburo*.

Consider for a moment the doctrinal framework in which propaganda operations are conceived. Distrust of the "ideological" can readily be derived from the stress put upon the primacy of "material" factors in history. This inheritance from Marxism was given a special twist in the lives of the chief conspirative leaders of Russian socialism. Lenin was only too conscious of being in a minority. His conceptions of revolutionary action reflected the helplessness that he felt in the face of the task of winning the Russian masses by peaceful persuasion. He saw in the ideological structure of Russian peasants and workers the imprint of the material ascendancy of the old ruling class. The sluggishness, stubbornness and stupidity of the Russian masses, against which Lenin railed at times, were ideological factors in history. But these gigantic icebergs were frozen into shape by the "material" forces at the disposal of the older elites.

And how were these ideological residues to be broken up and melted down? Not by persuasion, concluded Lenin. Only by sweeping material transformations. But how was this to be reconciled with the use of propaganda?[2]

It is not necessary to assume that Lenin solved the problem of the interplay of material and ideological factors in a manner free of contradiction or entirely in harmony with scientific knowledge. But the conspirative activists of Russian hammered out strategy and tactics that continue to influence Russian leaders. The making of propaganda is primarily a "material" activity in the sense that it depends upon the control of instruments of production, such as presses capable of turning out magazines, pamphlets and books; and it depends upon hours of labor devoted to processing and distributing the product. It is "material" in the added sense that it is possible to concentrate upon audiences who occupy disadvantageous material positions, and who are therefore susceptible to programs for the betterment of their material state. The number of such "susceptibles" depends upon the intensity of the contradictions prevailing at a given time and place. If the material instruments of communication are skillfully employed, a very small concentration of material factors can reshape the ideas of an ever-expanding aggregate. Eventually those in control of the expanded material resources may seize power, and control enormously enriched means for transforming mass ideologies on a colossal scale.

Once the workers have attained the new ideological perspective, they can make sure of perpetuating it intact by utilizing the material instruments of communication which can then be accessible. This is the background for the provisions appearing in Article 125 of the Constitution of 1936 relating to freedom of communication. The Article says that the rights of the individual to free speech (and such)

[2] Concerning the theory of propaganda used by Soviet leaders see Alex Inkeles, *Public Opinion in Soviet Russia* (Cambridge, 1950).

are secured by turning over to the workers and their organizations the printing establishments, stocks of paper, public buildings, streets, means of communication, and other material conditions essential for the realization of these rights.

The standing charge against the capitalist world is that the working masses are full of the illusions disseminated by the press, which is said to be under the control of the plutocracy. Obviously, the assumption is that whoever controls the material instruments of communication can imprint upon the passive mind of the audience images that protect the material relationships then prevailing or in prospect. Thus propaganda is viewed as an activity, low in material cost, by means of which the receptivities created by material contradictions can be made politically effective.

The disregard of persuasion on the part of the Russian elite is apparent in the dogmatic finality with which the eventual goal of policy is treated. The elite possesses a rigid, non-debatable conception of the future. In this future commonwealth man is within the realm of freedom and not of necessity (Engels). The gloss on the doctrine as applied by the Russians is that those who pursue this aim may deny freedom to others until such time as no material contradictions remain which are capable of imprinting ideas hostile to the functioning of such a free society. Not the least of the menaces that must be obliterated are the streams of communication directed toward Russian audiences from the material facilities at the disposal of foreign elites. The Russian ruling group has no hesitation in using whatever material means are at hand to seal off the Russian audience from such "subversive" exposure.

The directors of Russian propaganda do not ignore the sentiments and assumptions of their current or prospective audiences. But this is not for the sake of sharing with the masses the task of creating a consensus, through free discussion, concerning the aims, major policies and top leaders of the body politic. On the contrary, the scrutiny of the audience is a one-way affair in which the deviation of the audience from some leadership objective raises only a tactical problem: namely, what are the most economical means of overcoming such deviations? At moments Lenin was brutally frank about his contempt for the thoughts and feelings of the masses when they were other than he wanted them to be. In common with other modern tyrannies, the present leaders of the Russian garrison-police state recognize that so much candor is a source of weakness. Hence the Stalinists now congratulate themselves upon having the "most perfect democracy" on earth in which the will of the people is more fully expressed than anywhere else. Thus is revived the mystic conception of democracy which makes it possible for a tyranny to pretend to "intuit," free of representative mechanisms, the most profound sentiments of the people.

Within the framework provided by the secular revelation of the commonwealth of freedom, all questions are reduced to the level of tactical expedients. A decent regard for the opinions and sentiments of others in superfluous or worse; it is an act of pandering to the accumulated errors stamped upon the human mind by the weight of the material at the disposal of previous ruling classes. Honesty is of no value as an expression of rectitude; there is always the higher rectitude of whatever contributes to the ultimate goal.

The major task of propaganda strategy is proper timing in relation to the specific dangers and opportunities of a given set of circumstances for the power position of the Russian elite. It is possible to trace the prevailing offensive and defensive strategies of Russian propaganda. Many essential features were exhibited in the preparation by Lenin for the seizure of power in Russia. If we go back to the years of deepest depression for the revolutionary movement (after the collapse of 1905), we find that the first task of Lenin was to form primary nuclei capable of further expansion. Lenin and his followers provided the man-hours for propaganda work. They were often able to gain recruits by direct personal propaganda, often preceded and facilitated by the output of the party presses.

When the primary nuclei became sufficiently abundant to operate as a significant part of the power process in trade unions, in political parties and in parliament, a second task took shape. The problem was to find allies without losing independence. Now allies, whether inside or outside of the socialist movement, were full of danger to the towering ambitions of a Lenin (or Leninists). Without allies there is the threat of being crushed entirely by a combination of hostile elements whose strength is potentially overwhelming. The propaganda strategy of Lenin was to keep alive an attitude of suspicion toward allies, while at the same time lulling the ally into complacency, or diverting his attention to a common enemy, or fanning disunity. Propaganda has many means of contributing to the complacency of an ally. There is the direct declaration of mutual friendship and admiration. And there is the nullifying of hostile or disturbing manifestations. The propaganda goal of diverting attention to a common enemy is comparatively obvious, but the tactic of fomenting disunity is exceedingly complicated. Plainly the ally must not be allowed to weaken below a point where his usefulness against a common enemy is lost. But internal tension can absorb attention, and thus divert attention from inconvenient features of the Leninist-led group. The strategy of division paves the way for coöperating with minorities in wrecking or taking over the control of the ally at some future date.

The third stage is the seizure of power, and this sets a somewhat different propaganda task, which is to demoralize the potential opposition, and to gain support, by creating an impression that all further opposition, or noncoöperation, is both useless and immoral.

At any given movement the Lenin-led groups might find it necessary to assume a defensive posture, which consisted for the most part in masking all hostile potentialities of policy toward an ally; and in redoubling attempts to prevent or to break up hostile combinations by spreading complacency, fear of a common enemy, and disunity.

To recapitulate the strategic rôle of propaganda as a means of reducing the material cost of expanding and defending power (as exemplified by the Leninists, and followed subsequently by the Stalinists): *Stage one.* The creation of primary nuclei in which fully indoctrinated individuals provide the solid corps of full-time labor for the cause. *Stage two.* Coöperation with allies in the arenas of power accessible to the nuclei, who are by this time sufficiently strong to act as "parties," "unions," and the like. The propaganda task is to maintain the sentiment of having a distinctive mission (inside the party or "own" group), while at the same time fostering certain attitudes among potential enemies (including allies). The attitudes include complacency toward the party; the diversion of hostile attention to a common enemy; the spreading of disunity. *Stage three.* Seizure of power. Propaganda demoralization of the opposition and of noncoöperators: spreading fear or confidence in the inevitable triumph of the party, and of the hopelessness and immorality of further opposition or noncoöperation.[3]

Consider briefly the application of these strategic principles to the seizure of power in countries adjacent to Russia (the present satellites). The first task of propaganda in Hungary or Czechoslovakia was to win enough support to begin to play a bargaining part in the ordinary processes of local and national parliamentarism and administration. This was accomplished by penetrating the trade unions, and other private associations. The second task arose when the party was strong enough to join coalitions, and to work with allies at every level of government (including special attempts to permeate the ministries concerned with public order and information). The third stage came with the seizure and consolidation of power by *coup d'état* (within a "framework of legality"). It was during the second stage that the greatest versatility was required in the handling of Russian propaganda, since it was necessary to keep in balance the often contradictory tasks of fostering a distinctive sense of mission, complacency on the part of potential enemies (including allies), diversion of attention

[3] The seizure of power in Russia was but one step in the expansion of the Communist movement, though the most decisive. In relation to most of the world arena, the Soviet elite is at stage one or two. Stage three has been achieved piecemeal in adjacent states. On the internal transformations in Russia since 1917, see especially Barrington Moore, Jr., *Soviet Politics — The Dilemma of Power* (Cambridge, 1950).

to common enemies, and disunity. This was the period in which such illusions were useful as that Russian policy has at last "settled down" to peaceful coexistence and to the restoration of genuine coöperative effort. The third stage is less subtle and far more ruthless, since it involves the spreading of terror, often by means of close correlation and coöperation with acts of violence.[4]

Looking at the world picture as a whole, it can be said that Russian propaganda is best served at the first stage (penetrating a new community) by propaganda that possesses high doctrinal content. It is the function of propaganda during this period to provide a professional nucleus of revolutionaries to give skillful direction to ensuing activities. Suppose we ask ourselves why the propagandists of the Kremlin continue to repeat so many of the time-worn doctrines of the Marxist tradition. Clearly the answer is that most of the traditional doctrines are of demonstrated effectiveness in appealing to the disaffected of many lands, whether in the heartlands of modern industrialism, or among the peoples long subject to the economic expansionism of Western states. It is an old story that the dissolution of ancient loyalties and the break-up of old religious faiths and philosophical traditions have been signs of, and in turn contributory to, the vast transformations through which mankind is passing in our historical period. It is an old story that Marxist doctrine has provided a secular substitute for the universality of aim, of cosmic outlook, and of personal identification with destiny which were part of earlier systems. No doubt it is an old story that Marxism and liberalism were co-ideologies which were alike in attacking the institutions of a caste society, and in proclaiming the importance of renovating society for the sake of realizing human dignity in theory and fact.

Several of the doctrines carried forward from historical Marxism by the elite of Russia have a plausible ring to millions of human beings who live exposed to the material and ideological tensions of our time. (Note that I now speak only of plausibility, not of truth or falsity.)

Consider the familiar thesis that there is a tendency toward monopoly in capitalistic economies. Can the plausibility of this be denied in the United States, for instance, where monopoly trends have been the subject of lament for years?

Consider the thesis that the capitalistic system generates periodic crises of mass unemployment. In the light of "panics," "crises" and "depressions," can we sweep this entirely to one side?

Consider further the thesis that movements of protest arise among

[4] Consult these authoritative and concise case studies: Ivo Duchacek, "The Strategy of Communist Infiltration: Czechoslovakia, 1944-48," *World Politics*, vol. II, No. 3 (April 1950), pp. 345-72, and "The February Coup in Czechoslovakia," *ibid.*, July 1950, pp. 511-32; Stephen D. Kertesz, "The Methods of Communist Conquest: Hungary, 1944-1947," *ibid.*, October 1950, pp. 20-54.

the nonowners in capitalistic societies. This is not implausible in view of the vitality displayed by protest movements in the name of "labor," "socialism" and other political symbols.

Again, think of the doctrine that in parliamentary countries the owners abandon democracy in favor of non-democracy when they feel seriously threatened by movements of protest. Is this altogether implausible in view of the aid received from big industrialists and landlords in the formative stages of Mussolini's fascism, Hitler's Nazism, or Franco's falangism?

Think also of the thesis that imperialism is a result of capitalistic rivalries for the control of raw materials and markets. Obviously this gains plausibility from the scramble for colonies which enlarged the empires of England, France, Germany and Belgium, and which put the United States in the place of Spain in the Carribean and the Philippines.

Consider the thesis that imperialistic rivalries generate wars among imperial Powers. In this connection it is possible to point to the rivalries between England and Germany before 1914, and the German thrust for "living space" in the recent past.

Think finally of the revision which the "imperialism and war" thesis has undergone in recent years. I refer to the conception of capitalist encirclement of the "Socialist Fatherland," and the promotion of armament and war as means of preparing an attack upon Russia, particularly in the hope of diverting against an outside group the gathering rage of the unemployed masses of a collapsing capitalism. Is it not true that capitalistic countries have been stepping up their expenditures of arms? These doctrinal lines have an important place in the strategic balance of Russian propaganda appeals. Recruits continue to be sought by means of study groups devoted to the writings of Marx, Engels, Lenin, Stalin and other acceptable figures in the canonical list. That these study groups are effective instruments of Russian power has been demonstrated more than once. May I remind you that when the Canadian government looked into the spy ring in Canada, the trail led to study groups organized privately as recruiting stations for persons of high intellect and culture. Wherever Marxism-Leninism-Stalinism is ignored in the advanced educational systems of a country, or tossed aside with conspicuous prejudice by teachers who are obviously ignorant of the subject, the basis is laid for curiosities that may be gratified in private and faintly (or overtly) clandestine study groups. In these intellectual "speak-easies" the doctrinal system is expounded in a pious atmosphere free of the critical, deflating effect of vigorous evaluation on a comparative basis. Study groups are an important example of the tactical principle that it is possible to move toward effective power in an indifferent or hostile society by limited concentrations of superiority of books and man-hours in propaganda work. (The step from private study to espionage or sabotage is not too long for many persons to make.)

It is noteworthy that the greatest successes of Russian propaganda have been scored among nonindustrial peoples. This is a good example of the choice of audience anywhere in the world wherever material or ideological factors have created tension. These activities are vital at all stages of the power-seizing process, but create special resonances at stages one and two above. The Russian elite has become progressively clearer about the potential rôle of the "ex-colonial" victims of "imperialism," especially since so many of the "ex-colonials" live on the continent of Asia within the shadow of the Russian world. The new noncommunist elites of these countries are relatively weak, while the old elites are largely discredited. The sentiment of nationalism can be turned against former "oppressors" and directly toward complacent coöperation with Russia. Further, the resentment of ex-colonials is fed by the rankling memory of the indignities imposed upon them by the "white imperialists." In the traditional literature of socialism the link between race prejudice and capitalism has long been forged. The formula is that capitalists seek to divide the workers from one another, and to drive wages down, by setting black against white, yellow against white, and so on. Seizing upon these cleavages in the respect structure of the non-Russian world, the strategy of Russian propaganda is to identify imperialism and ethnic discrimination with capitalism. For this purpose the chief target is the strongest capitalist Power, the United States; hence, the distorted image of America as a land with Negroes hanging from the lampposts, lynched by miserable gangs of sharecroppers and unemployed workers, incited by ruthless agents of the plutocracy who are commissioned to keep the workers at one another's throats.[5]

The conspirative tradition of pre-revolutionary times has left an imprint upon the channels as well as the content and the strategic-tactical correlation of propaganda with total policy. Consider from this point of view the method of dual organization. This is the use of an open channel of propaganda which is closely paralleled by a closed, secret channel. The technique can be applied in many ways, as when one is labeled "governmental" and the other "party." If the upper corridor is closed for reasons of expediency, the basement is kept in operation (as when the Comintern was publicly extinguished in 1943). The secret channel can be a faction which is entrusted with the mission of controlling the policy of organizations which are nominally independent of party control. Hence the vast network of "come-on" organizations which are used by the party to permeate every national community, seeking to reach the armed forces, the police, the

[5] For the whole picture consult Frederick C. Barghoorn, *The Soviet Image of the United States; A Study in Distortion* (New York, 1950).

foreign service, business, the professions, trade unions, coöperatives, schools, publishing houses, radio-television, films, and the like. There is a slot for housewives who hate high prices, for mothers who hate war, and for humanitarians of every hue. Through these organizational networks a great number of special environments are made available for the restamping of minds, and for expanding the material facilities within the reach of the Russian leadership. The Russian technique parallels in a curious way the means by which in a capitalist economy the control of a gigantic network of private corporations is obtained through a series of minority stock ownerships. The parallel includes the use of "fronts" who are called "dummies" in the vernacular of capitalism, and something less complimentary in the private language of Russian propaganda.

Dual control was a congenial method in the hands of conspirator Lenin, who employed a small clique of disciples to continue to do what he wanted to do regardless of the formal prohibitions of his party. One striking example is the secret organization by means of which funds were raised through robbery, counterfeiting, seduction of rich women, and the like. To this day the channels of Russian propaganda continue to use the dual structure appropriate to conspiracy. In this way it is possible to conduct activities of the utmost unscrupulousness.

We can sum up the strategy of Soviet propaganda by saying that the chief strategic aim is to economize the material cost of protecting and extending the power of the Russian elite at home and abroad. Such propaganda is a struggle for the mind of man, from the Soviet point of view, only in the sense that it is a struggle for the control of the material means by which the minds of the masses are believed to be molded. Hence the purpose of Russian propaganda is *not* peaceful persuasion of the majority of the people in a given country as a prelude to the taking of power. Rather, the task is conceived as that of a minority that must remain an ideological minority until it succeeds in accumulating the material means of obtaining consensus. In the early stage of penetrating a new community, the basic task of propaganda is to assist in establishing and shaping primary nuclei of potential leadership at the next stages. When enough strength is assembled to admit of a strategy of coalition, the task is to maintain separatism, coupled with propaganda designed to prevent or break up potentially more powerful combinations. The fostering of complacency, the diversion of attention to common enemies, and the fomenting of division among potential enemies (including momentary allies) are part of the strategic tasks to be carried through. At the stage of power seizure the strategy of propaganda is that of demoralization, which is sought in synchronization with terror as a means of impressing all with the "inevitable" triumph of Soviet power and the hope-

lessness, and indeed the immorality, of resistance or even noncoöperation. Possessing a world-encompassing goal that is treated as beyond
the reach of discussion or inquiry, the ruling few of the Kremlin have
no self-limitations of principle upon the choice of message, channel or
audience. Soviet propagandists and their agents can lie and distort
without inner restraint, for they are largely immunized from the
claims of human dignity in any other sense than the dignity of contributing to the ultimate goal of the free man's commonwealth by
contributing to the present and future power of the Kremlin elite.

▲ PHILIP SELZNICK

*P*roblems of Counteroffense

Against International Communism

A complete program of anticommunist action must be based on a study of the conditions producing equilibrium in democratic societies. Such a study has not been undertaken here. Consequently, it must be emphasized that in this final chapter we are concerned with such conclusions regarding counteroffensive action as may be inferred *from this report*. It is believed that the foregoing analysis of communist strategy does suggest certain principles which are necessary for the intelligent formulation of policy. These principles, however, are not offered as a full "answer" to the problem of communism. They are relevant primarily to the context of political combat; and this context is only a part of that broad area — including measures enhancing the emotional and economic security of target groups — within which decisions affecting totalitarian threats to democracy are made.

The more we understand about the nature of communism, the more readily can we avoid (1) the failure to recognize its true aims and subversive methods and (2) those excessive reactions which threaten themselves to undermine the foundations of democratic society. Increased knowledge helps us to think concretely, to specify the problem in situational terms, to direct countermeasures to those areas where they are relevant and useful, and to avoid unsought consequences for the integrity of our institutions.

The problem of subversion has two aspects which are often confused. On the one hand, a group is considered subversive when it seeks to overthrow established authority by forcible means. It is here that the doctrine of "clear and present danger" most readily applies,

▲ This is the concluding chapter of Dr. Selznick's book, *The Organizational Weapon,* published in 1952 by the McGraw-Hill Book Company, and copyright by the RAND Corporation. It is reprinted here by permission of copyright holder and publisher. Dr. Selznick wrote the volume as a member of the social science staff of the RAND Corporation.

the assumption being that governments ought to punish acts and not thoughts, and that measures of restraint ought to be consistent with the seriousness of the acts committed. However, the problem is complicated when, as in the case of communism, subversion refers not only to a revolutionary program, but also to the manipulation of social institutions for alien ends, this manipulation being conducted covertly in the name of the institution's own values. It is this type of subversion which is meant when fear is expressed of the effect of communism in the schools, in the labor movement, and in liberal organizations. Such activities, and ultimate overthrow of the government, are of course related, but concern for the integrity of the institutions themselves leads us to seek modes of self-defense long before any clear and present danger to established authority is demonstrable.

We assume that institutional leaders, including those in government, have the right and the duty to defend the principles upon which their organizations are built. An inescapable corollary of this assumption is that the methods of action available to these leaders are limited. Since the goal is the defense of certain *values* (not simply of the power of an elite), the weapons used against subversion must be so fashioned as to preserve these values in the course of their defense.

These considerations, therefore, call for subtle and discriminating judgments, and can be given effect in policy formation only on the basis of detailed knowledge. This study has sought to contribute to our understanding of bolshevism in the hope that we may then be in a better position to make such decisions as would defeat the enemy without destroying ourselves. Given this perspective, the following conclusions deserve emphasis:

1. Each institution should be defended in its own terms. The appraisal of subversive threats to the integrity of institutions must take account of the differing conditions that affect the preservation of that integrity.

2. Anticommunist strategy should orient to the "intervening elites" through whom access to the mass is gained and who have the capacity to direct resentment into constitutional channels.

3. The denial of legitimacy is a key to the denial of access; but measures which seek to influence legitimacy must be adapted to the nature of the arena.

4. In the denial of access, the aim is to isolate the communists; but this counterstrategy has to do with *political* isolation and cannot be equated with formal exclusion from membership in unions or other organizations.

5. Reliance on organizational weapons is, for communists and anticommunists alike, a sign of strategic weakness rather than of strength. Hence countermeasures taken within the content of organizational combat are, from the standpoint of the over-all defense of democracy

against communism, of only tactical importance. Ultimately, only measures which contribute to long-term economic and political stability will be decisive.

THE NEED FOR SITUATIONAL THINKING

Although the *problem* of subversion concerns the entire society, effective countermeasures require that attention be focused upon specific arenas and targets. This seems scarcely more than a truism. Yet many proposals for anticommunist action ignore the fundamental principle that political combat, like other planned struggles, requires situational judgment; i.e., the nature of the arena must be taken into account when tactical decisions are made. Communist strategy is selective and elite-oriented. Effective counteroffense must take account of this strategy, recognizing the sources of weakness and strength in bolshevism, adapting itself to the conditions of combat in particular arenas.

The problem of denying to the communists such strategic objectives as legitimacy, access, and the neutralization of opponents *may* be considered from the point of view of the total society. But when this is done, there is a twofold danger: measures of intimidation and coercion may be introduced at many points where they are not justified by the actual subversive potential of the communists, resulting in a needless weakening of basic civil rights and in the strengthening of arbitrary methods; at the same time, such measures may be ineffective because they contribute to rather than weaken the strength of the communists among key elements in the community.

This general point will be clarified if we consider a few specific conclusions:

1. *Reliance on organizational weapons is a sign of strategic weakness rather than of strength.* In the general political struggle, organizational weapons provide the communists with important tactical advantages. But it must be remembered that these weapons have been developed precisely in order to overcome communism's fundamental weakness with respect to what is ultimately basic to political power — control over loyalties. Indeed, one of the general functions of organizational weapons is that of *eluding the need to win consent* as a condition for attaining or wielding power. When a power-oriented elite wishes to exercise authority beyond its ability to mobilize favorable opinion in its own right, organizational manipulation may be one method of doing so without the use of violence. The Leninists rely on organizational devices to gain power for a minority; and, indeed, any totalitarian government depends on such devices to control and mobilize the community.

In the United States, communist strength in the unions is dependent almost completely on the effective use of disciplined units of the combat party. This penetration and manipulation is abetted, to be sure, by the special circumstances of union organization, particularly (1) the ease with which one-party regimes are established within them and (2) the atmosphere of labor-management conflict, which binds the ranks to leaders under fire from the "enemy." Yet it is clear that the ideology of communism — either the traditional class-struggle variety or more modern stereotypes associated with Soviet patriotism — has with very few exceptions taken no hold upon the minds of labor's rank and file.

The situation among certain middle-class sectors is quite different, however. It is among these — especially professional and other groups who try to think for themselves and hence are accessible to ideological manipulation — that we find the fellow travelers of communism. Not necessarily accepting the doctrines of Marxism, these groups are seduced by Leninist activism and are drawn to the Soviet Union for the easy symbolic gratifications it offers. The party's peripheral organizations operating among these groups are more and more becoming devices for the mobilization of latent support rather than for winning power by the covert manipulation of groups basically unsympathetic to the movement.

Where communist strength is based exclusively on the effective use of organizational techniques, the problem of counteroffense is relatively simple, once the need to oust the party agents from positions of influence has been recognized. The need is to create and encourage devices to mobilize latent anticommunist sentiment. The strategic advantages are on the side of the anticommunists, and there need be little anxiety concerning the ultimate outcome.

2. *Effective anticommunist opposition is that which is relevant to the specific arena of combat.* The bolsheviks, in penetrating an organization, always seek to identify themselves with its aims — they become the "best workers" for whatever goals the organization seeks to attain. Occasionally, as in the case of their superpatriotism during World War II, affecting trade-union policies, the goals of the organization may be directly subverted. This is not ordinarily the case: what is usually at stake is the indirect consequence of communist control for the long-range character of the organization and for its role in the community. The struggle for the "soul" of an organization — its evolving commitments to modes of action and its basic loyalties — can be carried on only by participants. Efforts to intervene from the outside are usually self-defeating. This means that opposition to the communists in any given arena must come from within, led by men whose loyalty to the institution is unquestionable. Even this criterion, however, is not enough. Not only must the opposition come from within the arena, but to be most effective it should be able to appeal

to the same sources of support as do the communists, to meet them on their own ground.

3. *Defense against communism requires positive measures for the protection of institutional integrity, each in its own terms.* Institutions embody values, but they do not all do so in the same way. Therefore no uniform program can be devised, or is needed, which will protect all institutions with the same devices for, say, the denial of access or of legitimacy. Simple formulae, such as those calling for the formal exclusion of communists from all organizations and institutions, reflect a failure to think in concrete strategic and tactical terms.

There is no sure way of gauging the point at which communism becomes a clear and present danger to the integrity of an institution. This requires an estimate of the total situation, taking account of many symptoms. But it is at least possible to say that such estimates should be based on evidence available for each case rather than solely on inferences drawn from the general threat to society as a whole. Given a world situation in which democracy is under attack, institutional leaders will naturally wish to be on guard — in the sense of alert to — the sources and methods of totalitarian attack. But repressive measures, themselves consequential for institutional integrity, should be taken only when evidence shows that the particular institution is in danger.

This localization of the clear-and-present-danger doctrine will avoid the twin pitfalls of innocence and hysteria. On the one hand, the existence of a general communist threat is recognized; on the other, the faulty process of leaping from a general threat to repressive measures in specific cases is rejected. Innocence in this context fails to recognize the potentialities of communism and hence is blind when the threat is real; hysteria sees concrete manifestations of the threat everywhere, is unable to distinguish the possible from the actual. Both responses inhibit the application of intelligence to the formulation of policy.

The need for application of countermeasures according to the varying needs of particular situations will be evident if we compare a university, a government agency, and a trade-union. These institutions vary in function, hence also in relative vulnerability. Few ideas are too dangerous to be afforded a place in a university. Given proper safeguards, even the espousal of totalitarian doctrine — if done openly and not secretly or deviously — can be permitted, if only to function as a challenge within the intellectual community. Such participation can be controlled if the universities take account of the whole man, his entire background and prospective role on the faculty.

Administrative agencies, however, which must rely on the discretion of officials in action, face a different problem. Here there is no question of creating an environment most conducive to effective teaching and to the pursuit of truth, but of responsible and controlled decision-making. Therefore there can be no question of conscious toleration of elements inherently disloyal.

Labor unions face still other problems and have different opportunities for the elimination of communism. As voluntary associations, organized democratically, the unions are political arenas; the existence of anticommunist power groupings is the most effective way of dealing with the problem. At the same time, the special role of the labor movement as a target of communist penetration calls for the cooperation of such power groupings on a national basis in order to pool resources and concentrate forces at crucial points.

In other words, apart from general alertness, the methods proper in one institutional context are not necessarily justifiable (or effective) in another. Each must be dealt with in its own terms, due consideration being given to the intensity of the threat and to the special needs of each in defending its integrity.

THE ROLE OF INTERVENING ELITES

Apart from the state power of the Soviet Union, the most secure source of communist influence is not its own agitation, or its organizational effectiveness, but the unrest generated by stresses within society. This unrest calls forth its own leadership to create and man the machinery of social action — unions, pressure groups, political parties, newspapers. These heterogeneous and fluctuating leaders occupy a strategic role, for *the relation between the communists and the mass is mediated and largely determined by the prior relation of the communists to reformist organizational and ideological elites.* This, as we have seen, is very well understood by the bolsheviks themselves and effectively shapes their choice of targets and methods of action. Their use of "unity" tactics and of peripheral organizations is based on the assumption that leaders of mass organizations and those who mold public opinion are susceptible to manipulation. Through such activity, oriented to elites, the communists seek to gain access to the major sources of power in the society. In general, the *direct* relation of the communists to the masses comes only after considerable preparatory work among the "natural" leaders of workers, farmers, and middle-class groups. While these leaders give expression to rank-and-file resentment and to the desire for change, they also reflect the basic loyalty of their followers to the established institutional order.

Such intervening elites, standing between the communists and the masses, have always been regarded as the "main enemy" in bolshevik political strategy. Although this basic perspective has not changed, latter-day communism has adopted a more flexible and sophisticated approach to the "petty-bourgeois" leaders and publicists. Lenin stressed the need for a frontal attack upon these elites to isolate them from the masses. In this, however, he displayed too much faith in the potentialities of open communist agitation; his successors have relied more on deception, using the techniques he himself developed. This has required an attempt to gauge the differential vulnerability and potential utility of elite members for the movement, instead of writing them off as simple colaborators and defenders of the "class enemy."

The importance to the communists of neutralizing threats to the social base has been discussed. The greatest animus is generally directed against those who challenge the communists in specific organizational arenas. These threats come primarily from socialists and others who share certain strategic perspectives and modes of action with the communists. Some reformists, however, especially unattached labor leaders, professors, and publicists, do not threaten the communists directly or in any relevant organizational way. They do constitute an ultimate political threat as a group which can, in a time of crisis, help to divert the masses from revolutionary goals. Yet if approached "with patience and caution," these leaders can themselves be manipulated, hence treated as mass elements rather than as self-conscious elites.

Although it is true that socialists are among the "natural enemies" of the communists in the organizational battle, the socialists themselves are not invulnerable. This weakness has two important sources. First, the socialist organizations are themselves vulnerable to bolshevik penetration when they have failed to take a clear stand (as reflected in the indoctrination and selection of the membership) against the idea that capitalism is the main enemy, overlooking the threat to political democracy from sources not accounted for in the Marxian view of history.

When a socialist organization or a significant portion of its leadership is uncertain about its own character, it is possible for the communists to build a "left wing" within the organization. This left wing, composed of revolutionary socialists and secret communists, can then carry on a factional fight for control of the organization, either ousting the old leadership or itself leaving and thus weakening the party. Such activities are usually associated with strong feelings for "unity" with the communists. This process, which occurred in the United States during the mid-thirties, was evident in a number of European countries after World War II. As a result, the socialists have been weakened politically, although in many cases their antibolshevik stand has been clarified and firmly established.

It follows that socialist education, largely an elite-oriented operation, should be aided wherever possible.[1] The emphasis should be on

[1] Rules of this kind do not imply advocacy of socialism or other reformist movements. To the extent, however, that they do exist as significant political forces, their capacity to fight communism should be enhanced.

strengthening the differences between socialism and communism. Any propaganda which slurs over these real and potential differences, with the purpose of identifying communists and socialists, will subvert this task. This is one area where mass communication techniques are not necessarily relevant. The need is for educational work, through select-audience journals, books, and schools, which will strengthen anti-bolshevik understanding among the socialists and will lend assistance to those positive tendencies (including the Christian Socialists) which seek to ground the socialist movement upon a non-Marxian ideology.

The second source of socialist vulnerability is shared by any other reformist elite which champions social change while mobilizing mass resentment in the struggle for power. The socialists (and other reformist elites) must reflect, even while attempting to restrain, the sentiments of those who constitute their mass base. To the extent that this sentiment is congenial to (although not necessarily created by) communist programs, the reformist leaders may be forced into undesired positions. For example, pressure for "unity" with the communists may come from below, and the reformists may be forced into extremist positions which threaten social stability when general distress stirs the rank and file.

The political function of the intervening elites is to direct mass resentment into constitutional channels. The Leninists understand this very well, although, being interested only in the power relevance of group behavior, they identify this function of the reformists as their *only* role in society. It is precisely because the natural function of the intervening elites operates to sustain the established political order — while heading off the forces which may threaten it — that the communists devote so much strategic and tactical attention to them. This attention is divided between efforts to neutralize those who are direct organizational competitors and to win over those who, because of inadequate self-consciousness, can be treated as mass elements. An effective anticommunist program must also take account of these potentialities, strengthening the capacity of the reformists to enhance social stability.

The radicalism of the intervening elites, when it is manifest, reflects not so much a firmly held doctrine as it does the depth of the crisis. An upheaval within the labor movement, such as produced the CIO, will emphasize radicalism; so too will the problems of leading the unemployed. But as social conditions stabilize, the agencies of reformism become institutionalized, and the leadership, being more secure, reasserts its fundamental commitment to the established order.

This normal process is best exemplified in the labor movement. Indeed, of all the reformist elites, it is the labor leadership which is least vulnerable to the blandishments of communism. That is because an established union leadership has a stake in a going concern, seeks to minimize risks to the survival of its organizations, and readily adapts itself to what seems a viable, even if limited, mode of social action. In the United States, communist strength in the labor movement is not significantly due to the weakness of the labor elite; such strength as they have (apart from the penetrative powers of the combat party) is largely a residue of their capacity to fill a vacuum during the days of the great labor upswing of the mid-thirties. As the strength and stability of the labor leadership has grown, its ability to defend itself from — and indeed to take the offensive against — communist inroads has markedly increased. This was understood by Lenin, who counted the leaders of the "yellow" trade-unions among his primary targets.

Although modern communism has revised early Leninist doctrine to the extent of softening its verbal attack in order to take advantage of vulnerabilities as they arise, the basic orientation has not changed, nor has the validity of Lenin's insight. When trade-unions are strong, they are a bulwark against communism; but when they are weak, they are communism's opportunity. Lenin's heirs have understood better than he that elites become vulnerable to seduction when their institutions are weak. But this understanding, permitting greater tactical flexibility, does not alter the fundamental fact that the natural course of labor leadership is toward acceptance of the established order rather than rebellion against it. The labor leaders, Lenin would have said, seize upon social unrest and direct it into channels which are consistent with the continued existence of the constitutional order. This, as we have suggested, is an accurate judgment. We need not follow Lenin in his conclusion that this constitutes "betrayal of the masses."

Apart from the trade-union movement, reformism in the United States has had few strong institutional centering points. Its leadership has therefore been unstable, easily influenced by the shifting winds of doctrine, not bound by any strong ideological loyalties. This condition of chronic weakness has made the "progressive" movement an easy target for the communists, who have preyed upon its sentimental attachment to vague ideas, putting themselves forward as "the most vigorous fighters" for the values of democratic idealism.

As in the case of the socialists, a key problem for these institutionally unattached reformist elements is that of character-definition. The need is to sharpen their own self-image so that the basic difference between reformist liberals and communists cannot be obscured. This heightened self-consciousness in turn requires an appreciation of bolshevism's challenge to democratic constitutionalism on a world scale, as well as education in and reaffirmation of the democratic values themselves. Of course, everyone needs education along these lines. But where education is part of an anticommunist *strategy*, it must be designed to strengthen those who are "on the line," not only because of their own vulnerability, but because, newly armed, they are in a position to carry on the struggle where it can do the most good.

In mustering the intervening elites, it is wise not to abandon those who have a "communist element." We do not write off a military position when the enemy has penetrated with a patrol; yet in anticommunist tactics, this error is often encountered. It must be granted, understood in advance, that the communists will attempt to gain strength among the reformists; to identify the communist element is to *set* a problem, not to solve it. Just when a particular organization is to be written off as being hopelessly under communist control depends on the concrete circumstances, *including the possibility of competing for power within the organization.* In any case, the yielding of a particular organization should not be confused with the tarnishing of an entire social group as inherently subversive.

The essential point is that these intervening elites arise spontaneously under conditions of social stress and that they can perform the indispensable function of directing mass resentment into self-preserving channels. They are therefore both obstacle and target for the communists; it behooves an anticommunist strategy to maximize the size of the obstacle and the impenetrability of the target.

THE DENIAL OF LEGITIMACY

We have seen that bolshevism is sensitive to the need to legitimize its striving for power. Further, our analysis has shown that the bolshevik approach to legitimacy is situational, always adapted to the contest for a specific political arena. Thus Lenin tried to show that his ideas represented the true Marxist heritage, and to appropriate the symbols and heroes of Marxism for his movement. Similarly, the bolsheviks attempt to guard their role as participants in the general community of democratic idealism so that they will be thought of as simply one tendency among others within the liberal-labor movement. In doing so, they establish their right to participate in the organizations of labor and liberalism, an indispensable condition for the deployment of organizational weapons against key targets.

The opponents of communism are, in general, aware of the problem of legitimacy. Thus legitimacy is at stake in proposals to outlaw the communists as a legal party, and in efforts to treat them as pariahs, outside the pale of the community. Such efforts, however, are inadequate when they fail to take account of the special areas within which legitimacy is sought. The communists have been political pariahs with respect to this nation as a whole during their entire history; yet this has not kept them from extending their influence among disaffected elements seeking change, where communist activity is most effective. These elements, when access to them is won, offer the communists a base from which ultimately to attack the community as a whole. *The problem is to deny them this base,* to see to it that the groups to whom they appeal (not the society as a whole) do not accept them as legitimate participants in the movement for social reform.

As we have seen, the targets of communist penetration are vulnerable to the extent that they lose sight of ultimate character-defining values and consequently lose the capacity to apply any save superficial criteria to potential collaborators and participants. When liberals focus their attention exclusively upon goals, ignoring methods, they tend to accept the help of any proffered hand. Since, in specific areas, the strength of the communists may not be insignificant, this help may result in commitments which decisively alter the character of the reformist movements. But this process is not inevitable. Once the subversive potential of the communists is understood, it is quite possible for reformist organizations to eschew collaboration with communists and to become effective and self-conscious enemies of bolshevism.

If legitimacy in these key areas is to be denied the communists — for it is here, not in society at large, that they have been able to make significant inroads — then tactics must be adopted which will achieve that end. During certain periods, general legislation outlawing communism may be superfluous for the community as a whole; and precisely such legislation may have the consequence of strengthening rather than weakening the legitimacy of communists among those elements which provide them with an indispensable leverage in the body politic.

Legislative measures aimed at purging the labor movement of communist influence, but which actually operate to weaken noncommunist unions, serve to bolster the strength of the communists. Such action lends credence to their assertion that "what hurts us hurts labor." It follows that the communist issue should be clearly separated from general labor legislation. The rule is that nothing should be done tending to confuse communism with bona fide labor leadership, for it is precisely this confusion which the communists earnestly seek. The same holds for other reformist organizations and leaders.

These strictures as to the *misapplication* of the strategic principle of denying legitimacy do not, of course, impugn the principle itself. Indeed, one of the conclusions suggested by our analysis of communist organizational strategy may be formulated as follows: *Effective counteroffense calls for the denial to communists of legitimate participation in labor and reformist organizations.* This requires that educational activities on the communist issue be *elite-oriented.* The history of communist manipulation of target groups must be made available to such elites in specific terms relevant to their own problems and aims. In addition, these groups must be brought to see the general threat of communism to democratic values so that (1) the urgency of clarifying their own positions will be recognized and (2) the image of communism as a "left-wing" of democratic idealist tendencies will be destroyed. Such a program of reorientation cannot take place in an atmosphere which confuses the distinction between the vulnerable target and the aggressor.

The orientation to elites helps to refine a policy which is, indeed, already widely accepted. Anticommunist strategy does take account of the possibility that acute social distress may thrust large masses "into the arms of the communists." It is therefore generally recognized that effective strategy — whatever one's feelings regarding the moral status of the participants — clearly requires that a distinction be made between the seducer and the seduced. This principle should be extended to include the relation of communism to reformist ideological and organizational elites.

It is in this area, far more than in relation to the population at large, that educational activity can be extremely useful. The problem is not one of mass propaganda, but of training opinion-leaders within those centers that mobilize masses in times of crisis. It has been amply demonstrated in practice that such leaders become strong barriers to the power drive of the party when they come to a full understanding of the meaning of communism. Not only is vulnerability reduced by the anticommunist self-consciousness of these elements, but, more important, new weapons relevant to the arenas of action can be forged for use in offensive action against the communists and the areas they control. A good example is the effective work of the International Confederation of Free Trade Unions on such issues as forced labor in the Soviet Union.

A primary objective of this educational activity, thus directed, would be to deny to the communists their role as legitimate participants in the movements of democratic idealism. For it is the belief that the communists are only "more radical, perhaps even a little fanatical, but still part of the general community of those committed to democracy" which opens the door to their subversive operations. It must be recognized that this subversion is in the first instance directed against the reformist movements themselves, as a means of access to the society as a whole. To deny legitimacy is to deny access and hence to isolate and render politically impotent the bolshevik organizational weapons.

Historically, the labor movement has been associated with reformism; and the organization of labor has been a road to influence, not only for the communists, but for other political groupings as well. These other tendencies have for the most part been loyal to the basic interests of labor and have accepted, with many variations, its responsibilities to the entire community. At the same time, partly because of firsthand knowledge of bolshevism, partly because of the exigencies of seeking power for themselves, they have been the most consistent and effective barriers to communist expansion in the labor movement. These anticommunist resources should be broadened and exploited in the general counteroffensive. In order to do so, the common source from which these elements are drawn — the general radical and reformist tendencies in the country — should be made aware of the basic threat of communism, *not only to the status quo, but to the ideals of the reformers themselves.*

Such a program does not necessarily call for partisan support of the noncommunist left; it does suggest that where such forces exist their anticommunist potentialities should be recognized and aided. Such aid is not so much positive as negative: it is a matter of avoiding actions which would undermine the anticommunist leadership by insisting on politically irrelevant concessions. For example, employers who attempt to establish a docile union leadership will subvert the capacity of that leadership to sustain itself against communist-led pressure from below. In other words, the problem of legitimacy is faced by the anticommunists as well as by the communists: they too must retain their status as legitimate contenders for the ideals or interests of their followers.

We have emphasized the role of reformist elites, because the denial of legitimacy in the arenas they control is crucial in anticommunist strategy. The need for situational thinking on the question of legitimacy is more general, however. Particular institutions frame their own bases for legitimate participation, and any effort to deny legitimacy to the communists must take these variations into account. Thus the legal, scientific, and teaching professions, being especially sensitive to moral issues, must be permitted to approach the problem of legitimacy in their own way.

THE DENIAL OF ACCESS

The denial of legitimacy, when adapted to the needs of specific arenas, is a key to the denial of access. This is the point of much anticommunist activity. But it may be suggested that too much attention is devoted to the simple fact of whether communists do or do not exist within some organization. Of far greater importance is a question which does not raise such disturbing issues for democratic policy: Are there elements which accept the desirability of *political collaboration* with the communists? At first glance, this may seem to be much the same thing. But it is not necessarily so. The important point about unions, and other institutions accepting membership on nonpolitical grounds, is not that communists can become members. It is rather that noncommunist elements within these institutions can be used to conceal conspiratorial activity.

We have seen that the key tactic in the bolshevik strategy of access has been "unity." The communists have not gained very much from the simple ability to join other organizations, to have the narrow and literal access such a right affords. Their successes have depended on the capacity to induce other groups, through united action, to expose themselves politically as well as organizationally. It may be said indeed that organizational successes, in unity ventures, are empty unless they are accompanied by political victories, i.e., an actual gain in influence over the minds of the target elements. The most important such gain, a prelude to many others, is that which asserts the continuity of communist aims with those of noncommunist groups.

The acceptance of communists on this basis affords them significant access to the ranks and to politically naïve elements in the leadership. This is quite different from accepting the right of communists to belong to an organization when this right can be declared a derivative from the simple fact of citizenship. To debar communists from unions, or from the schools, is to raise questions of basic importance to the character of the constitutional order. But it may be suggested that formal exclusion solves nothing: it is not very useful when relevant, and it is unnecessary when irrelevant. If it is understood that the problem is not one of simple access, but of political collaboration, then we may conclude that the whole question of communist exclusion, with its constitutional implications, can be set aside. For then the problem becomes one of educating those who accept the "united-front" psychology — a task which may well be hindered rather than aided by repressive measures.

It follows that in the general attempt to deny access to the communists, the group to be given most attention is *not the communists themselves, but their collaborators.* This simply reverses the Leninist insight that given their objectives, the "main enemy" is not the capitalists, but those who sustain social order while seeking reform. At the same time, the anticommunists ought not to recapitulate the early Leninist experience, in which isolation and annihilation of reformists was conceived to be the appropriate strategic objective. Rather, an attempt should be made to discriminate among these groups, winning over some and isolating others, with particular emphasis on the organizational roles they play.

CONCLUSION

Our final point will serve to re-emphasize the *subordinate* role of organizational activity in the struggle against totalitarianism. Early in this study organizational strategy was defined as a derivative political strategy designed to maximize the utility of organizational weapons. To speak of organizational strategy and tactics is to define a special sphere of interest and action. It must not be forgotten that this sphere is limited, providing special increments of power to political elites whose fundamental sources of weakness and strength must be looked for elsewhere.

From the general political perspective, rather than the narrowly organizational one which has primarily concerned us here, the strategic advantages of communism include (1) its historic plausibility, as that is bolstered by its relation to the Soviet Union, and (2) the instability of democratic society. In its quest for a monopoly of power, bolshevik political strategy links a revolutionary elite to whatever social forces are set in motion against existing authority. We have been concerned to show the organizational dimension of this linkage, but ultimately success or failure depends on the ability of the movement to provide "answers" to felt needs within the body politic.

The historic plausibility of communism stems in part from its capacity to bring order out of confusion, to master (without destroying) the industrial system, to provide new (if false) hope of security to an anxiety-laden population. These advantages are real and not illusory. They must be faced, for it is clear that the cost in tyranny, war, and moral decay will be paid by the masses, if the alternative is continued and acute anxiety. This price, however, is paid with reluctance. When there is another solution, retaining traditional political and moral values, it will be preferred to the communist answer. The reluctance of the masses to embrace communism is a strategic advantage for democracy, but it can be exploited only if social stability is maintained.

We must conclude, therefore, that in the long view political combat plays only a tactical role. Great social issues, such as those which divide communism and democracy, are not decided by political combat, perhaps not even by military clashes. They are decided by the relative ability of the contending systems to win and to maintain enduring loyalties. Consequently, no amount of power and cunning, in the realm of political combat, can avail in the absence of measures which rise to the height of the times.

100 Titles for Further Reading

GENERAL REFERENCES

Berelson, Bernard, and Janowitz, Morris, editors. *Reader in Public Opinion and Communication.* Glencoe, Illinois: The Free Press, 1953.

Fifty-seven well-chosen articles, including section on research methods.

Bryson, Lyman, editor. *The Communication of Ideas.* New York: Harper, 1948.

Excellent lecture series on communication, including among others two papers by Margaret Mead on intercultural communication.

Hoban, Charles F., Jr., and Van Ormer, Edward B. *Instructional Film Research.* State College, Pa.: Instructional Film Research Program (mimeographed), 1950.

Annotated bibliography to 1950.

Lazarsfeld, Paul F., and Stanton, Frank, editors. *Radio Research, 1941.* New York: Duell, Sloan and Pearce, 1941.

Lazarsfeld, Paul F., and Stanton, Frank, editors. *Radio Research, 1942-43.* New York: Duell, Sloan and Pearce, 1944.

Lazarsfeld, Paul F., and Stanton, Frank, editors. *Communications Research, 1948-49.* New York: Harper, 1949.

These three volumes have consistently carried some of the most interesting research on communications.

Schramm, Wilbur, editor. *Communications in Modern Society.* Urbana: University of Illinois Press, 1948.

Papers written for the University of Illinois Institute of Communications Research. Authors include Hovland, Berelson, Lazarsfeld, Wilson, Casey, Hart, Dale and others.

Schramm, Wilbur, editor. *Mass Communications.* Urbana: University of Illinois Press, 1949.

Selections covering development of mass communication, control and support, process, content, audiences, effects, and an appendix on facts and figures.

Smith, Bruce, Lasswell, Harold D., and Casey, Ralph, editors. *Propaganda, Communication, and Public Opinion.* Princeton: Princeton University Press, 1946.

Annotated bibliography to 1945.

Waples, Douglas, editor. *Print, Radio, and Film in a Democracy.* Chicago: University of Chicago Press, 1942.

Includes, among others, papers on effects of radio, print, and film on public opinion, respectively by Lazarsfeld, Berelson, and Slesinger.

THE COMMUNICATION PROCESS

Hartley, Eugene L., and Hartley, Ruth E. *Fundamentals of Social Psychology.* New York: Knopf, 1952.

"Communication — The Basic Social Process," pp. 15-195.

Hayakawa, S. I. *Language in Action.* New York: Harcourt, Brace (1941).

A popular treatment of general semantics.

Merton, Robert K. "The Sociology of Knowledge and Mass Communication," in *Social Theory and the Social Structure,* 199-216. Glencoe: The Free Press, 1949.

Structuring of the field.

Miller, George A. *Language and Communication.* New York: McGraw-Hill, 1951.

A psychological approach to linguistics and verbal communication.

Morris, Charles. *Signs, Language, and Behavior.* New York: Prentice-Hall, 1946.

One of the classics of semantic analysis.

Shannon, Claude E., and Weaver, Warren. *The Mathematical Theory of Communication.* Urbana: University of Illinois Press, 1949.

Shannon states the theory in mathematical terms; Weaver discusses some of its implications for non-mathematicians.

Wiener, Norbert. *Cybernetics, or Control and Communication in the Animal and the Machine.* New York: Wiley, 1948.

Stimulating ideas from the pattern of thinking which has created the electronic "brains," the theory of games, etc.

ATTENTION AND MEANING

Allport, Gordon W., and Postman, Leo. *The Psychology of Rumor.* New York: Holt, 1947.

Full-length treatment of the material on rumor in this volume. Includes results of rumor studies during World War II.

Brandt, Herman F. *The Psychology of Seeing.* New York: Psychological Library, 1945.

Largely based on eye-camera studies.

Bruner, Jerome S., and Goodman, Cecile S. "Value and Need as Organizing Factors in Perception." *Journal of Abnormal and Social Psychology,* 42, 33-44 (1947).

Well-known article which has aroused scholarly controversy and stimulated redefinition of social perception. In general, the relationship is now thought to be more complex than this article postulated.

Katz, Daniel. "Psychological Barriers to Communication." *Annals of the American Academy of Political and Social Science* (March, 1947).

Excellent treatment of some of the perceptual problems of communication.

Krech, David, and Crutchfield, Richard. *Theory and Problems of Social Psychology.* New York: McGraw-Hill, 1948.

Chapters 3 and 4 on perception; 5, 6, 7 on beliefs and attitudes; 9 on persuasion through propaganda; 10 and 11 on groups and leadership. Viewpoint of Gestalt psychology.

Lucas, Darrell Blaine, and Britt, Steuart Henderson. *Advertising Psychology and Research.* New York: McGraw-Hill, 1950.

Pages 15-64 summarize much of what advertisers know about attention factors.

Ogden, Charles K., and Richards, Ivar A. *The Meaning of Meaning: A Study of the Influence of Language upon Thought and of the Science of Symbolism.* New York: Harcourt, Brace, 1936.

Standard treatment of the subject.

Osgood, Charles E. "The Measurement of Meaning." *Psychological Bulletin,* 49, 3 (1952).

Description of the "semantic differential" as a tool for quantitative study of meaning.

Postman, Leo, and Bruner, Jerome. "Perception under Stress." *Psychological Review,* 55, 314-323 (1948).

Effect of anxiety and stress situations on perceived meanings and structures.

CHANNELS AND AUDIENCES

Allport, Gordon W., and Cantril, Hadley. *The Psychology of Radio.* New York: Harper, 1935.

Partly superseded by later research, but still stimulating.

Beville, Hugh M., Jr. *Social Stratification in the Radio Audience.* Princeton: Princeton University Press, 1939.

The first full-length description of radio audiences by socio-economic categories.

Kayser, Jacques. *One Week's News.* Paris: UNESCO, 1953.

Comparative study of 21 major newspapers in 17 countries.

Kornhauser, Arthur. "Public Opinion and Social Class." *American Journal of Sociology,* 55, 333-345 (1950).

A study of class factors in opinion.

Lazarsfeld, Paul F. *Radio and the Printed Page.* New York: Duell, Sloan and Pearce, 1940.

One of the best treatments of differences between channels.

Lazarsfeld, Paul F., and Kendall, Patricia. *Radio Listening in America.* New York: Prentice-Hall, 1948.

Analysis of a national survey of the U.S. radio audience.

UNESCO. *News Agencies: Their Structure and Operation.* Paris: UNESCO, 1953.

Structure and operation of the chief news agencies of the world. This and the following book are based largely on the reports of UNESCO's Technical Needs Commission, which present detailed information on press, radio, film, and news agencies in different countries.

UNESCO. *World Communications* (edited by Albert Shea). Paris: UNESCO, 1951.

Summary of press, radio, and film in countries of the world.

White, L. W., and Leigh, Robert D. *Peoples Speaking to Peoples.* Chicago: University of Chicago Press, 1946.

Problems of international communication, discussed by staff members of Commission on Freedom of the Press.

ATTITUDE AND OPINION CHANGE

Bettelheim, Bruno. "Individual and Mass Behavior in Extreme Situations." *Journal of Abnormal and Social Psychology,* 38, 417-452 (1943).

Observations in concentration camps.

Cantril, Hadley. *The Invasion from Mars.* Princeton: Princeton University Press, 1940.

Analysis of panic effects of the Orson Welles broadcast.

Cartwright, Dorwin. "Achieving Change in People: Some Applications of Group Dynamics Theory." *Human Relations,* 4, 381-392. (1951).

Postulates as to how group relationships are related to attitude change and action.

Cartwright, Dorwin. "Some Principles of Mass Persuasion: Selected Findings of Research on the Sale of United States War Bonds." *Human Relations,* 2, 253-267 (1949).

Attempt to systematize "what worked" in war bond campaigns.

Charters, W. W. *Motion Pictures and Youth.* New York: Macmillan, 1933.

Summary of the Payne Fund studies on effects of motion pictures.

Coffin, T. S. "Some Conditions of Emotion and Suggestibility." *Psychological Monographs,* 53, 4 (1941).

Study of the qualities which make individuals "suggestible" to propaganda.

Cooper, Eunice, and Jahoda, Marie. "The Evasion of Propaganda." *Journal of Psychology,* 23, 15-25 (1947).

The "Mr. Biggott" studies of an anti-prejudice campaign that backfired.

Doob, Leonard. *Public Opinion and Propaganda.* New York: Holt, 1948.

Systematic treatment, represented by selections in this volume.

Festinger, Leon. "The Role of Group Belongingness in a Voting Situation." *Human Relations,* 1, 154-180 (1947).

Relation of group membership to voting decisions.

Festinger, Leon, and Kelley, Harold H. *Changing Attitudes Through Social Contact.* Ann Arbor: Research Center for Group Dynamics, 1951.

Study of what kind of social contact and communication appears to result in attitude change.

Goldhamer, Herbert. "Public Opinion and Personality." *American Journal of Sociology,* 55, 346-354 (1950).

Some of the personality factors in opinion formation.

Hovland, Carl, Lumsdaine, A. A., and Sheffield, Fred D. *Experiments on Mass Communication.* Princeton: Princeton University Press, 1949.

Summary of the Army I & E Branch researches, during World War II, on effect of orientation films. Represented in this volume by paper on "one side" versus "two sides" in presentation. Includes also studies on long-time versus short-time effects, effect of audience participation, effects on men of different intellectual abilities, interest qualities, and others.

Hovland, Carl, Janis, Irving L., and Kelley, Harold H. *Communication and Persuasion.* New Haven: Yale University Press, 1953.

Important volume, summarizing Yale communication studies through 1953. Represented in this volume by Hovland-Weiss paper on source credibility. Includes other material on credibility, also studies on effect of fear-arousing appeals, organization of persuasive arguments, on group membership as related to communication effects, on personality and susceptibility to persuasion, on participation as a factor in acquiring conviction, and on the retention of opinion change.

Hyman, Herbert, and Sheatsley, Paul. "Some Reasons Why Information Campaigns Fail." *Public Opinion Quarterly,* 11, 412-423 (1950).

Some of the requirements for effecting change through the mass media.

Jarrett, R. F., and Sherriffs, Alex C. "Propaganda, Debate, and Impartial Presentation as Determiners of Attitude Change." *Journal of Abnormal and Social Psychology,* 48, 33-41 (1953).

Comparative study of effects.

Klapper, Joseph V. *The Effects of Mass Media.* New York: Bureau of Applied Social Research (mimeographed), 1949.

Memorandum to Director of Public Library Inquiry, represented in this volume by summary papers on comparative effects of the media and on mass media as agents of persuasion. Includes, also, chapters on escapistic communication, and on the function of mass media in changing public taste.

Lasswell, Harold D. "Radio as an Instrument of Reducing Personal Insecurity." *Studies in Philosophy and Social Sciences,* 9, (1941). One aspect of the effect of radio.

Lazarsfeld, Paul F., Berelson, Bernard, and Gaudet, Hazel. *The People's Choice.* New York: Columbia University Press, 1944.

Study of the effect of mass media on voting decisions. Some of the postulates of this book were challenged by the election of 1948, and forthcoming studies will considerably modify our ideas of how the media function in voting situations.

Lazarsfeld, Paul F., and Merton, Robert. "Mass Communication, Popular Taste, and Organized Social Action." In Bryson, ed., *The Communication of Ideas* (95-118); also in Schramm, ed., *Mass Communications* (459-480).

Well-known article stating concepts of "canalizing" and "narcotizing dysfunction" by mass media.

Lewin, Kurt. "Group Decision and Social Change." In Newcomb and Hartley, eds., *Readings in Social Psychology.* New York: Holt, 1947.

Some of the basic concepts of group dynamic theory.

Lippmann, Walter. *Public Opinion.* New York: Harcourt, Brace, 1922.

Classic of public opinion literature. Developed concept of "stereotype."

Merton, Robert K. *Mass Persuasion.* New York: Harper, 1946.

Analysis of effect of Kate Smith war bond broadcasts. Represented in this volume by chapter on "Mass persuasion: technical problem and moral dilemma."

Newcomb, Theodore M. *Personality and Social Change.* New York: Dryden, 1943.

Effects of new environment on attitudes and values of students at a women's college.

Newcomb, Theodore M. *Social Psychology.* New York: Dryden, 1950.

Strong in its treatment of social interaction and group theory.

Sherif, Muzafer, and Cantril, Hadley. *The Psychology of Ego-Involvements.* New York: Wiley, 1947.

Systematic treatment of important topic in attitude formation and change.

Speier, Hans. "Historical Development of Public Opinion." *American Journal of Sociology,* 55, 376-388 (1950).
Useful perspective for studying current opinion.

Waples, Douglas, Berelson, Bernard, and Bradshaw, Franklyn R. *What Reading Does to People.* Chicago: University of Chicago Press, 1940.
Represented in this volume by selection on "Why they read."

Wirth, Louis. "Consensus and Mass Communication." *American Sociological Review,* 13, 1-14 (1948).
Consensus function of communication in a democracy.

INTERNATIONAL COMMUNICATION

Almond, Gabriel. *The American People and Foreign Policy.* New Haven: Yale University Press, 1950.
Stimulating treatment, important as background for understanding current international communication problems.

Bartlett, Frederick Charles. *Political Propaganda.* New York: Macmillan, 1940.
Systematic treatment.

Bruntz, George G. *Allied Propaganda and the Collapse of the German Empire in 1918.* Stanford: Stanford University Press, 1938.
Study of World War I propaganda.

Childs, Harwood, and Whitton, John B. *Propaganda by Short Wave.* Princeton: Princeton University Press, 1942.
Focusses on German radio propaganda.

Domenach, Jean-Marie. "Leninist Propaganda." *Public Opinion Quarterly,* 15, 265-273 (1951).
Incisive treatment of propaganda of a totalitarian state.

Inkeles, Alex. *Public Opinion in Soviet Russia.* Cambridge: Harvard University Press, 1950.
Most complete study in print of organization and activities of communication system within USSR.

Kecskemeti, Paul. "Totalitarian Communication as a Means of Control." *Public Opinion Quarterly,* 14, 224-234 (1950).
Analysis of how totalitarian state uses mass communication.

Kracauer, Siegfried. "National Types as Hollywood Presents Them." *Public Opinion Quarterly,* 13, 53-72 (1949).
The "world view" of our commercial films.

Kriesberg, Martin. "Soviet News in the New York Times." *Public Opinion Quarterly,* 10, 540-564 (1946).
Content study.

Krist, Ernst, and Speier, Hans. *German Radio Propaganda.* New York: Oxford, 1944.

Analysis of content, against apparent intentions of communicator.

Lasswell, Harold D. *Propaganda Technique in the World War.* New York: Knopf, 1927.

First of a series of publications on propaganda by Dr. Lasswell which have been widely influential.

Lazarsfeld, Paul F., and Knupfer, Genevieve. "Communications Research and International Cooperation." In Linton, ed., *The Science of Man in the World Crisis* (New York: Columbia University Press, 1945).

Some of the international potentialities of communication research.

Leites, Nathan. *The Operational Code of the Politburo.* New York: McGraw-Hill, 1951.

See also Dr. Leites' expansion of this volume, to be published by the Free Press in 1954.

Lerner, Daniel. *Sykewar: Psychological Warfare Against Germany, D-Day to VE-Day.* New York: Stewart, 1949.

The most complete treatment of Allied psychological warfare in Europe in World War II.

Lerner, Daniel, ed. *Propaganda in War and Peace.* New York: Stewart, 1951.

Excellent reader, focussed on political and psychological warfare, and including articles by Speier, Lasswell, Crossman, and many others.

Linebarger, Paul M. A. *Psychological Warfare.* Washington: Infantry Journal Press, 1948.

Easy to read, applied treatment, with many illustrations.

Lochner, Louis, ed. *The Goebbels Diaries.* New York: Doubleday, 1948.

See also the postulates derived from these diaries by Leonard Doob, "Goebbels' theory of propaganda," in this volume.

Lowenthal, Leo, guest editor. *International Communication Research.* Special issue of *Public Opinion Quarterly,* 16, 4 (1952).

Based on the research program of the VOA, this special issue is represented in this volume of papers of Davison and George, Glock, Smith, and White.

Nemzer, Louis. "The Kremlin's Professional Staff." *American Political Science Review,* 44, 64-85 (1950).

Describes the USSR organization for control of communications.

Schramm, Wilbur, and Riley, John W., Jr. "Communication in the Sovietized State as Represented in Korea." *American Sociological Review,* 16, 757-766 (1951).

How the Communists controlled and used communication in Korea.

Selznick, Philip. *The Organizational Weapon: A Study of Bolshevik Strategy and Tactics.* New York: McGraw-Hill, 1952.

Excellent treatment of Communist tactics.

U. S. Strategic Bombing Survey. *The Effects of Strategic Bombing on German Morale.* Washington: Government Printing Office, 1947.

U. S. Strategic Bombing Survey. *The Effects of Strategic Bombing on Japanese Morale.* Washington: Government Printing Office, 1947.

These two volumes are the results of surveys made immediately after the war.

MEASURING COMMUNICATION

Berelson, Bernard. *Content Analysis as a Tool of Communications Research.* Glencoe: The Free Press, 1952.

Most usable introduction to the subject.

Blankenship, Albert. *How to Conduct Consumer and Opinion Research.* New York: Harper, 1946.

Collection of papers on different research methods.

Cantril, Hadley. *Gauging Public Opinion.* Princeton: Princeton University Press, 1947.

Introduction to opinion study and measurement.

Dollard, John. "Under What Conditions Do Opinions Predict Behavior?" *Public Opinion Quarterly,* 12, 623-632 (1948).

Attempt to state postulates on this important topic.

Hyman, Herbert. "Problems in the Collection of Opinion-Research Data." *American Journal of Sociology,* 55, 360-370 (1950).

Suggestive notes from survey experience.

Jahoda, Marie, Deutsch, Morton, and Cook, Stuart W. *Research Methods in Social Relations.* New York: Dryden, 1951.

Useful handbook covering a broad range of research methods.

Lasswell, Harold D., Leites, Nathan, and others. *Language of Politics: Studies in Quantitative Semantics.* New York: Stewart, 1949.

Papers deriving from content analysis experience in World War II.

Lazarsfeld, Paul F. "The Controversy over Detailed Interviews — An Offer for Negotiation." *Public Opinion Quarterly,* 8, 38-60 (1944).

The problem of how to code and interpret detailed interviews.

Lazarsfeld, Paul F. "The Use of Panels in Social Research." *Proceedings of the American Philosophical Society,* 92, 405-410 (1948).

Some of the uses of panels.

Maccoby, E. E., and Holt, R. R. "How Surveys Are Made." *Journal of Social Issues,* 2, 45-57 (1946).

Useful introduction.

Mosteller, Frederick and others. *The Pre-Election Polls of 1948.* New York: Social Science Research Council, 1949.

Report of SSRC committee on polling "failure" to predict 1948 election.

National Opinion Research Center. *Reviewing for NORC.* Denver: NORC, 1945.

Useful handbook for interviewers.

Parten, Mildred. *Surveys, Polls, and Samples.* New York: Harper, 1950.

Useful text on the subject.

Stouffer, Samuel A., and others. *Measurement and Prediction.* Princeton: Princeton University Press, 1950.

Technical volume resulting from I & E experiments in World War II. Notable for its treatment of scaling practice and theory.

Stouffer, Samuel A. "Some Observations on Study Design." *American Journal of Sociology,* 55, 356-359 (1950).

Easy-to-read introduction to problem of measuring social variables.

Index of Names

Albig, William, 389
Allenby, General, 465
Allport, Gordon W., 61, 89, 141 ff., 218, 304, 564, 565
Almond, Gabriel, 569
Alverde-Friedrich, 464
Annis, A. D., 289, 292
Aristotle, 339
Asch, S. E., 119, 215, 310
Atkinson, J. W., 111

Barghoorn, F. C., 545
Bartlett, F. C., 154, 337, 569
Berelson, Bernard, 36 ff., 56 ff., 96, 292, 301, 303, 305, 306, 311, 317, 342 ff., 350, 352, 384, 391, 392, 469, 563, 568, 569, 571
Bettelheim, Bruno, 566
Beville, Hugh M., Jr., 565
Bigman, Stanley K., 402 ff.
Bird, Charles, 60
Blankenship, Albert, 571
Blumenstock, Dorothy, 355
Blumentritt, General, 463
Blumer, Herbert, 363 ff., 381, 382, 384, 385
Bradshaw, Franklyn R., 56 ff., 306, 307, 569
Braly, K. W., 195
Brandt, Herman F., 564
Brereton, Lewis H., 464, 466
Breslaw, Bernard J., 67
Britt, Steuart Henderson, 565
Brown, W. Norman, 171
Bruner, Jerome, 111, 117, 123, 564, 565
Bruntz, George G., 569
Bryan, J., 458
Bryson, Lyman, 58, 263
Buchanan, William, 191 ff.
Buswell, Guy T., 59

Campbell, Angus, 248
Cantril, Hadley, 37, 89, 131, 191 ff., 236, 248, 249, 321, 328, 348, 349, 351, 411 ff., 565, 566, 568, 571
Carnovsky, Leon, 59
Carroll, Wallace, 450
Cartwright, Dorwin, 360, 566
Casey, R. D., 489, 563
Cavell, Edith, 495
Chave, E. J., 250
Chein, I. J., 123, 249
Chen, W. K. C., 289, 292
Childs, Harwood, 569
Churchill, Winston, 183, 437, 451, 459, 528
Coffin, T. S., 566
Cook, Stuart W., 571
Cooper, Eunice, 291, 351, 355, 567
Cottrell, Leonard, 356
Coughlin, Father, 312
Creel, George, 437
Crown, S., 194
Crutchfield, Richard S., 110, 111, 116 ff., 211, 565
Curtis, Alberta, 347

Davis, Allison, 400
Davison, W. Phillips, iii, 433 ff.
Dean, Vera M., 179
Deutsch, H., 495
Deutsch, M., 249, 571
Dewey, John, 427
Diamond, Solomon, 67
Dollard, John, 65, 310, 571
Domenach, Jean-Marie, 569
Doob, Leonard, 138 ff., 321 ff., 517 ff., 567
Droba, D. D., 249
DuBois, Cora, 176
Duchacek, Ivo, 543

Duffus, R. L., 127
Duncker, K., 135, 136

Edwards, A. L., 249
Eisenberg, A. L., 383
Eisenhower, Dwight D., 522
Engels, F., 544
Erfurth, Waldemar, 465
Everett, Phoebe, ii
Eysenck, H. J., 194

Fair, Ethel M., 58
Ferguson, Leonard W., 224, 249
Festinger, Leon, 567
Fiedlander, K., 499
Fisher, Burton, 389
Fiske, Marjorie, 48 ff., 347, 433
Fitzpatrick, Richard, ii
Flowerman, Samuel H., 352, 383, 393
Foster, Jeannette Howard, 59
Freud, Sigmund, 495
Friedson, Eliot, 380 ff.

Gaudet, Hazel, 96, 292, 305, 307,
    309, 311, 312, 313, 317, 346, 347,
    352, 355, 391, 568
Gedalecia, Ben, ii
George, Alexander, iii, 433 ff.
Gibson, J. J., 154
Gilbert, Felix, 468
Gilbert, G. M., 203
Giraud, General, 528
Gladstone, A. I., 210
Glock, Charles, 469 ff.
Glover, Edward, 44
Goebbels, Joseph, 329, 437, 454, 457,
    463, 467, 480, 507, 517 ff.
Goering, Herman, 507
Goldhamer, Herbert, 567
Goodfriend, Arthur, 175
Goodman, C. C., 111, 117, 123, 564
Gorlitz, Walter, 453
Gosnell, H. F., 354
Graham, Milton D., 205
Greeley, Horace, 348

Green, Jeannette K., 52
Guingand, Francis de, 466
Gurfein, M. I., 505
Guttman, Leo, 233, 250

Hallowell, A. I., 478
Halsey, W. F., 458, 466
Handel, Leo, 383, 384
Hart, Clyde, 216 ff.
Hart, Liddell, 463
Hartley, E. L., 195, 216 ff., 249, 356,
    389, 400, 564, 568
Hartley, R. L., 216 ff., 564
Hartmann, G. W., 349
Hayakawa, S. I., 564
Heater, Gabriel, 347
Heider, Fritz, 135, 136
Helson, 132
Herskovits, M. J., 478
Herzog, Herta, 50 ff., 392
Hess, Rudolf, 463
Hitler, Adolf, 183, 329, 331, 439, 457,
    463, 506, 507, 523
Hoban, Charles F., 263
Holoday, P. W., 98
Horowitz, Clare Marks, 52
Hovland, Carl, 99, 213, 261 ff., 275,
    292, 293, 295, 296, 310, 392, 567
Hughes, Helen MacGill, 42
Hull, C. L., 310
Hungerford, Jean, 467
Hyman, Herbert, 249, 351, 391, 567,
    571

Inkeles, Alexander, 453, 539, 569

Jahoda, Marie, 249, 291, 351, 355,
    567, 571
Janis, Irving, 210, 213, 261, 567
Janowitz, Morris, 361, 392, 469, 501
    ff., 563
Jarrett, R. F., 567
Jodl, General, 468
Jones, H. E., 98

Kaplan, Abraham, 448
Katz, Daniel, 195, 243, 249, 565
Kayser, Jacques, 76, 565
Kecskemeti, Paul, 494, 569
Kelley, Harold, 213, 261, 567
Kendall, Patricia, 69 ff., 291, 292, 381, 566
Kenney, George C., 466
Kertesz, D., 543
Kilpatrick, F. P., 249
Kitt, A. S., 395
Klapper, Joseph, ii, 87, 91 ff., 289 ff., 385, 454, 568
Klineberg, Otto, 195
Kluckhohn, Florence R., 174
Knapp, R. H., 142
Knower, F. H., 289
Knupfer, Genevieve, 570
Koffka, K., 154
Kornhauser, Arthur, 565
Korzybski, Alfred, 59, 339
Kracaver, Siegfried, 569
Krech, David, 110, 111, 116 ff., 211, 565
Kriesberg, Martin, 569
Krist, E. E., 352, 489 ff., 570

Lasswell, Harold, 263, 355, 444, 448, 450, 489, 537 ff., 568, 570, 571
Lazarsfeld, Paul F., 37, 48, 50, 69 ff., 94, 96, 250, 263, 292, 299, 301, 303, 305, 307, 311, 312, 315, 347, 348, 350, 352, 355, 381, 384, 391, 392, 490, 565, 566, 568, 570
LeBon, Gustav, 363
Lee, Alfred M., Jr., 363, 381
Leigh, Robert D., 566
Leighton, Alexander H., 157 ff., 191, 206
Leites, Nathan, 352, 489 ff., 494, 538, 570, 571
Lenin, I., 456, 544, 546, 556, 557
Lepkin, M., 143
Lerner, Dan, 449, 450, 480 ff., 570
Leuba, C., 124

Levine, R., 123, 310
Lewin, Kurt, 568
Likert, Rensis, 61, 67, 249
Lima, Margaret, 60
Lincoln, Abraham, 348
Linebarger, Paul M. A., 570
Linton, Ralph, 171
Lippmann, Walter, 109 ff., 199, 342, 568
Lochner, Louis P., 517, 570
Lockhart, Bruce, 450
Lowenthal, Leo, ii, 175, 350, 433, 570
Lucas, D. B., 124, 565
Lumsdaine, Arthur, 99, 210, 215, 261 ff., 292, 293, 295, 296, 392, 567
Lundberg, George, 291

Maccoby, E. E., 384, 572
Mace, C. A., 195, 202
Mackintosh, Helen K., 65
MacLean, Fitzroy, 456
Mannheim, Karl, 390, 444
Mao Tze Tung, 172
Marks, E. S., 249
Martelle, Giffard, 466
Martienssen, Anthony B., 466
Marx, Karl, 461, 544
Maskelyne, Jasper, 466
Masserman, J. H., 492
McCarthy, Joseph, 254
McCarthy, P. J., 249
McClelland, D. C., 111
McCloy, John J., 247
McGarvey, 132
McLean, Philip T., 517
Mead, George, 220, 249
Meier, N. C., 249, 289, 292
Mendenhall, M. A., 65
Merton, Robert K., 292, 299, 301, 312, 315, 316, 349, 384, 390, 395, 424 ff., 564, 568
Micocci, Antonio, ii
Miles, Catherine C., 61
Miller, George A., 564

Mills, C. Wright, 347
Miner, Horace, 177
Mitchell, Margaret, 7
Montgomery, Field Marshal, 466
Moore, B. M., Jr., 542
Morgan, Frederick, 466
Morris, Charles, 564
Morton, J. T., 571
Mosteller, Frederick, 249, 572
Mott, F. L., 291, 348
Muenzinger, K., 117
Murchison, C., 249
Murphy, Gardner, 61, 67, 239, 249
Murphy, L. B., 239, 249
Murray, Henry, 62, 111, 122, 123

Napoleon, 437
Nemzer, Louis, 570
Newcomb, Theodore, 61, 67, 195,
    239, 249, 310, 347, 356, 391, 395,
    400, 568
Nixon, Lewis, ii
Northrop, F. S. C., 179

Ogden, C. K., 565
Opler, Morris Edward, 157 ff.
Osgood, C. E., 251 ff.
Otis, M., 490

Park, Robert E., 381
Parsons, Talcott, 397
Parten, Mildred, 572
Peak, Helen, 211, 249
Peterson, R. C., 291
Possony, Stefan T., 465
Postman, Leo, 111, 141 ff., 304, 564,
    565
Prescott, Daniel A., 62

Redl, F., 499
Ribble, Margaret A., 44
Richards, Ivar A., 57, 59, 565
Ridgway, Helen A., 58
Riesman, David, 393

Riley, John W., Jr., 383, 389 ff., 570
Riley, Matilda, 383, 389 ff.
Robinson, William, 348
Rommel, General, 525, 530
Roosevelt, Eleanor, 255
Roosevelt, F. D., 183, 347
Roper, Elmo, 36, 244, 249
Ross, E. A., 366
Rosten, Leo, 344

Sacco, N., 495
Sanford, R. N., 132
Saunders, H. W., 249
Schafer, R., 122
Schoenfeld, N., 194, 203
Schramm, Wilbur, i-iii, 1 ff., 29 ff.,
    71 ff., 87 ff., 109 ff., 209 ff., 359
    ff., 431 ff., 454, 563
Schreiber, Carl F., 517
Selznick, Philip, 548 ff., 571
Semmler, Rudolf, 450, 467
Shakespeare, William, 359
Shannon, Claude E., 564
Sheatsley, Paul, 351, 567
Sheffield, Fred, 99, 261 ff., 275, 291,
    293, 309, 311, 312, 317, 392, 567
Sheridan, Philip, 348
Sherif, Muzafer, 131, 215, 249, 295,
    296, 310, 568
Sherman, General, 348
Sherriffs, A. C., 567
Shils, Edward, 361, 501 ff.
Sinclair, Upton, 127
Sington, Derick, 450
Skinner, B. F., 310
Slesinger, Alfred, 301
Smith, Bruce L., 170 ff., 263
Smith, Kate, 300, 309, 311, 312, 314,
    316, 347, 350, 351, 424 ff.
Smith, M. B., 347
Smyth, H. D., 449
Sorokin, Pitirim, 311
Speier, Hans, 444 ff., 484, 490, 493,
    518, 569, 570
Stalin, Joseph, 463, 544

Stanton, Frank, 48, 50, 263, 348, 350, 384, 391, 392, 490
Star, S. A., 250
Stern, William, 238, 249
Stoddard, George D., 98
Stouffer, Samuel, 98, 217, 250, 451, 572
Strachey, James, 44
Strong, Edward K., 60
Strunk, Mildred, 202
Stycos, J. Malone, 175
Suchman, E. A., 250
Swing, Raymond Graham, 347

Taft, Robert, 451
Tannenbaum, P. H., 251 ff.
Terman, Lewis M., 60, 61
Thimme, Hunts, 450
Thomson, Charles A. H., 450
Thorndike, E. L., 510
Thurstone, L. L., 224, 250, 291
Titchener, E. B., 219
Toennies, Alfred, 174, 177, 478
Tolman, Edward, 118
Truman, David, 239
Truman, Harry S., 39
Tyler, Ralph W., 58, 59, 60

Van Ormer, E. B., 263
Vanzetti, B., 495

Wang, C. K. A., 250
Waples, Douglas, 56 ff., 306, 307, 563, 569
Weaver, Warren, 564
Weber, Max, 177
Weidenfeld, Arthur, 450
Weiss, W., 275 ff.
Welles, Orson, 411 ff.
White, David M., 71
White, L. W., 566
White, Ralph, ii, 180 ff.
Whitton, John B., 569
Wiener, Norbert, 564
Willkie, Wendell, 289
Wilson, Lord, 466
Wilson, Woodrow, 183
Wirth, Louis, 320, 569
Wolf, Katherine M., 48 ff.
Wolff, W., 291
Wollenberg, Erich, 453
Woodward, P., 248
Wulf, F., 154

Young, Desmond, 466

Zacharias, Ellis, 450
Zillig, M., 113, 136

Index of Subjects

Advertising
distinguished from propaganda, 377
nature of mass advertising, 372
Anthropology in psychological warfare, 157 ff.
Apathy, as effect of mass communication, 353
Atrocities, propaganda treatment of, 492
Attention, 29, 482
availability as determinant, 30
contrast as determinant, 30
reward and threat as determinants, 31
Attitudes, 11, 56, 61, 191, 216 ff., 251 ff., 359
active vs. verbal sanction, 319
and personality, 247
and suggestion, 209
change as modification or innovation, more often than conversation, 291
change in groups, 360
change related to environmental change, 214
change through mass communication, 209
change through use of one-sided vs. two-sided message, 261 ff.
civic, 318
congruity principle of change, 251 ff.
credulity and change, 260
definition, 209, 218
difference from opinion, 222
dimensions of, 229
direction of, 230, 251
effect of personal influence on, 402
effect of prestige on, 402
general or specific, 223
group origins, 239
how learned, 209
inference of, 221
intensity, 235
motivational components of, 226
perceptual components of, 226
salience, 238
scale analysis, 233
studying by method of "equal-appearing intervals," 232
studying by methods of summated ratings, 232
variation in degree, 231
Audience
and mass, 383
trust in the mass media, 82
Audiences
Brazil, 74
Bulgaria, 75
Burma, 33
China, 75, 78
Czechoslovakia, 75
Egypt, 74, 79
Ethiopia, 33
France, 33, 74, 79, 80
Greece, 33
Hungary, 75
India, 74
Italy, 74, 80
Japan, 74, 80
Mexico, 74
Philippines, 74, 79, 80
Poland, 75
Romania, 75
Syria, 74, 79, 81
United Kingdom, 74
United States, 33, 74
USSR, 75
book, 33, 69, 70, 81
magazine, 33, 69, 70, 81
motion picture, 33, 69, 70, 74, 81
newspaper, 33, 74, 78
radio, 33, 69, 74, 80
television, 33
Audience participation, effect of, 213
Audience tastes, 33, 34

Barriers to communication, 8
BBC
  and candor, 186
  reactions to, 187
Beliefs, nature and basis of, 161 ff., 191 ff.
Berliner Illustrierte Nachtausgabe, 518
Book audiences, 18, 33, 69, 70, 81
Borba, 77, 78
Broadcasting, 22, 33, 69, 74, 80
Bureau of Applied Social Research, 404

Canalization, 16, 308
Candor
  and BBC, 186
  in propaganda, 185
Capacity (of communication system), 5
Channels of mass communication (*see also* Media), 87 ff.
Chicago *Tribune,* 523
Colliers, 347
Comics, 48 ff.
  children's reading of, 48
  why they are read, 48
Commentary vs. documentary, 298
Communication, meaning of term, 3
Communication policy, 439
Communication process
  characteristics of, 5
  decoding, 5, 11
  encoding, 4, 12
  feedback, 9
  interpretation, 110
Communicator (*see* Source)
Communism, counteroffensive against, 548 ff.
Communist Party
  as a communication channel, 173
  use of agitators, 182
  use of fifth column, 182
  use of mass communication, 25, 87
Communist propaganda, 180, 181, 355
  as organizational weapon, 549
  counteroffensive against, 548 ff.
  dual channels in, 545

  importance of adequate policies in defense against, 562
  importance of denial of legitimacy to, 557
  importance of denying access, 560
  intended functions of, 540
  reactions to, 181
  role of intervening elites, 553
  strategy of, 537 ff.
  themes, 543
  three stages in, 542
Compensation, 330
Conformity, 333
Content of international communication, 170 ff., 180 ff., 439 ff., 458, 489 ff., 508 ff.
Conversion, 291 ff.
  conditions of likely success, 303
  difficulty of, 303, 453
Corriere della Sera, 77, 78
Credibility, 212, 275 ff., 418, 482, 525
  effect on change in opinion, 280
  effect on learning, 280
  effect on retention, 283
Crowds
  acting, 363
  casual, 363
  characteristics of acting, 365
  characteristics of expressive, 367
  conventionalized, 363
  expressive, 364
  formation of, 364
  how formed from public, 379
  steps in development of, 364
  suggestibility in, 365
  types of, 363 ff.
Cues, 29

Dagens Nyheter, 77, 78
Daily Telegraph (Australia), 77, **78**
Deception, forms of, 464
Decoding, 4, 11, 109 ff.
Destination (*see also* Audience), 3, 19
Deviant minority, 296
Deviant political behavior, its inducement, 454
Displacement, 328
Documentary vs. commentary, 298
Doubt, signs of, 10

Effects, 12 and *passim*
  apathy, 353
  forces in, 17
  long and short term, 354
  of Allied propaganda on German
    army, 501 ff.
  of communication on public opin-
    ion, 353 and *passim*
  panic resulting from mass com-
    munication, 411 ff.
  structuring political issues, 355
  types of evidence, 485
Ego-involvement and relation to
    panic, 422
Elites
  as targets of psychological warfare,
    448
  role of intervening elites in Com-
    munist propaganda and in de-
    fense against it, 553
Emotional appeal, effect of, 213
Encoding, 4, 32
Entertainment, effect of ent. content
    of mass communication, 353
Entropy, 5
Erie County study, 96, 347
O Estado, 77, 78
Evaluation of propaganda, types of
    evidence, 485

Face-to-face communication, advan-
    tages of, 102
Farm Journal, 347
Feedback, 9, 19
Film production in different coun-
    tries, 76
Filmstrips compared to motion pic-
    ture, 99
Focus of attention, 34
Foreign Morale Analysis Division,
    158
Fortune, 344
Frame of reference, 110, 131, 252
Frankfurter Zeitung, 529
Front und Heimat, 510

Goebbels' principles of propaganda,
    517 ff.
Grammar, 12

Groups, 15
  and public opinion, 389
  as origin of attitudes, 239
  attitude change in, 360
  bringing about disequilibrium with-
    in, 361
  characteristics of crowds, 363 ff.
  characteristics of mass, 363 ff.
  characteristics of publics, 363 ff.
  importance of primary group in
    Wehrmacht morale, 515
  in communication process, 359
  influence of prestige within, 361
  peer groups and communication,
    393
  primary group, 515
  reference group and communica-
    tion, 395
  resist deviance, 361
  statistical and functional, 359
  use of ingroup and outgroup atti-
    tudes in propaganda, 378

Haltung und Stimmung, 454
Humor, signs of, 10
Hurriyet, 77, 78

Identification, 63, 332
Indexing of communication, 29
Indoctrination themes used by Nazis,
    508
Informal channels of communication
    in different countries, 474
Institutions, 15
Intelligence, importance of access to,
    519
Intensity, 32, 235
International communication
  approaches to the study of, 436
  conditions of effectiveness, 440 ff.
  content, 439, *passim*
  difficulties in the way of, 432, 433
  relations to national policy, 437
  relation to political situation, 438
  special problems of, 431 ff.
Intervening variables, 11
Issues in public opinion
  crucial issues, 350
  peripheral issues, 350
  unstructured issues, 349
Izvestia, 78

The Jungle, effect of, 127

Kate Smith broadcast, 424 ff.

Labels, 213, 531
Learning theory and communication, 10, 11
Life, 347
Literacy
   and values, 174
   in different countries, 75
London *Times,* 78
Lying in propaganda, 184

Magazine, 18
   audiences, 81
Mass, 369 ff.
   and audience, 383
   characteristics of, 360, 370, 381
   definition, 381
   distinguished from society, 370
   mass advertising, 372
   nature of mass behavior, 24, 383, 384
   proletarian masses, 372
   role of individuals in, 370
Mass communication
   and attention, 23
   audiences, 19
   audiences in other countries, 74 ff.
   effects, 22
   effect on different kinds of people, 350
   feedback, 19
   importance of groups in, 359
   influenced by public taste, 342
   institutions, 18
   output-input ratio, 18
   process, 18
   source, 18
   use by Communists, 25, 87
   violence in, 25
Mass media
   advantages of supplementing with face-to-face communication, 103
   and learning of information and skills, 294
   and voting behavior, 96
   as disseminators of news and opinion in different countries, 74 ff.
   as instruments of persuasion, 95
   audience trust in different countries, 82
   comparative effects, 91 ff.
   comparative study in different countries, 74 ff., 470 ff.
   differences in participation among, 89
   differences in permanence, 90
   differences in speed, 89
   importance of specific coverage, 294
   persuasion by, 290
   retention of different mass media, 93
   space-time differences among, 88
Meaning (*see also* Perception), 12, 57, 251
   distortion of, 110
   effect of social structure on, 398
   interpretation in terms of experience, 111
   interpretation in terms of personality, 112
   interpretation in terms of wholeness, 112
Mediatory response, 7, 109
Message, 3, 13
   and group situation, 15
   and meaning, 14
   and personality needs, 14, 15
   constructive vs. destructive, 306
   documentary vs. commentary, 298
   effect of entertainment content, 353
   effect of "superiority," 189
   emotional appeal, effect of, 213
   importance of "positive" approach, 190, 212
   importance of specificity, 294, 296
   importance of what listeners know, 189
   labels, 213
   one side or two, 212, 261
   primacy, 213
   recency, 213
   reinforcement, 213
   repetition, 212
   slogans, 213
   variation, 212

Al Misri, 77, 78
Mob, how to prevent or break up, 366
Le Monde, 78
Monopoly propaganda and opinion, effect of, 299, 351, 540
Morale
  among Japanese in World War II, 159
  and morale indices, 486
  Wehrmacht morale as target of psychological warfare, 501 ff.
Motion picture, 22
  advantages of as channel, 102
  audiences, 81
  compared to filmstrips, 99
  compared with print, 98
  production in different countries, 76
Motivation, 226
Multiple channels, 9

Nachrichten für die Truppe, 512
La Nacion, 77, 78
Nation, The, 344
National Opinion Research Center, 225
Nazi use of mass communication, 352
Newspaper, 18, 22, 36 ff., 71 ff., 78, 476
  as influence on public opinion, 347
  coverage of world news, 76
  its use as a tool for daily living, 41
  its use for information and interpretation, 40
  its use for respite, 41
  its use for social contact and prestige, 42
  reading of, 36 ff., 71 ff.
  reading as an end in itself, 43
  ritualistic nature of reading, 45
  role of, 38
  "serious" use of, 38
Newsprint, use in different countries, 76
News selection for propaganda purposes, 186
New York *Daily News,* 43, 46, 77, 78
New York *Daily Worker,* 67

New York *Journal American,* 42
New York *Mirror,* 43, 47
New York *Times,* 42, 46, 78
Non-industrial countries
  audiences in, 177
  broadcasting to, 173
  class system in, 171
  communication networks in, 172
  politeness as a value in, 176
  problem of communicating to, 170 ff.
  religion as a value in, 177
  slow tempo as a value in, 175
  value profiles in, 173
Non-readers, 58

One side vs. two sides
  and attitude and opinion change, 261 ff., 316
  effect of education, 267
  effect of initial position, 266
Opinion (*see also* Public Opinion), 216 ff.
  comparative study in different countries, 469 ff.
  difference from attitudes, 222
  effect of personal influence on, 402
  effect of prestige on, 402
  intensity, 235
  scale analysis, 233
  study by method of "equal appearing intervals," 232
  study by method of summated ratings, 232
Opinion leaders
  and mass media, 404
  how to identify, 409
  indices of, 391
  nature of, 403
"Organizational weapon," Communist, 549
OWI, 444

Panic
  as effect of mass communication, 411 ff.
  nature and cause of, 422 ff.
La Parisien Libere, 77, 78
Peer groups and communication, 393

Perception (*see also* Meaning), 109
ff., 116 ff., 205, 226
  and individual need, 118
  and interrelations, 128
  and mental set, 123
  and mood, 124
  and needs, 122
  and social value, 117
  cultural cues, 134
  determinants of, 116
  functional factors in, 117
  how an impression of a person-
    ality is formed, 119
  is functionally selective, 121
  is organized and meaningful, 118
  of cause and effect, 135
  of nearby or similar objects or
    events as part of common struc-
    ture, 133
  of propaganda, 138 ff.
  of strange and bizarre, 119
  perceiving traits of individuals and
    groups, 130
  proximity and similarity, 133
  structural factors in, 116
Personal contact
  as influence on opinion and atti-
    tude, 402
  as influence on public opinion, 96,
    347
  effects on relationships, 205
  nature of, 405
Personalities, effect of mass communication on, 350
Persuasion (*see also* Attitude Change,
  Propaganda, Psychological Warfare), 289 ff.
  and prestige of spokesman, 313,
    530
  by mass media, 290
  effect of canalization, 308
  effect of offering real rewards, 310
  effect of prestige of source, 313
  in case of civic attitudes, 318
  moral dimensions of mass persua-
    sion, 424 ff.
Pravda, 77, 78
Predispositions as factor in public
  opinion, 355, 482

La Prensa (Mexico), 77, 78
Prestige
  as influence on opinion and atti-
    tude, 402
  of media, 313
  of spokesman, 313
Primacy, 213
Print
  advantages of as channel, 99
  compared with motion picture, 98
  compared with voice as channel,
    93, 95
Privatization, 493
Projection, 331
Propaganda (*see also* Psychological
  Warfare), 138 ff., 181, 376 ff.
  and action, 181
  and anxiety, 533
  and frustration, 534
  and interest of audience, 523
  and military deception, 466
  and use of censorship, 527
  attention, 482
  behind the Iron Curtain, 183
  black or white, 529
  candor in, 185
  Churchill as propagandist, 498
  conditions of effectiveness, 480, 482
  consequences to be considered in
    planning, 522
  credence, 482, 525
  definition, 376
  "democratic fallacy" in, 452
  difference between democratic and
    totalitarian propaganda, 496
  difference between World War I
    and World War II, 491
  displacement of aggression, 534
  distinguished from advertising, 377
  distrust of, 493
  effect of monopoly, 299
  environment, 482
  evaluation of effectiveness, 480,
    485
  functions of, 481
  Goebbels' principles of, 517
  handling defeats, 533
  impact of Allied propaganda on
    Wehrmacht, 511
  importance of credibility, 525

importance of declassified information, 523
importance of intelligence, 519
importance of prestige symbols, 530
importance of single authority, 520
importance of timing, 530
intended functions of Soviet propaganda, 540
in the non-Communist world, 184
lying in, 184
nature of policy goals, 480
neutralists' reaction to, 185
news selection for, 186
objectives of wartime propaganda, 490
of Soviet elite, 538
of the deed, 181, 348
perception of, 138
practical rules of, 377
predispositions, 482
privatization in, 493
procedures of, 377
reactions to U.S., 180
relation to enemy's policy and action, 522
relation to other stimuli, 516
resistance to, 180 ff.
summary of process, 487
to home front, 532
trends in twentieth century, 489 ff.
true or false, 525
types of evidence of effects, 485
typical aims of, 483
use of enemy material, 528
use of ingroup and outgroup attitudes, 378
what Goebbels thought propaganda could not do, 535
when to answer enemy, 529
Wilson's 14 points as, 183
Psychiatry in psychological warfare, 157 ff.
Psychological warfare (*see also* Propaganda)
ability and will to fight, 445
ability and will to work, 447
against Japan, 157

and the Japanese emperor symbol, 163
elites as targets, 448, 462
fighting population as targets, 450
forms of deception, 464
how will to resist may be weakened, 451
inadequacies of term, 444
inducing deviant political behavior, 454, 456
military elites as targets, 450
psychiatry and anthropology in, 157 ff.
range of planning, 459
shaping of expectations in target populations, 461
use of warnings, 457
will to obey, 450
working population as target, 449
Public
behavior patterns of, 374
characteristic features of, 373
definition of, 373
how changed into a crowd, 379
Public Opinion, 321 ff., 342 ff., 374 ff.
and group affiliation, 389
compensation as factor in, 330
conformity as factor in, 333
consistency of, 323
displacement as factor in, 328
Doob's principles of, 340
effect of communication on, 345
effect of communication on different kinds of people, 350
effect of communication on issues compared with effect on personalities, 350
effect of different conditions, 351
effect of purposiveness vs. non-purposiveness, 352
effect on communication, 343
effects of kinds of issues, 349
formation of, 340, *passim*
identification as factor in, 332
indices of leaders, 391
information as factor in, 351
kinds of effects, 353
Mannheim's focus of attention hypothesis, 390

Mannheim's interest hypothesis, 390
predispositions as factor in, 355, 482
projection as factor in, 331
rationalization as factor in, 325
relative influence of radio, press, personal contact on, 347
role of public discussion within, 376
simplification as factor in, 336
Public taste as influence on communication, 342

Radio, 22
advantages of as channel, 101
as influence on public opinion, 347
audiences, 33, 69, 74, 80
Rand Daily Mail, 77, 78
Rationalization, 325
Reading
and insecurity, 66
as end in itself, 43
by age, 70, 71
by economic status, 71
by education, 58, 59, 70, 71
differences between readers and non-readers, 58
differences by occupation, 59
differences by sex, 58
differences by social grouping, 60
effect of predispositions, 56
identification with characters, 63
motives for, 62
of comics, 48
of news, 71 ff.
of news pictures, 71
prestige of, 63
reasons for newspaper reading, 36 ff.
Recency, 213
Redundancy, 5
Reference group and communication, 395
Regression, 290
Reinforcement, 213
Repetition, 212, 316
Representational level, 12

Resistance to propaganda, 180 ff., 296
Response, 11
Retention, 93, 283
Rewards and persuasion, 310
RIAS, 456
Roles, 359
Rude Pravo, 77, 78
Rumor, 141 ff.
after Pearl Harbor, 141
assimilation, 150
embedding, 154
fear rumors, 143
hostility rumors, 143
leveling, 146
nature and process, 143
sharpening, 148
why rumor circulates, 143
wish rumors, 143

Safe conduct passes, 514
Sarcasm, signs of, 10
Saturday Evening Post, 347
Scale analysis, 233
Semantic differential, 252
Sieg oder Sibirien, 510
Sign, 6, 11, 14
Simplification, 336
"Sleeper" effect, 283
Slogans, 213, 531
Soap operas, 50 ff.
as source of advice, 51
reasons for listening, 52
Social structure and interpretation of messages, 398
Source (*see also* Communicator), 3, 18, 275
effect of credibility of (*see* Credibility)
effect of prestige of, 313, 402
Stereotypes, 113
adaptation to likes and dislikes, 203
as symptomatic, 204
change in, 202
generally held concerning Americans, British, Chinese, French, Russians, 192, 197
national, 191

national, expressed numerically, 200, 201

of other countries and themselves held by Australia, Britain, China, Germany, France, Italy, Netherlands, Norway, U.S., USSR, 193

Stimmung und Haltung, 454

Stimulus, 109

Strain, effect on communication, 396

Subversion, defenses against, 549 ff.

Suggestibility

conditions making for, 417

in crowds, 365

Suggestion

and attitude change, 210

and form of message, 212

and group norms and loyalties, 211

and perceived credibility of source, 212

and personality, 210

Surveys Research Center, 226

Ta Kung Pao, 77, 78

Television, 22

Textbooks, 22

Themes

Allied themes against Wehrmacht, 513

employed by Nazis for indoctrination, 508

fear as theme, 510

most effective on German troops, 513

of Soviet propaganda, 543

propaganda themes remembered by German POW's, 503

The Times of India, 77, 78

USIA, 2, 402

U.S. propaganda, reactions to, 180

U.S. strategic bombing survey, 160, 240

Values, 11, 173

Variation, 212, 316

Violence in mass communication, 25

Voelkischer Beobachter, 518

Voice, compared to print as channel, 93, 95

VOA, reactions to, 187, 483

Warnings, use of in psychological warfare, 457

Welles' "War of the Worlds" broadcast, 24, 411 ff.

classifying listeners to, 416

ego-involvement in, 422

why frightening, 413

why the panic, 418